MW01436076
June 2001
Tuesday
Wednesday
Thursday
Friday
7 Canadian Border Glacier Park, MT 3:45pm Started CDT - Belly River
8 Stealth camp overlooking Lake Sherborn on way to Many Glacier
9 Rain camp across from falls Cataract Ck on way to Piegan
13 Atlantic Camp grd
14 Flag Day Rain - Camp - Morning Star
15 E. Glacier whistling Swan motel
16 Twin Medicine Rain/Campsite Scenic Pt. → E. Glacier
21 Summer begins
23 From Round Park → Rock Ck
28 Start 6 AM
29 Lewis/Clark Pass
30 20 miles

Other books by Sunshine MacGregor Ferrell

BLAZE (Racing the Clouds II)

WHITE GOLD (Racing the Clouds III)

Racing the Clouds

BOOK I: Initiation

"Sunshine" MacGregor Ferrell

Racing the Clouds
First Edition, November 2021

Copyright © 2021 Elise Ferrell

Front cover, back cover and interior insert photos copyright © by Elise Ferrell
Book, cover and map design: Elise MacGregor Ferrell
Self-published and printed through 48-hour Books.

Manufactured in the United States of America

Website: https://racingtheclouds.com

Cover Photos: (front: afternoon fog in south-central, CO, back: Sunshine MacGregor Ferrell north of Lost Trail Creek in southern, CO)

Many Trail Names and Birthnames in this story have been changed. The events and geography are drawn from real life but may contain inaccuracies. This is not a guidebook.

All rights reserved. No part of this book may be reproduced in any form, or by any means electronic, mechanical, recording or otherwise, without written permission from the author (self-publisher), except for brief quotations used in reviews.

Library of Congress Cataloging-in-Publication Data

Ferrell, Elise MacGregor
        Racing the Clouds – First Edition
Text: Elise Ferrell
Photos: Elise Ferrell, reg. # VAu 1-400-912

ISBN: 978-1-7375331-0-8 Soft Cover
ISBN: 978-1-7375331-1-5 Hard Cover

*With gratitude to my family
Jeffrey, Ayla and Ariel Ferrell
and Malcolm and Eleanor MacGregor,
for helping me transform life into words.*

Special Thanks to First Edition Corporate Sponsors

Rebound AIR Trampolines
Cāblz Eyewear Retainers
48-Hour Books Publishing
Silver Mountain Vineyards

And Much Appreciation to all my First Edition Supporters

Thomas Shearman, Diane Davis, Willow M Dew, Marlen Shepherd, Carol M Biskupski, Ted Burke, Randall Ferrell, Brian Gidge, Debbie Glusker, Geneffa P Jonker, Mary Kline, Fabrizio Olsson, Thomas W Parker, Mark Pinto, Laurie Radovan, Elizabeth Posner, Kean Riekenbrauck, Eric Sarti, Frederick Schuller, Jackie Terry, Shelley Lynn Young, Colleen Wilson, Bonnie Merkin Wilson, Claire, Kimlin, Kathleen Brady, Philip Johnston, Brian Kimball, Greg Spear, Brian Staffa, Ben Kirkland, Stacey Kuypers, Anne, Esther Centers, Jeff Campbell, Nikki Lawrence, Kasie Talbot, Kristy, Ualtar, Liz Smith, Mike Long, Thaddeus, Ann Baier, Mitzi Condit, Andy Beck, Tony Becker, Patrick Vaughan, Jerome Verhasselt, Galt, John Everingham, Jeff Grudin, Alicia Booth Sprecher, James Williams, Ed Best, Jim Ansbro, Ken Capitanich, Eddie Clay, Ashley McDougal, Ana

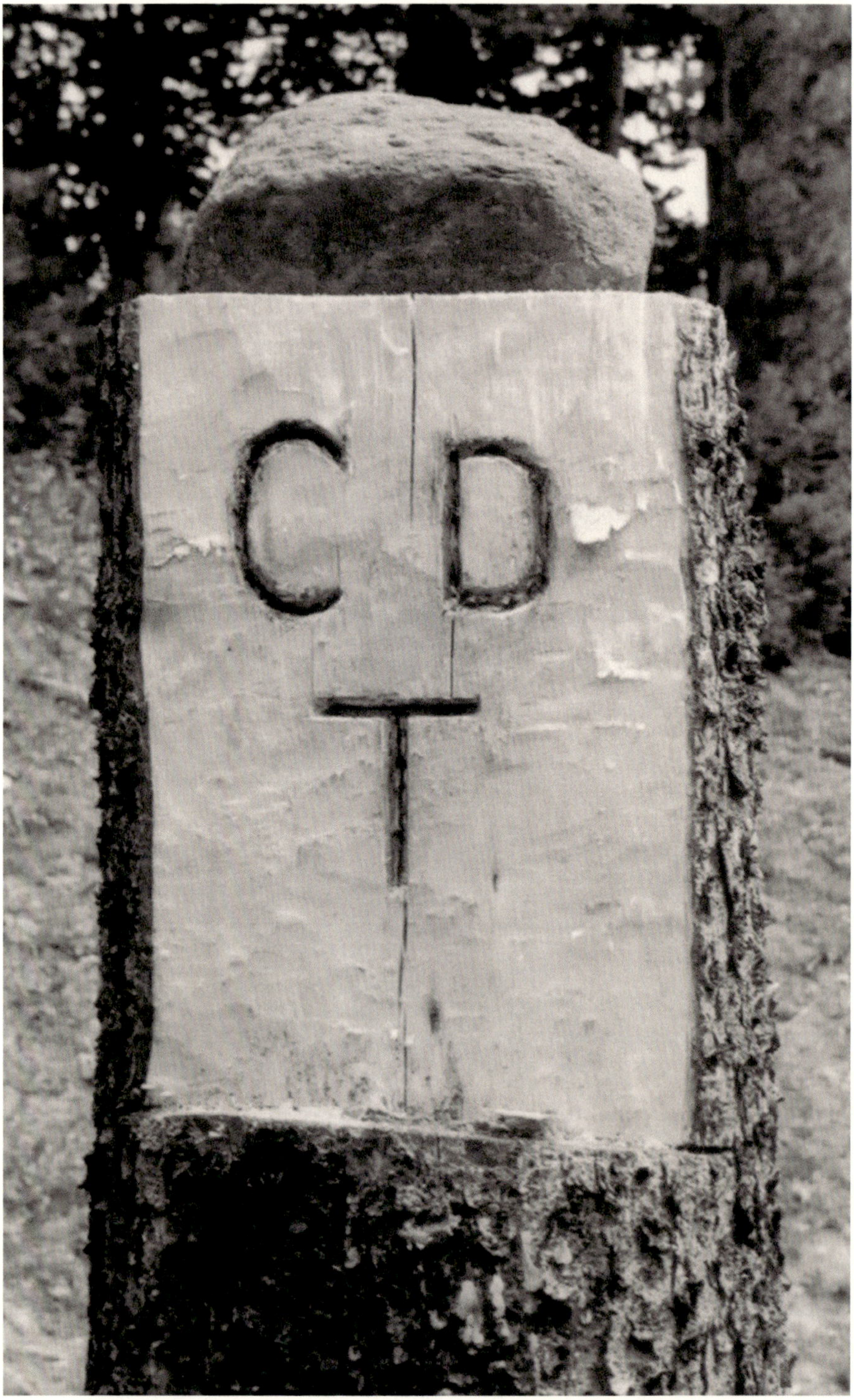
CD
T

CONTENTS

Chapter 1.	Before (Prologue)	p. 1
Chapter 2.	Becoming (PCT)	p. 9
Chapter 3.	Decision	p. 31
Chapter 4.	Countdown	p. 51
Chapter 5.	Initiation	p. 67
Chapter 6.	Drag	p. 139
Chapter 7.	Boom	p. 217
Chapter 8.	Heavy Glue	p. 235
Insert	Scenes of Montana	p. 305
Chapter 9.	Finding South	p. 323
Chapter 10.	Wisdom	p. 419
Chapter 11.	Coming About	p. 435
Chapter 12.	Perspective	p. 489
Chapter 13.	Beasts	p. 545
Chapter 14.	One Down	p. 573
Glossary	Hiking Terms	p. 589

S. FK. SUN RIVER TR. NO. 202
CONTINENTAL DIVIDE TRAIL
CDT
NATIONAL SCENIC TRAIL

Chapter I

Before

(Prologue)

One loses many laughs by not laughing at oneself...

— *Sara Jeannette Duncan*

My first brush with backpacking hurt so much that remembering it still makes me laugh. If I had been allergic to "character building," I would have quit on Day Two and gone home, end of story. Any sane person meeting my 21-year-old self would have deemed me poorly equipped to look wilderness in the eyes. Although, some people think sanity is overrated.

That first trip took place in 1987. My college boyfriend Dave was the joker who claimed people went backpacking in order to have fun. He promised to handle all the preparations for spending nine days in California's High Sierra Mountains. All I needed to do was fry chicken, bake cornbread and mass-produce chocolate chip granola cookies.

Naturally, we packed a lot more items for the trip than just food. Our "necessities" also included a bottle of red wine, one bottle each of blackberry and peach schnapps, a full tube of toothpaste, stick deodorant, blue jeans, thick wool sweaters, clean sweats for camp time, cotton sleepwear, and several changes of cotton t-shirts. Someone examining our finished pile might have thought we were going car-camping in Alaska.

The drive from Los Angeles to California's Eastern Sierras began with Dave lugging my backpack to the car because I could hardly lift it, let alone carry it on my back. We reached the Piute Pass Trailhead bright and early the next morning. There was parking space available. We could have whizzed right in and started hiking before noon except, whoops! Right after we paid for parking, I realized my hiking boots were still in Los Angeles.

"Okay, ding-dong, what a rookie-move," I chided myself before Dave could say it.

"No problem," he nodded, turning the car around.

Four hours of roundtrip driving to the nearest camping store got us back to the trailhead with our relationship intact and my feet wearing brand new boots.

As we drove through the guard gate, flashing the pass we had purchased four hours ago, we cheered, "Piute Pass, Take Two!"

There was no reason to feel stressed. We had plenty of daylight left for crossing Piute Pass and setting up camp at Golden Trout Lake.

My own next challenge was to remain standing while Dave hoisted my backpack onto my shoulders and fastened its buckles tight. My legs wobbled as if they might collapse. Hopefully, that was normal for newbies on Day 1.

In order to summon thrust for the takeoff, I pumped my fist into the air and shouted, "Piute Pass or Bust!"

Together, Dave and I waved to his dusty brown *Toyota Corolla*. Since posture was important, we squared up our shoulders before slowly taking off. I brought up the rear, staggering beneath my crushing load of toiletries, camping gear, liquor, and baked goods. Dave kept needing to restrain himself from pulling too far ahead. At the parking lot's end, I decided to pull over for a sock adjustment because I could feel my heels stinging.

Dave played the gentleman, never joking about city girls or princesses, while he helped lower my backpack onto a flat-topped boulder.

Once I got seated, freed my shoulders, and loosened umpteen shoelaces, I was able to pry off my stiff new boots, tug off my socks, and look under the hood. Imagine what went through

Dave's head, and mine, when my bare heels met the sunlight. Turns out, their stinging had been caused by something far worse than blisters. In fact, the blisters were already gone. Stage Two had kicked in and replaced my heels with two bleeding-red holes, no skin attached. Yes, this happened in the parking lot, and, no, it's not a fish tale.

Each next morning in the High Sierra Mountains, my heels were going to sting as if sprinkled with salt. Each next lunch break, airing out my feet was going to make the wounds crust over, doubling the pain I would feel every time I stuffed both feet back into their cages.

Does this sob story explain why Dave and I failed to cross Piute Pass that evening? Actually, no because, for one thing, my heels stopped hurting after we started climbing. It's true. Being covered in bandages and softened by sweat kept my wounds copacetic for the rest of the afternoon. We could probably have stuck with our original plan for the trip if my body had not manifested another factory defect.

Dave's itinerary imagined us crossing Piute Pass that first evening, setting up camp at Golden Trout Lake, and waking up in paradise early the next morning. Kudos to him because that was a sensible goal. The only reason we could not make it was because my skinny, knock-kneed legs used a different measuring stick. They thought three miles was plenty for our first day out, so that's where they quit. Rickety-rackety-putt-putt-conk. We failed to cross Piute Pass before the crash happened, and, what's worse—we had to pitch our tent right on the switchbacks because there was no other flat space and it was getting dark.

During our rush to stuff plastic tent-hooks into slippery eyelets, a katabatic wind shot over the pass and tried to tear the whole flapping mess out of our hands. Clinging desperately, we stabbed whatever into wherever, and that was that. It would have been impossible to fire up Dave's propane-butane gas stove. The wind was too strong. Instead of drinking hot chocolate to get warm, we sipped cold blackberry schnapps, gnawed on cold barbequed chicken, and shivered throughout a wild September night.

Thankfully, the next morning dawned tranquil and warm. We could take our time crossing Piute Pass. Never mind how loudly my hungover legs begged for rest and demanded to feel hands pressing against their knees. It felt marvelous to take a breather on the pass. My first eyeful of open mountaintop, echoed by more open mountaintops, helped me recover quickly.

Dave thought Day Two was just getting started, but wouldn't you know it? After dropping off the pass for just two miles, my motor decided it was finished for the day. This seemed like a pity. Why hang our hats while the sun was still high, right? Well, if someone else's legs had been attached to my hips, perhaps we could have kept going, but such is life. We had to set up camp at Golden Trout Lake, precisely where we had planned to sleep the first night.

Naturally, Dave started to worry about running out of food. He had reason to worry since the route we were attempting was a 9-day loop, not an out-and-back deal that could be cut short. In hopes of supplementing our food supply, he spent the whole afternoon fishing, only to establish that if anything with fins lived in Golden Trout Lake, its gastronomical cravings did not include drowning grasshoppers or *PowerBait*. That was a real letdown since we had expected fresh trout to round out our dinners, but no worry. I had baked plenty of cornbread and chocolate chip granola cookies. We could make do with a pouch of freeze-dried backpacker pasta, shared between us, which tasted pretty good washed down with hot chocolate. Looking ahead, though, we were hoping for better luck in the days to come, since fish was on our menu for the rest of the week.

After dinner, I lathered my armpits and gave them a quick shave. Obviously, this was necessary since we were backpacking, not having a gross contest.

Meantime, Dave dug out his buck knife and started whittling a yard-long stick. He created a spear sharp enough to scare rabid cannibals, but its purpose was to defend us from bears during the night.

Once I fell asleep, my imagination drifted into a nightmare. Nothing seemed wrong until I bolted awake to a frightening noise. It was not the commotion of our tent getting thrashed by a nighttime gale (also frightening). Nor was it the harrowing scritch of bear claws shredding our tent's rainfly. Rather, it was the unmistakable hack of projectile vomiting.

Feeling scared to look, I pried open our tent's flapping doorway, peeked outside, and saw something sad. Poor Dave was crouched on his hands and knees in the windy darkness. Pasta and cornbread were exploding through his mouth. He had not eaten anything rotten. The culprit was his propane/butane stove, which had been leaking gas near his face while he slept.

Then, came Day Three. Right out of camp, Dave complained about my snail's pace giving him intolerable back pains.

I did not enjoy being made to feel guilty, so I gave him permission to leave me behind.

Looking delighted, he kicked up his heels and trotted into the sunrise. *Sayonara Baby. See you when the bell rings.*

It only took ten minutes for me to lose the trail because, seriously, who could have guessed where a person should cross a wide granite slab? Fortunately, I knew better than to make a bad situation worse. After retreating to where the trail disappeared, I sat down and patiently waited to be rescued. I waited and waited. Finally, after an hour, Dave came back, apologizing profusely. Being a sensible boyfriend, he suggested we should stay closer to civilization for the rest of the week.

Back at Golden Trout Lake, we established a base camp, from which to take day-hikes to various scenic overlooks. During the same hour, a forest fire erupted somewhere and turned the whole sky dishwater gray. Refusing to feel discouraged, we spent the rest of that week bagging a handful of modest peaks, whose views looked lovely veiled in smoke. All we needed for utter happiness was a little fresh fish to round out our meals. Too bad the local dinks were still either fasting or waging a hunger strike.

By Day Seven, merely hearing the word chocolate, whether in relation to cookies, trail-mix, or steaming-hot beverages, made us cringe. Finally, we decided enough was enough. We grabbed our fishing poles early the next morning and went on a mission to find hungry fish who were ready to be eaten. I had a tricky time hopping across a wide boulder field, but Dave helped me out. We spent a couple of hours climbing steeply enough to sweat. The peak leveled off. Our heads punched through the smoke layer's ceiling, and there it was. A bald granite peak, covered in rocks. Aside from the sky's blue color, we appeared to be landing on the moon. Alone, in its center, sat a crystalline blue lake. Well, well, well. How about that? The rumors about water on the moon were true! Terrific because just think. How could the moon possibly be overfished?

Two sets of hungry fingers got right to work threading grasshoppers and *PowerBait* onto wire hooks. It was a lovely morning to relax above the smoke. We felt as if we could have touched the sky. Except, we were too busy baiting and casting to worry about sightseeing. After watching two hooks sink into the water, we started praying for nibbles. We visualized nibbles. We paced back and forth, trolling for nibbles.

No warning came before an easterly gale slammed into the moon and sucked 40 degrees out of its thin air. Shivering uncontrollably, we refused to stop fishing. When our hands froze, we used tube socks for mittens. The rest of that hour became a mental exercise in fending off hunger. Did we give up? Not in your life. Our bodies needed meat. Surrender was impossible. Fortunately, one good-sized trout was feeling ready to experience reincarnation. To this day, my memory of tasting its tender, pink flesh, stuffed with garlic salt and butter, still makes me smile.

Perhaps fish protein was truly all my body needed because the next morning I woke up feeling jazzed and ready to dash up to Honeymoon Lake. At least, I felt ready until I noticed tiny snowflakes dusting my cheeks. How bizarre, I thought, since I was still lying next to Dave, inside our tent. It took a moment to realize the snowflakes were made of his breath and mine, frozen across the tent's inner ceiling, detaching as flakes that fell onto our faces. For Heaven's sakes, that was the last straw.

Dave and I fled back over Piute Pass. Like two balls of fire, we hurried all the way down to where a dusty, brown *Toyota Corolla* sat waiting patiently in the trailhead parking lot. I obsessed the whole time about devouring a *McDonald's Big Mac*, even though I had rarely ever set foot in *McDonald's* and usually just ordered the soggy little French fries.

Back in Los Angeles, a bathroom scale verified that I had lost 10 pounds, during nine days of dividing every meal equally with my 180-pound boyfriend, who lost only 1 pound.

Fast-forward two years. This time, the setting was Kauai's Kalalau trail. No snow. No wind. A backpacker's paradise, according to some college friends who talked me into doing it. The trail crossed a sheer cliff, shaded by tropical fruit trees, with an ocean view made famous by magazine photographers. Everyone in our group immediately recognized who was going to be the slowpoke. Consequently, I had nobody to grab, when I tipped over and fell off the trail's beautiful edge. Fortunately, a tree trunk 30-feet below stopped me like a catcher's mitt. Nothing hurt because my fall had been checked by several intervening tree trunks. The cliff was vertical, but it was easy enough to peel off my backpack, lift it from one tree trunk to the next, and climb up after it. Once I safely reached the trail, I stood up, brushed myself off, and went back to hiking.

Later in the week, I also survived eating peeled, moldy bagels and salami that tasted strange, along with cooked bitter tree fruits that nobody in our group had ever seen before. When starvation set in, once again, I began to crave fish as if my life depended upon it—and, once again, nature provided. This time, a single fish got freakishly trapped inside a high-tide puddle, enabling itself to be caught with a hook and reel which had pulled nothing out of the ocean.

In the end, I finished that tropical adventure smiling. However, I also flew home feeling lukewarm toward the whole sport of backpacking. Perhaps, I would have written it off for good, if future thru-hikers could be easily discouraged, or if someone had sold me a bungalow on Maui.

Another two years passed before I met some friends who enjoyed backpacking less than 10 miles per day. Joining forces with them gave me an incentive to revisit the High Sierra Mountains. Gradually, I learned how to assemble my own camping gear, navigate bare granite and read topographical maps. However, using a compass and snow-camping were still pipe dreams when I met my future thru-hiking partner, in 1996.

Chapter 2

Becoming

(Pacific Crest Trail Flashbacks)

I dream of one day hiking north to south until you could no longer tell from the look in my eye whether I was still tame...

— Douglas Chadwick, Montana wildlife biologist

When Jeffrey and I first met, nobody would ever have expected us to become thru-hikers.

Jeffrey had grown up in rural Illinois, roaming freely through open farmland and sleeping alone in a backyard tent. After graduating from college and moving to Boston, he had car-camped with a shaman who taught him how to stalk and invisibly observe wild animals. He could legitimately have called himself an outdoorsman, but he never wore a backpack until we started dating.

Jeffrey's focus during 1996 was working at a California hypnotherapy clinic, helping stressed-out office workers stop smoking and lose weight. His long-term goal was to open his own private practice, using techniques derived from Neurolinguistic Programming, Hawaiian Huna Psychology, Pre-Mayan Shamanism, Reiki, and Transcendental Meditation. Essentially, Jeffrey had spent 34 years studying to become an urban monk. Therefore, it put a wrench in his plans to land a girlfriend and move into her house.

Our common interests included growing vegetables, cooking vegetarian meals, and practicing yoga. I windsurfed most afternoons, which reinforced Jeffrey's desire to try surfing. Also well-matched were his B.S. degree in botany with my B.S. in atmospheric sciences, and his former career in event photography with my career in freelance videography. Added together, all these similarities gave us a lot to talk about over dinner, and that was before we ever went thru-hiking.

The only subject that sometimes divided us was trying to discuss metaphysics. I felt amused by Jeffrey's belief that angels and animal spirits actively guarded human beings. It was fun to probe him for details since I had once seen my aura and therefore believed in more than flesh and gravity. However, Jeffrey felt antagonized by my logic-based questions. He always gave me intuitive answers, as if he could not understand what I was asking. Consequently, our discussions usually came out sounding like court trials with only one lawyer.

The good news was that out in nature, the two of us got along like peanut butter and honey. Our first weeklong trip into California's High Sierra Mountains began with me purchasing all the necessary maps and creating our daily schedules. Once the trip started, I cooked every meal. Jeffrey's jobs included setting up tidy camps and carrying more than his fair share of heavy food and water. This division of labor seemed to suit our respective superpowers, not to mention, our respective shortcomings. For instance, whereas I excelled at planning and multi-tasking, Jeffrey's first attempt to organize a surprise party had ended with him forgetting the date and double-booking himself at the last minute. Conversely, his excellence at lifting, balancing, and recognizing sneaker prints offset my weaknesses in all three areas.

As a team, Jeffrey and I happily joked about me being our Brains and him being our Pack Mule. These roles championed our evolution from taking weeklong High Sierra trips to summiting California's star attraction, Mount Whitney. The latter trip began with rain and more rain. We spent a whole day trapped inside our soggy tent, listening to *Volkswagen*-sized boulders cartwheel down the precipice we were waiting to climb. Sunrise dished up a window between rains, so we hit the trail at full speed and climbed as fast as our lungs would allow.

From atop the Continental United States' highest summit, we gained a 360-degree view of swirling gray clouds. Mercifully, Heaven's curtains swung open for a moment, giving us a peek at the glory we were missing.

Jeffrey wasted no time. Without making small talk, he fished a flattened wildflower out of his pocket and asked me to marry him.

I had not been expecting him to pop the question. In addition to feeling shocked, I wondered what my mouth was going to say. Incredibly, it said, "Yes!"

Apparently, Mother Nature approved, because the clouds responded by bursting apart. In every direction, we saw mountains upon mountains swaggering out to overcast horizons.

Jeffrey curled his arms around me and together we spun around in a slow circle, soaking in everything. That reverie lasted about five minutes before snow flurries and lightning sent us fleeing downhill, back to our soggy tent.

On paper, we returned home bright-eyed and promised, but that was all. Neither of us felt in any hurry to get married. At 41 years old, Jeffrey's top priority was to establish himself professionally as a private hypnotherapist. Likewise, at 33 years old, I just wanted to windsurf between video jobs. Certainly, neither of us had thru-hiking in mind, one sunny day, when we randomly took a walk through our city's outdoor mall.

* * *

Was it a coincidence? Or destiny? Either way, Jeffrey and I had no agenda when we strolled into our town's little hole-in-the-wall mountaineering store.

The Pacific Crest Trail Hiker's Handbook was humbly resting on a short shelf of books. I only noticed it because the word "Pacific" caught my eye. Jeffrey, on the other hand, already knew about the Pacific Crest Trail. Several years ago, while taking a long bus ride through Belgium and Holland, he had read a magazine article about the PCT. In fact, reading about thru-hiking had inspired him to scribble, "Hike the PCT," on a list of things he wanted to do during his lifetime. Ever since then, Jeffrey's pipe-dream had been gathering dust. Therefore, simply laying eyes upon *The Pacific Crest Trail Hiker's Handbook* made his heart leap.

Author Ray Jardine used simple language to describe how ultra-lightweight backpackers could travel extremely fast, by substituting intelligence and mobility for carrying all-weather camping gear. Jardine claimed that even novice backpackers could hike the entire 2,600-mile Pacific Crest Trail in 3-5 months if they followed his detailed pacing guidelines.

When I noticed Jeffrey's eyes sparkling, I joked, "Do you think we should hike the PCT next year?"

He would have enjoyed saying yes, if not for the sad truth. Working at a hypnotherapy clinic was failing to reduce his credit card debt. He did not keep any money under the mattress, or bury it in our backyard, so my question just made him laugh and change the subject.

Well, of course, shortly after buying a fixer-upper house, I was in the same boat.

Neither of us could afford a half-year vacation. That discussion should have ended right in the bookstore. And it would have, if not for Ray Jardine's seeds landing upon fertile ground. Somehow, *The Pacific Crest Trail Hiker's Handbook* reached into our wallets and left the store with us. Maybe we carried it home. Maybe it sprouted legs. Or flew through the air? Who knows? But once it landed inside our house, Jardine's seeds began to sprout.

Reading the book in cracks of time inspired Jeffrey to form a crazy notion. What if prolonged immersion in the wilderness could enhance his spiritual practices? Might he become a better hypnotherapist? Could such self-betterment help him pay off his credit card faster? Would such payment make thru-hiking a responsible career move? Seriously, and yes. Jeffrey actually thought we were going to begin each morning on the PCT doing yoga stretches at sunrise, and end each evening meditating in the sun's setting light.

I knew all along that thru-hiking was going to be exhausting. I just reasoned it might be worth getting to watch the weather all day long and hopefully feel a bit wild.

So, in a nutshell, that is how two financially challenged dreamers decided to save money, see fewer movies, and eat out less often while spending 5-months preparing for a 5-month hike.

* * *

It was easy to set our sights on thru-hiking, but gathering all the necessities turned into another story.

For one thing, Ray Jardine's philosophy diverged from athletic shoe fashions during 1999. Few companies were selling Gore-Tex-free fabric boots. Among them, only a couple catered to hikers with my skinny feet and Jeffrey's crimp-toed, mismatched, pontoon feet. Therefore, countless clerks watched the two of us leave empty handed, before we finally discovered the *Hi-Tec ATR Mids*—miracle of miracles—which only weighed 10-oz. and somehow fit both of us!

During the same year, Jeffrey and I also had trouble finding suitable lightweight backpacks. Most styles with external frames (skeleton on the outside) could hold a week's worth of food and all-season gear, but their hip-straps were positioned too low for swift walking. On the other hand, most frameless styles (skeleton on the inside) were just glorified tote bags, barely able to hold a tarp, jacket, and three days' worth of food. Jeffrey and I wanted to carry a few "luxuries," such as a free-standing tent, gas cooking stove, and winter-weight jackets. So, despite worshipping the "Ray Way," we decided not to aim for cult status. Instead, I ordered a well-padded frameless backpack from a garage manufacturer, and Jeffrey refurbished his big honking framer, whose bottomless capacity was going to save our hides.

After shopping with gusto, we got our gear dialed in, but what about food? Being gardeners and cooks, both Jeffrey and I wanted to prepare homemade meals for the trail. Or course, we knew it could take a long time to chop, puree, dehydrate, and vacuum-seal 450 entrees, plus 250 trail snacks. We were prepared to invest some elbow grease, but Egad! We did not expect the food preparations to keep us in our kitchen for three solid months.

Some tasks were simple. For instance, flipping half-dry banana slices and rolling up fruit leather could have been done by any monkey. It was more challenging to design delicious, high-nutrient dinners that could stay fresh for 6-months in storage. But even that chore would have been straightforward, if not for a certain few ingredients requiring exhaustive research, money for repairs, rhinoceros skin, and borderline insanity.

One problematic ingredient was brick cheddar cheese. Step one of attempting to dry 28-pounds' worth was leaning over a chopping block, crumbling the cheese with our fingers. Step two involved spreading all the crumbles onto plastic-mesh dehydrator trays. Once I got the machine plugged in, I left our kitchen feeling pretty buffed. Nothing seemed worrisome until a few hours later when yellow slime started pooling underneath the dehydrator. I conducted a short search and found more slime leaking through the dehydrator's motor lid, onto its heating coils. The result was a kitchen full of white smoke, as in, drop everything fast and call 911. I kept my cool and just unplugged the motor. It did not take long to scrub the heating coils. Voila! No more smoke. That was easy, right?

Except, there was still one problem. Standing idle during my scrubbing process had given 28-pounds' worth of half-melted cheese-crumbles time to harden into rubbery stalactites. Unfortunately, the stalactites had glued themselves onto and through my dehydrator's fragile mesh trays and micro-mesh screens. Removing the hardened rubber required a butterknife, followed by vigorous scrubbing with a sponge, my fingernails, and lots of twirled Kleenexes. All this rigamarole felt like a nightmare, but once the rescued cheese was back on scrubbed trays, everything seemed hunky-dory, until the same smoking mess repeated itself all over again. Because who could have known that drying halfway did not mean the cheese had lost all its grease?

Now, this is where borderline insanity took hold.

After realizing my plastic dehydrator could not effectively dry cheese, I decided to try using Teflon cookie sheets, stacked in my oven, at 200-degrees. Success seemed certain, until the crumbles I was drying suddenly changed color. By the time I yanked them out, ugh! The spoils looked like blood clots, not edible food.

It was depressing to have to purchase more brick *Tilamook* on a tight budget. Fortunately, my enthusiasm got rekindled by coming up with another bright idea. Windowscreen stapled onto a wooden frame, set over top of Teflon cookie sheets, might let the crumbled cheese drain better while drying in my mom's cooler 175-degree oven. Lo and behold, the new cheese stayed orange. Twelve cups of yellow slime oozed into the cookie sheets. Never mind trying to unsee 12-cups of cheese grease. My windowscreen contraption was a resounding success! Now, I felt ready to tackle tofu jerky.

One foodie magazine advised freezing brick tofu before thawing it on a slanted cutting board, to render out water for better marinade absorption. Unfortunately, the article's author neglected to warn dingbats about removing the tofu's packaging before freezing. After it was too late, I just unwrapped my thawed tofu, smashed it beneath a skillet full of books, and decided to accept the watery results.

The next steps were easy. Chopping the thawed tofu into bite-sized cubes. Applying teriyaki sauce. Any toddler could have spread marinated tofu across plastic mesh trays. Nothing appeared to drip when I plugged in the dehydrator. Everything seemed spiffy until smoke came pouring back into my kitchen. What in *Mori-Nu's* name? Was the motor burning? Did I need to call the fire department? Grabbing a hot pad, I cautiously unstacked all the plastic trays. Down underneath, I found the problem. While scrubbing off cheese grease, Jeffrey had accidentally splashed dish-soap onto the motor's heating coils. Okay, fine. I could just keep the motor running until the soap burned off. That solution got rid of the smoke, but then, something worse happened. Immediately after replacing the motor's lid, I saw its whole plastic surface start to bubble like hot pudding! Shock set in, before I yanked out the plug, opened every window, and gingerly lifted the bubbling plastic. Ah-HA! Well, of course. Jeffrey's heavy-handed cleaning job had also amputated some of the lid's stubby legs. Consequently, it had collapsed onto a few heating coils.

Fine, whatever. I fashioned a new leg out of smooshed aluminum foil. Did that fix the problem? Well, yes and no. Having cooled off, the lid looked fine, but now my dehydrator refused to turn on. What in asterisk-ampersand-number-symbol's name? Had overheating blown the motor's only fuse? Or had it simply died from feeling what I was feeling? Regardless, seeing a good machine die pushed me over the edge. I wanted to throw that freaking hunk of plastic good-for-nothing piece of garbage into the trash, call off our PCT hike, repurpose the money I had been saving, and just go on a long windsurfing vacation. Fresh air. Cool water. Salt on my tongue. No dehydration required. But, wasn't I being silly? Keep breathing, Sunshine. Slow, deep breaths.

After sobering up, I telephoned a neighbor to ask if I could borrow her dehydrator. She promised to bring it right over, as soon as she could find it. Of course, while waiting, I realized how to keep my drying process humming along. I could spread my rescued ("smoked") tofu back onto the dehydrator's plastic mesh trays and slip them into my 200-degree oven. Not being a ditz, of course, I stationed protective wooden cutting boards underneath the trays. That was smart thinking, but I should have done a beta test before filling the oven and going about my business. The next thing I knew, an odor of burning teriyaki sauce signaled the plastic trays were starting to warp, and there went another $60.

Sigh. Well, looking on the bright side, at least, having made every possible mistake meant I was done with that phase, right? Except, my neighbor's search took so long that it gave me time to cook up another bright idea. Could baking my salvaged ("smoked") tofu give it a nice roasted "jerky" flavor prior to dehydration? A short baking session at 200-degrees said, yes! My rescued tofu came out tasting yummy. Who could have guessed it would stick to Teflon like *Krazy Glue* sticks to paper? How could anyone imagine a soft, slippery substance like tofu ripping entire slabs of Teflon off my brand new cookie sheets?

If thru-hikers were quitters, that 48-hour day would have driven me to buy some expensive store-bought jerky. Instead, sheer willpower enabled me to smile when my neighbor's dehydrator finally arrived. And what do you know? Round Three of the Tofu Jerky Trials tasted fabulous until it turned chartreuse green after two months in storage. (Too bad thru-hikers don't carry pillows for screaming.)

One last story from my PCT test kitchen begins with *The Pacific Crest Trail Hiker's Handbook.* If Ray Jardine's description of his wife powdering dehydrated tomato paste was not a joke, then she probably used a *Vitamix*. Regardless, I decided to one-up the Queen of Powdering by pre-freezing my tomato leather for added stiffness. Success seemed imminent until the leather I had frozen proved tougher than my blender. Ditto for itty-bitty tidbits of dehydrated carrots, celery, and roasted garlic. My blender's sharp steel blades, which could nip off fingertips without the motor running, were no match for dried vegetables, frozen or room-temp. In fact, its plastic gear teeth disintegrated, instead of the vegetables. As a result, I needed to write, "new blender" on my shopping list that already said, "new cookie sheets." That was a crying shame, but I had more tools.

A short trip back to the freezer prepared my obstinate tomato leather to meet its match. This time, I pressed it into the jaws of a coffee grinder that could powder rock-hard beans. Ha-ha, take THAT, I thought. Until, Crap! Jeffrey almost sobbed when he saw the wreckage. I don't know why, since drinking coffee just gave me the jitters. Well anyway, Mister Caffeine Junkie could fret if he liked, but I was not going to miss that little noisemaker.

Next on my hit-list was an $80 hand grinder, designed for

pulverizing dried wheat and corn. Who could have guessed dried vegetables might be tougher than dried wheat and corn?

When Jeffrey walked into the kitchen, I told him, "People should really appreciate everything that goes into Top Ramen flavor packets."

Fortunately, the old saying "all's well that ends well" held true under pressure. My new $80 Osterizer boasted strong metal gears, capable of decimating every vegetable product that had broken my hand grinder and Jeffrey's coffee grinder. Better yet, it produced spaghetti sauce that tasted finger-licking good, and that was not all.

Out on the trail, each delicious meal Jeffrey and I had dried from scratch was going to remind us, time and time again, never to give up. Press on, regardless. Invite success by refusing to fail.

* * *

The final stage of assembling adequate gear for the PCT was dividing hundreds of meals and snacks, clothes for different seasons, refills of blister tape, mailable gas canisters, sectional maps, and umpteen other necessities into 23 addressed cardboard boxes. Each box contained specific instructions for when my dad should ship them to 23 post offices and wilderness resorts along the trail. By the time Jeffrey and I got all the boxes ready, only an asteroid could have prevented us from hiking the entire PCT. Or, perhaps we could have been stopped by our bus breaking down 2-blocks from the bus station, but not to worry. That little hiccup got fixed in two hours and then we were underway. Which means, the trip became real.

America's official *Pacific Crest Trail Association* expected roughly 100 thru-hikers to try finishing the entire PCT during 1999. Most of those hundred would travel northbound, following one of Ray Jardine's pacing schedules, which meant the majority would leave California's Mexican border during the first week of May.

Jeffrey and I were intentionally starting a week later. Therefore, we got to see most of that year's entries into the northbound trail register. A count of roughly 250 names made us feel lucky to have missed the parade. Nevertheless, it was still fun feeling like part of one big push, including another 300 thru-hikers aiming to complete America's Appalachian Trail, and 10-20 more braving the unfinished Continental Divide Trail.

Jeffrey and I had packed heavier camping gear than most ultralight backpackers carried. We should have spent more time learning how to use our compass. We should have learned how to snow camp before scaling California's Sierra Mountains during June, and before approaching Canada during October. If should-haves could have deterred us, we would never have succeeded in drying cheddar cheese or tofu jerky, which explains how we got right down to leaving the Mexican border.

Ray Jardine's handbook warned northbound hikers to avoid confrontations with starving Mexican immigrants. Jeffrey and I respected Ray's warning, and we tried to hurry, but alas. Trouble struck within the first 20-minutes. I was the heel who developed crippling back spasms and shoulder pains. The problem was my custom backpack sitting too low and crookedly on my hips. Back in those days, thru-hikers could not just whip out a cell phone and call Uber. The best relief we could manage was to transfer a few items from my backpack and into Jeffrey's, and press on regardless.

The next several weeks served as a critical training period. Jeffrey and I learned by trial-and-error how to relieve strain on various body parts. Essentially, the drill consisted of tightening our hip-belts until they crushed our butts, in turns with loosening our hip-belts enough to trade butt-crushing for shoulder-crushing, which worked nicely until the pain from both ends made us take a break and start over.

Hiking as such allowed me to speed through 105-degree heat in southern California's Great Mojave Desert. Everything seemed fixed in terms of ergonomics, until a cheap orthotic insert attacked my right arch.

Jeffrey was a real trooper, for willingly absorbing a few more items into his backpack, but we still finished Week-6 needing some deep rest.

It was traditional for thru-hikers to camp on the Big Bear fire station's lawn, before fetching their next resupplies and heading back to the trail. Sure enough, Jeffrey and I found several skinny, dusty, sneaker-wearing, ice-cream-guzzling transients letting their toes breathe on the indicated lawn.

I used a pair of borrowed scissors to chop my backpack's straps down to a 13" torso length. It took willpower to refasten them with crude hand-stitches because, boy, did that hurt my tender fingie-wingies. It was worth the pain, though, being able to raise my backpack's center of gravity.

One day's rest could hardly remedy Mojave-grade fatigue, but it would have to do. The next morning, Jeffrey and I trudged back to the PCT, feeling more determined than ever to reach Canada.

Atop California's High Sierras, Jeffrey played the hero by hauling my backpack over numerous log bridges that I could only cross on my tummy. Once, he even piggybacked me through an ice-cold river while I wore my backpack, so I could avoid wasting time changing blister bandages.

Some of the stormy heights we crossed required hiking on snow from dawn to dusk. Jeffrey's feet handled the cold well, but mine often felt stabbed by icy knives. Occasionally, I begged Jeffrey to press my bare feet against his bare tummy, and he lifted his shirt every time. Seriously, not only that but also, he tolerated hearing me cuss for pain relief until my feet stopped crying and his tummy cooled off.

If this description creates an impression that my partner was a saint, however, do not be fooled. Hour after hour, day after day, month after month, I put up with hearing Mister Picky Pants complain about heat, fatigue, thirst, toe-blisters, feeling tiny pebbles roll around inside his shoes, getting attacked by mosquitoes, and suspecting I had challenged his esoteric beliefs.

I stayed cool as a cucumber, no matter what he dished out. I told myself I could withstand anything until he really grew nasty in central Oregon. That was the last straw. Like it or not,

I needed to buckle down and fix my partner's attitude. Once I started analyzing what set him off, some of our circular arguments reached a point where, if a helicopter had dropped in to save us, we might never have spoken to each other again. Nevertheless, neither of us wanted to quit the PCT and go home. We both recognized it was just duress making us fight. Despite feeling angry, we were still in love.

Some days it helped to encounter other thru-hikers whose companionship broke us out of emotional gridlock. Two such saviors were Kevin and Colleen, a romantic couple who accompanied us through parts of California's Southern Sierra Mountains. We had the privilege of being with them, one sunny day in June when events unfolded that deserve a flashback.

The afternoon's weather was perfect for picnicking, swimming, or doing almost anything other than facing death. As a group of four, we all got surprised by a 30-foot snow-patch blocking the highest switchback beneath Mather Pass. Above and below the snow stood 400-feet of scree-covered mountainside, almost steep enough to be called a cliff. There was no obvious way to detour above or below the snow. Jeffrey and I needed time to assess the situation, but Kevin sized it up quickly and volunteered to go first. Daylong shade had been keeping the snow frozen. Fortunately, Kevin's boots sank in deep enough to provide secure footholds. None of us felt concerned about his safety until his trekking poles began stabbing wildly around his feet. Fear took hold when he realized the snow's softest section could not support his weight.

"Don't follow me," Kevin hollered over his shoulder. "I'm coming back."

That warning came just in time. We had all been preparing to march onto the snow, but instead, we held our breath, while Kevin carefully backstepped into the same boot holes he had made going forward. When he finally returned to Colleen's arms, she had to fight back tears of relief.

Retreating as a group, we all descended about 50-feet, around and back down to the next lowest switchback. From there, we started traversing sideways, searching for a line of ascent that might allow us to alight safely beyond the snow. The pitch we chose looked manageable but it was extremely steep, not to mention, crusted with loose granite scree.

I hung back, knowing I was the weak link.

My companions pooled their knowledge and came up deciding the route would be safe. We just needed to climb faster than our feet could slip.

Kevin and Colleen shared Jeffrey's and my determination to hike every last mile of the PCT. Like us, they had spent the previous winter drying five months' worth of food and dreaming about success. As a result, they shared our concerns about not wasting daylight and hurrying up to the summit. There had to be a splendid view waiting on Mather Pass. All of us could not wait to get up there.

Since Kevin and Colleen were experienced mountaineers, they volunteered to climb the scree first. Together, they scrambled straight uphill, reaching the upper switchback within a few minutes.

Jeffrey and I hesitated 50-feet below. Both of us knew I could never copy the same move until I got over feeling afraid. If there had been witnesses, some might have told Kevin and Colleen to go on ahead and let us catch up. Perhaps, we could have waited for the evening's cooler temperatures to firm up the snow. That way, we could have taken the upper trail, instead of climbing anything scary. Another option would have been for Jeffrey to complete the steep shortcut twice, once wearing his backpack and once wearing mine, while I climbed beside him on the second trip. Alternatively, he and I could have tied ourselves together with a food-hanging rope, to give me a false sense of security. A more cautious strategy would have been retreating into an extremely long detour, that would require us to severely ration our meals. Lastly, we could have followed Ray Jardine's advice to hitchhike out to the nearest town, check into a motel, and outwait the danger (thereby, substituting intelligence and mobility for carrying gear to address all emergencies). Altogether, this list makes clear that Jeffrey and I did not need to do anything rash. Kevin and Colleen were not going to unfriend us for failing to keep up. Consequently, the choice Jeffrey and I made serves to demonstrate how thru-hiking was beginning to affect our judgment.

Without warning, I shoved my trekking poles into Jeffrey's hands. I never wondered what he was going to do with an extra pair of poles to carry. I just figured my only chance to join Kevin and Colleen would rest upon climbing faster than vertigo could stop me.

Jeffrey struggled to grasp both sets of poles.

I lunged upward, onto the slippery scree. With one hand clutching my ice-axe, I used my free hand to steady my balance. It did not take long to realize the slope was steeper than I had thought. Nevertheless, I still felt in control. Nothing went wrong until I touched some bare granite, too slick to grasp. Freezing in confusion, I stared through a cloud of floating rock dust. My unblinking eyes began to sting. Clawing through the scree gave me no support. Nothing grabbed my kicking shoes. Nausea surged through my stomach in waves. How could I resist thinking about vertigo? My arms and legs began to feel rigid. Suddenly, my brain realized where I was and the void below turned into a vacuum. Climbing higher was out of the question. My brain simply would not allow it. Nor could I retreat because, if I glanced downward, I was going to faint.

"Help," I whimpered.

From somewhere far below, a faint voice hollered, "Keep going, Sunshine. You're halfway there."

Jeffrey's voice sounded incredibly distant. I could not estimate my height without glancing downhill. Last I could remember, Kevin and Colleen had been seated on a switchback straight overhead. They were probably wondering why I had stopped. My top-heavy backpack, holding a week's worth of food and camping gear, was tugging me backward. Dizziness began to rattle my eyeballs. My head seemed to float. I could not afford to think about falling. The scree was my friend, soft and supportive. I just needed to trust my friend until Jeffrey came up and saved me. Because, of course, he WAS going to save me. He always saved me. At least, he needed to save me now, because that was our only choice.

I wished I could take some weight off my kidneys, but leaning forward was out of the question, because staying upright was giving my backpack leverage against the granite. Oh, for crying's sake. When was this awful moment going to end? I took stock of my vital signs. Nausea. Scalp tingling. Fingers going numb. Eyeballs straining to roll upwards and backward. Eyelids drooping. Whole body weakening. Gravity increasing by the minute.

"Help," I repeated. "Please...I'm stuck."

"Just keep moving," Jeffrey's voice repeated. "Don't think about anything else, Sunshine. Just keep climbing. You'll get there soon."

"It's too LATE for positive thinking," I shouted. "If you don't come NOW, I'm going to FAINT."

Rivers of electricity tickled my scalp. I made some quick calculations. What might happen if I fainted and let go of the mountain? Could Jeffrey catch my falling body on the way down? Would both of us tumble together, from switchback to switchback, like the boulders we had seen cartwheeling down Mount Whitney? How would it feel to die? I knew I should not entertain such thoughts, but it was hard not to wonder. Hopefully, I would get knocked unconscious before hitting bottom because otherwise, ouch. Would fainting prevent me from feeling any pain? No, I decided, none of that could happen because I was not going to fall. Nor, was I going to faint, either. But what if crying weakened my grip? Hot, salty tears welled up, in my eyes.

"I'm sorry, Jeffrey. I blew it. I shouldn't be up here, but now that I am, PLEASE help me. I don't know what to do."

Cold sweat broke through my skin. Why was he not climbing up to help me? All I could hear was my own, stiff breathing. Was I hyperventilating? Trying to breathe slower, I realized something awful. Jeffrey had no idea that I was in real danger. He intended to stay down on the lower switchback and just coach me, for however long it might take until I finished the climb. He was not going to move before he saw me slipping, by which time it would be too late! I could scarcely hold on for another second. How could I convince him I was helpless?

From Jeffrey's vantage point 20-feet below, indeed, he thought I could stay up there for however long might be needed to recover. He never imagined that my arms were going numb. He failed to wonder if I was seeing stars. He only saw my shoulders hunched forward into a resting pose that looked fairly comfortable. He could not relate to what I was experiencing because his own body possessed the agility and balance of a cat. Literally, I had once seen him leap from our house's roof onto the crown of a 4x4" fencepost. He regarded the fear of heights to be just a trick of one's mind. He thought such fear could be cured with positive thinking, so he kept trying to embolden me with cheerful affirmations.

Kevin and Colleen knew I needed help. They just could not safely descend from where they were sitting. Besides, it seemed more sensible for my fiancé, who was closer, to take the initiative. Therefore, they stayed seated on the upper switchback, saying nothing, to avoid worsening my panic.

When Jeffrey finally realized I was never going to move, I had survived so many stages of fright that my brain and body were retreating into shock.

I could hardly believe it when I finally heard him say, "You can stop worrying now, Sunshine. I'm right behind you."

I wanted to let go of the mountain and collapse into his arms. However, I could not even afford to loosen my grip, let alone glance in his direction.

He arrived wearing his 70-pound backpack, with his trekking poles and mine all clenched together in one meaty hand, leaving his other hand free to assist with climbing. The reason he had brought up everything was that he only intended to perform the climb once. After dissolving my fear with optimistic suggestions, he figured I was going to finish the climb by myself.

His nearness warmed my legs like a gentle fire.

"It's okay now," he murmured. "GO! You're already halfway up. Just repeat what you've done and you'll get there in no time."

Suddenly, the warmth he had brought disappeared. Was he dropping downhill to give me more space?

"Don't leave!" I shrieked, "If you leave, I'll faint. You have to go up with me."

"I know," he murmured. "Just start climbing, Sunshine. I promise to stay right behind you. You're going to reach the top before you know it."

Convincing or not, his sales pitch was attractive. If only I had not been wearing a heavy backpack or clutching a bulky ice-axe. Darned, useless tool, it was getting in the way. I needed both hands free, to pull my weight.

"If only I could lose this backpack," I muttered. "If only I didn't have to hold this stupid ice-axe."

Cautiously, I raised my empty hand and fingered the uphill granite. It felt slick and dusty. Stabbing my fingers back into the scree, I decided that if Jeffrey could not save me, then, so be it. Fate would have to teach us a hard lesson.

Fortunately, Jeffrey finally realized his approach was never going to work. Playing along with my suggestion, he softly coaxed me to lift one arm, so he could remove my backpack and slip it onto his free arm. No doubt, his balance must have faltered when I thrust my ice-axe into his other hand, which had already been clenching four trekking poles, while his other arm carried my backpack like a purse.

Once I realized I was free to start climbing, I dug both hands into the scree and just enjoyed being alive for another moment.

Behind me, Jeffrey anchored his footing better, in hopes that I would make the next move. He was giving me one last chance to save myself.

I was going to need to finish the climb alone.

A few steady breaths helped me rise to the occasion. Hands over feet, I tore myself away from his warmth and began climbing. Immediately, I felt unprotected. My hands and feet raced one another. Unconscious. Unstoppable. Soon, Kevin's and Colleen's shoes popped into sight. That was enough. No need to look higher. Their perch looked narrow but safe. I crawled up beside them and had a good cry in Colleen's arms.

Meantime, Jeffrey continued struggling up the scree. One of his arms felt like it was carrying five sacks of potatoes. The other seemed to be choking a half-dozen loose golf clubs. He grunted with exhaustion, while flopping up next to our legs, and unloaded his luggage with a triumphant thud.

Just after we realized everyone was safe, another thru-hiker came bounding along the lower switchback. Without appearing to notice our group, his eyes located the soft snow Kevin had tried to cross. From there, he ran his eyes sideways and downward. Only one glance was needed for him to choose the same line of ascent we had all finished. Like a graceful ogre, he lunged straight upward, marching foot-over foot with arms dangling by his sides as if safety was not an issue. Everything about him spelled grassroots "thru-hiker." From his sun-fried skin and tree trunk legs to the bandanna handkerchief knotted around his shaggy blond hair, and frayed edges showing where scissors had chopped off his shirt sleeves, it appeared he had been "out" for quite a long time.

Once drawing near enough to notice me crying, thru-hiker "Sly" gave our group a polite nod and hurried on by. He was probably thinking to himself, Foolish girl, freaking out in a place where you don't belong.

Atop Mather Pass, we found him seated alone, smoking a hand-rolled cigarette. With knees spread apart and chin tilted toward the sun, he appeared to be enjoying a really fine experience.

There was nothing to be heard from atop the summit, besides our own shoes scuffling dry dirt. Even two crows flapping overhead seemed silenced by the mountain's tremendous sky. We gazed northward, from 12,100-feet, and saw a vertical granite fin curling halfway around Palisade Lake. The water's surface fractured miles of the sky into bluish-silver shimmers. One turquoise iceberg, floating near the lake's edge, seemed bent on befriending a lonely cluster of pine trees, loosely surrounded by patches of old snow.

Altogether, the splendor we found atop Mather Pass seemed

worth every hassle it had taken to get up there. In fact, I even wondered if overcoming fear should be as much a part of thru-hiking as enjoying pretty sunsets and bathing in ice-cold streams. Regardless, one thing was certain. Getting vertigo was no fun. I never wanted to feel dizzy in another steep, high place, ever again. But, of course, there was more steep terrain coming up ahead. For instance, a couple of weeks later, I was going to feel dizzy while crossing an icy snowfield above a half-frozen lake, with lightning striking close enough to make the snow flash yellow between my sneakers. That crazy feat was going to end with a downpour chasing Jeffrey and me into our tent during midday, only to have two other thru-hikers come along laughing that we could have bypassed the snowfield in the first place!

Again, in Northern Washington, we were going to encounter icy snow blocking steep mountain trails. Some slippery moments were going to scare us. None were going to kill us. Therefore, each challenge would progressively make us stronger, according to Nietzschean philosophy.

At the end of five months, we were going to reach Canada precisely on the date we had planned five months earlier, and board our homebound train without a hitch. We were going to achieve success without ever having "yellow-blazed" (skipped a few miles of the trail on wheels), or "slack-packed" (let someone drive our backpacks forward).

Some bad news was eventually going to reach us, through the thru-hiker grapevine, about Kevin spraining an ankle one week north of Mather Pass. He and Colleen were going to be sent home early, just like mountain-man Sly, who would allegedly run out of money farther up the trail and go home to paint houses, in hopes of finishing the PCT some other year. Many other 1999 northbounders were going to almost complete the entire 2,600-mile trail, only to get foiled 10-20 miles short of the finish line, by October's first big blizzard.

Words cannot explain what kind of shock Jeffrey and I felt upon learning that most of our speedier and savvier friends had never quite reached Canada. The comparison seemed incredible. Going into our last week on the PCT, we wondered how we could be faring better than many superior backpackers? The answer, of course, was simple—thanks to better timing. We had left Mexico one week later than almost everyone else. Therefore, we ended up approaching Canada 1-week after the big storm happened. As a result, we got to follow our friends' footprints through the snow, rather than cutting fresh tracks in freezing conditions, with poor visibility.

It was a heady moment when Jeffrey and I successfully tagged the Canadian border monument and raced to safety. Even we, barely made it to the finish line, during a short window between back-to-back blizzards, with snowflakes literally nipping at our heels. The victory we achieved sent us home forevermore believing in "Trail Magic."

In fact, our whole PCT experience had been extraordinary. We had seen fantastic things, met interesting people, lived to tell the tale, and that was enough. Our hometown friends and dog were glad to have us back. Our hearts felt satisfied. We were PCT-finishers. We had earned our badges. It was time to move on and do something else.

During the coming year, whenever somebody questioned us about thru-hiking, we agreed with Ray Jardine that achieving continuity made all the difference. Starting at Point A and ending at Point Z were just ways to earn bragging rights. Our strongest takeaway from 1999 had been discovering what really made thru-hiking satisfying. It was all about experiencing an entire range of mountains in one connected line. No gaps. No intermissions. One continuous dream.

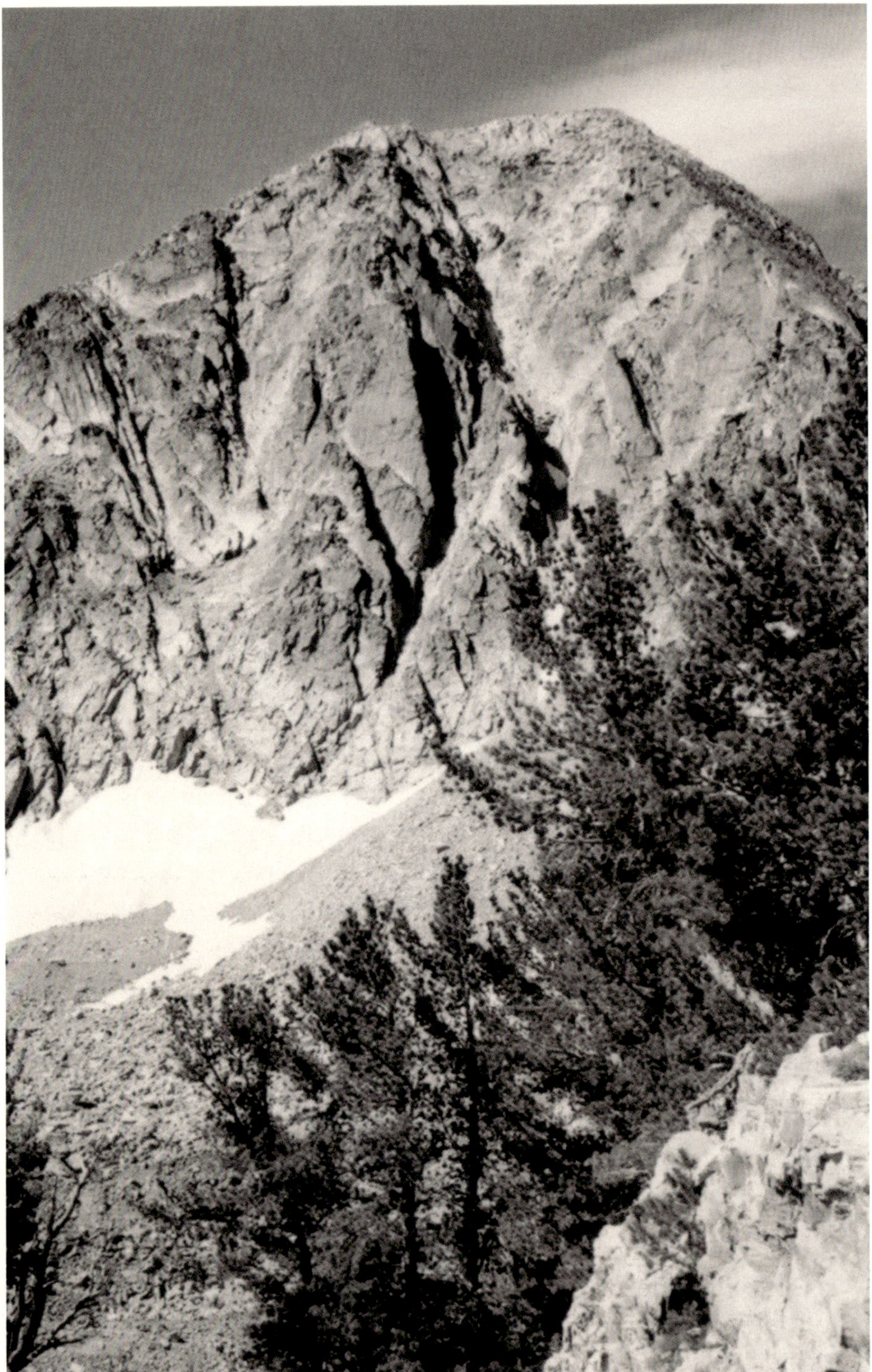

Chapter 3

Decision

Dreams come a size too big so that we can grow into them.

— *Josie Bisset*

    Six months after finishing the Pacific Crest Trail, Jeffrey and I spent an afternoon floating in my parents' backyard swimming pool. Its sky-blue water was heated to a tropical 90 degrees, warmed all around by peach-colored concrete, and cooled by a sea breeze coming off the Pacific Ocean. Palm trees were swaying. Lemon trees were fruiting. Nothing could have been farther from our minds than climbing cold, steep mountains. Therefore, it made no sense for a strange question to pop out of my mouth.

"Are we planning to go on any more thru-hikes?"

Jeffrey naturally assumed I was joking. His private hypnotherapy practice had been taking off like a rock. Our vegetable garden was going great guns but we could not thru-hike on vegetables alone. I had some decent videography jobs happening, but freelancing was barely paying my share of the bills. Furthermore, one of my jobs was a TV show threatening to go off the air.

Whenever Jeffrey and I talked about dining in restaurants and going out to see movies, nowadays it was always in the past tense. Neither of us could imagine taking another half-year vacation any time soon, and maybe not ever.

This was the reality we shared in the backs of our minds, but Jeffrey's assumption about me joking actually had nothing to do with finances. He just associated the word "thru-hiking" with all manner of personal discomforts, including mosquito bites, chronic exhaustion, shoulder strap pains, oppressive heat, nagging thirst, intense hunger, and hearing me cuss whenever my feet froze halfway across a snow-covered mountain. If Jeffrey had returned home from the PCT nursing any memories that did not involve pain, he kept all those gems to himself, while rehashing his worst miseries to anyone who asked. Not that people even needed to ask either. They could see for themselves that his cheeks still looked hollow, after spending a half-year eating homecooked meals.

My own hangover was mild by comparison. Sure, I still had an occasional flashback involving vertigo. Of course, I still cringed whenever my cerebrum dredged up some of our worst arguments on the trail. Fortunately, though, time was doing its job as a healer. Hot showers, easy access to ice cream, and nights spent sleeping on a soft futon mattress were all helping me cope with having returned to city life. In fact, the only times I ever considered tackling another Long Trail were when my brain chanced to think, *What if we just stay home from now on?*

Working as a freelance videographer was exciting. I enjoyed flexing my artistic imagination. Recording live music was always a thrill. There were downsides, though. In particular, I disliked spending long hours stuck inside dark conference rooms and television studios. Cave-dwelling always made me miss the Pacific Crest Trail's fresh air, starry skies, and ever-changing weather. Sometimes, I regretted never having felt "wild" enough to belong in the wilderness. Perhaps, despite having come home feeling satisfied, some little corner of my psyche still felt incomplete. But, make no mistake. The question I sprung on Jeffrey in the pool had nothing to do with scenery, staying fit, solitude, or any other aspect of thru-hiking.

Are we planning to go on any more thru-hikes?

The question had burst out of me, on a whim, and talk about feeling put on the hot seat. Once it hung in the air, I had to figure out where it came from. When the answer hit me, I felt so embarrassed that I blushed like a rose, while hurrying to explain, "...because if we are, we should probably keep in mind that...um...soon, I'll be too old for...you know...the kids we don't want to have anyway...or, I don't want, and probably you don't either, since you're eight years older than I am...so, if we're ever going to have them, soon would be the time...just in case we change our minds...because it would be important to finish thru-hiking first...just so having kids couldn't stop us from not having them anyway."

Jeffrey's outstretched body sank a bit deeper into the pool's warm water. His long eyelashes remained fixed shut. His brown hair floated around his face like seagrass.

I imagined his sparkly blue eyes gazing into mine. They recognized how much courage it was taking for me to speak the dreaded k-word. Jeffrey cared deeply about my feelings. Therefore, he did not mind hearing me break one of our unspoken taboos. In fact, his eyes were shimmering with compassion. It was fun to daydream because dreaming could be enjoyed without worrying about how he might react.

Meantime, though, in reality, I had to watch his face show no reaction at all. If anything changed, it was only that his body might have floated a little more sloppily.

Blushing fiercely, I clammed up and went back to minding my own business. My brain felt confused. My nose started to itch. Darned, my reckless mouth. It needed to shut up, already. Thank goodness, nothing more happened for the next few minutes, until, horror of horrors, my mouth resumed explaining, "It's not like I WANT us to have kids. I just said that for an example of what could PREVENT us from ever going thru-hiking again...on top of my parents and your mom needing more help from us in the future, and Tierra getting near a dog's lifespan, and Erik not being able to housesit forever, and our fruit trees maturing to a point where we won't want to leave home, and maybe getting jobs that wouldn't let us leave anyway...and, getting back to the k-word, I know the whole idea sounds like outer space, but wouldn't you hate if we waited until we couldn't have kids if we ever hiked again because I got too old, so we couldn't do both, and we ended up having to choose between one or the other?"

Jeffrey lifted his head out of the water and glided silently away, or around me, or something. He seemed to be supportive of my presence, in spirit, but his smile looked torn between defiance and panic.

Argh, why had I made a bad situation worse? What could possibly have been gained from fussing, about something I probably did not even want myself? There were so many downsides to having kids. Time would be subtracted from my personal hobbies. Kids were expensive. Planet Earth did not need any more babies. I might become boring and lose all my friends. My kid could turn out to be a video game addict, with no interest in nature or sports of any kind. Or else, on the flip side, it might turn out so cool that I would end up living life through the kid, instead of having a life of my own.

A former co-worker had once asked me, "Haven't you felt THE HUNGER yet?"

"No," I had answered, flatly.

Looking intrigued, she had described a biological craving completely outside my own experience.

I had joked about my "biological time clock" being broken.

She had concluded that giving her an intellectual response proved I was "definitely not ready" to have kids.

Flash forward to Jeffrey and me sitting in our living room, one cold winter night. We had decided to hold an official meeting about the k-subject, only because it seemed like we ought to before getting married. The meeting had opened with expectant silence. Jeffrey sat stiffly upon our couch, not saying a word, in hopes of being dismissed. Likewise, although I was usually a talker, I found myself at a complete loss for words. So, that was that. Meeting adjourned. Jeffrey and I agreed to revisit the topic before getting married, upon whatever unspecified date we might feel ready for another round of torture.

In the meantime, although our meeting had seemed fruitless, we came out of it knowing two useful facts: 1. Neither of us felt ready to have kids. 2. Neither of us had anything to say about it.

These conclusions had significance, for the reason that Jeffrey's motives were different from mine. Take, for example, his lack of negative arguments. He was not fundamentally opposed to becoming a father. He just feared that anything capable of hindering his spiritual practices might threaten his future success as a private hypnotherapist. For the most part, that was why hearing the k-word spoken in my parents' swimming pool made him swim around in clenched little circles. He started mumbling about it being nonsensical to thru-hike for prevention against letting a thru-hike prevent us from having kids. At the end of venting, his summary was, "Besides, we'd come home too broke to raise a family anyway, so why are we even having this discussion?"

"Well, you got me there," I sighed. "Okay, I give up. You win."

"Great," he smiled. "So, can we get back to swimming, now? I mean unless you've got a better farm to sell me?"

I thought for a moment, before coming up with, "How about staying in the wilderness long enough to experience a bit of what wild animals feel?"

"You mentioned that on the PCT," he recalled, "and we've already scared people with our looks and our smell, so I guess we can cross that thrill off our bucket list."

"Ha-ha," I frowned. "Stinking isn't the ultimate wilderness experience. I'm talking about maybe improving our sense of smell, or noticing more details besides trees and flowers.

"I'd love to feel wild," he admitted, "but that's not going to make me sign on the dotted line."

"How about taking a break from going broke trying to start your own business? Maybe stepping away from what's frustrating you would help you figure out a better plan, so you could earn some real money after we got back."

Wincing at my implication, Jeffrey snapped, "Thru-hiking is only good for thinking about thru-hiking, and that's it. Whether we stayed out for another half-year or ten years, or until the day we die, I'd still have to just watch out for rocks that could trip me. That's why nothing profound ever came to me on the PCT."

"You mean, rocks are why you never learned how to meditate on your feet?"

Peerrwww. Peerewww. A siren went off inside Jeffrey's head. He felt painfully aware of having failed to accomplish his number-one goal for our PCT-hike.

"Yes," he snarled, "because we were always too busy rushing from place to place."

"As beginners," I reminded him, "but now that we're pros, we could stay on schedule without losing sleep."

"Except that long miles would still be long miles," he argued. "Don't you remember how many hours we hiked each day? I do because I was carrying our wristwatch. We woke up around six each morning and went to bed around eleven-or-twelve midnight. That's hardly enough sleep, and the CDT's a much harder trail. Remember people saying it's not even finished yet?"

"Yes, but do you remember how fast we jammed through northern Washington?"

"That was totally awesome," he laughed, suddenly remembering. "Even after we sank through snow up to our shins, we were still hauling ass."

"Right, so just imagine if we had left Mexico in tip-top shape."

Jeffrey's smile faltered.

"I'm sure you could still learn how to meditate on your feet if you had more time. You just never got a chance to fully use your spiritual training. But, now that we're pros, you'd get to meditate, I'd get to relax, and we'd probably come home knowing for sure that we don't want kids, in which case you could jump right into building the kind of business you'll never want to leave, and when we're old fogies, sitting on our couch eating chocolate mousse with liver paté, we'll just look back and laugh about this whole conversation."

Jeffrey raised one clubby hand into the air. It looked as if he wanted to stop me from entering a crosswalk, but instead, he exclaimed, "Hold up there, Davy Crockett. If a little downtime is all we need, why can't we just skip the hike and make our decision right here at home?"

"We could, theoretically," I agreed, "but do we ever? Our last meeting was ridiculous. You never said a word, and I didn't really either."

"That's because I didn't feel ready to talk about it," he explained. "I'm sure when I feel ready, I'll have plenty to say."

"Before Mars gets *McDonald's*?"

"It won't take that long."

"Are you SURE?. If you think so, why not prove it right now? Come on, big talker. Put your money where your mouth is. Do you to want to...um...yikes...I can't even say it."

"Are you asking me to decide about having kids right here in this pool, sweetheart?"

"Yes. I'm daring you to quit dodging the issue and finally spill your guts."

"Daring. Rushing. Double-daring. Whatever you want to call it, I'm not going to participate because I still need more time."

"SEE?" I cried. "That's precisely why any discussions we have never amount to squat. Everything important we might have to say always gets put off by other stuff. That's why we seriously need to go on another thru-hike. Okay, I'm kidding, that was a joke. But, you get what I mean."

Speaking thoughtfully, Jeffrey suggested, "We could create more free time by building fewer hot tubs and doing less yard work. Ten minutes every day could make a huge difference."

Slyly, I retorted, "Does that include the ten minutes we just spent having this conversation?"

"...er, right," he frowned.

"See? Time is not the problem. We just had ten minutes, and we have ten minutes every day. Probably, even twenty."

"Not me," he objected. "I have zero minutes, ever because I'm always busy shoveling stuff or hauling rocks."

"Not right before breakfast, or right after dinner. What do you do during all those ten minuteses? Stare at the wall? Tidy up your sock drawer?"

"Whatever," he scowled. "I just think we could enjoy better talks if we did fewer house projects."

"Then, I guess you're more on my side than I am, considering that thru-hiking would eliminate every house project you've ever complained about, plus be easier than finishing our house."

"Hoh! That's a good one," he exclaimed. "Now you're presenting my model of the world, but stop right there because you're completely nuts."

"Which is a good thing, right? Since you like nutty women."

He almost smiled, before looking confused.

"Although, to be fair, we both know the thing you like most about me is not my personality."

"It's not?"

"No."

"Then, what is it?"

"My butt, wearing tight Levi's jeans."

Jeffrey froze, recognizing the truth.

"It's okay," I shrugged. "Since, we both know I only agreed to marry you for your long *Maybelline* eyelashes, your honking-big nose, those magical massage fingers, and the way you carry backpacks across logs I have to cross on my sexy-looking butt."

Finally, Jeffrey could not resist smiling.

"Look, can you please just forget our home lives for a minute? The single best reason for us to ever thru-hike again will be only for the love of wilderness, period. Money is no excuse. People can earn money if they really want to. Especially, resourceful people like you and me. So, if you could please just take a break from dwelling on negatives for a moment, and believe your job could succeed either way, would you ever want to go thru-hiking again?"

"You mean, tomorrow? Next year? Or ten years from now?"

"Any of the above. It's just a hypothetical question. Pretend we're living in a world where time and money don't exist."

"That's impossible," he scoffed.

"Not for people with good imaginations. Please, if you can, just try to stretch your mind a little. If you could fool yourself into thinking positive, would you want to ever try thru-hiking again?"

"Of course," he confessed.

"AHA!" I grinned. "See? So, if we actually DID live in a world where we could do anything we please, would you want to hike the PCT again? The CDT? Or the AT?"

"Not the AT," he felt sure.

"Me either," I agreed. "So, that leaves either CDT or PCT, and we've already hiked the PCT, so, basically, it would have to be the CDT."

A gleam of suspicion flashed through Jeffrey's eyes. "I'd like to hike the CDT someday, but I'm just not ready yet."

"How about the summer after this one? That's almost a year-and-a-half from now."

He swam away from me, aiming toward a fence surrounding the sparkling blue pool.

"Not until I get my business running smoothly, pay off my debts, and rebuild my savings account. I mean, if we ever are going to have kids, our top priority needs to be saving money, not going deeper into debt with another long vacation."

"So, we're ready to buckle-down for good and be done with thru-hiking forever, or, at least, until we're old enough to use canes in the grocery store?"

"Sad, but true," he confirmed.

"Okay, then, I guess you win. Please forgive me for trying to corrupt you. We've already had enough fun for one lifetime. Now, it's time to start saving money for a kid we'll probably never have, after taking so long to decide that our parents and dog will need us home anyway."

"I'm sorry," he groaned. "I wish you were marrying a rich man who could take you on all the thru-hikes you'd ever want, but the truth stinks, and I'm hoping you'll still marry me."

"I'll still marry you," I confirmed, "but please keep in mind that life's best opportunities often require getting a little crazy. Also, if you're really going to earn the kind of money you keep predicting, any money we'd spend on another thru-hike will seem like water under the bridge."

"Except for my bridge being logjammed by a credit card debt," Jeffrey sulked.

"Even that will seem trivial after your business succeeds," I promised. "Or else, if your business fails, then we won't be able to afford kids anyhow, so life will be cheap, and you'll pay off your credit card anyway."

Jeffrey could not help smiling at my logic. "You should go back to your old job working in sales," he suggested.

Then, rolling over onto his back, he resumed floating like a white-bellied otter. Several relevant memories percolated into his awareness. First, it was the train ride through Amsterdam, during which he had scribbled "Hike the Pacific Crest Trail" onto a notepad. Next, he saw himself opening *The Pacific Crest Trail Hiker's Handbook* and peeking inside to see what it was about. He could remember having first learned about Trail Magic. All the other PCT-hikers we knew took the phenomenon for granted. He loved that about thru-hikers. Also, he remembered loving how it had felt to walk through scenes from his favorite fantasy novels. He wanted to experience a real-life nature quest. What could be finer than learning how to converse with hawks and eagles? What could feel manlier, too, than playing the hero, every time I, his fair maiden, needed someone to thaw my frozen feet on his tummy or carry my backpack across a tippy log? These inspiring memories warmed Jeffrey's heart until he started seeing flashbacks of scorching-hot deserts, snow-covered peaks, and nobody's maiden cussing like a truck driver whenever her feet froze from hiking on snow. Feeling conflicted, he began to think. Could a second thru-hike really teach him how to meditate on his feet? Might spending another half-year in the wilderness further strengthen his connection with the sacred elements of air, fire, water, and earth? Could anything else in his lifetime be more important than strengthening those connections? Doubts took arms against his reptilian urges. Something inside him opened, like a door, and formed a question which escaped from his mouth.

"Do you really think it would be easier this time?"

"Absolutely!" I exclaimed. "I mean, not in terms of the weather or the terrain, but physically, yes. It's like we're baby birds who just got our wings, but somebody caught us before we could fly, and stuffed us into a cage where dreams turn to jelly."

Fixing on the word "birds," Jeffrey perked up and asked, "You really feel that strongly about going on another thru-hike?"

"Yes," I promised, even though, in truth, I had never given it much thought.

"Then, SO DO I!" he whooped.

Wait. Hello, Charlie? What had I just done? Uh-oh. Panic time. Could I take it back? Sure, it had been fun to give my fiancé a good sales pitch. I always enjoyed trying to sell people on ideas, but who would have expected him to throw caution to the wind, whip out a contract and buy right on the spot? Yikes, now the ball was in my court. Did I even WANT to go thru-hiking again? Hm, well, at least, one thing was certain. This was my only chance. If Jeffrey saw me hesitate, he would change his mind and that would be the end of it. Therefore, I had no choice.

Slapping the water hard, I cheered, "WOOHOO!"

Jeffrey added sternly, "But, you must swear. You must solemnly promise, this will be our last thru-hike for a very long time. I mean, unless we're planning to give up on regular jobs and just move to someplace where we can live cheaply."

"Hey," I interrupted him. "Is that a tear on your cheek, or just pool water?"

He was crying because he could not speak.

"What's wrong?" I asked.

"Nothing," he laughed. "I just can't believe we're going to do it again. I mean, I know it seems silly, but for some reason, I don't feel capable of crossing the whole country on foot."

"Even though you just did it six months ago?"

"Yeah, it's like the experience wasn't real."

"Maybe you were in shock. and it hasn't sunk in yet."

"Maybe," he agreed. "Maybe if I can do it once more, I'll stop thinking we got lucky and realize I really CAN do it. In fact, maybe that's what makes thru-hiking a sport. On the one hand, it seems impossible, but, on the other hand, you KNOW you can do it if you just keep pushing."

"Pushing is all well and fine," I said, "but please don't get attached to another perfect finish. The CDT is a much bigger challenge. We might not be able to finish the whole trail in one season."

"But, if we CAN finish, hooey, we'll accomplish some of our goals from last time that we couldn't pull off as beginners. Like, if the PCT was our dress rehearsal, this will be our chance to experience everything we missed."

Hearing my philosophy turned back upon me tripped some alarms. *He's getting carried away*, I thought. Okay, but who cared? I needed to keep feeding the momentum we had going, so I raised my hand and roared, "High-five, partner!"

That is how two lunatics agreed to thru-hike the CDT in 2001.

Unfortunately, our friends and family did not look excited when they heard the news.

"You're hiking across the country AGAIN?" one friend complained. "Why not do something different, this time? Like, take a long canoe trip down the Mississippi River?"

Jeffrey's mom flat-out begged us to change our minds.

My parents asked if we intended to skip the annual family vacation, and said they were going to worry the whole time.

Another friend protested, "Why do you have to hike so far? Wouldn't two months be long enough to see anything you missed the first time?"

Even our own inhibitions surfaced one evening while standing together in our kitchen, cooking spaghetti with red sauce.

I initiated the conversation, by asking, "Were we miserable during most of our PCT hike?"

Jeffrey almost choked on a tester noodle, before deciding I had meant sore and tired, not unhappy about being stuck with each other. After a quick recovery, he assured me, "Some days

Decision 43

were miserable but don't worry. It's just like you keep saying, this hike is going to be a lot more relaxing."

Correcting his assumption, my response was, "I'm not saying we were physically miserable. I'm remembering how often we argued on the PCT. Please, let's not ever relive southern Washington again. Otherwise, I'll feel scared to marry you."

Setting down the hot-pads, Jeffrey looked into my face and gasped, "You mean, you want to call it off?"

"No, silly," I laughed. "I'm just saying I want us to get along better on the CDT than we did on the PCT. That's all."

"Okay, Roger that," he agreed. "But, haven't we been getting along well, lately? I mean, when's the last time we argued?"

"Home is different from the trail," I reminded him. "That's why it might help to write down our biggest problems with each other before leaving home. Then, we won't hit the trail hauling any baggage bigger than our backpacks."

Jeffrey stirred the red sauce with unnecessary force. "What kind of problems do you mean?" he asked.

"Just, things we don't like about each other that might cause an argument."

"Oh, that's easy," he smiled, relaxing the spoon. "You can make the list, then. For my entries, just put hearts and smiley faces because I already like everything about you."

"Ha-ha," I laughed. "Don't be a fibber. Everybody dislikes something about their partners. If you repress what you resent, it'll just become a ticking time bomb, waiting to explode in some beautiful forest dripping with huckleberries and waterfalls and hawks."

"Okay, you're right," he winced. "We definitely don't want that to happen. So, go ahead, clue me in. What do you want me to write?"

"The worst stuff you don't like about me that drives you nuts."

"You never drive me nuts. I seriously can't think of anything."

"Then, why did you keep taking digs at me and acting ornery on the PCT?"

"Because I felt exhausted the whole time. Being a Pack Mule is harder than you think."

"I know it's hard, but that's no excuse to spoil a fine adventure."

"True," he admitted. "So, are you going to write down acting ornery as something you don't like about me?"

"Well, it's kind of a general term," I mused. "Maybe we should write down more specific things, like, how I really hate it when you take unnecessary risks. Remember that skinny log you crossed over the San Joaquin River?"

"Ouch," he smiled. "Sorry. I was being an idiot, showing off like that. You were smart to say I should have taken the big log, and I totally ignored you. But, I've learned my lesson, so maybe we can cross that bad habit off your list? Or do you still want to count it?"

"Hm, I'll have to think about that. But, in the meantime, we need two things from you."

Jeffrey set down the stirring spoon and glanced around like he wanted to leave the kitchen. "Two-for-two, huh?" he mumbled. "Tit for tat. That sounds like a fair exchange. Too bad, I don't have anything to contribute."

"Take your time," I offered.

"Probably, I won't have anything before dinner," he predicted, "and maybe never because I really like you just how you are, sweet vision of my heart."

Rolling my eyes, I replied, "Of course, ding-dong. If you didn't like me, I assume we wouldn't be engaged. But, liking someone doesn't mean you have to think they're perfect. Everyone has flaws. Just imagine how it would feel to have somebody claim they liked every single nose hair and fart you let out. Wouldn't that feel fake?"

"I don't know, since I've never had that experience," he shrugged.

"Smart-Alec!" I punched him. "Now you definitely owe me your two, for being sassy."

"Easy there, girl," he cowered, picking up the spoon again. "Sorry, I'm just not able to think while cooking. Why don't you ask me again after dinner?"

"You'd like me to spend my whole dinner wondering what you're not going to like about me, instead of just getting it over with now? Ergh. Can't you just use your brain for a moment? I mean, this is the perfect time, while all you're doing is stirring red sauce."

"Exactly, I'm stirring red sauce." He gestured toward the pot, whose bubbling contents were starting to look condensed. "As you can see, I'm busy."

"Busy with your hands, not your brain."

"Stirring may only require half a brain for good multi-taskers, like you, but for pack animals, like me, it's an all-consuming activity."

"Then, why not let me stir, while you think?"

"No!" he leaped backward, defensively clutching the spoon. "Just give me ten minutes of silence, okay? I promise to be thinking. In fact, I'm thinking right now."

Examining his eyes, I concluded, "No you're not."

"Okay, I'm not."

"Fine, then would you really like me to drag this out until after dinner?"

"No, no," he backpedaled.

"Okay, then, please. Just, give me your two problems now."

"I would if I had any."

"You'd have some if you were being honest. You're just afraid of hurting my feelings, but don't be because I promise I'll be fine with whatever you say."

"Okay look," he groaned, "if you can back off, for now, I'll promise to give you two things after dinner."

"Deal," I huffed, "but please don't forget. I just want to make sure. Do you remember your assignment?"

Jeffrey resumed stirring as if he had forgotten I was there until he lifted his head to ask, "Why are you still looking at me? Am I doing something wrong?"

"I don't know," I replied "Are you working on your assignment?"

"I don't know. Am I?"

"I can't tell. That's why I'm asking."

"Asking about what?"

"Whether or not you're doing your assignment."

"Oh."

"Do you remember what you're supposed to be thinking about?"

"Yes."

"You do?"

"Yes."

"Are you thinking about it?"

"Yes."

"Okay, good! Then, what are you thinking about?"

"Red sauce, obviously."

"Mm-hm, and...?"

"I don't know. Basket weaving? Ice hockey?"

"Aha!" I exclaimed. "See? I knew if I let you slack, you'd forget your assignment."

"I haven't forgotten any assignment."

"Really? Then, what is it?"

"Your two things."

"What two things?"

"The two things I don't like about you."

"RIGHT!" I cried, feeling genuinely impressed. "Okay, see? You CAN multi-task. Good, so now, if you can please just tell me your two things right now, we can get this over with, in a jiffy."

"You really promise not to care what I say?"

"Cross my heart, hope to die, make me scarf an apple pie."

"Okay," he agreed. "How's this? I want you to think less and ask fewer questions."

That deserved another punch in the arm.

"Hey, you can't censor my choices!" he whimpered.

"You're supposed to list stuff that bothers you on the trail, not just be a smart-ass."

"Ohhh," he nodded. "You mean, like talking while we're climbing?"

"BINGO!" I cried. "Excellent, now we're getting somewhere. Do you really think that's going to bother you on the CDT?"

"Definitely," he confirmed. "I don't think it makes sense to waste oxygen on chit-chat. We need all the air we can breathe just for climbing. Plus, dividing the mind makes us likely to trip and twist an ankle, which ought to be worse for you, since you do most of the talking."

Narrowing my eyes, I replied, "You should be so lucky as to receive the benefits of my fabulous entertainment. And also, keep in mind that talking helps me climb, by distracting me from feeling tired. But, if you don't like it...I don't know, maybe you just need more practice?"

"Practice? Practice at what? Developing bad habits? Dividing the mind? That's not something I want to strive for."

"It's a good talent to have when you need to spot landmarks at the same time you're keeping track of the weather."

"Those are your jobs, not mine, sweetheart. I'm just our pack mule."

"Hah, that's true. So, maybe I'm the only one who needs to multi-task. But, if you're aware of my job description, then shouldn't you support me practicing my job skills?"

"Yes—except when you talk during an uphill because if I can't figure out what you're saying, then I give you a bad response and get myself in trouble."

"Oh-ho! So, there's the rub. Okay, partner. That makes sense. So, shall I put down talking while climbing as being one of your complaints about me?"

"Sure," he agreed. "And here's another. I'm worried about you using that stubborn head of yours to push your body past its limits. Like, when you postpone eating, so we can keep hiking, but then your blood sugar drops and you get all shaky? Those situations really worry me."

"Fair enough," I admitted. "Although, I'm actually less of a risk-taker than you, since I fix my injuries as soon as they begin, whereas you ignore yours until they get nasty."

"Touché," he chuckled. "So, do you want me to think of something else for my second thing?"

"No, we can use it," I decided. "Unless you've got another gripe coming?"

"No, that's all."

Thus, we wrote down for Jeffrey's list:
> 1. *Talks while climbing.*
> 2. *Pushes body past limits.*

And, for mine:
> 1. *Ornery moods trigger arguments.*
> 2. *Takes unnecessary risks.*

Also, we designated Jeffrey's main personal goal to be:
> *Finish the whole CDT.*

And, mine:
> *Wants to feel at home in the wilderness.*

Lastly, we agreed upon a shared goal:
> *Money.*

The next day, I started drafting a budget.

Jeffrey shelved his struggling hypnotherapy business, in order to start selling Yellow Page advertisements.

I ditched several freelance video jobs and became the operations manager for a start-up software company.

Within six months, we gathered enough savings to cover all foreseeable expenses, minus replacing broken gear or spending unplanned days in town. Would that be enough money to get us all the way from Canada to Mexico?

Jeffrey wagered, "We're golden because the same planning skills you used to make our PCT-hike work will help us handle anything that comes up."

With thru-hiking fever coming on strong, Jeffrey resumed calling me by my trail name, "Sunshine."

I would have done the same, except for one problem. Somehow, five months had not been long enough for either of us to dream up a handle he liked. My first suggestion, "Walking Thunder," had been deemed too smelly. "Tiger" was too cutesy. "Pumpkin?" No way. And, in my opinion, Jeffrey's suggestions had been equally bad. For instance, "Hakoma" and "Hatama" would have been difficult for other hikers to remember, and "Ho-Ola" was tricky to pronounce. So, then, what were we going to call Jeffrey on the CDT? Just "Jeff" again? How boring. But, it seemed like Jeff was going to be it, until, one day, I noticed his habit of counting hawks perched on fences and telephone wires.

"Sees Hawks!" I suggested, meaning it as a joke.

"SeeHawk?" he repeated. "Huh...that's okay."

Whoa! This was the most enthusiasm he had ever expressed toward any name capable of gaining my approval.

"Finally!" I grinned.

So, from that day forth, he and I became team "SeeHawk and Sunshine."

As a team, we revived our training regimen of climbing stairs 2x week (accompanied by our dog, Tierra, until she realized she could just sit at the top and wait for us to quit yo-yoing up and down the stairs like a couple of furless fools). We also resumed day-hiking 1x week in some local mountains. SeeHawk did a lot of jumping on his mini trampoline. I went jogging. We both did yoga, and we surfed, which kept us limber in addition to getting exercise.

Hiking the PCT had already proven we could maintain an average of 18 miles per day. Our biggest concern about taking on the CDT was expecting rougher weather and route-finding challenges.

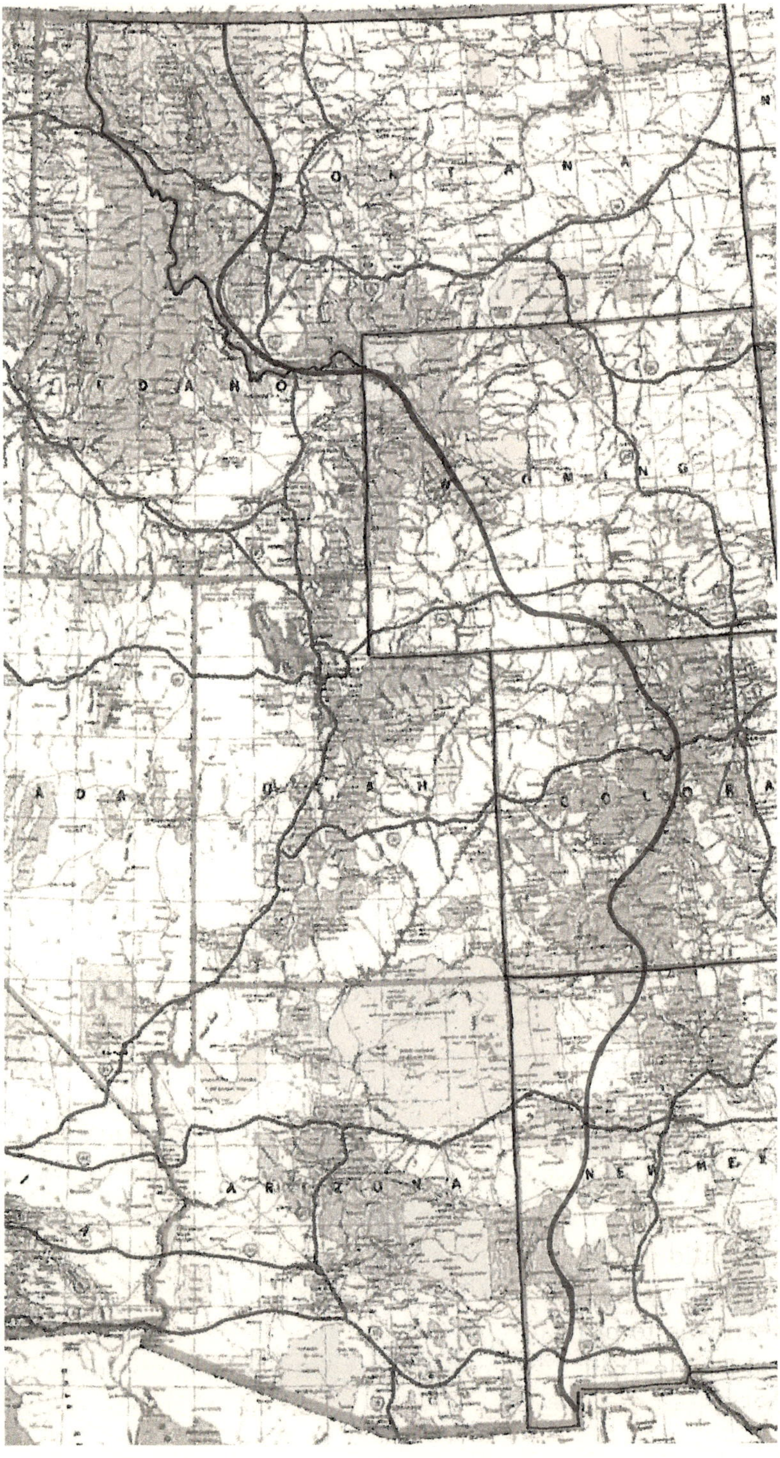
I D A H O
W Y O M I N G
U T A H
A R I Z O N A

Chapter 4

Countdown

Luck is what happens when preparation meets opportunity.

— *Lucius Annaeus Seneca*

Preparing for another thru-hike felt like reopening a used can of worms. The difference, this time, was that SeeHawk and I headed into the kitchen knowing how big the can was, and what it contained.

I calculated that a 6-month trip ought to require 540 meals, 180 fruit rolls, and 300 snack bars. That was a lot of dehydrating and vacuum-sealing for two working people to undertake again, but, at least, we had food-drying down to a science.

This time around, we did not break any blenders, coffee grinders, or grain mills. Nor did we melt anything made of plastic, and our Teflon cookie sheets stayed intact.

The final pile of food we assembled for our CDT hike weighed a grand total of 683 lbs. Divided into rations, it came to 28 lbs. per week, or roughly 2,900-calories per day for me and 3,500-calories per day for SeeHawk.

Were those rations adequate to keep us comfortable, averaging 18 miles per day? Probably, but if we got hungry, there were going to be restaurants at most of our resupply stops, and many would also have markets selling fresh cheese and fruit.

When it came to preparations outside the kitchen, our first concern was to purchase maps and guidebooks for the Continental Divide Trail. Unlike last time, it was not a one-shot deal. The CDT had two overseeing agencies, each offering four guidebooks apiece. The self-titled "official" guidebooks contained terrific maps, minimal directions for southbound hikers (e.g. us), and gorgeous photographs of a trail we were going to see anyway, printed on semigloss, heavyweight paper. Unfortunately, it would have been impossible to discard the photographs without losing critical maps and directions. Therefore, we deemed the whole series to be coffee-table guidebooks, and privately named them, "The Book of Beans."

By comparison, the other guidebooks for sale were cheap and flimsy. Their format included a few token black-and-white photographs, primitive maps, and outstanding directions for southbound hikers, printed on regular white typing paper. In other words, the cheap guidebooks were love at first sight. We even nicknamed their author, "Poppa Jim." However, when it came to forking out cash, we purchased both series, for a total of 8 guidebooks (cha-ching), because their authors oftentimes disagreed about where to route the unfinished CDT, and we wanted to pick and choose along the way.

Just for insurance against getting lost, we also purchased overview maps from the US Forest Service, Bureau of Land Management, Trails Illustrated, US Geological Survey, and deLorme's Atlas. Consequently, our finished pile of literature stood tall enough to start a bonfire. It burned our fingers, too, when we picked up scissors and started chopping every last page out of all 8 guidebooks, for bundling into 27 addressed resupply boxes.

When all that busy-work was said and done, once again, SeeHawk and I agreed that failing to succeed had become unthinkable.

* * *

The Continental Divide was rumored to be a snow factory. Nevertheless, we were still planning to carry 3-season gear (rather than 4-season), mostly purchased from our local mountaineering store.

When the store's clerk heard us mention thru-hiking, he perked right up and said, "I tried doing the Appalachian Trail last year, but I didn't get far because I busted my ankle. Tell you what, though, I don't ever want to go thru-hiking again."

"Why's that?" we asked him.

Most likely, we figured, he was either going complain about the dawn-to-dusk grind, or about moving too fast to enjoy the scenery.

Instead, he gave us a surprising answer, "Seems like everyone on the AT was totally obsessed with ultralight gear. Like, how much does your jacket weigh? How much does your water filter weigh? How much does your spoon weigh? After a while, it kind of drove me nuts."

"PCT-hikers are less obsessed," we assured him. "You might like the PCT better."

Without skipping a beat, he came right out and asked us, "What kind of stove do you carry? Will you be using down or synthetic?"

In truth, compared with most of Ray Jardine's disciples, SeeHawk and I were not authentic ultralight hikers. We spoke in terms of pounds and ounces, rather than fractions of ounces. Not only that but also (gasp), we carried "luxuries" like a free-standing tent, film camera, and propane/butane canister stove. Even though the PCT had taught us how much pleasure could be added by shaving weight, our packing list remained mostly unchanged.

Some of our PCT gear could be reused, but we did need to replace our worn-out tent, stink-infested t-shirts, ill-fitting backpacks, flimsy storm jackets, clogged water filter, and rock-eaten shoes. Once we finished assembling everything, new and old, our base pack-weights (minus food, water, and snow gear) came to roughly 20 lbs. for me and 35 lbs. for SeeHawk (minus sometimes carrying a 2 lb. bear canister).

Was this enough to ensure we could survive Rocky Mountain blizzards? Water-shortages? Snakebites? Ankle-sprains? Who knew? And, that was the beauty of thru-hiking. As an art form, it was like baking a cake from scratch. Things could go wrong from the beginning, in the middle, and even seconds before the timer went off. Structure and flexibility went hand-in-hand. Mistakes had consequences. Meticulous preparations could increase our joy or make no difference. The thrust came from within. It was a study of dancing with unpredictable forces. And the most important variable was choosing a lucky start date.

Toward the end of May, two different Glacier National Park rangers testified that Montana's snowpack had been unseasonably low. The reason was a two-year drought teaming up with a two-week heatwave.

"Although," one ranger warned us, "you never know what the park's weather will do at this time of year. It could snow three feet tomorrow and go back to being like it was several weeks ago."

Regardless, Jeffrey and I needed to buy train tickets.

Poppa Jim kindly answered his telephone when I called to ask about starting on June 4. He thought it might be safer to start on June 11, or even toward the end of the month, due to snow lingering on the Ahern Drift and springtime runoff flooding Strawberry Creek.

Feeling traitorous, I confessed our plan to bypass the Ahern Drift, in favor of following a Book of Beans route that would allow us to leave Canada earlier.

"The Belly River will take you around some big snowfields," he agreed, "but you'll still find a lot of snow in Glacier National Park, and you'll still have to ford Strawberry Creek."

I finished that phone call feeling persuaded to follow Poppa Jim's advice. Except, after hanging up the phone, I realized I had forgotten to mention Montana's two-week heatwave.

"Jim definitely knows about it," SeeHawk assured me. "He keeps in really close touch with the trail."

"Okay, but if he felt obliged to err on the side of caution...and doesn't realize how fast the park is thawing...maybe leaving just a hair sooner...I mean, we need to beat winter through the San Juan Mountains."

"When are we scheduled to reach the San Juans?"

"If we start hiking one week earlier than Jim recommends, we might get there by October first."

"Whoa!" SeeHawk winced. "October's late for Colorado. How long do you think it'll take us to cross the San Juans?"

"Maybe two weeks?"

"Then, we'll definitely get some snow."

"Unless we can start earlier than Poppa Jim says. We just need to decide if we're more scared of icy passes and flooded rivers or blizzards on the crest."

"Blizzards are worse, in my opinion," SeeHawk replied, "but I'm game for anything that'll put your mind at ease."

Priorities quibbled inside my heart until I stepped outdoors and got hit in the face with bright-hot sunshine. There were already baby doves hopping through our vegetable garden. Honeybees were buzzing through our lavender bushes. Hummingbirds were sipping cocktails from our salvias.

It was time to buckle down and call *Amtrak*!

In hopes that Poppa Jim's dates had been conservative, I told myself that I would be honoring his opinion by bumping our departure from June 4 to June 6.

When I picked up the telephone to dial *Amtrak*, I heard SeeHawk whisper, "Go for the sleeper car."

Curtly, I reminded him, "We can't afford a sleeper car."

That was true, and besides, who needed a sleeper car? It was going to feel heavenly just to plop down our bottoms in the train's big recliner seats and relax for the first time in months. There would be nothing left to vacuum seal. No more stairs to climb. I could hardly wait to watch our future unfold through the train's giant picture windows. In fact, perhaps I was looking forward to the train ride more than our destination.

When *Amtrak's* agent came on the line, she offered me a sleeper car discount for our second night on the train. The price was so cheap that it gave me no choice.

"Your wish is my command," I told SeeHawk, after booking the sleeper car.

"You've made me a happy man," he answered, looking very happy, indeed.

With our train tickets booked, I was able to complete our resupply schedule.

Town	Distance Off Trail	Date
START at Chief Mtn. Customs		June 6
East Glacier Park, MO	close to trail	
Benchmark, MO	4-miles off trail	
Strawberry Creek deep and fast		
Marysville, MO	4-miles off trail	
get rid of snow gear		
Anaconda, MO	29-mile hitch	July 5
Wisdom, MO	23-mile hitch	
Leadore, ID	13-mile hitch	
Mack's Inn, ID	close to trail	
Old Faithful Village, WY	close to trail	Aug. 4
severe thunderstorms		
Brooks Lake Lodge, WY	close to trail	
hot desert without much water		
Big Sandy Lodge, WY	close to trail	
South Pass City, WY	close to trail	
Bairoil, WY	close to trail	
Rawlins, WY	close to trail	
Steamboat Springs, CO	13-mile hitch	Sept. 5
end of water problems, begin steep ups and downs		
Grand Lake, CO	close to trail	
Copper Mountain, CO	close to trail	
Twin Lakes, CO	close to trail	
Creede, CO	18-mile hitch	Oct. 4
Pagosa Springs, CO	close to trail	
Chama, NM	8-mile hitch	
Ghost Ranch, NM	close to trail	
Cuba, NM	close to trail	
Grants, NM		Nov. 4
Pie Town, NM	close to trail	
Black Mountains dry and hot; Gila River might get lost		
Gila Hot Springs, NM	close to trail	
Pinos Altos, NM	close to trail	
Hachita, NM	close to trail	
FINISH at Mexican border near Big Hatchet Mtns.		Dec. 2

We seemed to be in good shape, preparation-wise. Or, at least, we thought so, until our local newspaper astrologer said everyone in the zodiac system (sign regardless) should stay "adaptable" during the week of June 6 because it was going to be a week of "changing schedules." Well, sure enough. Whether or not I believed in astrology, that lady must have been the real thing because, right on schedule, I got nailed with either food poisoning or a really nasty stomach flu. This happened the day before we were supposed to leave home. I ended up trapped in our backyard hammock, with 27 half-empty cardboard boxes sitting inside our house, waiting to be filled. The boxes were queued like train cars, from our dining room into the hallway, around our living room, over the woodstove and back, into a dark corner labeled "Hachita, New Mexico." I was supposed to finish stuffing all the boxes full of food, toiletries, seasonal clothing, and bundles of guidebook literature, but I could barely roll over without retching.

SeeHawk offered to finish the packing job for me.

"Thanks for the offer," I told him, "but you don't know which items should go into which box."

"Nope," he agreed, "and I'd feel awful if I accidentally put our trail directions or gas refills into the wrong box."

Nevertheless, he finally took his best shot because all I could do was keep clutching my stomach and praying for whatever had sickened me to end.

Later that morning, *Amtrak* took mercy and allowed us to postpone our train ticket by one day. They said it was a one-time favor, though, after which any further change would break our wallets.

While spending my sick day reading *Backpacker Magazine*, I noticed a solicitation asking readers, *Why haven't you renewed your subscription? Will you be out in the backcountry too long to read our magazine?* I smiled, thinking, yes!

The next morning, I woke up to find the storm had passed. My stomach felt normal. I was ready to catch a train.

My parents fetched SeeHawk's mom, and together we all drove to the bus depot, where the parents waited to give us a nice sendoff. It was dinnertime, so SeeHawk and I were clutching hot veggie burritos, ready to chow down onboard the train. Which is to say, phooey on the zodiac's "week of changing schedules," because we were achieving a perfect takeoff, just one day late.

Usually, superstition prevented me from counting chickens before they hatched, but things were going so well that I let my guard down and joked, "Now, all we need is for our bus to be working."

SeeHawk chuckled, remembering full-well how our bus to the PCT had broken down, two blocks from the bus station.

Feeling a twinge of nerves, I rechecked the bus depot's posted schedule, just to make sure everything was in order

"Right on time," I confirmed. "Apparently, the bus must be running late."

Ten minutes passed, while SeeHawk and I ran out of stories to amuse our parents and finally lapsed into silence. Eventually, the bus depot's attendant strolled over to ask where we were headed.

"*Amtrak*," everyone answered at once.

"Bummer," the attendant grunted. "Your bus left five minutes before you got here."

"What?" I gasped. "We CAN'T miss our bus. The next train to Montana leaves in THREE DAYS!!"

Looking apologetic, the attendant explained that *Amtrak's* new bus company had taken over running the buses without bothering to update their posted schedules. That news flash gave SeeHawk and me a shock. No way, in heck, could we afford to miss our train! Leaving three days later would not just be a matter of getting socked with *Amtrak's* hefty fine for ticket changes.

"You know the butterfly effect?" I told our parents. "On the trail, it's like, if we leave three days later, then, in every place where the weather was clear three days earlier, instead, it might be snowing, which could slow us down enough that we'd arrive even later to another place that was clear four days earlier, but now it's having a lightning storm, and so on."

SeeHawk sized up the situation by adding, "Just ask anyone who almost hiked the whole PCT during nineteen-ninety-nine, but then couldn't tag Canada because they got nailed by a blizzard on the last day."

"A blizzard we missed by being slower," I added, "so you just never know. Sometimes, it's better to be behind than ahead, but at least starting sooner gives you more options."

Noticing my worried expression, SeeHawk told me softly, "Don't worry, Sunshine. I know this seems like a bummer, but

The Universe always has a good reason for making people miss their buses. Maybe there's a crash on the highway or something."

"Do you really believe that?" I asked him.

"Who knows?" he shrugged. "But, you're definitely right about us needing to catch that train!"

My dad telephoned several taxi companies. Nobody could get us to San Jose within the hour. Several irrelevant buses came and went before we finally caught a bus due to reach San Jose one hour after our train.

"Cross your fingers," SeeHawk told me, while we climbed onboard the near-empty bus. "Trains can easily fall behind schedule. It happens all the time."

Well, guess what? Either, by the grace of freight-company politics, or maybe because it was the "week of changing schedules," *Amtrak's* Coast Starlight arrived at the station precisely one hour late! We dashed up the conductor's short plastic steps just in time to jump on the train, hauling our backpacks through doors that slid-shut behind us, triggering a loud horn blast.

I panted with amazement, "That's two close calls between our PCT bus and this one. Do you think we just have bad luck with buses?"

"Quite the opposite," SeeHawk beamed. "I think it means we have good luck with buses."

Dropping into a pair of open seats, we felt the northbound Coast Starlight sneak out of San Jose like a warm wind gliding on smooth steel rails.

Once we got comfortably settled, it was time to unwrap our veggie burritos. Never mind them having gotten cold—at least, we were eating them on the train.

Through the passenger car's big picture windows, I saw a full-moon gilding unreadable black hills.

At length, I asked SeeHawk, "Do you think tomorrow's sleeper car will have a double or two twins?"

"Either way," he replied, "it'll be our last chance to get naked without freezing or worrying about bears."

"Did you remember to pull our champagne out of the fridge?"

"Oh, yes," he smiled. "I've been trying not to shake my backpack, so it won't spray everywhere when we pop it open."

"We'll have to stop drinking early," I warned him, "because I don't want to hit the trail nursing a hangover."

Imagining what lay ahead, SeeHawk sighed, "Just think. Two days from now we'll be slumbering like logs in those deep, dark Montana woods."

As if drugged by his own fantasy, he fell asleep clutching a half-eaten burrito. In fact, he fell so deeply asleep that he did not even notice when a whiskey-reeking cigarette smoker brushed past his shoulder, spritzing his open mouth with cheap rose perfume.

Darned men's talent for sleeping anywhere, even sitting up. Envying SeeHawk was not going to help me sleep, and I disliked the rose stench lingering above our seats, so I climbed over my partner and took a long walk up the train's center aisle. Inside the glass sightseer car, I found several other passengers relaxing and conversing. Some sat alone, gazing at the full moon. I knew it was rude to eavesdrop, but who could resist listening to a middle-aged man brag about his recent vacation to Hawaii?

"My son-in-law claims Pele is some kind of god," the man reported, "so I said, off the cuff, 'To hell with Pele,' and you know what happened next? God's honest truth. The volcano erupted! It's like She heard me and got all pissed-off or something."

A short while later, another storyteller caught my attention by saying, "I think our government should put an end to all hunting. Wild animals shouldn't be allowed to multiply to the point where we need hunters to control their populations. Take your deer, for instance. When they start taking over residential areas, it's dangerous for children. We need stricter controls, so things don't get out of hand."

I could not resist butting-in, to ask the speaker how deer might endanger children.

"Because it happened to me, once," he explained. "I surprised a buck with eight points and it nearly charged me."

"But, it didn't charge you?"

"No, but it clearly was thinking about it. I still remember how angry that bad boy looked. All I did was catch it by surprise. You'd think it was gonna have gored me. Just goes to show how easily some little kid could get killed, just for walking in the woods. It's not safe to let our wild-animal populations get out of control. Don't get me wrong. I'm not some mean-old animal hater. In fact, I treat my dogs a lot better than this guy." He cast a teasing glance at a man seated next to him. "I probably treat my dogs better than anyone you'll ever meet. But, if they misbehave, you can bet I'm gonna shoot them before somebody gets hurt."

Changing the subject, I asked the two men where they were from.

"Iowa," answered the thinner one. "My friend here owns a pig farm."

Looking pleased for some attention, the pig farmer, who was quite obese, nodded, making his purple jowls jiggle.

I noticed that his eyes looked permanently bloodshot, although, they also looked kind to the point of seeming childish.

"He makes darned good money at it, too," said the friend. "Although, some people think pig farms stink."

"Do you know what pig farms smell like to me?" asked the pig farmer.

I shook my head.

"VEGAS!"

This answer sent both men into a fit of laughter, which lasted about a full minute. After the thinner man quieted down, for some reason, the pig farmer could not stop laughing. White spittle sprayed through his lips. Rising blood pressure reddened his purple cheeks.

I felt like it was rude to speak over his laughter, but curiosity made me ask, "Is pig farming really that lucrative?"

"Oh-ho-ho, yes!" he guffawed. "Pigs. Cattle. We grow corn and soybeans too."

"Do you mind me asking how much a cow is worth?"

"Well, that depends," he reflected. "From birth to six months, they're worth eighty-to-a hundred dollars. Beyond six months, they're worth about three hundred. After being on the fat farm for a year, they're worth about a thousand. Doesn't matter where they're from, price is a thousand, no matter what."

"Do all the cows we see in fields end up in feedlots? Or do some go straight to the butcher?"

"They all go to feedlots," he assured me.

"Even the super fat ones? Some look so huge you'd think they couldn't get any fatter."

The pig farmer chuckled. "Oh, don't be fooled. They can always get fatter. You haven't seen fat until you've seen a cow come out of a feedlot. The cows you see in fields are just heifers used for breeding. Say, do you know who's the expert on when to wean your calves?" He paused for effect. "The Farmer's Almanac, that's who! My wife told me a few years back to wait for the date they give in the Almanac. I didn't listen, and said, 'They're ready now.' She argued. I won. So, we took those calves away from their mamas too young, and oh, my god, did they bawl. Couldn't feed 'em nothin'. Couldn't make 'em quiet. They were just starving. Finally, we put 'em back on their moms and weaned 'em when the Almanac said we should. That did the trick. Not another peep. So, we've been sticking to the *Farmer's Almanac* ever since."

It was time to return to my seat and go to sleep.

SeeHawk was long since in dreamland.

Feeling jealous again did not help me sleep in a half-upright position, but, eventually, I managed to remember nothing more...until dawn revealed the Castle Crags towering above some familiar bushes.

"That's where we picked blackberries on the PCT," SeeHawk gushed, nudging me awake. "There's the closed Laundromat where we couldn't wash our clothes!"

I dug through my backpack and discovered I was missing my toothbrush, along with my birth control pills. Shoot!

When SeeHawk heard the bad news, he worried about it ruining our sleeper-car romance.

I worried harder about menstruating in grizzly bear country.

On the fringe of Klamath Falls, our conductor announced the Coast Starlight was running three hours behind schedule. "For those of you connecting with The Empire Builder," he specified, "we're going to put you on a bus. Please get ready to detrain."

Tossing SeeHawk a dry look, I asked him, "Now, do you think we have good luck with buses?"

He replied sensibly, "It depends what kind of drinks they're serving."

Well, it just so happened that *Amtrak* wanted to cheer us all up, by stocking the bus with a cooler chest full of ice-cold *Coca-Colas* and complimentary ham-and-cheese sandwiches. However, before the cooler chest appeared, we had to sit on the parked bus for a full hour, watching dozens of fellow passengers load in their baggage and climb on board. During that long wait, a young woman seated near us started gesturing through her window.

"There's money out on the sidewalk," she indicated. "Shouldn't somebody go outside and pick it up?"

SeeHawk and I had not dropped any money, so we ignored her and just continued our conversation. After a while, the woman repeated her announcement a bit louder. When, still, nobody responded, SeeHawk finally got up and marched outside. He thought if he flashed the money around while returning to his seat, somebody would claim it.

Outside, among all the bustling passengers, nobody seemed interested in a puny $1 bill lying on the sidewalk. Little did they know—as SeeHawk soon discovered—it was really a $1 bill, covering a $5 bill, covering a $100 bill! Now, SeeHawk felt unsure what to do. If he just went around hollering, "Who lost a hundred-and-eleven-bucks?" there was going to be some commotion. Instead, he quietly climbed back onto the bus and started asking individual passengers if they had lost any money. Nobody had, so, finally, he just handed the $5 bill to its original spotter, and deemed the remaining $101 to be "a gift from The Universe, for assisting with our journey's most wonderful and prosperous success."

Looking proud, upon returning to his seat he boasted, "See? We really do have good luck with buses!"

"Fair enough," I laughed.

But, privately, I wondered if this "good luck" was going to jinx us.

As the bus took off, a large woman stood up from her seat and announced she had first dibs on the sandwich cooler because she was diabetic. Soon, the whole bus came alive with the sounds of crinkling sandwich-wrappers and hissing pop-tops.

The bus driver mentioned Klamath Lake being 30-miles long, but only 10-feet deep on average, and how blue-green algae was harvested from the lake. This subject perked up SeeHawk's ears since he regarded blue-green algae to be a champion among superfoods.

An elderly lady shouted across the bus, "Tell 'em to keep their algae in the lake. I've got my ham sandwich, thank you very much." After everyone stopped laughing, she asked to watch a Lakers game on the bus's built-in television set. Several other passengers booed the Lakers, which triggered a formal vote, resulting in a screening of Meet the Parents, which led SeeHawk and me to forevermore call our drinking-valves "teats."

The rest of Oregon became a brown blur. Once entering Washington, the sky turned red.

The eastbound Empire Builder had our sleeper-car waiting. Its beds turned out to be stacked micro-bunks. Wishing to cuddle, we both squeezed onto a single micro-bunk and promptly fell asleep. There was no popping of champagne. No getting naked. Nor, did we even notice when somebody accidentally bumped our room's thermostat up to 95 degrees. However, we sure noticed it the next morning, when we both woke up drenched in our only set of clothes.

It was disorienting to get smacked in the face by Montana's

bold sunlight. Together, we gazed through our sleeper car's window, at rolling green pastureland, distantly edged with bare, brown mountains. A vigorous river, flowing close alongside the train, could only be seen by standing up a little.

"Seems like the river's flooding," I observed. "Maybe Glacier National Park's snow is melting fast."

Inside the Empire Builder's sightseer car, SeeHawk and I listened to a hired storyteller spin yarns about trains.

"Many years ago," he recited, "a freight train took this next curve too fast and dumped a whole load of corn on the tracks. Plenty of bears live around here, so when the bears smelled corn, they wanted to come and eat it. When the locals got wind, they started coming around to see the bears, which attracted big crowds, until the railroad started to worry about people getting hurt. So, leave it up to some genius, and here's what happened. Somebody realized they could just bury the corn underneath a load of gravel. Maybe that was smart, but you know what corn does when it spends a whole winter under wet gravel?" He paused for effect. "Yep, it ferments! So, after the snow thawed, the bears all got drunk. They kept having big parties, so the railroad had to truck-in heavy machinery and haul everything away."

Just as the story came to an end, like a warm wind blowing along bright, shiny rails, the eastbound Empire Builder pulled into Montana's Glacier Park Station and glided smoothly to a stop.

Never mind that SeeHawk and I had missed a bus to catch a late train, connecting to another bus, hurrying to make a late connection, which got us to Montana one day late. We were pulling into the station right on time.

"Trail Magic?" SeeHawk beamed.

"Definitely," I laughed, "before we've even seen the trail."

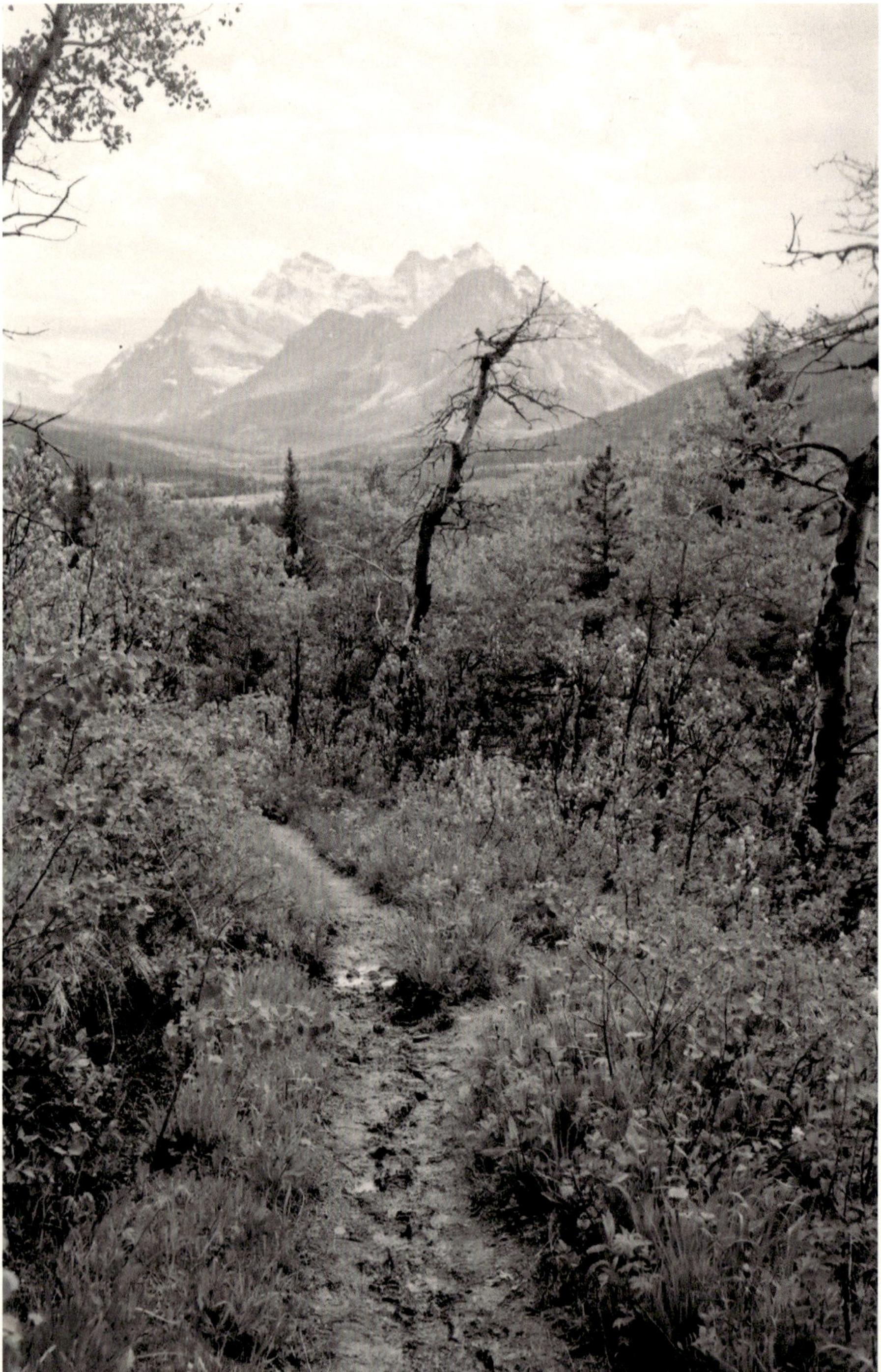

Chapter 5

Initiation

A woman is like a tea bag. You never know how strong she is until she gets into hot water.
— Eleanor Roosevelt

 Stepping from *Amtrak's* crowded train into northern Montana felt like an awakening. SeeHawk and I immediately noticed the change with our noses. Montana's mountains smelled cold and sweet, like wintertime laced with a spoonful of sugar.
 We had spent the past week fearing Poppa Jim's warnings about icy snowfields and flooded creeks. Expecting the worst made it doubly delightful to arrive on a calm, dry morning. Never mind the sun looking a little frosty. Cirrus clouds were common on fair-weather days. Being able to see our breath was also expected. And, feeling our legs sting? Meh, they just needed to get acclimated. Back in suburbia, we might have responded differently, by pulling on warm jackets and pants, but that was two days ago. Now, at almost 5,000-feet above sea level, we were stepping right into thru-hiker mode, which meant no time wasted on costume changes, unless the air temperature was extreme.
 Rather than rushing straight off the train platform, it felt stabilizing to pause and let everything sink in. The view fanned broadly across sprawling meadows and up forested mountains, whose greenness covered every horizon. Sleek, silver doors hissed-shut behind us. Two long rows of wheels groaned back into motion. Slowly at first, and then like a dream, the red-and-blue striped Empire Builder slithered away into the green mountains. One by one, a handful of fellow passengers scat-

tered like marbles off the train platform and disappeared into waiting cars.

Left to make our own exit, SeeHawk and I faced questions of surprise. Where were Glacier National Park's famous glaciers? What about *Backpacker Magazine's* photogenic crags? Where were the icy snowfields Poppa Jim had predicted? Every gentle, green mountain we saw could probably have been climbed wearing sandals.

I found myself struggling against disappointment. That is saying a lot, coming from someone who had been dreading a white welcome. And yet, my still heart beat faster because thrill-seeking had only been part of the equation. Even if Montana's scenery lacked drama, its powerful greenness was already enchanting.

Our agenda for this day started with hitchhiking up to St. Mary's to purchase a camping permit. Coming out of St. Mary's, we would need at least one more ride to reach the Canadian border by early afternoon. After that, it would be all walking for the next six months, except for resupply stops. Presumably, our first box shipped from home was already waiting at the East Glacier post office, where we expected to visit in five days' time. But, first things first. Our immediate focus was on *Amtrak's* rustic train station, assuming it might offer the luxury of flushing toilets.

An attendant locking the station withdrew her key when she saw us coming.

"Take as long as you need," she sang.

Upon returning from the washroom, I remarked about 9:00 a.m. seeming early to close the station.

The attendant explained with a laugh, "Oh, there won't be any more trains today. You're in the Boonies now, sweetheart. Where are you two headed?"

"Into the park for five days," I said, "and then, into the Bob Marshall Wilderness."

"Oh. Well, then, you'd best watch out for bears," she warned me. "Last year, my daughter-in-law and I got stalked by a sow with cubs for three days. Finally, we just gave up and hiked out."

The attendant's keys jingled loudly while she locked up the station and gave us a friendly wave.

"Anyway, you two be safe and have a great time, okay?"

Back outdoors on the train station's porch, SeeHawk and I eyeballed a garbage can. We had not intended to weigh down our backpacks with leftover Brie cheese, uneaten French bread, and two jars of leftover peanut butter and grape jelly. All this excess resulted from SeeHawk having lost his appetite on the train. Was it due to pre-hike anxiety? Or had he come down with the same stomach flu I had contracted a few days earlier? Regardless, now we needed to decide whether to waste all that delicious food or carry it on our backs.

Feeling ambivalent, SeeHawk joked, "We could use it for bear bait to get some good photos."

"Don't SAY that!" I scolded him.

Either because other people in the world were starving, or because our emotions were still attached to having a party on the train, SeeHawk dutifully tied our leftover brie cheese onto his backpack.

Meanwhile, I fixed all the other leftovers into a full loaf of PBJs, which could easily be tied onto my backpack.

Once everything was zipped-shut, I refastened my ponytail, just for relief from feeling my nerves flutter.

SeeHawk tilted his face toward the sky, feeling the sun warm his chin, before starting to grow a six-month beard.

Finally, I suggested, "Shall we mosey-on over to the golf resort? I've seen a few cars leaving their parking lot."

Hitchhiking was something I had done countless times. In addition to hitchhiking frequently on the PCT, I had spent a full winter commuting by thumb between my job in a ski resort town, the house where I had lived that winter, and the ski resort's mountain. Nevertheless, I still felt shy about climbing into strangers' cars. Usually, it took reminding myself that most people inclined to pick up hitchhikers were the friendliest people one could ever meet.

SeeHawk felt differently since he did not mind riding with strangers, but the challenge for him was feeling antsy whenever we needed to get somewhere in a hurry.

I strategically positioned us near the golf resort's exit lane, where drivers would have to approach us slowly, without any sun shining in their eyes. Unfortunately, we looked derelict, wearing the same clothes in which we had slept and eaten for two days, but nothing could be done since we only had one set of clothes.

The morning's heat spiked quickly inside our puddle of shade. It felt ironic to watch figurine-sized golfers enjoying a luxury sport, while we prepared to spend a half-year living without heat or showers. But, then again, taking a half-year off work might have seemed extravagant to them.

Only a few drivers glanced in our direction during a full hour of waiting, and nobody offered us a ride.

SeeHawk anxiously paced back and forth, trying not to say or think anything negative.

I gave him space to brood until, finally, we got picked up by a lawyer from Kentucky.

"I don't know what's come over us," his wife gushed while scooting us into her car. "We NEVER pick up hitchhikers!"

"Trail Magic," SeeHawk beamed as if this moment began our adventure.

Our hostess introduced herself as a schoolteacher and said her lawyer-husband also farmed tobacco, but he was considering a switch to growing native grasses. Their clean white sedan whispered through a stiff pine corridor streaked with shimmering aspen glades. The trees receded upon a high plateau, to make room for Blackfoot Indian cows, who could cross the highway anytime and anywhere they pleased. Within 20-minutes, the pleasant ride ended. We said goodbye to our journey's first Trail Angels, straightened our wrinkly shirts, and bravely marched into the St. Mary's ranger station.

A freckled-faced youth, wearing every ranger's uniform, hailed us in greeting, "Welcome! How can I help you?"

I lifted my chin, summoning confidence, and tersely explained, "We need permits from Canada to East Glacier. Here's our itinerary for the next five days. We'll cross Redgap Pass during the afternoon...ford Cataract Creek first thing in the morning...cross Piegan Pass well before dark..."

My plan prioritized avoiding high elevations during hours when their snowfields might be icy, fording deep streams first thing in the morning, and avoiding bald summits whenever lightning could be expected.

Glacier National Park respected my concerns, but its top priority was keeping hikers away from grizzly bears. This, it accomplished by enforcing strict campsite quotas, and by requiring campers to hang all their food, toothpaste, and sunscreen lotion.

I had debated using bear canisters with a Yellowstone National Park ranger before leaving home.

"You can bring a bear canister into Yellowstone," the ranger had informed me, "but you'll still need to hang your food because we don't officially recognize bear canisters."

"How can you not recognize the best method of food protection available?" I had objected. "Yosemite has the worst bear problems in the country and they require bear canisters, not pole hanging because bears just treat hanging food like pinatas. One swipe and boom! Down it comes. But bear canisters are purposefully made impossible for bears to carry. All they can do is bat them around, unless you add handles, by stuffing them into a hanging sack!"

"I understand," the ranger had sympathized, "but you'll still need to hang your bear canister if you bring it. And remember the Park's fines are huge."

In light of that conversation, I did not even bother mentioning our bear canister to Glacier National Park's young ranger. Instead, I just accepted the map he pushed toward me.

"You can choose from anything marked with a sticker," he explained.

The map displayed lots of campsites, but not many stickers.

I wondered if the ranger looked nervous because he feared my reaction, or if he was just a new hire. Regardless, my heart sank when I examined what he was offering. Few of the stickers matched strategic launch sites for avoiding icy summits, flooded streams, and afternoon lightning storms. They were also separated by extremely awkward distances, such as 4 miles apart or 25 miles apart. I might rather have shaved with tweezers than chosen our journey's first campsites from that list. But, sigh, there we stood. The clock was ticking. We needed to start hiking.

Feeling befuddled, I stepped away from the ranger's desk to put my fears on a chopping block. Which risks seemed most tolerable? Slipping down an icy slope? Drowning? Electrocution?

SeeHawk could not help me because he knew almost nothing about what lay ahead. He just stood off to one side, flipping through books about raptors, while I tore out some hair, gritted my teeth, and eventually handed my notes back to the ranger.

Machinery swallowed my input, made a little noise, and spat out a fresh itinerary.

Reading my own selections in print gave me the jitters. Day Two looked disastrous. We were supposed to cross 18 miles' worth of summits during their iciest hours. Day Three looked easier, so there was a fallback for any shortage on Day Two, but only if we could stealth-camp without getting caught. Days Four and Five looked equally dangerous, but the park's policy was inflexible, so we took the oath and pocketed our new schedule.

Next came a video, pamphlet, and oral test about pacifying grizzly bears. Essentially, the video told us to continuously make noise, in hopes of making the bears think, *Oh, it's just another pesky hiker whose meat, unfortunately, won't taste like chicken.* If our noisemaking failed and we startled a grizzly bear, we were supposed to freeze and not make a sound. The video warned us never to look into a grizzly bear's eyes, or run away because it would chase us if we ran. In the unlikely event of a chase, we were supposed to drop to the ground, curl up, cover our necks, and play dead. Unless we found a suitable climbing tree, in which case verticality might save us because grizzly bears are clumsy climbers, unlike black bears, which is why, if we ran into a black bear, we were supposed to do exactly the opposite. Look straight at them and make some noise. Act big. Unless, it was a momma bear with cubs, in which case we were supposed to use the grizzly bear protocol. Except, if the momma bear charged us, then we were supposed to run for our lives, and not just climb a tree because black bears (unlike grizzlies) are agile tree-climbers. Unless, we could neither outrun the bear nor climb out of its reach, in which case our only hope for survival would be pepper spray, deployed with good aim because bad aim, bad timing, or poor judgment could result in our hides becoming lunch-meat.

I finished the grizzly tutorial imagining how I might face off a bear in real life. First, I might think to myself, *Are you a black or grizzly? Do you have a humped back? Do your claws reach more than one inch past your toes? Do you have any cubs? Are they hiding nearby? Will you charge us if I sneeze? Should I pull out my pepper spray? Or should I drop to the ground and play dead? Raise my arms and make noise? Search for a climbing tree? Just turn-tail and run?*

The park ranger behind the desk concluded our lesson with his own personal warning, "A huge grizzly's been hanging out near the Atlantic Campground. Our rangers say it's one of the biggest they've ever seen." He spread his fingers wide to illustrate a gigantic paw.

I tried to look impressed, but my biggest concern was still all the likelier hazards introduced by our new campsite schedule. I asked him how much snow we could expect atop Glacier's highest passes.

Looking pleased to discuss something besides bears, he said, "People have reported a few snowfields near Piegan Pass, but the pass itself is dry, and there's not much snow in the rest of the park."

"Well, that's good news!" I exclaimed. "Can you give us a fresh weather forecast?"

Pulling up the latest, he predicted, "It's supposed to stay clear for the next two days, followed by a slight risk of thunderstorms...nothing unusual for June....then a slight cooling trend that could produce light rain."

Nodding, I said, "Given how early we're starting, that's good news."

So, now we were legal, which meant it was time to resume hitchhiking.

Back out on the highway, this time we got picked up quickly by a Canadian woman, who confessed, "I can't believe I'm letting you into my car. I NEVER pick up hitchhikers!"

Her jalopy's dusty windows showed us stout Douglas fir trees studding another long stretch of lodgepole-aspen forest. Midway up a crumbling rock cliff, we watched the aspens shrink with elevation. That second ride ended at a lonely intersection, where Chief Mountain Road branched off Highway 89. We were still 16 miles from the CDT's starting line. We needed one last ride, and nobody was turning toward Canada's border guard station.

This would have been a good moment to enjoy some tender and chewy PB&J sandwiches if only impatience had been compatible with hunger. Instead, we nibbled on dry cereal, while soliciting every southbound car approaching Chief Mountain Road. After a full hour of waiting, it was time to admit we needed to switch tactics. Not one, single car had turned in our direction. If we just started walking toward Canada's border-guard station, 16 miles of uphill would be added to our assigned 6 miles for Day One. In other words, failing to hike 22 miles before sundown might subject us to a hefty fine, and it was already getting on toward noon. But, if we could not thumb a ride, what other choice did we have? Sleeping at Canada's border guard station would add 6 miles to our agenda for Day Two because of our campsite reservations being fixed, and thereby land us in the same predicament one day later. Whereas, hitchhiking back to St. Mary's for new campsite reservations would just deposit us back at the same highway intersection one day later. Caught between a rock and a hard place, there was only one reasonable solution. We simply HAD to get a ride.

For the first time since getting dropped off, SeeHawk and I took interest in a cluster of dilapidated log cabins, whose storefront billboard said, *Last Stop in US. Motel. Ice Cold Beer. Store. Diesel. Propane.* Cars had been gassing up there, for an hour. The whole operation looked dodgy, but as the saying goes, desperate times require desperate measures.

SeeHawk volunteered to approach the store alone, while I stayed put, waiting for Murphy's Law to kick in. It only took minutes for him to reappear, followed by a lanky boy holding car keys.

Dressed in a t-shirt, despite the morning being long-sleeve chilly, the boy seemed shy until we got him talking about combing the local woods for elk antlers and deer antlers. After that, the boy grew animated, describing how both species habitually shed their antlers in the same locations year after year.

"What can you do with so many antlers?" we wondered. "Pile them on your porch?"

"Some flatlanders around here buy them," he explained.

It would have been fun to chat a while longer, but shortly, Canada's border-guard station appeared through the trees.

"This is as far as I usually go," our driver muttered.

I gave him a curious look. Had he ever gotten in trouble with the law?

"No problem," I said. "We can jump out here. But, just for the record, I don't think they would mind if you drove right up to the guard booth."

The boy shook his head, "I'm not old enough to drive. I just know how."

My mouth fell open.

SeeHawk muttered as the boy drove away, "Trail Magic."

After all, if we had known our driver was underage, ethics would have compelled us to refuse his help, and who knows how things might have turned out differently?

* * *

Around the lazy hour of 3:30 p.m., SeeHawk and I finished photographing each other at the Canadian border monument. My backpack's contents were well-organized, but standing on the CDT's starting line reminded me how annoying it would feel to get constantly poked or tugged sideways by anything asymmetrical. Therefore, I spent a moment unpacking its entire contents and repacking everything more evenly. Once my backpack was strapped shut again, I stomped its frameless body square with heel.

Then, came the ritual of deploying my trekking poles. It felt comforting to lock them into the same extension notches where they had stayed locked on the Pacific Crest Trail. Little by little, my thru-hiker identity was slowly coming back. That felt comforting, in a place where I recognized nothing besides my partner.

SeeHawk and I both felt giddy while adjusting our packstraps for a comfortable fit. Together, we paused and breathed deeply. This was our last chance to experience the CDT living up to our dreams.

I stared into a forest whose trees essentially all looked the same. My brain was still in city-mode from two days of constant traveling.

"Are you going to pick up a pebble?" SeeHawk wisecracked. He was referring to an Appalachian Trail tradition of symbolically carrying one select pebble all the way up or down the whole AT and then dropping it at the trail's other end.

Laughing, I fired back, "Only if you can wait for me to saw off my toothbrush handle."

SeeHawk began reciting esoteric prayers.

I squatted down to tighten my shoelaces because just thinking about starting to hike made them feel loose. One retied shoelace came out tighter than the other, so I loosened it again, but, oops, too much, so I tightened it again, and so forth until I needed to quit trying and just calm down.

When I finally declared myself ready to start hiking, SeeHawk announced that he felt hungry for the first time in days.

"We can eat a PBJ, quickly," I consented, "and thanks for lightening my load, but then we'll need to hike nonstop all the way to camp because I don't want to learn how to set up our new tent in the dark."

"With giant grizzly bears standing around watching us," SeeHawk dramatized.

"Cut that out!" I scolded him. "Don't you dare jinx us before we even start hiking."

Our sandwich conversation began with SeeHawk reminiscing back two years, to the day PCT-hiker Robert had told us he felt guilty about stepping on hundreds or thousands of ants.

I remembered our first time meeting Robert. He had come speeding toward our camp in total darkness, with one ear glued to a transistor radio broadcasting an *NBA* playoff game. Nighttime hiking (combined with afternoon napping) was a popular custom in southern California's thirsty deserts, as a tactic to avoid heatstroke. Therefore, we had not been not surprised to see a backpacker approaching through the darkness, but we had definitely giggled into our elbows because, poor Robert. His sneakers must have been caked with cow poop, thanks to SeeHawk and me paving the way behind a herd of cows.

SeeHawk's recollections of Robert drifted to the industrious young African-American's vehicle for financing both his AT and PCT hikes; reportedly, Robert had walked door-to-door in Ohio, selling glow-in-the-dark home address numbers.

"He really killed two birds with one stone," SeeHawk summarized, "getting his legs in shape while earning the money."

I recalled Robert being the only other thru-hiker we knew who carried a fly-fishing rod in his ultralight backpack. Being a kind fellow, when Robert found an abandoned fly-rod lying on the PCT, he had passed it to a female hiker who promised to leave it for us in Yosemite, thinking it was ours.

Those memories led us to reminisce about PCT-hikers Kevin, Colleen, and Sly (our companions going over Mather Pass), Team Onfire (two speedy youths who ate mashed potatoes with dehydrated hamburger almost every night, before they ran out of steam in northern California), mountain-man Pigpen (who kept leap-frogging us because he hiked faster but spent more time relaxing), Alaskan fisherman Foxtrot (who routinely chugged cartons of milk side by side with orange juice, while gnawing on a 2 lb. brick of cheese), and Bob and Jane (seasonal partners, with whom we expected to soon cross paths in Wyoming, while they section-hiked part of the CDT northbound).

Altogether, doing the PCT had been a "social" experience, compared with SeeHawk and me now undertaking a trail whose estimated attendance, during 2001, was only 10-20 total thru-hikers per year. We feared luck might be required for us to meet anybody else traveling border-to-border, let alone spend time with them.

"But, we can at least increase our chances by wiping that peanut butter off our cheeks and getting our butts in gear," I urged SeeHawk while repacking our uneaten PBJs.

It felt silly to bend down and readjust my shoelaces again, but I had to loosen them because either nerves or adrenaline had caused my feet to bloat during our snack break.

SeeHawk stayed busy readjusting pack-straps that were already readjusted until I pronounced myself ready to return to the trail's starting line.

A ceremonial kiss made our starting procedure official.

SeeHawk mumbled another round of sacred incantations… waved his arms in the air…asked his personal "Awaikus," plus the Spirits of every mountain along America's Backbone, plus The Universe in general, to grant us a safe passage from Canada down to Mexico.

I beseeched any hypothetical Beings who might exist or not, listening or not, to teach us whatever we needed to learn without making us suffer.

SeeHawk ended his preliminaries by asking, "Can I please check my wristwatch?"

"Argh!" I groaned. "Just tell time by watching the sun, okay? This is a nature hike, not a business meeting."

SeeHawk flashed me a pouting look, but rules are rules. Even before setting foot on the PCT, he and I had agreed to forego electronics while hiking. He knew I was not going to budge on that issue, so he left his beloved timepiece stowed in a handy pocket and gave up on pinpointing our exact time of departure. (Unless, he slyly checked the time, which is possible since our agreement included a clause that anything was fair game so long as I never saw it or heard about it, or if we were hurrying to reach a post office.)

Meantime, my own departure ceremony ended with grabbing my trekking poles like I meant to get some use out of them.

SeeHawk did not bother unstrapping his poles since the trail's entrance looked flat and easy. He just recited the words of philosopher Lau Tzu, "Every journey of a thousand miles begins with a single step."

Crunching the numbers, I deduced, "Does that mean our first step needs to be three steps?"

SeeHawk chuckled, "Why round down? Let's play it safe and start with four."

Together, we roared, "Mexico or bust!"

Interlocking hands and with our shoes side-by-side, we officially marched forth. The adventure was underway!

Right off the bat, our shoes found rapport with the familiar texture of hard-packed earth.

SeeHawk quickly released my hand and moved into position behind me because the trail was too narrow for romance on the move.

Montana's boundary forest contained two distinct layers. Upwardly, its pine canopy blocked out the sun completely, as in shutters closed, blinds down, no leaks anywhere. Inwardly, its bare-naked branches were crushed into tangles like an old rotten hairbrush.

"This place must hold a lot of snow during most of the year," SeeHawk supposed.

"Probably, Glacier National Park's tourist season peaks from July to August," I agreed.

The easygoing trail gave us leisure for peering into deep, dark shadows. Frightened minds could have filled them with eyes, claws, and teeth, but our minds were at ease. Even though the trees looked shabby as individuals, their collective appearance was smooth, which had a pacifying effect. Likewise, our nerves got soothed by the monotonous rhythm of my trekking poles clanking between four thumping shoes.

The first change of scenery appeared where a moist pocket of forest transported us into springtime. Green leaf shoots were popping through fibrous pine mulch, which anchored elastic goldenrod, odorous cow parsnip, and stiff white yarrow. More diversity appeared as we descended through pines with a bit more elbow-room, which reached out and tickled dapper Englemann spruces.

I spent a moment wondering if my own personality aligned more with the unruly pines or with the tidy Englemann spruces. My knock-knees, warped neck, and fan-shaped left eyebrow suggested unruly, but my trip-planning skills were tidy, except for leaving some things to chance.

SeeHawk, on the other hand, had more in common with the Douglas Fir trees we had seen driving up to the Canadian border. His chest was thick. His hands were square. His calves could rival picnic hams. Even his character was robust, thanks to having gotten stabbed five times in the stomach by a mugger from Boston, hit by a car at age 5, walloped on the head by a dropped board that cracked his skull during the same year, been run over by a hay wagon full of people at age 14, and survived a rollover car crash in his twenties. Genetics contributed to SeeHawk's toughness, in the sense that he could build muscles sitting in a chair, whereas I could lose muscles during a walk home from exercising. Blah, blah, blah, my mind kept chattering about stuff and nonsense until a rogue sunbeam slapped me back to attention.

We were entering a stretch of roomier woods, letting in enough sunlight for its lodgepole-pine trees to grow tall and straight, like their name said they should. In fact, some pines grew straight enough to humble the Englemann spruces. Arboreally speaking, the party came to life where both species got joined by my favorite aristocrats, the glamorous grand firs—who stole the runway with their long, slender cones, star-shaped needle clusters, and whitish-silver bark.

Several small clearings were splashed like painter's palettes with common yellow dandelions, yellow arnica, shrubby goldeneye, red Indian paintbrush, purple asters, and pink shooting star lilies. The last clearing folded into another deep-shade forest, whose hodgepodge greens were mixed like a salad. Budding columbine, feathery angelica, and low-spreading clover dramatized the broader leaves of palmate thimbleberry and whorled corn lilies, whose bulk gave the understory structure and loft.

Along with increasing visual interest came a new soundtrack, starring one piledriving woodpecker beating its head in time with a mountain chickadee, who kept whistling 4- and 6-note reels. Countermelodies and percussion were added by some mysterious warbler SeeHawk nicknamed the "Reverb-Bird," plus another bird whistling a tropical minuet, some creature imitating a household smoke alarm, and a spring-loaded doorstopper getting twanged in slow-motion. Overall, we could have been listening to a preschool jug band.

I hated to break the momentum we had going, but nature pulled me over for a quick whiz. While squatting in some deep grass, I discovered a can of pepper spray lying beside my shoes. Probably it had fallen off somebody's backpack.

SeeHawk thought I should pick it up and wear it. That way, I could defend myself against bears, instead of relying on him to carry our only can of pepper spray.

I complained in response, "Now you've totally jinxed me because not taking the can will invite Murphy's Law, but it weighs close to a pound."

"You don't have to follow every suggestion I make, Sunshine," he reminded me. "And anyway, jinxes aren't real. They're just a fun thing to worry about when you're a kid."

"Says the guy who believes in angels," I snorted, while resentfully pocketing the dirty old can.

The downhill vegetation receded and grew softer inside a fluttering aspen glade. Midway across an underlying terrace, we gained our first view of the southern skyline. Several of its distant skyscrapers looked snow-white from their tips to their timberlines.

"Now that's more like it!" I rejoiced. "Sorry for doubting you, *Backpacker Magazine*."

Geologic history spoke about earthquakes violently upheaving the Rocky Mountain range. As construction jobs go, their work had been coarse. The demolition crews left behind a mess of crooked and broken peaks. Fortunately, the glacier crews coming in after them had followed up with extensive chiseling and polishing. 75-million years later, the end result was a row of gingerbread village roofs. Snow should have slid off the roofs in a jiffy, so why did they all look bottom-up white? Was this Poppa Jim's reason for warning thru-hikers not to leave Canada until later in the month? Well, anyway, it was too late now. Our window for rain-checks had come and gone.

The trail's next meadow received a fresh breeze coming in from the west. Glancing across a border of windward trees, my eyes caught sight of a bluish-silver oval. Strangely, it was floating all by itself, in an otherwise sunny sky. Technically speaking, it was a "lenticular" cloud. Children might have called it a UFO because of its smooth flying-saucer shape. Meteorologists might have predicted a snowstorm coming within two days, but that was not possible. The park's current forecast had said nothing about snow. It had to be a fluke; although, something had caused it to form. Regardless, before I could even show the cloud to SeeHawk, poof! It disappeared. Had my eyes tricked me? I decided to start watching the sky more closely.

Delving back under the cover of deep woods, I got startled by a shrill whistle ricocheting through the trees. Nothing moved to identify its source. Another shrill whistle shot by, and then another until SeeHawk started joking about Pan playing his flute.

"I bet you'd be the happiest man alive if we met Pan, for real," I teased SeeHawk.

"Don't egg me on, or I'll start hoping to meet all the heroes of my favorite fantasy novels," he laughed, resurrecting one of my usual jokes.

Changing the subject, I pointedly asked him, "What do you want for dinner tonight? Barbequed elk? Stewed reverb-bird? Some kind of boiled starch with rehydrated tomato-leather?"

Cringing SeeHawk groaned, "Don't even talk to me about food, please. I'm still too full of PBJs to think about eating anything else. Plus, my stomach's not feeling great right now."

It was normal for SeeHawk to feel queasy while adjusting to high altitudes. Currently, though, we were only at 5,000-feet. Could his discomfort have been caused by contracting my recent stomach flu? Uh-oh. Was he going to be able to keep up with our ambitious campsite schedule? I sure hoped so since darned if we were going to leave the woods for anything short of outright vomiting.

Within the next hour, dusk dialed the forest's brilliant greens down to grays. It had been a long day. Between the train ride, visiting the ranger station, hitchhiking three times, and backpacking six miles since morning, we both felt ready to call it a night. Therefore, we experienced a flood of relief when the Gable Campground finally appeared.

Another party of backpackers had already set up camp near the trail. They were busy eating dinner, so we just threw them a wave and strode on by. The campground's rear boundary offered a lovely tent site fastened close against the Belly River, whose rushing was quite loud.

"It'll be nice not to hear our neighbor's conversations," I remarked, "but also, we won't be able to hear any bears come visiting tonight."

"Psht," SeeHawk shrugged. "Who cares? Since we're going to hang our food anyway."

Accepting that logic, I flung down my backpack, and, together, we got right to work figuring out how to pitch our brand-new freestanding tent. Its un-labeled hooks, holes, and sleeves were designed to accept insertion from three curvy poles that were almost, but not quite, the same length as one another. Once we produced a lopsided dome, the next step was covering it with a slippery rainfly, lashed to the same crooked tent stakes we had bent two years ago, along with some handy logs.

Then, came a frenzy of unloading our backpacks. Separating wads of mashed clothes from dinner utensils led me to discover that our whole loaf of PB&Js had gotten squished into one gigantic ball of bear bait. The resulting goo looked worse than inedible. That was problematic since not eating it would mean carrying it, day after day, without having enough room for it in our bear canister each night, unless we wanted to risk some of our home-dried meals.

"Can't you please drink a little soup, if nothing else?" I begged. "How about split-pea? That's always your favorite."

"Not in a million years," SeeHawk insisted, pushing away the spoon. "Hopefully I'll feel better in the morning.

I always hated eating alone, no matter if I was on the trail, at home, or flying solo in a restaurant. Therefore, rather than exceed my own ration, I just dumped both SeeHawk's leftovers and mine into the same plastic bag containing our smashed PB&Js and rotting Brie cheese.

Once our food supply was tidily returned into its stuff sacks, then it was showtime. Inside the campground's designated food-hanging area, four curious neighbors watched SeeHawk and me forget how to do something we had done every night on the Pacific Crest Trail. We remembered that counter-hanging involved tying two food sacks onto each end of a rope. We also remembered that the suspension arm (usually a tree branch, but currently a high metal hanging pole) needed to be twice as high as a bear could reach because counter-hung sacks would end up hanging at half the suspension arm's height. Furthermore, we remembered something about needing to see-saw one sack upward before attaching the other sack. But, why had we brought one long rope and one short rope? Also, how were we supposed to retrieve both sacks the next morning? Unfortunately, I had forgotten about looping the shorter rope through one sack's bottom strap, in order to create a pulldown that would slip-free if a bear tried to rob us because no bear would ever think to grab both ends of the rope. Clever, huh? Except, for one problem. My mind went blank while staring at two mismatched ropes in my hands, with four curious faces witnessing my confusion.

SeeHawk kept his mouth shut as he stood by, patiently waiting for instructions. Like me, he felt groggy from having spent 2-nights sleeping on trains, fatigued from our first day of hiking, and tired from not having eaten a proper dinner.

The forest was getting dark. This was all so ridiculous.

I just wanted to lie down and sleep, but our food...the bears...I wracked my brain...were we supposed to push up one sack with a stick? That operation seemed familiar. But, which sack? Attached to which rope? Short or long? Was I confused because we had brought the wrong ropes? Would it help to splice a section of the long rope onto the short-rope, in order to make them more equal?

I felt nervous about asking SeeHawk for his buck knife.

"Are you sure?" he frowned.

Trying to ignore the peanut gallery, I nervously admitted, "No, but if I'm wrong, I guess we could always re-tie them."

Schoop!

As soon as the rope's cut-ends fell apart, I recognized my error. *Darn, darn, darn!* I wanted to scream, jump around and curse, but with four campers watching it was like being on TV.

"Sorry," I apologized to SeeHawk. "I know this little knot will drive you nuts every time it snags a tree branch for the next six months, but..."

He refrained from answering. It was bad enough just to stand there watching me triple-square-knot the rope back together.

Finally, one audience member stood up and introduced himself as the group's hired guide. He wanted to know why we were even bothering to counter-hang since it would be easier just to stuff everything into one sack, throw a single rope over the pole and lash it around a tree as his party had done.

I curtly explained, "No offense, but where we come from? The bears would cut down your food faster than we're having this conversation."

The hired guide laughed. "Thank goodness, Montana bears aren't that smart!"

Now it was my turn to feel surprised. Could I believe this jovial stranger, just based on his aura of confidence? He looked awfully clean by wilderness-guide standards. Furthermore, could Montana's bears really be significantly dumber than Yosemite's bears? I felt skeptical, but exhaustion convinced me to let fate take its course. Together, SeeHawk and I hung our food from a rope any bear could sever in one swipe.

Back at our campsite, we shoved both backpacks into our tent's small vestibule, for overnight protection from salt-licking deer. Next, we set about soaking the bandanna handkerchiefs we had worn around our necks all day in cold Belly River water. The wet pieces of cloth made good scrubbers for freshening our faces, necks, and feet until all the day's heat evaporated into pleasure. Miniature pack towels finished the job nicely. Our tired arms and legs fairly screamed to slip into silky nylon longjohns. With teeth on the verge of chattering, we chose familiar sides of our shared sleeping quilt and dove undercover. Lying side-by-side, it felt blissful to watch moonlight glow through our tent's sheer ceiling. *Thank you, Mother Nature. It's great to be back.*

The river made noise. Its embankment felt sturdy. Our bones sank heavily onto inch-thick sleeping pads. Nothing could have felt grander than simply lying still, after a whole day of constantly being in motion.

* * *

SeeHawk awoke in the Gable Campground feeling like a child on Christmas morning. The sun was still sleeping when he unzipped our tent, crawled outside, and ran over to check on our food. Much to his relief, he found everything hanging right where we had left it, still tied off by a single rope. No bear tracks showed in the dirt underneath. If Montana's bears were dumber than Yosemite bears, that theory would have to be proven some other day.

When SeeHawk returned to camp, boasting success, he sheepishly confided, "I kind of wish they'd taken the Brie, or at least that purple ball of whatever we're not eating."

"We could bury it six inches under," I suggested.

But, of course, we were too environmentally correct to do any such thing. Instead, SeeHawk just tossed the smelly goo-ball into a pile of other things assigned for his backpack.

While striking camp, we wished a shadow glued onto us would please move over and let the sun thaw our fingers, but it did not budge.

When SeeHawk noticed me shivering, he launched into one of his timeworn speeches about mornings being coldest just before sunrise.

As usual, I gave him my timeworn answer, "According to one of my old college professors, it's coldest at four o'clock in the morning. That wind chill you feel at sunrise is just a localized thermal breeze, triggered by sunlight hitting the coldest air."

"Exactly," he beamed, "it's colder at sunrise."

"It's cold but not as cold as at four o'clock," I told him. "If you don't believe me, check your keychain thermometer."

"I don't need to," he claimed, "because I already know the answer."

"But, you're not getting up at four o'clock to check."

"Are you asking me to wake up in the dark, just to prove something I already know?" he laughed.

"If you already knew, you'd agree with me.".

"No, I wouldn't," he protested, "because it's something I've observed over a long period of time, not just something I thought of today."

"Except, your observations have been based on limited data."

"Actually, my data comes using from my keen powers of observation. Don't forget that I was a paperboy. Four a.m. is when I woke up every morning to check our kitchen thermometer and decide what to wear. By the time the sun came up, that's when I usually finished delivering papers. So, if you're asking for experience, I have firsthand experience. But that doesn't even matter because it's the same now as it was back then. If you'd felt what I felt an hour ago, you'd understand what I'm saying."

"I do understand, and your perception was correct, but you were feeling wind chill, not the absolute coldest temperature."

Around and around we went, having our first circular argument on the CDT. Okay, correction. It was really just an annoying (not to mention, erroneous) conversation. The problem was, we could not seem to end it. And then, when something came along to distract us, we still were not happy because that distraction was an abdominal cramp, which sent SeeHawk sprinting into the woods.

As I watched my fiancé disappear, I worried again about him having caught my recent stomach flu. Time would tell but, at the moment, we just needed to hurry up and get cracking.

While sitting alone in the unmoving shade, I unfolded a wad of loose guidebook pages and skimmed through a mixture of paragraphs, charts, and maps. I was searching for the highest and lowest elevations between the Gable Campground, where we had slept, and the Many Glacier Campground, which was our goal for the day.

When SeeHawk returned, I reported uneasily, "The park's computer thinks it's eighteen miles from here to our next campsite.

"Sounds doable," he nodded. "That's about what we figured yesterday, right?"

"Right, but guess what? Poppa Jim thinks it's twenty-two miles."

"Twenty-two versus eighteen? Our guidebooks disagree?"

"Right."

"That's weird."

"Weird, as in, disturbing because we've got a big climb ahead, and if we don't reach Many Glacier before dark, the park might really take us to the cleaners."

Scowling, SeeHawk inquired, "What does the Book of Beans say?"

"Nothing specific enough to be useful. I guess we'll just need to hike fast and hope for Poppa Jim to be wrong."

"Well, in case he's right, we'd better put in our order for clear weather."

Agreeing that a little prayer couldn't hurt, I said toward the sky, "Okay, listen up, all you Trail Gods. Please melt any snow between here and Many Glacier. Tell the bears not to bother us, and please let today be an easy day of hiking."

In his turn, SeeHawk politely thanked the Spirit of the Mountain for providing us with a safe and comfortable place to rest. Then, he glanced around our campsite, making sure not to leave anything behind.

Finally, he and I resurrected a ritual we had performed every morning on the PCT, by simply saying, "Thank you spot," to our first campsite on the CDT.

That was a rap. Without further delay, we took off sprinting into our first full day on the Continental Divide. Come hell or high water, we were sworn to complete either 18 or 22 miles before it got dark, whichever might apply, depending upon whose mileage estimate was correct.

SeeHawk followed me up a gentle incline, tunneling beneath trees that hid most of the sky. Shortly past our campsite, a missing chunk of forest revealed a mighty spectacle called Dawn Mist Falls. Its focal point was a broad ribbon of whitewater, collapsing squarely over a thick stone bench. Along its forward edge sat heaps of glistening-wet boulders, getting thwacked by rubbery spruce boughs, themselves bouncing upon exploding mist. The whitewater's impact sounded like cannon fire. Boom after boom played over a steady roar. Altogether, we felt reminded of a miniature Niagara Falls, except for the waterfall's odd location making it seem added to the woods by Photoshop.

Wistfully, I mumbled, "It sure would be nice to eat breakfast here."

"But, brrr, no way," SeeHawk agreed. "Just imagine how cold this place must feel at sunrise."

"NO!" I wailed. "Please, don't start THAT again."

Beyond Dawn Mist Falls, we traversed through a wreckage of dead and toppled trees. Nothing looked burned, so the cause must have been either an avalanche or a violent windstorm. Booms from the waterfall followed us downhill, like echoes of wartime until we entered a fresh enclosure of living trees. From there on downward, greenery funneled our attention toward a picturesque valley containing Elizabeth Lake.

Once we touched bottom, the lakeshore provided front-row seats for watching insects cast circles across the silver water, and fish casting circles around the floating insects. It was a scene fit for silence. Too bad, we needed to make a bunch of noise chomping hard strawberry granola, barely fazed by our rehydrated milk.

After breakfast, we began a long, steady climb toward Redgap Pass. The first overlook reminded us to think in all directions. There was beauty at every turn, but it was too soon to start taking photos because we knew grander views were waiting uphill.

Once our food felt digested, it would have been nice to speed up, but our legs balked because we had done most of our pre-hike training at sea level. Soon, I began to resent carrying a bunch of smelly food trash. Why, in the name of birdbrains, had SeeHawk and I both snubbed the train station's garbage can?

Two hundred feet above Elizabeth Lake, the photo opportunities began. We appeared to be scaling a miles-long glacier valley, excavated by the Ice Age into a giant halfpipe. The valley's opposite wall was zebra-striped with conifer trees and vertical grass chutes, pouring all their various greens into Elizabeth Lake, where they mixed with the sky's blue reflection, to create a vortex of tropical-looking water.

Standing opposite to us, the valley's southern mountains formed a cul-de-sac of teeth, enameled with shining snow. Cornered against the teeth stood hulking Mount Cleveland, impersonating shattered cream-filled chocolate. Next, in line came a red-and-purple ridge, whose color matched the dirt beneath our feet. This last coincidence made us curious. Had the opposite ridge ever been connected to Redgap Pass?

My gaze headed north until it landed upon a sight that made my skin tingle. Seen through the Belly River's watershed, Canada should have looked tiny in the distance. Instead, my eyes could not even find it. *Bon voyage*, I thought. *This journey is turning real.*

We could not afford to dally, so, after taking in the view, we got right back to climbing. My trekking poles clanked like pocket-change, still keeping time with our four thumping shoes.

Hiking in the rear, SeeHawk's shirt kept making a ripping sound every time he opened his Velcro chest pockets. Eventually, hearing rip after rip made me wonder what he was up to. I kept spinning around to look, but I could never catch him doing whatever he was doing.

Meanwhile, my hat's floppy brim kept brushing against my backpack, "fsh...fsh...fsh...fsh," until it started to drive me crazy.

Inside a gap between two converging slopes, we ran into a sign saying the Ptarmigan Tunnel was closed. An off-branching trail might have aimed toward the tunnel. I felt puzzled because I could not remember reading about any tunnel in our guidebooks. Of course, that made sense since why would a guidebook mention features unrelated to the trail it was describing?

We climbed for another 15 minutes before a disturbing thought struck me. If the park's computer had expected us to pass through the Ptarmigan Tunnel, but Poppa Jim's guidebook (assuming a June departure) had expected it to be closed, perhaps that might account for the 4-mile mileage discrepancy?

When SeeHawk heard my theory, he concluded gruffly, "We'd better speed up."

As it was, though, neither of us could climb any faster.

Above the valley's timberline, the CDT narrowed enough that we had to walk with our shoes banging together. Mincing steps across a paprika red peak, shaped like an egg, we started running into smooth, acre-wide snowfields. Late-morning sunlight had already softened the snow, making it easy for us to stomp secure footholds. There was no danger of slipping any distance. Nevertheless, SeeHawk comfortingly reminded me about the St. Mary's ranger reporting no snow atop Piegan Pass and only isolated patches on the mountain's shoulder.

"Really," he summarized, "I think it's obvious that Poppa Jim overestimated this year's snowpack."

"Or else, there was a lot of snow before the heatwave, but it's been thawing like mad ever since," I suggested.

"Well, if that's true," he replied, "it just goes to show The Spirit of the Mountain wants us to succeed."

Laughing skeptically, I replied, "You think the Cosmic is purposely melting Glacier National Park for our benefit? How can you be so...so...ack! Don't you think other people have weather needs, too? If Mother Nature tailored the weather for every one of us, we'd all have to live in separate universes."

"That's true," he agreed, "but most people don't put in their orders, so maybe we don't have much competition."

"Oh, for Pete's sake, never mind."

The Belly River valley looked gorgeous from 2,000-feet above Elizabeth Lake. Not only that, but even just the plain-old dirt surrounding our shoes looked gorgeous. There were little scarlet-orange, pink, purple, and teal-colored stones scattered everywhere as if a jeweler had tripped and spilled a bucket of beads.

Maybe the National Park's local grizzly bears had a treasure fetish because in the same location we started seeing fresh grizzly tracks pressed all over the dirt.

SeeHawk examined the spacing between one pawprint's toe-holes and claw-holes, and he thoughtfully concluded, "No wonder bears can cut a rope with one swipe. This big kahuna must look like Edward Scissorhands."

I encouraged my partner to keep talking because his banter distracted me from the effort of climbing, but when he caught on, he snapped with annoyance, "Let's stop all the chit-chat, okay? I need to focus on where I'm stepping."

Redgap Pass turned out to be a saddle separating two sentinel peaks. One peak looked back across the Belly River valley; the other looked forward across turquoise-blue Poia Lake. Our maps showed the CDT bypassing Poia Lake, so we decided to eat lunch on top of the scenic saddle. Luckily, although mountaintops can be windy, that hour remained so calm that we could hear ourselves chewing Swiss cheese and vegetarian pepperoni.

After a long spell of chewing, SeeHawk remarked, "Hm."

Gazing at everything, I added, "Huh."

"...boy..."

"...man..."

Why did splendor often cripple our vocabularies? We just could not find words to describe what we were seeing. Thankfully, though, our powers of speech returned when two cute chipmunks darted out of a huge rock cairn marking the pass. The feisty little monsters tried to steal our lunch. They sniffed our toes. Finally, we got fed up and started chucking pebbles at them, which only made them snicker.

"Now, we know how that cairn got so huge," SeeHawk remarked. "It's from people throwing rocks at the chipmunks."

The sun passed through its zenith during the next hour that we spent skirting Poia Lake. We had only progressed 8 miles since morning. Given this figure, we had to evaluate. Could we, realistically, hope to complete another 14 miles before dark? One element working in our favor was Montana's long daylight. During June, we could expect the sky to remain bright until about 9:30 pm. Nevertheless, more speed would be required for us to honor our campsite reservations.

Slightly below Redgap Pass, we noticed some rare whitebark pine trees infiltrating a community of subalpine firs. The youngest pines had wrinkly bark, like children dressed in big adult clothing. The elders had multiple trunks, which was normal for whitebark pines and also common among other pines at high altitudes. The whitebarks, in particular, captured our interest because seeing them warned us to expect harsh weather.

On the backside of Swiftcurrent Ridge, we entered a forest steeped in gothic shadows. Suddenly, from out of nowhere, a powerful wind whooshed through the trees. The air temperature turned mitten-cold. Sporadic wind gusts came and went. During the same half-hour, my blood sugar crashed. It began with a bout of irrational sweating. Next, came dizziness and a vague floaty feeling.

SeeHawk smiled when I asked if we could sit down somewhere. He felt a little queasy, himself, and could easily have been talked into a nap. However, when he snuck a peek at his wristwatch, he realized we could not afford to stop for long.

I knew full well that it was getting late. There were already slivers of golden skylight peeking through the trees. I wanted to keep moving, but, first, I needed to rest until my blood sugar normalized.

Luckily, within a few minutes, poof! A perfect sitting log appeared. It even came packaged with Swiftcurrent Ridge Lake, whose choppy blue water had no business hiding inside the deep woods, but there it was.

Hoping that my body just needed a generous helping of calories, I smeared moldy Brie cheese onto a hunk of stale French bread and devoured it like a wolf. The food went down easily. Instead of jumpstarting my engine, though, it sent blood rushing from my head down to my stomach, which made me feel sick. Apparently, I really just needed to rest, but, shoot. The forest's interior was starting to fade. Its air temperature was dropping fast. I tugged on a windbreaker jacket and snuggled against SeeHawk, trying to glean some warmth through his layered nylon clothing. Gradually, he and I sank into a shivering trance. Strong wind gusts kept shifting the lake's color back and forth between silver and blue. Wind chop was common to see on open-air lakes, but inside the enclosed woods, it took on the appearance of magic.

When I noticed the western trees losing their color, I felt a pang of alarm.

"Come ON," I urged my body. "Get UP. Get MOVING."

When SeeHawk heard me speak to myself, he responded by jiggling his legs, to release them from sitting and get psyched for the last push.

Suddenly, inky shadows came spilling through the trees and threw a black cloak over Swiftcurrent Ridge Lake. The forest's visibility dimmed like a stage. Leaping to our feet, we flung on our backpacks and charged. The lakeshore's trees helpfully pulled back, exposing a gentle downslope that coaxed us along. We made good progress, but there was no chance to reach Many Glacier before dark.

"At least, the park rangers should give us credit for getting close," I hoped, "because we might have made it all the way if the Ptarmigan Tunnel had been open."

"That makes sense," SeeHawk agreed, "but if they find us stealth-camping, you do the talking."

Further downhill, we watched twilight's last wildflowers melt into blackness. Stars crept in. The moon came up. Cold silver sparkles outlined alien shapes, drawing our eyes toward a flat-topped bluff. My legs were kaput. They could hardly walk another step. The bluff looked hospitable, so we pulled off the trail two miles before reaching our goal.

SeeHawk helped me whap-together our tent poles, while I pondered what to say if night-prowling rangers caught sight of our camp. Would they let us off the hook if we told them the park's computer had failed to account for the tunnel being closed? Was the closure even relevant? If not, might we be able to bribe them with some moldy Brie cheese?

Once our tent stood stiff, SeeHawk wandered out into the darkness, searching for a suitable food-hanging tree. He needed one with a snag-free limb 20-feet off the ground, thick enough to support heavy food-sacks, but thin enough to eject a hungry bear-cub. After finding the right limb, he would pitch the longer of our two counter-hanging ropes over the limb's midsection, using a rock tied onto the end, for added inertia, and then finish the job after dinner.

Tonight's entrée was home-dried lasagna, boobytrapped with rubbery Mozzarella clots that challenged SeeHawk's queasy tummy. Somehow, he managed to eat his full ration, and afterward, he even performed his usual "dishwashing" routine, which was never a pretty sight to watch. The routine began with pouring a little water into the cooking pot we double-purposed for eating. Then, he scrubbed the pot "clean" with his index finger, drank the scrub water, and, finally, wiped the pot dry with a few squares of toilet paper. All of this, he had done every night on the Pacific Crest Trail, and I always felt grateful, while looking the other way.

Once we got everything neatly packed away, we flopped onto our sleeping quilt, switched on our headlamps, and got to work.

SeeHawk sorted through our next day's maps.

I read through our just-finished guidebook pages and presently confirmed, "Poppa Jim's guidebook says we hiked twenty miles today."

"Not bad, for day two," SeeHawk responded.

"Although, none of the numbers I'm reading quite match each other," I added.

Moving on, to some of the new maps SeeHawk had organized, I calculated that we needed to complete 16 miles the following day (including two makeup miles), which was a reasonable goal. My only concern was waking up farther away from Cataract Creek than I had originally planned. The increased distance would give a little more time for the creek's water to rise before we got there.

My last trip outside confirmed what I had suspected, which was, brrr. The air temperature was dropping fast. As soon as I finished brushing my teeth with retched-tasting baking soda-mint-powder, I dove back into our tent and clenched SeeHawk's and my shared sleeping quilt tightly around my chin. It took a few minutes to stop shivering. Then, a familiar heatwave came on strong. It felt delicious to get high on hypothermia. Nothing could have excited me more than spending another six months in the great outdoors.

* * *

SeeHawk and I awoke to a faint pattering sound, like sand being sprinkled onto the ceiling above our heads. It took us a moment to realize we were hearing gentle rain.

My waking reaction was, "Hooray, if it's going to be cold today, maybe there won't be much snow melting upstream, and Cataract Creek won't flood before we get there."

"Um, rain creates floods, and melts snow," SeeHawk reminded me.

"Well, true," I frowned. "I guess, we'd better tell the weather gods to stop the rain, but keep the clouds."

I did not realize our true situation until I climbed outside and looked up, at which time I laughed, "SeeHawk, you won't believe this. We're camped beneath the only rain cloud in sight!"

There were other clouds standing by, of course, but none of them looked worse than fluffy little cumulus.

"Still, though, it's a bit of a walk from here to Cataract Creek," I said, "so we'd better make like a banana and split."

Our first task of the morning was to finish the last two miles' worth of trail approaching Many Glacier. It took diligence to keep every piece of our camping gear dry while striking our rain-dampened tent. Once that task was accomplished, we took off hiking in a lingering drizzle.

As usual, we spent the first mile gnawing on pre-breakfast fruit rolls, which were almost a meal in themselves. The fruit rolls' purpose was to delay our meal schedule, making 4:00 pm feel like lunchtime, which helped us stay perky during the afternoon's groggiest hours. Today's flavor was blackberry-banana-coconut, sweet and tangy, with an especially nice chew.

Once the drizzling rain stopped, borders of pink geraniums and yellow goldenrods sprang to life alongside the trail. The cumulus clouds we had seen at daybreak were still immature, but some were inflating like baking biscuits. Down at trail–level, the air warmed enough for our damp clothes to dry by the time we reached the Many Glacier picnic area.

It was too early for breakfast. We had just finished our fruit rolls, but whatever. We decided to eat in the picnic area anyway because, considering our destination, who knew when another good opportunity might come along?

While unscrewing twin mugs of soak-and-eat rice pudding, we saw a few timid sun rays sneak through clouds. Their splendor lasted about five minutes before an incoming stratus layer slid the sky shut. Gloom resumed, but even in grayness, the picnic area looked intoxicating. Its pocket of open space was wide enough to feel roomy, between walls tall enough to block out the world. Straight lodgepole pine trees and flouncy black cottonwoods shielded fountains of shiny beargrass scattered across the ground.

We had the whole picnic area to ourselves, with no more weather happening and the air holding still. Therefore, we should have been able to hear the nearby campground, but we heard nothing. Wasn't that strange? Where was everybody? How come we could not hear any laughter or conversations? What about cars, coming or going? Where was the guard gate that usually preceded campgrounds? Pondering these questions made me realize we were lucky not to have hiked into the dark, trying to reach the campground last evening because we would only have ended up sleeping illegally in the picnic area, where bears and rangers might have found us in a snap.

By the time we finished eating, things were drying up. Nevertheless, we kept wearing our rain-ponchos, just for protection against Murphy's Law, and sure enough. Midway through packing away our breakfast utensils, a fresh drizzle prodded us to hurry.

I sealed up my backpack, before speculating uneasily, "Is this enough rain to flood Cataract Creek?"

"Probably," SeeHawk guessed.

"Wrong answer," I told him.

"How so?"

"Because that's not what we want to happen."

Looking confused, he stated, "But, you like realism. I'm the one who's too optimistic."

"Realism is good whenever we have a choice," I corrected him, "but, today we don't."

"We don't?"
"No."
"Why not?"
"Because we can't afford to get fined for not reaching our next campsite."

"Oh, right," he agreed. "So, how far is it from here to Cataract Creek?"

"Five or six miles. That's probably two or three hours."

"And then, how much farther to Piegan Pass?"

"Another three-and-a-half miles, which could be a crapshoot, depending on what's in those miles.

"Gotcha," SeeHawk nodded. "So, we'll cross that bridge when we get there."

"A bridge would be nice, but I think we'll be getting our tootsies wet."

Before leaving the picnic area, we fastened thigh-high rain chaps onto our shorts, to cover the gap between our poncho skirts and shoes.

Last, of all, I tried to drum up some verve by asking SeeHawk, "Are you ready for an adventure?"

"Ready like Freddy," he confirmed.

Wanting more verve, I asked him, "How ready is Freddy?"

"Ready when you are."

"That'll do," I nodded, and off we went.

A short traverse around Swiftcurrent Lake chilled us with a breeze that seemed limited to the water. We felt glad to get rescued by an orange clay trail, heading into a spruce-pine forest teeming with fresh greens. Poppa Jim's guidebook gave names to the glistening foliage of wet corn lilies, ferns, alders, leafing thimbleberry, serviceberry, gooseberry, ground roses, pearly everlasting, fireweed, angelica, harebell, asters, and mountain maple. Upturned leaves cupped raindrops which jiggled like rubber rhinestones when our ponchos brushed past them. Pillows of velvety moss advertised vacancy for comfort-loving bugs, if they dared come out of hiding. Higher-up, in the forest's broad canopy, reclusive grand fir trees hid between clumps of hardier pines and spruces.

It was the kind of forest in which nobody should speak unless they have something to say. The gentle rain kept tickling our ponchos. The curving trail kept us in suspense.

After a long silence, I remarked, "Coyote."

SeeHawk answered, "I love you, too."

Chuckling at his error, I explained, "No, the scat. It's behind us, now. Didn't you see it?"

Frowning, he apologized, "Sorry, Sunshine. With this poncho hood swishing across my ears, I can't hear what you're saying."

No wonder we rarely talked in the rain.

Josephine Lake welcomed us into her fold with a cheerful doormat of yellow arnica flowers. The sky added a burst of full sunlight, as we began to circle the lake's leafy shoreline. Within minutes, it grew warm enough for t-shirts, but we kept wearing our ponchos, still for defense against Murphy's Law.

SeeHawk was first to notice some interesting objects coming up ahead. From a distance, they looked like jumbo-sized toilet paper tubes. Had some litterbug carelessly dropped their potty trash on the trail? Nope. We soon realized what the tubes were, but it took another moment to piece everything together. Fat scats. Wet berry thicket. Lake containing fish.

"We're in Bear Heaven," SeeHawk gasped.

"Maybe we should put our video training from St. Mary's to good use?" I suggested.

Liking that idea, SeeHawk joined me in butchering post-boomer rock songs. We clapped our hands and yipped as if trying to wake up guests in the faraway Many Glacier Lodge. Perhaps, nothing with hooked claws and blood-stained incisors heard our commotion, but, in any case, we felt relieved to depart from Josephine Lake without having peed our pants.

The next surprise was a crosswise trail, appearing where we should have found an uphill trail.

"Tails or tails?" I joked since our destination was supposed to be straight ahead, not right or left.

SeeHawk read the posted sign and deduced, "So, we can either go back the way we came, except now on this side of the lake, or else visit some other lake that's nowhere near the CDT?"

"Exactly," I nodded, appreciating his quick comprehension. "Or else, option three is just to sprout wings and fly up to Cataract Creek."

"Don't get loopy yet," he warned me. "It's not even lunchtime."

A fat wad of guidebook pages and maps confirmed we were supposed to climb straight away from the lake.

"The turnoff must be ridiculously close," I felt certain. "It's just a matter of choosing which way to turn."

"We should turn right," SeeHawk decided.

"What makes you think so?"

"My internal compass."

"What's it referencing?"

"The knowledge I'm receiving."

Frowning, I argued, "You're being influenced by not wanting to go backward. I know that's a drag, but with the junction being super close, it could be either way."

"Except, my hunch is really strong," he emphasized.

Rolling my eyes, I tried to be diplomatic about saying, "It's excellent that you're participating in helping me navigate, but nobody's hunch should overrule a person who reads maps."

Ouch, that had probably been the wrong comeback.

Sure enough. SeeHawk hitched up his chest and insisted that for once in a friggin' million years, I should respect his opinion.

My shackles flew up, saying no way in heck would I ever turn right because I was our team's Chief Navigation Officer and my word was law.

SeeHawk felt chagrined, but he respected the law. Without saying another word, he followed me onto a flat trail, looping back toward Many Glacier. It was a pleasant stretch of woods, casual and easy. I hated having to bum a good high by admitting it was time to turn around.

"Say what?" SeeHawk gasped, looking as if it had never occurred to him that my leadership could be wrong.

"It's time to turn around," I repeated, "and, don't you dare rub it in."

Did he dare, anyway? Not at all. In fact, he did not even gloat in silence, while we retraced our steps and, this time, left the junction going his way.

All the while, both of us kept glancing uphill. Time was-a-wasting. Where was the Piegan Pass trail? It could not be mistaken on our maps. They were lacking in detail, but, come on. A fork leaving the groomed trail ahead could hardly be missed.

Another quarter-hour vanished before my brain must have hiccupped because, suddenly, we ran into Grinnell Lake.

"About two miles," I told SeeHawk, when he asked me how far we had overshot our mark.

He gave me a hard stare.

I stared back at him.

It was drizzling in spurts. We had fallen behind schedule. We were seriously bungling the start of a critical approach. What should we try next?

The Book of Beans mentioned an alternate trail adding 1-2 miles to the distance between Grinnell Lake and Cataract Creek. Given our error, might the alternate route now be faster than turning around? Hoping so, we proceeded toward Grinnell Lake. Before long, we ran into a 2-foot-thick snowbank, hardened stiff by thawing and re-freezing. Mounting the snow required chopping out steps. I felt shocked enough to recheck our guidebooks, which confirmed we were only 5,000-feet above sea level. Yeesh, how odd. Maybe thick snow could resist thawing in shady places, but we were fully 2,500-feet below Redgap Pass, which had been mostly dry, and the supposedly dry summit of Piegan Pass was even higher.

Feeling puzzled, SeeHawk and I angled away from Grinnell Lake, now heading inland. We made slow progress across the lakeshore's hard snow. Before long, we ran into a third surprise. A trench full of thundering rapids cut through the snow. Beside it lay a rolled-up plank bridge, probably taken down each winter. We halted because the trench blocked us from proceeding. Also, we halted because the trench did not have any right to be there. Its location was impossible. In order for it to be there, we would have needed to cross a bridge. Poppa Jim's ford was 200-feet higher. Cataract Creek showed clearly on our maps. Moreover, the Book of Beans' brief description of how to get there from Grinnell Lake did not mention any seasonal bridge. Had its author deemed the bridge not worth mentioning because she came through during midsummer when the bridge had been operational? Either way, one big question hung in the air.

"Should we ford, or turn around?" SeeHawk asked me.

"Wow," I replied, "this looks scarier than Sundays at a waterslide park."

The rapids were spiked with mini-logjams, poking into the air like tipi-poles. The distances between each logjam measured roughly a leap-and-a-half. Wading seemed feasible if we could hunt upstream for a safer location, but would such research be worth our time?

"I'd feel more eager if we could see a trail leaving the opposite bank," I told SeeHawk.

"There must be one because there's a bridge," he assumed.

"Unless, the bridge is just a convenience for summertime tourists visiting the lake, and not part of a trail," I debated. "You know, like those little bridges at *Disneyland*?"

"Good point," he agreed.

Turning partway around, I curiously gazed through the upstream woods.

When SeeHawk saw where I was looking, he groaned, "Oh no, Sunshine, please..."

"Just, bear with me," I requested. "This seems like a longshot, but if we can bushwhack up to Poppa Jim's ford, maybe we could arrive on the dry side and just keep going."

Looking astonished, SeeHawk inquired, "How far would that be?"

"Two hundred vertical feet, which our guidebook calls a mile, depending on if we'd run into many blockages."

"You're kidding, right?" he hoped.

From what little we could see through the upstream trees, there was a cliff of some kind hidden behind them.

Deciding I needed redirection, SeeHawk suggested, "Maybe we should go back to Josephine Lake."

"You really want to do that if this might be a shortcut?" I protested. "What do you think will happen when we get back there?"

SeeHawk reflected, and came out mumbling, "Well, I suppose it couldn't hurt to just see what's upstream, but only for a little way. Let's not make a bad mistake worse."

The first barricade we encountered was a soggy willow thicket. After shoving through the willows, we ran into several rotten logs heaped across the creek's muddy bank. Patiently and clumsily, we heaved our backpacks over each log in turn, progressing slower and slower, until every few yards felt worthy of a cheer. Had we lost our minds? Still refusing to quit, we blundered through another cheek-whapping willow thicket, got our pants soaking wet, and had to squeeze ice water out of our shoes. The clincher was when our ankles sank into half-frozen mud.

I did not speak a word.

Neither did SeeHawk.

Seeing the rolled-up bridge again gave me license to cut-loose, ranting, "If this is some downstream extension of Cataract Creek, who the heck decided to call it a creek? Creeks are where kids play. This is a river. And, why would anyone name a creek after an eye affliction? Couldn't they have chosen Drown When The Bridge Is Down Creek? Or Come Back During July Creek?"

"Are you saying we should go home and spend the rest of the summer surfing?" SeeHawk winked.

If looks could kill.

"No, no, no," he laughed. "Sorry, Sunshine. I was only joking. Rain and snow are awesome. Mud is awesome. Adventure is what I live for. Bring it on, baby. Let's have some more!"

Despite the ongoing risk of Murphy's Law, we removed our damp ponchos, but we still kept them handy, just in case. It took the rest of an hour to trudge all the way back to Josephine Lake. Along the way, we kept our eyes peeled for any slightest trail forking uphill. Nothing came forth before we stopped to stare at the same darned sign which still neglected to mention Piegan Pass.

"Looks like the odds are back in your camp," SeeHawk submitted.

Saying nothing, I stomped through the junction and repeated our first walk toward Many Glacier. This time, we hit payday!

Chewing upon the irony, I estimated, "We turned around fifty yards too soon."

SeeHawk sympathized, "It's a bummer to reach Cataract Creek later than you planned, Sunshine, but look on the bright side. At least, the rain has stopped. It's staying cold, so there won't be any flooding. Which means, it shouldn't matter what time we get there, right?"

"Just keep moving," I commanded him.

Turning straight uphill, we climbed into a tangle of leggy cow parsnip, and prickly gooseberry bushes, feeling compressed by the mountain's gray sky. A blind wall of aspen trees, grand firs, and spruces loomed up ahead. The bushes thinned. The ground grew rocky. A tighter enclosure of trees smoothed out the trail.

A bit higher uphill, I began to wonder. Had Grinnell Lake's deep snow been some kind of freak phenomenon, caused by the local topography? Everything ahead and above looked green. Maybe SeeHawk was right. Despite our initial two hours of blundering, now that we were back on track, things did seem to be looking up. At least, our future was looking brighter until a frosty wind burst through the trees and blew straight into our faces.

"That's coming from Piegan Pass, isn't it?" SeeHawk hollered, from a good distance ahead.

My guts took a drop. "Unfortunately, yes."

Tiny raindrops began to sting my cheeks. The droplets looked small enough to be called mist, but they must have been arrow-shaped, judging by the way they hurt.

Stopping some distance ahead, SeeHawk paid no attention to feeling his face sting because he found a tattered crow feather, which he plucked out of a mud puddle.

When I caught up and saw him pressing the feather back into shape, I whined, "Ew! What do you want that for? Crows are everywhere. I'm sure we're going to see nicer feathers for you to keep."

Ignoring me, he rinsed his treasure in a clean rain puddle, stroked it smooth enough to shine, and held it up for me to admire, saying, "This feather is very auspicious, Sunshine. Crows bring magic, and this feather is wet. Maybe we can expect some magic involving water."

I raised one eyebrow. Lord help me, but whatever. Promising to marry a weird guy had signed me up for some weirdness.

After doing a bit more climbing, we reached an elevation where the wind backed off and ran out of arrows. The Piegan Pass trail responded by leveling-off, onto a snow-covered meadow littered with old plant stalks. If the weather had been hot, we might have found ourselves post-holing, so it was lucky to be arriving on a cloudy day.

The meadow's far end met Cataract Creek, roughly in the location of Poppa Jim's ford. I estimated that we were directly upstream from Grinnell Lake, via the 200-foot cliff we had glimpsed down below. That was something to keep in mind because, just downstream from the long-awaited ford, Cataract Creek whipped around a bend and plunged out of sight. Its rapids probably dropped over the cliff, which meant, we could drop over the cliff if we lost our footing and fell into the rapids. But, of course, we were not going to fall because we were going to take our time and proceed with caution.

Several fallen trees came close to bridging the creek.

After ruling out a few, SeeHawk sighed, "It's too bad, close only counts in horseshoes and hand grenades."

Thinking about midsummer, I reasoned, "Probably those logs go all the way across when the water is lower."

In the throes of wondering how to proceed, SeeHawk and I trotted up and down the creek's snowy bank like nervous dogs.

Questions of comparison kept looping through our heads. Does this shallow section look easier than that smooth section? How deep are those rapids? Does this short log look safer than that tippy log? Eventually, we settled upon the creek's centermost rapid. Perhaps, if we quit stalling, we could wade right through it.

SeeHawk thought its water might reach up to our thighs.

I guessed knees, which was still deep enough to be taken seriously.

A dip-test would be required.

We glanced at one another.

"Do you want to draw straws?"

"We don't have any."

"I could go back and grab some plant stalks."

One problem was the cold wind. Even though it was no longer raining, our cheeks were still frozen. Plunging bare feet from the snowbank into the ice-cold water would be torture. Wearing shoes into the water did not seem smart either, with everything uphill looking as white as a Hallmark Christmas. Sure, I had a pair of dry boots stashed inside my backpack, but SeeHawk only had the pair he was wearing, (because he had mistakenly shipped his sneakers ahead, apparently thinking northern Montana was a mountain in Alaska). Of course, See-Hawk was a pretty tough guy, but even tough guys know where to draw the line, and crossing a snowbound pass wearing wet boots seemed to cross that line. So, what other choice did we have? How about wading through the water wearing socks, without shoes? That seemed like a good compromise, in terms of warmth, but what if the creek's slippery cobblestones jammed our sliding toes, or caused us to fall and float toward the downstream cliff?

All dangers aside, what worried me most was sensing that the day was getting on. There was snow everywhere. Even if we could ford Cataract Creek safely, what then? Might we get trapped camping on hard, cold snow, somewhere between Piegan Pass and the creek? What if the sky's overcast clouds coughed up a storm? What if that storm dumped enough rain to flood the creek, as well as enough snow up higher to bury Piegan Pass, and we woke up unable to escape forward or backward? Just in case, would it be smart to set up camp where we stood, ford Cataract Creek the next morning, and give ourselves a full day for crossing Piegan Pass? Then again, though, it could be argued that getting the ford over with before making a low camp could be safest because then we could enjoy drier shoes while having more time to cross the pass. And, really, what were the odds of a giant storm happening during June? Although, would our shoes really dry overnight, inside a tent surrounded by snow? Rumors existed about hardcore backpackers stuffing wet shoes into their warm sleeping bags, but eek. That form of shoe-drying did not sound cozy. Besides, we probably needed to respect the risk of getting trapped between the pass and creek.

Finally, I just heaved a long sigh and told SeeHawk, "The rangers will just have to understand that we haven't fallen behind schedule for lack of trying. That sign near Josephine Lake...the park computer's error...it's like a conspiracy...if they're at all human...if anybody even comes up here in wet weather."

Feeling sure that we were making a smart decision, but also disconcerted, I helped SeeHawk pitch our tent on an island of wet needle duff, sheltered beneath some pine trees. The surrounding ground was littered with miniature scats shaped like bee-bees and quail eggs. There were still a few hours of daylight left, so we decided to kick back and enjoy Cataract Creek's beautiful surroundings.

Straight across the water stood a naked rock cliff called Feather Plume Falls. Perhaps 1,000-feet from base to crown, its height was such that we had to lean backward and keep moving our eyes to take in all of it. Water pulsing over the top exploded into clouds that vanished up high, exploded again 300-feet lower, and exploded a third time nearer to the ground. Altogether, the effect was like a three-tiered display of aqueous gun smoke. Nobody witnessing what we were seeing could justify complaining about coldness, snow, scheduling, or anything else that had bothered us earlier in the day.

The clouds ceased glowing as we sat together on a damp log, rehydrating my mom's version of classic tuna casserole. Pan the flutist serenaded our dinner. First, he performed as a soloist. Then, many of his fellow goats joined in until the forest sounded full of whistling referees. We never physically saw anything with hooves, so we could not judge their distance. However, we immediately knew when dusk broke up the party because the resulting silence enabled us to hear murky thunderclaps rumbling in the distance.

"Piegan Pass?" SeeHawk guessed.

"Of course," I nodded.

After dinner, SeeHawk launched into his usual routine of finger-and-toilet-paper dishwashing. Luckily, he finished that chore in time to escape from a sprinkling rain.

Once we hunkered down inside our cozy tent, it felt exhilarating to peel off damp clothes and drape them over a clothesline spanning the tent's inner ceiling.

SeeHawk cuddled me underneath his arm, and together we heard Cataract Creek' rushing through the darkness. Raindrops pattered on the meadow's hard snow. Once in a while, the last party goat who refused to go home let out a whistle, to see if anyone else wanted to start things up again. Distant thunder rolled off Piegan Pass. Our brains relaxed, letting go of thoughts, but then beginning to ask questions. For instance, how might this day have turned out differently, if we had found the Piegan Pass Trail immediately after leaving Josephine Lake? Where would we have ended up camping? On a blanket of snow covering Piegan Pass, with lightning flashing above our tent? In a dry campsite, somewhere beyond the pass? My head juggled theories while SeeHawk lay beside me, quietly admiring his beloved crow feather. It had found a home, duct-taped onto a carabiner that would dangle from his backpack for the next six months.

Lovemaking would have been a nice dessert, but sleep became a drug too sweet to resist.

Just before conking out, SeeHawk rolled his red balaclava into a hoop. Midway through pulling the hoop over his head, he noticed a familiar-looking, wiggly brown hair. Immediately, flashbacks of throwing tennis balls for our dog made his eyes burn. He whispered to me in a cracking voice, "Tierra sent this gift, to say she misses us and to keep ourselves safe!"

My last emotion before sleep was feeling glad not to have pushed our luck by hiking another two miles after dark, no matter what any park ranger might have to say about it.

* * *

When the sun rose at 5:30 am, its diffused light cast a silvery glow across our tent. Fearing what that could mean, I unzipped the front door and peeked outside. Sure enough, the sky was overcast and that's not all. There was a ragged gray unibrow concealing Piegan Pass.

Nudging SeeHawk awake, I told him, "Remember that lenticular cloud I spotted a couple of days ago? Well, guess who was right about what it meant for today?"

"The park's computer forecast?" he guessed.

"Nope. Yours Truly. But, shoot, I wish I been wrong."

Sitting up to lace on his boots, SeeHawk assured me, "Don't worry, Sunshine. It might look cloudy now, but we're going to see the sun before this day is over."

"Argh, not that again," I groaned. "Your theory about Sundays is cute, but seriously, you know as well as I do that Mother Nature does not read calendars."

"Just watch," he insisted. "We'll see the sun today, or my name isn't Sees Hawks."

"Well, just in case you're ready for a name change," I told him, "we'd better hurry up and ford Cataract Creek before it starts raining."

"Right behind you," he yawned. "But first, I'd like to boil some water, just in case it gets cold going over Piegan Pass."

"I know you love our thermoses to death," I acknowledged, "and, yes, it's going to be cold today, but do you think we might be able to survive without hot chocolate? This isn't really the right kind of day to sit around waiting for water to boil."

"It'll only take a minute," he promised. "You'll thank me later for making you wait."

After striking camp quickly, we ceremoniously said, "Thank you, spot," to our third campsite on the CDT.

It only took a few minutes hurrying over to Cataract Creek, so we could check on the flood situation. Lo and behold, good news! The creek's water level had dropped about a foot. Its rapids still looked vigorous, but not dangerous like yesterday.

Wasting no time, I plunged one dry sneaker and clean sock straight into the current. Paralyzing coldness cut through my sneaker, bloomed into my wool sock, and drilled through my foot, faster than I could think.

Blowing on my knuckles, I stomped in and out of the water, slowly getting acclimated and all the while complaining, "No matter how many times we do this, I'll never get used to it."

Poor SeeHawk. He tried to look manly about plunging his thick leather boots in after me, but it turned out that "waterproofed" was another word for "sponge."

Marching into the creek's central current allowed the water to yank our ankles sideways. Deepening rapids splashed up to our knees. Unseen cobblestones wobbled beneath our shoes. Trying to plant trekking poles between the loose cobblestones was a gamble. Sometimes, the poles stuck and gave us needed support; other times, one pole slipped and sent us reeling off-balance. Twice, I got overzealous, lunged too far, tipped over, and had to squat in order to avoid taking a swim.

Within ten feet of reaching the creek's opposite snowbank, a barricade of willows forced both SeeHawk and me to halt. Our shinbones were screaming. Driven by panic, we sloshed back and forth, searching for a clearing through which to leave the water. It all became a blur until we gratefully stumbled back onto "dry" snow. Cursing and throbbing, we stomped around in circles, trying to work more blood into our feet. Movement helped. Forging ahead, we clawed through the branches of a dense willow thicket. Once breaking free, we ran into a sight that overshadowed our pain.

"Holy cow!" SeeHawk gasped.

"Is this a dream?" I scowled. "Please, tell me this is a dream."

In front of us flowed two additional creeks, both roughly equal in width to the one we had just forded. Their currents looked a little slower. Their water looked a little deeper. Maybe slowness and deepness were related, or not. Either way, we thought the fords looked safe, if more painful. But, all of that was beside the point because, ark! Neither of the two creeks had any right to exist!

"This is crazy," I stammered. "Our maps show a single blue line, not three."

SeeHawk fixed me with a questioning look.

This was one of those moments when I did not necessarily enjoy being our team's Chief Navigation Officer. I mean, it was totally unfair. First, some random creek down by Grinnell Lake had the nerve to ambush us from a weird direction. Now, this? Of all the silly hijinks. SeeHawk and I did not deserve to be taunted on the same day we had to deal with snow. Our feet had done what they were asked. Now, they deserved a chance to warm-up, before returning to the creek farther upstream. Nature needed to play by the rules. What was this nonsense about seeing two more forks?

Out loud, I complained, "What's going on?"

Nature responded with a sprinkle of rain.

Reacting quickly, SeeHawk and I dug out our ponchos and took cover. Creeks or no creeks, we could not afford to moisten our under-layers at the start of a long, cold day.

Once reassembled, I grimly told the creeks, "Okay, you two probably don't show on our maps because it would have looked messy for the cartographers to draw you all smushed together."

"Which means, what?" SeeHawk asked.

"We're screwed."

"Okay," he nodded. "I can accept that, and my feet aren't getting any warmer just standing here, so is it time to seize the bull by the horns?"

"Aye-aye, captain."

A few deep breaths. A bit more prancing. By the time we felt ready for another cold plunge, the sprinkling rain turned into a steady drizzle.

Glancing upstream, through intervening trees, I mumbled uneasily, "Do you think it'll be safe to cross Piegan Pass?"

Usually, SeeHawk gave me optimistic responses, such as, "Absolutely," or "Safer than tying our shoes together," but not this time. Instead of saying anything, he just snugged my poncho tighter around my backpack and turned around for me to do the same.

Between having our ears covered by swishing poncho hoods, hearing a breeze hiss through the rain, and preparing to enter rushing water, there was no use in trying to talk or be heard. Fording the second creek was purely about sensation. It started with, *Ouch, this is water is even colder.* Next came, *Thank goodness, it's gentler, unless deeper water just feels gentler.* Time disappeared for a moment before our feet were suddenly climbing onto the next snowbank, and that was a green light. We were primed to keep going.

Fork number three turned out to be the easiest of the bunch. It was almost deep enough to make us lift our backpacks above our waists, but, at least, its temperature felt mild, thanks to our feet going numb.

With all three fords vanquished, I felt tempted to swap out my wet sneakers for dry boots. However, our maps said tough beans because we were going to have to re-cross Cataract Creek farther upstream.

At least, circumstances had the decency to provide us with a linear dent in the snow, which left no question about where to aim. We headed upstream for over a mile, staying alongside the water while gradually entering a crude timberline. Disbanding spruce trees, mingling with lopsided and multi-trunked lodgepole pines, made us appear to be entering the cheap end of a

Christmas tree farm. Flat terrain kept our pace steady. The light drizzle stopped. Four wet feet smashed inside wet socks, caged inside wet shoes, thought it might have been nicer to stay zipped inside our tent and sleep-in.

Once a skosh more elevation caused the snow to thicken, the trail we had been following got buried and disappeared. There, we stopped to examine our surroundings. According to our maps, we had probably reached the place where we were supposed to re-cross Cataract Creek. It was now just a single channel, not three forks, but ai ai ai.

"People can't just cross here," I assumed, "There's got to be some clue we're missing."

Splitting-up, to search upstream and downstream, we scrutinized the creek's opposite snowbank. Any among dozens of widely scattered trees could have born an ax-blaze. Any broad openings between them could have contained a snow-covered cairn. There were lots of possibilities, but without any evidence, what could we do? Cross Cataract Creek anywhere that looked safe, and worry later about rejoining the trail? Maybe, but a lot was going on upstream. Starting less than a mile away, the lowest tier of mountainside supporting Piegan Pass could have posed for a *Backpacker Magazine* centerfold. Its central attraction was Morning Eagle Falls. Stunningly vertical, and impressively huge, the waterfall's sheer liquid spilled like a bridal veil, over and down henna-colored cliffs. That whole upper section almost seemed motionless but, once hitting ground, the waterfall's outflow took off like a rocket. Topography funneled its rapid water into a deep-water channel, confined between 6-foot walls of vertical ice. Competent swimmers might easily have drowned trying to reach the opposite snowbank. Our eyes followed the current's rollicking whitecaps downstream, to a point where they smoothed off but still looked dangerous.

"This is where I draw the line," I said. "I know how to swim, and I know how to backpack, but, as far as I'm concerned, they should be two separate activities."

Ignoring my remark, SeeHawk pointed upstream, saying, "Looks like time to find out if we've been eating too many fruit rolls."

He was referring to a snow bridge we had been pretending not to notice. Roughly 4-yards wide and 1-yard thick along its presenting edge, the bridge must have emerged from an uneven thaw, judging by how it hovered higher than the surrounding snow. Probably, the recent heatwave had compacted its snow crystals into ice. That was a comforting image since ice could be strong. However, ice could also contain holes. If we tried mincing steps across the bridge, might we plunge through a hole and fall into the channel's powerful rapids?

Visualizing success, SeeHawk declared, "I think this might be Piegan Pass's winter entrance."

"If it is, CDT-hikers ought to leave Canada super early, not late, like Poppa Jim says," I reflected.

"Except, for needing to cross the rest of Glacier National Park," SeeHawk reminded me.

"Well, true. So maybe tween-season hikers should bring a rubber raft?"

"Or a human catapult."

"I'd prefer a personal jetpack."

"Hey, look!" SeeHawk exclaimed.

Looking where he pointed, I saw a trail of deer tracks puncturing the snow. The small, shallow holes appeared to cross the snow bridge along its thickest edge.

"Smart animal," SeeHawk muttered.

Wanting to be our safety tester, he approached the bridge like a monster, stomping hard to spring any trap doors before fully transferring his weight. Halfway across the bridge, he found a clean hole, melted all the way through. Peering into it, he saw intensely blue water rocketing 4-feet below his shoes. If he slipped and got flushed, he would find himself caged between 6-foot ice walls, fighting to stay afloat while being swept downstream.

I saw his posture stiffen and protectively called out, "Be careful, sweetheart."

He hollered back, "Don't worry, Sunshine. Two different palm readers have told me I'm going to live to a ripe old age."

Ha-ha, well, okay then. Several times in the past, he had described getting his fortune told by a flamboyant, *NBA*-sized Turkish Canadian palm reader, as well as an English translator for an Indian palm reader whose office had been crawling with lizards.

Laughing out loud helped me summon courage for taking the next step. Before mounting the snow bridge, I tightened my backpack's shoulder- and hip straps, for prevention against anything shifting. Then, came the big leap of faith. Planting my sneakers into each fat stomp hole created by SeeHawk's boots, I stayed well behind him, as he passed the halfway point. After all, the only thing worse than either of us falling through the bridge alone would have been falling through together, without anyone left to save us. However, I did not let him get too far ahead either because safety in numbers was a comforting illusion.

How long I held my breath, I do not know. Regardless, stepping onto the opposite snowbank, having survived the bridge, was cause for both of us to break into a happy dance.

"Looks like we're headed to Mexico, come hell or high water," I cheered.

"Having already beaten the high-water," SeeHawk added.

"Pshht!" I scolded him. "No jokes that might jinx us."

Glancing around, he proposed, "So, before we spend the next coon's age climbing switchbacks, is this a good place to sit down and eat?"

"You want to sit on the snow in your wet boots?"

"No," he decided. "I'd rather find someplace dry enough to keep my butt warm while I put on dry socks."

"I'm really thirsty, though," I realized. "Can we please drink some water, before we keep going?"

SeeHawk waited for me to drag a few sips, but he did not drink much himself, in case we might need it later. The icy liquid paralyzed my throat. I nearly had to spit because it hurt too much to swallow.

Once we felt ready to leave the creek, all we needed was a cairn, blaze, or any other clue to point us in the right direction. Too bad the CDT still refused to cooperate. Finding nothing, we eventually threw precision to the wind and just struck out aiming toward Morning Eagle Falls. About 100 yards upstream, we spied a trail of human footprints scaling an adjacent foothill. The footprints were not really aiming toward Piegan Pass, but half of me wanted to follow them anyway, in case they had been made by a local hiker with knowledge about an indirect route. However, I should have checked our maps before angling away from the pass. Instead, I spent 15 minutes leading SeeHawk up the wrong foothill, only to realize we needed to turn around.

By the time we returned to the snow bridge, it was starting to feel like we had wasted a lot of time. SeeHawk could hardly wait to eat. Our fruit rolls were still rock-hard frozen.

"If we can put off eating until we cross the pass," I told him, "we should be able to sit on the dry ground since it will be south-facing, but it's up to you. Which would you choose? Eating right before a long climb? Or going hungry a little longer, to eat on dry ground?"

"I'd choose eggs, biscuits, and gravy," SeeHawk answered, "but if we can't eat first, let's, at least, drink our hot chocolates."

"A toast to the hot chocolates," I laughed, making an air-fist. "Okay partner, you win. Thanks for making me wait for the water to boil."

A small cluster of pine trees provided enough shelter that we could comfortably sit on damp needle mulch, admiring a stunning profile of Morning Eagle Falls.

SeeHawk wasted no time. First thing, before servicing his wet, cold feet, he screwed-open his thermos and started licking melted ghee off the hot chocolate.

I gratefully removed my frozen sneakers, swapped soggy wool socks for a dry pair, and hastily stuffed one foot at a time into dry Gore-Tex boots I had been saving all morning.

Poor SeeHawk. Having no spare shoes, the best he could manage was to exchange his wet socks for a dry pair. As soon as the dry socks entered his waterlogged boots, they got soaked on contact, but, at least, they did not become wringing-wet. Before leaving the trees, SeeHawk strategically stashed two homemade macadamia-nut-chocolate-cherry bars inside his anorak jacket's kangaroo pouch.

When I noticed him squirreling, I said, "Good thinking, partner, but please don't count on us stopping again before we reach the top."

"Never, in a million years would I expect such a thing," he smiled. "This is just for insurance, in case your body or mine turns out to have less horsepower than our heads."

An incoming drizzle wetted our ponchos as we came out from hiding. Snow covering the whole upper mountainside gave us no clue where to aim. It took several minutes to find a linear depression that could pass for a snow-covered trail. Following it diagonally upward, we entered a maze of spruce trees, studded with mysterious white lumps of snow. A gentle breeze scraping our faces kept us aware of not being on vacation. Soon, the linear depression doubled back above itself, proving that we really were on a trail. Steepening terrain pushed the spruce trees apart, exposing wider panes of hard-packed corn snow, followed by chutes of fluffy powder. We seemed to be passing underneath some kind of impasse. The next opening ahead was a double-black-diamond powder chute. Our trail ended where the powder snow began.

"Interesting," I mumbled, looking uphill.

"Looks like fun, if we had downhill skis," SeeHawk noted.

"Or if we had plastic cups and maple syrup."

Pulling out my primitive snowshoe crampons immediately felt silly. The clumsy contraptions had three metal toe teeth, dull enough to be used for opening bottle caps or loosening screws. Being intended for snowshoeing, they did not have any teeth on their heels or sides. Nor, did they provide the snowshoe part of the snowshoes. They were just three cojoined teeth, attached to interlocking plastic straps—which was the reason I had bought them because they could be securely attached to fabric boots—but, oh my word. The sensation of wearing them gave me a shock. With heels floating several inches above the snow, it felt like I was wearing spike-heels on backward. Nevertheless, as silly as the weird little toe-elevators seemed, they worked like a charm. My boots stuck fast with every kick. All I had to do was keep my head together.

SeeHawk protectively stayed close below me, just in case of anything going wrong.

Methodically, I kicked one foot above the next. My trekking poles added thrust to each step. The crampons chomped deep and held securely, so long as I kicked them fairly hard, but they were not designed for real mountaineering. They could never have penetrated real ice. Nevertheless, during that brief moment in time, I felt bionic. It was like being a James Bond movie villain scaling an Alp with booty on my back, until the grade grew steeper. After that, I just felt a dead weight pushing through my chest, threatening to topple me over backward. Leaning forward to compensate made me feel tippy, especially because I was balancing on my tiptoes. Still, I kept climbing and never looked down. In the end, I was rewarded with an upper switchback to land upon. So far, so good. I sat down, peeled off the silly plastic crampons, and packed them away because traversing sideways on tiptoes would have been exhausting, and there was no need.

Back in motion, now traveling horizontally, I noticed tiny snowflakes dusting my rain-poncho. Also, I noticed little patches of exposed earth dotting parts of the trail. This development seemed strange. Was the snow getting thinner as we gained elevation? If, by some miracle, Piegan Pass could flip storms upside down, might its summit still be dry? Naw, I decided. Everything we had seen up to this point guaranteed the summit was going to be white as Santa's eyebrows. Still, I felt encouraged to see wider bits of ground peeking through the snow. Some wide openings even revealed small rock chips, glued together with gloppy-looking mud. I could not help wondering if a few hard stomps might collapse that whole section of the trail. My concern seemed reinforced by a few tiny spike-holes perforating the mud, which implied someone had worn real mountaineering crampons up to the pass.

Shortening switchbacks lifted our hopes to be getting near the top. At the same altitude, we saw no more holes and the snow became solid. Each next step required more physical effort. As we angled out of the highest spruce trees, a landscape unfolded which looked uniformly white, except for fragments of gaunt shrubbery and weathered spruce "krummholz."

Starting into another long lateral, I wondered if we had accidentally left the CDT. Instead of checking our directions or maps, I took orders from a long crease in the snow, extending off the switchback we had just left. We seemed to be making a beeline for an overlook. Judging by its sharp rim, the drop below must have been scary-steep. Was it positioned above Morning Eagle Falls? Approaching the rim made me fear getting too close, in case its snowpack might be unstable. Our exact location was vague, but one helpful clue was seeing Cataract Creek's forested valley come into view, 800-feet below. The rim's perspective invited us to gaze into the valley like a fishbowl. Something was happening down at its far end. White fog, spilling in from Josephine Lake, was rapidly swallowing the valley's interior trees. One after another, they were vanishing like quarters on a busy sidewalk. Within minutes, half the valley was gone. Then, two-thirds. The next thing we knew, there was syrupy white fog washing over our boots. Wait, hold on, now. How could any fog scale the precipice so fast?

SeeHawk and I exchanged a look of concern.

"Are we about to go blind?" his eyes asked me.

"This seems to be changing our tune," my eyes told him; and, also, "We should probably figure out if we're still on the CDT."

Taking stock of our surroundings, I wondered if the snow crease we had been following could be hiding a mud fracture, instead of the CDT. If that was the case, might our weight break the mud loose and send us careening down Morning Eagle Falls? Probably not, I decided, since nothing else in sight resembled a snow-covered trail—but, just in case, I resolved to keep scanning the uphill terrain.

We made good progress paralleling the rim until, seemingly from out of nowhere, a 50-mph wind barreled through the valley and slammed into us. Our eyes practically got forced-shut. Fortunately, we both had trekking poles clutched in hand, so we were able to jam them into the snow, for resistance against getting blown backward. Still, we found ourselves in a tricky situation. With snow spattering our eyes, we could not see far in any direction. Moreover, with our poncho skirts flapping like scarecrows in a hurricane, we could not even see much of the trail in front of our shoes. Hearing and speaking became nearly impossible. Altogether, we found ourselves hugging a cliff, half-blind, and the worst thing was, we could not do anything about it. Our hands needed to hold our trekking poles, which prohibited subduing our flailing ponchos. Some of the wind's strongest gusts kept freely jerking us backward and sideways. On the bright side, though, at least we were getting pushed diagonally uphill. We just needed to tolerate being tossed around like kites until we could reach a wind-sheltered landing.

All this struggle was foremost on my mind, but SeeHawk was, meantime, facing a different problem. Back when changing his socks, he should have fastened rain-chaps over his hiking pants. Tragically, the wind now seemed to think he was not even wearing pants. His private parts felt seared by dry ice. He tried to use my body for a wind-block but drafting only reminded him that any proper gentleman would have been hiking in front of his lady. That's right, sheesh. Had he been raised in a barn or something? Feeling guilty, he tapped me on the shoulder, to let me know he wanted to pass.

I stepped aside, trying to create all the passing room I could manage, which was not much.

While shuffling past me, he saw my mouth spell out, "Must be...near the top. Can't believe...two miles."

He could not read my lips, so he just shook his head.

It was time for us both to hunker down and focus. Like two mechanical robots, we concentrated on putting one shoe in front of the next, over and over again.

During a stolen glance uphill, SeeHawk happened to notice a tall corridor of snow, edged with haggard krummholz. Its shape seemed to imply some kind of gully. Probably, its center-line drained snowmelt from Piegan Pass down to Morning Eagle Falls, or at least down to whatever lay below us.

Gazing higher uphill, the gully's smoothness made SeeHawk wonder. Was he seeing a shortcut to the pass? Somehow, he forgot that trails never aim straight-up anything steep. Without mentioning his plan, or even tapping me on the arm, he stared climbing uphill as if following an angel.

I shouted after him, to no avail.

The higher he climbed, the more futile my shouts became. Finally, I quit trying. It was no use. He could not have heard me. Nor, could I have run up and caught him, unless he slowed down. Heavens to Betsy. Had he forgotten about having a partner? I watched him disappear into the windblown snow. What was the right thing to do? Chase after him until wherever I might catch him? What if we both ended up lost, without being able to see each other? Neither of us would know if the other person was still climbing or going back down. However, losing sight of each other was not safe, either. Therefore, I had to weigh SeeHawk's opinion against mine. Might the gully really be a shortcut? Might it be safer than progressing along the rim? More fog kept spilling between my legs. Drifting snowflakes kept tickling my eyes. I needed to hurry up and reach a decision

All right, fine. Since my partner seemed to have lost his mind, I would go up and fetch him. But, wow. The moment I turned uphill and lifted my trekking poles off the snow, I got pushed so hard that it almost felt like I was riding a chairlift. Soon, I caught sight of SeeHawk in the distance. He looked like a tiny, smudged silhouette, framed with billowing white curtains. Riding the chairlift toward him felt like a daydream until I drew close enough to hear him gasping for air, and had to get his attention by tugging on his poncho.

He was panting hard, having stopped for a reason that I recognized when I looked uphill. He had run into a barricade of impassable crags. Dream over. The gully was not a shortcut.

Neither of us wanted to turn around, but it had to be done. Thrusting our faces straight into the gale, with eyes and cheeks stinging, we retreated down to the horizontal rim. Upon finding what was left of our footprints, we watched their last traces get erased by blowing powder. Gazing off the rim, we found that Cataract Creek, all of its trees, and its fishbowl valley were all completely gone. Now, all we saw in that direction was blinding whiteness.

Had this situation become dangerous? Maybe. Would it have made sense to retreat to Cataract Creek and wait for safer conditions before crossing the pass? Probably, but SeeHawk and I were willing to bet that going forward could be equally safe. The distance from Cataract Creek to Piegan Pass was three miles or less, most of which already lay below us. We had to be extremely close to the top. If a big storm moved in overnight, camping to leeward might be warmer and less perilous than camping to windward, near Cataract Creek. Either way, though, there was no reason to panic. This day was still young. We were not under pressure to do anything crazy. We just wanted to escape from the wind as soon as possible because our faces were freezing and our eyes kept watering.

Suddenly, we noticed that it had stopped snowing. There was still a lot of snow hitting our faces, but now it was powder blowing off the ground, not snow falling from the sky. Within a few minutes, the clouds straight above split partway open. Fissures of bright blue popped out to greet us. There now, see? Just like we had hoped, the flurry was ending. It was too soon to uncork any champagne, though because most of the sky was still full of clouds, and they were racing like mad toward Piegan Pass.

Before carrying on with our original traverse, we ducked behind some krummholz, to undergo a little costume change.

I traded my hazardously flapping poncho for a lightweight fleece sweater, layered underneath a paper-thin, 5 oz. windbreaker jacket.

SeeHawk could have finally Velcroed rain-chaps onto his hiking pants, but he decided not to bother. After all, it had stopped snowing, and anyway, the chaps (being designed for wearing with our ponchos) did not quite reach his private parts.

This moment in refuge could also have been used to raid SeeHawk's snack stash, but both of us cared more about hurrying over the pass than eating. However, we did take a pit stop, where the wind could not blow pee onto our legs.

After remounting my backpack, I glanced toward the sky and felt my heart sink. The fissures of blue sky were already gone, having gotten swallowed by swirling gray clouds. Oh, well. Easy come easy go. Together, we shared a blue-lipped kiss and plunged back into the wind's bracing cold. Once again, our ears got deafened by the noise. It seemed even louder. Was that possible?

Upon regaining the rim, we got slammed by a wind gust that nearly flipped me off my feet. Throwing my bodyweight forward, I stayed standing but recovered with my heart racing and muscles ready to fight. Okay, point taken. Maybe it had been foolish not to eat something when we had the chance. Well, too bad because now there was no turning back.

A subtle curve coming up ahead made us appear to be heading into space. The trail's shifting snowdrifts were subtly growing wider. Their gritty crystals gave our boots good traction, but the width of them was also squeezing us toward the trail's scary edge.

When we reached a pullout that looked relatively safe, we swapped our gangly trekking poles for ice-axes that could be chopped securely into hard snow.

After making that exchange, SeeHawk took the lead. He used his giant size-11E boots to kick through each snowdrift that refused to grab our ice-axes, as if his feet were a pair of wet-leather snowplows.

Trudging along behind him, I started to worry about getting vertigo. It would have been disastrous to glance toward the trail's outer edge. Instead, I pretended the trail had no edge. Meantime, I noticed myself running out of breath. Pausing to inhale deeply did not help. The problem seemed to be caloric exhaustion. Also, my thin outerwear was not cutting the mustard. I missed my waterproof poncho. Its insulating airspace had kept me cozy. Without it, raspy ice collected between my windbreaker-jacket and rain-chaps, which rubbed my thighs raw.

Each time we turned a corner, I managed a little smile. It felt good to change directions, so we could get pushed the other way, for a change. The only bummer was having to keep traversing across the switchbacks' midline, where each of the trail's rungs seemed narrowest and slippery. I kept wondering how many more switchbacks remained above us. Wondering and waiting became an obsession. Nothing changed until, suddenly, the unthinkable happened. My entire body ran out of adrenaline. It happened the same way a car runs out of gas. My arms and legs lost coordination. The air grew thin. As if that wasn't bad enough, at the same time, it started snowing. Not just little sleeve-dusters, either. Big, flat flakes started falling from the sky. Every ounce of my body yearned to collapse, but there was no secure place to even pause. Besides, constant climbing was keeping us warm. My body simply needed more fuel. With an empty tank and no adrenaline left, the only thing keeping me going was sheer, glorious willpower. My limbs felt operated by someone else. My hands kept mechanically flicking snow off my jacket. Windblown fog reduced my vision to the closest few feet. This limitation helped me ignore the white abyss lurking alongside my shoes. My head stayed calm until a shrieking wind gust hit me from the rear and blasted part of a snowdrift off my boots. Was the blizzard coming unhinged? Could wind, alone, knock me off the trail? My lungs felt like they were starving. I needed more oxygen. I needed the wind to shift a little and make the climb easier. My calves felt useless. They were only being propelled by my straining thighs. Tugging wet boots out of knee-deep snowdrifts was too much work. Each sinking step felt like dropping a piece of lead. Ice stuck to my pants, sandpapering my skin. Seams inside my brain began popping loose. I wanted to speak, but my lips refused to move. Was my brain going numb? Was this a symptom of hypothermia? Was I too hungry to think? How dangerous could it be to lose concentration?

"SeeHawk?" I croaked.

He was too far ahead to hear me.

I did not have enough energy left to shout louder. I needed to conserve. There was no telling how much farther we might need to climb. Therefore, I just fixed my eyes upon my shoes and kept going. Except, staying calm was difficult with my legs turning rigid. This was not an imagined threat. The stiffening was real. *Keep moving*, I commanded my legs. *If you stop, you'll take our brain down with you.* Was my brain powering my legs or the other way around? *Keep pushing,* I commanded. *The top is getting close. We'll get there soon.* It helped to pretend I was seeing Piegan Pass. It helped to imagine my legs spinning faster. Never mind if I was barely moving because, at least, I was moving. The snowdrifts were getting drier and fluffier. Our boots were floating through them as if kicking feathers. They were easier to march through, but, for some reason, slipperier in a way that felt dangerous. Meantime, the mountain started running out of air. This was even with the wind supplying more air than anyone could breathe.

SeeHawk remained several yards ahead. He was chanting Mayan nature words and Hawaiian prayers under his breath. His focus was solely on ignoring the pains seared into his private parts by each new wind-gust. If it had been safe to stop, he would have rummaged through his backpack for an extra shirt to tie in front of his waist. Instead, he just kept climbing until one backward glance caused him to forget his own misery.

I did not look good. Backtracking to my rescue, he pulled out a hunk of macadamia-nut-chocolate-cherry bar and firmly said, "Eat."

No way, I thought. Experience had taught me that eating heavy, rich food while climbing could make me feel faint. However, every inch of my body begged for fuel. Therefore, I begrudgingly obeyed. Good thing, too, because I felt a little zing from the sweet and tangy bars. In fact, they helped me force a crooked smile, through lips that did not feel attached to my face.

"Let's get there," I faintly hollered.

My brain felt determined to succeed. That's right, I was not a quitter. Even though I could not lift my legs anymore, I could still drag them, two steps at a time; Step, step. Pause. Step, step. Pause. *Come ON, legs,* I silently shouted. *This is RIDICULOUS. We're only climbing THREE stinking miles. The pass is only seventy-five-hundred-feet high. That's PEANUTS compared with the High Sierras.* I could hardly see anything past my arms. Was the fog floating into my mouth made of laughing gas? How else could it be erasing my memory of whatever we had done that morning? What time of day was it? How long had we been climbing? My knees kept sinking into snow so fluffy that it floated through the air. How could kicking fresh-fallen snow feel like booting a soccer ball? My eyeballs kept leaping back and forth. Which snowdrifts could be bypassed safely? Which ones ought to be kicked-through for prevention against slipping? How deep was the abyss bordering our shoes? A hundred-feet? A thousand-feet? If we slipped and fell, would the distance matter? Suddenly, I heard myself think, *After this trip, I might decide never to speak again.* The idea shocked me. I seemed to be growing delirious. To fend off panic, I reminded myself that vertical mountains often have gentle summits. The Saint Mary's ranger had called Piegan Pass dry, so probably it could not be deep under snow. Although, come to think of it, had the ranger said dry? Or Poppa Jim? Was my memory playing tricks on me? I could no longer remember who said what. Most important, though, was not to worry because Piegan Pass was going to appear any moment. As soon as I saw the top, my head was going to recover. A sob welled up inside my chest.

How much longer? I dared not cry, for fear of weakening my legs, which were already trembling.

SeeHawk, being in front, could not monitor my condition. When he reached a switchback wide enough for passing, he motioned for me to sidestep around him. I felt my head clear as soon as I took the lead. It had been counterproductive to think about reaching Piegan Pass. I needed to just focus on the here and now. Each switchback was becoming shorter and steeper. Soon, we changed directions every few minutes. No doubt, the pass was going to appear any moment. I felt tempted to glance uphill, but there would have been nothing to see anyway. The fog was absolute. The farthest we could see in any direction was just a few yards. I wished the fog would peel open and give us a peek at our surroundings because it felt claustrophobic not being able to see anything. Although, one advantage of hiking blind was not being able to get vertigo. I felt better when the switchbacks began to seem shorter. Perhaps, we were finally getting near the summit. I imagined myself crawling... climbing...gliding over the pass. Hopefully, there was still a chance for the mountain's leeward side to be dry. Of course, it might not be dry at the top, but maybe lower down, where the wind could not reach. My lips could hardly wait to smile. I felt euphoric. Also, nauseous. My head could not control many sensations inside my body. This frozen, exhausted person, still climbing long after she should have reached the pass, could not be me. At least, the part that used to be me felt like someone else, just before we ran into a sheer wall of ice. My tired brain stared. How could it be possible? After spending the whole morning negotiating creeks that should not have existed, and pushing our bodies farther than they could stretch, we had run into a dead-end. There was no conceivable way to climb over, or around the ice. We were not mountaineers. Without backup, our ice-axes could not even apply for the job. The ice looked glossy and bluish. It was one giant crystal, covering the whole trail. Not just covering, either. It also bulged off the trail's edge. There might as well have been a sign saying, *Piegan Pass Closed Until Further Notice.*

SeeHawk and I turned to face each other and thought, without speaking. What other choice did we have? Retreating? No way. Even if I could have emotionally coped with trudging for hours back down to Cataract Creek, physically, it was out of the question. I would either have fainted or frozen before reaching the bottom. My only choice, now, was to cross over the pass because reaching its other side was going to re-start my engine. I knew that as surely as I remembered my name. But, how could we keep going? My blood was losing heat. My feeble snowshoe crampons could not penetrate real ice. The tool I needed was irrational courage. My head started spinning. Stabbing my ice-axe into the glossy ice barely made a dent. Pooh. It should have been called a snow-axe, not an ice-axe. Suddenly, I thought, *Are we still on the CDT?*

Thinking backward, I struggled to remember. When had we last seen the mountain's shape? Turning around to look backward, I came face-to-face with a rocky embankment, looming through the fog. Could it support a trail? Were my eyes being influenced by wishful thinking? Probably, since I could only see a few feet upward. Who knew what could be waiting up higher? Lots of embankments looked capable of supporting trails. However, I did need to consider the possibility, in case we had mistakenly bypassed a switchback. Unless the switchback we needed was hidden behind the ice? That scenario seemed most likely. Although, what if a bypass trail did exist? Could there be two summit routes? As in, one trail people used before the spring thaw, and one after? Could two routes explain why the St. Mary's ranger had called Piegan Pass dry, even though the ice we were seeing had not budged for months, or even longer? Regardless, there was no point in guessing. We needed to just backtrack and search for an alternate route. Except, my face was freezing. And what were our real odds of finding anything we had missed? Although, taking any action seemed better than just standing there, getting colder by the minute. Argh, this was beyond frustration. My overloaded brain felt ready to explode. The embankment stood right beside me. Its embedded rocks were probably loose since the dirt holding them in pace was soggy. Using loose rocks for handholds would be a terrible idea. Every option, forward and backward, seemed as crazy as the next. Time was running out. I needed to quit thinking and just act. So, I did. Throwing caution to the wind, I grabbed the biggest rock I could reach above my head and tugged my body upward. My backpack sluggishly followed. I was hoping to scale the embankment like a gecko. Wherever the upper trail might wait, I was hoping to reach it faster than I could get vertigo. This was a bold move, without being able to see what lay above. I refused to consider how foolish I was being. The alternatives were worse. I needed to gamble.

Something flattish felt hard and slippery. My forward hand groped. Was it the summit? An upper switchback? Another impassable blob of ice? One terrifying lunge gave me the answer. Leaning all my weight forward, I fell onto a level pane of snow. It felt hard and slick, like polished marble. The wind sanding it slick was beyond gale-force. I imagined myself getting shoved across the ice like a hockey puck. Could I safely unhook my legs from the embankment? If I let go, would I start to slide?

Where was SeeHawk? Had he climbed underneath me? Or was he still standing on the trail below, thinking I was nuts? What if his heavier backpack prevented him from repeating what I had just done? What if the embankment could not support his weight and a poorly anchored rock came loose in his hands? Or, what if he tried climbing the ice, instead of the embankment? Might he land a short distance away and be unable to find me, in near-blindness? Or, what if he could find me, but, then, we could not find the pass?

I clenched my teeth, praying for his scruffy face to appear. The fog poured in like vaporized milk. It filled my eyes. I could hardly see anything. The suspense was terrible. What had I been thinking? Charging up to the summit, without saying a word. How careless was I?

Suddenly, a wet, red face, mostly hidden behind snow-crusted eyebrows and beard stubble, surfaced underneath my boots. Next, came an ice-covered backpack that forced me to scramble out of its way. Following the backpack came two painfully chapped legs, scraping across the snow like seal flippers. I wanted to hug my icicled partner, but we could not hesitate. The storm had no mercy for thrill-seeking fools.

Taking the lead again, I maneuvered onto my feet and staggered across the snow. It was slow going. I needed to halt between every step, for fear of the wind lifting any weight off my shoes. If I started to slide, I might not able to stop. How far could the wind push me? What might be waiting on the other side of Piegan Pass?

The wind chill felt arctic. Fortunately, its grit seemed buffered by pushing against our backs instead of our faces. The summit's shape emerged kinesthetically. It began with a faint curve, angling slightly uphill. Next, came a slight sinking feeling. Had we crossed over the summit? Could Piegan Pass have a simple dome shape? Hoping for the best, I kept expecting to drop out of the wind any moment. Where was the mountain's backside? In my mind, it harbored a wet trail, built of dirt or rock, lightly dusted with windblown powder snow. Just imagining the trail almost made me smile. We had to be incredibly close. My hopes kept mounting until I stepped out of the fog.

SeeHawk stepped out behind me and stopped.

The view straight ahead rendered us speechless. Indeed, we had reached a south-facing slope. Its exit plummeted 1,200-feet down immeasurably long switchbacks. The landing below intersected a flat yoke cojoining two valleys. Both valleys looked completely white. Everything looked white. Below and into the distance, snow covered everything for as far as we could see. There was no way to tell which valley received the CDT. It would have been reckless to pull out our maps. The wind was too strong for us even to keep standing there, looking off the edge. Fortunately, Piegan Pass only had one exit. We could hardly go wrong by trusting the only trail in sight. Whatever might follow could wait until we got there.

"Snow shmow!" I roared.

My body felt renewed. Never mind the past. It was safely behind us. Shelter lay ahead.

"You take the honors," SeeHawk offered.

We did not share a kiss. Not even a high-five.

I went first plunging, headlong down the snow-covered trail. Thank goodness, its fresh-blown powder felt sticky. Our shoes did not slip. Joy swelled inside me. SeeHawk and I were going to live to tell our tale. We had not careened down Morning Eagle Falls. We had not triggered a mudslide and slid to our death. Nor had we lost any toes from spending hours hiking on snow in wet boots.

The south-facing trail took its time about descending. Its first long switchback kept going and going, sometimes feeling horizontal. We were almost sheltered by the upper mountain, but not completely. Now and then, a cannon-ball wind gust slammed into us so hard that we needed to jam our ice-axes into the snow. Otherwise, we might have gotten blown off the trail.

One convenient calm spell permitted SeeHawk to pull out his camera and photograph the valleys waiting below. Unfortunately, he took too long. Before tucking his camera away, he got sucker-punched by an incoming wind gust. The impact knocked him to his knees, clutching the camera in one hand while grabbing the trail with his other hand that was also holding an ice-axe.

I was too far ahead to notice him flailing. When the same wind gust hit me a few seconds later, I got knocked off my feet and ended up clinging to my ice-axe, with both legs dangling off the trail. It took a mighty hoist to lift my combined body and pack weight up to where I could brace one leg against the trail. When I finally managed a backward glance, I could not find SeeHawk anywhere.

I called out his name and got no answer. "SEEHAWK?"

Had he fallen too far downhill to hear me? Might yelling louder trigger an avalanche?

Regardless, I needed to get ready for the next wind gust. Chopping my ice-axe into some firm snow, I wiggled onto my knees and prepared to stand up. While placing one leg forward, I heard a voice approaching.

"Sunshine? Do you want me to hike in front, for a while?"

Just like that, Mister Unbreakable was back. He had not seen me fall. I had not seen him fall, either. We agreed to stay closer together, from now on.

Descending swiftly to an elevation where fewer wind gusts could reach us, we started rounding a bulge in the mountain's south face. Our expected landing point, far below, disappeared for so long that I started wishing to have checked our maps while the valleys were visible. Still, I did not feel worried. There was only one trail and we were on it. In fact, gliding down the trail's shock-absorbent snow was a hoot. It almost felt like flying, until we ran into a gully sheathed in translucent ice. If the day had been warm, no problem. The ice would have softened and been easy to cross. Instead, we found it frozen so firm that if a wind gust hit us, we might slip and take a nasty ride down rib-breaking ice chunks.

I lifted my ice-axe and gave the ice a hard tap. Just as expected, it did not budge. Bringing my axe down hard, I created a small dent, still too shallow to stop boots from slipping.

"SeeHawk, this is your department," I announced.

He confidently stepped forward.

"If you're worried about getting hit by the wind, it's okay," he reassured me. "There won't be another big gust until after we get across."

Raising one eyebrow, I replied, "How do you know?"

"Because I've put in my order for us to reach our next campsite safely," he explained.

Sigh. Leaving that alone, I set about calculating that 30-40 steps would be required to cross the ice. With that goal in mind, I dug out my silly plastic snowshoe crampons.

SeeHawk pried the flippety devices out of my hands and knelt to fasten them onto my boots as if I was a toddler.

"Fifty-two fire-breaths," he estimated.

That was the kicker. Marching onto the snow, he officially took breath number one. "HA-kom-a..."

Without thinking, my legs fell right into step behind him.

The drill consisted of plunging my ice-axe into every hole he vacated, two at a time, while calling forward, "Okay, next."

Stab, step, step.

"Okay, next."

The reason for this regimen was to be ready, in case the wind gods' office might be overwhelmed with orders, causing SeeHawk's order not to receive prompt attention.

Each lift of SeeHawk's ice-axe signaled me to take another step, lift my ice-axe and transfer it into the next empty hole.

Stab, step, step.

"Okay, next."

Stab, step, step.

"Slow down a little, please. Next."

Considering how slowly we were moving, I felt amazed there were no more wind gusts.

Stab, step, step.

Toward the gully's midline, I became hopeful for a safe finish. Then, suddenly, it was happening. We both stepped back onto soft powder snow. I had crossed all the ice and never gotten vertigo!

SeeHawk assured me this was a big advance toward overcoming my fear of heights.

I told him I would settle for just being stoked.

Our stomachs wanted to celebrate. Where was that delicious macadamia-nut-chocolate-cherry bar, which had become our only meal of the day?

SeeHawk raised his bar into the air and toasted, "These are now, and forevermore, dubbed our official Piegan Pass Bars."

Tearing off a chunk, I toasted, "Thanks for keeping them in your pocket, Chief Snack Officer, and for not letting me stop you from making hot chocolate."

Within the next half hour, we landed upon the yoke between two linked valleys. I had been hoping the CDT would show us where to go from there, but it just disappeared beneath deeper snow. Glancing right and left, we searched for a cairn, cleared logs, blazed trees, or any evidence to indicate which valley contained the CDT. Finding nothing, for the first time since leaving Cataract Creek, I reached into my pants pocket and dug out that day's guidebook directions. They had gotten mashed into a tight wad during several hours of not being touched. When I tried to unfold them, Crud! I discovered the whole wad was soaked! Worse than that, all the Book of Beans pages had melted into one shapeless lump of preschool paste. Truly, they were not even paper anymore. Poppa Jim's pages could still be gingerly peeled apart, and they were still legible, but reading them did not help us figure out which valley to enter.

SeeHawk recalled what Poppa Jim had told us about Montana's snow season, and he speculated, "Maybe guidebook authors don't bother including snow-directions for people who ignore their recommended start dates."

"Well, anyway," I shrugged. "We're alive, so I'm not complaining."

Privately, though, I felt my body's core temperature dropping fast. This was partly due to exhaustion, but mostly due to seeing the overcast sky grow darker. It was getting late. My body craved shelter. I tore off another chunk of Piegan Pass Bar and chewed it like steak. What I really needed, though, was to peel off my backpack and get cozy inside our tent.

"Should I refrain from cracking jokes about flipping a coin?" SeeHawk asked me.

"I'm pretty sure we should turn right," I asserted, "but if we don't find the trail quickly, we should probably start looking for an emergency camp."

"On the SNOW?"

"Only as a last resort. I mean, it would be better than blundering around while we're tired."

Fortunately, within minutes of turning right, sheer luck rewarded us with a trail of human footprints. Fresh enough to show clearly upon the snow, they led us straight into the right-hand valley's forest. Without such help, nothing else we could see would have given us any clue about which valley to enter.

"Hold up," SeeHawk warned me, before losing our backward view. "Remember what happened after we crossed the snow bridge? How do we know this person is on the CDT?"

"Who cares?" I shrugged. "Even if they're not, we're eventually going to end up at some kind of road. We could hitchhike back to Kansas if the storm doesn't end tomorrow."

"That's probably true," SeeHawk agreed. "So then, what's our next landmark?"

I had been waiting for him to ask, and took delight in saying, "Going to the Sun Road."

He grinned with surprise, "Right on, Sunshine! Let's get to that sun and start experiencing some Sunday."

It felt marvelous to follow someone else's footprints for a change. After a full day of being on high alert, we finally had the leisure to amble along, enjoying some casual conversation. Ironically, though, it turned out that neither of us had anything to say. Every recent memory inside our brains was already known by the other person. Therefore, instead of saying anything, we just shared a good cry and giggled through our tears.

The forest's snow-flocked spruce trees and grand firs let in just enough visible sky to show us bits of golden sunlight starting to leak through the clouds. Was it earlier in the day than I thought? Might there still be a couple hours of daylight left?

The ongoing footprints led us through another two miles of dense woods before their impressions softened into melting slush. Holes, where the slush had melted, revealed a groomed and muddy trail. Another transition occurred where the forest's homogenous conifer trees gained company from gregarious black cottonwoods, aspens, alders, and willows. In the same location, the air turned balmy and the slush completely disappeared. It was like stepping through an invisible doorway, from wintertime into springtime.

Green foliage exploded through the next mile of woods. Familiar eyes could spot the leaves of mountain maple, thimbleberry, gooseberry, cow parsnip, corn lilies, asters, and budding columbines. Soon, we ran into a stripe of hard asphalt, whose name made us smile.

"I guess if the weather wasn't better already, we could have followed this road to get warm," SeeHawk joked. "But, hey-hey, LOOK! There it is! Just like I told you, sweetheart. Sooner or later, the sun always shines on Sunday."

Indeed, as much as I wanted to roll my eyes, never before

had I felt so happy to see the sun shine on Sunday. It did not matter, either, about needing to prove SeeHawk wrong, since I still had almost six months' worth of Sundays left, in which to set his thinking straight.

After crossing Going to the Sun Road, we entered a looser spruce forest. Once again, the trail's banks were teeming with foliage, belonging to leafing boxwood, serviceberry, Solomon's Seal, pink shooting stars, and Indian paintbrush flowers. It had been a long day, and we felt ready to retire, so logic cannot explain how we missed seeing the turnoff to Reynolds Creek. Fortunately, after backtracking a quarter-mile, we found the campground and it was deserted. We could pick any campsite alongside the creek's raging rapids, with plenty of daylight left for pounding-in tent stakes and kicking-up our feet.

Come 10:00 pm, the sky remained bright enough for a headlamp-free feast of sundried-tomato-pesto pasta, followed by camp chores under a darkening sky. The last thing we saw, before zipping our tent shut, was millions of twinkling stars creeping into the darkness.

It felt divine to collapse onto our inch-thin sleeping pads. Once again, I inhaled SeeHawk's armpit pheromones for dessert. They were good and stinky, just how I liked them.

While waiting for sleep to take me away, memories from the day caused me to reflect. High-elevation warm-season blizzards were probably a ho-hum event in Montana. The nearest townspeople probably cared more about whatever was happening on TV, at their jobs, or on the golf course, than about Piegan Pass turning white again. Perhaps, even Glacier National Park's rangers hardly gave such weather a second thought. But, even if someone had told them about two newcomers struggling to cross Piegan Pass, they would probably have just replied with a shrug, "Yeah, weather reports mean nothing around here. One minute, it's snowing. The next minute, it's sunny. That's why we always carry gear for all kinds of weather, no matter what the season."

Anyhow, the two of us slept like logs until the next morning's sunrise rolled in too early. When I groggily unzipped our tent, my face got blasted by blinding heat. A sagging-wet roof, fogged-up windows, and all the trees surrounding our tent were dripping with sparkling, rainbow-filled dewdrops. When I reached out retrieved my soggy sneakers, I discovered a tiny frog sleeping inside my shoe.

"SeeHawk, you won't believe this!" I cried. "Aren't frogs a symbol of good luck?"

He reverently explained, "The frog represents ascension and shoes relate to your feet, so maybe your entire soul, from feet on upwards, is ascending towards a greater state of magnificence."

"Maybe so," I laughed. "Anyhow, it's a fabulous day for making up some fast miles. Let's try to get back on schedule, so the park rangers will feel less inclined to bust us."

Little did we know, the footprints which had guided us away from Piegan Pass belonged to the same park ranger who had booked our campsite reservations.

Additionally, two days prior, another pair of CDT thru-hikers, coming through before us, had gotten lost in the same location. With no footsteps to follow, they had shivered throughout a long, miserably cold night, just like we might have done, if not for getting lucky.

Chapter 6

Drag

"My mind does not waver; my body maintains its balance. With such an attitude, how can I fail?"

— *Benjamin Hoff, The Te of Piglet*

Melted snow was dripping like rain through the forest surrounding Reynolds Creek. It was barely sunrise and already the sky looked late-morning blue. Sunbeams poking through holes between the trees were sipping water from shrinking puddles. Four boots resting on a soggy log had been drying, slowly, in the morning's muggy heat.

SeeHawk and I made short work of striking our tent and rainfly, rolling them up tightly, and smashing them into undersized stuff-sacks.

Our first goal for the day was to hike 14 miles by midafternoon. After taking a breather at Red Eagle Lake, we hoped to cross 7,400-foot Triple Divide Pass before the evening's cooler temperatures could make the pass icy. This plan was ambitious. Neither of us felt sure we could cross the pass before sundown. We just wanted to try, for the sake of honoring our campsite reservations.

"But if we can't reach Two Medicine tonight, I'm sure the rangers will forgive us, since we got hit by a blizzard their computer forecast didn't even know about," SeeHawk reasoned.

"Plus, delayed by a missing sign near Josephine Lake," I pitched in.

"Plus, now with all the snow, we're probably almost the only people camping, so who cares if we occupy a specific site one day later than our reservation?"

"Care Bears care," I reminded him.

"Well, right," he chuckled, "but I'm pretty sure the Atlantic Campground Grizzly is not pink, yellow, or blue. Anyway," he added, puffing up his chest, "he's not going to get our food because your number one counter-hanger man will find the perfect hanging-branch to prove brains are mightier than the beast."

"Okay, then, Number One Counter-Hanger Man," I replied, "while you're in superhero mode, could you also, please fly up and super snow blow Triple Divide Pass? Because I'm hoping to see some triple-dividing headwaters up there, not just a bunch of snow."

"Why, of course," he grinned. "Don't know if I can get to the whole job today, but if you give me enough time, I'll melt the whole mountain."

Donning his backpack, he thought to add, "Seriously, though, I want some awesome photos of those headwaters, so let's try to get up there well before sunset."

A blaze of wildflowers trumpeted our takeoff from Reynolds Creek. Soon, we began passing postcard waterfalls. The first one hissed down a red rock chute, artistically streaked with fluorescent green moss. Saint Mary Falls thundered into a simmering azure pool, spanned by a horse bridge that smelled freshly oiled. Virginia Falls spilled down an 80-foot cliff, framed with evergreens costumed in shadows. SeeHawk and I had a tradition of making love near waterfalls, but we knew better than to expect privacy in day-hiker territory, so we did not let our hair down. Good thing, too because we found a sociable cigarette smoker loitering near Virginia Falls, who was eager for someone to hear his funny stories. Deciding to give him an ear, we took off our backpacks and shared some good laughs, before dashing onward, whistling *Peter and the Wolf*.

Unfortunately, finishing the waterfall tour left us high and dry for distractions. The forest closed back up. Everything seemed to be in order, as far as knowing where to aim and being generally comfortable. We were pretty much entering the Land of Milk and Honey, and, strangely, that is why we fell into some old bad habits.

SeeHawk stirred the waters first, by claiming the morning's beautiful weather proved The Universe was kind.

I knew better than to contradict anything he ever said about Divine Benevolence. Nonetheless, triggers are triggers. I could not resist arguing that The Universe does not care one whit whether or not people like the weather they are given and that anyone who thinks otherwise is overvaluing human beings.

SeeHawk insisted that The Universe most certainly cares about individual desires, and does address peoples' requests if they are submitted with focused intention.

I kept trying to talk sense into him, which merely strengthened his conviction.

If we had been sitting down together, none of this conversation would have amounted to much. However, discussing an esoteric subject while hiking full tilt across tree roots and trip holes made SeeHawk feel increasingly unreceptive. Gradually, he quickened his pace, hoping to put some distance between us.

I nearly jogged, trying to keep up with him, while doggedly insisting, "Maybe you just think The Universe is kind because you want it to be true, like with reincarnation, where a comforting story seems more appealing than the sad alternative."

He smote me by saying, "Whatever you think, Sunshine."

Hearing those words made me recoil in shock. Nothing could have been more insulting than the same generic put-off he used every time.

Fortunately, he sensed a storm was brewing and twirled around to face me, clutching two banana-blackberry fruit rolls as a gesture of peace.

I selected the thinner fruit roll, as a means of saying, "Thank you for not mentioning any more about this."

Fortunately, we did not need to brood after we got back to hiking because our next forward view contained Saint Mary Lake. Huge, serene and edged with sandy beaches, the lake's hilly basin looked like vacation heaven.

The trail, itself, remained far less interesting, but it did supply a nice variety of trees. Giant Douglas firs had dropped their tasseled cones all over the trail, the balance of which dangled from their shaggy branches like Christmas ornaments. Intermixed between the space-hogging Douglas firs were petite grand firs, subalpine firs, and erect lodgepole pines, all keeping the forest's canopy intact, between seasonal gaps imposed by leafless aspens, black cottonwoods, and rare broad-leaved maples.

The trail was flat in an overall sense, but we kept having to climb and drop, climb and drop, over small speed bumps, with no extra reward for our effort. Growing vaguely agitated, our attention shifted toward a cluster of bare sandspits jutting into the water. It would have felt sublime to peel off our damp shoes and socks, wriggle clammy feet into the sand, strip off our dusty clothes and enjoy a short swim. Why did thru-hiking have to be puritanical? Was it worth having quit our jobs just to keep walking, day in and day out, if pleasure could not be part of the equation? We felt tempted, but our consciences said no. Carousing in a full-blown lake would be too extravagant, compared with the pragmatic stream-dips we enjoyed at strategic times. Triple Divide Pass was waiting. Our top priority was to snap some great photos of water diving atop the pass, toward Hudson Bay and the Atlantic and Pacific Oceans. Besides, it was an axiom of thru-hiking that speed bumps needed to be taken in stride, so we just kept plodding along, finding contentment in steadiness and birdsongs.

A bend in the trail eventually redirected us through a ratty pine forest, full of whining mosquitoes. We crossed Red Eagle Creek on a wooden suspension bridge, whose slats rippled elastically beneath our feet, daring us to bounce like kids on a trampoline. Strangely, the bridge's cables felt cold to the touch, even in full sunlight. I noticed some filmy cirrus haze drifting across the sun and felt a whisper of concern, but that was all.

Yesterday's storm was still moving out, Now, in all fairness, it was the sun's turn to shine.

SeeHawk was first to step off the bouncing bridge.

When I dismounted after him, he started licking my cheeks like an affectionate puppy.

Realizing his purpose, I cringed, "If you're acting like a dog after just three days, how gross are you going to be, by the time we reach Mexico?"

"Not grosser than a face covered with sticky purple fruit-roll," he winked.

"Ouch," I laughed. "Okay, but maybe next time, you could just tell me I'm a slob, instead of cleaning the mess yourself?"

We skated right up to Red Eagle Lake but still arrived too late for a final push over Triple Divide Pass. The last 5-mile ascent was introduced by an upward sloping drainage valley, walled with patchy snow, which looked best suited for the start of a new day. Seriously, that is why we stopped. It had nothing to do with wanting to camp at Red Eagle Lake. However, prudence did not deter us from enjoying our consolation prize.

Red Eagle Lake was a five-star destination. Its orange clay shoreline made the conifer trees overhead look intensely green. A few dozen rice grains floating near the water's edge reminded us to appreciate being ahead of Montana's tourist season. Once we got our tent set up, I could not wait another merry minute. Off came my clothes. Straight into the water went two dusty feet. A chill ran up my spine. Senses suppressed during our hiking hours bolted awake and smiled. I waded out farther, dunked my bandanna, and squeezed dribbles of cold water down my back. Ooh, that felt cringy. A glacial breeze ricocheted through the trees, prodding me to hurry but phooey on that. Stinging chills were something to be ignored, or even enjoyed, depending upon one's attitude. I kept splashing my arms and stomach until the cold became bearable. That was my cue for a full body drop. Shoulders, head, and all. Mission accomplished. I whirled around fast. It was time to flee-the-heck out of that freaking cold water.

Rapture embraced me upon the lake's sandy shore. I hurried to fetch my pack towel from a lichen-crusted tree branch. Clumps of squishy moss created a plush bathmat, rigged with puddles that swallowed my toes. I blotted my arms and legs partially dry. Nature could do the rest. Euphoria was kicking in. The air smelled sweet. I could have stayed beside the lake forever, just breathing in everything, if only my crotch had not gotten stabbed by something sharp.

"Auggggh!" I screamed.

It hurt too much to think. What in the devil's name was happening? Oh shit! Could it be? Yes. Of all the vile, horrid creatures. I knew by instinct. It was a tick. Pinching around until my fingers could grab hold, I yanked the little bastard and out came its body. Plump full of blood. Head intact! Gross. I hammered it flat with a rock. That was not enough. I ground its deflated, blasphemous little carcass into smithereens. No amount of grinding could overkill a tick. I had to exterminate all its future lifetimes.

Back in camp, I got busy cooking dinner and forgot about the bite. Therefore, I never wondered if my attacker had been trying to tell me something.

A light rain shower sent SeeHawk and me into our tent right after dinner. Assuming our usual sides of the tent, we folded smelly clothes into makeshift pillows and quickly fell asleep, without noticing the moon's failure to appear.

I dreamed about flying home to visit friends and getting stuck in California, unable to return to Montana because the airline's ticket price had risen by $10,000. Later, I dreamed about waking up one sunny morning...seeing gray daylight ooze into our tent...discovering that I was awake in real life. Except, how strange. The daylight seemed awfully dim. Nothing could be heard outside my ears. No birds were chirping. No breeze was stirring. Did such deep silence mean we were in for a stagnant, high-pressure day? Might heat setting in early thaw Triple Divide Pass before we got there, and camouflage the headwaters we were hoping to photograph? That would sure be a letdown. Not to mention, it would be no fun climbing through melting slush. Except, wait. Didn't the morning sound a little too quiet? Such deep silence could only mean one thing. Starting to worry, I did not want to peek outside our tent. Could I just go back to sleep? Well, of course not. Curiosity made me look. I scarcely breathed while unzipping the front door. Sure enough, there it was. Pure white snow had covered every inch of ground and flocked all the trees. Yesterday's views we had enjoyed while swimming were gone and buried, and that's not all. It was also the worst kind of snowfall. Not just tiny granules hitting the ground and vanishing, its flakes were the size of *Wheaties*. They could have covered a trail while we looked the other way.

When SeeHawk crawled outside, his first remark was, "At least our food is still hanging where we left it."

"That's good," I grimaced, "since we might be camping here for a while."

In truth, though, I had no intention to stay put all day. Triple Divide Pass was only 5-miles uphill. Surely, the snowstorm was going to break soon.

Trying to stay positive, I gaily observed, "At least it's not windy."

SeeHawk stared at the approach to Triple Divide Pass. Its patchy snow was gone. Now, everything uphill was just solidly white.

Noticing my partner's knitted eyebrows, I acknowledged, "Yep, it's probably snowing like hell on the pass."

Our top priority was to keep everything dry while striking camp. Fortunately, we had purchased a tent built by brainiacs. Its inner body was designed to be collapsible from underneath the rainfly. Thus, we were able to stay sheltered while packing everything besides the rainfly into stuff-sacks. Our lunches got slipped into baggies strapped on our backpacks, where the food could be reached without unzipping anything. It took another few minutes to shimmy rain chaps over our knee-high snow gaiters. We anchored loose poncho corners under any available straps, just in case of the pass getting windy. The last step was lacing on my sneakers and SeeHawk's boots. Then, we emerged from beneath our rainfly, still fully dry.

People residing in far northern climates might sometimes see snowflakes reach the size of quarter-dollars, but probably not often. SeeHawk had spent 25 years living in Illinois and Boston, without ever seeing snowflakes rival the platters that welcomed us into the cold.

Commencing a march toward Triple Divide Pass, our shoes sank into fresh, soft powder. We marched side-by-side, loosely following where the trail had aimed before it got covered with snow. Our initial destination was obvious, so there was no reason to worry about route-finding or maps.

Both of us kept expecting to hear the other person say, "So much for taking those headwater photos, eh? We'll be lucky just to leave the pass with all our fingers and toes." Therefore, it gave us both a shock to blurt out in unison, "Let's get out of here!"

We practically jogged from Red Eagle Lake back toward St. Mary's. It felt important to hurry, for prevention against changing our minds. The falling snow grew wetter with decreasing elevation. Soon, its broad flakes melted into slush-clods, which soaked our sleeves on impact. One sodden meadow contained hundreds of delicate, pink shooting star lilies, bowed from wearing heavy slush bonnets. Decreasing elevation turned the falling slush into liquid rain. From that elevation downward, we could have been experiencing any normal day in June, except for all the ground and trees being flocked.

At the end of retreating 7-miles down and sideways, we reached the same ranger station from which we had obtained our camping permits six days earlier. Inside its wooden fortress, the same freckled young ranger greeted us, looking quite surprised.

"Hey!" I complained. "You told us the weather was going to be clear, or perhaps a little rainy, not dumping snow in buckets."

He replied with a shrug, "Yeah, what a surprise, huh? The forecast changed ten minutes after you left."

A short conversation revealed the ranger deserved credit for rescuing SeeHawk and me from snow-camping two days earlier.

He had gone into the woods to search for something, without checking the weather before he left. When the blizzard sneaking over Piegan Pass caught him by surprise, his flight had created the trail of footsteps that saved SeeHawk and me from getting lost.

After the park ranger recovered from feeling speechless, he changed the subject by asking, "Have you seen any grizzly bears?"

"No," I reported, "and we have no idea why because we've been carrying stinky peanut butter-sandwiches and Brie cheese this whole time."

"Well, you'll probably meet the Big Guy if you pass through the Atlantic Campground," he warned us. "That bear's been making trouble again. Apparently, he's not too scared of humans."

"No offense," I said, "but grizzlies are the least of our worries right now. Can you please give us a fresh weather forecast?"

The ranger ripped a stiff sheet of paper out of his computer and methodically reported, "Colder temperatures for the next few days. It might snow enough to get us back to where we were three weeks ago. Do you want to change your campsite reservations?"

My mouth fell open. Did he mean the snow level was going to revert to its height before the recent heatwave? As in, its height during May?

"Too bad we don't have a slush-fund for unplanned motel stays," I remarked.

"Ha-ha," SeeHawk groaned. "Slush money for laying over until the slush melts."

Seriously, though, going back to town would mean paying for food and lodging with my credit card, until whenever returning heat might take the snow back down a few notches.

SeeHawk pulled me aside and softly mumbled, "Take your time, Sunshine. I know it's hard to sacrifice all the great planning you did to get us here early, but it doesn't sound like the weather's going to cooperate. You don't need to feel guilty, though because it's not your fault. I still have total faith in your excellent planning skills. Just do whatever you think is best. I promise I'll be fine with it."

I wracked my brain, paced back and forth, and finally decided, "Well, if we have no choice, then screw it. Let's find a motel with a bathtub, have sex, order a pizza, and get a good night's sleep. Tomorrow, we can decide what to do after we see how the weather shapes up."

"Atta girl," SeeHawk laughed.

Over my shoulder, he told the ranger, "We'll see you tomorrow morning, if not later in the week..."

* * *

One might expect motorists driving through a blizzard to avoid drenched hitchhikers wearing soggy backpacks, but as it turned out, SeeHawk and I got picked up by the third car to come along Highway 89. Through the car's dripping windows, we saw Blackfoot Indian cow pastures revert from springtime back into winter. It was a magical scene, for anyone not wishing to cross tall mountains and sleep outdoors.

Upon arriving in East Glacier, we found comfort inside a warm Mexican restaurant, which satisfied all our immediate needs with a basket of crisp tortilla chips, spicy homemade salsa, and sweet Moose Drool ale. Best of all were the juicy Chili Rellenos. Last, but not least, I was about to attack a pillow of key-lime pie, when into the restaurant strode two CDT thru-hikers.

A brief introduction revealed they were the pair who had gotten lost leaving Piegan Pass and ended up snow-camping. Of course, that was before the ranger had left footprints, so they had been on their own. Both lads looked shaken by their recollection of becoming disoriented shortly before dark. Running into some flooded creeks had convinced them to pitch camp on the snow. It would have been a cold night for anyone, but more so for them because being ultralight hikers, they were sleeping underneath a tarp, instead of a tent.

That trial by ice had occurred within days of a much bigger disappointment that was still feeding upon them. Initially, they had begun their CDT-hike northbound, starting from the Mexican border. Recently, they had flip-flopped, to restart their hike heading southbound from the Canadian border, because their northbound hike had gotten a bad start.

As one of the pair explained, "We got rained-on EVERY SINGLE DAY in New Mexico. I don't know how a desert can be so wet. We rarely ever got to dry out our clothes. Plus, we had to wait on the road for TWO WHOLE DAYS before catching a ride to Reserve. Can you imagine what it feels like to spend TWO WHOLE DAYS trying to catch a ride? That was before we ran into a wall of snow in the San Juan Mountains. There was no way to keep going, so we decided to flip-flop up to the Canadian border, but now it's snowing here, too. We're kind of...um...not having the experience we hoped for."

SeeHawk mentioned having seen tiny holes perforating the switchbacks approaching Piegan Pass.

Both men confirmed they had worn mountaineering crampons up to the pass.

One proceeded to describe their latest misfortune, getting marooned in East Glacier. "

We decided to pitch our tarp at Two Medicine," he began. "It seemed like a nice place to wait out the storm because of their store and bathrooms. But then, the rain came down hard. Our tarp collapsed and soaked all our gear. Even our sleeping bags. That's why we're back in East Glacier for a while. We need to dry out and get warm before we can even think about getting back on the trail. We're so sick of rain. I think we're starting to lose our morale."

I noticed desperation glimmering in the young man's eyes. His heart was aching for one more chance. If only, tomorrow's sun would come out and keep on shining. He envied SeeHawk and me for being bright-eyed newcomers, who still felt enthusiastic, despite our recent trials. Also, he shared a guilty confession.

"I'd like to go home and see my girlfriend."

The restaurant was getting ready to close, so we had to all say goodnight and, "Maybe we'll run into you again down the trail."

Back in our motel room, SeeHawk and I reveled in luxury. Not only did we fill our room's deep jacuzzi bathtub with drinkable hot water and soak in it for an hour, but also, we scrubbed our fingernails with strong-smelling bar soap. After drying off like royalty, with full-sized bath towels, playtime was over and we got down to business.

The discussion began with me telling SeeHawk, "If we hike back to Red Eagle Lake, we'll be able to start from where we left off and keep our thru-hike continuous."

"Sounds good," he nodded. "So, our plan is pretty simple?"

"Well, it depends upon what happens with this storm. We can't afford to spend too long in Glacier National Park and fall way behind our deadline for entering the San Juan Mountains."

"You're talking about the wall-of-snow place that made those rain-guys flipflop?"

"Exactly. Our big scenic climax of this whole trail. We don't want to miss the San Juans for anything, but I've thought of another idea. Instead of returning to Red Eagle Lake, maybe we could hitchhike to the other side of Triple Divide Pass and go backward from there."

"You mean, cross the pass backward? Why would we do that?"

"No, just listen. We could sleep in the Atlantic Campground. Wake up early. Leave our backpacks on the campground's food-hanging pole. Approach Triple Divide Pass from the south instead of the north, which wouldn't take long without our backpacks, and then connect the dots back to Red Eagle Lake with our eyes instead of our feet. After that, we'd just turn around, grab our backpacks and keep going."

SeeHawk replied uncertainly, "Hm, I don't know about connecting the dots with our eyes, Sunshine. Wouldn't that disqualify us from doing the whole CDT?"

"Technically, yes, but this is not a small snowstorm. If it sets us back by more than a day or two, you know as well as I do what that will mean for Colorado during October."

Understanding my concern, SeeHawk inquired, "How many miles of dots would we connect with our eyes?"

"It's hard to tell exactly. Our guidebooks aren't quite precise enough, but I'd say five-to-eight by foot measure, or maybe four as the crow flies."

SeeHawk made a sour-milk face.

"I know," I agreed, "that sounds like a definite last resort, but if the weather doesn't clear soon, it might be our only way to see both Triple Divide Pass and the South San Juans."

SeeHawk almost nodded, before exclaiming, "Wait, are you saying we should camp where they've been seeing that giant grizzly bear?"

Laughing, I answered, "Yes, but don't worry. He'll be no match for our bear canister. We have good ropes, even with the knot I added for decoration, and our Pack Mule is the world's best counter-hanger, ever. Plus, if you want some extra insurance, we can eat a cold dinner."

"Sounds smart," he accepted. "So, should we hitchhike back to St. Mary's and change our campsite reservations? Or just gamble on not meeting any rangers?"

"Probably gamble," I replied. "It's a long hitchhike. Nobody was camping besides us before it snowed, and now the park will be empty, so I bet the rangers will give up on being nitpicky."

"Great, so, when do you want to start?"

"As soon as the weather clears up."

"Okay, I'll put in my order for good weather," he concluded brightly.

"Well, as long as you're ordering, please ask the weather gods for free overnight shipping."

The next morning, we sauntered into the Two Medicine Grill, grabbed two seats in the dining room, and ordered a pair of steaming three-egg omelets.

A young man seated nearby introduced himself as a local rock-climber. When he heard our plan, he warned us to expect lots of snow on Pitamakan Pass.

"How close is Pitamakan to the Atlantic Campground?" See-Hawk asked.

"Very close," he said, "Just watch out for one icy section that's pretty steep. You can cross anything if you just take your time. The main thing is, not to go up high until it stops snowing. Do you both have crampons?"

"I have snowshoe crampons," I told him, "but SeeHawk just has his boots."

"No problem," the climber promised. "I'll loan you my crampons. Just return them whenever you get back to town."

I finished that conversation quaking in my chair. Any kind of ice that might force a rock climber to take their time was probably going to scare the pants off me.

SeeHawk reminded me that no sane climber would loan crampons to somebody who might fall and not come back.

"Good point," I laughed, "but I'm still scared."

We were digging into wedges of fresh huckleberry pie when the climber returned, carrying his promised crampons.

Anxiety gripped me when I saw him hand SeeHawk 2-pounds worth of savage steel spikes. My snowshoe crampons were an absolute joke by comparison. Nevertheless, my crampons would have to do because, now that serendipity had stepped in to help, we were doubly committed to crossing the pass.

As luck would have it, serendipity also did us a second favor, by clearing up the weather just after lunchtime. Which is to say, a few sunbeams poked through the clouds. That was fair weather, by local standards, during June in Glacier National Park.

Both SeeHawk and I experienced heavy déjà vu while trudging back to the same golf resort which had provided our first ride after stepping off the train. This time, every passing driver ignored us. After a half hour of rejections, we started to feel discouraged. The sun was sinking fast. Few cars were leaving the golf resort and fewer remained.

"We could try again first thing tomorrow," SeeHawk suggested.

He did not mean it, though because just think. Another motel room? Unloading our backpacks? Paying for another restaurant meal? Re-loading our backpacks? Walking back to the golf resort and standing in the same place, all over again? Uh-uh. No way. Time was of the essence. We needed to get back into the race, pronto. This frame of mind made it hard to stay composed when a shiny white sportscar pulled to a stop in front of us.

Out hopped a fashionable young lady, who giggled nervously, "I can't believe I'm doing this. I NEVER pick up hitchhikers!"

As it turned out, she was hurrying like mad to reach East Glacier. It made no sense for her to have picked us up. The only possible explanation was Trail Magic.

Feeling extremely grateful, we asked our Trail Angel to deposit us at Cut Bank Creek Road. From there, we expected to walk 10 miles, in hopes of reaching the Atlantic Campground before dark. This plan felt increasingly ambitious as we gazed westward through the car's closed windows, watching a low golden sun disappear and reappear, disappear, reappear, and so forth, between the highway's bordering mountains. It was going to get dark within a matter of hours. We needed to start hiking right away. Therefore, I gritted my teeth when I saw an appropriate-looking dirt road fly past our window.

"No problem," chirped our driver, when she heard us groan.

Without hesitation, she whipped a U-turn and sped us back to the dirt road we had overshot. It was a little disconcerting not to see any road sign marking the junction, but whatever. Everything looked right, geographically speaking, in terms of the road heading into a gap between two westward foothills.

Immediately upon starting to walk, SeeHawk's borrowed crampons, clipped onto the carabiner holding his crow feather, started to clank like prisoner's chains.

I spent several minutes getting used to the noise, before deciding we were on the wrong road.

"WHAT?" SeeHawk gasped.

The sun was preparing to set, for real.

"We need to go back to the highway," I admitted, "and then...well...I don't know if we should turn right or left."

Things could have gone from bad to worse. Luckily, our intrepid Trail Angel, who was still hurrying to reach West Glacier, came back to fetch us after having spied the real Cut Bank Creek Road!

As we climbed into her car for the second time, she hurriedly explained, "I just couldn't bear to leave you here. It seemed like you'd come back if I parked and waited."

Feeling overcome with gratitude, we reached the real Cut Bank Creek Road within a few minutes. Our Trail Angel threw us a quick wave, and then, off she whooshed, vanishing right before the sun winked out of sight.

"Ten miles," I told SeeHawk. "That means, no stopping for anything until we smell giant bear-scat."

"Are you sure we should start walking ten miles this late in the day?" he asked.

Gesturing around, I answered, "Ha-hem?"

"Got it," he nodded.

Together, we took off walking at top speed. Much to our surprise, before long, a family from Alabama drove up to us from the highway, cheerfully announcing, "We'll give you a ride to the trailhead if you'll help us spot bears."

Well, gee, that was not a tough decision because Cutbank Creek Road was not part of the CDT. So, yes!

A squirmy little boy, we joined in the backseat, claimed to have spotted two black bears and two grizzlies since morning. While he bombarded us with animal stories, his parents fawned over a pair of wild turkeys bobbing through the woods.

The mother guffawed when she heard SeeHawk and I claim to be thru-hiking the entire CDT. "Why'd a couple of people walking THREE-THOUSAND MILES wanna hitchhike five miles to a trailhead?" she demanded.

SeeHawk and I looked at each other and laughed. We knew the answer, but there were no words to explain it.

Upon reaching the trailhead, we stepped back into Mother Nature's arms. The infamous Atlantic Campground lay five miles ahead. A warm breeze swept us from the evening's graying glow into murky conifer woods. Bland scenery kept our brains on mute, until we started encountering fresh grizzly tracks. Presently, a short break in the trees revealed distant Flinsch Peak, masquerading as a frosted Egyptian pyramid. Babbling alongside us, Cut Bank Creek framed our progress up to an elevation where snow patches appeared.

Stars were coming out by the time we reached the Atlantic Campground. There was still enough skylight left for a cold dinner of hummus on crackers before sprinkling rain drove us into our tent for the night.

Lying on my back in inky darkness, listening to the raindrops patter above my head, I dreamed about getting chased by zombies...SeeHawk decided to quit the CDT and go home early...I woke up feeling sad...fell back asleep...experienced a recurring dream about pulverizing criminals with my bare fists...and finally woke up inside a dark tent slowly turning blue. It was still twilight. Our second attempt to reach Triple Divide Pass could wait until the air warmed a little.

Somewhere in the distance, referees were blowing whistles at a smoke alarm. Of course, it was really a bunch of mountain goats, whistling at an "alarm bird." Suddenly, I remembered last night's rain. When had it stopped raining?

SeeHawk was first to peek outside our tent. When he saw our food still hanging from the campground's lofty pole, his whole body sagged with relief.

"Guess Mister Grizzly's found a good series on *Netflix* or something," he reported, ducking back inside.

When I poked my head through the door, I saw passive stratus clouds, leftover from the rain.

"Mother Nature is giving us the green light because she wants us to see Triple Divide Pass," SeeHawk happily confirmed, based on what he had seen.

I scrutinized the overcast sky more carefully, and said, "Maybe, but let's hope that green light isn't the start of her playing Red Light Green Light."

We ate breakfast quickly before striking camp, and then hung everything we had, besides water, so we could climb unburdened to Triple Divide Pass.

Walking away from all our gear and food felt irresponsible. We might as well have left a baseball bat lying on the ground beneath our backpacks, with a note saying, "Hello, Your Eminence, Mister Atlantic Grizzly. Would you care to partake in a little game of piñata whacking? Go ahead and invite your friends, but make sure you all get turns with the bat and share the candy." Realistically, though, our sacks were hanging so high that only Jack in the Beanstalk could have reached them.

The campground's exit led us onto the midline of a huge glacier bowl, whose trail traversed its perimeter wall. When I peered off the trail's edge, I lost my sense of perspective. Everything deep inside looked tiny, but the bowl's circumference was huge. A lake resting at its bottom looked shrunken to a puddle. An entire forest down below looked reduced to green lumps. Conifer trees clinging to the bowl's lower walls divided meadows striped with miniature shrubbery. Snowy ledges bracing its midriff were overhung by antlers of forked deadwood. An opposite set of cliffs, underscoring Triple Divide Pass, was decapitated by flat stratus clouds.

SeeHawk and I followed the bowl's perimeter trail in one direction, as if stuck on an endless switchback. The scale of everything was so huge that we seemed to be traveling in a straight line. After perhaps an hour, we ran into a snowfield whose aggressive angle brought us to a halt. The refrozen snow felt slick and hard. Nothing was going to soften it until the sun appeared. Glancing off the trail's edge, to where a hiker would fall if they slipped, I saw a bare talus chute offering no mercy. This was a job for my snowshoe crampons. However, the snowfield was only about 20 steps wide. That was too short to bother putting them on.

SeeHawk went first, stomping toe deep holds, except where he could only produce shallow dents.

Gingerly, I placed one sneaker after the other into each hold or dent. The snow felt so slippery that I broke into a sweat. Clinging to my ice-axe, I struggled to remember how I should use it for self-arrest. By rolling onto my belly? And then, as I recalled, either stabbing one end or the other into the ice? Which end? The sharply pointed end? The flat chopping end?

"We should probably have practiced using our ice-axes a few more times before leaving home," I told SeeHawk, in mid-crossing.

"Just like I should have learned how to read our maps and compass," he called back to me, "but at least it won't be springtime much longer.

After safely crossing the snowfield, we ran into several more snowfields in quick succession. Altogether, our little Triple Divide Pass excursion was becoming a full-blown adventure, and the day was just getting started.

Beyond the last snowfield, several things changed. The CDT's tread grew skinny. The glacier bowl's perimeter wall became nearly vertical. Icy raindrops blew in and forced us to put on windbreaker jackets. Above 6,000-feet, the trail became glazed with granular corn snow, formed by repeated thawing and refreezing. At first, light rain kept the corn snow soft, but after we gained a tad more elevation, the same rain had an opposite effect and began hardening the corn snow, instead of making it soft. My sneakers began skating. I tried not to dwell upon the trail's vertical edge, but it was hard not to look because the talus underneath offered nothing for brakes.

"Aren't you glad we didn't cross Triple Divide Pass in the dark?" I asked SeeHawk.

"If it had come to that, we could have camped on the pass," he reminded me.

"By building an igloo out of the snow on top?"

"Yes, with me, your hot-blooded man, keeping you warm all night."

We were not in a situation anything like Piegan Pass. It was just lightly raining. There was no wind to speak of. We could see where we were going. Nevertheless, I started to feel threatened in a different way. Small waves of dizziness tickled my temples. The air temperature snuck toward freezing. Soon, we spied a topless summit coming into view. Thick clouds still blocked us from seeing Triple Divide Pass, but the mountain's shape made clear that we were getting close. Maybe another mile? Maybe two? How awesome was it going to feel, standing on the pass, looking off its other side? Hopefully, Red Eagle Lake would not be hidden by the clouds. And, hopefully, the dividing headwaters would be free of snow.

Within a few minutes, I noticed the rain had stopped. Things were looking up. Except, then, it started lightly snowing. Darn. Well, at least, fluffy snow was less slippery than freshly hardened ice. We had no reason to panic. Although, one prominent cloud above the summit did deserve to be watched. It was sprouting fingers of lanky scud that seemed to be pointing in our direction. At the same time, I noticed the trail getting skinnier. How was that possible? Had whoever built the trail designed it for mountain goats or people? I wished I could drop onto my knees and crawl. How silly was that? If I crawled, we were going to reach the summit tomorrow. Okay, but shoot. What else could I do? Cave in and faint? No joke. My peripheral vision was getting blurry.

When SeeHawk glanced backward, his eyes seemed to say, *PLEASE don't wuss-out, Sunshine. We're almost to the top. Just keep your head together for another twenty minutes, okay? Please?*

Examining the cloudy summit made me worry out loud, "Are we even going to SEE anything up there? I mean, the whole reason we're doing this is to spot Red Eagle Lake and photograph the headwaters, right? But, the headwaters will probably be hidden under snow, and those clouds won't let us see anything from the top."

"Who knows?" SeeHawk groaned. "Let's just get up there and find out."

It took courage for me to ask, "Will you be mad if I can't make it?"

SeeHawk stopped hiking and turned around to face me. His facial expression made him appear to be choking.

"I knew it," I cowered. "Never mind. Keep going."

Part of me wanted to say SeeHawk should finish the climb without me, but I feared I might faint if I got left alone. Besides, it was our rule never to split up, for any reason. I tried urging my legs to climb faster, but the effort just made my head feel dizzier. Suddenly, a sharp chill cut through my clothes. It was the first of several wind gusts, neither frequent nor strong, but directional enough to make the clouds close ahead start swirling. My limbs began to shiver. *Keep moving, Sunshine*, I scolded myself. *Don't you dare chicken-out, after having risked your neck to cross all those snowfields.* But, my conscience argued back, *What the heck? This climb is taking forever. I feel miserable. See-Hawk is not having fun either. We aren't going to see Red Eagle Lake. The dividing headwaters will be hidden under snow. If we had skipped this climb, we could be halfway to Pitamaken Pass by now.*

In these circumstances, SeeHawk and I practically jumped when a bright apparition popped through the swirling clouds ahead. Descending briskly toward us, the apparition grew into a young man wearing a cherry-red ski suit. He carried a small daypack and was swinging his trekking poles like a holiday skier.

"Ahllo!" he called out, in a thick European accent. "You won't tsee anyfing from ze top. I'f just come over and ze wint was misserable. I couldn't see anyfing but my two hants." He grinned broadly. "Af goot day."

Swerving to avoid us, as if rounding a mogul, he bounded off the trail's edge and vanished. We did not hear him scream.

I grabbed SeeHawk's arm and peered off the edge. Shockingly far below, the red-suited hiker was carving jump turns down a boulder chute spiked with broken trees. He might as well have been skiing the Swiss Alps.

"I guess agility comes with the accent," I joked.

"His name must be Pierre," SeeHawk agreed. "Pierre The Mountain Goat, who descends tall cliffs in a single bound."

"Pierre the Ladies Man, who skis all day, and retires at night to sip white wine and eat cheese fondue."

"I am Pierre," SeeHawk bragged, pretending to ski.

From that moment onward, "Pierre" became a symbol of immortality in our minds. Every time we headed down something steep, we were going to cry out in terrible European accents, "I am Pierre. Women adore me. I drink Chardonnay. I eat cheese fondue."

This was all before we learned the hiker's name truly was Pierre!

After sobering up, I asked SeeHawk, "Does knowing we won't see Red Eagle Lake, or the dividing headwaters, make any difference?"

"Difference, in what way?" he asked.

"Difference in terms of convincing you that we should, or shouldn't go all the way up. Considering we won't be able to see anything, how much do we value just being able to say we did it?"

SeeHawk spent a moment imagining how much longer it might take us to reach the pass. At length, he admitted, "We should probably turn around."

"Yes!" I rejoiced. "Thank you, Pierre!"

Somehow, retreating across the corn snow happened a lot faster in reverse. Once I gained headspace to think freely, a years-old memory bubbled into my awareness. It was the story of how I had first dented my brand-new pickup truck.

"Seeing it felt awful," I explained to SeeHawk, "because the repair would have been expensive, and my truck was only a few months old. But, then, I realized something cool. Getting that first dent set me free to stop worrying about it."

"You mean, breaking our continuity has set you free from worrying about breaking our continuity?" SeeHawk surmised.

"In a way, yes. But don't worry, partner. We're not going to skip anything else, unless hellfire and tornadoes drive us off the trail."

I wanted my words to hold, but, privately, I wondered. Was missing Triple Divide Pass going to weaken our morale? Could we still hope to reach Mexico feeling successful? Or had copping out labeled our whole thru-hike as a failure, no matter how well everything else might turn out?

***

Back in the Atlantic Campground, SeeHawk triumphantly lowered our backpacks from the campground's high food-hanging pole. The dirt underneath showed no large footprints other than ours.

"Mister Atlantic Campground Grizzly must be back in his cave, watching Netflix," SeeHawk speculated.

"Pshht!" I hissed. "Don't get cocky while we're passing through his neighborhood."

Before leaving the campground, we zipped off our pantlegs, because last night's clouds were starting to break apart and things were heating up.

Our first stop of the morning was Atlantic Creek. A wooden footbridge beckoned us to stand above violent rapids and snap a few photographs. Directly upstream, engorged snowmelt was blasting through a gash between wooded snowbanks. We tossed in some leaves and watched them joyride downstream like miniature kayakers. Nobody else seemed to be around. We had all the beauty of springtime to ourselves, inside Montana's short window between stone-cold winter and bikini-tourist season.

Uphill from Atlantic Creek, we found snow covering a gradual incline thinly severed by Cut Bank Creek. Poking through the snow stood an early crop of yellow flowers, fighting to keep blooming until whenever it might get hot again.

Farther uphill, we started seeing bear tracks 2-inches deep. They merged onto the trail in front of us, and proceeded to lead us up the mountain.

SeeHawk compared one pawprint to his clodhopper of a hiking boot and confirmed the bear's paws had exceeded size 11-E.

When he stomped onto the pawprint it had no effect, which meant the bear had probably weighed upwards of 210 lb.

"We should probably hike slower," I concluded. "Those tracks don't look more than one-hour old."

"Is your bear spray ready?" SeeHawk asked.

"It's in my side pocket."

"Make sure you remember which pocket."

Following the bear, we entered a shady corridor pinned between close-knit conifer trees. Mister Big Paws had strode through the corridor so recently that we feared we might overtake him from behind.

"Just in case, let's review what to do," I said. "First, we need to unlock our safety clips...then, aim our sprayers into the bear's eyes..."

"...rather than our faces," SeeHawk clarified.

"Yep, and then hope for the bear to hate pepper spray, unlike my first dog, who used to lick it out of the air."

Together, we teamed up and sang songs about bears, backpacking, and foods we had not packed for the trip. Perhaps our noisemaking helped, because nothing with bigger-than-size-11-E paws gave us any trouble before we reached Morning Star Lake.

The bear's tracks continued, heading across the lake's scenic campground, before they disappeared into the next uphill woods.

"Looks like Mr. Grizzly's planning to do a little ice-climbing," I noted.

"Let's hope he brought his crampons," SeeHawk agreed.

"Maybe if we can't find the CDT under all this snow, we can just follow the bear's tracks over Pitamakan Pass."

"Are you joking?" SeeHawk frowned.

"Not entirely," I admitted. "Bears like following human trails, so this one might keep us on the CDT."

"For how far?"

"It's three-point-four miles from here to the summit of Pitamakan Pass."

"That's too far to rely on a bear for prevention against getting lost in the snow."

"Yeah, so we'd better hope for some of those trees to be blazed."

Our future looked unsettling, but for the time being, we had it made. Morning Star Lake was a feast for sore eyes. There was nobody else around, so we could camp any place that was free of snow. Granted, we had enough daylight left to keep going, but only by dry-trail, go-getter, hiking-into-the-dark standards, which did not apply to an icy pass requiring mountaineering crampons. Besides, within minutes of stopping, we got hit by a cold breeze that forced us to put on our hats.

Feeling glad to have played it safe, SeeHawk imagined, "If The Big Guy's crossing Pitamakan Pass right now, he must be freezing. Even though, of course, he's wearing a bearskin rug."

I pointed through a hole in the sky's low stratus layer and showed SeeHawk, "Those clouds look like they're inside a washing machine."

Tumbling, swirling and bumping into one another, several upper level clouds peeking through the hole seemed to be getting blown by conflicting winds.

"Hopefully, their rinse cycle won't last beyond this evening," SeeHawk shivered, looking a bit worried. "But, hey, what about this campsite, eh? Not a bad place to get stuck overnight."

"Or even for a week," I agreed, "knock on wood."

The campground's central attraction, Morning Star Lake, looked small and mysteriously deep. Its water underpinned a vertical stone cliff, tall as any skyscraper, to which snow could not stick and neither could most trees. Time fell away while SeeHawk and I got lost in examining the cliff's miniature details. There was so much to look at that we forgot to take off our backpacks, until another blast of cold wind slapped us in the faces. Suddenly, it started snowing. The flakes were not quarter-sized, but they had enough oomph to remind us of the blizzard at Red Eagle Lake. Fearing to keep our gear dry, we hastily unpacked our tent's standalone rainfly. Instead of ditching our backpacks, we kept wearing them, while stretching the rainfly into shape. Clipping it, full circle, onto our tent's small ground cloth required squatting and standing numerous times. That exercise should have been difficult wearing backpacks, but I found it so easy that my mind reeled. Just days ago, I could never have stood up from even one squat while wearing my backpack. Now, my legs hardly noticed the extra weight.

SeeHawk strictly followed instructions, until I ducked underneath the rainfly, to start pitching our tent's interior walls. After that, SeeHawk anchored down the rainfly by attaching its long strings to peripheral rocks and logs.

Not until zipping the tent's door shut did we dare to un-cork a laugh attack. Incredibly, every piece of gear besides the rainfly, our ponchos, and our shoes, was dry. This morning, we had evaded the notorious Atlantic Campground Grizzly. Best of all, our sweat-stinking lair smelled like home.

A couple of minutes later, the snow stopped falling.

Feeling bewildered, we climbed back outside to have a look around. Sure enough, the coast was clear.

"It looks like we can cook outside, so let's do it," I decided. "Better to not leave any food smells near our tent, in case Mister Grizzly has a midnight snack attack."

"You're right, he might do a U-turn before crossing Pitamakan, if he wasn't expecting it to snow," SeeHawk agreed.

Morning Star Lake looked exquisite through a veil of bubbling pasta steam. Add to its elegance the delicious aroma of spicy Thai peanut sauce and things could not have been nicer in a chef's choice restaurant.

While eating, we watched eight white dots frolic back and forth across the opposite cliff. They were mountain goats, playing an astonishingly polite game of Follow The Leader, without any apparent regard for gravity. Each leap demonstrated by the herd's esteemed Leader (or, at least, by its athletic champion) got copied, one at a time, by each member of the herd, in their turns. No goat ever tried cutting the line. Nor did any showoff ever hog the spotlight after finishing its turn. Occasionally, one bobby dazzler or another would try for extra style-points, by adding a lope, curve, or secondary mini-jump, but such bravado was only exhibited after completion of the original move.

While watching from the peanut gallery, I remarked, "Who needs TV?"

SeeHawk reflected, "This probably was the Sports Channel for Native Americans two hundred years ago."

No more snow fell from the sky's darkening clouds before we retired into our tent for the night. Any bear coming down from Pitamakan Pass should have smelled our dinner while passing through the campground, but we heard nothing besides the cold wind blowing into our dreams.

Next morning, SeeHawk got awakened by an urgent need to "nature stop." Unfortunately, when he tried unzipping our tent's rainfly, the zipper got snagged and refused to budge. Desperation drove him to shove one arm underneath the rainfly and yank its exterior flap outward. At the same time, he tugged hard on the zipper's inside handle. Eventually, the zipper moved, only to get snagged again. Breaking free, it got snagged again, and so forth, until my partner's face turned beet-red and he had to slither outside on his belly.

While hurrying away, he grumbled half-jokingly, "Let's hope we'll never need to shoo-away bears by waving bye-bye underneath a stuck rainfly."

When I climbed outside to join him, my eyes narrowed.

The sky looked like a mess. Broken and disorganized cumulus clouds were zooming over trees concealing Pitamakan Pass. Windblown snow was spray-painting the trees and sneezing white mist through spaces in-between them.

SeeHawk and I snuggled together for warmth while sitting inside our tent's flapping doorway, masticating hard granola steeped in cold milk.

It was impossible to see much sky from our tent. There were trees all around, so we could only guess what might be happening on Piegan Pass.

Dreading to discuss our plans for the morning, I waited until we finished striking camp, sealed our backpacks, and tightened our shoelaces, before breaching the subject.

"It's less than four miles from here to the pass," I told See-Hawk, "plus another eight miles to the Two Medicine Campground. In clear weather, we could make it there by midafternoon, but today..." I noticed my partner giving me a hard stare. "...if Pitamakan Pass is going to be dangerous..." My voice faltered. Oh, dear. How was he going to take this? "Just so you know, we could potentially hitchhike down to Two Medicine Lake instead of walking. I mean, not saying I want to, definitely not. That's the last resort, only for the worst-case scenario, but...IF, and only if, we end up not being able to cross the pass today...and IF we have to come back down here again...we'll be falling behind schedule even more..."

SeeHawk tensely interjected, "What are you trying to say, Sunshine?"

"Just that we need to think responsibly," I mumbled, "because doesn't that sky kind of look like Piegan Pass?"

"You're asking me?" he shrugged. "I have no idea. You're our weather expert. I'm just our pack mule."

"Yes, but I can't make an expert forecast without seeing more of the sky."

"We're going to see a lot of sky on the pass, right?"

"Assuming we can cross the ice and get there, yes. Although, by the time we get that far, we'll be home-free, regardless."

"Great, so let's get up there and enjoy that big sky," he encouraged me.

"Except, you know what'll happen if we go up there, and then, the weather turns nasty?"

"No...what?"

"You saw it yourself, yesterday. We'll tackle the ice, even if it's dangerous."

"We will?"

"Yes, and I'm sure we'll be fine, but, just for the record, my bucket list does not include winning a Darwin Award for crossing crampon-grade ice during a storm."

"I sure hope not."

"But, I am, for sure, willing to go up there and take a look. Just, please, let's agree to turn around early if it looks dangerous, so we won't be tempted to do anything stupid."

I expected SeeHawk to slap me a high-five and take off marching into the uphill woods. Instead, he replied with a frown. "If you're worried enough to mention Darwin, maybe we should just play it safe and hitchhike down to Two Medicine Lake."

Feeling shocked, I protested, "No, no. If we can still get over Pitamakan Pass, I'm totally up for it. I mean, that's our hike, right? It's the whole reason we're out here. I was just asking for your opinion because this is not a cut-and-dried situation. I really have no idea what to expect."

"Okay, well, I gave you my opinion a moment ago," he reminded me. "Didn't that count?" Then, he added with annoyance, "Oh, for Pete's sake. Nothing I say matters anyway, since you always make every decision for us, so why are we even having this conversation?"

"What do you mean?" I cried. "I don't always make every decision for us."

"Argh, never mind. Forget that. Just, please decide for yourself, okay?"

"SeeHawk, it's not my decision to make alone. We need to decide together, so we can be equally responsible for whatever happens. That way, no matter how things turn out it'll be our shared decision, with no guilt involved."

SeeHawk threw back his head and roared, "Oh, THAT'S your game, is it? Fine, then, do you want my opinion? I think we should cross the pass. That's my opinion. Ice schmyss. We'll get over it."

"Even if it's snowing and super-windy?"

"Yes."

"You're not worried about needing to save me if I slip?"

"No, Sunshine. Ack, I mean, yes, of course. Look, if you're that worried, why did you even bother asking?"

"Because I wanted to know your opinion."

"Great, well now, you got it. So, what are you going to do with it?"

"Combine it with mine, I guess. Reach an intelligent decision, obviously."

"...which is?"

"Probably different from whatever you might decide since I'm a little worried and you're clearly not."

"Um-hm. So?"

"SeeHawk, don't you get it? The problem is, you not worrying makes me have to double-worry for both of us, half for you and half for me, which makes it twice as hard to make good decisions, with you just kicking back fondling your feather collection."

SeeHawk let go the feathers, saying nothing.

"Okay fine," I huffed. "Tell you what. I'm going to make this decision without you, for once because today I'm feeling strong. So, today I'm going to say that...I think we'll probably be safe going over the pass if we just take our time...like the rock climber said...if we don't lose the trail..."

Hearing some hesitation in my voice, SeeHawk objected, "Look, Sunshine, you honestly don't need to go up there for my benefit. If you think it's too risky, we should turn around."

I opened my mouth to argue. 98.99% of me wanted to cross the pass because I figured we had at least a 90% chance for success, but the words stuck in my mouth. My brain refused to cooperate. Did some deeper part of me truly feel scared to cross Pitamakan Pass's notorious icy passage in stormy weather? Or did I just feel scared, period?

Regardless, the next thing I knew, SeeHawk started leading me back downhill, toward Cut Bank Creek Road.

My eyes widened. I did not want to go downhill. I did not want to hitchhike. No way. No how. Our thru-hike would be ruined. SeeHawk needed to stop and turn around. I wanted to make him stop. Somehow, though, I kept following him, like a dog who knows its owner is going home too early but has no choice. Above us, turbulent clouds kept speeding overhead. It looked likely to start snowing any moment, but it was not snowing. The air we breathed was still clear. With every next step, we were intentionally, needlessly, tragically getting farther away from Pitamakan Pass. Our dream was being ruined for no valid reason. We could still turn around. SeeHawk's precaution was overzealous. We needed to see the pass, firsthand, before deciding whether or not it was safe. I needed to shout at my partner to stop. The longer my jacket stayed dry, the sadder I began to feel. We were putting another 8-mile gap in our continuity. The whole point of thru-hiking was to achieve, enjoy, and worship continuity. Even touching Mexico at the end of six months might have less importance than staying connected the whole way (minus Triple Divide Pass). My sadness deepened into misery by the time we regained Cut Bank Creek Road. I had never spoken the whole way down. What was wrong with me? How could a person claim to want something their mouth would not defend? They could not claim anything. I was a loser. SeeHawk was a loser. We were both losers. Sad, but true, our epic journey was becoming a sham before we had even reached our first resupply stop. It was all my fault, too because I was the traitor who had voiced hesitation. I should have kept my chicken-mouth shut. Without me saying anything, we might now be enjoying a fabulous view from atop a bright-white mountain, promising to lead us into a bright-yellow future. *And, we still can,* my brain argued. *This day is still young. We could still turn around.* Realistically, though, staging a full return to Morning Star Lake would have worn us out too much to charge right up and over Pitamakan Pass. We would have needed a long rest before tackling the pass, and possibly gotten stuck waiting overnight. The implications seemed grim because, even though it had stopped snowing, the air still felt cold enough to snow. Peak wind gusts blasting through the trees were showering us with snow picked up from the ground. Pitamakan Pass might have gale-force gusts. Any ice lurking up there might take a while to cross. Our shoes would be soaked (waterproofing regardless), and if it did resume snowing, oof. So, yes, even though we still had an option to turn around, our reward for another pass-attempt might not be worth the risks. Therefore, I just kept plodding along behind SeeHawk, still saying nothing and silently feeling miserable. Nothing changed until we got far enough past the Medicine Grizzly foothills to take a long look backward. Much to our surprise, the view was an eye-opener. Angry gray storm clouds were rototilling Pitamakan Pass. Any ice lurking near the summit had to be dangerous, crampons or no crampons. More than likely, SeeHawk's decision had saved us from mortal peril.

Roughly 2,500 vertical feet below Pitamakan Pass, we started getting clobbered by gale-force wind gusts. Time and time again, our feet kicked each other as if they were having a boxing match.

Suddenly, the air temperature dropped sharply. My teeth started to rattle—not just chatter—they made creepy skeleton noises.

Trying to stay warm was burning so much energy that, wind or no wind, we need to pull off the road for an emergency lunch break. Lacking access to trees, we sat right on the open road, beside a small herd of cows who also looked cold. Sliced cheese and crackers seemed like an easy lunch to eat inside our ponchos, but nope. The wind kept flipping crackers out of our hands. When we tried to drink water through our spill-proof bite-valves, just the slight parting of lips needed to bite the valves allowed wind to reach in and blow some water out of our mouths. It was a fruitless effort, so we finally quit packed everything away and got back on our feet.

About five minutes after we resumed walking, a momentary pain stabbed my left kneecap. It ended so quickly that I barely had time to wince. Thank goodness because wow. What could possibly hurt like that? A pinched nerve? A small tear? Something sharp poking my patella from the inside? Like, maybe a bone spur? Or a loose bit of cartilage? Whatever had caused the pain, its timing made no sense. We were just walking along a flat dirt road. I had not stepped into any potholes, tripped over any rocks, hyperextended my leg, or even scuffed a foot. Nevertheless, there it was again. Pain so sharp, I could barely breathe. This time, it lasted longer, making every next step torture.

I refused to tell SeeHawk. Limping along behind him, I just fumed in silence because the pain did not deserve to be recognized. It heeded to go away. Any long-term injury during the first week of our six-month journey, for which we had given up our jobs and dried a half-year's worth of food, was unthinkable. Perhaps I could have coped with injuring an arm, but a leg? No way. I needed my legs to be invincible. They were invincible, too. The pain had to be a fluke because my kneecap was healthy. In fact, both my legs were becoming Herculean. Hadn't I just proved it the previous evening, while squatting numerous times, wearing a fully loaded backpack? Indeed, I had. So, if my legs were getting burly, why was my left kneecap smarting with every step?

Just 100-feet short of Highway 89, the afflicted knee locked up completely. I stopped walking and froze. My brain could not figure out how to react. Pressing on the front of my knee felt fine. The only thing that hurt was trying to bend it.

Steeped in frustration, there I stood. SeeHawk was pulling ahead and I could not catch him. There were another 3,000 miles' worth of mountains waiting to bring us joy, if only I could solve whatever was happening. The implications floored me. Panic crept in. How was this going to work? Could I carry my backpack all the way to Mexico with one knee held stiff as a board? I urged myself to calm down. Any injury that had surfaced 15 minutes ago could easily disappear just as fast. If I hobbled the rest of the way to Highway 89, after we caught a ride to the Two Medicine Campground, surely some focused experimentation was going to fix anything resulting from a road walk.

Eventually, SeeHawk noticed there was empty space behind him and began to slow down. If he noticed me limping, he said nothing about it.

Upon reaching the highway, I could hardly believe our luck. We got picked up almost immediately, by a man from out of state with his eleven-year-old son. The boy had no arms. It was a birth defect. He had never experienced throwing a baseball or eating spaghetti with a fork. He had never been able to hug his mom or dad. Yet, like any normal boy, he happily described to us all the wonderful animals and trees he had been seeing in Glacier National Park. His equally cheerful father offered to drive us an extra 10 miles, just so they could drop us off right at the Two Medicine Ranger Station. That was more than a casual favor because, on our way there, Montana's sky opened up and started pouring cats and dogs.

"Thank you from the bottom of our hearts, both of you," SeeHawk gushed while climbing from the Trail Angels' car into a deafening downpour.

I hurried out after him, feeling revived. Sure, it still sucked that our thru-hike's continuity was broken, but in the greater scheme of life, we were lucky to even be capable of backpacking.

After piling into Two Medicine's ranger station, all dripping wet, we had to shake our arms dry before proceeding to the permit desk. Not until that moment did it occur to me that I had sprinted through the rain. Wait, hello? Was my kneecap fixed? Yes! When I tried bending it, the pain was gone! What had just happened? I felt confused. Further exploration was needed, but not right now.

A handsome young ranger, wearing a shoulder-length ponytail, stepped around the service counter to give us a friendly welcome.

I requested permission for us to camp at Two Medicine, before picking up our first box of re-supplies, in East Glacier, and then exiting the National Park via the Bob Marshall Wilderness.

The ranger looked agreeable. Pulling out a pen, he asked me to specify every campsite we had occupied during the past week.

I loosely described the flawed trail sign which had prolonged our departure from Josephine Lake, before we spent a whole day crossing Piegan Pass during a blizzard...got ejected from Red Eagle Lake by a second blizzard...returned to the CDT via Cut Bank Creek Road...thought it might be dangerous to cross

Pitamakan Pass during a windstorm...and finally hitchhiked down to Two Medicine. These episodes were easy to recall because we still had emotions attached to them.

By the time I finished speaking, the ranger looked disturbed.

I avoided his eyes while explaining in detail why SeeHawk and I had not updated our campsite reservations. One reason was to avoid extra hitchhiking. Another was being in a hurry to leave the National Park. A third was thinking the dates hardly mattered, with nobody else camping in the sites.

Looking increasingly distressed, the ranger probed us for more details about every individual campsite, going back to Day 1.

SeeHawk helped me piece together a list. Partway through, we got confused by forgetting about Cataract Creek.

The ranger looked as if he thought our confusion was a ploy. The longer we scratched our heads, the more agitated he became.

Conversely, his agitation unseated us, by making us worry about getting the Saint Mary's ranger in trouble. During a weak moment, I slipped into mumbling about the St. Mary's ranger failing to inform us that the Ptarmigan Tunnel had been closed. As soon as I spoke, I wanted to take back my words and run away screaming, but it was too late.

The Two Medicine ranger demanded to know, specifically, what the Saint Mary's ranger had said.

No way, in heck, was I going to finger the savior who had rescued us from getting lost in the snow beyond Piegan Pass. Besides, we had not even established if the Ptarmigan Tunnel had any relation to the CDT. Perhaps its closure was irrelevant. Now that things were taking a bad turn, though, I dared not ask. Instead, I redirected the conversation toward our experience on Piegan Pass.

In turn, the ranger asked me again about the tunnel. Was he trying to bust the Saint Mary's ranger? That could not happen. If anything, our Trail Angel deserved a medal for rescuing us with his footprints. My head began to spin. SeeHawk and I had already admitted our crimes. We could not afford to get slapped with a huge fine, charged to my credit card, which we could not pay off before December, if even then.

Glancing out the ranger station's window, I saw a downpour flooding the Two Medicine campground.

SeeHawk shuffled over to stand beside me.

We listened anxiously while the ranger telephoned some rabid superior who spit hellfire into his ear. Twenty minutes dragged on. The conversation seemed to be taking forever. A teensy little voice kept bellowing into the telephone's receiver. When the ranger finally hung up the phone, out came his verdict. The National Park was going to let SeeHawk and me off easy, with a pair of $10 fines for having set foot on Cut Bank Creek Road (owned by the Blackfoot Indians), plus a warning that violating any other rule within the next 7 years would cost us one week's pay after we got home.

On our way out the door, I asked if the ranger knew anything about snow conditions on Scenic Point.

"You've got nothing to worry about," he assured me. "Plenty of locals have gone up there this year, and there's no snow worth mentioning."

SeeHawk and I sagged with relief.

Back outside in the pouring rain, we witnessed a semblance of what two other, discouraged CDT-hikers had recently seen before their tarp collapsed, taking their morale down with it.

We could not pitch our tent without getting everything drenched. Instead, we fled into the campground's empty gift shop. Through its giant picture window, we watched the storm claw Two Medicine Lake into shreds. Even under siege, the whole scene looked beautiful

As SeeHawk's tensions from the day began to melt, he philosophically suggested, "Let's just polish off this last section in the park, pronto. After we get past all the rules and regulations, we'll be able to start fresh and stay on track from here on out."

"Great idea, Chief Mental Health Officer," I agreed.

Glacier National Park had been spectacular, but we both looked forward to entering a true wilderness. After tomorrow, nobody would monitor where we camped, and we could tailor each day's mileage goals toward safety and comfort, rather than just avoiding grizzly bears.

* * *

SeeHawk and I felt speechless when we unzipped our tent and saw Two Medicine Lake's bright yellow sunrise. Never, had we seen such intense blueness paint an entire sky. The lake itself looked completely transformed. Yesterday, it had been a gray cauldron of boiling rage. Today, it was a slick blue mirror, neatly framed with green conifer trees.

Three central mountains clustered behind the water ranged in color from silver to reddish-orange. Their shapes evoked a wizard's cap paired with two dinner-buns, one plain and the other frosted. Facing all three stood a lone standing peak, which reflected the sunrise as if producing its own heat. Most beautiful of all was the water itself. Every last detail of trees, sky, and mountains was preserved upon its glassy surface, except where ripples lazily kissed its shoreline.

"Never mind getting a fresh start in The Bob," SeeHawk summarized. "I'm feeling refreshed right now!"

Inspiration spurred us to strike camp in a hurry. Our next agenda started with climbing 2,000-feet, hopefully before lunchtime, so we could cross Scenic Point before any afternoon winds kicked in. This was because the Book of Beans talked about 80 mph winds roaring like "jet planes" over the summit and creating a real threat of blowing hikers off the edge.

When SeeHawk heard the author's description, he worried, "Could we get blasted up there, even though it feels like a terrarium down here?"

"We could," I confirmed, "but it probably won't blow eighty today, and not even twenty because this high-pressure system seems pretty mellow."

"How's your knee feeling this morning?" he wondered.

Startled into laughter, I replied, "Knee? What knee? I've forgotten all about it. Who knows why it went berserk-o yesterday?"

Last thing before leaving camp, we debated whether to dress for how the lake basin looked, or how it felt. Judging by the sun's early brightness, it was shorts and t-shirt weather. However, if the air we were breathing was not 32-degrees by mercury standards, it sure felt close. For efficiency's sake, we decided to leave camp wearing t-shirts and shorts. Presumably, climbing steeply right from the get-go would save us from turning purple. However, it turned out that the ascent began inside a shadowed ravine, whose interior felt like a walk-in refrigerator. Climbing up a slope tiled with bare rock chips, the only trees we passed were geriatric limber pines and all-but-dead junipers, whose birth could have predated Jesus. Some of the skeletal "trees" were naked to windward, with decrepit branches jutting to leeward like tattered flags. Others looked head-pruned into clusters of wiggling snakes.

The CDT took a businesslike approach toward zigzagging up the ravine's east wall. Rung by rung, we gained evolving views of Two Medicine Lake, gradually shrinking from a vacation-sized flood into a shrinking blue oval, and then into a puny blue squiggle. One prominent overlook faced a gang of snow-frosted, vividly orange mountains, clustered in the distance framing Two Medicine Lake. Sandwiched between the mountains sat a pure white saddle, professing to be Pitamaken Pass.

"That view would have been gorgeous," I sighed, "but probably not safe in yesterday's weather, and maybe we wouldn't even have been able to see anything."

"Too bad I didn't get to try out that guy's crampons, though," SeeHawk let slip, before he caught himself and laughed. "Ha-ha, just kidding. I'm totally with you, Sunshine. Going up there yesterday would have been a huge mistake. Like, Darwin Award stupid. Good thing we bailed."

My heart felt lighter as we resumed climbing away from Two Medicine Lake. It was time to enter our journey's next chapter. Sure, I regretted having broken our continuity, but the CDT was a serious undertaking. If we wanted to succeed down the line, it was important to recognize when to cut our losses and move on.

A shift in the trail's angle exposed it to full sunlight. From that point upward, rock chips paving the trail sent up radiant warmth that made us feel like we were climbing into Summer. Everything seemed casual until the CDT bumped into a giant ice blob. Translucent and vertical, it was too steep to cross without real mountaineering crampons, sharper ice-axes than ours, and well-anchored ropes. In rough weather, we could have been in for a replay of our ice encounter on Piegan Pass. Instead, clear visibility helped us spot an easy detour heading straight uphill. The only caveat was that we needed to balance on our tiptoes due to the slope being too steep for our heels to touch the ground. At the top, we made an easy U-turn and headed back downhill to resume our traverse, safely beyond the ice.

"No snow worth mentioning, say the rangers?" I snickered. "Okay, I get it. Around here, no snow means less snow than January, and some snow probably means like the North Pole."

Indeed, we were soon going to hear a local man say, "Ha-ha, THAT old ice field? Yeah, we all know about it, but it doesn't really count because it's almost always there."

The sun floated toward its zenith while we completed the climb that had lasted all morning. Rather than encountering a ferocious wind, we found the upper mountain's air calm enough to keep a candle burning. Was Mother Nature making amends for our rough start leaving Canada? Or was She trying to appease the two waterlogged thru-hikers whose tent had collapsed during a rainstorm at Two Medicine? If the latter was true, Her gesture came a day late and a dollar short, because the two discouraged partners had just decided to quit the CDT and go home early. Regardless, though, SeeHawk and I felt darned lucky to be given a smooth ride where others had crawled through frightening windstorms.

Scenic Point topped out at 7,522-feet, bald and gentle. We had all the time in the world to slowly spin around, soaking in the works. Every mile of land between Canada and the Missouri River, as well as a good percentage of Glacier National Park, could be seen from that one location. Northward and eastward, it was all green and rolling, like an ocean made of mountains. A few metal rooftops floating on the ocean stood in for rowboats. Westward and southward, the park's interior was a jigsaw puzzle of complex, dramatic, and exquisite land shapes, glamourized by fresh white snow.

SeeHawk and I could have lingered on the summit for hours, examining its fossilized sea creatures and petrified sandbars, savoring its panoramic view, or even just lessening our sock-tans, but nope. Thru-hikers are always on the clock, so we had to keep moving.

Being one day away from reaching Marias Pass, we were nearing the end of our time in Glacier National Park. Tomorrow, we would hitchhike back to East Glacier, grab our first resupply box and then catch a ride back to the trailhead, hopefully, all before dark. The next morning, we would enter the Bob Marshall Wilderness, in which backpackers could set their own schedules and camp anyplace they pleased. I could hardly wait to get there. Freedom was almost within smelling distance. Consequently, I felt horrorstruck when my kneecap pain returned, partway down the switchbacks. This time, it hurt worse than before. I tried tilting my knee from side to side. I walked with my leg rotated at different angles. Nothing helped. The pain was unbearable, but not constant. It came and went, lasting for seconds and vanishing in-between, as if operated by a faulty toggle switch.

"WHAT'S GOING ON?" I hollered. "My kneecap hurts. Then, it doesn't. Then, it does again. Is it injured, or not? What did I even DO to it?"

Having no choice, I started using my trekking poles for crutches. It was slow work, hobbling down the rest of the switchbacks mostly on one leg, but, at least, I was able to keep going.

SeeHawk kept shooting me helpless frowns, each time he turned around and saw me limping absurdly, or stooped over my trekking poles, or squeezing my kneecap from side-to-side. Time and time again, he asked, "Do you need to rest?"

"No," I insisted. "Please, let's keep going. All I need is a big plate of French fries and a hot fudge sundae."

* * *

Another crystalline-blue sky shined through a crack between the curtains of our window at the Whistling Swan Motel.

SeeHawk observed happily, "It's just like I always tell you, Sunshine. No matter if the sky stays gray from Monday to Saturday, you can look forward to enjoying a little sunshine on Sunday."

Right on cue, I got rescued from answering by Amtrak's eastbound Empire Builder. Our room's floor shook during its 9 a.m. horn blast. Presumably, there was a fresh batch of Californians, Oregonians, and Washingtonians pulling in to the Glacier Park station.

After the rumbling noise subsided, I asked SeeHawk for today's date, so I could enter it into my notebook.

"June seventeenth," he reported. "It's Father's Day, so while we have access to a phone, you might want to call your dad."

"You mean, it's taken us TEN days to hike a distance that was supposed to take FIVE days?" I wailed. "At this rate, we'll reach Mexico by the middle of next year."

"Yep, we'd better get cracking and find a doctor who fixes knees," SeeHawk agreed. "Er, no pun intended."

I glanced around the motel room we had rented from former thru-hiker Mike, who also owned the Two Medicine Grill. It was a comfy little den, but my heart was already aching for the Great Outdoors.

Unfortunately, my kneecap was feeling a different kind of ache. Every time I stepped off our motel room's stoop, sharp, stabbing pains assaulted my patella.

"Something must be misaligned," I concluded. "It can't be a torn ligament or a strained tendon because it doesn't hurt inside the main joint."

If only I could have flown home to my Tui-Na practitioner in California. He had once relieved me of an out-of-joint ankle by simply pulling hard and setting it back correctly. Another time, he had realigned my hip in the same manner (and boy, did that hurt). However, I could not afford a round-trip plane ticket home to have my knee fixed. Hitchhiking to Kalispell or Missoula seemed unlikely to summon a Tui-Na. Chiropractic care was yet a different animal, and my faith in orthopedists had been ruined by one who advised me to hike the whole CDT wearing a gel pad, before the Tui-Na just fixed my ankle. Nevertheless, I could not deny needing to take this injury seriously. Seeking efficient options, I scrutinized our upcoming maps.

The next section of trail was infamous for keeping thru-hikers far away from civilization. Reportedly, we were going to travel 123 continuous miles without encountering any mapped jeep roads, let alone highways. Snow could be expected after the solstice, so we might suffer delays from both land and sky. At the end of completing that whole section, resupplying in the boonies, and continuing onward for the balance of sixteen days, we were going to reach a town large enough to house some kind of bone doctor. In other words, all things considered, we could not afford to leave East Glacier before fixing my injury.

But, argh! Gazing toward the west, I saw the sun shining like a new baby's smile.

"Our door of opportunity does seem open," SeeHawk agreed, not daring to say more, for fear of putting me under pressure.

Of course, I felt pressured of my own accord. Trying to balance ambition with precaution, I thoughtfully told him, "The CDT stays flat between here and Marias Pass. Since it's close to the highway, maybe we could use that stretch of trail to test out my knee. If it keeps hurting, we'll come back and look for a doctor, without feeling guilty because we'll know we don't have a choice."

SeeHawk replied soberly, "I trust your judgment, Sunshine. Your determination to come on this trip has been so focused that I know you aren't going to do anything foolish."

End of discussion. The acid test was scheduled to begin. Its results would tell us whether I could safely enter the Bob Marshall Wilderness. But, first things first. East Glacier's small grocery store sold exceptionally good ice cream. While milling through aisles stocked with canned food and moose sweatshirts, we ran into the same rock climber who had previously loaned SeeHawk his crampons.

"You're the Alfred Hitchcock of East Glacier," I laughed.

"Are you guys FINALLY leaving?" he teased. "Don't come back here any more, okay?"

Blushing, SeeHawk and I had to admit we would be back the following day, to fetch our first resupply box from the post office.

Outside the store, I privately told SeeHawk, "After tomorrow, we'd better make like bananas, before the locals start plugging us into their campfire stories."

Armed with espresso-fudge-ripple-chocolate-chip ice cream cones, we hustled back into the afternoon's bright sunlight, feeling ready to roll some dice. My kneecap felt fine. Maybe it was going to hurt going uphill or downhill, but there were no hills on the way out of town.

East Glacier's golf course ushered us into a leafless aspen glade whose canopy looked like tree roots flipped upside down. Giant Douglas fir trees, mixed with smaller conifers, shaded flocks of wild roses, serviceberry, geraniums, lupins, yellow asters, and budding white yarrow. The air smelled ripe with chlorophyll and honey. Also, it smelled like French onion soup.

"Can you believe we just did laundry?" I complained. "My armpits already stink again!"

The bittersweet aroma came from eating copious amounts of dehydrated onions and roasted garlic, which flavored all our homemade soups and dinners. Its refusal to wash out of our clothes stemmed from wearing synthetic t-shirts, about which one *Backpacker Magazine* tester had claimed made him stink before leaving his tent.

The CDT's exit from East Glacier looked flat on paper. Therefore, we did not expect a pump-track experience. Downhill and back uphill, downhill and back uphill, the forest's humped micro-gullies quickly lost their charm. One saving grace was starting to see grizzly bear tracks, which took our minds off feel tired.

Shortly beyond the eighth or tenth, or maybe gazillionth, micro-gully, we ran into a roadblock, where a huge Douglas fir tree had fallen across the trail. Without thinking twice, I kicked up one leg and used both hands to cartwheel my legs over the tree's mighty trunk.

"Smooth maneuver," SeeHawk chuckled, looking impressed.

I felt rather impressed, myself, considering that I was wearing a backpack. Unfortunately, though, stepping away from the tree sent a familiar pain shooting through my kneecap. Trying to stay positive, I reminded myself that I had returned to the woods expecting this to happen. The next step was testing my injury, to see if I could fix it. First, I tried shaking my leg, while bending the kneecap back and forth. Nothing much changed during our next mile of walking. After that, the pain grew sharp every time we aimed downhill.

By the time we reached Marias Pass, the results of my test could not be denied. Like it or not, my kneecap was unfit to enter the Bob Marshall Wilderness.

A Campground Host stationed at the pass gave SeeHawk and me a cheerful welcome. He launched right into apologizing for his campsites being closed, due to contamination of the local water supply. The upside was that we could dry-camp for free if we did not mind sleeping near a ranger who was tranquilizing and tagging the local grizzly bears. The host's eyes gleamed while describing one clawed hooligan who still made his nightly rounds, even though most of the campsites were unoccupied..

"You'd best keep your eyes peeled in The Bob," he summarized. "Our woods south of here are chock-full of grizzlies."

"Welcome to deregulation," SeeHawk chuckled.

Bears or no bears, I fell asleep dreaming about watching storm clouds overtake the sky. When I woke up the next morning, it was time to pack up our camp and start hitchhiking.

Northbound Highway 2 was a blur of high-speed traffic. Never mind its only good pullout being fixed beneath the only dark cloud in sight. SeeHawk and I stood underneath the cloud and pumped our thumbs toward every passing car. Unfortunately, nobody stopped before the cloud ran out of patience. Big wet raindrops plopped onto our heads. Would donning our ponchos discourage drivers from wanting to pick us up? Probably not more than letting our clothes get soaked. We decided to go with the ponchos, and just waggled our thumbs harder. Now, anything with wheels became fair game. Overcrowded compacts. Gleaming sports cars. We even thumbed big-rigs that could not safely stop on the highway. One 18-wheeler faked us out by passing so close that its tailwind doused us with dust. Watching the dust stick to our wet ponchos seemed like a bad omen. It rained a bit harder.

"Nobody's going to pick us up soaking wet," I groaned.

"If it stops raining, we'll take off our ponchos, so only our legs and shoes will be wet," SeeHawk suggested.

But, in the meantime, there we stood, with nothing else to do besides keep trying.

After several more minutes, the same 18-wheeler which had coated us with dust reappeared, speeding in the opposite direction. Suddenly, it U-turned across the double-lane highway. That was strange behavior for a giant, wobbling, dust-spewing tractor-trailer. The next thing we knew, it aimed straight for us. We could hardly believe our eyes. The giant vehicle slowed down and stopped on the highway's wet shoulder.

A beefy driver climbed out of his lofty cab and laughed, "You two look like you could use a ride. Hurry up. It's about to start pouring!"

* * *

The word embarrassed cannot do justice to how SeeHawk and I felt upon reentering the Whistling Swan Motel. I could scarcely bear asking former thru-hiker Mike for our third motel room in less than a week. However, this time we had a valid excuse.

The first thing we did was take a stroll through East Glacier's Native American trinket shops. It took about an hour to sift through all the blankets, dream catchers, turquoise jewelry, fake turquoise jewelry, and huckleberry flavored sweets a small town could hold. After popping into the minimart, we returned to our room carrying postcards, snacks, and Gatorade, for an afternoon of not being sure how else to address my knee problem.

SeeHawk got busy manning the TV's remote control, while I fiddled with my kneecap, trying to realign it as my Tui-Na would do. Unfortunately, all I accomplished was making the kneecap pop loudly every time I bent or straightened my knee.

Meantime, SeeHawk concluded that our only choice for a decent movie was *Into Thin Air*—a story about climbers freezing to death on Mount Everest.

The next morning, we moseyed back into the Two Medicine Grill, kind of wishing we could wear bags over our heads. A depressingly familiar table in the smoky dining room offered menus we almost knew from memory.

Several familiar faces piled in after us. One buxom blonde woman, decorating the arm of a burly construction worker, came in with a local park ranger/nature photographer who waited tables at the grill. After the trio sat down together, the blonde commenced blowing cigarette smoke into the park ranger's face, while keeping him entranced by whatever she was saying.

Two potbellied men, coming in next, received the park ranger's greeting "How's it going?"

One man replied, "I had a good bowel movement this morning."

That got a laugh out of everyone who knew him.

All heads turned when five lookalike cowboys sauntered into the dining room, five-way twinning in stiff denim-and-leather. Their costumes included Montana's requisite bandanna handkerchiefs and cowboy hats. Also, they wore matching jeans that needed to be hitched up before they could sit down together, knees splayed apart, wearing smiles that could have given Charles Bronson the hiccups.

By this time, the dining room was getting too noisy for SeeHawk and me to hear each other talk, so we decided to move to the grill counter. Alfred Hitchcock, the crampon-loaning rock climber, was already there sucking on a cigarette butt, beside the grill's street-facing window.

Motel owner Mike was frying stuff behind the counter, while his girlfriend waited tables inside the dining room.

When Mike became available, SeeHawk and I ordered three-egg omelets, hash browns, and buckwheat pancakes, dressed with a side of huckleberry jam.

Our chef was a master of talking while cooking, so we asked him about East Glacier's crime rate.

"You know?" Mike answered. "This town is completely safe. That's why we think it's funny to see tourists locking their doors just to drive through town. We can't understand why, since it's so nice to live here."

He went on to explain the town's reason for lacking a local newspaper. "It's not because nobody who lives here knows how to write or take pictures. They just don't want stuff printed about them, either good or bad. Any news about East Glacier has to come from reporters outside of town." Laughing confidentially, he added, "I've often thought this place would be excellent for a Coen Brothers' movie, except, it'll never happen because they'd have to draw upon local gossip, and whoever spilled the beans would have to move after their neighbors found out."

Later in the conversation, Mike revealed, "We've been having a lot of trouble with bears coming down from the mountains lately. People who work at the golf resort are carrying pepper spray just to walk from there to here."

"It's ridiculous," another local chimed in, "as if people were getting eaten or something."

By the time SeeHawk and I finished conquering our breakfasts, most other customers had left because they had people to see and places to go.

While gazing through the grill's front window, I saw a sunbeam push through the Continental Divide's fractured clouds and felt my heart being pulled. I had to get back up there. I had to fix my knee. Some way, somehow...

The rock climber lit a fresh cigarette.

Mike re-filled my third glass of root beer.

A local deliveryman marched up to the grill counter, delivering fresh bread. Once unburdened, he sank onto a barstool like sinking into an easy chair.

The rock climber launched into a story about a local Native American man getting struck by lightning three separate times. Before his story ended, its punchline got cut off by an ambulance screaming past the grill's front window. All eyes turned to look out the window, while the ambulance's screams faded into the distance.

Mike had the best vantage point for gazing down the street, and when he saw the ambulance take the corner too fast, he cringed like a sports fan, "Oooh, near miss!"

"Something must have happened," he and the butcher agreed.

Feeling eager to keep chatting, the rock climber launched into a fresh story about some local hikers being afraid to write their names in a particular mountaintop register because it repeatedly got struck by lightning. After that story came his alarming report that grizzly bears disliked eating their victims' toes, which made SeeHawk and me wonder if he was pulling our legs.

Soon, another four ambulances came screaming past the window, causing all heads to whip around again.

Somebody commented with amazement, "They're going faster than the last guy."

Even the bread truck driver looked interested.

Again, the sirens faded out of earshot, leaving us all to wonder what was happening south of town.

Mike launched into saying he had recently elected himself treasurer for East Glacier's first city council meeting in eight years. "Because," he explained, "we had an eight-year period of inactivity, where all our city council members moved away except the president. So, in our first meeting, somebody suggested installing benches along the new bike path. I picked up the ball and asked everybody which three people would like to research benches. Everybody liked the idea, but nobody volunteered. So, finally, I just selected three people of my choice, and the weird thing is, after I did that, people started volunteering by themselves!"

Another ambulance came screaming by, this time headed the other way. Behind it, followed a whole parade of wailing ambulances, chasing the first in hot pursuit.

Suddenly, the same park ranger/photographer who had finished eating earlier and already left the grill barged back in, bearing gruesome news. "A van carrying nine people crashed outside town. They needed ambulances to transport all the crash victims, but one ambulance crashed leaving the scene, so they had to call for backup to rescue victims of the ambulance crash."

SeeHawk and I left the Two Medicine Grill comparing civilization's dangers with Glacier National Park's natural hazards. Snowstorms, ambulance crashes, gale-force windstorms. What did it all mean, in relation to everything?

We slept without starlight, behind blackout motel curtains, and woke up feeling mired in too much indoor time. Our heads craved emptiness. Our hopes reeked of uncertainty.

"I'll just take some aspirin or vitamin I, so we can get going," I told SeeHawk. "If the pain returns, I'm sure I'll be able to walk out of anything I walked into. I mean, I'm not totally crippled or anything. My knee doesn't hurt like it did on Cut Bank Creek Road. In fact, it's probably getting better as we speak."

"Are you SURE?" he demanded. "You promised to see a chiropractor."

"One-shot chiropractic would probably just make it harder for us to afford ice cream," I wagered. "Besides, any day now, my kneecap's going to pop back into place and that will be the end of it. I just need to figure out how to reverse whatever happened."

SeeHawk wanted to believe me, but sobriety made him reply, "I hope you're not letting desire overrule what's best for you in the long run, Sunshine."

"Time will tell," I shrugged, "but staying in town longer isn't going to help."

After checking out of the Whistling Swan, we bought one last round of espresso-fudge-ripple chocolate-chip ice cream cones, and decisively told the locals, "REALLY, this is our final goodbye. If you ever see us again, you'll be at least a year older, and we'll be driving up in a car."

Back on the shoulder of Highway 2, we smiled like street vendors at every passing car. In return, the drivers acted like we were selling $10.00 zucchini. Nobody even glanced in our direction. After 15 minutes of feeling invisible, we started to wonder if people truly could not see us.

"What was in that ice cream?" SeeHawk pondered.

"I mean, they could at least smile or pinch their fingers to show us they aren't going very far," I complained.

But, wait. Our eyes widened upon spying a pickup truck decorated with painted pawprints. Its camper shell was made from some kind of animal hide. A black Labrador retriever, leaning through its passenger's side window, flashed us a friendly smile.

We are dog people, too, we telepathically informed the driver.

Sure enough, she pulled over!

While watching the woman climb out of her truck, we could not help noticing her colorful ensemble of green fleece legwarmers with turquoise-blue tights and matching blue water shoes. Altogether, she looked a little strange, but, then again, she was probably thinking the same thing about us.

Without hesitation, the driver stowed our backpacks inside her truck's rear bed and gestured for us to squeeze in beside her dog, who slobbered ice cream off my cheeks while buffing SeeHawk's face with its wiggling rump. We laughed through floating hair. The driver apologized. Slowly, we rolled onto southbound Highway 2.

I earnestly told our driver, "Dogs don't bother us. In fact, maybe if we soak in enough dog smell, it'll help keep the grizzly bears away."

"Grizzly bears," she repeated. "I house sit a ranch just up the highway. The owners don't come around anymore because they're so afraid of grizzlies. We've got the densest population of any place in the country. You'll see 'em going through Marias Pass." Her expression grew animate. "You know those bad bears you hear about in Glacier? The kind that harass folks and steal their food? Yep. Well, you know where they bring 'em? Right here to The Bob. Yes, indeed, we've got all the bad bears. So, don't plan on going wherever you're headed without running into a couple of close encounters."

Suddenly, changing the subject, she asked us where we were headed.

"Into The Bob," we grinned.

She frowned while saying, "Three days ago, I drove to that big creek you're gonna have to cross. You know about Two Medicine Creek? It's a couple of miles in."

"We're not going that way," I said. "We're going over Elk Calf Mountain,"

"Good thing," she nodded, "because the creek was so flooded three days ago, I couldn't drive my truck through it. You'd probably have a hard time swimming, even if you tried carrying your packs instead of wearing them."

Hearing that warning caused me to recall Poppa Jim's warning about Strawberry Creek. Was there a correlation between the two creeks, in terms of high water? Rather than ask our driver, I got distracted by noticing how she kept glancing at our shoes.

"You know, I'm an inventor," she finally explained. "I invent shoes."

Henceforth, she gave us a thorough education about her latest design for moccasin-style boots, which allegedly could outperform both my *Adidas* trail runners and SeeHawk's leather boots, by reducing foot fungus along with toe-cramps.

The industrious shoemaker dropped us off at Marias Pass, precisely where we had gotten picked up the day before by a semi-truck driver. She ran her eyes from my knock-knees down to my skinny ankles, and then up SeeHawk's slender frame, before asking about our previous hiking experience.

"We finished the entire PCT two years ago," I told her. "And we've taken a lot of short backpacking trips in California's High Sierras."

Smiling as if impressed, she concluded, "You two must be tougher than you look!"

* * *

"Aloha Mother Universe," SeeHawk mumbled, inside the dark confines of our tent. "Hello, Blackfoot Indian Spirits of the Mountain. We have a humble request to ask of you. We wish to cross Elk Calf Mountain tomorrow. We know it is the Blackfoot Indians' sacred ground. We promise to stay on the trail at all times. We will not disturb any animals who live there."

"Except for ants," I interjected.

Ignoring my interruption, he continued, "In return, we ask you to grant us safe passage across Elk Calf Mountain. Hatama. Thank you, and good night."

Having filed the order, SeeHawk fell into a long and peaceful sleep, thinking we were going to receive a warm welcome and hospitable passage through The Bob.

* * *

I bolted awake sometime after midnight and stared into the darkness. What had awakened me? The sound of an animal sniffing our tent? All I could hear was a gentle breeze.

Somewhere in the distance, a freight train rumbled. Faint in the beginning, its noise kept getting louder. Perhaps I had only imagined hearing sniffing. Louder still, the train thundered toward Marias Pass. Its wheels kept pounding, "Tha-thump. Tha-thump. Tha-thump." All at once, the rhythm grew deafening,

Drag

"THA-THUMP. THA-THUMP. THA-THUMP." My head conjured Huey Lewis's song "Heart of Rock and Roll." How annoying. That song drove me crazy. I fell asleep trying to get it out of my head.

* * *

When I awoke again, it was a calm, cold morning. Little gray birds were pecking for bugs outside our tent. Cars kept whizzing up and down Highway 2. Shreds of Parmesan cheese left on our picnic table overnight had not been touched and no new bear prints had been stamped across our campsite.

"What's today's forecast?" SeeHawk wanted to know.

"Just patchy clouds," I recalled from the day before. "No blizzards, if we can believe the National Weather Service."

"Excellent," he nodded, "Then, it's looking like time to play some rock-and-roll, baby."

Before setting off, I read him a paragraph from Poppa Jim's guidebook that made the Elk Calf Mountain Trail sound awfully tedious.

SeeHawk responded, "Coming from Poppa Jim, you know it must be really bad because he usually has good things to say about almost every part of the trail. Is there any other route we can take?"

"We could ford Two Medicine Creek."

"The dangerous flood that inventor lady warned us about? Yeesh, no thanks. I'd rather stick with the viewless slog. At least, we'll be back in the mountains soon. I can't wait to stop hearing highway noise and feel like we're finally getting somewhere."

"Just help me watch for the Elk Calf Mountain turnoff," I requested, "because we don't know if it'll be signed."

"What does Poppa Jim say?"

"Nothing specific about its appearance, but I can see Trail One-Thirty-Seven on our atlas."

"Okay, then. I'm ready when you are."

My kneecap felt fine as we strode out of camp. I could have jumped for joy, if only it would have been obvious how to leave Marias Pass. The best exit we could find was an unmarked jeep road which roughly matched Poppa Jim's description. Following it into a substantial forest, we started sideswiping lookalike jeep roads, some of which crossed our winding path, as if we were trying to navigate boiled spaghetti. I grew worried about getting lured off-course. Overall, though, our aim seemed correct. Good thing, too, since our attention soon got diverted by seeing fresh grizzly tracks take the lead in front of us.

"Momma bear and cub," SeeHawk observed.

"They look too close for comfort," I added nervously.

Another few minutes passed without incident, before See-Hawk murmured, "I smell bear."

Sniffing the air, I only smelled dry forest, and my nose was usually sharper than his.

Continuing onward, we met a slight breeze ricocheting through the close-growing woods. Then, I smelled it. Moist. Fetid. The odor was like concentrated urine mixed with rancid cheese and moldy sweat. Was that how grizzly bears smelled? I had no idea, but whatever could produce such a potent stench had to be large.

Minutes later, SeeHawk remarked, "I hear a dog barking."

"What gives?" I scoffed. "Usually, I hear and smell stuff before you, but today you're Mister Keen Jeans, and I don't hear any dog barking."

Listening carefully, though, a vague sound entered my awareness, but only for an instant and then it was gone, but then it was back.

"That's not a dog," I decided. "It's just people talking. Maybe hunters? Or people from the ranch where the shoe-inventor housesits?"

"Maybe it's the ranger who tranquilizes grizzly bears," See-Hawk suggested.

"Ooh, you're right. Or, maybe Blackfoot Indian spirits."

"Speaking of Blackfoot Indian spirits, how much farther to the turnoff?"

"Two miles from camp,"

"Have we hiked that far?"

"Probably. It's hard to know for sure, after curving all over the place without any view, but I think we'll see the turnoff soon. If we miss it, we'll run into Two Medicine Creek and realize we need to backtrack half a mile."

A grassy clearing signaled the jeep road's handoff, from which we turned onto a skinny single-track. Halfway through the clearing, we spied a perpendicular footpath forking toward Elk Calf Mountain. The footpath was almost too skinny to hold a pair of shoes, and its tread contained an inch of standing water. We stopped at the junction and asked ourselves. Could an officially numbered trail be so primitive?

"We might have to walk sideways, or with our feet in single-file, to make our shoes fit," I joked, half-seriously.

"Isn't that just a deer trail?" SeeHawk supposed.

Before we could decide, another round of voices floated out of the nearby woods. This time, they sounded quite close. Perhaps the speakers were located along the clearing's edge. After listening for another moment, I agreed with SeeHawk that we were either hearing a dog bark at someone talking, or else two people talking over a barking dog.

"Maybe hunters train their dogs around here," SeeHawk speculated.

"If you're right, let's hope they don't practice shooting while they're training," I replied.

"Well anyway," SeeHawk said, "it looks like momma and baby bear don't think this is the turnoff."

Indeed, the two bears' tracks continued across the clearing, without turning onto the waterlogged footpath.

"So, shall we keep going straight, then?"

SeeHawk shrugged, "Why are you asking me? You're our Chief Navigator."

"True, but can you please, just say yes or no? Sometimes, it helps having something to react to."

Instead of cooperating, SeeHawk pretended to find interest in some tiny flowers dotting the meadow's tall grass.

Feeling dismissed, I grumbled, "Fine, if I have to decide on my own, then, okay. I'm going to bet this is not the Elk Calf Trail."

"It's just a deer path," SeeHawk agreed. "Come on, let's keep moving."

Upon exiting the clearing, we entered another stretch of darkly shaded woods. Their enclosure opened onto another damp meadow, similar in size to a soccer field. A few steps in, we discovered some brown fur mashed into the meadow's tall, soft grass.

"Did somebody kill an animal here?" I wondered.

SeeHawk squatted down to inspect the oily fur.

"There's no blood," he observed, "and no bones either."

Simultaneously, the answer hit both of us.

"We'd better keep walking," I snapped.

I did not feel afraid, but, ugh. The stench! My nose needed to get out of there, fast.

Before SeeHawk stood up, we heard another dog barking. Except, it was neither a dog nor a person talking. In fact, it was not even a laryngitic seal. It was a perturbed grizzly bear, ordering us to get the heck away!

The barks gained urgency while we scanned the meadow's perimeter. Where was the bear hiding? Hm, well anyway, we were not stupid. Hurrying away and out of the meadow, we quickly entered the next stretch of woods.

"I never saw her, but I can still feel her watching us," SeeHawk reported, after catching his breath.

"Just keep going and don't look back," I advised him. "We should probably make a little noise, to let her know we're leaving."

Liking that idea, SeeHawk started belting out an impressive-sounding Hawaiian chant.

Progressing through the trees made the barks gradually fade until we only heard silence separating our footsteps. Once again, we commenced feeling safe, for about 1 minute, before unexpectedly running into Two Medicine Creek.

"Huh?" I stammered. "Maybe that skinny footpath really was the Elk Calf trail."

"Maybe so," SeeHawk agreed, "but, now that we're here, let's keep going. I don't want that bear to think we need some etiquette training."

Whatever kind of flood the shoe-inventor had encountered three days earlier, on the morning we arrived, Two Medicine Creek could barely wet our ankles. In fact, its only hazard was feeling incredibly cold. Shivering uncontrollably, we knocked off the ford cursing and howling. Fortunately, it only took a short couple of minutes to land on hot pebbles, which thawed our feet quickly.

SeeHawk experienced a surge of joy while relacing his boots. He started babbling about the Spirit of the Mountain sending momma grizzly as a gift to discourage us from crossing Elk Calf Mountain.

Naturally, his premise made me wonder about my kneecap pain. Was it serving any cosmic purpose? Such as, trying to delay us from reaching Strawberry Creek too early in the season?

Regardless, one nice development was that the trail leaving Two Medicine Creek looked flat and easy. The sun was rising. It was time to count our blessings. Strawberry Creek was still days away, during which time many things could change.

* * *

Two Medicine Creek's bordering trail cut through a flat pine forest which smelled damp and dusty at the same time. Packhorses and ATVs had widened the tread, allowing SeeHawk and me to hike side by side without bumping shoulders. We gazed along a riverbank gnawed into scallops by violent flooding and felt convinced the shoe-inventor had not exaggerated its potential to be dangerous.

Interestingly, Poppa Jim's guidebook did not make a big deal about fording Two Medicine Creek, and called Strawberry Creek a few inches deep during July, even though on the phone Jim had warned us about Strawberry Creek being dangerous during June. Likewise, the Book of Beans called Strawberry Creek peaceful during August, but very dangerous earlier in the season. So, our takeaway was that Strawberry Creek and Two Medicine Creek were both subject to extreme fluctuations caused by upstream snowmelt and rain, which made good timing especially important.

After making quick calculations, I told SeeHawk, "If we really bust butt tomorrow, I think we could camp right at Strawberry Creek and knock off the ford first thing the next morning."

"Hooray," he nodded, "except for the busting butt part. If we're going to go all-out again tomorrow, could we please start taking it easy afterward? I mean, the weather's getting so nice. Isn't this the window you keep promising, where we get to relax in camp more often?"

"Amen, partner!" I laughed. "That's exactly why I keep explaining everything whenever we need to hurry, so you won't think I'm just a glutton for punishment."

"The proof is in the pudding," he asserted.

"Fair enough," I smiled. "Anyway, I really don't think Strawberry Creek will be dangerous. I'm just being extra cautious so we can't end up in another Cataract Creek situation, waiting overnight for the water to go down."

Perking up, SeeHawk exclaimed, "Hold up, now. If we had to wait overnight, wouldn't that give us an excuse to catch up on some sleep? Plus, eat some of the extra food we've been carrying for a storm that'll never happen? And, you know, other fun activities...?"

"Chht! Bite your tongue," I scolded him. "Just because Two Medicine Creek was shallow doesn't mean we're out of the woods yet. You've seen how fast Montana's weather can change. The forecast I got yesterday has probably already expired. Don't forget, we're only three weeks into June. It's still blizzard season."

Flat terrain allowed us to knock off some fast miles alongside Two Medicine Creek. However, our overall progress was slowed by stopping every 20-30 minutes to take off our shoes and cross shallow feeder streams. This was not orthodox thru-hiker behavior. I was only being a princess for the sake of keeping my orthotics dry. But, what was SeeHawk's excuse? Poor guy. He still had not received his water-friendly mesh sneakers in the mail. Fortunately, we had June's long daylight working in our favor. While spending up to 17 hours completing each day's mileage, we still had 4-6 hours available for sleeping, which felt like enough for now.

Right on the verge of dusk, we reached North Badger Creek and got our tent pitched by 10:00 pm.

I woke up the next morning feeling rested and cheerful, if still a bit fatigued from the previous day's sprint.

SeeHawk, on the other hand, woke up feeling so hungover that he hardly spoke a word while striking camp.

We kicked off the morning with a 500-foot climb through rolling woods, which collapsed into a series of flood-damaged valleys. Mud and deadfall obstructing the trail imposed frequent slowdowns. Our patience got tested by increasing heat.

SeeHawk felt his backpack-straps digging into his shoulders. His legs were struggling to balance a crushing load of food and winter gear. It did not help to also be carrying a bulky, 2-pound bear canister. His body ached for rest. He wanted to take a breather, but he knew I would say we could not afford to stop before lunchtime, so he did not even ask. Feeling helpless seeded some resentments inside him, which germinated as the sun rose. I had no idea until his temper exploded inside an indeterminate meadow called Lost Horse Camp. The explosion began with a few snarky comebacks, like, "If you say so," and, "that's one way to look at it."

I kept my temper in check. Hard as it was, I stifled every urge to react, until I simply could not resist shouting, "If you're going to keep jabbing me with snarky little digs, prepare to RE-LIVE NORTHERN WASHINGTON!"

SeeHawk's eyes glittered with recognition.

That was my cue to watch out for him getting ornery.

Reacting quickly, I bellowed with alarm, "You'd better fix your attitude right now, Mister Mean Jeans, or this trip is going to fail, and you know what that'll mean?"

Connecting my words to our upcoming marriage, he refused to speak another word.

I felt like clobbering him. He should have apologized. Instead of demanding an apology, though, I switched tactics and cried, "Penalty toes!"

Thank goodness, he broke into a laugh.

"Okay, Sunshine," his mouth conceded, "you've earned a foot-rub after we get to camp, but please don't call it penalty toes. Just think of it as a nice favor from me, your most wonderful life partner."

Somewhere around noontime, we officially entered the Bob Marshall Wilderness. The boundary was marked by three broken signs collectively spelling out, " B   HALL   NESS. M KR ASS. CONTINENTAL DIVIDE. ELEVATION 6,10 muskrat cr tr 147." The sign's southbound arrow was missing, but we still figured out where to enter a boggy meadow littered with rotten logs. At the meadow's end, we climbed onto a deer path whose skinny tread made us scratch our heads. Had we lost the CDT? Following the tread uphill, we merged onto an ancient-looking human trail, camouflaged by erosion. More steady climbing hoisted us into a rustic spruce-fir forest, crammed full of dry brush tangled in living trees. We needed to slow down to squeeze around the tangles. It was frustrating to have to keep slowing down, but fun to bust through all the rubble because the forest's medieval appearance made us feel swarthy.

By the time we regained the Continental Divide, both of us were in a happy state of mind. It helped to encounter a nice change of scenery. The trail speared straight across a vast stage of yellow grass, called Badger Pass Meadow. Behind the stage stood an equally wide backdrop of snow-capped peaks. We reveled in openness for about twenty minutes, before turning to enter a gently descending forest. Thin streams snaking through the trees turned our trail into a slalom course. The streams were shallow at first, but with decreasing elevation, they swelled enough to make us prioritize camping at Strawberry Creek. It was a worthy goal, but we only reached Grimsley Creek before twilight persuaded us to leave our last three miles for the morning.

I made short work of tiredly cooking ginger-carrot soup, to sip with something else we tiredly swallowed for dinner. Restless dreams carried us into a bright sunrise. Strawberry Creek was waiting, and that was not all. When we opened our eyes, it was the first day of Summer.

SeeHawk consulted his calendar before rejoicing, "Today is the solstice!"

"It's also the longest day of the year," I reflected. "So, from here on out, we'll need to hike faster but, at least, we'll be getting more sleep."

Nature was celebrating her longest daylight of the year with blue skies and bird songs. Apricot-yogurt fruit rolls gave our departure from camp a zesty flavor. Spruce, pine, and fir trees shaded our eyes, while we took off angling toward the rising sun. Before long, a small break in the forest revealed Pentagon Mountain's snow-streaked summit. Thick tree roots, protruding through short gooseberry thickets, threatened to trip us for not looking where we were stepping. Fresh spring flowers curtsied toward our shoes, urging us to slow down and give them a smile.

I felt confident we could reach Strawberry Creek quickly, until a familiar pain reared its ugly head.

"What the—?" I gasped. "How can my kneecap hurt on a totally flat trail, after not hurting at all since Marias Pass?"

Feeling bewildered, I pushed on harder, refusing to slow down.

Upon reaching Strawberry Creek, my gut reaction was neither one of relief nor alarm. The creek could have been 30 feet wide, give or take. Its depth was disguised by millions of sunsparkles dancing off the water.

"Shin deep," SeeHawk reported, when he poked a trekking pole out as far as he could reach.

"Sounds good," I nodded, "but what about the middle?"

He replied with a shrug, "Who knows? We'll just have to cross that middle when we get there."

After removing our shoes, we each plopped two bare feet into the biting-cold water. Our feet slipped, folded, and stuck into awkward positions, groping around for traction on polished round cobblestones. I screamed like a wildcat when the cold pierced my shinbones. All I cared about from that moment onward was reaching the opposite shore, like, yesterday.

SeeHawk cringed every time I screamed, but he never glanced backward. After all, he was used to hearing me scream under torture. As he waded into the creek's powerful central current, his feet deciphered cobblestones his eyes could not separate.

Meantime, my agony transitioned from piercing to stinging. The worst phase was feeling skinned by knives. What was wrong, for pole-stomping, forehead-wrinkling, roaring-from-the-gut sakes? Why were my feet refusing to go numb? Well, of course. I had neglected to step into and out of the creek several times before forcing my feet to stay underwater. Still, they should have gone numb by now. Why did the pain keep getting worse?

Two-thirds of the way across, I had to admit there was no turning back. Less water remained ahead of me than behind.

SeeHawk had already reached the far shore. He was triumphantly stepping onto sun-warmed pebbles.

I was still just exiting the creek's deepest channel when my feet started to hurt worse than I could bear. Stings and knife pokes had been tolerable, but maddening aches from deep within my bones? OwwooOOO! Feeling desperate, I lunged onto a lone boulder sticking out of the water. Its width could barely hold both of my feet. Hot diggety dog! That was good enough to save me from fainting. My rigid toes struggled to grip the slippery rock. After a few minutes, my shins stopped aching. The numbness that followed gave rise to euphoria. My breath returned in gasps.

Gazing upstream, I watched the creek's central rapids tumble toward me, fat and beautiful. Shingles of skylight glanced off their ripples. Golden, yellow, and pink-colored cobblestones wiggled like melting rainbows. Their motion was hypnotic. My senses became polarized. I forgot what I was seeing, forgot about SeeHawk, and just zoned out while my brain transcended.

Upon taking another glance toward shore, I happened to witness SeeHawk with new eyes. Sometime during our past week of constant togetherness, he had changed from a smooth-faced salesman into something resembling a disheveled gold prospector. Now, as he stood near the water's edge, with sunlight twinkling through his light-brown hair, he looked willing to let me stand on my little two-foot island for as long I wished.

Unfortunately, though, my feet were starting to regain some feeling. Re-entry was going to hurt like thumbscrews. Like it or not, I could not afford to wait. Three, two, one. I breathed like a swimmer and stepped off the boulder. It took willpower not to panic. Wobbling and lurching, I looked like a caffeinated oil rig, stumbling through the last 10 feet of rapids. Gratitude summoned a whimper when I finally landed upon dry pebbles. Sharp, whatever. At least, they were hot.

SeeHawk let me lean on his arm, to paw through a thicket of face-whipping willows. Once in the clear, we collapsed onto a soft, sandy beach, and spent a minute taking a little power vacation. The sun dried our feet. Ahh, that felt nice. Vacation finished. On went dry shoes. We stood up and, click, a door shut behind us.

"So long, Glacierville," SeeHawk waved.

"Bye-bye, Highwaterville," I chimed in.

"Hello, Easy Street."

"Almost. Except, we haven't crossed the North Wall yet."

"The what now?" SeeHawk asked, looking confused.

I conjured the Book of Beans and read to him a few lines about sub-standard switchbacks on rocky terrain with lots of ups and downs, as well as avalanche chutes being dangerous during the snow season.

He responded without concern, "That sounds bad during winter, but we're almost into summertime, so I don't think we'll have any problem. What's our ETA?"

"Day after tomorrow," I predicted, "assuming clear weather and having my knee cooperate."

* * *

The CDT's exit from Strawberry Creek climbed gradually through a forest fluted with stream-fed gullies. Their spattering water kept giving SeeHawk and me quick, cold showers, providing relief from the morning's early heat. Gradual climbs should not have bothered my kneecap, but the pain came and went all morning long.

At 5,800-feet, we entered a vast tableland named Grizzly Park. Its cropped grass was backed by a picket fence of close-growing spruce trees. If Montana's Rocky Mountains had wanted to host a golf tournament, Grizzly Park would have been the place.

My kneecap stopped hurting upon entering the park as if all it had wanted was flat terrain. However, a couple of miles later, where the land grew uneven, it still felt fine. That was confusing. Many things seemed confusing lately. My injury. The unsettled weather. Creeks that might or might not be flooding. Mountains that might or might not be covered in snow. With so much to think about, SeeHawk and I appreciated having a shallow stream appear, just at the perfect time. We lay down flat to dunk our whole bodies and emerged feeling refreshed for a long push through the sun's hottest hours.

While stepping back into my clothes, I noticed a flock of cumulus clouds approaching from the north. They looked harmless, but experience had taught me to always pay attention.

Beyond Grizzly Park, the CDT led us into a machine-cut firebreak. For some reason, its steep incline pacified my kneecap, even though any slightest incline had hurt like crazy two hours before. Good grief. What did so many mood swings indicate? A misalignment (easy to fix)? Strained connective tissue (slow recovery)? A misfired attack by some knee-obsessed witchdoctor's voodoo doll?

Regardless, nothing hurt on our way up to Sun River Pass, where the Continental Divide rested 6,350-feet above sea level. That was the whole deal. Tag the pass. Move on. We had been expecting a view from the summit, but it was covered in trees.

Thick conifer mulch made the peak's whole backside resemble a rake pile. Lunch was calling, but we had no place to sit. Back at the stream, it had been too early to eat lunch. On top of Sun River Pass, lacking any view had felt too confined. Now, we needed to eat without delay. My brain felt tipsy and SeeHawk's stomach was growling, but who wants to eat on a rake-pile? Besides, we were too busy swatting mosquitoes, clawing spiderwebs off our faces, and brushing away gnats. The whole backside of Sun River Pass seemed plagued with flying insects. Moreover, it was heaped with rotting deadwood, which kept forcing us to detour onto primitive animal paths

After finally outdistancing all the flotsam and flying fauna, we started seeing good lunch sites within easy reach. So, could we finally pull over? Not yet because a bear started barking at us from the nearby woods. *Move along. Don't stop. This is not your picnic area.* All the caterwaul sounded like a neighbor shouting at us over a sidewalk fence.

Eventually, the CDT struck flat ground, where it met a tidy meadow called Round Park. Pink shooting-star lilies gave us a cheerful welcome. Unfortunately, so did thousands or millions of bloodthirsty mosquitoes. When their sharp little siphons smelled us coming, they staged a full battalion attack. At the same instant, we got avalanched by an icy wind pouring out of the uphill forest. Which is to say, we got hit by a drainage wind coming off the North Wall. Its peak gusts smashed the mosquitoes into helpless piles, which tumbled past us, unable to fly until a lull set them free for a return attack.

SeeHawk and I were beyond needing to eat lunch. Alarm bells were ringing between our ears, but how could we eat in a scathing windstorm laced with mosquitoes?

Glancing upward, I happened to notice several suspicious clouds turning gray. The mosquitoes must have noticed, too because they responded by upping their attack. Arms, legs, faces, you name it. Every inch of our bodies became fair game, without regard for placement or finesse.

Glancing desperately everywhere, we fixed our sights upon one fat spruce tree. Like a boulder dividing a river, it was splitting the wind in two. Downwind of its thick trunk stretched an invisible island of calm, in which we could literally sit undisturbed, with mosquitoes thwarted on both sides and hardly a breeze ruffling our hair.

Once we got situated, I thoughtfully told SeeHawk, "We should probably cook dinner now, and eat one of our cold lunches tonight. That way, if the North Wall turns stormy, there won't be any issue of cooking after dark."

Liking my logic, SeeHawk flopped onto his back and took some deep breaths, while I boiled cheese-sauced corn macaroni, and simultaneously kept one eye on the sky.

Our guidebooks claimed the North Wall lifted hikers to 8,050-feet. Theoretically, that was 1,000-feet higher than The Bob's typical snow level during June, and we could believe it, having seen snow covering Pentagon Mountain.

"If the North Wall trail still has some snow, we'll be fine, as long as the sun comes out to soften it," I told SeeHawk, "but, if these clouds don't break, tomorrow could be a knuckle-biter."

Casting me a hard look, SeeHawk demanded to know, "Would you consider bailing out again?"

Shrinking away from him, I cried, "Are you kidding? Why would I have rushed us up here, if I didn't want to keep going?"

He shrugged but did not retract his question.

"Argh," I groaned. "Would you rather have me pretend everything is hunky-dory, no matter what I see in the sky? Or would you rather be forewarned when I might smell trouble?"

"Suit yourself," he shrugged. "Personally, I'm looking forward to some really fine views tomorrow."

"Me, too," I assured him. "Probably more than you, since I'm the one who made us miss Pitamakan Pass and Triple Divide Pass."

Inside my head, I begged whatever Beings might be listening to make tomorrow's situation cut-and-dried. If the morning could not be hot enough to soften any snow slickening the North Wall, then I wanted to get hit by a storm so powerful that nobody in their right minds would refuse to turn around. Either extreme seemed better than ambivalence until I realized the North Wall's orientation would hide any oncoming storm until it was too late to escape. Oh, for Pete's sake. We just needed the clouds to give us a break for 24 hours. Well, at least, it was not presently raining or snowing. There was no reason to untie any rowboats before seeing pirates.

Lunch remained comfortable inside our little island of calm. After packing up everything, we thanked our wind-blocking spruce tree for its most excellent shelter. Then, we strode back into the wind's raging maw. About fifty steps upstream, our shoes sank underwater. Apparently, Round Park's grass had gotten flooded by snowmelt draining off the North Wall. Seeking drier ground, we bushwhacked through a sidewall of trees, soon reaching a trail cutting into the uphill forest. I had totally forgotten about my kneecap during lunch. Therefore, it caught me by surprise to feel a sharp twinge the moment I started climbing. A few more twinges led to my tendon feeling sawed over an ill-fitting bone. Uh-oh. This was getting bad. Had my stubborn streak created a serious injury? Should I have rested longer in town? Should I have seen a chiropractor? Was I being an idiot, by continuing to climb? All I knew was that I could not let anything short of pure, wreathing agony deprive my fiancé of the world-class view we were both hoping to enjoy atop the North Wall. I owed him that much, at least, considering how much I had put him through during the past two weeks.

During snatches of unwatched time, while climbing behind SeeHawk, I started fiddling with my kneecap. Sideways. Bent. Held straight. Which knee position might lessen the pain?

SeeHawk eventually noticed my antics, and inquired stiffly, "What's the matter, Sunshine?"

"I don't know," I whimpered. "It doesn't make sense. My kneecap hasn't hurt since we entered Grizzly Park, but now I can barely walk."

"Do you need to sit down and rest?"

"REST? We just finished resting. We rested for, like, half an hour. We need to keep MOVING. Have you noticed the clouds?"

Suddenly, I experienced a horrifying thought. What if my injury was PSYCHOSOMATIC? Could it have been triggered by my fear of crossing the North Wall? And, earlier, by my fear of crossing Pitamakan Pass? Or even by some fear of fording Strawberry Creek? If so, I wanted to die from shame. Not only from shame. Also, from despair because imagine another five months of having my knee go to pieces every time we faced something scary? Gadzooks, talk about working off some karma. Had I really done anything that bad in my lifetime?

Apprehension gripped me, while I struggled to keep up with my partner, limping as if I had a wooden leg. *FIX YOURSELF, KNEE, JUST FIX YOURSELF.* I gave my body firm commands, but nothing changed. In fact, soon, my whole knee began to stiffen up, like it had done on Cut Bank Creek Road. Once that happened, the game seemed over. Could I even climb another five steps? Was some connective tissue tearing? What was going to happen higher up the North Wall, upon a narrower trail that might be steep? How about, going down a set of backside switchbacks that were not "up to the usual Bob Marshall standards?"

Suddenly, I noticed SeeHawk bending over to examine something heaped on the trail in front of him. When I got close enough to see what it was, I yelped in disgust. He was examining a partially collapsed, giant animal skeleton. It lay squarely on the CDT, blocking our path toward the North Wall. Its teeth looked grizzly-bear huge. Brown fur clung to portions of two skewed hipbones. An intact jawbone, topped with other assorted bone segments, had been ripped off the skeleton by partaking scavengers.

SeeHawk flung off his backpack and started dashing around, toughing various bones. He was trying to visually reconstruct the living animal.

My eyes defocused. What was I seeing? A Divine Message, sent to warn CDT hikers about dangerous snow-conditions on the North Wall? Or sent to warn me, personally, not to overtax my knee? Nope, such ideas were ridiculous. Over the top, woo-woo. Dreamer-grade *Looney Tunes*. But, for sure, I was being offered a golden opportunity to sell SeeHawk on the idea of turning around, since he was a sucker for anything that supported his belief in animal guides. Although, shame on me for even having that thought, since I still wanted to see the North Wall more than I wanted hot fudge, crutches, or anything else that could be bartered with destiny.

Eventually, SeeHawk interrupted my thoughts to ask, "Can I take the skull?"

Reading his eyes, I roared, "Are you out of your MIND? Even if you don't believe in jinxes, how could you possibly consider taking something that's like...like a caution sign, warning hikers to watch out for the North Wall being dangerous? I mean, isn't it enough to look, without taking? Or, like, what if it's diseased? I know that sounds paranoid, but what else, besides old-age or disease, could kill a bear up here? Plus, the skull probably weighs more than you think. Would you really want to carry it all the way to Marysville? That's a least a week-and-a-half away. Ack! I can't believe we're even having this conversation. You've got to be kidding me. Please, tell me you're kidding."

SeeHawk knew he was cornered, so he wisely responded, "Of course, Sunshine. I was totally kidding. How about if I just leave that heavy old skull here, and take two teeth instead?"

Cringing with disgust, I examined his eager face and sighed, "Okay, if you must, but two is the max. And, remember, I'll be afraid of your trophies jinxing us."

SeeHawk replied with complete assurance, "Don't worry, at all. This bear died of old age. Its bones are good medicine.

"Now listen," I added, while watching him eagerly reach into the bear's skull, "you can only take two teeth IF they fall into your hand. If they won't come loose, it means the bear wants its teeth. In that case, leave them alone. We don't need to invite bad luck. Plus, you have to promise not to take more than two because our risk of getting jinxed will increase if you hog. Remember to leave some teeth for other hikers. I'm sure you're not the only...ugh...collector of dead animal bones."

"Two's my limit," he promised, in mid-struggle with the bear's rigid jawbone.

I averted my eyes because watching him try to loosen a tooth was horrid.

At length, he mumbled, "Darn, it's stuck...I can't...get it out..."

"Then you have to give up," I insisted. "Obviously, the bear wants its teeth. *Yogi's* Souvenir Shop is closed for today."

Fretting in silence, SeeHawk obeyed my order. It took great inner strength for him to say goodbye to the skeleton and walk away, empty-handed. Hoisting on his backpack, he resumed climbing, without saying another word.

Once again, I scrambled to keep up. When I saw the space between us growing, eventually, I had to confess, "Forgive me...I'm sorry...really hurts...maybe a pulled tendon...I'm just a wimp...either way..."

Descending back to where I had stopped, SeeHawk responded gently, "That's okay, Sunshine. We don't have to see the North Wall if it would ruin your knee. Let's just go back down and sleep in Round Park tonight. If we need to take some kind of detour tomorrow, at least we'll have gotten to see a bear's skeleton. Hooey, what a gift!"

I stared at my fiancé in surprise. Had a pile of stinky animal bones really touched his heart deeply enough for him to forgive me?

As we both turned to abandon the North Wall, I hoped the pain in my kneecap would disappear when we started descending. Sadly, though, it hurt just as much going downhill as going uphill. I told myself this was all a big mistake. The Bob was about to fulfill SeeHawk's and my dreams. Colorado's San Juan Mountains were going to be spectacular. All our painstakingly dehydrated meals were going to be eaten, right down to the last crumb, before we went home. My brain set to whirring. Mistakes could be corrected. Suddenly, I heard SeeHawk speak.

"What if I just take the whole jawbone?"

Shocked back into awareness, I shouted, "UGH! Can't you please leave that poor bear ALONE?"

"Okay, okay," he laughed. "I was just kidding, Sunshine."

"No, you weren't."

"Okay, I wasn't. You're right, I would have taken it if you'd let me, but I knew you wouldn't, so I just wanted to make sure."

"That's obnoxious," I scowled. "And, it's equally obnoxious to test my superstitions at a time like this. I mean, don't you think maybe The Universe is trying to tell us something?"

"Absolutely," he agreed. "We're being told not to climb the North Wall tomorrow. I know because I've been seeing bears in my dreams. Did I ever tell you the brown bear is my Aumakua?"

"No," I chuckled, "but it figures."

* * *

My kneecap hurt before I fell asleep, but upon waking, it felt dandy. In fact, I might have considered disobeying SeeHawk's Aumakua and heading back up to the North Wall, if not for an influx of storm clouds making my partner suggest a full-scale retreat. Seriously, he wanted us to walk all the way back to Marias Pass and hitchhike back to East Glacier, so I could get my knee fixed. Obviously, any knee doctor would have seconded his motion, but, come on. A few gray clouds never hurt anybody. Most likely, I could still hack going forward, if we found a low bypass around the North Wall. Pulling out our maps, I pinned new hopes upon Trail 110. At least, it looked flat and stayed low the whole way.

"We'll still get to see the North Wall's nearest relative," I told SeeHawk, "and our guidebooks say the Chinese Wall is even more spectacular."

Despite wanting to honor my injury, SeeHawk loved that idea. He decided my knee was going to be okay and went full-tilt helping me strike camp.

Not until after we left Round Park did I recall having seen an official bulletin posted at Marias Pass. In my memory, it had mentioned something about 15-20 wilderness trails being closed due to fire damage. I had neglected to take notes at the time because none of the listed trails coincided with the CDT, but now the names "Lick Creek" and "Trail 110" began to sound familiar.

Sure enough, just where Trail 110 bent toward the south, we ran into a hellish landscape. Every eastward mile of forest looked black from head to toe. Rootless trees stood leaning against each other and lay collapsed across lattices of toothpick shadows. Fallen logs, hauled partway off the trail by maintenance workers, made us maneuver between them like human pinballs. The only greenery we could find was a few blades of grass peeking through the black soil. And yet, the North Fork Sun River remained intact. Tinted yellow by whatever it contained, the river's cool water was bubbling gaily around invincible boulders.

As Trail 110's view expanded, we lost all hope for an easy detour around our messy detour. The burn's vast acreage touched every horizon. Aside from turning around, there was no escape.

Glancing toward the west, we saw the Continental Divide caged behind thousands of wooden jail bars. That was one way to look at it. Another way was to regard Trail 110's tremendous view as being created by the destruction of intervening forest.

"Backbone of America," SeeHawk intoned. "I guess, right now, we're crossing America's ribcage?"

"You mean, walking across some rib meat?" I construed. "With barbecue sauce? Yum. Too bad, I've stopped eating beef ribs."

Inside a thicket of lodgepole pine saplings, whose seed-cones had been hatched by extreme heat, we saw evidence of the burn favoring certain species. However, favoritism clearly did not guarantee longevity. Eventually, massive regrowth was going to make some saplings die, so others could become full-sized pine trees. Otherwise, their entire generation would grow up malnourished, like the stunted old pines we had seen crowding the CDT's Canadian entrance.

A gradual color shift, changing everything ahead (both trees and land) from black to gray, coincided with where trail-maintenance crews had stopped refurbishing Trail 110. Beyond the color shift, parts of the trail became blocked by logs as thick as wine barrels. Some logs reached so far to both sides that we crossed them by doing slow-motion kickovers. Others could be skirted via handy animal paths.

Squeals erupted when a row of green treetops peeked over the southern horizon. Maybe before lunchtime, this labor was going to end! We just needed to—pant, pant—endure another 4-7 miles through all the wreckage.

In the meantime, though, we were becoming a mess. Sweat making our shirts sticky caused each charred log we vaulted to smudge us with soot until we began to look like chimney-sweeps.

A shallow swale, connecting Lick Creek and Wrong Creek to the North Fork Sun River, happened to coincide with a page-break on our atlas. It was difficult to connect wiggling lines across the pages, but that hardly mattered, since the swale's surrounding landscape was open. Of more interest was realizing we had entered an oasis. All three rivers converged into a central pocket of moisture, giving life to vigorous grass and cheerful yellow dandelions. One river was bridged by a sturdy log, whose transport saved us from needing to go swimming.

That was all a nice change of pace, for fifteen wonderful minutes, after which we landed right back in jail, facing grayness in every direction. Especially toward the west, dark cumulus clouds skulking away from the North Wall looked guilty of mischief, but their lips were sealed. All we could make out was that they looked tired, which we could understand on this long, hot morning.

My stamina felt stretched, but everything seemed better after SeeHawk volunteered to say, "Good thing we didn't tackle the North Wall, Sunshine. Your knee matters more than seeing every possible view on this trail."

Appreciating his gesture, I sincerely promised, "But, that is absolutely the last high view we're going to miss, even if I have to crawl over the top in some places."

Beginning where Trail 110 intersected Trail 111, the green trees ahead appeared within reach. Increasingly damp soil implied water leaching from an underground spring. Horizontal wicking had created a layer of firm mud, preserving every detail of paw- and claw-prints belonging to bears, wolves, coyotes, elk, deer, bobcats, raccoons, skunks, and squirrels. All these various creatures had followed Trail 110 for distances up to 1-mile, detours and all. That includes tiny animals like mice, whose low perspective should have prevented them from knowing about trails, and yet they had followed Trail 110 around logs and through seasonal puddles.

By midafternoon, we felt extremely grateful for the chance to enter a living forest. Strangely, it contained a wild wind we had never noticed until that moment. Even more strangely, the wind was savagely rustling its treetops, but having little impact down below.

Another dramatic change met us at the entrance to a rippling grassland called Gates Park. Fixed within the grass stood a white-rumped mule deer, posing for anyone who might have a camera. Also, out in the open stood one lonely ranch house, reachable only by airplane, horse, or foot-travel, since no roads came within miles of the park. The trail we were following passed near the house, while not seeming to fully agree with our maps. Deciding to diverge, we ran into a swamp containing several enormous birds.

"Ostriches," I guessed.

"Or emus," SeeHawk suggested.

"Have we made a wrong turn into Australia?"

"If we have, I'd like to order an ostrich burger," he imagined, licking his lips.

"Ugh, would you really eat it?"

"Maybe, if I was hungry enough."

Feeling disoriented, we kept alert for side trails, before heading down switchbacks dropping into a rocky streambed. At the bottom, we enjoyed splashing our arms, legs, and faces clean from accumulated soot and dirt. The continuing trail climbed back out of the streambed, via switchbacks my knee did not mind at all. Wait, seriously? Jumping Jehoshaphat! What was up with my kneecap? Had it suffered any real injury? Or was it true about the pain being psychosomatic?

Toward evening, we pitched camp between some random trees, ate another sleepy meal, and promptly retired.

SeeHawk started snoring the moment his head hit whatever he had folded into a pillow.

For a while, I lay awake, wondering if my kneecap was going to hurt every time we approached something scary.

Several days' worth of hiking on dry trails had given us a false sense of security regarding snow. Therefore, early the next morning, we were caught unprepared for the CDT to disappear underneath a blanket of thigh-deep corn snow. The coverage began around 6,500-feet, sticky like wet cement. Drab stratus clouds doubled the insult by casting a gloom over our labor. Ho-hum. La ti dah. It was still a good morning. My kneecap felt fine and my body felt strong.

We reached My Lake before breakfast time and paused there to admire bright silver clouds beautifully reflected upon silver water. Deciduous larch trees framed the water's edge, re-growing needles they had lost over winter. One presiding peak turned physics upside-down, by having a bare chest above its white snow skirt, so that we climbed out of the snow on our way up.

The Continental Divide celebrated our return with a banner of yellow buttercups and white globeflowers. Flat snow hid our trail from that point forward, but we did not care because the Chinese Wall made it obvious where to aim.

SeeHawk claims to have had "a religious experience" when he met the ancient limestone reef.

I experienced something closer to amnesia. Or, at least, I forgot my earlier troubles while trying to figure out where to put my attention.

Thrusting 1,000-feet skyward and six miles into the distance, the monstrous cliff dwarfed its audience of baseline trees. Being similar in color to expired lunchmeat, its vertical face was streaked with black drip-stains as if leaking oil. Thin layers of snow icing both its skyline and a middle-height ledge gave the appearance of a cross-sectioned layer cake. Birds in flight might have examined fossils embedding the cake's top layer, but down below we only saw two muscular elk grazing on scant shrubbery. There were other traces of life, though. For instance, a trail of hoof tracks stamped across the snow proved we were not the season's first tourists. Our predecessors must have come a long way, considering that Poppa Jim's guidebook placed us 20-miles away from the nearest recognized road, which was said to be as remote as one could get within the Continental United States. Naturally, such imagery made us wonder what was happening in California during our absence. Earthquakes? Terrorist attacks? Plagues? Locusts? My mind flipped through a Rolodex of possibilities before—gasp—I caught myself ignoring the Chinese Wall! Well, come on now. Let's be truthful. No matter how impressive an edifice might be, minds will wander wherever imaginations take them.

The rest of the day became a timeless glide between vertical limestone and baseline trees. Silver clouds above and white snow below made us appear to be walking through a pale snow globe, which hardly changed between afternoon and camp time.

More surrealism greeted us the next morning when a light snowfall scooted us out of camp. Fortunately, the flurries turned out to be short-lived. By the time we reached the CDT's departure from the Chinese Wall, bits of the sun were peeking through fractured silver clouds. Except, wham! Right at the same turning point, we got flash-frozen by an icy wind. Dashing into a snow-sugared forest, we found shelter between loose cover of trees. The air grew warm while we followed grizzly cub tracks down to an elevation where the ground dried up and everything was calm. For one glorious instant, full sunlight anointed our dunk in a babbling stream. Then, just as quickly, the sun retreated behind another cloudbank, while we twisted open our thermoses to enjoy a hot lunch.

SeeHawk's appetite had recently ballooned. After emptying his thermos, he nearly pilfered our storm rations, before I caught him in the act.

"Probably, we won't need any spare food before we hit the next town," I told him, "but the sky is still gray, so let's not try to channel Edward Murphy."

The sun reappeared as we got back on our feet, providing some gaiety to coax us into action. However, the moment I squatted to pick up my backpack, a crippling pain shot through my kneecap. Feeling stricken, I wailed, "How could I hurt my knee just from eating LUNCH?"

SeeHawk gave me a blank stare, not knowing how to respond.

Confusion drove me to think backward. Was there any commonality between what I had just been doing and my previous flare-ups? Well, let's see. We had just finished eating lunch, the same as in Round Park. Could the two meal breaks be related? What about our stream-bath? Had dipping my knee into cold water had some effect? Come to think of it, though, we had not bathed near Round Park. Okay, so then, what about removing my backpack or putting it back on? Did my on-and-off technique involve some kind of knee-twist? Nah, that seemed unlikely because the pain did not always recur after taking off my backpack. So, what else, then? My sitting posture while eating? Exploring that theory, I sat down cross-legged to observe what my legs did upon standing. It seemed like my knees angled outward while passing through a wide squat. Was that how I had squatted numerous times when we pitched our tent at Morning Star Lake, wearing a backpack because it had been snowing? If so, could performing a reverse-squat fix the injury? I tried to squat with my knees turned inward. Erk, no mirror was needed for me to know that I looked like a klutz trying to poop in the woods. Then, I remembered a trick once demonstrated to me by my Tui-Na. Following his instructions, I bent my left leg and stood like a flamingo, using my left hand to pull my left ankle upward and outward. This awkward pose forced my knee to rotate inward. Gingerly, I gave the raised ankle a little tug. It would have been wonderful to hear a satisfying crack, but nope. Nothing happened. Darned, how disappointing. I jerked the ankle harder, and, Whoa! There, it was. A satisfying POP shifted my kneecap back into place! Hey now, was it fixed? Yes! I could feel it. My injury was fixed. As in, really and truly FIXED!

"It WORKED!" I shouted, dancing around. "See? See? I told you my kneecap was just out of joint. That's all it needed. Just, the right kind of pop!"

SeeHawk's whole face relaxed into a smile.

"No more detours! No more delays!" It was hard to contain my joy for shouting, "Look out, Mexico, here we come!"

Mother Nature must have approved, because She whisked away the clouds by afternoon's end and replaced them with a sky full of glittering stars.

We awoke to find summertime singing on our doorstep. Sweet forest blossoms were perfuming the air. Another omen of summer was seeing an outfitter lead about 50 pack-mules toward the Chinese Wall, where he would pitch a group camp for seasonal tourists who would soon arrive on horseback.

"We're escaping just in the nick of time," SeeHawk muttered, throwing the outfitter a friendly wave.

Halfway across the Sun River's horse bridge, a familiar scent instantly transported me back to the Pacific Crest Trail. It was the scent of sunbaked creosote, oily and earthy, soaked into hot wood, and always packaged with beautiful summer days. Taking deep whiffs gave me a deep sense of leisure. The time had come for SeeHawk and me to slow down a little. I needed to honor my promise about pulling into camp earlier and spend a bit more time relaxing. This month and next would be our window of opportunity. Aided by midsummer's long daylight, we were past the worst delays of Spring, and far ahead of Autumn's impending challenges.

Of course, though, being in the free zone did not mean we could afford to slack. Thru-hikers are always on the clock, every single minute of every single day. Once set into motion, the race became continuous, and it would stay continuous until we crossed the finish line.

Chapter 7

Boom

When a cow endeavors to scratch its ear,
It means a shower is very near.
When it thumps its ribs with angry tail,
Look out for thunder, lightning, hail.

— *Weather Folklore*

By the time SeeHawk and I reached the Benchmark Wilderness Guest Ranch, we could hardly form a sentence without mentioning pancakes. It was reassuring to find our resupply box waiting for us at the ranch, but disappointing to get denied pancakes because the ranch was one week away from opening for the season. Sympathetically, its owners let us cook dehydrated chili on one of their cabin's porches. As a bonus, we got entertained by a fully costumed elementary-school cowboy, pushing a wheelbarrow at breakneck speeds, who nearly dumped his baby brother into our laps.

"Howdy li'l podners," SeeHawk drawled.

The cowpoke gave us a spaghetti-western nod.

His baby brother stared at our odd-looking food.

SeeHawk dug out a grungy deer antler he had recently found and presented it as a gift.

The cowpoke tossed the antler into his wheelbarrow, spun baby brother around, and raised dust back to wherever he kept other treasures found in the woods.

Overcast clouds subdued our mood while road-walking back to the CDT. Our eyes grew sleepy, but our mouths stayed awake and happy because the ranch-owners had given SeeHawk a freshly fried chicken leg and me a crisp red apple to munch while we walked. Having loaded our new re-supplies quickly, we got back to the CDT with a full afternoon left for exploring Lewis and Clark National Forest.

The next section of trail traversed beneath spruce, fir, and pine woods bordering the South Fork Sun River. Wide like a country highway, the whitecapped river bounded close alongside us, cutting a clean path between banks dotted with saxifrage and shaggy yellow groundsel. Sporadic wind gusts pushed bright yellow pollen out of the pine trees, tossing it through the air like cannon smoke.

With an easy trail to follow, drinking water close-at-hand, clear weather, and four happy knees kicking our feet forward, SeeHawk and I felt carefree. All we had to do was maintain a steady pace and enjoy the sights whizzing past our eyes. If only life could be that simple, the rest of the afternoon would have melted into a blur. However, as it turned out, the end of one struggle permitted a new struggle to emerge. In fact, the new struggle was directly created by outdistancing the struggles we were leaving behind. How this came about was that no longer having our speed checked by any rocks, deadfall, snow, or navigation exacerbated the difference between SeeHawk's natural walking pace and mine. This was a tough nut to crack because the equation was not simple.

SeeHawk neither had long legs nor an unusually long walking stride. The reason he could haul ass in ideal conditions was that, unlike most people, he had been born without an internal speedometer. Literally, the man could not tell if he was walking swiftly or slowly unless someone gave him a reference for comparison. Consequently, hiking behind me on flat ground sometimes caused him to ride my heels, especially if he was daydreaming or deeply absorbed in scenery. On this particular day, I had to ask him to back off so many times that we finally decided to switch places, putting him in front, which made me beg him to slow down, making it hard for both of us to decide which was worse. When the controversy degenerated into mild quibbling, I decided to seize the reins and perform a test.

First, I dramatically lengthened my walking stride. The result was that my legs got tired and started to hurt in unusual places. Abandoning that idea, the next strategy I tried was to increase my stepping speed. Unexpectedly, that plan also backfired because hearing my sneakers speed up behind him just made SeeHawk instinctively walk even faster.

Eventually, we decided to switch places every 20-30 minutes, which was a good compromise, but we still reached the South Fork Sun River feeling long overdue for Lullaby Lane.

Dusk set in as we pulled off the trail to examine the river's lumpy shoreline. Both of us felt eager to remove our backpacks, but we could not seem to agree about where to pitch our tent.

SeeHawk's favorite flat area looked too rocky for my taste.

Mine had the disadvantage of being covered in tall grass.

Finally, SeeHawk started yanking up boulders, in hopes of making his choice more appealing.

When I noticed him remodeling, I called out to him, "Don't move anything. We can sleep over here."

"They're not heavy," he muttered, without looking up.

"It doesn't matter about the weight," I countered. "Why move anything, when there's a perfectly good spot right here?"

"Because this spot is better," he explained.

"Not, if you have to rearrange Mother Nature's furniture. That would be kosher in an emergency, but we've got plenty of choices, so let's keep looking."

"This is only temporary, Sunshine. I promise I'll put every rock right back where it was, tomorrow morning."

Planting my hands on my hips, I protested, "But you're ruining the houses of every ant, worm, and whatever-else lives beneath those rocks."

"Don't worry," he insisted. "I already checked for ants and grubs. There aren't any. Plus, like I said, I'll put everything back first thing in the morning."

I still disagreed, but he won, and perhaps Mother Nature approved because we did not incur any bad bear karma during the night.

The next morning, it felt like we had only slept a few hours when the first glow of daybreak urged us to get hiking. The air temperature felt near freezing. No sun appeared for the whole first hour. We stayed submerged beneath loose woods, endlessly bordering the South Fork Sun River. Around 6,000-feet, we merged alongside trickling Straight Creek, whose banks sloped every which way, as if designed by a haphazard planning committee.

SeeHawk focused on keeping an even stride because his top-heavy backpack tilted painfully whenever he neglected to keep it in balance. His feet were smarting from constantly wearing boots. Why, oh, why, had he not shipped his sneakers to Benchmark? What had made him think the ground would still be covered with snow on June 27th? He felt hot, despite the sky being overcast. No amount of water could quench his thirst.

I, on the other hand, was feeling spry. My only complaint was wishing for something more interesting to look at than trees and more trees. By and by, I randomly wondered, "Do you think the command 'yaw' came from a contraction of 'yee-haw,' like in, 'giddee-haw,' which might have originally been, 'get thee haw?"

Startled out his own ruminations, SeeHawk mumbled, "That's a far-out thought, Sunshine."

Sensing no interest, I turned my attention to a mountain chickadee whistling rounds of a 3-4 note song. Its notes nearly matched those of a similar song whistled by all mountain chickadees along southern California's Pacific Crest Trail, but not quite. Apparently, different chickadee populations had their own dialects. This observation led me to wonder. Could chickadees living in a mid-zone between two different regions sing in mixed dialects? Or, did their dialects change abruptly, like European languages across country borders? This question led me to suggest, "Someday, let's hike east-to-west and find out."

SeeHawk kept on with his own thoughts and did not bother answering.

Feeling mentally stranded, I became acutely aware of my backpack straps cutting into my shoulders.

SeeHawk had been feeling strap pains all morning.

During the same hour, the air temperature hit 90 degrees, beneath solid cover of clouds. A final climb toward Straight Creek Pass ran us into a burn that had killed every tree in the visible distance. Neither prominently black nor gray, all the spoils had faded into colorless driftwood, dreary like the overcast sky. Leathery chaparral provided greenness on the ground, and it looked vigorous but matched us for thirst.

By early afternoon, our hats felt scorched. Dry heat had toasted our skin raw. Our brains felt like boiled noodles.

Sweat kept making my sunglasses slip down my nose, pinching my nostrils together, which forced me to keep pushing up my sunglasses, over and over, until the constant hassle got on my nerves.

In the distance, ahead nothing changed. Consequently, we could hardly believe our luck upon spying a crystal-clear spring bubbling through the burn's naked soil. Not only was it a miracle for the spring to exist, but furthermore, it was ringed with succulent green moss. Feeling awestruck, we dropped onto our knees and refilled every water bag tight enough to bounce. Next, we plunged our faces straight into the cold water and slurped like we might never drink again. The final step was soaking our hair and hats, before we took off feeling refreshed, in hopes of hiking faster.

Unfortunately, having fresh eyes failed to make the landscape come alive. Its spoilage continued into the distance. No more springs appeared to give us another drink. The sky looked bleak in every direction. Once our hats and hair evaporated, monotony resumed, until a fire-shaved summit appeared in the distance.

I made some calculations that led me to predict, "Lightning could be a problem tomorrow when we go up high."

"Okay," SeeHawk replied.

Resenting his lack of interest, I added, "Do you want to know WHY?"

"Not while we're climbing," he admitted. "Let's talk about that in camp."

"After it's too late to adjust our plans?"

"Sorry, Sunshine. I know planning is important, but I'm just too hot to think right now."

"Mm-hm, well, maybe I'm too hot also, but if neither one of us thinks, we're going to be in trouble."

"Maybe so," he agreed.

"And, that's okay with you?"

"Sure."

Sensing that my partner was not really listening, I replied slightly louder, "So, if I start making decisions without your input, are you going to get mad or peacefully comply?"

"It depends," he shrugged.

"Okay, so, what if I decide to make us hike into the dark?"

"Then I'll probably get mad, knowing me, or at least I won't be happy. Why, Sunshine? Is that what you've been getting at by asking me all these questions?"

"GETTING at?" I snorted. "This isn't a nag session, See-Hawk. I'm talking about stuff that should interest anyone who wants this trip to succeed."

"Well, obviously I want this trip to succeed, but right now my head is boiling, so please, just decide whatever you need to decide, and I promise I'll be fine with it, okay?"

"Fine as in Julie Andrews fine? Jumping over the moon fine? Or just grit-my-teeth-and-shut-up-so-I-won't-get-in-trouble fine?"

"Yes, all that," he laughed.

"Okay, then I'm going to decide we should push to reach the second ford of Dearborn Creek tonight."

"Sounds good," he nodded. "There, see how happy I am? Why were you even worried? Er, wait, should I be worried?"

"Only, if you don't want to hike into the dark."

"Into the dark? Ha-ha, no problem. What's a little lost sleep, with November coming up? It won't be long before we'll have plenty of long nights to turn in early."

"Are you being sarcastic?"

"No. I'm just saying that having longer daylight will force you to let us go to bed at a decent hour."

"LET us?" I echoed. "You think I voluntarily stretch our limits just to give us more exercise or something?"

"No, Sunshine. I'm sure all your decisions are justified."

"Then why were you just sarcastic?"

"I wasn't sarcastic."

"Yes, you were."

"No, I wasn't. All I meant was, why should we hike farther than the day is long, before even knowing if there's anything to worry about?"

"Before even knowing? What do we not know? You want to see trees explode into flames before you'll believe in fire? Is that a brilliant strategy? Is that how we finished the PCT?"

"No, Sunshine, of course not."

"Then, how did we finish the PCT?"

"By you being an excellent planner and me being your pack mule."

"Right. So, do you think we should stick with a winning strategy, or change it up whenever we're feeling sleepy?"

"Definitely, stick with it, Sunshine. Look, I know lightning is dangerous, okay? I'm just not worried because I know we're going to be fine tomorrow."

"Based on what? Being some kind of fortune-teller?"

"No, sweetheart. There are just certain things in life a man knows."

"Like, that he can trust his immortality complex?"

"Exactly. No, that's not it either."

"Really? Then, why does being a man make any difference? Can your unit be used for a weather antenna?"

"No," he laughed. "It's really just got two functions."

"Okay, well, maybe you could teach it to read maps if you tried, so we could stop needing to have these discussions."

"Okay, but why would I want to steal your glory, Sunshine? You're the best navigator a pack mule could wish for."

"Except when you don't want to hear my opinion."

"Pack mules aren't perfect."

"Okay, but they don't need to be obtuse, either."

"Mules are stubborn by nature. But, that's beside the point. I get what you're saying about planning, Sunshine. I just wish we had more time to relax in camp."

"Okay, well, if we had more time, how would you use it?"

"Oh, I don't know. Maybe I'd clip my toenails. They're getting pretty long. Or, if I may be so bold, maybe I'd want to enjoy a little afternoon delight?"

"In BEAR country?" I gasped. "Let's get farther south first."

"Okay, then how about doing a little focused meditation?"

"We've talked about that before and it's coming up soon. But, in the meantime, haven't you often said you want to learn how to meditate on your feet?"

No response

"Anyway, we're right on the verge of having more time, so please keep the faith a little longer, okay?"

"Okay," he whined, "but, even after we get back on schedule, there still won't be any time for fun activities, because if it's not storming, some river will be flooding or a post office will be closing, or some other sh—."

SeeHawk's abrupt change of tone startled me into asking, "What other sh— are you referring to, specifically?"

"Just the same sh— as always."

"Are you talking about me? Am I the sh—?"

"No, not you. Forget I said anything."

"How can I forget you having a grudge?"

"I guess you can't. Forget it. Never mind."

"If you have a grudge, SeeHawk, we should solve it."

"There's no grudge. I'm just feeling grumpy because it's hot."

"I'm hot too, but I don't call you a sh— just because I feel uncomfortable."

"It wasn't calling you anything, Sunshine. You're taking my words out of context."

"Maybe, but if you care what I think, why don't you say something loving and flattering to let me know everything is really okay?"

"Loving and flattering let you know is okay," he sloppily repeated.

"Jerk!" I hollered. "Don't mock my effort to help you make peace."

There was too much sunlight drilling into my skull. Sweat kept trickling down my forehead. My sunglasses kept slipping, no matter how many times I pushed them back up my nose.

"Please stop acting snarky," I pleaded, "and just tell me what your grudge is, so we can get this over with."

"I promise I would tell you if I had a grudge, but I don't," SeeHawk insisted.

"Except that, apparently, you do, and, apparently, we need to find out what it is because grudges are like poison. They kill good relationships. In fact, let's stop hiking right now and solve this, okay? Can you please stop for a moment and turn around to face me?"

"No," he snarled. "I can't stop because we can't afford to waste any time, or we'll end up hiking into the dark."

"AHA!" I declared. "There, see? We found your grudge. And now you're proving it, by being a total jerk."

"Jerk, nothing."

"Trust me, SeeHawk, pulling into camp ten minutes later will be a heck of a lot more pleasant than what's going to happen if you don't stop hiking and face me right now."

Blatantly refusing, he sped up, to put some distance between us.

"You're only making me madder," I shouted after him.

"Getting madder is your choice," he shouted back.

"Do you think I'm choosing to make you have a grudge?"

"If you're not choosing, you'd better realize you're creating one by having this conversation."

"Oh, great. So, now you have TWO grudges?

That was the last straw. SeeHawk whirled around to face me. His expression looked tempestuous.

"Okay, good!" I panted. "Thank you for realizing this is important. Now, please stay calm and just be honest. Why do you think we'll never get any free time on this whole trip because, if it's not a flood or a post office, it'll just be something else? "

"I never said that."

"You used different words. "
"Right, which means I didn't say it."
"If I misquoted you, please correct me."
"Correct you how?"
"By repeating whatever you said five minutes ago."
"How can anyone remember something they said five minutes ago?"
"I still remember."
"You do?"
"Yes."
"Then, you tell me."
"I just told you, and you said I got it wrong. That's why I'm asking you."
"Well, too bad I can't remember."
"Maybe, but it's still in your subconscious memory bank. That's how grudges are, which worries me."
"You're getting weird on me, Sunshine. I probably just forgot because I have amnesia."
"You don't have amnesia. You're just annoyed because you don't like me being right that you have a grudge."
"If I had a grudge, I promise I would tell you."
"Admission is the first step toward solving, SeeHawk. Haven't you heard how they do it in *AA*? Just be honest and come clean. I promise not to get mad. Just admit the sh— you mentioned was me."
"I didn't call you anything because you overextend us on purpose."
"Aha! See? Now, we're getting somewhere. you're acting passive-aggressive because you don't want to openly call me a slave-driver, but you think I am one."
"You're not a slave-driver."
"Sorry, wrong word. I'm an over-extender."
"You're twisting my words."
"You specifically said overextend."
"If I did, I meant something different."
"You did? Then, what did you mean?"
"Who knows?"

"I do."

"You do?"

"Yes."

"Well, thank goodness for that, since you're the one doing the talking."

"Wise-ass," I snarled. "If you talked at times when you should, I wouldn't have to talk for you."

"Look, let's just forget whatever I said and move on, okay? Because I take it all back."

"Take what all back?"

"Everything I've said."

"Honestly?"

"Yes."

"Is that supposed to make me feel better?"

"Yes."

"According to whom?"

"According to you. Or, er, me. According to me, and God, and Nature as my witness."

"Fine, SeeHawk, if you can please just admit you have a grudge and promise to act nicer from now on, I'll forgive you, okay?"

"Great!" he beamed. "So, we're finished? Now, can we get back to hiking?"

"Not so fast, buster. First, you have to admit you have a grudge."

"But, I don't have a grudge. I just hate talking while I'm climbing, that's all."

"O-HO! So, THAT'S the deal. We're back to the climbing while talking thing, eh? Okay, great, well, that's already on our list of things you didn't like before we left home, so, fair enough."

"Look, please just drop the whole grudge thing, okay?"

"After we just hit payday?"

"Please."

"SeeHawk, I'm female. You know how much we hate having grudges come back to haunt us."

"Fine, if we have to talk about it, let's at least wait until we get to some trees."

I gestured all around. We were surrounded by trees. Dead trees, everywhere. No living trees in sight.

"This is ridiculous," SeeHawk sighed. "Let's quit wasting energy and use it to hike super fast, so you won't need to push me into forming another grudge." With that resolution made, he took off like a rocket.

I hurried after him, trying to catch up.

His big blue backpack faced me like a wall.

I pleaded, toward his backpack, "But the grudge you already have isn't fixed yet."

"Nope," his voice confirmed.

Tightening my cheeks, I hollered in anguish, "Do you realize how much this argument sounds like all the stupid arguments we had in Oregon and Washington?"

That reminder must have struck an artery because the words flying over his backpack grew downright vicious.

Together, we spiraled into the same verbal dogfight which had tainted our memories of the PCT.

Close to Straight Creek Pass, I began praying for us not to disturb any other hikers, or even animals, with our godawful noise. Of course, I did not feel seriously worried about infringing upon anyone. The last time we had seen another human being on the CDT was 2½ weeks earlier, at Virginia Falls. Furthermore, The Bob was not exactly Tourist Central.

During the same loaded silence, SeeHawk's backpack turned into a load of bricks suspended from his shoulders with binder twine. Dammed if he was going to give in to some squeaking female voice tagging along behind him. He sped onto Straight Creek Pass like he was hoping for an escape. He seemed to have forgotten that we always stuck together.

"Jerk," I yelled, hurrying to keep up with him. "Asshole."

"I just want to hike," he hollered back.

We halted on top of the pass. Neither of us wanted to meet each other's eyes. Our argument had lost focus. Still, neither party felt ready to give in.

Descending from the pass in angry silence, we followed the CDT into another burned valley that looked mercilessly bleak.

Eventually, I growled, "Are you really going to keep blowing me off until I go completely ballistic?"

"Okay," he grunted.

"Okay, meaning you DO want me to go ballistic? Okay, then, if that's what you want, here I go..."

Before I could go anything, SeeHawk's radiator blew and his mouth sprang open. Like a maniac on steroids, he vomited every particle of air his lungs could hold, expelling THE YELL to end all yells. It crashed through the surrounding valley like a shockwave. Its energy ricocheted off burnt-bare mountains. Afterward, came silence as heavy as death. No listening animals dared to make a sound. Hawks and eagles probably stopped flapping their wings. Bobcats must have frozen stiff in their tracks. Even ants underground might have stopped building their nests. Every living creature for miles felt every ton of agony crammed into poor SeeHawk's head, heart, and soul, by punishment of being stuck with me!

Lord knows what would have happened if we had not run into Welcome Creek.

SeeHawk dropped onto his knees and plunged his whole head into the creek's icy water. Immediately, sharp pains pierced his skull. Keeping his head submerged, he gargled, asking the forest to forgive him for having disturbed its beautiful creatures with his ugly Yell.

Then, he sat down beside me, helped me refill our water bags, and drank handfuls of water straight from the creek.

Soon, we managed to speak in normal voices. Our flushed skin cooled off. Our heart rates relaxed.

Eventually, I stood up and announced, "We should probably keep hiking."

"Yeah," he agreed, still with an edge of tension.

While repacking our backpacks, both of us got spooked by a slender, bearded, 40-ish looking man descending toward us from Straight Creek Pass. He was dressed in a fitted t-shirt and shorts, wearing a white cowboy hat which shaded his whole face, and carrying a frameless rucksack on his back, which looked too small for holding overnight gear. He wore black dress socks, peeking over flimsy white tennis shoes which seemed to give him uncommon speed. In one bony hand, he carried a two-gallon water jug, loaded full enough to feel like a bowling ball, and yet, somehow, dangling casually from his hand, like it hardly weighed anything. Altogether, he had to be a thru-hiker.

As soon as I saw him, I wanted to disappear.

Had he heard The Yell? Or worse, had he also heard See-Hawk and me arguing before we reached Straight Creek Pass?

I told myself that any hiker moving at his speed must have been out of earshot before we crossed the pass, and even during. However, it also stood to reason that he could have hung back to give us privacy. After all, his timing seemed awfully perfect. Was it just a coincidence? Or was he deliberately pretending not to have heard us fight?

I searched the shade underneath his hat brim, finding no clues.

"Good day," he exclaimed, as he pulled up beside us. "I'm Devin. You'll probably see Karen coming along soon. I guess I'll just stop here if you don't mind me joining you?"

Nobody materialized in the distance behind him.

"She's probably back-a-ways," he explained. "I'm sure she'll catch up quickly, though. I came down here pretty fast."

Aha! So then, if Devin had not intentionally hung back, perhaps we could assume he had not heard us arguing? Hoping so, I let go of some embarrassment.

"When did you leave the Canadian border?" SeeHawk asked.

"During the middle of June," Devin recalled.

"So, a week after us," I nodded. "Did you run into much snow in Glacier?"

"Oh no," he replied. "The passes were all clear. It was easy hiking, mostly, except for the Ahern Drift, and really, even that was no big deal. I just chopped steps for Karen. We were able to go across wearing tennis shoes."

My ears did a double-take. This unassuming thru-hiker, plus some superwoman named Karen, had crossed the infamous Ahern Drift wearing tennis shoes? They had accomplished this one week after SeeHawk and I left Canada via the Belly River route because we feared the Ahern Drift might be dangerously slippery, even if we used our ice-axes and I wore snowshoe crampons?

While marveling at the difference a week could make, I asked Devin, "Did you run into much snow going over Piegan Pass and Pitamakan Pass?"

"Not enough to shake a stick at," he recalled. "There was hardly any snow covering the trail."

My mind reeled again. Had most of the snow SeeHawk and I saw in Glacier National Park melted within a single week? Did that mean we should have strictly heeded Poppa Jim's advice? Or was Devin simply defining "snow" in the manner of an East Glacier local?

He spent a moment topping off his water jug with refreshment from the creek, before settling into a comfortable slouch. Then, he merrily remarked, "You two are probably happy to have some company for a change. I know how it can feel, being stuck together on a trail for too long. Sometimes you get to where you want to kill each other."

My cheeks burst into flame. Had this friendly gentleman heard The Yell after all? His smiling eyes offered no answer.

Before SeeHawk or I could change the subject, Karen popped into sight, bounding off the pass. She had impressively long legs and a muscular build, downplayed by wearing a floppy sun hat.

"Are you the gal who crossed the Ahern Drift wearing tennis shoes?" I cried in greeting.

She laughed like it was no big deal.

We all chatted briefly. That was a long time, by thru-hiker standards. Getting back to business, Devin and Karen hauled up and dashed away, vanishing as quickly as they had appeared.

"No amount of training will ever make me able to hike that fast," I mumbled, zipping my backpack shut in preparation to leave.

"Me either," SeeHawk agreed, and he meant it.

Welcome Creek and the CDT wove braids across each other heading downstream, except in places where the creek and trail became one. We descended merrily through rails of twiggy shrubs, around fractured boulders, and right through the water wearing our sneakers because that is what thru-hikers normally do, and Devin and Karen were doing it.

During the afternoon, living trees finally came to our rescue, just in time to save us from the day's peak heat. The trail arced over several small foothills, before landing alongside the sluggish Dearborn River. We followed the river's knee-deep current along a white, sandy beach held together by willows. Presently, our attention fixed upon a squall descending toward us from the western mountains. It was visibly accelerating, and growing darker.

"Look what your Yell created," I told SeeHawk.

"See?" he grinned. "I told you human beings can influence the weather."

Suddenly, the squall's fury came alive. Thunder boomed. Sheet-lightning flashed. Forked yellow daggers attacked the Dearborn River. Fat raindrops turned everything into a blur. Plants got smashed along the water's edge. Hailstones pounded the sand so hard that shouting became necessary in order to be heard. The streambed melted into a swamp. Our socks and shoes puffed out like water balloons. There was no place to hide. We could not even find a patch of high ground on which to sit and ball up inside our ponchos. Instead, we just squinted through the hail and kept sloshing back and forth, struggling not to lose sight of the trail, until eventually, I decided it was not ours.

"What happened to the CDT?" SeeHawk stammered when I gave him the news.

"No idea," I admitted, "but I think we've been following animal paths for a while now."

"What makes you think so?"

"Nothing specific. Let's hope I'm wrong."

Bears, deer, and whatever else had forged paths all over the waterlogged beach. None of them appeared to have been following the CDT. Pulling out maps would only have gotten them soaked. Besides, the river was an obvious landmark, so we just stuck to it, letting faith be our guide.

The storm seemed to be centered above us, judging by having lightning flash on our right, left, ahead, and behind. Fortunately, it was only a show of lights and water, not also a windstorm. We felt cozy inside our ponchos, even with our pants soaked and shoes overflowing. However, things took a frightening turn when a second squall latched onto the first. Its stronger convection sucked 20 degrees out of the riverbed's humid air. SeeHawk and I started shivering. The Dearborn River overflowed. Every animal path got swallowed when the entire beach went underwater. On paper, this situation seemed dangerous, but we did not care. The fresh aroma of airborne ions tantalized our senses. Deep, booming thunder drummed us into a state of rapture. The storm was a celebration of life itself, and we were living, oh boy and how!

Of course, we still had to navigate. Therefore, we kept our eyes peeled for any exit trail leaving the river.

"Keep moving," I urged SeeHawk, "because if don't find the CDT soon, we might float past it and get carried out of the chocolate factory."

"Gotta go, Julia. We've got cows," he fired back.

Joking made it easier not to feel worried.

The rain kept coming for another 20 minutes. Then, suddenly, everything changed. An angel's bright sword speared through the clouds, igniting every water-droplet dangling from every branch, leaf, and ripple of water.

SeeHawk and I stared at our sopping-wet pants...mud sloshing out of our shoes...a spongy wad of maps and guidebook directions (somehow soaked underneath my poncho), which could not be unfolded without destroying the pages, and all we could do was laugh.

"Maps? Who needs maps? We don't need no stinking maps."

That was true. Why? Because the same sunbeam lighting up the willows also splashed a small wooden sign saying "CDT."

"High-five, Chief Navigator!" SeeHawk exclaimed.

The storm's violence had washed away our anger. We both felt revived, inside and out. Ballyhoo finished.

Race still going.

Chapter 8

Heavy Glue

Flee to the wilderness. The one within, if you can find it.

— Utah Phillips

It was still the 27th day of June, but it seemed like a whole new day because SeeHawk and I were finished arguing, and finished getting drenched by a passing thunderstorm. The CDT's departure from the Dearborn River headed into a border of living trees, thus ending our long passage through the burn consuming Straight Creek Pass.

Inside a merry meadow, we came face-to-face with two mounted park rangers, leading four horse-riders, leading three loaded pack-mules in our direction. The mule team had right of way, so we stepped aside to give them passing room, but that was not enough. The mules still balked and stamped around, lurching against their jingling harnesses.

The mounted rangers, sounding a little panicked, hollered out to us, "You'll have to step all the way back to the trees. These mules aren't used to seeing backpackers."

Obediently, we strode a good distance backward, feeling astonished that an entire horse-and-mule team could be intimidated by two puny human beings.

"Although, we do smell pretty bad," SeeHawk noted.

"It must be all the dried onions," I agreed.

"Plus, the garlic grenades in our lasagna."

After getting past the mules without any mishaps, we focused on our goal for the day, which was to camp at the CDT's second crossing of Dearborn Creek. Reaching the creek by nightfall would have given us a nice jumpstart on racing the next day's thunderstorms across six miles' worth of mountains topping 8,000-feet. However, we ended up pitching camp one mile short of goal when dusk overtook us near Whitetail Creek.

It was a nice compensation that the creek's rocky shoreline remained warm after dark, allowing us to comfortably cook dinner and eat beside the water. We slept beneath hissing conifer trees, swishing cottonwoods, and fluttering aspens, whose flattened stems made their perpendicular leaves shimmer in every breeze.

Food-burglars could have used the river's noise to mask a midnight raid, but in the morning, we found everything hanging right where we had left it, and our bear canister untouched.

While helping me strike camp, SeeHawk lifted his chin and announced, "I smell smoke."

Turns out, Devin and Karen's camp was only 100 yards away! Neither they nor we had sensed each others' presence because little could be heard through the river's constant noise. Our friends were extinguishing a small cooking fire when we arrived. They had just fixed and eaten hot cereal for breakfast before we even tasted our fruit rolls.

As a group of four, we all set off together, chatting about our various approaches to camping. I praised Devin and Karen for being early birds, who slept 2-4 hours longer than we did, hiked 2-3 hours less per day, and still got to build campfires almost every night and morning. Their secret for success was hiking extremely fast, without seeming to expend more energy. Clearly, they were going to outdistance us quickly, but I still appreciated leaving camp with them because Karen looked confident about navigating the CDT's first two miles beyond Whitetail Creek. Sure enough, she made clean work of guiding us through a rough patch of unfinished trail, beyond which we found a ladder of switchbacks easy to match with Poppa Jim's guidebook.

SeeHawk and I paused where the switchbacks began, to take off our jackets and pack them away.

That was Devin and Karen's cue to start climbing. They had already stripped down to t-shirts and shorts before leaving camp, so they threw us an apologetic farewell and bounded up the switchbacks like caffeinated jackrabbits.

I mumbled as they climbed out of sight, "Yes, partner, I know what you're thinking. If we could climb that fast, we'd get to build campfires every night, too, and you could meditate while I was cooking."

Being a good partner, SeeHawk replied, "But, how often are they getting to really enjoy the scenery?"

After regimentally climbing 1,600-feet, the two of us landed upon a grassy crest crowned with a single green-egg peak. White bog orchids and starry parnassia framed a rogue summit stream, flowing into the trees from which we had emerged.

Devin and Karen were nowhere to be seen.

We sat down, scooped water out of the creek, and used it to soften our rock-hard granola because skipping breakfast was not an option. Today's agenda called for topping 8,000-feet right after breakfast and then staying atop the crest without cover of trees for another six miles. Devin and Karen were already underway. My eyes needed a moment to adjust before spotting their ant-sized figures, scaling the green-egg peak.

SeeHawk spent much longer locating them, before observing with awe, "They sure are carrying the mail this morning."

"They're probably planning to eat lunch after finishing this whole high part," I figured, "while we're still stuck in the middle, channeling Ben Franklin."

It was typical to see cumulus clouds form before lunchtime, so we felt lucky to be starting this long race on an unusually clear day.

Recalling somebody's statistics, from somewhere, I told SeeHawk over breakfast, "Remember that lightning only kills seventy-three people a year. Of course, that's not including three hundred who survive, but still, it's not a huge number, considering how many storms there are."

"But, you have to factor in that you and I are currently in the same category with golfers and telephone-pole repairmen," SeeHawk reminded me.

"Does that make you scared?"

"Not at all," he grinned. "Especially, not today."

Racers on your marks, the sky announced.

Both of us took a last sip of water.

Get set...

My heartbeat quickened. Yesterday's hailstorm, lightning, and flash flood were still fresh in my memory. Currently, I did not see any danger, but if yesterday's weather had overtaken us on the crest? Whoa, Nelly!!

When SeeHawk saw the look in my eyes , he cheerfully announced, "This is going to be a dynamic move."

Both of us tightened our backpack straps.

GO!

We took off chasing Devin and Karen. Scaling the green egg swift and steady, our legs and lungs complained about surpassing 8,000-feet without ever stopping to catch our breath. Finally, we had to pause atop the summit. With our heads surrounded by fair-weather clouds, we gazed across mountains stacked beyond mountains, all repeating a color scheme of brown, green, and pink. A few of the tallest peaks still wore caps of snow. None of them rivaled the crags we had seen in Glacier National Park. This was a new version of Montana. Massive. Summery. Superficially repetitive but probably concealing different surprises.

The CDT's descent eased onto a narrow catwalk, displaying one cluster of dead trees fixed in the distance.

Devin and Karen were nowhere to be seen.

Proceeding horizontally, we bored through a side-on southwesterly gale, feeling like some earwax from our right ears might get blown out the left.

I shouted over the wind, "At least, there isn't any snow left."

SeeHawk nodded without answering since he could not hear me.

Heavy Glue

It was impossible to open our eyes if we looked anyplace except straight downwind. Glancing even slightly to windward made our eyeballs get smashed—as in, we could physically feel our eyeballs flattening, which felt unbearably creepy. Therefore, we kept our eyes riveted on the trail, which made it impossible to keep tabs on the windward sky.

When we reached the catwalk's cluster of dead trees, we found they were bent into parabolas, hoops, and spirals, like a wooden playground built for ghouls. Maneuvering over and under them became a game, which helped us forget about the wind for a moment. Then, we realized the wind had eased because we were inside a localized wind shadow. This protection allowed us to peek toward the west, where we saw a handful of cumulus clouds drifting toward us. None looked dangerous, but we still had 6-miles of high trail left before dropping to safer ground.

A bit farther along, the crest widened into a boulder-studded meadow whose grass swallowed the CDT in one gulp. Smack in the meadow's center stood a podium-sized cairn. Was it marking the CDT, or just inviting preachers to give sermons to the sky?

Suddenly, something dark swooped toward my head. Instinctively, I ducked. It looked like a low-flying bird. Then, I realized it was a cloud shadow, moving at roughly the speed of a bird. Was the weather changing? Not knowing where to aim but thinking we should keep moving, I rolled the dice and led See-Hawk toward the left. Lucky guess! The trail found my shoes before my eyes found the trail.

Next up was a 1,000-foot ladder of switchbacks, whose top landing almost touched the clouds. From high within the sky, we gazed across another hundred colorful mountains, getting massaged by a thousand moving cloud shadows. It was a view worth savoring if only the wind had not wanted us to fly.

Shielding my eyes, I squinted toward the west. Some half-mature clouds were drifting toward us, none of which looked dangerous yet.

Out the corner of my eye, I spied a red-tailed hawk.

"Look!" I shouted back to He Who Sees Hawks. "Your favorite bird is doing a little windsurfing."

"What?" his response warbled through the wind.

"A HAWK," I shouted.

"Where?"

"TURN around and LOOK."

"WHAT?"

"STOP hiking and LOOK where I'm pointing!"

By now, the hawk was soaring away.

"STOP?" he repeated. "I can't stop now. Just tell me where to look, Sunshine."

"Ack! Never mind. It's gone. You'd have to have looked sooner."

Finally, he stopped hiking, long enough to shout into my ear, "WHAT do you want me to LOOK at?"

"Never MIND," I groaned. "It was just a nice-looking hawk, that's all. Doesn't matter because it's gone now."

"A HAWK?" he exclaimed. "Shoot, why didn't you tell me where to look?"

"I did, but you couldn't hear me. You were supposed to look backward and see where I was pointing."

"Why didn't you tell me what o'clock on the dial?"

This was such a frequent request that I reflexively gave him my usual answer, "Trying to visualize a clock while I'm watching something move gets me all confused."

"Sunshine," he growled, "you can't expect me to find something unless you tell me where to look. That's why the clocks are so useful. Just try it, okay?"

"Using the clocks might save you energy," I acknowledged, "but for me, it's a brain drain, if I have to visualize a clock while I'm trying to show you something."

"Well, if you won't be precise, then don't expect me to find whatever it is you want to show me, next time," he huffed. "Do we have an understanding?"

I sighed loudly enough to be heard over the wind, "If it means that much to you, I'll TRY using the clocks, but if I can't picture one fast enough, you'll just have to look where I'm pointing."

"Deal," he agreed.

Case closed. Although each of us had only understood half that conversation, we resumed hiking.

Only another few minutes passed, before I noticed some blue forget-me-nots fluttering, up ahead.

"Pretty, huh?" I shouted.

"What o'clock?" SeeHawk shouted back.

"Oh, heck...they're on the ground...like, maybe eleven-thirty, or eleven?...actually ten...just look beside you, you're walking right past them!"

Finally, my partner's eyes found the blue flowers, and he shouted approvingly, "Very good, Sunshine. Those ARE nice flowers. See how easy that was?"

"Easy for someone who checks his wristwatch all day long, whenever he thinks I'm not looking," I snorted.

"It's digital, not the dial kind," he reminded me.

"Never mind," I grumbled. And then, pointing into the distance, I added, "Check out those big mountains. If it wasn't so windy, I'd find their names on our maps."

Of course, he responded, "What o'clock, Sunshine?"

"Oh, for Pete's sake! They're taking up a whole quarter of the sky. Just look where I'm pointing."

Crazy as it seems, we continued squabbling back and forth like this all the way to the midsection of our 6-mile skywalk. After that, our attention got diverted by an abrupt wind shift, from southwesterly to southeasterly, which mercifully changed the direction our backpacks were getting pushed. The change felt good, but my shoulders still needed a break from being crushed by weighted straps. Despite being unable to hide from the wind, I decided to remove my backpack for a moment.

When SeeHawk noticed me pumping blood into my arms, he decided to make it an official time-out and joined me in peeling off his backpack.

I spread my arms into a flying T-shape. The wind shrink-wrapped my jacket around my chest. It felt like being a skydiver. When I leaned forward, facing a 1,000-foot drop into empty space, the wind almost supported my full weight. Before and below me, the eastern lowland rolled up and down like a motionless sea. Its brown and green mountains were dappled with moving sunspots and cloud shadows, creating a groovy kaleidoscope effect. Far in the distance, the eastern horizon looked trimmed with tiny cauliflowers, standing in for clouds. My eyes looped from the horizon up to a fan of bigger cauliflowers, expanding across the sky. They grew into the clouds above my head, from which I looked down, finding some blue forget-me-nots clustered near my shoes before I started the loop all over again. The first trajectory was looking back across the waveform lowland. Then, seeing the horizon again, I traced the cauliflowers back toward myself, and so forth, around and around in circles. I was trying to taste all of Montana's beauty in one gulp. The exercise felt hypnotic, but satisfaction was impossible. I was going to have to settle for a group of snapshots on film.

Back in action, SeeHawk followed me onto Peak 8,655 (pragmatically named for its height above sea level), where we began traversing across a snow-seamed cliff. From there, we got relayed to a wraparound ledge, whose reverse aim caused us to realize we were being tailed by floating gray roses, made of stuff that could eventually rain.

The next stretch of crest sideswiped a scaffold of twiggy dead brush, serving as a high-rise apartment complex for hyperactive prairie falcons. Two minor peaks, framing our passage through a wide gap, watched us run smack into a rogue snowfield and stop. Resting on flat terrain, the snow could easily have been crossed in about 100 steps. Its endpoint led our eyes toward a bristle of burned treetops, peeking out of a small valley shortly past the snow.

SeeHawk shrewdly observed, "If Devin and Karen came this way, why didn't they leave any footprints on the snow?"

Taking interest, I discovered he was right. The snow looked untouched. That was odd, since detouring around it would not have made sense.

Heavy Glue

Our maps showed the CDT keeping a straight course, up to an important left-hand turn. Without having a more detailed map, we could not tell for sure if that turn would happen near the valley ahead, or closer to the peak on our left. While sifting through a small stack of literature, I happened to glance down and realized we were no longer standing on a trail. Thinking backward, I could not remember having followed any trail from the prairie falcons' high rise over to the snow. Oops! Had we mistakenly left the CDT? But, how? The terrain had been straightforward, offering few choices, and it precisely matched Poppa Jim's text.

"Should we backtrack to look for the CDT?" SeeHawk suggested.

"No," I decided. "Everything else has made sense, so far. The trail has to be right around here, somewhere."

Craning his gaze across the snow, SeeHawk speculated, "Did you notice if Devin and Karen had wings? That would explain how they didn't leave footprints."

"As well as, their speed."

"And, the fact of us not seeing them, even when we could see way far ahead."

"Maybe they are witches," I agreed, "but I think we should probably assume they're terrestrial. Which means, judging by how well Karen navigates, we should probably be concerned about her not coming this way."

"So, are you changing your mind about backtracking? Or, what do you want to do?"

"Hey!" I huffed. "That's the wrong response. You were supposed to say, 'Oh, poor Sunshine. Are you feeling insecure because Karen navigates better than you do, and now you look stupid for losing the trail? Don't beat yourself up, sweetheart. She's a good navigator, but, so are you.'"

SeeHawk stared at me, in complete bewilderment.

"I mean, can't you butter me up, sometimes?" I explained. "It's not easy being a Chief Navigation Officer at times like this."

Backpedaling immediately, he apologized, "No, no, Sunshine. I have complete confidence in whatever you say. Sorry, I shouldn't have opened my big mouth. Go ahead and lead us wherever you think is best. You're doing a fine job."

"Okay, that's overkill," I laughed, poking him in the ribs. "I was just pulling your leg. For sure, it's disturbing to not see their footprints, but maybe they just pulled off the trail to eat lunch and came back a different way."

SeeHawk frowned a little, not buying my theory.

Pulling out Poppa Jim's directions again, I read a passage describing cross-country travel around Summit 8655, possibly following trail markers.

Thinking out loud, I asked SeeHawk, "Does not seeing the markers mean we might be on a different trail from what Jim took?"

"When were those directions published?" SeeHawk asked.

"Two years ago."

"Then, you could be right."

"Although, it's possible the markers are just hidden underneath this snow," I added.

Perusing the text further, I singled out many potential landmarks, including a deep cirque containing Bighorn Lake, a spur ridge, Caribou Peak, a gravelly descent, and a footpath disappearing near the Valley of the Moon. Altogether, the guidebook provided a loose description of a loosely arranged landscape, which made perfect sense but left me feeling confused. In an effort to start somewhere, I tried to focus on specifics. Was the burned valley ahead, and beyond the snow, Poppa Jim's cirque? Was the minor peak on our left Caribou Peak? Or part of the spur ridge? Not feeling sure, I noticed that we were supposed to lose track of a trail while approaching the Valley of the Moon. Also, we were supposed to descend steeply. Suddenly, I realized the valley's rim resembled a moon crater if I ignored its burned trees. Also, its surrounding terrain looked moonlike. A comparison between the valley and our map's topographical lines almost gave me confidence, but not quite. There were too many angles and not enough landmarks. I felt tired and hungry. We were overdue for lunch. The wind's constant noise made it hard to think. We were still 2-miles away from exiting the crest.

Heavy Glue

Clouds were piling in that could storm at any moment. It was no fun reading the same directions over and over again. Even though I knew better than to act in haste, I pocketed our maps and asked SeeHawk to follow me across the snow.

Looking doubtful, he fell into step behind me.

Of course, my purpose was to find the CDT. I was hoping to find it immediately after stepping off the snow. I remained hopeful and, sure enough. A dry trail fetched us right off the snow. Furthermore, it aimed straight toward the valley. Which was great, right? My assumption had been correct. So, why did I feel surprised?

SeeHawk followed me to the valley's rim, where we leaned forward together, sharing a moment of surprise.

The valley did not contain anything green. Nor was it empty. In fact, it was full of burned trees, reaching all the way down to a pretty blue lake resting at the very bottom. Sturdy switchbacks descending toward the lake seemed to match what our guidebook described.

Putting two and two together, SeeHawk rejoiced, "Way to locate the CDT, Chief Navigator! Pardon moi for doubting your most excellent judgment. I was just feeling anxious to escape from that horrible wind."

I still felt skeptical, but SeeHawk's praise spurred me to quit thinking altogether. It was as if I had gotten bumped on the head or drunk some hallucinogenic creek water. Downhill, he and I went, without first deciding whether we were approaching Bighorn Lake or entering the Valley of the Moon.

Soon, a resurgence of doubts caused me to mutter, "This descent is starting to look awfully steep."

SeeHawk responded, "Yep, just like Poppa Jim says."

Wait, what? Had my partner paid attention when I read him the directions?

"It's got to be the CDT," he went on recalling, "because the only thing missing is the trail markers, and you already explained why they're missing."

Holy Toledo! Here was proof that my partner could be taught to help me co-navigate! Witnessing his potential inspired me enough to quit caring where we were going. I just wanted to enjoy being part of a team.

As a team, we accelerated faster down the switchbacks. I was feeling a little winded when it occurred to me that the valley must not have looked like a moon before it burned. Had somebody changed its name, after the fire? Thinking backward, I realized we had never been told to enter the Valley of the Moon. Poppa Jim had only mentioned peeking into it.

Spinning around, I halted SeeHawk with a look.

He whimpered unhappily, "No way, can I climb back to the top before we eat."

The overhead clouds were starting to look darker. Too bad, I thought, because skinny hikers need frequent refills. Fortunately, our assigned lunch was PBC sandwiches (graham crackers stuffed with peanut butter and dark chocolate), which could easily be eaten on two feet.

One hour later, we regained the snowfield, now approaching it from an opposite angle. Lo and behold, there it was! A half-buried wooden sign stood, poking out of the snow. It should have been easy to spot from any direction. What the heck? Why had we failed to see it the first time? Lethargy? Snowblindness? In any case, what did the sign SAY? Stepping up to get a closer look, we found that it said, yes! There was the CDT's southbound turnoff.

"Duh George," I blushed.

"Oopsie-daisy," SeeHawk rolled his eyes.

"Bonkers."

Well, at least, we could celebrate being back in the race.

SeeHawk followed me onto a weather-beaten footpath, faintly approaching another, shallower valley. The new valley's rim seemed to match Poppa Jim's description, but not entirely. Instead of supplying switchbacks, its entry plunged down a gravelly drop, toward nothing that looked like any moon. In fact, it was floored with living pine and fir trees, verdantly framing another small lake. However, if moons are strange, then "Valley of the Moon" was a proper title, because, jeepers! The CDT cut straight through the lake. Meaning, we could see its tread heading underwater, but not follow it without swimming or jumping into a boat.

"Is this somebody's idea of a practical joke?" SeeHawk frowned.

"Maybe aliens have a weird sense of humor," I shrugged.

Anyway, we decided to walk around the lake, regretfully trampling its fragile vegetation, but only for a moment. Then, we came to our senses. ripped off our clothes, and did what lakes are made for doing.

Never mind, if Devin and Karen were getting farther ahead. Today's whole race had turned into a false alarm. No storms were happening. We had plenty of time.

While swimming ashore, I told SeeHawk "From now on, I promise, I'll read our maps better. I'll keep wearing my thinking cap, even when I feel lazy."

"Okay," he nodded, "and from now on, I hereby give you permission to veto anything I say about navigation.

"Ooh, can I get that in writing?" I teased him.

"Here's a coupon," he replied, giving me a fat kiss.

* * *

Several miles past the Valley of the Moon, evening time's low sun watched SeeHawk and I get trapped inside another massive burn. We needed to pitch camp, but all the flat spots we could find rested between dead trees that looked ready to fall if a camper snored.

My mind resurrected a two-year-old memory, of having once heard a tree fall on the Pacific Crest Trail. Its descent had not been announced by any Hollywood-style splintering noises. It had just crashed straight down. BAM! Tough luck for anything too slow to move out of the way.

Now, as we wandered through a maze of fragile deadwood, I had to admit. Any slightest breeze would have scared me into saying we had to exit the burn before making camp. My only rationale for stopping sooner was that the afternoon's windstorm seemed blown itself out, like a child sleeping after a long tantrum. The ensuing calm felt stagnant by comparison. It was as if the air had ceased to exist. Every now and then, I took a deep breath just to break the tension and feel my lungs work.

Such utter calm could have kept everything silent while we pitched camp. Instead, somehow, the dead and motionless trees uttered spooky creaking noises, as if practicing how to say "timber" before putting the word to use. Many were covered with bullet-sized woodpecker holes that showed off their deadness. Others leaned at precarious angles or lay collapsed across heaps of their fallen relatives. Silhouetted, those that remained standing turned the melting sun into an egg yolk getting pressed through an egg-slicer.

Our tent only had room for one occupant to change clothes at a time, so I crawled inside first. Without asking, I knew See-Hawk would march away to find a food-hanging tree. If I overheard him sighing in the distance, that would mean his rope had snagged over a high branch and would not fall back down for him to catch it. On this particular evening, though, his motive for sighing was not finding any branches, because the dead trees had lost them.

After changing into my nightclothes, I stowed my day clothes, toothbrush, and headlamp into handy tent pockets, the same way as always.

When SeeHawk returned, he felt eager to begin his usual routine of "washing" his feet and face with a wet bandanna handkerchief, before slipping into the long silk underwear he used for jammies.

Normally, SeeHawk's washing commotion sent me into our tent's open vestibule, where I fixed hot soup with ghee, or hot chocolate with peanut butter, before cooking dinner. However, this particular evening's late warmth lured me out to a burnt log, where I set water to boil for cream-of-mushroom soup and started scribbling notes in my daily journal.

SeeHawk stashed a bag of drinking water on his side of the tent, before climbing outside to join me for dinner. Once he got situated, he began sifting through nine different flavors of maps and guidebooks, searching for descriptions of the coming day's hike. After assembling them, he began stacking them into order, for whenever I might get around to reading them.

Phantom breezes tried to sneak by us, unnoticed, but we could hardly miss hearing the dead trees whistle. Sometimes, we also heard loud crackling noises, even though nothing appeared to be moving.

After extinguishing our stove's blue flame, it was time to chow down on spicy peanut-sauced pasta. The challenge was not to head-butt each other while leaning over our shared pot, and not to splash hot rice noodles onto our laps.

That evening's dinner theatre featured four industrious ants, comically demonstrating why pilfering bits of noodle required more than teamwork. Not far away, stood a dark brown moth, trying to tow a white moth back to its kitchen, or else prepping it for burial.

When both of us finished eating, SeeHawk loosened the pot's last food scraps with his index finger and drank the dirty dishwater.

Meantime, I bagged whatever food would not fit into our bear canister. Therefore, I was preoccupied when a sharp pain caused me to shriek, "EEEAUGH! Not AGAIN!"

This time, the tick was biting my leg! Yanking it loose, I hurled it asunder, legs still wiggling. Where was something heavy? I used my water bottle to pound it, flat. Deader than a doornail. Blotto. Kaput.

Glancing suspiciously around the burned woods, I recalled my previous tick bites and briefly wondered. Was there any connection? Had this tiny messenger from the Devil been trying to warn me that SeeHawk and I might get crushed in our sleep? Ha-ha. No way. It was just a tick bite. We did not need to repack our whole camp and relocate in the dark.

As expected, nighttime passed uneventfully. Although, just before dawn, we awoke to the sound of hooves snapping branches next to our tent.

SeeHawk peeked outside and gasped, "Why didn't we see that mud puddle last night? It's only twenty yards away!"

Talk about feeling guilty. If thirsty deer needed to come within a stone's throw of our tent, we were probably trespassing upon the only water source for miles around.

It might have felt good to fall back asleep, but before we could relax, our wristwatch alarm chirped at 6:00 a.m. Ready or not, we had to hop to it. Nature was imploring us to start pawing over and around each other, searching for jackets and shoes, so we could exit the tent before our sphincters gave way.

Once outside, we ran in separate directions. The first task was urgently hunting for rock shovels. Sometimes, uprooting a small rock exposed an entire ant colony. Other times, a bit of tugging revealed we had grabbed an immovable boulder.

The absent sun seemed to be sleeping in. Well, who could blame it? The cold before dawn sent us diving back into our tent, where we both tried to change clothes at the same time.

Being the smaller occupant, I scooted backward to give See-Hawk extra space for pulling flailing arms through his shirt's wrinkled sleeves. Unfortunately, the tent's diagonal ceiling blocked me from scooting completely out of his way.

"Sunshine, could you just—?" he growled between flails.

"I'm trying. Could you hold on a minute?" I begged on repeat.

While ducking away from his back-jabbing elbows, I managed to slip on several shirts and leave the tent without any black eyes. My finished costume included pockets bulging full of hard candy, sunscreen, Chapstick, our compass, and thickly-wadded guidebook pages. SeeHawk's kangaroo pouch always bulged much larger, containing who-knows-what items he might not even have known were in there.

Our tent strike came next, followed by brushing teeth with gag-flavored tooth powder, a good-morning kiss, and finally saying, "Thank you, spot," to our latest home for the night.

In regards to all of the above, June 29 began like any other morning on the trail.

Our first goal of the morning was to refill several water bags at Alice Creek. There was a turnoff coming up in a few miles, from which we could reach the creek by detouring seven miles around an unfinished section of the CDT. The high route was slated to tag Blowout Mountain, before banking a ninety and dropping into a saddle called Lewis and Clark pass. We would have preferred staying high, but we did not have enough water left to withstand serious route-finding challenges.

The burn's end gave way to an utterly bald crest. Our legs had not shifted past third gear before the morning's heat began to feel intense. One long glance backward showed us the Chinese Wall, diminished to a smidgen of rock, wedged between ninety miles' worth of miniature mountains. That surprise kept us talking, while we strode between exotic green gentian plants, whose lime-green flower cones wore tutus of sword-shaped leaves.

The turnoff to Alice Creek was flagged with buttercups, decorating the mouth of an old dirt road that dove steeply off the crest. Much to our surprise, the junction was marked with a brand spanking new CD-sign, encouraging hikers to head on over and check out the new high trail.

"Seems like there's been some construction here, since Poppa Jim wrote his guidebook," I surmised.

Catching my drift, SeeHawk objected, "But, we're almost out of water and we know there'll be water at Alice Creek."

"In addition to a thousand-foot drop, waiting to laugh at us when we have to climb back up to Lewis and Clark Pass," I informed him.

"A thousand feet?" he whimpered. "Suddenly, that high trail is looking pretty scenic."

"It is," I agreed, "but keep in mind that I only have one sip of water left."

"I have about three sips," he reported.

"Plus, we don't know for sure if the spring at Lewis and Clark Pass will be flowing."

"So, what are you trying to say, Sunshine? Should we head down this road, or keep going?"

"No idea. I'm just giving you the facts, pro and con."

"Mm-hm, but how do you interpret those facts?"

"You mean, what do I personally think we should do?"

"Yes. What does our highly esteemed Chief Navigator personally recommend?"

"She recommends the Sauvignon Blanc. But, if you're talking about choosing between the low road and high road, that's a tough call. Maybe our CNO should punt, and forward this question to our Chief Water Officer."

"Our Chief Water Officer is vacationing in the Bahamas."

"Really? Could we call him on the phone?"

"If we called, he would probably say he'll accept whatever verdict you recommend, as long as it's wet and there's a lot of water.

"Okay, then, what do you think our Pack Mule would say?"

"He'd probably vote for Alice Creek, but you know mules, they're kind of shortsighted. "

Suddenly, my tongue felt desperately dry. Right then and there, I needed to drink water.

"Can I finish my last sip?" I begged SeeHawk.

Looking surprised, he grunted, "You don't need my permission to drink your own water, Sunshine."

"Yes, I do," I corrected him, "because if I get thirsty after I run out, I'll need to beg for yours, so you would have to be okay with that."

Before he could answer, my last sip went down the hatch. Poof! It was gone because I simply could not wait any longer. Ahh, and wow, it tasted delicious, like a really good appetizer.

Rolling his eyes, SeeHawk reached out and handed me his water teat.

Gratefully, I took another small sip, leaving the two last sips for him.

"It sure would be nice to have a cold *Cherry Pepsi* right about now," I sighed.

"Or a cold *Cherry Coke*," he agreed.

Despite being essentially out of water, we decided to gamble upon taking the new high trail. Within a matter of yards, we were given a red-carpet welcome, starting with velvety purple delphiniums, and then, baby blue forget-me-nots, more yellow buttercups, and more green gentians. Progress along the crest kept changing our perspective until the mountains shrinking behind us revealed their snowy northern faces.

Where the CDT grazed Blowout Mountain's shoulder, it vaulted a rocky high point dribbled with lodgepole pine trees. From there, it dipped through a smear of thirst-defying grass, and even passed sprays of pink shootingstar lilies whose gaiety seemed to say, *Keep going, team. It's a beautiful day for taking chances.*

I smiled because it truly was a fine morning. I would have enjoyed sprouting wings, flying 2,000-feet off the crest, and splashing my toes through a couple of sideline lakes, which shined provocatively in the distance below.

Upon reaching the new trail's end, without having dropped onto our knees from thirst, we descended into loose timber overlooking Lewis and Clark Pass.

Feeling greatly relieved, SeeHawk threw up his hands and sang, "Score one for the high trail, baby! Great job, Chief Navigator. Way to make the right choice."

Laughing, I reminded him, "We just got lucky."

Moohaha! I imagined the dead tick saying. *Hello, my pretties. Wasn't that easy? Watch out for bliss and don't get cocky.*

A large historical sign marked where thirsty thru-hikers could boomerang from Lewis and Clark Pass down to a nearby spring.

Leaving the crest felt like a journey back in time. Our shoes wobbled over fat mud-ridges created by pioneers' wagons 200 years earlier. Which is to say, wagon ruts older than *Little House on the Prairie* had withstood two hundred years' worth of rain and thawing snow. This tangible experience of history made us wonder. How had the Continental Divide looked back in 1804 when President Thomas Jefferson commissioned Captains Meriwether Lewis and William Clark to find a waterborne trade route between the Louisiana Purchase territories and the Pacific Ocean?

SeeHawk and I had read some of the region's history. We knew that both captains, traveling with their 26-man Corps of Discovery (including volunteers and army men), had left Saint

Louis, Missouri during May, with no idea what to expect west of the Continental Divide. Our book said members of the Corps had been satisfied with a wage of $5 per month, in addition to receiving a land grant upon their successful return. The expedition had included a French trader and his Shoshoni Indian wife, Sacajawea, who facilitated communication with the local Native Americans. Their first batch of food supplies had included 50 kegs of meat, 14 barrels of cornmeal, 20 kegs of flour, sugar, salt, coffee, dried apples, biscuits, and 100 gallons of whiskey (some for drinking and some for trading). They had eaten 5-7 pounds of fresh buffalo meat per day, while traveling 15-20 daily miles up the Missouri River, hauling a 55-foot keelboat, with a 29-ton capacity, which could be sailed, rowed, or towed upstream by hand-ropes. The costumes they wore for hauling their keelboat had been long linen frocks or fatigue jackets, with snug trousers, tarred gaiters, and wool caps, tall riding boots, half-high leather boots, or soft-soled moccasins. Comparing all of this with our own outfits and supplies made SeeHawk and me feel, not only privileged but also, futuristic.

We had no problem finding the spring promised in Poppa Jim's guidebook. It was spraying straight out of the Continental Divide, as if from a broken wall pipe. Refilling our water bags only took seconds, after which we did an about-face and marched right back up to Lewis and Clark Pass.

It was just after noontime when we reached a loose shale peak, almost too steep to be climbed wearing backpacks. Charging straight up to its 360-degree view, we paused at the top to admire a circumference of white gift-bow clouds, capping pink-tinted mountains, which floated airily upon supporting green forests. No roads or towns, or even a single rooftop, could be seen anywhere in the distance. We might have been seeing a view similar to what Captains Lewis and Clark saw two centuries earlier.

Descending from the overlook, pint-sized cairns led us down to an unmarked footpath. There, I perceived a choice, which made me stop to look around.

As SeeHawk pulled up behind me, he opened his mouth wide and exhaled a big, glassy-eyed yawn.

"Cairns or footpath?" I asked him.

"Huh?" he mumbled.

Well, shucks. How could I blame him for not paying attention? The sun's constant glare was weighing upon our eyes. The afternoon's heat was making us both feel groggy. It was that sleepy time of the afternoon which SeeHawk often liked to call "heavy glue."

I felt sluggish too, but Chief Navigating Officers must always be on duty. Therefore, I dutifully reread Poppa Jim's directions. Essentially, we needed to descend more-or-less southward, while staying on or near the crest. There was no mention of cairns or any specific footpath.

"This might be a deer trail," SeeHawk suggested.

"Maybe," I agreed. "So, what's worse? Possibly going the wrong way on a deer path? Or, possibly going the right way, following cairns that we know will end because they always do?"

"You just answered your own question," he replied.

Cairns, it was.

Descending briefly through a sparse section of forest, we entered a small meadow ringed with shade trees. Sure enough, partway across the meadow, we ran out of cairns. It happened early enough that we could still have turned around and gone back to explore the deer trail. But, did we? Or course, not. Instead, we allowed ourselves to be lured across the meadow by the promise of more shade trees. From where they ended, we strolled across another meadow, and so forth, as if we were not on a tight schedule and mistakes could be taken lightly.

A few meadows in, we happened upon an explosive spring, gushing straight out of the grass, as if from an underground fire hydrant. This discovery gave us a wake-up call because neither of our guidebooks mentioned any spring.

"Are we lost?" SeeHawk inquired.

I answered him by pointing toward a manmade trail, whose aim just happened to coincide with ours.

"Whoa," he grinned.

"Pshht," I warned him, "Don't jump to any conclusions before we make sure." However, I soon admitted to thinking we were on the CDT. "But, only by dumb luck," I insisted, for superstitious reasons.

"Dumb or smart, this means we'll be able to pick up my sneakers tomorrow," he beamed.

"Only if we hike fast and don't make any wrong turns," I cautioned him.

Late in the afternoon, we followed a flat jeep road up to a small dome-shaped peak, which presented us with another riddle. Poppa Jim advised climbing over the peak, but a new looking CD-sign told us to circle it. We decided to trust the new CD-sign, and were rewarded with a lovely jeep road, circling the dome beneath cooling shade trees. Everything seemed to be going smoothly, until the jeep road ended, in a place that made no sense for either jeeps or hikers.

"What were we thinking?" I swore, adding some unprintable punctuation. "Never EVER disregard Poppa Jim."

By this time, we had circled far enough around the dome that our best option was just to keep going and traverse around across its backside. The rear slope was sandy, brushy, extremely steep, and curved just enough to keep us blind the whole way.

Waxing philosophical, I remarked, "At least we're not the only boneheads who ended up back here."

SeeHawk examined another set of footprints stamped through the sand ahead of us, but he could not profess to know who had made them.

Upon regaining the CDT, we climbed onto a ridge scored by another jeep track. Its parallel ruts guided us onto a narrower ridge, whose handover jeep track led us to a red-painted iron gate, inset with two wagon wheels, in front of which we stopped and stared in surprise. The gate stood alone. As in, there was no fence attached to the gate. It just stood by itself, offering us a choice to go around, either to the right or left.

"This trail is weird," I muttered, for lack of a better explanation.

"Very weird," SeeHawk agreed while following me around to the right.

Yet another jeep track led us up a rocky peak. Its switchbacks were narrow but quite sturdy. Midway up the climb, I started to feel a little nervous about the sun's low angle. Could we still hope to reach Rogers Pass and climb another 1,200-feet before dark?

SeeHawk kept glancing from side to side, trying to spot any place flat with a food-hanging tree.

I had to flog him along, by sternly reminding him, "If we don't hurry, the Marysville post office might close before we get there and leave us stranded all weekend without your sneakers."

"Say no more," he nodded and took off like a racehorse.

Struggling to catch up, I followed him over a low ridge, beyond which we dropped onto a precipice overlooking a dark forest. Rogers Pass had to be straight below. We knew it was down there, but the forest hiding everything in between blocked us from seeing Highway 200.

According to Poppa Jim's guidebook, dropping straight down to the highway would have been slow going and possibly dangerous. Instead, we were advised to follow a ridge of some kind sideways, toward a cairn marking a descent with fewer trees. Did this directive mean we needed to turn around and climb back onto the ridge we had just come over? The Book of Beans mentioned cairns and survey stakes. Where were they? We saw nothing poking up from the ridge's visible skyline. Nevertheless, we could easily imagine where Poppa Jim meant to send us. Instead of climbing back uphill, though, could we just traverse sideways, in hopes of intercepting the descent? Our only deterrent was a lone snow patch guarding the adjacent forest's entrance. Lots of trees standing below the snow could catch us if we slipped, but, argh. Late evening was a bad time for undertaking new adventures. Did we need to just buck up and climb back onto the ridge? Feeling undecided, my brain got stuck wondering what to do. Nothing entered my head for so long that, after a while, it began to feel ridiculous. Heavy glue was setting in again. SeeHawk and I needed to hurry, but we could not seem to act.

Suddenly, the skylight dimmed several notches, signaling the sun's disappearance.

SeeHawk hardly noticed any change, because his eyes were trained upon a flock of black crows making a great commotion with its 15-20 pairs of wings all flapping toward us.

"Is that a BALD EAGLE?" he exclaimed, squinting toward one of the silhouettes.

"I don't know," I replied. "How can you tell the difference between an eagle and a crow when they're all far away?"

SeeHawk started blathering about wing-shapes and wing-spans.

My eyes drifted across all the flapping wings, trying to find one pair that looked different from the others. As the flock approached the ridge behind us, I spied a minuscule bump peeking up from the ridge's skyline.

"Is that a cairn?" I squealed.

SeeHawk remained so fixated on the eagle that it took him a moment to comprehend why I was shouting.

"It is! Hooray! That has to be a cairn!"

When it sunk in that the eagle had found our trail, SeeHawk became agog with gratitude.

Once we climbed back onto the ridge, it was easy to spot a trail of cairns heading in the direction we wanted to go. The cairns led us over to some robust switchbacks, providing a safe descent toward Rogers Pass. By this time, the sky was fading toward gray. We started off descending between Douglas fir trees, gangly Jeffrey pines, and weather-beaten lodgepole pines thinly covered with dust. Lower downhill, most of the trees stepped back to make room for red and yellow sunflowers, leafing green snowberry, gooseberry, beargrass, lupins, Oregon grape, cow parsnips, common junipers, flowering red columbines, goldenrods, geraniums, yarrow, knapweed, pearly everlasting, purple asters, mullein, and pink wild roses. Altogether, the flowers seemed to be having a last hurrah before dusk would snuff out their colors for the night.

It was a happy moment when we finished descending and there found a huge CD-sign shouldering Highway 200.

"One last climb," I promised SeeHawk, "If we can finish before dark, we shouldn't have any problem reaching the post office tomorrow, weather regardless, knock on wood."

"Great, so now what?" he asked.

Straight across the highway, we saw a solid wall of trees.

"Er, well, we just need to find the southbound CD-sign," I muttered. "How strange, that it's not straight across from here."

Feeling unsure which direction to turn, we ventured a short distance toward the left, and then, a short distance toward the right, peeking as far as we could around the highway's gradual curves. There was no time to waste. With a big climb ahead and the sky getting dark, we needed to find the southbound sign, pronto. So, where the heck was it?

Eventually, frustration drove SeeHawk to ask, "Could we just camp down here and knock off the climb early tomorrow morning? Or, would that put us at risk for missing the post office?"

"You want to camp inside the coldest pocket of shade in the Continental United States?" I asked him.

"Say no more," he nodded.

We needed to search farther toward one side or the other, so, after a moment of debate, we decided to gamble on turning right. It took several minutes of walking along the highway's narrow shoulder to discover that, phew, we had made a lucky guess. The southbound CD-sign was well hidden amongst the highway's opposite trees.

Within a few minutes of dashing across the pavement, we ran into a creek flowing through a jungle of aspen trees, alder bushes, willows, and wild strawberry plants. Being in a hurry forbade us from staying for supper, but we could not resist slurping some water out of the creek like thirsty dogs, as well as indulging in a little armpit-splashing and forehead-mopping.

Feeling thoroughly refreshed, we used our last ounces of energy to climb back up to 7,000-feet, watching time roll backward all the way. It seemed like a miracle when we stepped through the timberline and saw the long-gone sun shining in full capacity. Not only had its full glory been reincarnated, but also, its goldenness turned every western mountain into silhouetted shockwaves.

Normally, camping on top of the crest might have seemed risky, but with the evening's last clouds exchanging goodbyes, we decided to go for broke and pitch our tent right then and there. Incredibly, enough daylight remained for us to watch the sun's second departure while eating Mac N' Cheese for dinner. First, the golden orb itself turned red. Then, its horizon turned black, before every cloud edging the gray sky burst into flames of orange, golden, and pink.

"This whole evening is just...like a dream," I babbled, between eating bites of macaroni. "How could the crest be so calm? And, we're still wearing t-shirts..."

"We truly are lucky," SeeHawk agreed, while absentmindedly flicking a few ticks off his socks.

Suddenly, we realized that all the grass surrounding our tent was crawling full of ticks. We had to brush the wiggly little porkers off our pants, before fleeing into our tent for the night.

Once safely zipped indoors, we stared through the tent's sloped plastic window at orange sheet-lightning flickering toward the west.

"It's just heat-lightning," I assured SeeHawk. "Nothing to make a fuss about."

Collapsing onto our backs, we instantly felt chronic exhaustion leak out of our bones.

SeeHawk fell asleep mumbling to himself, "I keep thinking I feel ticks crawling on me, but that's probably just because we saw so many outside."

* * *

The terrain south of Rogers Pass relaxed into cow pastures rolling between stands of domestic lodgepole pine trees. Nothing looked dramatically different from what SeeHawk and I had been seeing for weeks. Nevertheless, we felt transported from the realm of alpine mountains into pastoral countryside. This feeling was partially caused by an intensifying odor of sundried cow pee. Mingling with the scents of airborne dust and fragrant grass, it collected inside our sinuses and dripped onto the backs of our tongues, producing a flavor reminiscent of mescal or smoked tea leaves.

Accompanying the pastureland's taste were increased sightings of slatted steel cattle guards. No thru-hiker worth their salt should have shied away from hopping over a cattle guard, but yours truly always needed help. Why? Because during my youth, I had accidentally jumped through a playground's tire bridge, creating a trust issue that was hard to shake. Consequently, every cattle guard south of Rogers Pass obligated me to whimper until SeeHawk stopped and held out his arm.

He always obliged, but with his usual reminder, "You should try crossing these on your own, Sunshine, so you'll learn how to do it without my help."

Okay, but in all fairness, I never leaned on SeeHawk's arm. I just touched it lightly for a spatial reference, the same way I sometimes touched blades of river grass, for help with crossing tippy logs.

We spent the rest of the afternoon crossing more cow pastures decked with toasting grass. Stratocumulus clouds stippled the lazy sky. One golden field contained a natural spring boxed inside an A-framed log fence. Outside the fence rested an open water trough, installed to service cows and wildlife.

SeeHawk and I wasted no time, peeling off our clothes. A quick splash-bath revived our spirits for squeezing in a couple of last miles. Lingering warmth kept us comfortable without making us sweat or drying our hair.

Sweet-smelling grass inspired SeeHawk to reminisce, "I remember on nights after my family finished dinner, all the kids in our neighborhood would play Ghost in the Graveyard and Ditch 'em."

"Never heard of either," I confessed.

"Ditch 'em is like tag, except bigger," he explained. "Whoever's 'It' counts to ten, while everybody else runs all over the block, trying to get away."

"All over the block?" I questioned. "Wouldn't it take forever to tag someone? I bet you had a million places to hide."

"Our neighborhood wasn't like what you're thinking," he clarified. "None of the houses where I grew up had fences."

"Whoa," I exclaimed. "That's hard for a California girl to imagine."

"Anyway, Ghost in the Graveyard has to be played after dark. It's pretty much like Ditch 'em, except you play it in somebody's yard, not the whole neighborhood, and it has to be dark so you can't see each other."

I recalled, in my turn, "Our block's kids headed over to the elementary school's front lawn, if it stayed warm after dinner, or else we just threw green almonds at each other."

"Ouch," SeeHawk shuddered.

"Yeah, almond wars weren't fun, but you should have seen our ball games. This one huge football player would march across the field with half of us hanging onto his arms and legs like monkeys. That was until he mysteriously disappeared and people started saying he murdered his grandma with an ax. I don't know if that story was true. Maybe he just went to jail or something."

Back and forth, SeeHawk and I swapped stories, until the evening's orange clouds slowly began to fade. We had no specific destination in mind. Therefore, we could afford to camp anywhere, beneath a billion or more stars creeping into the sky. Soft yellow grass made a comfortable seat for sipping hot minestrone soup with oily pesto pasta.

The air stayed warm after it got dark, lulling two weary minds into comfortable dreams until a tick sunk its mandibles into one of SeeHawk's testicles. Any man who has gotten bitten downstairs will understand what flashed through my partner's head when he bolted awake. He needed to find his headlamp. Where had he left it? Feeling around in the darkness, he could not find anything round with straps. Giving up for the moment, he tried to pinch the little ball-biter between his fingers, but it was difficult to feel until his fingers caught hold. One focused yank ripped Satan's tiniest minion out from hiding in the pubic forest. Now, SeeHawk needed to open our tent's sticky door-zipper. How could he accomplish that with one hand? Trying and failing, he went back to groping around for his headlamp. Finally, he found it, only to realize that twisting the dial would have required two hands. Growing desperate, he dropped the headlamp and resumed battling the zipper. When virtue prevailed, out went Mister Pervie, flattened like a frisbee flying into the darkness.

By the time I woke up, SeeHawk was busy inspecting a pinhead-sized hole in his testicle.

The next thing I knew, the sun was rising. It was July 1st. That was obvious. Our brains began to boil before we ate breakfast. Such early heat usually summoned thunderstorms, but today we did not care. Hooray. Hurrah. We were on our way to Marysville.

Setting a good pace along flat dirt roads, we sang, to the tune of "Row, Row, Row Your Boat."

*Hike, hike, hike the trail
under sunny skies.
We are off to get the mail,
for our re-supplies.*

Normally, SeeHawk and I could tell we were getting near a town by seeing windblown litter, broken glass, domestic weeds, barbed wire fences, utility lines, railroad tracks, car-tire tracks, and drainage ditches. We were not expecting Marysville to be a metropolis, but Forest Road 136 looked so tidy that we started wondering who lived in the town.

Plenty of time remained for reaching the post office before they closed. We had no reason to rush, so we decided to sit down and eat breakfast beside the road. While munching on cold banana granola, we got startled by a car rolling into view. Its riders were two men in the front seat, and one in the back sitting with a young boy. They were just out for a drive, judging by how slowly the car was moving.

Suddenly, SeeHawk and I stopped chewing and ducked. A pellet gun was sticking out the car's rear window. Its barrel slowly traced a line across our foreheads! Breathing hard, we needed a moment to recover before realizing it was okay. The boy in the back seat was just hunting squirrels.

Jeffrey and I spent the rest of our walk to Marysville practicing heat tolerance. No amount of shade could have kept us cool. There was little to look at besides trees and more trees. The first evidence of town was a giant two-story house, guarded by stately cottonwood trees, preceding a block of summer cottages.

Unnatural silence hung over the town's main drag. There were no engine hums. No machines whining. Not even a banter of faraway voices. Visually, too, the center of town looked abandoned. Nobody was doing any building repair or construction work. In the town's modest suburbs, there were no retirees lounging on shady porches. None of the houses we passed smelled like frying bacon, or roasting garlic, or frozen pizza coming out of the oven. In fact, many of the town's peripheral buildings were just collapsing miners' shacks. There were also a good number of modern houses, but some had backyards landscaped with rusting cars, unremoved tree stumps, and propane tanks. Altogether, it looked like we were walking into a ghost village, either vacated by some historic catastrophe or gutted by an old-fashioned bank robbery.

The real story of Marysville had begun during the late 1800s. Back then, an Irish immigrant's discovery of gold had triggered a population boom that reached almost 5,000 residents. Urban expansion had then added two railroads, three newspapers, several saloons, an astonishing variety of churches, a large schoolhouse, an opera house, and a tailor to help dress up the town. Prosperity reigned until the 1950s, when the Drumlummon Mine closed and sent most local residents packing. Henceforth, the town's cobblestone and Barnwood storefronts had spent half a century vacantly staring through openings that should still have been windows. Above the abandoned stores sat a few modern billboards, spouting irrelevant messages. Nobody was using the coin-operated telephone, which meant SeeHawk and I could be first in line.

While striding up the town's main street, we spied a paper plate advertising "cabin" above hand-sketched flowers.

"Maybe whoever owns the cabin can give us directions to the post office," I reasoned.

We turned and soon reached a gingerbread-type house. The front porch held a wide-eyed toddler curiously watching our approach.

Feeling silly, we asked the toddler slowly, "Can...you...tell us....how...to get...to the post office?"

The little boy frowned and ran into his house.

Out came a young mom, pretty enough to stop a train. While scooping up her boy, she cheerfully asked, "Can I help you?"

Not surprisingly, proprietor Linda was eager to show us Marysville's only guest lodge. She took us inside to see her "cabin's" clawfoot bathtub, ornate bed, fancy soaps, and well-stocked kitchen, plus a shelf full of books about Montana. The clincher was promising to do our laundry overnight. Hooey, that was naïve. Our clothes were two weeks into an odor that even smelled gross to us. With the next southward town being nine days away, we had to accept, before Linda could change her mind. However, first, we asked her for directions to the post office.

Linda sourly warned us, "Don't go inside, whatever you do. Just stay on the porch and ask them to bring your package out. The place really smells."

SeeHawk and I chuckled, "Worse than us?"

"Trust me, it's bad," she emphasized.

Well, maybe, but, in terms of cute points? Marysville's homespun post office took the cake. Its whitewashed front porch was decorated with Fourth of July ribbons, potted pansies, and a miniature Dutch windmill. How could such a charmer ever be called smelly? SeeHawk and I found out when we opened the front door. Whoosh! Out came a blast of airborne mouse urine that practically forced breakfast into our throats. Proceeding anyway, we got escorted into the lobby by an adorable 88-year old woman named Ruby, and her thirtyish-looking daughter, Marilyn, who both looked unaware of anything smelling bad. Their lobby was hardly large enough to hold a table and chair. Nevertheless, right in its middle sat our giant resupply box, getting used as a dining table for Ruby's half ham-sandwich and daily *Pepsi Cola*. She had been eating on our box for the whole past month because it would not fit into her usual storage area.

Ruby wore a crayon-striped smock with bright blue sweatpants and shin-high boots. Her eyes fairly laughed when she sweetly asked, "Are you coming to take away my table?"

As it turned out, the postmistress and her daughter loved receiving mail for thru-hikers, because it gave them more business. In fact, the post office needed revenue so badly that sometimes Ruby sold stamps to a neighboring post office, just to stay afloat.

SeeHawk and I wanted to help, so we mailed off a few unplanned postcards, before escaping back to our cabin's sunny porch.

It felt extravagant to cook home-dried Asian noodle soup on an electric stove, and then pour it into individual serving bowls. Never mind needing to discard a couple handfuls of green tofu jerky.

Later that evening, we bathed like royalty in the cabin's clawfoot bathtub. Then, we got down to business, organizing a new stack of loose guidebook pages and maps, which kept us awake into the wee hours of the night.

The next morning, Linda offered to drive us back to the CDT. Since visiting Marysville had been a side trip, we could accept her offer without any qualms. Only after climbing into Linda's pickup truck did we find out she was a closet drag racer. Our skulls nearly bashed the cab's side windows, while flying over bumps in the graded dirt road. Thank goodness, it was a short ride. We stepped back into the heart of cattle country feeling recharged for another day of hiking.

* * *

SeeHawk and I felt excited to get back on the CDT, but we could not take off quickly with our backpacks fully loaded. Nine days' worth of food plus all the tap water our screw-lidded bags could hold was enough to be daunting, and that was not all. Add an extra sack of bagels and a bottle of juice from Linda, plus several bags of corn chips strapped onto our backpacks, and how did SeeHawk and I look? Like a couple of mobile snack vendors being crushed by our own inventory.

My legs kept threatening to buckle during our first hour of crossing rolling cow pastures. Fortunately, the terrain stayed mostly flat. We did not need to hurry because nothing in the sky looked threatening. Our only major concern was failing to have found Poppa Jim's updates in our resupply box.

"Still not getting the updates means you didn't just drop them into the wrong box, while I was puking in our hammock," I told SeeHawk.

Feeling guilty anyway, he suggested, "Maybe they got sucked into a black hole."

"Maybe so," I agreed. "Anyway, for this leg, it means we'll need to follow the Book of Beans more often."

"Which is almost like not having directions," SeeHawk sighed.

"Actually," I conceded, "the Book of Beans gives plenty of details for this next section. The problem is, they recommend a new route that sounds super confusing. I'm torn about whether to try it or just stick with Poppa Jim's old route."

Nothing got decided before we reached a freshly installed CD-sign, telling us to merge onto an old jeep road. Feeling encouraged by the new sign, we entered a scraggly pine forest in which the jeep road handed us off to another jeep road, which intersected another jeep road, and so forth. Eventually, we came across a historical meeting site used by Montana's Freemasons during 1862.

Poppa Jim's guidebook talked about three stone posts being grouped in a "precise east-west alignment." Spying an opportunity to play Girl Scout, I whipped out my compass, but no matter what I tried, I could not make its needle align from east to west.

"Is the needle broken?" SeeHawk suggested.

"Worse. I think it's operator error."

"Oh boy," he groaned. "I hope we aren't heading into banjo country."

"Well, if you're worried, next time we're in camp, why don't you read the user's manual and enlighten me?"

"Oh no," he laughed. "I'm just a pack mule. We only read manuals written in horse language."

Beyond the Freemason's meeting site, The Book of Beans gave explicit directions for southbound hikers. We were supposed to expect little or no signage, lots of distracting trails, and difficulty figuring out if we were going the wrong way. The same text also led me to suspect that Poppa Jim's original directions were obsolete. Since we did not have his updates, it seemed like we should probably merge onto the Book of Beans route at some point, but where?

Lacking sureness, I told SeeHawk, "Let's just keep both guidebooks handy and be prepared for anything. We need to stop talking, so I can focus, or this could get messy."

Despite looking worried, SeeHawk gaily replied, "You're preaching to the choir, Sunshine. My lips are sealed." And, he happily drew a zipper across his lips.

Soon, we ran into a steep mountain preceding the Mullen railroad tunnel. There were three choices available. Either, we could bushwhack around the mountain's thickly forested baseline. Or, we could climb up aways and follow a game trail around its skinnier midsection. Or else, we could climb straight over the top, via an extremely steep, machine-cut firebreak underscoring a high-voltage power line.

The Book of Beans told us to ignore both a game trail and a visible trail, but I was not sure how those directions corresponded with the mountain.

A short debate led us to choose the firebreak because it was easy to identify.

SeeHawk summarized our choice by saying, "A bird in the hand is worth two in the...uh...er..."

"...oven, or something..." I added vaguely.

Uh-oh. We were getting drugged by heavy glue again, and that was not all. Just a few steps into the firebreak, my kneecaps started complaining that its grade was too steep. I tried to lean hard onto my trekking poles, but taking weight off my knees just crushed my wrists. Still, I kept climbing until I glanced downhill and noticed that we had only gained about 50-feet of elevation. Crud. There was a lot more mountain left above us than below. Was it time to retreat and circle through the baseline forest, instead?

Before I could decide, SeeHawk called down from slightly above, "These might be Devin and Karen's shoeprints."

I climbed uphill to join him and, sure enough. His finger pointed toward two pairs of shoeprints, turning onto the kind of game trail that we were supposed to ignore. Considering that Devin and Karen were consulting Poppa Jim's updates, which we did not have, it made sense for the trail to look different from what we were reading, and also for it to diverge from the Book of Beans. Therefore, we decided to gamble on following Karen.

Turning sideways, we traversed from the firebreak into a deciduous forest whose leaf mulch immediately smothered the footprints. Still, we kept going, because the game trail soon widened into a manmade trail. Meantime, it began twisting and turning all over the place. My sense of direction got thrown out-of-whack. I did not want to waste time re-reading our directions because we were probably taking a different route anyway, but my head remained full of unanswered questions. Were we following Austin Creek? If so, would that mean we were on the CDT? Everything seemed roughly correct until we reached the old Mullen railroad tunnel, whose orientation made me wonder if the Book of Beans' author had misidentified the new CDT.

Across from the tunnel stood a matchstick pine forest, whose congested trees had never found room to grow bottom branches. Could hikers wearing backpacks squeeze through all the congestion, without getting stuck or being unable to find an exit?

The Book of Beans mentioned new trail construction, but we could not even find an old trail.

Poppa Jim said it would be difficult to follow the area's mess of trails and better to just use our compass. He supplied a heading, but without knowing precisely where he had entered the trees, I feared we might end up a bit off course.

"At least, though, Jim calls his number a 'true bearing,'" I told SeeHawk, "which, I think, means we don't need to adjust the declination. That's nice because if I accidentally twisted the dial twelve degrees the wrong way, we could end up three-quarters of a mile off course."

Upon pulling out the compass, I quit speaking and lapsed into silence because my brain felt muddled. Once again, it was that "heavy glue" time of the afternoon. Despite being past the solstice, Montana's long afternoons seemed to be getting longer. Not to mention, hotter. It was hard just to keep my legs moving throughout the afternoon. Add any kind of mental challenge and Foosh! The glue's viscosity doubled. Sometimes, it even caused me to do silly things, like tinker with adjusting our compass for declination right after I had agreed to follow a true bearing.

During this instance of me acting silly, SeeHawk passed the time peeling bark off a stick.

When his idleness grew annoying, I grumbled, "Why do you never worry about stuff that should worry you?"

He grumbled back, "Actually, I do worry. Right now, I'm worried about our water situation. You said there's a spring on the other side of Priest Pass?"

"Yes, and we'll get there soon if I don't screw this up."

"Do you want to go back and grab some water from Austin Creek, just for insurance?"

"You mean, backtrack? Of course, not."

"Is there any chance we won't find the spring?"

"Always, but, not if we don't get lost—and, if we do get lost, finding water will be the least of our worries."

"Are you trying to make me feel better?"

"No. I'm trying to get this compass heading right, so please stop breaking my concentration."

Speaking louder, SeeHawk begged, "Look, I think we should really go back to Austin Creek and play it safe, okay?"

Responding in haste, I twisted the compass into a position that felt correct and snapped its lid shut.

"No, we're good," I declared. "The heading is close to one hundred-and-fifty-five-degrees. Maybe that's not spot-on, but it's close enough for government work."

"Government workers carry radios," SeeHawk reminded me.

"Radios are for wimps."

My heart started thumping as we headed into the trees. Within 30 steps, we lost sight of the Mullen Tunnel. There was no rewind button to hit if we chickened out. Our shoes left no footprints on the forest's dry mulch. Tangles of deadfall steered us around, over and into slight hills and dales, making it nearly impossible to follow our compass heading. Sometimes, we struggled to figure out whether we were ascending or descending. Occasionally, we could only distinguish the ground's angle by feeling our backpacks lean backward or forward. Rogue sunbeams, spearing through the trees, cast psychedelic sunspots onto their flaky bark, merging repetition into a dizzying collage.

SeeHawk discovered he could freak out his eyes by staring sideways at the close-growing tree trunks while hurrying past them.

I copied his experiment and felt like I was traveling at warp speed.

Each time we climbed an imperceptible hill, the temptation to angle off-course became an experiment in awareness. Likewise, each anonymous trail popping out of nowhere challenged us to stick with our compass heading.

As the adventure wore on, lengthening shadows changed how we perceived uneven ground. When Douglas fir trees, with thick green foliage, entered the mix, it became impossible to keep track of time. A thickly mulched knoll asked us to choose between two entering trails. Both aimed more-or-less where we wanted to go. The left-hand trail dipped into spooky-looking woods, whose appearance convinced us to choose the right-hand trail. Partway up a modest incline, thinning trees admitted a faint, blue glow.

"Daylight!" SeeHawk shouted. "It looks like we're almost out of the woods!"

Four overworked eyes strained for confirmation. Sure enough, beyond the glow, we stepped into full sunlight.

SeeHawk opened his mouth to congratulate me, but I raised one hand, saying, "Not so fast. For all we know, this could be Idaho."

My gaze glissaded down a yellow grass slope. At the bottom sat a frying-pan valley, scored with a perpendicular, thin brown line.

"Is that a road?" I wondered.

SeeHawk stared where I was looking and saw nothing but yellow grass.

"It IS!" I rejoiced. "That's got to be Priest Pass!"

Accepting my word, he hooted, "You know what my Uncle Fred always says. Luck is where preparation meets opportunity."

"Normally, that could be true," I agreed, "but, in this case, I think it was mostly just luck."

"Not just any luck," he corrected me. "It was luck guided by your divine intuition, which is a form of preparation, in the sense that you've learned how to use it."

"Oh, boy," I rolled my eyes. "Earth to SeeHawk. Beam me up, Scotty."

Beyond the valley's end, we followed a livestock trail into a roomier forest, whose long-needled Jeffery pines and few-odd limber pines mingled with common lodgepole pines and stout Douglas firs. Poppa Jim's guidebook made it easy to find a fenced spring and stock trough that should have given us water. Unfortunately, though it turned out to be dismantled, as if by someone scavenging for spare parts.

"WHY do we NOT have Poppa Jim's updates?" I lamented. "Argh...well...do you think we should look for a digging rock, to see if the water table is shallow? Or, just keep going?"

Ignoring my question, SeeHawk exclaimed, "Hey, look. Here are Devin and Karen's shoeprints!"

"Really?" I laughed. "Well, if they came here, too, I guess we would have ended up here even using the updates."

Updates, schmupdates and shoeprints regardless, we still needed water for cooking dinner. With the sky overhead turning golden, I reviewed Poppa Jim's description of some upcoming "water seeps" and a cattle-fouled pond 2-3 miles ahead.

"Hm, should we drink seeps or cow pee?" I debated.

"Seeps, hands down," SeeHawk voted.

"I guess this is one of those beggars can't be choosers situations," I summarized. "Either seeps or pee sounds better than digging here with a rock."

Continuing up the wooded incline, we began to feel drained in a sluggish sort of way. We had only logged 13 miles since morning, but each mile had felt doubled by wearing freshly loaded backpacks. Neither of us felt ready to take a pop-quiz. Therefore, it was annoying to have the CDT vanish inside a meadow carpeted with tall grass. Its acreage spanned roughly the area of a football field. Dense timber walls should have made its exit obvious, but, inexplicably, there were no visible openings, all the way around. We spent ten minutes scanning every sidewall for a blaze, cairn, CD-sign, saw-cut log, or inconspicuous break in the opposite trees. When nothing emerged, finally, we split up to perform a roaming search, which ate up another ten minutes, before we discovered an exit hidden off to one side.

That first pop-quiz turned out to be one several, appearing in quick succession, each of which involved a meadow whose exit could not be found without a search. We kept our cool, but another thru-hiker coming along after us was going to spend half an hour stuck inside one meadow, shouting expletives at the top of his lungs.

The sky turned pink by the time we reached a radio-and-cellular tower flagging MacDonald Pass. Feeling relieved to be finished climbing for the day, we thirstily downed our last sips of water. A last set of switchbacks took us back downhill, with the overhead sky fading from pink to gray. Halfway down the switchbacks, we found Poppa Jim's mentioned water seeps spilling through a pair of culvert pipes underneath the trail. SeeHawk got right to work filling several empty water bags, which did not take long since "seeps" were pretty vigorous.

In the process, he mused, "I wonder if somebody installed these pipes after Jim wrote his guidebook."

"Who knows?" I shrugged, "But, next time we go into a big town, please remind me to get some *Kool-Aid* powder."

"Cherry or grape?"

"Yes, and orange."

After resealing our backpacks, it was easy to descend the rest of the way to U.S. Highway 12. Our future looked bright until SeeHawk got overexcited about crossing the highway and forgot to use his ears. He glanced both ways before stepping onto the pavement but that was all. Without noticing a blind curve on our left, he dashed into the nearest empty traffic lanes, leaving me behind.

Confusion ensued when I found myself alone. After hesitating for a moment, I hurried to catch up. Within seconds, though, two fast-moving cars whooshed around the curve, heading straight for us! Thinking fast, I grabbed SeeHawk's arm and yanked him backward. We barely got out of the way in time to avoid getting run over.

Needless to say, some words were exchanged about paying attention, whose fault our demise would have been, and humans hopefully being smarter than roadkill. But, in the end, the moment passed without harm.

Starting from the highway's far shoulder, we got busy searching for a public campground that was said to rest 2-miles down the highway. Most of the landscape in that direction was

Heavy Glue

wide-open pasture, leaving few places for a campground to hide. We walked and walked without seeing a turnoff. Nor did we see any tents, RVs, or parked cars. Finally, we gave up and just pulled into a "vista point" shouldering the highway. Which is to say, we pitched our tent beside a radio tower surrounded by cows, on a dry stretch of dirt heaped with fresh cow pies.

In the midst of unpacking, SeeHawk shrieked.

Whirling around, I saw water spill onto his camping gear and sleeping clothes.

Of all the hair-brained mistakes. His water bag's lid had come slightly unscrewed. What made the accident hair-brained was when he yanked the leaking bag out of his backpack, causing the lid to fall off completely and dump a cupful of water into my shoes!

I stared at my fiancé.

He stared at his backpack.

My stare had no effect on him since my shoes could dry out, but, horror of horrors, he had just wasted an entire bag of water!

Silken moonlight glowed through our tent while we lay with our eyes closed, waiting to fall asleep. Soon, I grew restless. Maybe one last trip outside would help me sleep better. Of course, I took a headlamp. After all, our tent was surrounded by fresh cow pies. My headlamp's yellow beam transformed the platter-sized turds into beached jellyfish or giant water blisters. Soon, it became apparent that daylight had not emphasized how much cow poop was covering the ground. Tiptoeing through the darkness seemed hazardous until my headlamp located a pie-free space in which to whiz with the wind at my back.

While squatting, I noticed a 20-foot row of yellowish dots hovering before my eyes. They looked like miniature bicycle reflectors. Shifting my headlamp toward them gave me an inkling of what I was really seeing. Nevertheless, it took another moment for me to fully catch on, because only their unblinking eyes showed through the darkness.

All the cows were seated in one neat row, watching me squat as if I was on TV. Perhaps, they had lined up outside our tent thinking it was some kind of temple or feeding station. In any case, when I stood up from squatting, Holy Cow Pies! The entire herd leaped up and bolted away, kicking dust through my headlamp's narrow beam.

The next morning, every cow was gone. Had they had all relocated to a pasture whose grass tasted more like breakfast? Regardless, the cows who had witnessed me peeing last night were probably having a hoot this morning, telling their fellow cows about having seen a glow-in-the-dark alien in their dreams.

* * *

First thing after leaving our camp beside the radio tower, SeeHawk and I visited Poppa Jim's cattle-fouled pond. After giving our water filter some exercise, we embarked upon a daylong tour of vanishing roads, forgotten trails, aimless meadows, and nebulous foothills. The route was a cakewalk in sunny weather. Plenty of trees stood by the wayside, offering to give us shade on demand. The afternoon drifted smoothly into evening, without any clouds trying to become thunderstorms.

Shortly after sundown, we rock-hopped across several shallow streams shaded by conifer trees, cottonwoods, and maples. A final climb through open sagebrush ended upon one dominant mountain, belted around its waist by a lateral jeep road. Marking the jeep road stood a weathered CD-sign, telling us to turn right. So far, so good, we thought—except, oops! Poppa Jim's directions told us to turn left.

"Old versus new CDT?" I speculated.

Cringing like usual, SeeHawk joked, "Gee, I sure wish some bonehead hadn't dropped Poppa Jim's updates into the wrong box."

"Well, you're off the hook here," I told him, "because this sign looks older than Poppa Jim's guidebook."

Visibly relaxing, he replied, "Okay, so which is it, then? Right or left?"

"I don't know," I admitted. "Right obviously looks correct at face value, but maybe turning left would lead us to a trail doubling back up higher, to give hikers more of a road-free experience."

"That's an interesting theory," he acknowledged. "What does the Book of Beans say?"

"Nothing I can match with Poppa Jim's directions, although they are pretty complicated."

"Well, we can't just stand here," he sighed. Should I pull out our *Ouija* board?"

"Definitely not," I snapped. "*Ouija* takes like an hour. And, please, don't ask me to flip a coin, either, you goofball. It's getting near camp time. We can't afford to make any wrong guesses."

Stepping backward to give me thinking space, SeeHawk started sniffing some green-tipped sagebrush.

I skimmed through Poppa Jim's directions one last time, before caving in and joking, "Do you HAVE a coin?"

His face lit up. "Actually, I have quite a few. Would you like a quarter, a nickel, or a penny?"

"WHAT?" I cried. "WHY are you carrying so many COINS, when we're supposed to be hiking lightweight? Couldn't you have traded them in for dollars? Or just given them away to someone?"

"I could have," he admitted, "but since they're in my pocket, do you want to flip one?"

"NO!" I scowled. "And stop looking like you wouldn't even care if I decided to trust a coin toss."

"Okay, okay," he chuckled, and went back to sniffing his sagebrush.

I stared hard at the weathered CD-sign.

It stared back at me, saying nothing.

"Fine," I mumbled. "Let's go with the sign because, come on, it can't be the worst decision we've ever made."

SeeHawk immediately took off, heading toward the right.

"HA-HEM!" I hollered after him. "That wasn't my final answer. I just threw it out there to see how you'd react."

"What?" He marched back, demanding to know, "Why would you do that?"

"Because my hunch is telling me to turn left, but I don't have the guts to defy an official trail sign."

"Argh. Well, do you want to go the other way, then?"

"Do you?"

"Why are you asking me?" he shrugged. "I haven't read the guidebook or seen our maps. Besides, it's your job. You're our Chief Navigator."

"I know, but right now, I can't take the heat. Maybe we really should flip that coin."

"Do you want to?"

"NO! Eesh, let's just go your way. The sign says turn right, so it can't be totally wrong, right?"

"MY way?" SeeHawk reacted. "What do you mean, my way? I only went that way because you gave me the order."

"True, but your speed indicated full congruence."

"Say WHAT?"

"You took off so fast that your subconscious mind thought it was the right way to go, which means it probably is."

"But, my hunches keep being wrong."

"Well, assuming the law of fifty-fifty applies to you, that means your odds of being right are improving every time. Look, just play along with me, okay? I'm tired of making every decision by myself. It's getting late. The directions are super confusing. I'm hungry. Therefore, I'm copping out and passing the buck."

Visibly hesitating, SeeHawk objected, "You mean, instead of employing your superior wisdom, you want to follow some clueless pack mule who doesn't worry about anything, and let him decide for you?"

"Exactly!" I laughed. "Is that better than flipping a coin?"

Weighing my comparison, he nodded, "Okay then, follow me."

Turning right at the sign, we followed a deteriorating jeep road into and out of one gully after another. If ever jeep drivers needed to test their barf-tolerance, that would have been the place. In terms of elevation, though, the jeep road stayed virtually flat, despite cutting across extremely steep terrain. We seemed to be circling a mountain, whose girth was impossible to estimate with all the gullies steering us inward and outward. Occasional gaps between the downhill trees gave us glimpses of foothills rambling into the distance. As dusk set in, we pitched our tent right in the middle of a blind curve, without fear of getting run over since the old road was clearly out-of-service. There was still enough warmth left to eat dinner in our short sleeves. Afterward, we fell asleep having no idea if we were on the old CDT, the new CDT, or just some forgotten jeep road decaying into a hiking trail.

The next morning's sun got us up early to finish circling halfway around the broad mountain. Its backside gave us a choice that demanded our full attention. Either we could continue following the same jeep road, or we could merge onto a newer, graded dirt road of unknown identity. DeLorme's atlas portrayed a whole mess of variously angled roads, all too small to be numbered and virtually inseparable from one another. After some debate, I made an executive decision to choose the road located nearest to the mountain. Soon, we began passing new-looking road signs, none of whose destinations appeared on our atlas. Hoping, nonetheless, to still be on the CDT, we kept following the same road for another several miles. Toward morning's end, we ran into a collection of rusting machinery and collapsing wooden shacks, presumably belonging to the old Monarch Mine.

"Everything has sort of matched what I expected," I told See-Hawk, "but not quite. Do you suppose Poppa Jim's route could be above us?"

"Are you saying you want to climb up and look?" he frowned.

"Maybe."

"What if it's not up there?"

"Then, we'll burn some extra calories for nothing."

"Is that a strong possibility?"

"Yes, but more likely, we might cross the trail without recognizing it."

"Ouch, double jeopardy," he acknowledged.

"I don't think that'll happen, though, if we can keep our noses to the ground and focus," I assured him. "Just, please don't look up, even if you hear hawks, eagles, and griffins screeching your name."

He promised to stay focused, as we began climbing.

My gamble gained support when we struck a perpendicular jeep road angling across the mountain. Following it briefly, we got handed over to a narrow stock trail, this time aiming straight uphill.

"Why would anyone drive pack horses straight up a mountain, where it's easy to build switchbacks?" I wondered.

"They wouldn't," SeeHawk said. "This trail must have been built for some other purpose."

Nevertheless, we jumped on board and headed straight up the grade, chewing on horse dust all the way. Within minutes, we reached a nonsensical dead-end.

"Time to turn around?" SeeHawk hinted.

"Heck no," I said. "Finding weird trails down here doesn't mean the CDT isn't up higher."

Continuing to climb, but now cross-country, we soon ran into a neatly carved, small wooden sign, clearly intended for hikers. That was encouraging, except, instead of naming any specific destination, or even having a name of its own, the sign simply said, "Trail."

Scratching my head, I complained, "WHICH trail?"

Well, of course, no matter which trail it was, now that a sign implied we were getting somewhere, we had to keep going. Turning right, we traversed southward until we felt sure of having found the new CDT.

Breakfast time soon arrived, according to one thick Douglas fir tree which offered to be our backrest. We accepted its offer, pulled off the trail, and commenced slathering gooey cashew-butter and honey onto whole-wheat crackers.

SeeHawk snuck a peek at his wristwatch before announcing with surprise, "Hey, can you guess what day it is?"

"Not a clue," I admitted.

"I'll give you a hint," he winked. "Tonight might be good for making a little fireworks."

* * *

Long daylight, combined with frequent confinement by unremarkable forests, made it difficult for SeeHawk and me to avoid spacing out in central Montana. We welcomed any entertainment provided by exciting weather, snacks, and even temporary route-finding challenges. However, there was no way to sugar-coat our first mass encounter with Rocky Mountain mosquitoes.

America's early explorers had foiled mosquito attacks by smearing their skin with animal fat. PCT-hiker Sly had smeared his whole body with *DEET*. SeeHawk and I just gritted our teeth and sped through the mosquito-infested forest approaching Thunderbolt Mountain.

The Book of Beans warned us to expect a "lung-bustingly" steep climb, terminating with a choice to either cross the mountain's shoulder or take a side trip onto its scenic 8,632-foot summit.

Glancing upward, I saw a collage of overhead clouds oozing together like runny pancake batter. Uh-oh. No wonder the mosquitoes were going crazy. Even our ultralight jackets, worn for mosquito protection, knew it was going to storm, judging by how their thin sleeves sagged against our skin.

"We've probably got one hour left to complete this climb and tag the summit," I told SeeHawk. "After that, we'd better hurry down to the orchestra pit and grab good seats."

We tried to quicken our pace, but the pursuing mosquitoes just flew faster.

SeeHawk had the misfortune to have been born with delicious skin. Therefore he needed to constantly whip his hat across his face, shoulders, arms, legs, and anywhere else he felt tiny stings. Each whip of his hat sent clouds of the bloodsuckers whirling away, only to have them return within seconds. This drill went on for so long that his arm grew fatigued, forcing him to keep switching the hat from one hand to the other.

I, meantime, had been born with bland-tasting skin, so I only had to worry about SeeHawk's hat-strap making me blink whenever it whipped past my eyes.

"I'm sure you realize, we won't be stopping for lunch until after we cross Thunderbolt Mountain," I told him during a moment when I was not ducking.

"Suits me," he replied. "It's more fun to eat when I'm not being eaten."

"Right, but I'm talking about the weather."

"If there's weather coming, let's hope it's mosquito-killing weather."

"I think today you're going to get your wish."

Upon reaching the trail going up Thunderbolt Mountain, we found a trail of pink plastic ties flagging a detour that would allow us to stay low. According to the Books of Beans, it was a new shortcut still under construction.

"A trail through Mosquitoland?" SeeHawk shuddered. "Ugh, no thanks. I'll take the climb any day."

Following his decree, we ignored the pink-plastic ties and hurried past them. Uniform coverage of lodgepole pine trees made it difficult to see much sky after we started climbing. With no easy means to gauge our progress, my mind started wondering how insects with only a two-week lifespan could know backpackers aren't able to slap their shoulder blades.

"Collective consciousness," SeeHawk guessed. "It's like the hundred-monkeys phenomenon, converted into evil."

Above 7,000-feet, we grew impatient to bust out of the trees. The lodgepole pines were shrinking, but we still needed to climb another 1,500-feet before reaching the mountain's timberline. When we finally touched open daylight, it was because we had reached a three-way junction of trails. On paper, the CDT passed through that junction in its water over Thunderbolt Mountain's left shoulder. If we stayed on the CDT, we could stay shielded from any approaching storm, but we would miss seeing the summit view touted as "a shame" to miss. Before reaching any decision, we suddenly realized the mosquitoes were gone. Gone, as in, GONE gone. Hot diggety dog! We had finally climbed high enough to save our skin. This discovery made us goofy with relief. Wasting not another lazy minute, we hoisted on our backpacks and jogged up to the lookout.

From Thunderbolt Mountain's utmost tippy-top, we gazed full circle around a bird's-eye view of forested mountains. The view was anticlimactic for southbound CDT-hikers (having recently experienced Glacier National Park), but it was certainly a breath of fresh air.

"No wonder they call this state Montana," I observed. "It's covered with mountains every place you look."

The summit's wooden sign simply said, "Thunderbolt Mountain Elevation 8,632-feet." We patted ourselves on the backs for bagging an extra peak that did not belong to the CDT. A last glance around used all the time we had before a thunderhead looming two miles in the distance commanded us to skedaddle.

Hurrying off the lookout, we fled down Thunderbolt Mountain's backside, reaching the cover of trees precisely when the storm arrived. The rest of our descent became a blur of noisy hailstones, lightning, thunder, and streamers of floodwater racing alongside us. We ate lunch sitting on the trail's raised bank, staying dry inside our ponchos, and waited for the lightning to end before standing up again.

Next in the queue was Thunderbolt Mountain's neighbor, Electric Peak. A steady ascent through vigorous foliage lifted us through a maze of clear running streams. The climb ended upon a flat summit, roofed with broken clouds disbanding into twilight. Sparse cover of trees would have discouraged us from camping atop the peak in stormy weather. Therefore, we deemed ourselves lucky to be able to pitch camp in the clouds' central traffic lane.

Within minutes of getting settled, we saw a giraffe among men march onto the summit. His angular joints seemed attached to his torso by strings. His stomach had been replaced by a flap of loose-hanging fabric. He wore blue mechanic's coveralls, color-coordinated to match his blue fanny pack, blue-and-white-striped umbrella, mismatched blue and black gloves, matching blue-and-white sneakers, and camouflage-colored army cap displaying his name in big block letters.

"Hey, where's the water?" Blue Man demanded, in some kind of hybrid east-coast accent.

SeeHawk and I glanced at each other, thinking, *Dummy, why didn't you fill your bottles at the last stream before you came up here?* It took us a moment to realize he was just making conversation.

Marching straight to our campsite, he peeled off his featherweight, frameless backpack and politely asked permission to camp with us for the night.

We barely had time to accept, before he yanked off his army cap and replaced it with a purplish-blue beanie, indicating a done deal.

SeeHawk exited the conversation long enough to finish changing into his nightclothes.

Meantime, I watched Blue Man circle around our campsite, methodically deciding where to pitch his tarp. He did not have much of a sleeping cushion. Instead, he relied upon finding smooth ground, which was hopefully soft. Also, he needed to find secure anchorage for suspending his tarp across trekking poles, to form a makeshift tent. Once that chore was accomplished, he hunkered down and entertained us with some hilarious recollections. First, came his memory of spending half an hour circling around a meadow with no obvious exit. The expletives he shouted at the top of his lungs had been heard by nobody since he was thru-hiking alone. In a big, booming voice, he proceeded to rant about Thunderbolt Mountain's irascible mosquitoes, the Book of Beans' useless directions, and its author's constant warnings about "bear sign." Lastly, he berated Thunderbolt Mountain's low bypass route, marked with pink plastic ties, for luring him into a boobytrap of impenetrable dry brush.

Stars sugared the twilight sky while Blue Man poured cold water into his cooking pot and started sponge-bathing himself with an orange bandanna handkerchief. Next, heating water for dinner, he lit an alcohol-burning stove self-made from a soda-pop can.

"Food is IT, man!" he raved. "Food makes all the difference. If I'm hungry, I might be walking through some woods thinking 'F--ing rocks, f--ing trees, f--ing trail...' But then..." his tone grew rosy, "...I remember this one time when I was feeling grumpy. I went into a restaurant and ate a pizza. Then, a Hoagie, and another Hoagie to-go. I walked outside after eating all that food and felt really good. You know? Like, after that, I was passing through the same damn forest thinking, 'Beautiful rocks, beautiful trees, nice trail...'"

While Blue Man polished off a potful of steaming pasta, he told us about having hitchhiked with a gal driving a jeep through northern Montana. Her offer to pick him up had inspired him to ask, "You know? You're all alone, and with my hair looking like this and me wearing this outfit, I don't exactly look harmless, so why did you pick me up?"

"Because you needed a ride," she explained. "I wasn't worried, since I have a gun."

On that note, Blue Man bid us goodnight.

The summit's starry sky fell silent. However, while SeeHawk and I used our headlamps to sift through and organize tomorrow's guidebook pages, we heard a familiar voice speak into the twilight.

"Damn, it's past ten-thirty and still too light to sleep. Can you believe how Montana hardly gets dark before the sun comes up? I can't fall asleep, but I have to try. New Mexico's gonna be awesome. Shorter days and fourteen-hour nights."

A full moon rose, while SeeHawk and I prepare for our own effort at sleeping. We made a lot of noise arranging our swishy sleeping bag, so when we finally lay still the silence seemed profound. Gradually, we relaxed into a slumber that felt like a long, cool drink. Our muscles sank into the unmoving earth. Our thoughts floated upward...our perceptions went blank...our ears got drilled awake! What in abomination's name was that monotonous little whining noise? A mosquito? Darned! Either it had snuck inside our tent, or else gotten trapped between our tent's rainfly and interior walls, unable to bite us, but also safe from being killed. Either way, SeeHawk stood no chance of falling back asleep before watching the little noisemaker die, preferentially by his own hands. Unfortunately, switching on his headlamp would have required reaching for his headlamp, which would have required swishing our sleeping bag, whose noise would have sent the mosquito back into hiding. Instead, he lay still, waiting for the crafty little stealth-bomber to regain confidence. Once it resumed whining, he quickly switched on his headlamp and tried to spot it, only to hear it stop whining again, and so on, for increasingly longer intervals. One especially long silence allowed me to slip into a fragile sleep, which telepathically signaled the mosquito to realize SeeHawk was hogtied and start dive-bombing his ears,

"...nneeEERRROWRrrr... ...nneeEERRROWRrrr..."

Eventually, SeeHawk swatted hard enough to yank the sleeping bag off my neck, which caused me to bolt awake and shout, "CUT THAT SH-- OUT AND GO TO SLEEP!"

That was the beginning of a long night for my poor fiancé. He might never have slept at all, except for one lucky swat finally enabling him to "facilitate the next step" in the mosquito's "divine evolution."

Afterward, he and I both drifted away, to better places in the universe, never noticing how many additional mourners swarmed in to avenge their comrade's death.

The next glow of daybreak illuminated a scene from the apocalypse. Somewhere near 1,000 teensy, winged bodies were peppered all over our tent's interior, nylon-mesh ceiling. Their combined noise sounded like a miniature violin orchestra, endlessly tuning for a macabre concerto. Within three feet of our noses (reduced to inches, after we sat up), we saw thousands of kinked twig-legs, tissue-thin wings, and thirsty syringe-noses struggling to penetrate the transparent mesh between us. This scene might have fascinated children dressed in combat gear, but it was terrifying for adults who had full bladders and back doors rattling. The act of unzipping our tent's vestibule felt like firing a starting pistol. Both of us simultaneously dashed outside to pull down our long johns, exposing fresh meat in places we could not see.

While sprinting back to our tent, we noticed an empty space where Blue Man's tarp no longer stood. *Another rooster*, we thought. *Just like Devin and Karen.* Perhaps, if we had been roosters, we might have finished our pit stops before the mosquitoes awakened, but so it goes.

"Never dwell on what-ifs," SeeHawk reminded me, "unless you're fighting a traffic ticket, or trying to get into Heaven."

Not only had we risen too late to beat the mosquitoes, but also, after crawling back inside our tent, we discovered a few dozen hitchhikers riding in with us. While we started converting them into blood smears, the violin orchestra stationed above our heads played faster and louder. The morning was heating up, signaling the musicians to prepare for takeoff.

Once every hitchhiker lay dead between our sleeping bag's slippery folds, we decided to stay put until full-strength heat cleared the runway for us to start hiking. In the meantime, we enjoyed a rare pre-hike breakfast, listening to songbirds regale with the orchestra.

SeeHawk reflected, "I love this time of day, between dawn and nine or ten, when birds are more active. Bees are more active. Even mosquitoes. It's like rush hour for the animals. I remember when I was a paperboy. If Big Ben failed to wake me up at dawn, I never worried about oversleeping because every morning the same old blue-jay landed in my window and always woke me up."

Storytime was over when the tent grew stuffy. We thought it might be safe to climb outside, and, sure enough. The mosquitoes were gone.

Being freshly fed, we had no reason to leave camp eating our usual fruit rolls, so SeeHawk Ziplocked them into a plastic baggie with two caramel-apple snack bars, for deposit into his bottomless kangaroo pouch.

I never saw him pocket the snacks, and even if he had, I would never have expected them to cause a kafuffle later in the day.

During our first hour of hiking, the morning's early heat could have poached an egg. When snack-time arrived, SeeHawk handed me a strawberry-banana fruit roll, limp from being warmed inside his kangaroo pouch. The delicious sugary fruit made us feel euphoric as we sped through a series of tall grass meadows spritzed with pink shootingstar lilies. Insects were springing like popcorn through the grass. Clouds of them whizzing through the low sunlight resembled sprinkler mist. A woodpecker kept knocking holes into a hollow-sounding tree, alongside the Reverb-Bird's warbling prelude and a Warm-Up Bee revving its heat-fed metabolism. All across the ground, flowers painted the grass with mixtures of bright colors. Among the mixtures were deep-purple delphiniums paired with pale-purple asters, purple lupines mixed with yellow sunflowers, and golden sunflowers, yellow yarrows, and yellow buttercups mixed with sprigs of red Indian paintbrush.

Toward noontime, thick gray clouds socked in the northern sky. A labyrinth of dirt roads, compacted heavily by ATVs and jeeps, guided us into a darkly shaded forest. We lost sight of our surroundings for about 20 minutes, before running into an off-branching road whose sign said, "Restricted to Administrative Use Only."

Having expected the sign, I pulled out the Book of Beans and did a little reading before telling SeeHawk, "Well, at least one out of two ain't bad. We're missing the blue-and-white CD-sign, but we've found the Restricted Admin sign. I do think it's weird, though, for us to leave this road before crossing the ridge."

I was referring to a ridge that had spanned our forward horizon before we lost sight of it upon entering the trees.

Agreeing that it had looked like we were supposed to cross the ridge, SeeHawk suggested, "Do you think maybe this isn't our turnoff?"

"No idea," I admitted, "but do you want to ignore the sign?"

"Not really," he frowned.

"Maybe this road heads sideways for a while before swinging around to cross the ridge in a more scenic way than if we stayed inside the forest," I suggested. "Maybe the trail builders wanted to give us a better hiking experience."

"Okay, so are we turning here, then?"

"I guess so."

"You sound hesitant. Are we just testing the water, or going for a swim?"

"Maybe both, because it's about to rain."

What followed was an exercise in optimism. Gradually, the primitive sideroad we had chosen deteriorated into a worn pair of tire ruts, divided by weeds, which kind of looked like a hiking trail if we pretended not to notice it being surrounded by re-planted trees.

Eventually, SeeHawk suggested, "If this is an old logging road, should we turn around?"

"Not necessarily," I told him. "The Book of Beans only says we should avoid several old logging roads, not shun them altogether."

"So, we don't really know what we're looking for?"

"Right because the text is super cryptic and we don't have time to sit around solving word puzzles."

Scud was starting to protrude from the clouds trailing behind us. I glanced over the top of saplings on our left and noticed we were hiking parallel to, rather than toward, the southern ridge. Was it time to admit we had messed up and turn around? I might have said so, if not for being egged-on by a low point farther down the ridge, which looked capable of being a pass. That theory went up in flames, though, when we ran into a dead-end wall of trees.

"Damn!" I roared. "We KNEW this was a logging road! Why did we keep going?"

And, down came the rain.

Hurrying into our ponchos, we spun around and grumpily trudged back to the CDT. Upon regaining the perpendicular road we had left, we vowed never to stray from it again until we crossed the southern ridge.

This was my stomach's cue to start growling. I did not want to stop hiking yet, so I asked SeeHawk for a caramel-apple snack bar.

He reached into his kangaroo pouch, dug around for a moment, and lifted out...an empty Ziploc bag!

"SEEHAWK!" I shrieked. "Did you eat ALL our SNACKS?"

"I...er..." he stammered, looking confused. "I guess, after I finished my fruit roll, I just kept going. I didn't notice myself eating the bars. I guess they were just in there..."

Smoke puffed out my ears. Apparently, it was time to start keeping a closer watch on my partner, not only to prevent him from filching snacks but also to make sure his mind was functioning clearly.

* * *

From atop the Continental Divide, a gigantic valley containing the sister cities of Butte and Anaconda looked filled to its brim with chicken consommé. The atmospheric haze creating that consommé floated beneath a ceiling of clear blue sky. Through the blueness, SeeHawk and I walked as if belonging to a different world. We had fun pretending to smell pizzas and hear distant traffic, but we were still 1-week away from descending into the valley. That's right. One entire week from now, we were scheduled to finish circling a valley we could already see, and drop into Anaconda for re-supplies. How was it possible to progress so slowly at thru-hiking speeds? Well, for one thing, the valley's mountainous border required a lot of ups and downs. Secondly, that section of "America's Backbone" was anything but straight. Hence, we were probably going to spend the coming week feeling stuck on a treadmill, as well as underwhelmed by industrialized scenery.

Already, we saw the Continental Divide losing some of its wild character. Most noticeable was a change from heritage forests to domestic timber forests, dotted here and there with historic miners' cabins collapsing into ruins. Like time-travelers, we felt ourselves being swept back to an era when horse-drawn wagons and steam locomotives had rolled across the Continental Divide, transporting food, livestock, and mining equipment from one lowland to the next. Gold prospectors finding ore on Butte Hill, in 1864, had triggered a migration of merchants, followed by tradesmen whose heyday lasted nearly a decade. Then, had come an exodus, during which most of Butte's new residents decided the gold mines could not meet their needs and left in droves, reducing the city's population to less than 60 people. Later, someone had realized bigger profits could be made from mining silver than from mining gold, and the town's population slowly rebounded. A third mining boom occurred in 1884 when people realized copper could be more profitable than silver. This third wave inspired the construction of 300 copper mines in and around Butte, along with 9 quartz mills, 4 copper smelters, and a fleet of entrepreneurs scavenging valuable ore remnants from the copper train's tracks and mining companies' waste piles. By the century's end, Butte was producing almost one-quarter of the world's mined copper, plus 72-million ounces of gold and silver per year, leading into a decade of its copper mines earning something like 2-billion dollars in revenue, from roughly 10,000 miners excavating 20,000 tons of ore each day. The city's reputation for hard labor eventually earned its nickname, "The Richest Hill on Earth." However, legend says the town's riches came packaged with skies blackened by flying beer bottles, due to roughly 25 beer-wagons hawking booze up and down its city streets every summer, of which the Atlantic Bar spanned one city block. Miners were said to arrive at work carrying beer in their lunch buckets, greased with lard to keep down the foam. One copper company, located in Anaconda, built tract-homes near its smelters, with bars on every corner, so laborers could easily stop for a beer on their way home. (Incidentally, this was back in the days when respectable bars did not serve liquor to women; men were allowed to beat their wives once a month; prostitution, cockfights, and bar brawls were considered business as usual; charity towards poor people was common, and immigrant laborers were welcomed from all corners of the earth.)

SeeHawk and I began to feel connected with the valley's colorful history as we watched Anaconda's twin smelter-stacks loom through the haze. Once again, we felt reminded of being lucky to breathe fresh air 24/7 and eat delicious organic food (even if it was dehydrated), instead of working all day inside dark, dusty mines, whose above-ground temperatures sometimes dropped below zero. We had no right to complain, but it still felt like a crisis when our water supply ran low, shortly after sunset.

We had just stepped out of a sandy pine forest, artfully glazed with fading pink skylight. A flat gravel road, curving through a narrow valley, took over leading us toward a full-service campground, where we were expecting to get water and sleep overnight. Everything was going according to plan, except for dusk beating us to the campground. We did not want to switch on our headlamps because their narrow light beams would have given us tunnel vision and possibly made us miss seeing the campground's entrance. Therefore, we just let our eyes get used to the darkness.

After a spell of cautious walking, SeeHawk started asking, "Where's the full moon, when we need it?"

I kept mumbling, "We should see the turnoff any minute now."

Soon, we lost sight of the roadside trees. Next to disappear was the hard-packed gravel beneath our shoes. Not being able to see where we were stepping made it difficult to avoid rocks and potholes, but the road was in good shape, so we just walked slowly. In an effort to keep track of each other, we made small-talk and stayed close together. Complete blindness introduced an odd sensation of feeling our feet push toward the earth and the earth push toward our shoes, sometimes with enough force to catch us by surprise. Eventually, we could not resist switching on our headlamps, but, as predicted, they blinded us to everything outside their narrow beams.

While proceeding as such, we got approached by an old pickup truck grinding along the flat gravel road. Stepping aside, we tried to imagine. What might our glowing headlamps look like to its driver? Two giant fireflies? A pair of bobbing monster-eyes?

As it turned out, the truck contained a father and son, searching for firewood to haul back to the same campground we were trying to reach. They looked incredulous when we refused their offer of a ride.

"Thanks," I said, "but if we ride to the campground, we'll have to come back tomorrow morning, just to connect the dots. We'd love to know, though, are we almost there?"

"You're going the right way," the driver assured us, "but it's still a bit of a walk from here."

Seeing that we were determined to keep walking, he reluctantly drove away, still looking puzzled.

It became easier to relax after we knew, for sure, that our aim was correct, and we started to laugh about our clumsiness in the dark.

Within ten minutes, the same driver returned, hauling firewood back to camp. Again, he looked astounded when we refused his second offer.

After watching him drive away, I asked SeeHawk, "Is it stupid for us to pass up a favor from The Universe?"

"Maybe," he admitted, "but, maybe we're being tested to see if continuity is still important to us."

Another few minutes passed, sightless and soundless, before everything outside our headlamps' little bubbles of light began to seem like The Void.

At length, SeeHawk ventured to ask, "How much longer do you think it'll take us to reach the campground?"

I hesitated to answer. It was starting to haunt me that the driver had not estimated the distance, or told us exactly what to look for.

"Probably not far," I hedged, "but I'm kind of surprised we aren't hearing voices. Maybe nobody else is camping tonight, besides the driver and his son."

"Hah!" SeeHawk snorted. "On Fourth-of-July weekend? You can bet the campground is full to its whiskers. Maybe we were foolish to turn down that ride. We should, at least, have asked him for some water, just in case we end up dry-camping."

Fifteen minutes later still, I began to feel genuinely concerned. Our headlamps kept glancing off a split-rail fence running alongside the road. Shouldn't we have seen some kind of gate by now? Or, maybe a driveway coming up ahead? I kept hoping, but the fence remained solid. We seemed to be rounding an extremely long curve. Coming out of it, the road headed straight into a forbiddingly thick forest. That change alarmed me. Our headlamps displayed two solid borders of trees shrinking into the distance. No campground gates. No intersecting driveways. Had we missed a fork in the road somewhere? Where could it be hiding? Suddenly, I heard muffled laughter. Next, came a sound that I usually loathed, but temporarily felt relieved to hear, which was the noisy rumble of RV generators. The noise grew louder. Then, fainter. It seemed that we needed to vault the split-rail fence in order to reach the campground. After taking off our backpacks in order to cross the fence, we shuffled carefully through a grassy forest, feeling like ghosts approaching unsuspecting humans. Country, pop, and soul music guided our approach toward the holiday weekend smells of cheap beer, vehicle exhaust fumes, campfire smoke, BBQ lighter-fluid, and burning chicken grease. Soon, we spied several groups of seated RV campers, eating plates of food beneath floodlights diluting the glow from their bonfires. We continued to feel invisible, sneaking up like ghosts, until a barking dog confirmed our smell to be unmistakably human (heavily seasoned with onions and garlic).

There was a vacant campsite available, so we plunked down our gear and launched right into setting up camp. After weeks of being alone, it felt strange to talk in whispers, for fear of encroaching upon neighbors close-at-hand. Shortly after mid-

Heavy Glue

night, almost everyone shut off their RV lights and switched off their boom-boxes. When somebody took in the last barking dog, we recognized our cue to lay down in the darkness. It felt marvelous to spoon without moving a muscle...listening to the campground's noises peel away...falling silent...until, a faint scratching sound grabbed our attention. Something slid down our tent's thin roof. Something small hit the ground, "SsshhhhhhhKLUNK!"

"Mouse," SeeHawk whispered.

He knew that sound like the back of his own hand. It sounded the same as it had in some of the PCT's most popular campsites.

"Tap, tap, tap..." Tiny feet climbed our tent's slippery roof. "...ssshhhhhhhKLUNK!"

The mouse hit the ground with another dull thump. Apparently, our tent had become a carnival attraction.

I sighed, "Go ahead and have your jollies, Mr. Camp Mouse. At least, we have walls, instead of just a tarp."

The next morning's entertainment included an entire family of people riding their ATV back and forth to an outhouse stationed 100 feet from their campsite.

We could hardly wait to leave all the commotion. Upon returning to the same gravel road we had left in darkness, we found it bathed in warm sunshine. The coming hours gave us disproportionate pleasure in watching swallows feed their young beneath Interstate Highway 15 and black ants commute across our dusty trail.

Dirt Road 78154 forged a 15-foot corridor through dense conifer woods. Unexpectedly, we got surprised by one impressive cobweb strung all the way across, at a height that made us catch it in the chins. In the midst of wiping web gunk off our faces and shoulders, we marveled to think. Had the spider crawled up a tree alongside the road and farted its web across 15-feet of thin air? Had it performed an Evil Knievel-style jump, expelling web juice through the air behind it? Or had it attached its web onto a tree, crawled down, crossed the trail, and climbed an opposite tree, reeling-in slack, before anchoring its web at chin-height? We had no idea, but it was sure fun guessing.

Upon reaching Nez Perce Creek, we stripped down and rinsed the campground's fire smoke out of our hair. Who would have expected Ninja mosquitoes to be up and about during midday? Neither of us felt or saw anything, until, 15 minutes after the attackers flew away, our arms began to itch like poison ivy.

Scratching and cursing, we climbed onto an incline that the Book of Beans called "Switchback Hell." It was a ladder of uniformly long, nearly level switchbacks, heaped with dead trees toppled by windstorms or repeated snowslides. Each new blockage forced us to debate which was worse, climbing over arm-gouging deadwood or climbing without seeming to gain elevation. Finally, we landed upon a level bench, partially timbered with disorganized trees. It was as if Nature had started building a respectable forest but then lost interest. Aiming straight uphill from where we landed, an unmarked jeep road left the bench at an angle almost too steep for jeeps.

"Do you think that's a shortcut, for people who just can't face another switchback?" SeeHawk hinted.

"Possibly, if it aims toward Whitetail Peak," I replied.

"You mean, you agree with my hunch?" he concluded, looking oddly pleased.

"Er..."

Before I could say more, he said, "Well, okay then," and lunged uphill like he had swallowed rocket fuel.

Scrambling to catch up, I climbed swiftly, until the incline lifted my heels off the ground.

"This is definitely too steep for jeeps," I noted. "Even if they could drive up to it, their engines would overheat."

"It's also too steep for some hikers to carry all their stuff," SeeHawk observed.

His finger pointed toward a rusty cooking-pot, rusty coffee pot, and weathered but unopened package of tea crackers, which he picked up and started to peel open.

I could not believe my eyes. "Are you crazy?" I shrieked. "Who knows how long those crackers have been lying there? Am I not feeding you enough, for god sake?"

With obvious reluctance, he forced himself to set down the crackers, but only because he feared my wrath more than he feared hunger.

We climbed steeply for another 20 minutes, before reaching a second landing that we mounted on trembling legs. The flat ground ahead was geometrized with evenly spaced trees, virtually uniform in size and appearance. Beneath the trees, a crosshatched tangle of unsigned jeep roads ran to-and-fro, seeming to correspond with a confusing mess of red lines on our atlas.

"Hm," I frowned. "No sign of Whitetail Peak."

"Uh-oh," SeeHawk worried. "I'm sorry, Sunshine. My bad, for getting us into this mess. But, why didn't you stop me?"

"Because those switchbacks drove me nuts, too," I admitted, "and since you made the suggestion, I couldn't get blamed for whichever way it might turn out."

SeeHawk rolled his eyes. "Well, anyway, what should we do now? Turn around and go back down?"

"So you can snag the crackers again?" I snorted. "Fat chance, Polly. No, we don't need to go back down. We just need to figure out which of these jeep roads leads to the CDT, and then also recognize the CDT when we get there."

Selecting a dirt road was like choosing the best orange out of a pile of oranges. I knew how to do it, but only by means of intuition. SeeHawk agreed to trust my hunch, so off we went, following my gut choice. Several intersecting dirt roads vied for our allegiance. Sticking to our guns, we snubbed them all. Never mind seeing no evidence of Whitetail Peak or the CDT. We acted like someone had made a law against doubting hunches.

This whole endeavor was like a blip on the scale of important incidents. We could easily have turned around. Even if retreating past the crackers would have been hard on our knees, we could have taken our time because we had plenty of water and daylight left. And, yet, we acted like victory was all that mattered. In fact, we danced for joy when we ran into a southbound footpath. Never mind that it bore no sign. These days, I could recognize the CDT like smelling my own shirt. Perhaps, I would even have kissed its dirt, if not for disliking the taste of horse manure.

SeeHawk swore, never again, to suggest another shortcut.

We crossed fingers behind our backs and shook hands.

Clearly, we were in a fragile state of mind regarding inefficiency.

It felt glorious to hike at full speed for the first time in hours. We followed the CDT back and forth, uphill and downhill, before topping out upon the summit of Whitetail Peak. Its view overlooked lots of trees. That was all. Heading off the peak, we wound elaborately down the mountain's backside, brushing against smooth boulders, crossing terraced clearings, and finally coming to rest inside an elongated marshland called Halfway Park.

All I could do by then was plop my bottom onto a fallen log, smell muddy grass and hear water gurgling.

SeeHawk trotted away to do something that could not wait for an explanation. During his absence, he found a tremendous hipbone rotting in the grass, beside a fractured jawbone and various scattered leg bones.

Coming over to check out his finding, I quickly looked away. The bear's remains were fascinatingly huge, but also creepy. At least, I did not like being reminded of the skeleton we had seen guarding the North Wall.

Perhaps, SeeHawk felt creeped-out too because he did not try extracting any of this bear's teeth, or packing up any of its bones to mail home.

After returning to the trail, we left Halfway Park feeling numbed by a long afternoon of hiking. This was not a good frame of mind in which to have to choose between several unsigned jeep roads, all matched in appearance, by virtue of descending extremely steeply and being warped and rutted by water erosion. The sun looked near to setting when I whipped out the Book of Beans and confirmed that, sure enough, its author had gotten confused in the same location. Fortunately, I knew for certain that we were approaching Delmoe Lake.

"All we basically need to do," I told SeeHawk, "is just aim downhill until we run into water, and after that, I've got clear directions for leaving the lake."

Unfortunately, aiming downhill became tricky when our chosen jeep road buckled into a V-shaped, cross-furrowed trench. The steep grade thrust our backpacks so far forward that my knees wobbled like rubber hoses, making me use my trekking poles for brakes.

At length, SeeHawk said, "These roads aren't useable for jeeps anymore. They've probably turned into a giant playground for ATVs and dirt bikes."

"Yes," I agreed, "and their usage might have changed this whole area since our guidebooks were written."

It gave us some relief to spy Delmoe Lake shimmering two miles in the distance. Knowing exactly where to aim would have made it easy to get there fast, if only we could have flown, but descending via the rutted trench was slow-going. Then, to our dismay, the trench suddenly bent sideways, depositing us onto a lateral jeep track, which seemed to have no interest in the lake. This new development did not look good. For one thing, I had secretly been plotting to fix SeeHawk a nice lakeside dinner before it got dark. Already, my mind had imagined him saying. *Wow, baby! You told me we'd get to relax on this trip, and here we are, living the good life.* Instead, I had to watch the lateral jeep track diminish into a skinny single-track, overlooking a forest choked full of boulders and obstreperous deadfall. In other words, we lost our option to bushwhack downhill if the single-track never turned toward the lake. Still, we kept going sideways because backtracking up the ruts we had just come down seemed like the worst option of all.

A bit farther ahead, the lateral trail entered a Douglas fir forest whose foliage totally hid Delmoe Lake. Suspicion turned to dismay when the trail angled diagonally uphill. Gazing downhill during the climb, we felt like passengers boarding the wrong train.

In hopes to stay cheerful while digesting bad news, I wise-cracked, "Looks like tonight's dinner won't be boiled in fresh lake water."

"Is it time to look for an emergency camp?" SeeHawk worried.

"Let's keep the faith for another fifteen minutes," I told him. "Then, we can panic."

Following the trail uphill, before long we heard water rushing.

"Camp!" SeeHawk assumed.

Trotting toward the rushing sound, we ran into a rocky waterfall, crossing the trail beneath a wooden plank bridge. Our tent could not fit onto the bridge, and, anyway, sleeping above a waterfall would have felt weird, but we did appreciate being able to refill our water bags.

While flipping through Poppa Jim's directions, I noticed the treetops overhead turning dark. Apparently, we had reached International Creek. A ravine lurking downstream might have coincided with Poppa Jim's cross-country approach to Delmoe Lake, but it was getting too late to consider any such adventure before the next morning.

Feeling glad to have found a landmark, SeeHawk rejoiced, "See, Sunshine? It's just like I always tell you. Wherever we go, we're always protected. If we can't find the trail, it will find us."

Instead of responding, I just gave him a cockeyed look.

Twenty-paces past the footbridge, SeeHawk announced, "Looks like we're home!"

Sure enough, standing inside a dark hollow, roofed with Douglas fir trees, sat a curiously situated old wooden cabin. Its border of juniper shrubs and wild pink roses created a homey appearance. A gentle creek trickling alongside outlined a flat space perfect for camping. Above the flat space sat an old treehouse, watching over a dilapidated outhouse, a rusting bed frame, and a spring-fed pool that had once fed the cabin's kitchen sink. If ever a historical hideaway had stories to tell, this was it, and we had it all to ourselves!

Heavy Glue

While pitching camp, we imagined some bygone gold prospector occupying the cabin all by his lonesome. Had he spent his evenings reading books? Smoking cigarettes? Writing letters? Had he finished each day's dig wondering if he should have kept on, lest the gold might be a few inches deeper? Did he ever dig all day without finding a cent? Had he ever felt afraid to get snowed-in, for weeks at a stretch? Had loneliness threatened his sanity? Or had silence been his favorite companion?

Our speculations got interrupted by eight thirsty cows bursting through a border of trees near the creek. Seeing humans near their watering-hole seemed to surprise the cows as much as seeing cows inside a steep forest surprised us. Once both parties recovered from the shock, the cows resumed ambling down for their evening drink.

The next morning, SeeHawk and I descended through a tumbledown playground of boulders, glistening water pools, and tree-covered rock chutes. At the bottom, we found Delmoe Lake, centered inside a frame of pretty much nothing.

All I could think of to say was, "Now I feel better about having camped with the cows."

Climbing away from the lake, onto a series of hot gravel roads, we kicked up dust as the morning wore on. Seedling cumulus clouds hovered alongside, teasing us by refusing to cover up the sun. It would have felt nice to take a break from climbing, especially each time we passed a nice shade tree, but nope. We climbed nonstop, hoping to reach Homestake Lake early enough for a nice midday swim. Eight miles out, we started getting buzzed by exhaust-spewing dirt bikes, ATVs, and pickup trucks. Time and time again, SeeHawk clamped a bandanna handkerchief over his nose and mouth, until he became downright grumpy.

Trying to cheer him up, I declared, "It must be *Cherry-Pepsi-thirty*."

Normally, he would have voted for *Cherry Coke*, but he did not even smile, which had to mean he was feeling miserable.

Eventually, I joined him in pulling a long face because, come on, the dusty gravel road just kept rolling over one small hill after another, like someone had forgotten to turn off the duplicating machine. Every new horizon unveiled another horizon. Meantime, our eyes grew tired from squinting toward the sun. Sweat dripping down our backs seeped low enough to make our butts feel slippery. The hot, hilly road seemed to go on forever. Suddenly, a hawk screeched close by. Glancing toward the screech, we noticed a train track running low alongside and toward Homestake Lake.

SeeHawk perked up and sang, "Hello shortcut! Thank you, Mister Hawk, for showing us the way."

I pointed toward a trestle bridge and protested, "Couldn't a train run us over if it caught us in that section?"

"We could dash to safety in time," SeeHawk wagered.

"Wearing backpacks?" I scoffed. "Nah, forget it. I'm not THAT desperate to swim while it's hot."

Feeling disappointed, SeeHawk sulked right into that "heavy glue" time of day which always bummed our mojo. The gravel road's relentless humps and dips sapped what remained of our enthusiasm. By the time we reached Homestake Lake, getting there almost felt like a surprise. Then, came the real surprise.

Homestake Lake was experiencing an algae bloom. Its lukewarm water had turned into something resembling a green-slime smoothie. Not to be dissuaded, I stuck one bare foot into the slime, stirred up some chunkiness, and smiled. At least, it felt warm enough for a good long swim.

SeeHawk took the lead, jumping in first. He and I both paddled offshore wearing our hiking clothes, like a couple of crazy fools. Within minutes, we got joined by four giggling mini-fools, shrieking and happily splashing each other.

Glancing at the shoreline, SeeHawk happened to notice the mini-fools' parents lugging a giant cooler chest up to a pair of beach chairs. Out of the chest came two ice-cold cans of cold *Pepsi Cola*.

"Land-ho!" he exclaimed.

"Shush. Don't you dare," I scolded him.

Ignoring my warning, he splashed out of the lake and marched straight up to the unsuspecting parents, looking like a swamp monster covered in green algae.

"Hello," he said in greeting. "Would it be possible to purchase two of your ice-cold *Pepsis*?"

"Why sure, you can just have them," the wife answered. "We always bring plenty. My husband's a real *Pepsi* fan. Before I married him, he used to drink seventeen *Pepsis* a day."

Whoa, call the doctor!

After thanking the couple and getting back on the trail, sipping cold *Pepsi Cola* with salty garlic croutons, we had no problem powering through the day's last heat.

Directly across Interstate Highway 90, a new stronghold of dusty mountains lifted us into a firebreak roofed with high-voltage powerlines. Midway through the firebreak, SeeHawk spotted something that startled him to a halt.

"Chief Navigator, do you want us to keep going straight? Because it looks like Devin and Karen turned off here."

Looking where he pointed, I saw two pairs of shoeprints descending into a perpendicular clear-cut.

Poppa Jim's pages told us to climb underneath a power line, follow another power line and then angle back toward the first power line. We were more or less doing that and the shoeprints did not match our aim, so I had doubts.

"Are you SURE these tracks belong to Devin and Karen?" I queried SeeHawk.

"As sure as pigeons drop their lunch," he confirmed.

Darn. The timing was bad. I just wanted to enjoy my sweet-and-salty snack. Without doing any serious thinking, I hastily decided we might as well trust Karen.

Following our friends' shoeprints into a perpendicular clear-cut felt like dropping into a downhill ski run. Soon, we ran into a huge boulder whose underlying slope looked intimidatingly steep. Much further downhill, where the land flattened out, we saw a road that appeared to be our next destination. It would have been nice to fly down to the road by parachute but, instead, our only choice was to drop over the boulder. I felt a bit scared—unlike SeeHawk who, after a moment's hesitation, just bounded right over the boulder and disappeared. Within seconds, he reappeared, scuttling downward until he vanished into some lower woods.

"How am I supposed to get down there?" I hollered after him.

Eventually, he came back up to help me.

Peeling off my backpack, I listened to him give me a speech about how to manage the drop safely, culminating with, "Don't slide down on your butt. Face the rock, so you can keep a good grip."

Silently, I thought, *Right-o, buddy. Not in your life.*

Knowing what would work best for me, and in complete disregard for mountaineering wisdom, I slid down the boulder on my butt. It was impossible to see the landing. Therefore, I got surprised when my shoes struck a pile of sun-bleached animal bones!

SeeHawk scrunched up his face and laughed, "I guess some of our predecessors could use rock-climbing lessons."

Following Karen's shoeprints into the downhill forest, we soon landed upon the flat dirt road we had seen from above.

It gave me a sense of freedom to pocket Poppa Jim's directions for a while, knowing we probably were not going to need them until the next morning.

No cackling could be heard as we strode peacefully along the flat road. However, perhaps if we had listened harder, we might have heard a dead tick say, *MooHAHA! Good evening, tenderfeet. Got your thinking caps on? Hopefully so, because this hide-and-seek game is just getting started.*

Scenes of Montana

June 7– August 2, 2001

306 *Racing the Clouds*

Launch Day at the Canadian Border

Belly River Entrance into Glacier National Park

Scenes of Montana

Dawn Mist Falls, GNP

Redgap Pass, GNP

308　　　　　　　　*Racing the Clouds*

Morning Eagle Falls, Glacier National Park

View from Cataract Creek Plateau, GNP

Scenes of Montana 309

St. Mary's Falls, GNP

Approaching St. Mary's Ranger Station, GNP

Cut Bank Creek, GNP

Skyline South of Triple Divide Pass, GNP

Scenes of Montana 311

CDT South of Triple Divide Pass, GNP

Grizzly Tracks Approaching Morning Star Lake, GNP

Climbing from Two Medicine to Scenic Point, GNP

Trees Playing Charades (4-letters, rhymes with twinned)

Scenes of Montana 313

View of Two Medicine from Scenic Point, GNP

Lunch in Round Park, Bob Marshall Wilderness

The Chinese Wall, BMW

Scenes of Montana

Overlook Scapegoat/BMW

Lightning Charred Crest, S/BMW

316   *Racing the Clouds*

Scenes of Montana

Pick-Up Sticks, Helena National Forest

Beargrass, Anaconda-Pintlar Wilderness

conovers
Trading Post
conovers
SPORTING GOODS
JEWELRY
ANTIQUES
BUY SELL TRADE
TRADING POST
BUY SELL TRADE

Scenes of Montana 319

Hawkweed and Lupin, Centennial Mountains

Arrow at N. Fork Sheep Creek, Beaverhead Mountains

Beargrass, Beaverhead Mountains

Artwork of Trail Blazer Joe Phillips

Scenes of Montana

Overlook, Beaverhead Mtns.

Near Lehmi Pass, facing Salmon-Challis Nat. Forest

Mail Drops Along the Continental Divide Trail

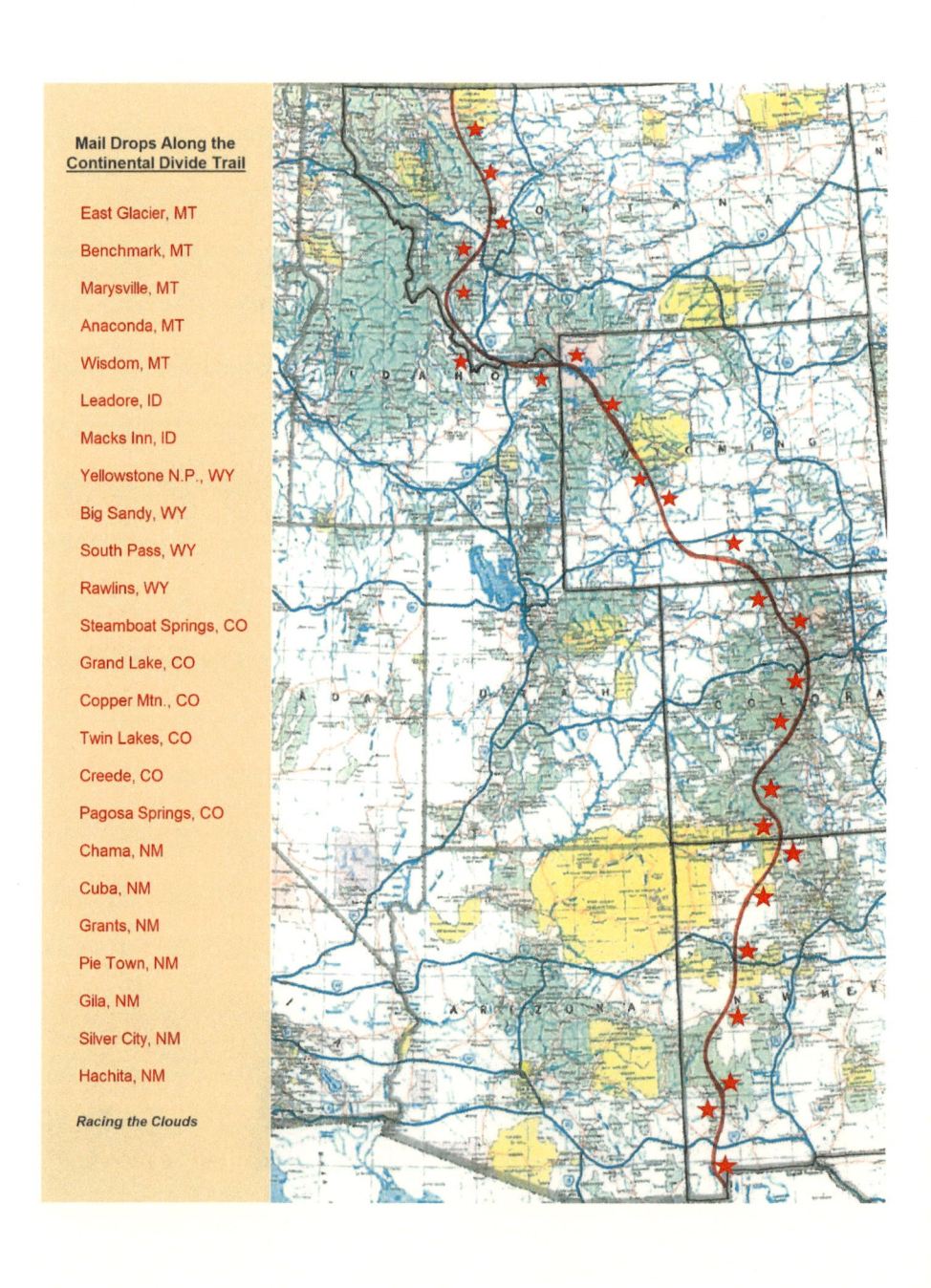

East Glacier, MT

Benchmark, MT

Marysville, MT

Anaconda, MT

Wisdom, MT

Leadore, ID

Macks Inn, ID

Yellowstone N.P., WY

Big Sandy, WY

South Pass, WY

Rawlins, WY

Steamboat Springs, CO

Grand Lake, CO

Copper Mtn., CO

Twin Lakes, CO

Creede, CO

Pagosa Springs, CO

Chama, NM

Cuba, NM

Grants, NM

Pie Town, NM

Gila, NM

Silver City, NM

Hachita, NM

Racing the Clouds

Chapter 9

Finding South

"Not all those who wander are lost."

— J.R.R. Tolkien

    Coming out of southern Montana's dry conifer forests, SeeHawk and I noticed the Continental Divide taking on a western flavor. It began with arid foothills covered in twiggy sagebrush. Clouds playing peek-a-boo with the sun kept shifting the sagebrush's color back and forth, between green and silver. Cows scattered everywhere chewed on sinewy grass. Tiny white flowers hiding beneath the sagebrush envied hardier Lupins for boldly exposing their purple flower stalks.

    We were still three weeks away from reaching Wyoming. This timeframe seemed baffling, after having already spent five long weeks crossing Montana, but the explanation showed clearly on paper. The CDT folded back upon itself, first steering hikers due-west for 150 miles, flipping them 180 degrees around a hairpin curve, and then launching them due-east for another 150 miles, before entering Wyoming through a smidgen of northern Idaho. In other words, the next 300 miles of trail extended along and doubled back along Montana's state line.

    As SeeHawk surveyed the lower ground ahead, abstract emotions caused him to remark, "If there's any section of the CDT that tests peoples' commitment to hike the whole trail, this must be it."

I chuckled ominously, "You'll say the same thing when we get to the Great Basin."

The trail's descent from Red Mountain led us over and down melting foothills until we struck bottom amongst grazing heifers, who looked up in surprise when they saw us coming. Several surly bulls tried to scare us away with intimidating stares. When that effort failed, the entire herd gathered together and bolted away, as if we had fired a pistol.

I picked a blunt-tipped sage leaf and smashed it between my fingers. The oil barely showed, but it smelled pungent. Rubbing some onto my lips, I shuddered while its fumes exhumed my demons.

There was little else to think about in terms of scenery. Blue sky. Silver sage. Green sage. Back to silver sage.

Suddenly, I spied something that made me cry out, "Is that the Continental Divide, or a petrified dinosaur!"

SeeHawk looked where I was pointing and saw a chain of freakishly isolated, miniature volcanic peaks. "Stegosaurus Rex," he laughed. "Maybe that's how America's Backbone got its name?"

"Semantics bedantics," I laughed. "Yeah, why not? America's Backbone sounds a lot catchier than if they had called it America's Dorsal Plates."

A quick lunch break drew us to notice white stratus clouds slipping across the sun. Before we finished eating, our meal got adjourned by a battery of wind gusts, not too strong, but definitely cold enough to prohibit sitting without long sleeves.

Rising back to our feet, we forged ahead, entering a flat landscape whose sole attraction was the Stegosaurus armor.

SeeHawk did not mind hiking in silence.

I was alone in wishing for conversation, so I tried to bait him with a little pop-quiz.

"Would you rather be a pro surfer, golf pro, or tennis pro?" I asked first.

"Pro surfer," he replied automatically.

"That was too easy," I decided. "How about, if you could only eat one kind of food for the rest of your life, which cuisine would you pick?"

"Italian."

"Not Mexican?"

"Sure, Mexican's good too."

"But you chose Italian, so it must be your favorite. Okay, what about, if you could be born in another country, what country would you choose?"

He thought hard, before coming up dry.

We needed a new subject. How about old beer jingles? I burst into singing, "It's *Miller* time...This *Bud's* for you... *Hamm's* the beer refreshing, *Hammmmms*."

It was fun singing like nobody could hear us, with nobody around to hear us. However, our mouths clamped shut when we ran into a swarm of eyeball-kissing gnats, which hovered in front of our faces as if holding a tip jar. Watching them float set me to thinking.

"Are we staring at their faces or their butts?"

"Huh?" SeeHawk mumbled, through a frenzy of eye-blinking and face-fanning.

"Because, if we're staring at their faces they would have to be flying backward."

Catching on, he groaned, "Who knows if they're flying backward or forward, Sunshine? I can't look that hard while I'm trying not to trip over rocks."

Mercifully, after some length of time, a freshening breeze came along and blew all the gnats out of our hair. Unfortunately, the same breeze also forced us to put on long sleeves. Even after our arms were covered, we still shivered while climbing onto a bluff whose view required us to establish new bearings.

The name "Deer Lodge Pass" had led me to expect cute little *Bambis* grazing in a meadow, or at least some kind of grassy area framed by an enclosure of trees. Instead, we saw a vacant wasteland, four-miles huge, which looked inhospitable for anything larger than rabbits and snakes, let alone deer. What's more, there was a dark squall cloud spilling into its far southwest corner.

"Will that squall be able to reach us before we get all the way across?" SeeHawk worried.

"Let's see…" I told him.

Using our guidebook for a reference, I traced our anticipated 1-mile walk alongside a stinky drainage marsh, followed by turning westward to head straight across the wasteland, and finally reaching a forested mountain four miles in the distance. The squall would, meantime, be trying to head-us off from a distance of several miles.

"Those trees will be our finish line," I said, pointing toward the faraway mountain.

"Looks pretty straightforward," SeeHawk nodded, glancing uneasily toward the squall.

"So, in terms of our odds? I'd give us fifty-fifty."

"Sixty-forty if we hurry?"

"Nope, I'm already assuming we'll hurry."

As we commenced walking alongside the marsh, it was difficult not to wish for some company taller than waist-high sagebrush.

Vultures placidly soaring overhead seemed to think we were entering their food chain.

At the end of one mile, we took a last squall-check. In our imaginations, the starting gun fired. We stepped off the pavement. That made it official. Almost immediately, we ran across four fresh deer legs, stacked into a neat pile presumably by a hunter.

"Well, what do you know?" SeeHawk exclaimed. "It looks like Deer Lodge Pass really does have deer."

Bluntly, I added, "Or, at least, it used to."

The breeze picking up made me shiver in fits. My long-sleeved t-shirt felt thinner every minute.

SeeHawk must have felt the same because he suggested pulling out windbreaker jackets and zipping pantlegs onto our shorts.

Finding South

While I fastened my shields, a familiar sensation caused me to ask SeeHawk, "Is your skin tingling?"

Looking startled, he reported, "Yes. Just now, I felt a few tingles."

Usually, we found it thrilling to feel tingles ahead of a big storm, but, for some reason, this day felt different.

Before long, the triple whammy of tingling, shivers, and vulnerability combined began to gnaw on SeeHawk's nerves. As the squall drew closer, his discomfort turned verbal. It began with just a few petty digs, which grew into insults before he clammed up and refused to apologize.

I did not want to argue with a squall approaching, but I did not appreciate being vented upon, either. Perceiving a choice, I rose to the occasion and urged my assailant to explain what was eating him.

In response, he curtly barked over his shoulder, "If whatever I said was so bad, clearly it means I need to shut up and quit talking."

"Right, but not before you explain what you meant," I insisted.

"Meant?"

"By saying all those mean things."

"What mean things?"

"Come on, SeeHawk. You're the one who said them, not me. Do you really want ME to list them all back to you?"

"Only if you want to."

"SeeHawk, this is YOUR mess to clean up, not mine!"

Getting no response, I bellowed louder, "Don't you CARE about hurting my feelings? Surely, you don't think I'm trying to clean this up just because I enjoy arguing?"

"Who knows?" he fired back.

So, away we went, quibbling ourselves into another circular trap, with me literally jogging to keep up with him.

Every wind-garbled sentence that reached SeeHawk's ears caused him to chant over his shoulder, "Can't stop now, Sunshine. We have to get to camp."

I pleaded desperately, "Why are you ignoring me? Why are you turning something that might be easy to fix into a major argument? Please, stop long enough to help me solve this."

"Talking will just waste energy we need to beat the storm," he protested.

"But anger uses MORE energy than talking," I reminded him. "Can't you please, at least, start being nice?"

Speeding up faster, he pulled farther ahead, saying nothing more.

I jogged after him faster, hollering words twisted by the wind into senseless garbage.

Finally, he got fed up and spun around to face me. However, instead of making amends, he yelled a lot of unprintable adjectives.

Even though I hated getting yelled at, this was better because now I could look him in the face.

Neither of us spoke during a long moment of him glaring at me and me waiting for my feminine charm to soften his anger. When nothing softened, I gave him hell.

Just as my tirade was reaching its crescendo, both of us turned our heads in surprise. Far in the distance, what did we see? A mirage? A rip in the fabric of reality? Holy head trips! It was a cyclist. Racing through the middle of nowhere, he was heading straight for us. Could he not see the squall speeding toward him? Did he not fear any romantic attraction between electricity in the clouds and his metal bike?

SeeHawk and I had not seen another human being since meeting Blue Man, several days earlier. The odds of a cyclist coming along precisely during the climax of our argument were staggering. It was almost like a replay of thru-hiker Devin overtaking us beyond Straight Creek Pass. Except, on that occasion, Devin had hung back until we stopped fighting, whereas, now, this lunatic-on-wheels was timing his appearance to break up our fight! Was he even real? Or just a shared hallucination? He sure looked real, judging by his skimpy spandex outfit and overloaded bike-trailer rattling to a stop beside us.

"Hi," he introduced himself.

Tilting the bike over enough to balance on one leg, he proceeded to explain that he was a CDT thru-biker. Apparently, this meant he was traveling cross-country, the same as us, except paralleling the hiker trail on sideroads. Sheepishly, he confessed to having just nailed a cow coming off Red Mountain. As if needing to offer proof, he rolled up his shirt sleeves and displayed several large road rashes, still oozing blood.

"Probably hurt the poor cow more than me," he reflected, sadly "Anyway, I'd better keep moving. Those clouds look like rain."

SeeHawk and I hovered between surprise and envy, while we watched the intrepid thru-biker peddle away. Probably, he was going to reach the opposite forest before we could even get back up to speed.

Within five minutes, the squall slammed into us. Somehow, we got taken by surprise and could barely yank off our hats and sunglasses in time not to lose them into the sagebrush. With the unsteady wind buffeting our backpacks, we got jerked in different directions, which made it difficult to extract and shimmy into big, floppy rain-ponchos. After successfully mashing our heads through the top-holes, then we had to fumble around hunting for the armholes. Fat bullets of water stung our eyes. The dirt surrounding our shoes looked covered in thumbtacks. As the wind grew stronger, the rain's circular splatter marks stretched into ovals. During all this time, we were still struggling to find our ponchos' freaking armholes! From a distance, we must have looked like a pair of Highland Houdinis experiencing straightjacket failure. Once we got the holes figured out, then it was time to wrestle hysterical poncho skirts over each other's backpacks. Cramming flapping corners underneath straps that kept letting go became an exercise in futility. By the time we resumed walking, it was challenging just to kick our feet forward instead of sideways. Lightning flashed a mile toward the south. The nearest trees waited two miles ahead. Could we still hope to reach them before the squall's epicenter reached us?

As the rain beat down, I noticed SeeHawk smiling and realized he was enjoying the squall's raw power. Likewise, I felt thrilled beyond words. We were both having fun, but it was tough not to feel anxious after lightning started flashing too close for comfort.

At the end of four miles, we felt more than ready to dash across the finish line. Stepping into a forest felt like punching through a magical forcefield. Tall conifer trees marshaled in around us, diminishing the wind into distant white noise. Aspens whispered about the coming of human beings. Our own self-awareness returned, bringing to light one lingering question. Were we still arguing? The answer seemed to be, not anymore. Everything we had quibbled about seemed like old news.

"Peace?" SeeHawk offered, extending an open hand.

I examined his guileless blue eyes. They were sparkling with hope. His brown-gray-and-orange calico beard paired strangely with his salt-and-pepper mustache. One prominent shock of white hair, permanently fixed above his temple, still commemorated his childhood hay wagon accident. Altogether, he looked like a used car with a good engine, or maybe sturdy blue jeans with authentically frayed edges. In statuesque terms, he looked fitter than ever, but completely unlike the smooth-faced salesman I had agreed to marry before we left home. And, hey now, was he shamelessly grinning, beneath all that calico facial hair?

Addressing the outstretched hand, I told him, "Before we shake, first you have to admit you caused that fight by being a jerk."

"I caused that fight, by a jerk," he admitted.

"Good," I smiled. "Then, can this argument not count as breaking our agreement not to argue on this hike?"

"What argument?" he frowned. "All I remember is getting my face blasted by a hecking-ton of wind, and not being able to find my friggin' armholes."

"You DON'T remember us ARGUING?" I gasped. Then, I realized he was teasing and cautiously added, "Okay, you win. Peace, brother. What happens at Deer Lodge Pass stays at Deer

Lodge Pass. But, from now on, please help me watch out for you becoming a menace whenever it's cold and we're feeling thirsty."

"Also, whenever we're hiking through a burn," SeeHawk added, recalling our fight on Straight Creek Pass. "Fire and water are positive transformational elements, but too much fire can make a person angry. Plus, wind feeds fire, so whenever the weather gets nasty, I need to keep flowing water."

"That's very esoteric," I teased him, "but if it'll help you be a gentleman in Wyoming, keep that water flowing, baby."

* * *

Hours after leaving Deer Lodge Pass, SeeHawk and I rolled into a deserted campground and kicked off our shoes. It felt cozy to hunker down inside our thin fabric nest and sit still, listening to leftover raindrops drip from the trees onto our sagging fabric ceiling. Everything piled around us stank to high heaven, and that was okay. We relished the odors of our French-onion armpits and musty sleeping bag, mixed with pine needles crushed inside our tent's drafty vestibule because it all smelled pleasantly familiar.

As relaxation softened our mood, SeeHawk began squeezing my shoulders with his sensitive fingers. In synchronicity with the rain, he nibbled my arms, hips, and legs, like a lion cub chewing on its littermate. Finally, he turned himself into a pounding ocean wave.

When our lovemaking ended, I felt like rolling over and going to sleep, but instead, I switched on my headlamp and began my nightly navigational duties.

SeeHawk listened while I recited what the Book of Beans had to say about a confusing, unmapped route that was supposed to be marked with a little spray paint.

At the end of listening, SeeHawk wanted to know, "What does Poppa Jim say?"

"Nothing similar," I recalled while rummaging around trying to find Poppa Jim's directions. "I think his route might be less scenic but easier to follow."

"Can you please read me the directions?" SeeHawk asked.

"I'm looking for them. Hold on..."

Fighting off drowsiness, I searched and re-searched a thick stack of pages for any mention of the name Jerry Creek. Meantime, questions kept drifting through my head. *What might tomorrow's weather be like? How had Jerry gotten a creek named after himself? Was there also a Tom creek?*

After a short period of waiting, SeeHawk dozed off until my voice woke him up.

"Oh shit! Oh shit! I think Poppa Jim's directions fell out of my pocket!"

"What?" he gasped, bolting wide awake.

"I'm sorry...I can't believe it...I think I've lost...Poppa Jim's directions!"

"For avoiding the whole mess you just read to me?"

"Only the morning part. We still have his pages for the afternoon."

Continuing to rifle through everything I still had from the Book of Beans, deLorme's atlas, and the National Forest Service, I finally zeroed in upon one fat, green line.

"See this?" I showed SeeHawk.

His eyes followed my finger along Road 8251, which showed clearly on the Forest Service Map.

"It's the CDT's sidecar. If we take it, we'll see similar views without getting lost. Then, we can follow this obvious fork back to the CDT, and pick it up from where I still have the directions."

"Getting back at what time?"

"Maybe early afternoon?"

"Okay, that sounds reasonable, considering the alternative. Maybe we can even use the road to bust out some fast miles."

After getting a good night's sleep, the next morning, we had an easy time finding Forest Service Road 8251. It truly was a superhighway among backcountry roads. Ho-hum scenery and a couple of ear-grinding ATVs came with the territory, but otherwise, going mainstream gave us a nice intermission from constantly checking maps and guidebook directions. In fact, we found unusual interest in common lodgepole pine trees, ordinary blue sky, and regular giant boulders planted next to the road.

"This must be how Blue Man felt after leaving the restaurant with a full belly," I imagined. "Stuff we don't normally care about looks beautiful today.

SeeHawk proposed, "Let's keep that good feeling going after we're back on the CDT."

Midway through a curve around Delano Creek's headwater valley, a low peak called Starlight Mountain blocked us from seeing the Continental Divide. Numerous dry feeder-gullies began pinching the roundabout road into kinks. It felt like the valley's perimeter was getting doubled in length. Beyond Starlight Mountain, the Continental Divide started peeking over the uphill trees. Everything seemed to be going as planned until the gullies ended and the Forest Road straightened out. The next roadside attraction we saw was a buried culvert pipe, channeling water underneath the road. Its outflow formed a thin waterfall, spilling into a creek whose colorful pebble floor was mounded into islands. Top-down sunlight made the decision easy. We stopped to skinny dip and have a quick drink. While drying off, SeeHawk checked his water supply.

"Do you want to fill 'er up while we're here?" he suggested.

"Not right before climbing back to the Divide," I reminded him. "The turnoff ought to be really close, and, once we get up there, it won't take us long to reach Poppa Jim's spring."

"Let's hope it's flowing, though."

"Fingers crossed."

"How many miles, from here to the spring?"

"Maybe four, altogether?"

"Hm," he reflected. "Four miles is long enough for things to go wrong. We should probably refill one bag, just in case."

After stashing just one spare water bag, SeeHawk followed me back onto Road 8251's sun-washed straightaway. At one point, the road began to lose elevation. This development helped us pick up speed. I noticed the valley's adjacent treetops rising past our heads and felt puzzled. Why were we significantly descending where the road was supposed to fork uphill? Checking our atlas made me wonder if we had overshot our mark. Yikes, how could that be possible? The uphill forest had been visible all the way around. Any road cut into it could hardly have escaped our notice. Well, maybe I was reading the map incorrectly because, what other explanation could there be? Erasure of the uphill road, for erosion control? Or to prevent jeeps and ATVs from driving up to the Continental Divide? That would have been a lot of machine work for such a lightly traveled area. In any case, I said nothing to SeeHawk before he invited me to sing…

Good day, Sunshine,
Dum-da dum-da,
Good day, Sunshine,
Dum-da dum-da,
Gooood day, Sunnnshine.
I took a walk,
Down a windy, er, calm road.
Iyy looked around and there was
no one around.
I don't know, the wor-herds
of this song.
Buuut I'm singing 'cause there's
No one around.
Good day, Sunshine…

Singing plumped out my fiancé's hollow cheeks and made his eyes dance with happiness. How could I bother him with an annoying little newsflash about things not adding up correctly? Eventually, though, I had to ask.

"Don't you think it's a little strange for us not to be seeing our turnoff yet?"

"I haven't even been looking," he confessed. "Do you think we passed it?"

"No idea, but our map makes the upper road look as big as the one we're on."

"Then it's going to be obvious," he declared and went back to humming nostalgic *Beatles* tunes.

We lost altitude for another ten minutes, before plunging downhill so steeply that no singing fool could deny we were aiming toward the valley's floor.

"Dang," SeeHawk sighed when I delivered the bad news. "This is like getting a C-minus on a pop-quiz about what we learned yesterday."

Turning around, we began carefully scanning the road's uphill shoulder for any kind of turnoff concealed by vegetation, erosion, or mechanical bulldozing. After 20 minutes, we decided the map's cartographer must have chewed some bad pinesap.

Feeling duped, I ranted toward the sky, "Doesn't the Forest Service need accurate maps to put out forest fires? How am I supposed to lead us out of Montana, if I can't even trust the Forest Service to map their own roads? And, the Book of Beans...hardly any signs...Poppa Jim's updates, where the heck are they?"

Catching a side glance from me, SeeHawk scowled, "Hey, don't blame me for today's little detour!"

"Sorry," I sighed. "It's just really frustrating to still be missing those updates when we're down to our atlas and a compass I can barely use."

"Plus, a GPS we never look at, which I can barely use," SeeHawk admitted. "But, check that out!"

Looking where his finger pointed, I saw a new wooden sign labeled, "Libby Creek Trail No. 80." Despite the sign being small, it was plainly visible from the road.

"How on EARTH did we miss seeing THAT?" I gasped.

SeeHawk shrugged, looking proud to be of service.

The name "Libby Creek" sounded familiar. Summoning Poppa Jim's text, I confirmed that he mentioned a signed jeep track labeled Libby Creek Trail No. 80.

Putting two and two together, I told SeeHawk, "Apparently, Poppa Jim saw this trail drop off to the left when he hiked along the Divide. Which means, following it uphill should take us to the CDT."

"Right on!" SeeHawk grinned. "Show me where to aim. I'm ready to start climbing."

We searched every yard of roadside trees growing within eyeshot of the sign. Many small entryways between the trees looked enticing, but none contained any kind of footpath, game trail or even human footprints. Instead, we found some discouraging rock-formations and piles of deadwood from an old fire. Lacking encouragement, I returned to the road's open corridor, for another look over its uphill trees. The flat crest above had a prominent central bend, which could serve as our North Star. Maybe if we just bushwhacked uphill, we could sort things out after we reached the timberline. Although, what was I thinking? Blundering 1-2 miles through dark woods boobytrapped with deadfall and rock formations?

SeeHawk thought we should split up to search for a trail farther from the sign. While being separated, I heard him holler, "Bingo!"

His search had uncovered an old-looking trail, which we followed for fifty-or-a-hundred steps until it ran into an impassable ditch.

Frowning, I led him back to the Libby Creek sign, saying, "There's only one thing left to do."

"Start bailing?" he guessed. "Find something to sacrifice? Book tickets to Hawaii?"

"Nope." Reaching into my pocket, I gave him the instruction, "Now, remember to always put red in the shed."

When SeeHawk saw me start fiddling with our compass, he nervously suggested, "Before we get embroiled in whatever you're planning, should we go back to the waterfall and fill a couple more bags of liquid insurance?"

"You mean, in case we need to make an emergency dry camp on a forty-five-degree angle in the woods?"

"Er, something like that," he blushed. "Not that I'm doubting you, but, just saying."

"Don't worry," I assured him. "We'll reach the crest within a couple of hours, even if I can't figure out how to use this dang-blasted device."

Still looking worried, he timidly suggested, "I know this sounds crazy, Sunshine, but would you consider backtracking to where we camped last night and starting fresh tomorrow morning? I mean, might the Book of Beans' route be easier than all this mess?"

"Are you KIDDING?" I laughed. "Please, tell me you're kidding."

"Ha-ha," he fake laughed. "Of course, I was kidding. You know I'm a kidder. Fell for that old joke, did you? Ha-ha, sucker."

End of discussion.

Barnstorming into the uphill woods, I kept the compass dangling from my neck, with full intention to use it. Never mind that I had not adjusted its declination to account for the difference between magnetic north versus true north. Who cared about a worst-case error of 12 degrees, within the scope of 1-2 miles? If such nitpicks could bother me, my Native American name would not have been Flies By Seat of Pants.

Once SeeHawk set aside his concerns, he started helping me improvise detours around heaps of fallen trees, dry brush, and living shrubs. It was the kind of bushwhack that could best have been accomplished with a machete, chainsaw, and flask of whiskey. Nevertheless, we tried hard to follow the compass, until we stumbled across a very old footpath.

"Well, whaddya know?" SeeHawk beamed. "Hello, LCT! Where've you been all these years?"

Observing the Libby Creek Trail's condition, I wryly added, "It looks like the Forest Service doesn't need to worry about job security."

Growing reflective, SeeHawk asked, "Why would they install a brand new sign before making the trail ready to use? Just to help work crews know where to start?"

I dryly reminded him, "Why didn't we find a road where there's a big road fork shown on our map?"

"Ah, yes," he laughed in agreement.

Unfortunately, the LCT had no intention of letting us off easy. Within a hundred yards, it dove beneath so much deadwood, leftover from an old fire, that we seriously considered turning around...only to have the trail reappear long enough to regain our trust...only to have it disappear, and so forth, until we could hardly guess how far we had traveled from Road 8251. Weaving back and forth made our compass heading useless. I finally just stuffed the dizzy little whirligig back into my pocket and switched on my internal radar. The mood of the hunt grew tense, but we breathed easier after emerging from the wreckage, onto a clean trail.

SeeHawk's mood grew positively chipper when he started spotting deer, elk, and bear tracks stamped all over the trail.

Our luck held out until we ran into a clear-cut as wide as an airstrip. Its legacy was a minefield of tall grass, tree stumps, and potholes, through which we had to mince steps, searching for an exit.

When SeeHawk noticed the skylight fading, he worried that we might run out of water. This notion caused him to get terribly excited about seeing a few tablespoons of brown-colored liquid gleam from inside a deer's hoof print.

"Do you think we should treat it and pack it?" he suggested.

"Are you kidding?" I snapped. "We're not desperate enough to drink water from a HOOF PRINT! We just need to find the trail. Come on. Let's keep looking."

Eventually, we did find an exit from the clear-cut, which led us through suspiciously thick overgrowth. It was probably a game trail but that was okay. Game animals often intercepted human trails. Sooner or later, it might lead us to a trail heading toward the Continental Divide. At least, that was our hope, until it dumped us into another clear-cut, which appeared to have no exit.

"This must be where the loggers went home for Christmas," SeeHawk muttered.

"Never mind," I decided, "because we know where to aim from here."

Bushwhacking out of the second clear-cut, we soon reached a snowmobile trail climbing into the spoils of a different logging operation. For some distance on both sides, the mountain's whole timberline had been lowered by machines, turning its highest 200-feet into a minefield of tree stumps buried under grass.

"Finally!" SeeHawk grinned, fixing his eyes upon the top of the climb.

"Not so fast," I warned him. "What about over there?"

Together, we turned to examine a forested incline, angled kitty-corner to the rubble above us, which intercepted the crest around its central bend.

"What do you think?" I showed SeeHawk. "Going that way would add an extra mile, but also save our ankles."

Our spare bag of water was half-empty. Camp time was approaching, and we had still not eaten lunch.

Starting to have regrets, SeeHawk remarked, "I should have bagged some water from that hoofprint."

"Well, it's too late now," I stated. "So, which do you want to prioritize? Climbing less distance? Or saving our ankles?"

SeeHawk agreed that our ankles took priority.

Veering sideways, we mounted a terrace of skinny cow trails, climbing steeply through the right-hand trees. It took 15 minutes to reach the upper crest. Trees grew over the top, but there was lots of open space between them. With plenty of room for walking, and with the summit being so narrow that we could almost look off both sides at once, the CDT should have been obvious. We had not crossed any manmade trails on our way up. Nor, could a trail have been hiding behind the crest, whose backside plunged into a pit trap of brushy woods. Clearly, the CDT had to stay atop the summit if its builders were not daft, so where was it?

SeeHawk threw me a questioning look.

"This is... really... strange," I mumbled.

"Could another crest be hidden behind this one?"

Staring at the pit trap's formidable vegetation, I said, "If it's that way, we're definitely not taking a shortcut."

"Okay, so what are we doing?"

"Feeling sure the trail has to be right under our noses because everything else has made sense until now."

"Except for, the big road fork we never saw," SeeHawk reminded me.

"Well, true, but we found the Libby Creek sign, so we couldn't have been way off-base."

"Until we left the road, anyway."

"Well, if all we've done, since then, is climb into Nowheresville, I'm going to need a brain scan, some aspirin, and a pizza."

"Plus, a tall glass of water to wash it all down," SeeHawk crooned.

That remark floored me. It was my fault we had not packed more spare water before leaving the road. Personally, though, my own greater concern was having skipped lunch.

While SeeHawk waited for me to choose our next move, he paced back and forth, searching and re-searching the same visible crest.

I reviewed our literature long enough to feel certain that we were standing in the right place, but shoot. What good was certainty without a trail?

"Just in case my head is screwed on backward," I decided, "let's descend back to the snowmobile trail and try climbing through all that logging rubble. At least, then we'll end up closer to Poppa Jim's spring."

SeeHawk openly laughed, "Are saying you want to BACK-TRACK, sweetheart?"

"Yes," I admitted, "and don't give me any grief, or I might change my mind."

Returning downhill and readjusting our aim, we tiptoed from the snowmobile trail into a mess of tree stumps buried in tall grass. I kept my head down, trying not to feel pressured by long golden sunbeams tilting toward the sky. At the top of the climb, and roughly 1-mile past the crest's central bend, we ran into a half-eaten CD-sign.

"Well, what do you know?" I chuckled, experiencing both delight and embarrassment. "At least, DEER know where to find the CDT. And, of course, it had to be here. I mean, where else could it be?"

Exhaling fully, both of us flung our backpacks onto a patch of soft turf and gratefully collapsed. Only then did I notice tiny flutters leaving my nerves. I had not been afraid of getting lost; it had just been disturbing to question my own sanity. But anyway, thank goodness, that moment was over.

SeeHawk lay back and closed his eyes, while I got right to work putting out lunch. The turf's yellow buttercups and flowering dandelions made a beautiful platter for spreading cashew butter and honey onto whole-wheat crackers. By the time we finished eating, most of Montana's residents were probably washing their dinner dishes beneath golden windows.

SeeHawk felt like calling it a day and finding a place to camp, but tough luck. We still needed water, so he lumbered back to his feet and refastened his backpack's sweat-stained straps.

Not until revisiting the half-eaten CD-sign did I realize it did not indicate whether we should turn right or left.

When I mentioned the choice to SeeHawk, he chuckled, "Um, Earth to Sunshine? Doesn't a sign facing toward the right make it pretty obvious?"

"Not necessarily," I corrected him. "It's a two-directional trail."

"How so?" he frowned. "There's no sign facing left."

"Hello, tired one!" I laughed. "Earth to SeeHawk? All trails are two-way, by definition."

"Oh right," he blushed.

"But, you do bring up one good point. The CDT has so many northbound signs, and so few southbound signs, some people might think it's a one-way trail."

"No kidding. Well, anyway, we know which way we're going, so would you like to do the honors?

"First, I need to make sure we really do know where to aim because I've lost touch with the crest, so I can't be sure we're not on some weird wiggle where the crest doesn't aim south."

"Should we check our maps?"

"They don't provide enough detail to help in this situation."

"Even though they got us up here?"

"You mean, even though they got us to where we couldn't find the trail?"

"Well, right, " SeeHawk frowned. "So, should we check our compass, then?"

"Yes, but keep in mind that, no matter if it says east, south or west, we'll still try going left first because that's the direction of the spring."

"So, you really don't care what our compass says?"

"I'll care if it points to Mars."

Digging out the indisputable instrument, I held it level in my hand and patiently waited for its needle to stop wiggling.

"There, now see?" I showed him. "This section of the crest actually does run north-south. It's just like I thought. North is on our right. South on our left. We're supposed to turn left."

"What?" he protested. "Nuh-uh, Sunshine. Look where the needle is pointing. Left is west."

"No, silly," I laughed. "The N isn't where north is. Sorry, I neglected to rotate the dial. But, just so you know, the dial is superfluous. You can find magnetic north just by looking where the needle points."

"But, the needle isn't lined up with the N," he showed me.

"Right, but you can still tell where magnetic north is, just by looking at the needle."

"But, what about the N?"

"FORGET the N! Can't you understand? The red needle and the dial are totally independent. You don't have to use the dial to find magnetic north."

"What's wrong with the dial?"

"Argh, never mind. Look, I'll fix it your way if you want. There. Are we done? Now the needle is marking magnetic north."

"Thank you," he beamed. "Now, I can clearly see where north is. Why didn't you do that before?"

"Because I wanted you to understand how the red needle works. That way, if you ever need to operate our compass, you'll know how to find magnetic north."

"But, I already know how the needle works. You just put red in the shed—"

"ARRGH," I wailed. "You DON'T HAVE to do that! Sheesh. Never mind. Let's just decide which way to turn and get on with finding the spring."

"I thought we already decided on turning right."

"You mean, left.

"Right, left. Not here, though. First, we need to follow the sign, right?"

"Eeaugh! SeeHawk! Didn't we just go over this? FORGET the sign. It doesn't MATTER which direction the sign is facing. By definition, all trails that could ever exist in the universe are TWO-WAY TRAILS...unless..."

In mid-rant, my eye fell upon a Road and Area Restrictions sign, which had been patiently standing alongside the deer-eaten CDT sign. Its list of regulations suddenly made me think. *What if this is a trailhead made for snowmobilers trying to find the CDT, and it's not the actual CDT? In that case, only one sign would be needed, for people going outbound, not for people coming back.*

When SeeHawk heard my theory, he argued, "But, what about snowmobilers leaving the crest in a different place from where they came up?"

"Going out of bounds is people's own choice. It doesn't justify installing extra signs," I reasoned.

Suddenly, he grinned, "Wait, are you saying we should turn right, after all?"

"Maybe," I admitted, "but, can you please not rub it in? I don't want to start bickering like an old married couple."

"Okay, okay," he chuckled. "But, you DO want to turn right, right?"

"Correct, and hopefully not by mistake because, if right turns out to be wrong, we aren't going to find the spring before dark."

"Which means, you're putting my money where my mouth is? Okay, got it," he winked, not even looking worried, as he followed me toward the right.

Immediately, we entered tight conifer woods, whose enclosure focused our view straight ahead. The effect was like entering a dark green tunnel. We kept going straight, past a point where I thought we should have rounded the crest's central bend. What did that mean? Did the bend not match its appearance from below? I started to feel uneasy until the green tunnel finally did begin to curve. Phew, okay then. I was not going crazy. However, the tunnel just kept going and going, as if it was never going to end. No peepholes appeared. We could not gauge our progress. Within a few minutes, the uneasy feeling returned because, cripes. Where the heck were we? Aiming toward the loosely wooded crest above the cow paths? Merging onto a parallel, second crest, hidden behind the pit-trap? If so, was it time to turn around? We still needed water. Every minute of daylight remaining might be needed to help us find the spring. I felt pressured to intervene, but at the same time, I felt increasingly curious. Because my intuition said we were aiming toward the cow paths. Any minute now, the trees were going to loosen, and we were going to find ourselves on the same crest where, previously, we had not found a trail. This made no sense. I had to know the explanation. Otherwise, I was going to feel tortured for the rest of my life. Therefore, I led SeeHawk onward through the green tunnel for another quarter-hour, desperately hoping to find the answer at any moment. *Please, oh please,* I kept thinking. *Trees break away.* But, nope. Finally, I just had to blow the whistle. Enough was enough. We needed to turn around.

"Are you joking?" SeeHawk demanded.

"I wish," was my answer.

Neither of us spoke while struggling to contain our separate disappointments.

My itch had not been scratched.

SeeHawk felt thirsty, but also afraid to drink the water left in his bag.

We had turned around without ever seeing anything outside the green tunnel. Heading back toward where we had eaten lunch, we saw shadows flooding the crest and worried about the time. It took us half an hour to get back to square one. As soon as we arrived, our eyes landed upon something that rendered us both speechless. Next to the deer-eaten CD-sign adjoining our lunch site, and positioned way-high up a tree, floated a tiny little CD-sign, meekly soliciting low flying birds.

"That must be the height where snowmobilers travel, during a heavy winter," SeeHawk imagined.

"We ate lunch practically beneath the sign we couldn't find?" I groaned.

"Apparently," he nodded.

Narrowing my eyes, I suggested, "Shall we agree never to speak about this again?"

Laughing, SeeHawk and I shook on it.

Then, onward we went, past a soiled placemat of buttercups and dandelions, now definitively aiming toward Poppa Jim's spring.

A quarter-mile farther along, we spied an ancient wooden sign saying, "Libby Creek Trail No. 80." Stopping to have a look downhill, we could not find Poppa Jim's jeep track entering the lower forest. Again, that seemed strange, since Poppa Jim never made mistakes or omitted important details. It was obvious where the trail should have left the crest, and that whole section was underlaid by thick vegetation.

"I guess, it's a good we broke our pact not to bushwhack anymore," SeeHawk concluded, "or else, we might never have made it up here."

"Right," I agreed, "so the lesson we've been learning this whole month is never to bushwhack, except when we should."

"Er, what does that do to our pledge not to bushwhack. Are we still committed?"

"Totally," I grinned.

A silhouetted mountain kept its mouth shut and just slurped away the sun. Thankfully, we still had enough daylight left to fill several empty bags with fresh, clear water from Poppa Jim's long-awaited spring

One last climb carried us near eight enormous elk, who got spooked and bolted as soon as we caught their eyes.

The climb ended upon a balmy mountaintop, housing the defunct Hungry Hill Mine. Weather-beaten and collapsing, the abandoned mine's ruins lent historical ambiance to our twilight dinner. The hour was getting late, so we did not bother reading any guidebooks, before laying down for a short power sleep. There was not much to prepare for tomorrow anyway. After spending a full week circling the valley containing Butte and Anaconda, tomorrow we were finally going to drop into the valley and fetch our next resupply box. Of course, we were also hoping to do laundry, eat ice cream, read newspaper comics from home, and otherwise replenish our strength for a speedy passage across the rest of southern Montana.

* * *

Bright yellow sunlight blasted my eyes open at 4:45 am.

When I saw the glare, I complained in confusion, "Didn't we just go to bed?"

Woken up by my voice, SeeHawk groaned, "Ouch, that's bright. Is the Mother Ship landing?"

Sometimes, sleeping only four hours at a stretch made us cringe whenever Apollo came knocking. Being only one short descent and one hitchhike away from Anaconda, it would not have been negligent to sleep in. We only bolted awake because few things could get us onto our feet faster than escaping from early heat to the promise of ice cream.

Heading away from the Hungry Hill Mine, we followed a graded logging road steadily downhill, aiming to reach Highway 274. Once again, whistling *Peter and the Wolf,* we spoke about nothing that mattered to anyone. One jubilant wildflower meadow forced us to pull over, sink our bones into its feathery grass and let our eyes dance across cake-sprinkle flowers, colored pink, lavender, bright white, buttercream, and egg-yolk yellow. My personal favorites were the white Mariposa Lilies, whose whisker-thin stems each supported a flower goblet cradling three dregs of Merlot.

Around the meadow's edge ran a border of pine and fir trees flecked with golden sunlight. More goldenness flickered off a gentle stream, tinkling through the meadow like liquid windchimes. In its center stood an old log cabin, floating upon the grass like a primitive wooden arc.

Altogether, SeeHawk and I felt steeped in poetry, lounging beside a hedgerow of shrubs, feeling the grass suck miles out of our feet. The flowery meadow was our little hideaway, disturbed only by our own teeth chomping jam-sweetened granola, until two panting dogs shot through the hedgerow, licking the air, with their tails wagging. Behind the dogs appeared a plaid-shirted gentleman, probably in his 60's, whose blue jeans sported a hefty pistol and sheathed 6-inch knife.

I had rarely seen weapons worn casually, so I shrank back as the intruder approached.

"Good morning!" he announced. "Where you headed this morning?"

SeeHawk did not hesitate to say, "Anaconda."

The man stared blankly.

"To get resupplies for hiking the CDT."

Still, no bells rang, but the intruder looked interested.

Deciding to give him a full explanation, I described how the Continental Divide Trail circled Butte and then the Big Hole valley, before heading southward into Wyoming.

In the listener's turn to speak, he pointed to a clear-cut overlooking the meadow and reminisced, "Back when I was a logger, I used to work up there (cutting trees) on days like this... I've always been fond of coming back to visit..."

He segued from logging to talking about Montana's fickle weather...then, his dogs...which sparked a conversation about our dog...which ended with goodbyes before the man rounded up his dogs and resumed climbing the road we had just come down.

By this time, SeeHawk and I were finished eating, so we packed up quickly and got back on the road. Never, for a moment, did we think to question the logger's alibi for being in the woods that morning.

A short distance farther down the road, we met a much smaller man, climbing toward us, who could have been in his 70's. He wore farmer's overalls, beneath an external frame backpack whose storage compartment was a plastic kitchen wastebasket. Stretched over his wastebasket was a perforated tarp, doing double-duty as both its lid and an emergency rain-poncho. In one hand, he clutched a gallon juice jug containing a few tablespoons of red *Kool-Aid* powder. Altogether, he looked glad to be alive and happy to say hello.

"I'm going to meet my son from Louisiana," the man proudly announced. "We're on a mission to scout elk."

This news cautioned SeeHawk and me to seal our lips because we were not willing to fink on the proud beauties we had spooked last night.

Trying to change the subject, I casually remarked, "We just saw another man go the way you're headed. You'll probably catch him if he takes a break soon."

"I've already met him," the elder man replied, "and I don't know why he's here."

"Oh, we do," I offered, gaily recapping the logger's story about visiting his old workplace.

The elder man grunted disapprovingly, "He said the same to me, but I don't believe him."

SeeHawk and I caught our breath. Why such mistrust? With no explanation offered, it would have been rude to ask.

As the mysterious little man strode past us, he gave us a salute with his juice jug, and declared, "You'll see my pickup truck parked behind a gate you'll be coming to shortly."

That was his farewell, after which, off he went, climbing toward the elk whose location was safe with us.

We did, indeed, find the promised pickup truck, parked at the road's end. It was blocking an official-looking wilderness gate as if nobody might ever need drive-through access. Two ruby-red garters dangling from its rearview mirror implied ownership by a teenage boy, circa 1970. All this strangeness returned us to wondering about the elder man's mistrust of the logger. Were the two going to bump into each other higher up the mountain? Was either man going to find the elk we had spooked?

After finishing one last descent, SeeHawk and I finally reached Highway 274. The asphalt was radiating such intense heat that we could feel our chins baking while spending a full hour flagging down a ride. This time, we got picked up by a man wearing blue jean cutoffs with an old white t-shirt, who described himself as a self-made millionaire. His jalopy of an old pickup truck, which barely looked capable of reaching highway speeds, nearly skidded to a stop when he saw us jumping up and down like chimpanzees. Obviously, the ride was not going to be pretty. Given our condition, it was a match made in Heaven.

The driver did not bother to ask about fine china before chucking our backpacks into his open truck-bed as if he was pitching haybales. Once inside the cab, he started asking questions, like a paid tour guide. Who were we? What had brought us to Montana? Where did we want to go? While listening to our answers, he ratcheted his jalopy into first gear and roared up the highway, using sports car maneuvers to compensate for the old girl's sluggish acceleration.

SeeHawk and I leaned around every curve, discreetly clutching the cab's springy bench seat, for fear that clutching the dashboard might look rude.

Our driver launched into reverently praising Anaconda's beautiful countryside. Then, he explained about himself, "I got started working in the metal industry, down in Southern California. Now, owning a small airplane means I can spend two weeks, out of every year, entertaining my friends who like the outdoors. Today, I dropped a few folks in the Big Hole. I'll pick them up later after they're finished rafting."

He went on to summarize Anaconda's turbulent mining history. Beginning with a copper boom that financed two iconic smelter stacks, the city had suffered an economic recession that shut down its copper company, resulting in its smelting equipment being auctioned off, while almost everyone below retirement age packed up and left town.

"But now things are starting to pick up again," the driver reported. "We've got a new wave of youngsters coming in from other states. It's like this place is a well-kept secret just starting to leak out. You've got your mountains, rivers, skiing, hunting, fishing, rafting...anything you could possibly want for recreation. Plus, an old movie theater that's a real masterpiece. Fifth-grandest cinemas in America. All painted fancy in copper and gold. You've got to see the place while you're in town, even if you don't have time to watch a movie."

Indeed, Anaconda's outskirts did transport us back to an era when cookie-cutter lawns fronted square stucco houses. The main boulevard's traffic was gridlocked with big rigs, grinding their motors between dusty cars all jockeying for access to gas stations and restaurants. We could no longer converse until we cranked up the jalopy's rolling windows because of all the street noise.

While driving past a supermarket that had seen better days, we asked our driver where to find a Laundromat and a cheap motel.

"Oh, that's easy," he grinned. "Anne's got the cleanest rooms in town. I'll drop you right on her doorstep if you can wait for me to get gas first. My favorite Laundromat's just down the street. They've got a bar inside, so you can order a G-and-T while your clothes are washing."

Anne turned out to be a sweet, older lady, with neatly curled hair and smiling blue eyes.

I was first to greet her, by enthusiastically saying, "We hear you've got the cleanest rooms in town."

She whispered like an aspen leaf, "Yes, I believe I do."

In support of her claim, she showed us an available room that could have passed the White Glove Test. While letting us pay cash, she was probably thinking, *I hope these two stinkers will jump into the shower immediately.*

We stank, plain and simple. However, in our defense, the longer we lived in nature, the dirtier civilization seemed by comparison. Nowadays, funky motel carpets, smutty bedspreads, traffic smog, restaurant grease, public toilets, and chlorinated tap water had come to seem more or less revolting. Equally objectionable were heavily perfumed fabric-softeners and laundry detergents which people used to make themselves smell "fresh." Of course, we could not deny needing some powerful bar soap and industrial-strength machine suds to clean away our funk, before we might try entering any public eating establishments.

Inside our motel room's spotless bathroom, I got surprised by a face looking back at me in the mirror. Its moon shape was familiar, but what about those slightly thinner cheeks? Visible jawline? A few new highlights in the same brown hair? Altogether, I saw a face resembling one I had seen in Marysville, four weeks earlier, except for its eyes, which looked shockingly alert.

SeeHawk waited until I handed over the bathroom before he took a turn insulting Anne's shower.

Once we were both presentable, we bundled up armloads of dirty clothing, newspaper comics, and ice cream, for a quick stroll across Anaconda's main drag.

It was Wednesday on a sunny afternoon, and the Laundromat's cocktail bar was in full swing. Muggy cigarette fog greeted us at the door, making us ask a grim question. Would spin-drying improve how our clothes smelled, or make them reek worse? Throwing caution to the wind, we filled two washing machines, before cracking open our ice cream and sitting down to enjoy the latest adventures of *Doonesbury*.

Presently, a local resident sat down beside us to start chewing the fat. He was lean and short, with feisty eyes, and a muscular body for being over 60. His self-introduction began with a recent move from Butte to Anaconda, which seemed to him like a significant relocation.

Curiosity prodded us to inquire about the man's childhood growing up in Butte.

He looked pleased to recollect, "When I was a kid, I used to work in the mines as a mucker. Know what a mucker is?"

We shook our heads.

"My uncle'd blast out big old chunks of rock. Then, it was my job to get down and shovel ore into all those cars they'd send up the chute, and have 'em weighed. My uncle'd get paid by the pound. Didn't matter how much copper was in the ore. Me, I got paid two bits an hour. Didn't matter how much we shoveled. You know how much two bits is?"

SeeHawk and I shook our heads.

"Well, you figger there's eight bits in a dollar. Forty bits in five dollars, so that makes...can you figger out how much two bits is?"

"Twenty-five cents?"

"Bingo!" The mucker winked. "I was paid twenty-five cents an hour. But my uncle, his pay varied, depending on how much we could shovel, so he worked us pretty hard. My uncle was a real fella. You can believe this or not, but I'll tell you. My uncle used to take me out hunting. Fishing, too. Whenever we went fishing or mining or hunting, he never spoke a word. That was his rule. No one was allowed to speak during fishing, hunting, or mining with my uncle. Speak one word? He'd never invite you again. He didn't say it. We just knew. So I kept my mouth shut and we didn't speak until we got to the car. Well, this one time, we went out elk hunting, and, there was snow all over, so we were snowshoeing, and my uncle shot an elk, but he didn't kill it, just wounded it. So the elk took off, and my uncle took off after it. Chased it down in his snowshoes and killed it because he didn't want it running around in the woods all wounded. So he chased it down in his snowshoes, no kidding. The two of us had to haul that big elk all the way back to the car, which by now was a long ways off, 'cause he'd chased it a long way, and the whole time my uncle didn't speak one word. Not 'til we got back to the car. Yep, that was my uncle."

I asked what it had been like growing up in Butte.

"Oh, it was great fun," the man chuckled. "Back when we were kids—I guess that was just after World War Two—we used to go down to Silver Bow Crick." He saw us smile in confusion, and helpfully explained, "That's 'creek' to you folks. Anyhow, Pee Wee Lake drains into Silver Bow Crick. My mom used to tell us never EVER go in Pee Wee Lake or we'd get in big trouble. But, you know, we were kids. So, all of us used to go down to where this big ol' drainpipe, maybe fifteen- or twenty feet across, used to drain out of the mine. Let's see, I guess that would be the Travonia Mine. Anyway, the pipe used to drain water from the mine into Pee Wee Lake, so it was all full of arsenic and heavy metals and such as whatever else they was flushing out of the mine. Pure poison, my mom said. We didn't care, 'cause we were kids. So, every day they'd flush out that mine. Same time each day. Four o'clock in the afternoon. Seven days a week. Us kids would go down and get ourselves some truck tire tubes. Then, we'd go in that drainpipe at three-thirty and climb as high as we could go, hauling them big truck tire tubes. Then, we'd wait 'til come around four o'clock, when you'd hear a click, and that click would tell you it was time for the water to come down. So, we'd all climb onto our tubes and hold real tight, 'till suddenly, the water would come rushing down—fsssheww—and there we'd go! Smack to the end of that twenty-foot pipe and land in Pee Wee Lake," the man concluded with a laugh. "I cut my foot, once, in that lake. There was an old stove sitting right in the middle. Course, my mom told us not to swim, but we went anyway, so I cut my foot diving off that old stove. It bled really bad, but I was afraid to show my mom, so I just wrapped it up in a sock and hid it from her. You know, nobody ever cleaned the cut or nothing, and it healed just fine."

"Maybe there was enough arsenic in the water to sterilize your wound?" I suggested.

"Maybe so," he chuckled. "Anyway, I remember another thing we used to do was ride the electric train from Butte's mines to the smelter in Anaconda. We'd hang on 'til just before the ore cars dropped in the chute to dump their loads. Then, we'd jump off and run 'cross the tracks to jump on an empty car heading back to Butte."

"Are there still any active mines in Butte?"

"Oh sure," he nodded, "but it's all pit mines now. Back in the day, they dug trenches like ant tunnels. Kept tunneling deeper and deeper 'til they couldn't go no farther. Stopped when they hit underground water. So, they started pit mining instead. Dug a big ol' pit that took the roof off all them mines.

That's when the trouble with the water started. You heard about the hassle pumping water outta Butte?"

SeeHawk and I shook our heads.

"It's been all over the papers for years. The environmental agencies were trying to do something about it, but nobody can figger out what to do. See, all this water drains off the mountains around Butte and pools underground, so when they first dug them ant tunnels, they had to pump out the water to keep 'em clear. After they stopped pumping, the tunnels filled up, which was okay 'cause they weren't using 'em anymore. But, when they dug out that pit mine, they put a huge hole in the roof and started letting out all that underground water. Once it started coming, nobody could stop it. Now, they have to keep pumping all the time. Send the water into evaporating ponds instead of flooding Butte. 'Parently there's no way to plug the tunnels. I think if they ever turned off those pumps, South Butte would go right underwater!"

SeeHawk and I struggled to imagine the entire city of Butte going underwater, while we finished our laundry and hurried outside to escape from the smoke.

During a quick visit to Anaconda's run-down supermarket, we bought cheese and other perishables, before realizing we had no place to store them overnight.

Anne volunteered her refrigerator, but she warned us in a whisper, "It'll be safe with me unless I get hungry."

Once we were out of earshot, I curiously asked SeeHawk, "What is it about Anne that makes her seem unusually humble, or playful or something?"

He answered without thinking, "It's her confidence. I'll bet you any money she used to be a schoolteacher."

We were gone from the lobby when two other CDT thru-hikers sauntered in and asked Anne for a room. She forwarded them to us, even though her prices ended up sending them to a different motel.

When SeeHawk heard a knock on the door and went to open it, he found himself facing a tall stranger, who introduced himself as "String Stick." Smooth olive skin and a lean, muscular build made the stranger appear less than 30 years old. Another ten years were added by the man's neatly clipped beard, banded straw hat, and intelligent brown eyes.

A second young stranger was introduced as "Dutch," before he melted into the background of String Stick's opening remarks.

I story-swap ensued, during which I noticed some curious things about String Stick. For instance, every time he talked about thru-hiking, he slouched. Whereas, every time he talked about his "real life" job marketing high-tech products in Seattle, Washington, he straightened up to his full height. When standing erect, with shoulders spread apart, he looked capable of carrying large loads, but, of course, being a thru-hiker, he wore an ultralight backpack. His Trail Name derived from a small stringed instrument touted to be his only "luxury" of the trip, which he used for entertaining friends in camp. Whenever String Stick talked about art or music, he fingered a charm dangling from his neck, which he never touched while speaking about computers. His own self-description further revealed him to be a meticulous trip-planner, who had pre-printed a full set of CDT maps before leaving home and annotated them with information from Poppa Jim's guidebooks.

Dutch, by comparison, looked barely 20 years old and likely to stay ageless for the next 30 years. His physique was pure vanilla, with milky, smooth skin and vertical blond hair. He covered most of the hair with a brown cowboy hat—given to him by a Trail Angel from New Mexico—which sat squarely on his head like a sheriff, rather than tipped back like a cowboy. A small teddy bear strapped on his backpack kept him connected with his girlfriend from Holland. His long-sleeved shirt and thin synthetic pants conformed to typical thru-hiker fashions, but, instead of wearing sneakers, he wore stout leather boots. Also, upon speaking with him, I found it quaint to hear that growing blond chin-whiskers made him feel "adventurous," and that his girlfriend kept begging him to shave before returning home.

In a thick Dutch accent, the young traveler described his first month spent hiking the CDT northbound, before he had met String Stick, and before SeeHawk and I reached Glacier National Park.

"I'f already finished hiking frough New Mexico," Dutch recalled. "Me and tsis other guy, Redbeard, wass hiking in May. He'ss an American I'f met on the Internet. We'f plan to hike tse whole trail, but now Redbeard iss with his friend and I'm with String Stick."

"If you and Redbeard started off heading north together, what made you flip-flop?" I asked him.

Dutch groped for appropriate words to explain, "We'f come frough New Mexico, no problem. Tsen, we got to the San Juan Mountains. You know tsoss mountains?"

"Only by reputation."

"Well, tsey deserff what tsey say," he smirked. "We hit so much snow it wass like runnink into a wall. Snow everywhere. Too much. We try to hike but iss no good. Finally we chuss gayf up and say, 'Forget it. We go to Montana and try heading south.'"

I felt my stomach tighten. If this fit young buck—whose capabilities were sure to exceed mine—had failed to cross the San Juan Mountains during late May, how were we going to enter them during October?

"Did you get much rain in New Mexico?" I asked him. "Because, we met a couple of thru-hikers in Glacier National Park who started around the same time you did, and apparently they got rained on every single day in New Mexico."

Dutch looked quite surprised. "Rain?" he exclaimed. "Wass not raining. No, I like New Mexico ferry much. Nice sunsets. Ferry colorful. I like to watch them."

So, there it was—proof of how much difference a few days or weeks could make, toward shaping one's experience of any given mountain.

String Stick and Dutch wanted to accompany SeeHawk and me for a walk to Anaconda's fancy movie theater, so we all went together and bought tickets for the movie Pearl Harbor. A couple of hours later, we headed back out to see the movie, but this time it was raining cats and dogs. String Stick wore his slim, homemade brown nylon poncho, beside SeeHawk and me wearing our tent-shaped store-bought $20 navy-blue and forest-green ponchos, with Dutch outshining all of us in his stylish red Gore-Tex jacket. Along the way, we watched blue-edged lightning splinter the rain into fiery sparkles. Thunder clattered the sidewalk's windowpanes like dish carts. A set of electrical power lines failed to scare the menfolk, but I bent over while passing underneath them.

Having paid $3 for admission seemed like a steal when we entered the theater's palatial gallery. Velvet curtains, suspended from a grandiose copper-and-gold ceiling, set the stage for something big, like an opera or a Broadway musical. Consequently, even just finding our seats felt exciting.

Before the gallery's lights went down, I met a lady in the restroom who was from my original hometown in California. Hearing her mention familiar placenames made me ponder the distance between Montana and California...California and Seattle...Canada and Mexico...Holland...Japan. How could anyone truly comprehend such distances without being in every place at once?

When the movie Pearl Harbor began, pictures flashed across the screen of dangers that nobody in our group had experienced.

After the movie ended, my brain naturally started comparing things that seemed scary in my own life (steep cliffs, loose scree, grizzly bears, earthquakes, car crashes, muggers, giant ocean waves, nuclear power plants) with the events of Pearl Harbor. Such reflections, in turn, made me wonder who was presently safer. People thru-hiking the CDT? Or people living in my hometown? As I waited to fall asleep, I could not decide.

* * *

First thing next morning, Anne cracked a joke about having eaten our cheese. Then she gave us a wink and fetched the cheese from her refrigerator.

The motel had vacancies, so Anne gave her housekeeper permission to drive four needy thru-hikers back to the CDT. As an added perk, the housekeeper persuaded Dutch to mail her a pair of wooden shoes after returning to Holland.

It was 7:30 a.m. when our group got dropped off at the Mount Haggin Wildlife Management Area. Ultimately, we were all aiming for the same skyline, belonging to the Anaconda-Pintlar Wilderness, but our intended routes of approach were different.

SeeHawk and I were planning to follow the Book of Beans' cross-country route across a flat grassland, first heading westward, taking a jog southward, and finally following a flat gravel road toward the wilderness boundary.

By contrast, String Stick and Dutch were planning to follow Poppa Jim's high route over and down to a talus cliff alleged to be the CDT's worst hazard.

Obviously, that cliff was not meant for me, so, feeling a bit sad to see our friends go, SeeHawk and I had to wave goodbye and wish them good luck.

Left alone in the parking lot, we both needed a moment to clear our heads. Echoes of Anaconda's traffic noise, along with conversations from that morning's car ride and flashbacks from the movie Pearl Harbor kept cycling through our minds. Both of us had difficulty shifting back into wilderness mode until a cool breeze slipped in and gave us a nudge. Glancing upward in surprise, we saw a fleet of cumulus clouds sprouting early bubbles. The breeze they carried smelled suspiciously moist. The grassland ahead offered no place to hide. Goodbye, brain fog. It was time to get moving.

Our first waypoint was a small cluster of cabins called Mule Ranch. Heading cross-country into the grassland beyond, we started running into streams that were impossible to spot from any distance because the grass was quite tall. Fortunately, borders of willows growing along the streams' banks gave us some advance warning, wherever their tip-top leaves peeked through the grass. Several of the streams were almost skinny enough to permit hopping across them, but not quite skinny enough, and fording them would have gotten our shoes all muddy. Therefore, we sought to avoid the streams by following interconnected cow paths, which could randomly be followed from one to the next.

After bypassing the last stream, we merged alongside a torpedo-shaped ridge whose aim showed clearly on our maps. Following the ridge gave us the freedom to stop worrying about navigation and start paying attention to the sky. This was important because the sky seemed to be up to something. Its eastern clouds were visibly darkening from pale-silver to purplish-gray. Their position posed no threat to us, being on our leeward side, but if storms could form downwind they could also form anywhere, and the ridge blocked our view of the windward sky.

At length, the ridge running alongside us tapered down until its height could have been double to ours. In roughly the same location, a rogue stream corralled us tightly against the ridge. We could no longer see any hint of the sky to windward until an intervening bog forced us onto the ridge. Once regaining an open view, we thought we might spy the gravel road that was our eventual goal but instead, gadzooks! We saw a giant thunderhead speeding toward us from the Continental Divide. Lightning flashed. Thunder boomed. The interval was about 10-seconds. Simple math indicated the storm was approximately two miles away. That was all we needed to hear.

Fleeing toward the south, we outdistanced the bog, before dropping back off the ridge and crouching against its leeward side.

"Isn't it awfully early in the day to be having lightning?" See-Hawk complained.

"Yes," I confirmed, "and it's not going to end quickly either, so let's hope those horny electrons think ridges and streams are sexier than humans."

Gazing toward the east, with our backs against the ridge, we jumped in surprise when a jagged yellow thunderbolt struck Highway 274. The bang that followed nearly loosened our socks. Within minutes, we found ourselves pinned between one active thunderstorm to leeward and another to windward. The clouds overhead remained quiet, but we still felt worried because collisions between thunderstorms were known to produce the worst lighting on record.

I visualized the metal things resting beside us: aluminum tent poles, titanium, and stainless steel cookware, aluminum trekking poles—eek!

"We need to ditch our backpacks," I told SeeHawk.

There was no use in panicking. Proceeding methodically, we dug out our rain-ponchos, along with a couple of green apples to munch during the show. Then, we rested our backpacks 50-feet away, resumed squatting, and anxiously waited for nature to take its course.

First to arrive was a gust front, coming over the ridge, whose violent wind gusts whipped our ponchos back and forth. Lunging to pin them down, we seemed to be squinting through a shower of garden slugs.

"Keep your butt off the ground," I warned SeeHawk, "so you won't be vulnerable to a three-point shock."

After a while, though, our legs got tired from constantly squatting.

Close toward the east, we saw a fleet of gray rain-shafts pressing toward the highway. At the same time, a series of explosive booms marched toward us from behind. Suddenly, it was as if whatever had been said by the rear storm's booms made the highway's thunderstorm get pissed-off and go totally berserk. Three simultaneous lightning bolts flashed at the same time. Their triple thunderclap might almost have shaken China.

I chomped into my green apple and hardly tasted its sour juice. Watching the storm rage caused me to ponder some bizarre questions. *Are insects on the highway getting burned to a crisp? Can lightning melt asphalt, or turn it into glass?*

"Plant your feet closer together," I warned SeeHawk. "We need to reduce the potential difference between our feet."

Obeying my order, he shifted his feet together, while also jiggling his thighs to relieve the strain from squatting.

Our heads whipped up when lightning struck again, midway between our protecting ridge and the highway. This time, the boom reached our ears within seconds.

"Rounded down, I figure that strike was zero miles away," SeeHawk shouted through the wind and rain.

"Yes," I shouted back. "We should move farther apart, so if one of us gets struck, the other one can perform CPR."

Crab-walking away from SeeHawk, I lifted my hands often to avoid getting a four-point shock if lightning struck any wet grass nearby.

The rear storm was moving fast, but its trajectory carried it far enough sideways for the heaviest action to spare our lucky souls.

During an interval of things calming down, SeeHawk and I cautiously climbed back onto the ridge to have another look around. Some distance toward the west, we saw either the gravel road we wanted to reach or a good imposter. Descending to windward, we met a pair of conflicting breezes. At the same time, I experienced a hunger attack.

"Darn it," I told SeeHawk, "I know this is bad timing, but my stomach is growling like the Atlantic Campground Grizzly."

"Okay, then," he nodded. "We should pull out a snack as soon as we reach some trees."

"That'll be too late," I whimpered. "I need to eat now."

"Seriously, Sunshine?"

"Serious as a toothache."

The only snacks I could reach without digging deep were a bag of cheese puffs and a bottle of *Cherry Coke,* intended to have been a special treat for the afternoon.

"Sorry, partner," I whimpered again, before ripping open the bag.

With surprise and horror, SeeHawk watched me start stuffing orange cheese globs into my mouth like nobody was watching. Next, I twisted open the *Cherry Coke,* which still felt cold from Anne's refrigerator. I twisted it without noticing a loud hiss that should have given me fair warning. Once the seal broke, brown sugar-water sprayed me from head to toe.

SeeHawk stood by, muttering under his breath, "Fool me once, fool me twice."

When I peered into the crumpled snack bag, I saw orange cheese globs floating in brown fizz.

"Ugh!" I wailed. "The Anaconda-Pintlar Wilderness is supposed to be full of bears, and now I'm a walking candy bar."

"A clown candy bar, with orange cheese lips," SeeHawk shuddered.

"Quit judging and help me lick my arms," I ordered because we did not have enough extra water for a splash bath.

It was officially lunchtime when we finally reached the anticipated gravel road. Its bordering trees offered to shelter us from any further lightning, but there was no need. Just before making the turn, we spied two distant figures speeding toward us from the highway. Curiosity made us halt to watch them approach. Even from a great distance, we could hear their trekking poles clanking against the gravel like chainmail. Gradually, the figures grew into a pair of stocky young men.

First to introduce himself was the leader, named Redbeard. As soon as SeeHawk and I heard the name, we realized we were meeting Dutch's original thru-hiking partner, with whom he had attempted hiking the CDT northbound. Pulling up behind Redbeard came Teach, a hometown friend who was accompanying him down to Yellowstone National Park. Both friends looked glad to make new acquaintances, but they were also on a mission to keep moving quickly. We tried to fall into step with them, but it was difficult, with them huffing and puffing away like steam engines, and, man, they were fast!

In terms of getting to know each other, Redbeard did not have to tell us he was Irish. We guessed it from seeing his dancing blue eyes, freckled red cheeks, and flaming orange beard. For character, he had a heavy aura of yang, spiked with good cheer. His self-described occupations were writing, storytelling, wandering and beer-drinking, combined with a willingness to speak about anything and, purportedly, nothing to hide. His blue eyes flashed whenever he laughed, which was often, and the laughter coming out of him filled the grassland's open space. At the same time, the smell coming out of him verified that he disliked stream-bathing, even though he was a hardcore nature enthusiast. His clothing, too, defied thru-hiker norms—being a flower-print Hawaiian shirt with baggy, knee-length standup shorts. He had barbells for muscles, and when SeeHawk and I mentioned knowing a PCT-hiker with a similar build, it turned out the two had backpacked together in the past, as well as worked together on fishing boats in Alaska!

"Plus," I added, "we've just met your original partner, Dutch, during our stop in Anaconda."

Redbeard laughed. "Oh yeah, Dutch and I hooked up on the CDT website and agreed to be partners. It was going well when we started in New Mexico, but then we got cut off by snow in the San Juan Mountains. After that, we kind of got thrown off track. Now, I'm hiking with Teach and Dutch is hiking with String Stick, but Teach is only out here for a month, so I'll probably join those guys after he goes home."

Speaking for himself, Teach explained, "School starts at the end of August, so I'll need to go home and prepare my lessons."

Unlike Redbeard, the soft-spoken young man was difficult to size up while in motion, but I could immediately tell he was a good friend to Redbeard.

Teach had silky brown hair, sweet chocolate eyes, and pudgy cheeks that jiggled whenever he laughed. His gentle smile, perhaps resulting from vegetarian parents who washed him with *Dr. Bronner's* soap since the day he was born, probably made it easy for him to befriend women. He was new to thru-hiking, so he carried a heavy backpack, wore stiff leather boots, and retained 30-pounds more bodyweight than most thru-hikers could sustain. He also had a short walking stride but made up for it by stepping fast enough that he had no trouble keeping up with Redbeard.

After talking further, Redbeard got a notion to ask SeeHawk and me, "How did you two meet?"

Startled by the question, I felt hesitant to answer.

"Not on the Internet," SeeHawk chuckled.

"Okay, I confess. I went to SeeHawk for hypnosis."

"Ahhh," Redbeard grinned, lifting a trekking pole and swinging it slightly. "Look deep into my eyes…"

"Yeah, yeah," I laughed. "I know what you're thinking, but it wasn't like that. I got driving phobia from three consecutive car crashes. I was hoping for a quick fix, but..." Glancing at See-Hawk, I comically demanded, "Hey, what went on during those sessions, anyhow? I can't remember..."

"She's kidding," SeeHawk asserted.

"Did it work?" Redbeard asked.

"It helped," I confirmed. "Plus, I got a fiancé out of the deal, so you could say I got more than I paid for." Throwing SeeHawk a playful glance, I added, "The first time I saw him come into the waiting room, he was wearing a white collared shirt with blue slacks and some kind of weird Arizona belt covered in silver disks. I looked at him and thought, 'Wow, there's Barry Manilow, if he was short with brown hair.' That was the clincher because, as a kid, I had a big crush on Barry Manilow."

"Because of his big nose?" Redbeard guessed.

"You bet. I've always loved big noses. How could I resist some guy with a big honker sitting me down in a cushy hypnosis chair and gazing at me with those long-lashed blue eyes?"

Searching for some resemblance hiding behind SeeHawk's wooly mustache and beard, Teach remarked, "He doesn't look like Barry Manilow to me."

Yes," I agreed, "but he would if you saw him shaved. Right now, he's almost unrecognizable."

A sharp thunderclap returned our attention to the next round of thunderstorms queuing up for action. Fortunately, the trees running parallel to our aim kept safety just a few steps away.

"Round Two, coming up!" Teach announced.

Hearing another clap of thunder, I glanced toward the north, feeling vaguely concerned about String Stick and Dutch. Were they still negotiating Poppa Jim's hazardous cliff route? Or had they already entered the Anaconda-Pintlar Wilderness? Thinking about them stirred me to ask our new companions, "How'd you guys enjoy that giant lightning show, an hour ago?"

Redbeard exclaimed, "Holy smokes! We were out on the highway when it hit. Can you believe how fast those clouds were moving? By the time we smelled danger, we were already caught between lightning on both sides. Super scary. We just dropped our backpacks and ran."

Redbeard segued from there to describing his recent purchase of a 35 mm camera. "It's got automatic everything," he bragged. "All I need to do is point and click. When I get home, I'll be giving a slide show to Teach's class."

The word "school" reminded me of having once found a deflated balloon atop California's High Sierra Mountains. A note tied onto it had been written by elementary school kids 60 miles away, from whom it had floated 3,000-feet upwards, to be found by hikers like a message in a bottle.

Before I could finish telling my balloon story, one especially loud thunderclap sent us all scurrying into the road's adjacent forest. We ate lunch together, but then split up because SeeHawk and I wanted to get back on the road, but Redbeard and Teach thought it might still be dangerous.

The gravel road's end met up with a trailhead whose footpath tunneled into fairytale woods. The ground became carpeted with tender spring grass, mounded with mopheads of lanky, green beargrass. Each mophead sent up a few tall stalks, each supporting one lightbulb-shaped flowerhead, whose hundreds of tiny, cream-colored petals magnified the forest's interior light, making the footpath seem lined with glowing streetlamps.

Ambient mist, leftover from the rain, still carried an invigorating scent of moist earth. Through all the freshness, SeeHawk and I trod upon soft orange pine-mulch, stitched together by tree roots as thick as our wrists. Some of the trees' bark had been clawed into shreds by bears or rough weather, exposing underwood that matched the ground's reddish color. Altogether, we felt too enchanted for regular conversation, until after we finished a modest climb.

The trail leveled off inside a disbanding forest, where a localized gale, draining off a rocky peak, covered Storm Lake with a fleece of whitecaps.

Redbeard and Teach caught up and passed us, just as we began to circle the lake. We had not even started discussing where to camp when the other two selected a small, wind-sheltered tent site. Not wanting to invade their privacy, we continued onward, hoping to find another wind-sheltered site. Unfortunately, every hollow we could find rested beneath a precipice clutching rocks that looked capable of killing us in our sleep. It took a long time to find a safe-looking campsite, but we finally succeeded, and, hooray for that, because we spent the rest of the night hearing rocks break loose and tumble down to the lake.

Rocks were still tumbling the following morning when we began climbing steeply toward the Continental Divide.

Teach and Redbeard had overslept, in hopes for String Stick and Dutch to catch up and hike with them. Therefore, we strode past their tent without saying goodbye, assuming we might see the whole group later in the day.

A misty sunrise welcomed us onto 9,300-foot Goat Flat. There, we paused, between splotches of sunbaked snow, to inhale sips of clean mountain air. Our eyes danced across neighboring white peaks, scattered throughout the mist like islands in the sky.

The summit's ecosystem was a collage of molting tundra grass, mixed with bald rock. Its weathered spruce krummholz stood far apart, like lopsided flags. One prominent footpath tried to lure us off-course, but we knew better. Dropping steeply off the summit, we entered a dusty chute sprigged with red and yellow wildflowers, whose bottom stair ran into a shallow creek.

"Rock hop? Or wet sneakers?" SeeHawk debated.

"Dry socks get my vote," I answered, "but some of these wobblers might soak our shoes anyway."

It seemed like time to deploy my trekking poles. While strapping them onto my wrists, I temporarily stopped paying attention to SeeHawk.

He was busy examining an ice-crusted log. Bridging the creek, it overhung a short waterfall into which nobody would ever want to land. SeeHawk knew better, but his impulse took over. Without deploying trekking poles, he blithely hopped up, expecting to cross the log faster than he could slip. Instead, whoops! Halfway across, he lost traction and crashed into the waterfall, with a loud WHOMP. His cap fell off...floated over the waterfall...plopped into a muddy pool...got impaled by a branch and stopped, floating just out of reach.

"WHAT in the name of DING-DONGS?" I gasped. "Why didn't you use poles, if you were going to try something stupid?"

SeeHawk grunted with embarrassment, "I didn't need poles."

"Um, Earth to Klutzhead? You just fell?"

"I should have been more careful," he admitted, while awkwardly retrieving his cap.

"More careful AND more willing to use your poles." I drove home.

"Yes." His voice faded, while I led him away from the stream.

It did not seem clear that my partner had learned anything, so I repeated anxiously, "Why carry poles if you're not going to use them at times when you need them?"

Getting no response, I spun around and caught him stroking a hawk feather he had found on the trail. He was straightening its nap. Admiring its shape. *Darn, you!* I thought. *Just give me some better assurance that you're not going to fall off another log tomorrow and possibly get hurt.*

He glanced up and happily explained, "It's a gift from my Amakua. Go ahead and keep walking, Sunshine. I'm right behind you."

I wanted to do exactly that, but first, I needed him to acknowledge my distress.

"If you don't care about hurting yourself," I huffed, "then, at least think about me for a moment. If you sprain an ankle, how will I get us out of here? Carrying you on my shoulders? Wearing your backpack over mine? Letting you lean on me for support? We'd have to chuck a lot of gear, and for what lame reason? Just so you could show off your incredible balancing skills for the eight-thousandth time? Why prove something we already know? There's nobody else around to give you a blue ribbon."

SeeHawk may have privately agreed but, instead of responding, he just kept stroking his precious hawk feather. Even though he wanted to add it to his growing string of assorted feathers, he finally let it go, by wedging it into a soft-barked tree.

"Okay, Sunshine." he murmured, "I get your point."

This time, his tone sounded convincing, so I let the matter drop and we got underway.

Another 4,500-feet of climbing took us through woods that loosened upon a summit clasping Warren Lake. Complete stillness made the lake's smooth water perfectly reflect Warren Peak. A chain of half-submerged boulders falsified the look of rotten pilings from an old boat pier. A small red fox, watching our approach, leaped aside and skedaddled when its eyes met ours.

We paused beside the lake, to give up on camping with The Boys.

Had String Stick and Dutch gotten delayed, while crossing Poppa Jim's cliff during yesterday's thunderstorm? Or had they rejoined Redbeard and Dutch, but failed to overtake us because their group was taking it easy?

Missing our friends' company, we selected a quiet campsite framed with yellow arnica, glacier lilies, red-stemmed marshmarigolds, tiny yellow buttercups, spiky louseworts, purple lupins, white pussytoes, and spongy mats of pink-blossomed heather. Oh, and besides that, our campsite had a spellbinding view of the lake.

One cloud sticking fast to Warren Peak burst into flames after the sun went down. Its reflection seemed to set the water on fire. Not only the water. Also, an orange glow crept up and spread across the lakeshore's deciduous larch trees, green-needled spruces, firs, and whitebark pines.

I sidled up to the lake's edge, dipped in one toe, and smiled. The water felt lukewarm. Dinner could wait for bliss to come first. SeeHawk and I floated above submerged boulders, trying not to disturb the lake's murky bottom. Farther offshore, we lounged inside sitting holes, saturated with joy. Time left us alone until the cloud capping Warren Peak grew impatient and detonated a loud BOOM.

We splashed back to safety, dried off quickly, and gulped down a meal of gingery squash soup. There was not enough time to wipe-off our chins before a light rain sent us dashing into our tent. That was our dismissal. Another day finished. Warren Peak's clouds wished us sweet dreams.

***

The next morning, SeeHawk greeted The Boys in single-file. I was busy squatting between some overlooking trees, so I could not just poke up my head and shout, "Hello."

After I came back down, SeeHawk filled me in on everything I had missed about String Stick and Dutch. As we had guessed, indeed, they had gotten chased by lightning coming down Poppa Jim's steep talus cliff, the day before. Thankfully, the good news was, they had suffered nothing worse than a few raised hairs.

SeeHawk and I were still finishing camp chores, so we figured we might never see The Boys again. This notion felt sad, but we took it in stride. After all, comings and goings were a natural part of thru-hiking.

A low ceiling of smooth stratus clouds kept our departure from camp unseasonably cool. The air smelled restless. Our skin felt damp.

"This can't be typical weather for midsummer," I assumed. "It's almost like the clouds are stuck in limbo because somebody forgot to hit their reset button."

"What does limbo mean for this afternoon?" SeeHawk wanted to know.

"No idea," I admitted. "Either the clouds will have another party like yesterday, or else they'll just poop out and move on."

Inside a forest concealing Fishtrap Creek, SeeHawk added a new hawk feather to his growing collection of hawk, crow, and owl feathers.

Soon, we entered an old burn dotted with saplings sprouting from its ashes. Tangles of dead and living trees blocked us from seeing much of our surroundings. With gloom overhead, disorganization everywhere, and nothing, in particular, keeping us focused, our mood grew edgy. We knew it by comparison after the forest returned to life and we could feel its green trees and streams restoring our good humor.

Five hundred feet of nonstop climbing hoisted us from the lower forest onto Rainbow Pass. Our welcoming committee was a community of pine trees whose tiny orange cones glowed like candles. On the summit's far side, we reached an overlook that seemed to reveal a whole different world. Gazing 1,000-feet downward, onto a quilt of exotic colors, made it obvious how Rainbow Pass got its name. Starting from the left, peach-tinted cliffs plunged down to a lime-green meadow, preceding an isthmus of dark green trees. The trees divided an emerald green lake from a sapphire blue lake, whose neighboring foliage had turned permanently orange after a recent burn. That shock of orange underscored foothills that graduated from pink to blue, entering a sky full of shining silver clouds.

SeeHawk and I feasted our eyes, exclaiming and marveling until we descended into the rainbow's right-hand corner. Immediately, our eyes were met with a riddle. How could trees which had looked bright-orange from above look utterly black from below? Of course, the explanation was bottom-up charring, but, still. Why could we not see even a hint of orange peeking through the blackness? Literally, every tree looked cast in black iron, along with every root, follicle, and square inch of topsoil burned in-between.

Persistent overcast kept the burn trapped underneath a tight lid, while we strode through its bowels in mute fascination. Nothing whispered, fluttered, or otherwise moved. Before long, the blackness transitioned into a pseudo-living forest, whose green trees were technically alive, but still conveyed an aura of death.

We should probably have taken a quick swim in Johnson Lake. Cooling our engines would have been smart before beginning another hot, dusty climb. Silly as it sounds, though, we had seen enough horror movies to dread even touching a haunted lake.

With hats gone dry and faces turning red, we mounted the next switchbacks feeling overheated. The higher we climbed, the hotter we felt. Fatigue crept in. So, did malaise. Each discomfort could be tolerated alone, but combining several miseries was a recipe for trouble. SeeHawk, in particular, resumed dwelling upon the scolding I had given him for slipping off an icy log. Even though he would have denied it, deep inside, his resentment had been growing into a ticking time bomb. All it needed to achieve detonation was a little more heat or a little more thirst.

Before long, my partner started saying unpleasant things. Naturally, I felt obliged to defend myself.

Instead of apologizing, he responded by acting meaner.

I responded by crying until he pulled over and stopped.

Inside a small patch of shade, we recovered our wits. Peace was restored for a few, sweet minutes. Then, another round of bickering erupted, like a dying spark bursting back into flames. Back and forth, around switchback after switchback, we yelled until we both ran out of angry words. Silence followed for only one minute before we stepped onto 8,750-foot Pintlar Pass.

Leaping lizards! Why did it look as if String Stick, Dutch, Redbeard, and Teach had fallen out of an airplane? They were lounging all over the summit, surrounded by pieces of clothing and gear scattered everywhere.

Oh, no! I thought. *Can they tell I've been crying*? I wanted to run away and hide. There they all were. It would have been ridiculous to flee. I had to just hitch up my cheeks and smile.

They all smiled back as if nothing seemed wrong.

Point taken. It was time for SeeHawk and me to forget our differences and get back to work.

Methodically slicing Swiss cheese, for piling onto thick rye crackers, helped me calm down enough to start enjoying Pintlar Pass's dramatic view. It was just cascading trees dropping into more trees, but the trees covered irregular peaks that formed interesting patterns.

The Boys went on a lark, reciting funny stories from their past thru-hikes. Laughing and listening kept all of us distracted from watching the sky. Mostly, it was just overcast anyway, so long as we ignored a couple of sleeper clouds marching in from the wings. Suddenly, one of the sleepers puffed up its chest and belched thunder.

The Boys grabbed their backpacks and fled off the pass.

SeeHawk and I had to spend another few minutes stuffing crackers and cheese into our pockets, before diving down after them. By the time we reached the mountain's backside, our friends were gone. Not until dropping into a sparse timberline did we come upon String Stick,. He had stopped there, to quickly tell us why his companions had left in a hurry. Apparently, they were all planning to follow Poppa Jim's high route past Oreamnos Lake. Their motive was to enjoy better scenery than the Book of Beans promised while avoiding a gratuitous 1,000-foot plunge off and back onto the Continental Divide.

When SeeHawk and I heard what The Boys were planning, our mouths dropped open.

"You're not worried about staying high the whole time, in this weather?" I asked String Stick.

"Maybe," he admitted, "but the new trail you're talking about requires an extra thousand feet of climbing, and it's a mile-and-a-half longer."

Plus, infinitely safer, I thought, but there was nothing more to say since our friends were already committed.

While watching String Stick disappear in the direction of Oreamnos Lake, I recalled Redbeard and Teach hiding from yesterday's lightning storm longer than SeeHawk and I had hidden.

Sympathetically, I reflected, "You can bet Redbeard and Teach are shitting bricks right now. They're just going with the flow so they can stick with their friends. What do you think? Does that make them brave or stupid?"

"Yes," SeeHawk answered.

It took at least an hour, but felt much longer, for the two of us to zigzag down 1,500-feet worth of switchbacks. The trail lost elevation at such a gradual rate that, perhaps, hikers coming up the trail might hardly have known they were climbing.

Lightning struck within a mile on both sides, keeping us threatened all the way down. We stayed safely below the timberline, but wide spacings between the trees enabled us to see trees flashing from a fair distance, and each crackling thunderclap sounded dangerously close.

After perhaps one hour of descending, we entered a wooded ravine whose dense coverage gave us real shelter. Its floor hosted a footbridge spanning Pintlar Creek. Since bridges and creeks are easy to find on topographical maps, I pulled out a wad of folded pages and gave SeeHawk an updated report.

"There's a major switchback near the top of this next climb," I told him. "We can't afford to miss it, so let's keep a stream-count on the way up."

"I'll follow you," he agreed.

And, up we went.

* * *

One thousand feet worth of switchbacks was a lot of climbing to attempt, all in one shot, at the end of a long day. See-Hawk and I started counting streams from the moment we left Pintlar Creek. This was to ensure we could not overshoot a turnoff onto the southbound Continental Divide. We assumed that counting would guarantee our success, but wouldn't you know it? After counting the last stream we ran into another one, without seeing any turnoff.

I had to vent a few expletives, before calming down enough to admit, "Maybe we counted some seasonal streams that don't exist year-round."

SeeHawk needed to catch his breath before he could respond, and then, all he said was, "Please don't tell me we're going to go back down and start counting all over again."

"Are you kidding?" I snorted. "Not in your lifetime. Don't worry, I'm sure the Continental Divide will be obvious. It's supposed to be the highest land elevation around, and the southbound trail stays right on top."

"Good," he nodded, "because it's starting to feel like camp time."

After climbing for another ten minutes, we reached a pair of old wooden signs, planted right below the elbow of a switchback. A narrow trail forking off the elbow headed southward, onto an open ridge. The next straightaway above undercut a sandy rim, probably offering a rewarding view to hikers going all the way to the top.

SeeHawk gestured toward the rim and shouted. "Hooray! We're almost there!"

"Not so fast," I warned him. "These signs look important. Let me check our maps."

My partner fidgeted and sighed with impatience, waiting for me to unfold two different maps and skim through two sets of guidebook directions.

At length, I muttered, "What's wrong with this picture?"

"Huh?" the fidgeter frowned.

"There are two signs, but it's a three-way intersection."

Staring at the closely paired signs, he laughed, "Well, yeah, of course. One is marking the CDT for northbounders. The other is marking a turnoff that goes someplace else, but it's not for us, right? Because we're going up there." He pointed, again toward the rim.

Examining the narrow trail that forked off the switchback's elbow, I said, "Normally, I would agree with you, but see how the signs are facing?"

Moving into my spot, he saw what I was seeing.

"Gosh," he agreed, "it's hard to tell if the sign on the right is pointing uphill or off the corner."

"Mm-hm, and also, it's also strange that none of these destinations listed appear on our maps."

"Why do you think that is?"

"They must be super far away."

"Which means?"

"They're not part of the CDT."

"Then, why are we still standing here?"

"Because we've overshot our expected stream count, and this intersection looks significant."

"Can you see where we're standing on our map?"

"Maybe, but there's more than one trail junction. That's why we were counting streams."

"Oh," SeeHawk's body sagged a notch. "Well, if you want my opinion, I think we should keep climbing because it looks like we're almost to the top."

"You're probably right," I agreed. "Maybe we should go up and check out the view before we waste any more brain juice standing down here guessing."

"Sounds good," he nodded. "but just so I understand, does this fork even stand a chance of being the CDT?"

"It looks awfully skinny, but it does merge onto a southbound ridge," I acknowledged. "If this was the top, I'd think, for sure, it was the CDT. But, since there's more above, we should probably keep climbing, even though our stream-count came out weird."

Having said that, I hitched up my backpack in preparation to take the lead. However, before I stepped forward, SeeHawk threw up his hand.

"Check this out," he exclaimed. "Somebody drew a little arrow on the sign!"

Looking where my partner pointed, sure enough, I could see it. Someone had used a small pocketknife or ballpoint pen to carve "CDT" next to a cartooned arrow, pointing...well...either downhill or off the switchback's corner.

"Ack," I complained. "Even the drawing meant to clear things up is confusing."

Frowning, SeeHawk agreed, "Yeah, it really could be pointing either way."

"So, let's try to imagine what went through the artist's head. You'd think if they wanted us to turn here, they would have drawn the arrow sideways, and it's pointing upward."

"Telling northbounders to go downhill? That wouldn't make sense, since it's already on the official sign."

"Exactly."

"So, the arrow has to be pointing off the corner?"

"Probably. In which case, we should turn here."

"So, this IS the CDT?"

"Only if the rim up above doesn't reach high enough to add a topographical line. In that case, up there and down here might look the same on paper."

"Ooh, that's tricky," SeeHawk acknowledged. "You might be onto something, but do you want to hear a different theory?"

"Sure."

"Maybe Mister Art Person thought the CDT turned off here, but later they found out they were wrong and didn't come back to fix their mistake.

"That sounds plausible, coming from someone who couldn't draw a better arrow," I agreed. "Although, if they went the wrong way, why wouldn't they come back?"

"Maybe they got eaten by a grizzly bear while they were lost?"

"Ooh, ten points," I laughed, "but, I can one-up you."

"Really?"

"What if we're climbing the completely wrong switchbacks?"

"Er, what? How could that be?"

"Maybe the artist was trying to tell people, 'Hey, if you're looking for the CDT, this is not it, but here's a shortcut.'"

"But, we know we're on the CDT because the downhill sign says so."

"It might be saying, 'Go down these switchbacks to FIND the CDT once you get to the bottom.' I know that seems unlikely, but it would explain why our stream count was off."

"Also, it would explain why only one of these signs mentions the CDT, even though they were both installed at the same time," SeeHawk assumed, based upon their matching appearances.

"True. Although, this whole theory is just nonsense because we only saw one trail leaving Pintlar Creek."

"Okay, so, now that our heads are totally screwed up, what do you think we should do?"

"Keep climbing and check out the rim. If we don't like what we see, we can always come back down and try the fork instead."

"Sounds like a plan," SeeHawk nodded. "Just tell me when it's time to start cooking dinner."

Together, we climbed through thinning conifer trees, on substrate that evolved from dirt to coarse sand. After several minutes of climbing, I began to feel suspicious. Why were we still not seeing the top? Also, why did the trail keep aiming north? Our maps showed the CDT turning south from the switchbacks, to begin a long haul of staying on the crest.

I felt hungry, tired, and annoyed with myself for not being able to solve everything faster.

SeeHawk just wanted to eat dinner and sleep. He pretty much zoned out, until I delivered the unwelcome news that we needed to turn around.

Back down at the three-way junction, we carefully reexamined two wooden signs that still had us baffled.

I noticed the western sky turning golden. It would have felt marvelous to sit down, flash our signal mirror, get picked up by a helicopter, have the transport company's attendant serve us Gatorade in martini glasses, and be whisked off to some luxury motel equipped with an electric stove and hot shower. Instead, I told SeeHawk, "Let's just see where this fork trail leads. If it doesn't look promising right away, we'll turn around and think of something else."

SeeHawk said nothing in response. He just obediently followed me from the well-constructed switchbacks onto a thin trail etched across a hard, crusty ridge.

All of a few trees populating the ridge were leaking long, gray shadows. Overall, the surrounding landscape seemed pretty generic. We searched into the distance for anything recognizable.

After a few minutes, I told SeeHawk, "So far, so good. It doesn't look like we're on the highest land around, but we are staying high, and we're still heading south."

"So, what would you call our odds? Sixty-forty? Fifty-fifty?"

"Probably forty-sixty, but, at least, that's better than zero."

A bit farther along, lush pine and spruce trees welcomed us into a full coverage forest, whose canopy hid the sinking sun. One small meadow, dotted with blue forget-me-nots, displayed a fresh ax-blaze, from which a better footpath entered its opposite trees.

"Seems like our odds of success are improving," SeeHawk beamed.

"Don't speak too soon," I warned him. "Right now, I'd say we're still at fifty-fifty."

Striding easily along the better footpath, we agreed that it did look wide enough to be part of a National Scenic Trail.

SeeHawk's shoulders visibly relaxed, allowing a smile to play upon his lips.

I loved seeing him smile. It was easy to feel encouraged in beautiful surroundings.

"If we keep up this pace," I dared to say, "we'll be cooking mushroom soup before it gets dark."

"That's the best news I've heard all day!" he sang.

Not long after exiting the meadow, we entered a tavern of slender grand fir trees, massive Douglas firs, and common spruces, furnished with knobs of coarse granite rock. Reaching a cluster of alder bushes, we stopped to scratch our heads.

"That's two extra streams," I tallied, "although our count probably became moot when we left the switchbacks."

"Want to check our compass?" SeeHawk suggested.

"Sure…" I pulled it out and confirmed, "SSE. At least, that part seems correct."

The woods grew rustic with decreasing elevation. Massive Douglas fir trees towered to a height that dwarfed ordinary full-grown spruces. The ground's damp mulch became laced with boa-constrictor tree roots, choke-holding boulders covered in moss, which piggybacked clumps of dormant beargrass.

Thinking critically, I mumbled, "You know, we really shouldn't be losing this much elevation. I mean, our maps show the CDT staying almost level."

"Do you think we've left Kansas?" SeeHawk worried.

"Let's just say, if we don't turn uphill soon and veer toward the right, you won't want to hear what I'll have to say."

"Are there any specific landmarks we should be watching out for?"

"Just, anything to help us locate the crest. I wish we could get a view past all these trees."

As if granting my wish, suddenly the forest ahead split open. Before us, sat an overlook, facing a 1,000-foot drop into a mile-wide valley. Its entrance was overgrown with vines tangled between conifer trees and bushes. A steep set of switchbacks dropping through the overgrowth looked wide enough to accommodate pack mules. Heading in that direction would have carried us farther south, but dropping into a giant hole was not on our agenda.

Searching for other options, I scrutinized an adjacent mountainside blocking our view toward the west.

Following my gaze, SeeHawk also examined the blockage, and his conclusion was, "Don't you kind of feel like we're not on the highest land elevation around?"

"Yes," I confirmed. "Nothing we've been doing for the past hour has really matched what I see on our maps."

"So, we've been going the wrong way this whole time, and now we've reached a dead-end?"

"Possibly."

"Do we need to turn around?"

"Hopefully not."

"Do you think we could have missed seeing a turnoff coming down here?"

"Possibly. Do you want to go back up and take a look?"

"Not really. It's getting near camp time. I'd rather start drinking that hot mushroom soup."

My eyes glanced back and forth, trying to comprehend everything I was seeing.

Suddenly, SeeHawk exclaimed, "Hey, wouldn't this be a perfect time to try using our GPS?"

Chuckling with amusement, I scoffed, "Go ahead, Mister Gadget Head. You paid a hundred bucks for that cyber piece of baloney. Might as well use it once on this trip."

With obvious glee, he dug through his backpack and produced the space-age device he had been carrying, without using, ever since we left Canada.

I used the same period of time to reexamine several pages' worth of maps and directions I almost knew from memory.

The GPS took a while to link with at least three different satellites, cross-referenced for accuracy before its digital screen reported our current elevation being 8,100-feet.

"Say that number again?" I gulped.

"Eighty-one hundred feet," he repeated. "Is there a problem?"

"Actually, that's exactly right," I admitted.

"Great!" he grinned.

"But, how weird because eighty-one hundred-feet is supposed to be the highest land elevation around here, and we've been descending for almost an hour. Just now, I thought we were at, more like, seventy-one hundred-feet, but, huh. Maybe the descent wasn't as steep as I thought. Because the GPS can't lie, can it?"

"Not with information coming from three different satellites."

"Okay, well, maybe a couple-hundred-feet feels like a thousand when you're worried about following the wrong trail. I guess that's good news. But, I have to admit, if the GPS had said anything starting with a seven, I'd have turned around and dragged us back to that crazy arrow sign."

"Okay, but we're here now, so what should we do next?"

"Apparently, just aim west, until we run into the Continental Divide."

SeeHawk took another hard look at the brushy mountainside blocking our western view.

"Is that a joke?" he hoped.

"Not entirely," I said.

"You want to launch into some big adventure with the sun about to set? That terrain looks steep, Sunshine. Please, tell me you're joking."

"Do I look like I'm joking?"

"No. That's why I'm quaking in my boots."

Before he could say more, I exclaimed, "Look!"

His eyes followed my finger to a thin footpath, traversing across the westward slope. It barely looked wide enough to fit both our shoes, but it was aiming in the right direction.

"No, Sunshine," he objected. "That's only a deer path, not our pot of gold."

"Yes, but maybe it's been earmarked to become the CDT-in-progress."

"You're grasping at straws, sweetheart."

"Totally, but even if it's not the CDT, it might still be a shortcut back to the CDT."

"A deer shortcut, not a shortcut for backpackers with fear of heights."

"I'm only afraid of crossing slippery logs and cliffs without trees underneath. This slope is dry, with trees to catch us if we slip. So, how about a little less talk and more action?"

"Hey, that's my line," SeeHawk chuckled, as he followed me onto the deer path.

Within a short distance, we started running into small erosion chutes. Lunging across them put us at risk for slipping pretty far before any trees might catch us. I sought traction from rudely stepping on prostrate Oregon grape bushes, huckleberry branches, and creeping juniper. There was less vegetation where the incline grew steeper, exposing treacherous washouts that looked risky to cross.

"Apparently, this is where the deer hang a U-turn," SeeHawk observed.

"You're probably right," I agreed.

So, why did we keep going? Because the earth is round? Because eagles have wings? More likely, we kept going because the thinning trees ahead gave us some encouragement. Viewed in silhouette, against a darkening yellow sky, their farthest skyline loomed five miles toward the west. We had seen similar skylines often enough to know them like the backs of our own hands. Moreover, we were running out of options. Nothing else made better sense than to assume the visible western skyline was the Continental Divide. It looked reachable, too. Hooray for that, although its distance away shocked me. How could we have strayed so far off course? My brain felt punchy from a full day of trying to piece confusing things together. We were running out of daylight. Finding someplace to camp and get a good night's sleep would help us wake up thinking better and feeling less confused.

Taking charge of the situation, I led SeeHawk diagonally uphill. In time, it became hard on our ankles to stay bent sideways. My legs got tired too and started arguing that we needed to either quit bushwhacking or get our heads examined.

Glancing downhill, I felt my throat go dry. The adjacent valley was too steep and brushy for emergency camping. If we could not find a flat clearing uphill, with darkness coming on, where were we going to sleep?

"Sunshine?" I heard SeeHawk inquire from behind me. "What's happened to our trail?"

"Don't worry," I grunted. "As long as we're able to keep heading west, we're good. There's no mistaking the Continental Divide."

Twice, I needed help negotiating small washouts. Both times, I refused to look my partner in the eyes. Of course, I was being stubborn. Obviously, I might have been leading us into deeper trouble but, come on. What could be worse than backtracking all the way to...to...where? The same two wooden signs we had faced several hours ago? Just to spend another half hour wondering, all over again, where the hand-drawn arrow was pointing? No way, José. Pressing on seemed better than any alternative we had been offered.

It helped lift our spirits to enter a lusher stretch of woods, whose twiggy needle mulch gave our shoes good traction. Soon, a new deer trail popped out of the mulch. It was blazed, here and there, by some hunter's pocketknife.

Seeing blazes encouraged SeeHawk to cheer, "Full steam ahead!"

He gained confidence from feeling his legs move faster. More knife-blazes surfaced close ahead. I felt pleased to see my partner looking happier, but also jarred by his enthusiasm. After all, we were still following a deer trail flagged by hunters, not a human trail used by deer. We could not afford to get giddy and go on a wild goose chase with the sun about to set. Case in point, before long, the blazed trail vanished, just like all the rest.

SeeHawk tried to remain philosophical, but it was no use. A man can only take so much disappointment. With trees blocking our view of the western sky, we held our course until a third footpath appeared, marked with pink plastic ties.

"Hunters again," SeeHawk concluded. "Probably they came through here during pre-season, scouting for paths made by deer and elk."

Golden skylight flickered through every crack between the western pine and spruce trees covering a broad bench. Its gentler incline allowed our ankles to relax. We could no longer see the western mountains, but that did not matter with the flickering skylight making a good compass. Heading due north, we stepped over fallen logs and skirted small potholes.

Eventually, I dared to say, "If both our maps and your GPS are right, then why are we still climbing? I mean, doesn't it feel like, by now, we've climbed more than the distance between two topographical lines on a map?"

Catching my implication, SeeHawk stammered, "What are you trying to say, Sunshine?"

"I have no idea. It's all just so weird."

My eyes felt relieved when the westernmost trees finally stopped flickering. But then, I put two and two together and realized the sun had gone down. Bummer.

Another few minutes passed before the forest's interior visibly grew dark. This change happened with unnatural speed. Were we entering some kind of Alice in Wonderforest, where time could accelerate and mountains could grow taller?

A bit more climbing took us onto level terrain. We seemed to be nearing the mountain's summit. There was no proof, under the solid cover of trees, but my intuition told me we were finished climbing.

"Looks like we've probably reached the top," I dared to tell SeeHawk. "It's time to start heading west again. Maybe we'll still find the CDT before dark."

He opened his mouth to protest, but no words came out.

"Don't worry," I assured him. "I've got our compass handy, just in case we get confused."

"What about finding water?" he worried.

"I think we'll find a refill by tomorrow morning."

As we kept pressing onward, the woods became littered with spruce branches and beargrass straw, transformed by dusk into heaps of black skeletons. Suddenly, we ran into a northbound footpath. Not just a deer path. It was a formal human trail. The kind that might lead us back to the CDT!

SeeHawk broke into a victory dance, suggesting, "Do you want to camp here?"

"Yes," I admitted, "but if we keep going, we might find the CDT tonight. I don't know about you, but I'll sleep a lot better if we can go to bed knowing where we are."

"But, it's seriously getting dark," he pleaded.

"Mm-hm, but just imagine yourself waking up wearing a big, fat smile."

As it turned out, though, merely having found the good trail was enough to make us smile. From there on out, we thoroughly enjoyed watching inky tree roots slither past our shoes and shadowy phantoms slide past our heads. The trail whisked us right along until it ran into a gurgling creek. There, it stopped like a half-finished sentence. Marching upstream and downstream, we searched for any connected trail leaving the creek's opposite bank.

Finding nothing, I wryly remarked, "Well, well, well. Isn't that disturbing?"

"It's too dark to keep going anyway," SeeHawk declared, "but, at least, now we've got water. Do you want to camp here?"

"Of course, not," I replied.
"You'd rather keep walking into the dark?"
"Of course, not."
"So, we're camping here?"
"Of course."

SeeHawk sagged like his tires had gone flat. After taking a deep breath, he timidly inquired, "Are we lost?"

"You tell me."

* * *

Sometimes, when easy trails let my mind wander, I had wondered what it might feel like to get lost in the woods. Such wonderings were just romantic whims. I had never once wanted to find out the hard way. And yet, here I was, having the real experience. With darkness setting in, I learned that getting lost felt like a mild asthma attack.

For a while, it kept me calm to perform routine camp chores, like pitching our tent and unpacking the food. No angst emerged until after SeeHawk wandered away to find a bear-hanging tree. Then, sitting alone inside our tent, listening to the nearby stream gurgle and blurp, I was forced to face some unpleasant questions. For instance, in my role as our team's Chief Navigation Officer, was this my worst failure ever? Did I deserve all the blame for getting us lost, or had the CDT contributed, by being poorly marked? What was the last definite landmark I could remember seeing? The wooden signs marked with a hand-drawn arrow? The unsigned bridge spanning Pintlar Creek? Aside from all that, what about The Boys? Had they safely skirted Oreamnos Lake? If so, where were they camping, on this short, dark night?

When SeeHawk returned, he looked elated. He had found a perfect bear-hanging tree and pitched our long rope over one of its high branches without getting a snag.

I calmed down quickly after he climbed into our tent and started jabbing me with his elbows, changing into his nightclothes.

Scrunched into a corner, with arms guarding my face, I skimmed through a small library of maps, hoping to estimate our location.

Once SeeHawk finished changing, he started fiddling with his beloved GPS unit. Some moments elapsed before he blurted out, "Sunshine? Er…I think I might have…um…f…fouled up that last reading."

"WHAT!?"

Embarrassment made my partner struggle to explain, "The GPS, I just checked it again. It says we're still at eighty-one hundred feet. That's kind of weird, isn't it? I mean, for both readings to be exactly the same after we did so much climbing?"

Of all the—eagh! I could have smashed that confounded electronic device. I could also have blamed my partner for bringing it in the first place. Instead, though, I just answered calmly, "Yes, that's totally weird. I would also call it strange, and highly unusual."

An awkward silence hung between us.

Finally, SeeHawk realized what to do. Leaning forward, wearing a bright smile, he offered, "Want some toes?"

Narrowing my eyes, I chuckled, "Smart thinking, Chief Butt-Saving Officer. At least, a foot rub will help me sleep better, so I can navigate like a champion tomorrow."

Sometime after midnight, I dreamed about riding coach class on a disabled airplane flown by a loony pilot…swimming out of a donut-shaped ocean current…hearing our tent's stubborn door-zipper get stuck again.

When SeeHawk noticed my eyes opening, he stopped cussing long enough to explain, "I HAVE to take a nature stop."

Resuming his wrestling match versus the door, he cursed and gyrated for another couple of minutes, before finally crawling underneath the door on his belly.

I heard struggling noises outside and called through our tent, "Are you okay?"

"No," he gasped. "I can't…open…my darned kangaroo pouch. Its freaking zipper's stuck. I can't get my toilet paper."

Shoving a fresh roll underneath the door, I watched it get snatched by vanishing hands.

The ensuing silence left me alone in the faint glow of daybreak, wondering how I ought to go about finding the CDT. Yesterday's ideas felt stale. I needed to start fresh. After patiently unsnagging the door's stuck zipper, I crawled outside to start looking around for new information.

Once SeeHawk returned, we struck camp together, stuffed peach-yogurt fruit rolls into our pockets, and hoisted on our backpacks.

"Thank you, spot," we spoke in unison, to wherever-the-heck we had spent the night.

"Hasta luego," SeeHawk added. "It's time to get this show on the road."

"So long, and thanks for all the fish."

"Sayonara, baby. Catch you on the flip side. Actually, no. We're moving on and never coming back here again."

First thing upon setting off, we returned to the stream which had terminated our trail.

"I think that, in general, aiming west should be our main strategy," I told SeeHawk.

"West is best," he agreed. "East is least. South is out. North is where we came from. Please, anything but north."

Fixing my eyes upon the western trees, the first thing I noticed was that being lost at sunup felt a lot different from being lost after dark. The difference was delightful. I felt more at ease. Getting down to business, I whipped out our compass and prepared to put my noggin to the test. First, though, I took a good look at everything.

The brightening forest seemed totally virgin. If appearances rang true, it had never gotten defiled by bulldozers, chainsaws, packhorses, bike tires, or even many campers traveling on foot. Its understory was shaded by a solid ceiling of pine, spruce, and fir boughs, tinseled with lichen, like a witch's Christmas tree. Boulders thrusting through spongy needle mulch wore tree roots for scarves and moss for toupees. Fallen logs, rotted by funguses, had birthed new saplings which fed upon their flesh. Bursts of common huckleberry, gooseberry, beargrass, and creeping juniper looked exotic snuggled into hollows between the logs. Altogether, it was a magical underworld, discreetly hidden amongst recreational mountains, like a spy blending into a sidewalk crowd. Even the outside weather was barred from entering the space through which SeeHawk and I walked. This was our precious moment, in which to explore the forest's innermost secrets. Ethereal. Camouflaged. No longer frightening.

I was walking in front when a melodic stream lifted my awareness into a new dimension. Starting from the ground, I noticed my shoes compressing cushiony moss without leaving any footprints. Was I becoming weightless? I pretended to be a light-footed animal, striding nimbly on dainty little hooves. My legs felt capable of loping and leaping. Maybe I could spring sideways in order to escape from a hungry mountain lion. My heartbeat quickened. Muscles inside my legs felt whittled by speed. Every slightest sound seemed able to reach my ears. My nostrils inhaled. The forest's language became clear. Momentarily, I almost belonged there.

Meantime, SeeHawk drifted into a completely different experience. Where I saw plants, trees, and hollows, he saw energy fields, both friendly and threatening. He did not perceive us to be swerving around cobblestones. He saw the cobblestones guiding us around localized dangers and magnetic vortexes. Wherever he spied especially bright energy, he herded me toward it, in hopes of feeding my navigational intelligence with fuel for finding the Continental Divide.

As we came alongside a big heap of boulders, I reached out to touch one, thinking it would be warm. The shock of it being cold startled me out of daydreaming. It was time to wake up and assess our situation. We seemed to be generally heading west, but precision was impossible. More heaps of boulders and impenetrable shrubs kept steering us sideways and around in half-circles. One small clearing gave us a partial view of the sky, which felt like an offering, but all we saw was a blank canvas, made of overcast clouds.

"I guess, we won't be navigating by the sun today," I remarked.

SeeHawk responded suspiciously, "Why are we heading east?"

Caught off guard, I laughed, "Hello, Mister Whirlybird? Got your glasses on backward? I think we're heading almost straight west."

"I'm not wearing glasses, and we're actually heading east," he insisted. "I can tell because I've been paying attention this whole time."

"Me too. So, are you hallucinating, or am I?"

"I think, this time it's you."

"Well, I know you won't believe me until I show you, so hold on..."

Reluctantly, I dug out our compass, flipped open its mirrored lid, and set about putting "red in the shed." The wobbling needle gave me a new heading. I read it twice, questioning my eyesight. How could this be? My brain felt flabbergasted. According to geomagnetism, we were heading east!

"Traitor!" I cried. "Wrong. This is wrong!"

"How can a compass be wrong?" SeeHawk chuckled smugly.

"It can't, but it has to be because we're not heading east. I swear, we're heading west."

I knew something had to be wrong because, come on. How could the Queen Of Intuition be 180-degrees turned around backward? It did not make sense. Sure, we had detoured sideways in places, but never for long, and definitely not halfway around a circle without correcting our aim.

"We're heading east, or my name isn't Indiana Jones," SeeHawk insisted. "If your intuition disagrees, maybe we'd better examine that fruit roll you've been eating."

"No way," I cried. "I'm telling you the truth. This compass has got to be messed up or something. If we could see the sun, I swear, I could prove it to you."

Tilting the compass back and forth, I tested to see if its needle was stuck. When the needle rotated freely, I felt disappointed, even though, of course, I did not really want our compass to be broken.

"Compasses can't lie, sweetheart," SeeHawk repeated.

"Just like GPS-thingies can't lie," I fired back. "Except, we both know one did recently, so how's that for a miracle?"

I hated acknowledging that he had to be right. After all, admitting my error would mean accepting that my brain had malfunctioned, which would not be okay because if such a thing could happen once, then it could happen twice. I felt like a driver losing control of the steering wheel. Inside my head, the ground flipped upside down. Everything I had trusted was acting irrationally. My conscience rebelled. This could not be happening. Snapping back to attention, I complained, "There's got to be something we're overlooking. We aren't heading east. No way. No how."

"Majority vote wins, Sunshine. I think you're outnumbered, by me plus the compass."

"You can't even read the compass."

"Touché," he laughed. "But why are you getting all huffy? Isn't your goal the same as mine?"

My head felt nauseous, but it was no use. Circumstances had me cornered. Two against one. I had to give in.

SeeHawk looked triumphant as he led me across the clearing, aiming in the direction his "majority" called west.

Upon reaching the clearing's edge, I felt an urge to check the compass again, just for hoots. Much to my surprise, its reading drove me to holler, "SEEHAWK! You won't believe this! Now, the compass says we're heading east!"

"That's impossible," he scowled. "Is the needle sticking?"

"Definitely not," I confirmed. "It swivels all the way around. I don't know what happened back there, but now everything's lining up correctly. Am I going crazy? Or has our compass become demonically possessed?"

SeeHawk and I stared at each other.

"Could you have read the needle upside down?" he suggested.

That theory startled me into a fit of laughter. "Joker, you can't read a compass upside down. It swings in a full circle. It works in any direction." Groping for another explanation, I added, "Could there could be something weird about this place, like an underground meteor reversing its magnetism?"

"Probably, it's just Kwalaka," SeeHawk decided (referring to chaotic energy). "This place is full of bliss. We'd better move on before it messes with our focus."

I would have enjoyed performing a scientific study, but time was of the essence. We needed to keep moving.

Throughout the rest of the morning, our compass consistently verified we were still heading west. Several more portholes of open sky showed us unchanging clouds, still concealing the late-morning sun.

At length, SeeHawk reminded me, "You realize, we still haven't eaten breakfast?"

It was a rhetorical question. Neither he nor I wanted to stop for anything before finding the CDT, especially without proof of even being on the right mountain.

Thinning tree cover gradually expanded our views, allowing us to see more trees ahead. At the same time, progressively flatter ground enabled us to aim in any direction. This improvement stirred up some excitement. Were we finally getting near the Continental Divide? Our eyes scanned every opening for a north-south trail. When no trail appeared, we settled for targeting a well-defined ridge. At least, from a distance, with lots of trees in the way, it looked capable of being the Continental Divide, except for one problem. It was burned to smithereens. Literally, we had never seen such an all-consuming burn since leaving Canada. Its blackness resembled a sky without stars. As in, velveteen black, or freshly dug coal; not even a smidgen of green remained. No regrowing trees, nor even one living branch appeared to have survived the catastrophic burn. It was all just black, farewell, and good night.

The implications were troubling. If the CDT had burned, could Montana's harsh storms have erased its tread overwinter?

Might any surviving tread have gotten buried underneath heaps of charred trees?

SeeHawk nervously fingered his drinking teat, saying, "We don't have enough water left to last beyond dinner tonight, even if we ration."

"Then, let's find the CDT quickly," I resolved.

As soon as we reached the burn's entrance, I marched right on in, without hesitation.

Fearing that a tree might fall on me, SeeHawk dashed around to shield me with his body—so that, if a tree did fall, who knows? Maybe he could catch it with his hands, growl super loudly and heave it asunder like a Las Vegas wrestler?

"Well, there's one advantage of being engaged to a midwesterner," I laughed. "Thank you very much, kind sir."

It was fascinating to notice a dramatic mood shift, from all the fertility we were leaving behind, to something profoundly different. Here, instead of a legacy, we found anticipation. Stripped of its usual tree cover, the burned mountaintop was hibernating. Plans were being made to create new saplings, whose birthdates had not yet been established. The soil expected to feed them was still learning how to negotiate daylong sunlight and unimpeded winds. SeeHawk and I were intruders, arriving before the regrowth committee was ready to receive visitors, like spectators arriving too early for a parade. Conversely, though, we were also providing entertainment to some other beings, judging by how many animal tracks imprinted the black soil.

Suddenly, I realized something useful, and mentioned to SeeHawk, "If The Boys already came this way, shouldn't we be seeing their footprints?"

"Yes," he agreed, "four sets of footprints should be easy to spot, and I've been looking this whole time."

Yipes. That sounded like a red flag. If The Boys had not come through the burn, did their absence mean we were on the wrong crest, and possibly nowhere near the CDT?

Starting to carefully examine the ground, I noticed nearly invisible blades of grass timidly puncturing the topsoil's ashes.

Their scant greenness could only be seen by leaning forward and looking very hard. While looking, I also noticed black blister beetles waddling drunkenly toward nothing in particular. Diving underneath the burn's charred topsoil, my imagination found earthworms, seeds, newborn roots, and sprouts, all pushing up against the pull of gravity. Pink-blossomed fireweed was probing toward the daylight. Huckleberry seeds and fire-loving lodgepole pinecones were preparing to germinate a whole new forest, destined to grow taller each season. But, shoot, stop it, Sunshine. We could not afford to daydream. We needed to keep searching for the missing trail. Our eyes needed to rove everywhere at once. No distractions. Constant focus. My brain felt undisciplined. What was I missing? How often did I miss things? How often did I lose focus? Mostly, I lost focus when I was under pressure. Why did being under pressure matter? Was I impatient? Maybe. Not usually, but sometimes I got careless. At least, that's what happened yesterday, right? I had left the signed CDT, in favor of trusting a puny game trail, without even checking all the way uphill. Granted, I had tried pretty hard to figure things out before taking that gamble. But, once it became clear we were going the wrong way, why had I refused to turn around? Was I utterly stupid? Might that stupidity still doom us to wage a full-scale retreat? Back to where? Our campsite? Or, further back, to the overlook where SeeHawk's GPS had given us a bogus reading? Or even, all the way back to the switchbacks where this trouble had started? Worries kept ping-ponging through my head. The crest's right-hand precipice sucked my eyes downward and lured them toward a shiny lake coming into view. We could have reached it by butt sliding several-hundred feet down a raw cliff covered with dead trees. Beyond the lake sprawled mountains upon mountains, each burned as badly as the next.

    I gazed toward the overcast sky and decided it was time to strike a deal. "Please, Great Spirit," I begged, "if we can find the CDT today, I promise we won't do any more bushwhacking. SeeHawk, you're my witness. Mountains, do you hear me?"

"I hear you, Sunshine," my partner confirmed. "We'll just stick with good trails from now on, no matter what."

"Unless we're absolutely sure we couldn't possibly get lost."

"What? No," SeeHawk snapped. "Why don't we just stay on the trail, period?"

"Okay, okay," I conceded. "No more bushwhacks at all, ever."

It felt uncomfortable to sign on the dotted line, but after rebelling for a moment, then it felt good.

Literally, within the next two minutes, a crosswise trail appeared from out of nowhere. Happy tears spilled from our eyes. The trail was imprinted with fresh sneaker tracks. I could not recognize the tread patterns, but nobody needed to tell me who had made them.

"A blaze!" SeeHawk shouted. "Holy sh--. There's a sign!"

Looking where his finger pointed, I saw a black exclamation mark, carved into an equally black tree trunk. Directly below the carving hung a black wooden sign, from a nail that looked ready to drop if we sneezed.

"CD," the immortal sign proclaimed.

Together, SeeHawk and I thanked the Spirits of the Mountain for having mercy on our foolish souls.

Then, we hurried southward, following the blackened trail with a sense of urgency because storm clouds were brewing in the overcast sky.

* * *

"It's all well and fine to hurry," SeeHawk panted, "but we're still going to need to eat breakfast somewhere because it's getting near lunchtime."

He wanted to sit down someplace that was not black, and, speak of the devil. We found a sunken oasis tucked alongside the crest—miraculously spared by the fire that had burned everything else for miles.

It felt divine to collapse onto a blanket of soft grass, surrounded by living shrubs and trees. Songbirds were singing romantic jingles. Woodpeckers were bludgeoning bugs out of trees. Fish were strafing a pond ringed with grasshoppers. None of the local residents seemed bothered by two smelly homo sapiens scooping water out of their hunting ground.

When SeeHawk tossed his sweaty socks over a log, they got mobbed by frenzied black buzzers.

"Goodbye, mosquito season. Hello, black fly season," I chanted, not feeling sure if this changing of the guard was something to celebrate.

There was no need for SeeHawk and me to recap anything while we ate. It felt satisfying just to sit together, on a patch of living grass, noisily chewing sticky banana granola.

Before we knew it, our mugs were empty and young thunderheads were bulging in the wings. Climbing swiftly out of the oasis, we regained the crest in a terrible place to get chased by lightning. It was an elongated catwalk, straight for most of the next 8 miles, entirely burned and completely exposed, except for a few pinches of dead trees. Most of its length could be seen from the starting line. At its opposite end, the finish line was a central peak, crowning a band of perpendicular mountains posing as the catwalk's Olympic watchtower. We were going to need to climb over the watchtower to reach safety on the other side. Meantime, we had few choices besides hiking fast. Several dark clouds overshadowing the finish line looked ready to explode without provocation. In terms of escape routes, the catwalk's right-hand edge was out, due to a huge vertical drop. Its left-hand edge could lower us toward a living forest 1-mile in the distance, but fleeing in that direction would require a good head-start.

Feeling, at once, scared and excited, I reminded myself that our whole reason for coming to Montana had been to enjoy wide-open spaces, not to mention beautiful stormy weather.

Out loud, I told SeeHawk, "Just aim for the watchtower. Hook your energy to it. Tell the weather gods all we need is to get over it, and we'll have no other requests for today."

Feeling a little nervous, SeeHawk proposed, "Couldn't we just camp inside the forest on our left and go over tomorrow morning, when the weather might be safer?"

"Sure," I answered, "If we're willing to gamble on running out of food before we reach Wisdom, but if we can finish this part today, our prize will be leisurely hiking for the rest of the afternoon."

"You call that a prize?" he scoffed. "I'll tell you what I call a prize. How about two large pizzas and a keg of ice-cold beer?"

"How about dinner in Wisdom tomorrow night?" I countered.

"Say no more," he grinned and fell into step behind me.

When I hit the gas, I expected SeeHawk to stay on my heels, but after a few minutes, I noticed an odd silence. Turning around, I spied my partner stooping over to examine several sneaker prints stamped into the trail's soft dirt.

"Looks like The Boys made it this far," he shouted when he realized he was being watched.

"That's awesome," I smiled. "Glad to hear they survived Oreamnos Lake. Now, hup to it!"

Despite trying hard to speed up, both of us felt sluggish. The problem was being hungover from yesterday's emotionally draining, overnight adventure. Fortunately, nothing cures a hangover like a strong shot of adrenaline, which both of us received the moment we smelled rain."

I hollered back to SeeHawk, "Three hours to *Miller Time*. One hour to rain. Do you know what that means?"

"Shower first. Beer later?" he guessed.

"Right, and you can sing all you like, but there won't be any soap-on-a-rope."

Running my eyes down the catwalk, I analyzed its orientation in relation to the clouds. Trajectories mattered. Which among the nearest clouds were moving toward the crest? How fast were they moving? Which clouds looked dangerous? Suddenly, a disturbing question struck me.

"Do dead trees attract lightning, the same as living trees?"

SeeHawk had no idea.

"If they do," I reasoned, "staying alongside them might be smart, but my guess is that they don't, and going near them might give us is a false sense of security.

"Trust me, Sunshine, dead trees or no dead trees, I'm not feeling secure."

"Good," I nodded. "Then, let that fear factor make you hurry, so we won't have a bunch of electrical charges building up underneath our shoes."

"Did you read about that in one of our guidebooks?" SeeHawk asked.

"No, it's just my own theory, but you never know. It could be true."

"Well, in the meantime, if you don't want to get wet, I'd suggest pulling out your rain-poncho."

I barely had time to heed SeeHawk's warning, before a sharp gust of wind plastered hair across my eyes. The next instant, it felt like we got hit from behind by a carwash. The wind came roundabout, first hitting our backs and then shoving us sideways. The rain stung our exposed faces and legs. There was no time to escape. No place to hide. We just took off, running. Poor visibility made us thank the crest for being so narrow that we could not possibly drift off-course. Soon, the downpour transitioned into hail. One especially dark southwestern cloud seemed to be training its sights upon us. I clutched my poncho to stop it from flapping and silently prayed, *Any spirit who's listening right now, never mind if I didn't believe in you before. Please keep us safe.* My mind rehearsed emergency measures, like what to ditch if we needed to descend, and how to administer CPR.

Suddenly, I noticed the rain tapering off. Was my prayer being answered? Could we still hope to reach the watchtower in one straight shot?

"Mushrooms!" SeeHawk shrieked.

Whirling around, I stammered, "Huh?"

"Look, Sunshine. These are morels! We can eat them!"

His finger was pointing toward a cluster of spongiform fungi tucked beneath a burnt log.

"Are you CRAZY?" I gawked. "How can you think about MUSHROOMS at a time like THIS?"

"Because I think we can eat them."

"You're probably right, but guessing and knowing are not the same thing. Are you out of your MIND?"

"No, I'm just hungry, and I like morels."

"Have you ever picked a wild mushroom before? You're not even positive those are morels, are you?"

"No, but they look just like in the store."

Feeling aghast, I tried not to laugh. There was no time for scolding. I grabbed SeeHawk's arm and pulled him back into action.

More mushrooms peeked at us from beneath more logs. We raced past them all, with SeeHawk pointing, exclaiming, and begging me to let him pick some.

I felt like a meanie until lightning struck a mountain next to the watchtower.

"Whoa!" he hollered. "Don't stop running, Sunshine. We're almost there."

The rain dispersed into drifting mist. Feebler wind gusts implied the storm was petering out. Ahead and to our left, lightning kept flashing. With a vertical drop close on our right, the only way we could escape was by turning around, but retreating did not look foolproof either.

A slight incline boosted us high enough to see a bit farther over the watchtower. What did we see peeking up from behind its summit?

"Living trees!" I squealed, pointing at a fringe of tiny green triangles.

For once, danger affected SeeHawk and me the same way. We gunned our engines like there might be no tomorrow. A slight downturn buckled into a shallow notch wedged against the watchtower. The notch was only a stone's throw wide. Beyond it loomed one last climb sloping toward the summit we could no longer see. This was our moment of reckoning. We needed to race uphill, cross the watchtower, and drop into safety among the green triangles.

I pulled SeeHawk over to assess the sky. We felt safe about stopping because, miraculously, the notch contained a patch of living trees. That was sure lucky because before we could peel off our backpacks, the sky simultaneously turned blacker and brighter. Reacting fast, we planted our fannies onto a low embankment and hunched forward to make ourselves short.

"It looks like we're going to be stuck here for a while," SeeHawk grimaced.

"Which means we might as well have a party," I decided.

The party consisted of ripping open a bag of crispy parmesan croutons. I should also have dug out pantlegs and a fleece pullover while my backpack was open, but, too late. It started to rain, which meant my backpack had to stay underneath my rain poncho.

Shivering slightly, I snuggled against SeeHawk. The croutons we were eating turned into a game when we started passing them through our ponchos' armholes. At the same time, we watched Heaven's light show double in violence. Metallic pink flashes zinged across the sky. Spidery pitchforks stabbed peaks too scorched to care. Thunderclaps sizzled above kettledrums and cymbals, building the whole orchestra into one big climax. The showstopper was a single pink flash, striking the length of crest we had just evacuated.

"Good thing we didn't pick mushrooms!" SeeHawk admitted, clenching his knees.

"Thanks for saying so," I purred, "because I've been feeling pretty guilty about depriving you of your jollies."

"Just think, though," he added, "right now we could be roasting mushrooms by skewering them on our poles and pointing them toward the sky."

I expected the storm to end quickly because it had formed quickly, but it kept on raging for another full hour. Wearing wet shoes underneath our wet ponchos started to feel yucky. My legs turned clammy but my core temperature seemed okay until an arriving wind chill switched on the air conditioner. From then on, I would gladly have bought a Norwegian pineapple farm from anyone who could promise me a steaming-hot bath.

SeeHawk interrupted my shivering to suggest, "I'll lead us over the top, whenever you're ready, Sunshine."

Examining his eager face, I could tell he had lost all fear of the storm.

To be honest, I had never felt phobic of polarized electrons, but I did respect them, partly because I personally knew two lightning survivors. My own relationship with thunderstorms included a summer of tracking downbursts for Colorado's National Weather Service, plus three decades of vacationing on Canada's Great Lakes. Despite having scientific knowledge about storms, I was a firm believer in folklore, originating from both hearsay and my personal observations. For instance, I staunchly believed that whenever my arm hairs stood on end, I truly was in danger of electrocution. I also believed that every thunderstorm ends with one distinguished Final Strike, coming shortly after the storm's end, like an electrical Badum-Pah. This latter belief drove me to insist, "It won't be safe to climb until we hear the last strike."

SeeHawk thought the storm was already finished. Feeling antsy, he fidgeted beside me, flicking sourdough crumbs off his poncho and prying dirt from underneath his fingernails. After a while, he blurted out, "The storm HAS to be finished, Sunshine. It's been a long time. Besides, look over there."

A cluster of fresh thunderheads was approaching from the west. If we did not cross the watchtower immediately, perhaps we really were going to get stuck down there for the rest of the afternoon. Heaven forbid if that happened, where were we going to camp? Certainly, not inside the notch. Its little pocket of trees could hardly shield a tent rigged with bits of metal. Possibly, we could camp inside the living forest a mile away, but if we did, reaching Wisdom tomorrow was going to be a long shot. All things considered, our best bet was still to climb over the watchtower, and our window of opportunity was shrinking fast. But, would it be safe to come out of hiding before the Last Strike? Stewing in indecision, I felt a cold draft waft underneath my poncho. Its raspy breath whispered into my ear, *Climbing will make you warmer.* My skin answered, *Yes.*

Out loud, I told SeeHawk, "Let's just start climbing a little way and test the water. If it seems safe, we'll keep going, but if we hear thunder, even if it's two miles away, we'll come right back down, okay?"

"Okay," he promised.

"Pinky swear?"

We locked pinkies and shook.

"Also, how about shoulder squeezes for anyone who doesn't chicken-out?"

SeeHawk laughed, "Last one's a rotten egg!"

It felt thrilling to jump back into the game. Stupid or brave, together we mounted the watchtower's ghostly face. Burned trees that looked transplanted from Hell sidelined the switchbacks in oddly-spaced bunches. The watchtower's ceiling was formed of unpredictable clouds, curdling and dissolving with no apparent focus. Climbing steeply from straight below, we could no longer see the summit that was our finish line.

This is crazy, I thought. *Should we climb faster, or turn around?*

The nearest clouds overhead looked flat. Meaning, they were horizontal in shape, but their textures looked rough. That was a cryptic combination. My brain sounded alarms when my arms begin to prickle. At first, it felt like getting stung by tiny bees. I knew what those stings meant. It was time to check my personal voltage meter. Pushing up both sleeves of my windbreaker jacket, I confirmed that, sure enough, my arm hairs were standing halfway up. *This is not scary*, I told myself because *halfway is only halfway, not all the way, or even three-quarters.* In fact, it occurred to me to wonder if my arm hairs ever laid completely flat. I could not remember ever having checked on a day without storms. One thing for sure, though, was that my hairs were not being raised by a chill because my entire body felt warm from climbing.

A bit farther uphill, I started to feel tiny bees stinging my legs. Still, I did not panic because nothing will make a person itch more than wondering why they itch.

SeeHawk was hiking in front when we rounded a wide switchback whose higher rung redirected us toward the summit.

I felt afraid to even glance uphill. The thing I feared most was seeing lightning strike me between the eyes. Also, I wondered if acknowledging the clouds, by looking at them, could attract them to notice me, in an energetic sense. Just in case, I kept my head down and stared at the trail in front of my shoes.

At this point, it seemed silly to bother rechecking my arm hairs. We had passed the point of no return. Increasingly short switchbacks lifted our hopes for the summit to appear any second. It should already have appeared. Dang, where was it? We had climbed high enough, already. Couldn't the mountain give us a little help? Our situation was beginning to feel critical. Every upward step was increasing the danger. I still thought we could make it all the way, but summits are notorious for giving false hope. Several times in the past, receding summits had strung us along, to the point of thinking they might go on forever.

I gained strength from chanting inside my head, *We WILL reach the summit...we WILL reach the summit...*

SeeHawk started grinning before he saw trees. He felt absolutely sure we were getting near the top.

I spent those same few minutes trying not to scratch a fresh outbreak of bee-stings. Sternly, I told them, *Bees go away. You are a psychosomatic figment of my imagination.*

Fully 30 minutes after leaving the notch, we heard a muffled boom roll off the summit. It came from exactly where we were aiming. Both of us froze. Had we just heard the Last Strike, arriving fashionably late? Or had a new storm emitted its first thunderclap? If the latter was true, might that new storm greet us atop the watchtower?

"RUN!" I hollered. "Don't wait for me to catch up. Just GO!"

Hunching forward to be short, I felt myself sprinting in super-slow motion. It felt like being a parody of somebody climbing in slow motion. My legs were spent, but we could not afford to stop, in case the clouds might get a lock on our position.

Soon, the summit popped into sight. There, was our finish line. Oh, so close. We just needed to climb another 30 steps...20 steps...10 steps. That was all I could manage before my legs gave out. I hunched forward, gasping for air. It was the worst place possible to stop, but I had no choice.

"Sorry," I panted, laughing in horror because my legs would not move.

SeeHawk halted a few steps above me, also gasping, while he waited for me to recover. I could see by his face that he was screaming inside, *Come ON, girl. COME ON!*

Finally, we hustled over the watchtower together. For just a split second, we each got to be the tallest object around. Then, over and down we went, crossing gentle terrain.

The next ecosystem we entered was a green alpine forest which leveled off near 8,300-feet. Remaining high, suspended amongst the clouds, we thanked every living tree for its valuable gift of shelter, while enjoying a beautiful skyline traverse.

My wits gradually fell back into place. Strung-out limbs relaxed. Suddenly, I burst into uncontrolled laughter.

The grade began to drop. Its rocky dirt surface eased into hardpacked clay. Peering through occasional breaks in the trees, we gained glimpses into a tremendous, sheer-sided valley, whose interior looked full of soft-whipped cream.

"That's the Big Hole!" I exclaimed. "We're almost finished heading west."

"Which means?"

"We're about to head south for a couple of days, before heading east for as long as we headed west."

"Wait a minute," SeeHawk responded. "Are you saying, we're going to spend another whole week going sideways, instead of toward Mexico?" Pressing a hand over his heart and reaching his other hand toward the sky, he playacted, "Get ready, Elizabeth. This is the big one. I'm coming, Elizabeth. I'm coming to join you."

Rolling my eyes, I told him, "It won't last forever. We'll be in Yellowstone two weeks from now."

Breaking into a grin, SeeHawk declared, "Now, that's more like it, baby!"

The tree cover thinned as we lost elevation. Exposed orange clay showed evidence of violent rain. Perhaps, it had even hailed, judging by the clay's deep golf ball dimples.

Soon, we came upon four sets of sneaker prints, jammed into the mouths of four muddy toe holes.

"Looks like The Boys skidded down here at full-tilt," SeeHawk observed.

"They must have seen some really big lightning," I assumed.

At 8,200-feet, Surprise Lake was overflowing its grassy banks. Impressionistic tree reflections striped the water's surface. Every passing breeze dragged the reflections into fractals. Underwater stones, chinked with rotting wood, peeked through shallows stitched to the air by aqueous reeds. A band of white mist blanketing the water kept clotting with every passing breeze. Above the mist, a layer of clear air was capped with low clouds, chopping the Continental Divide's scalp clean off.

All in all, SeeHawk and I could not have imagined a better place to fix an extremely late lunch. Never mind that it was almost dinnertime. We sat together on a rain-softened log and assembled a full bag of chocolaty PBC sandwiches. Packing them to-go made sense because, having already taken a long break during the storm, we could not be sure of reaching Wisdom the following day unless we hurried.

A light drizzle coaxed us back into our ponchos before we left Surprise Lake. Once back in motion, our ears heard little besides swishing nylon hoods, overriding the softer squish of sneakers sloshing through muddy grass dotted with soggy wildflowers. The rain's end was prolonged by droplets falling inside spruce and pine groves whose saturated limbs created their own rain.

Our next stop took place at Hell Roaring Creek, where it seemed prudent to bag enough water to last through breakfast the next morning.

While sealing up his backpack, a yearning came over SeeHawk and he wistfully mumbled, "I wish we could just camp here tonight. It's so lovely. It's peaceful, and we've had a long day."

FOOM! I shot down that idea faster than a Ninja mosquito could have bitten him and flown away.

At 8,500-feet, we breathed air that tasted like a water popsicle. Foggy to the point of sticky, its chill bored into our sweat-soaked clothing, reminding us that, even though we felt warm from climbing, our energy reserves were running on empty.

Both guidebooks warned us to watch out for the CDT becoming difficult to follow atop the crest. Indeed, they were right because its tread vanished precisely where the trail leveled off. After that, humongous cairns directed hikers to cross open ground. We had to keep pausing in order to site each next rock pile. Progressively fewer trees stood by the wayside, most barely matching us for height. Soon, SeeHawk and I became the tallest objects in each other's company. This felt unnerving after the crest shrank to a ribbon of raised earth. The only trees remaining were haggard limber pines, torched by lightning and otherwise flogged into the shapes of hunchbacked gargoyles.

With fog encasing our bodies inside a blank white shell, we got goosebumps from seeing our ribbon-shaped course acquire cliffs on both sides. Fortunately, in the same location, the CDT's "trail" of cairns solidified into a real trail, whose guidance saved us from stepping into empty space. The spook factor remained, though, each time we approached a rogue limber pine, reaching out to poke us like a cloaked gray ghoul.

With increasing density, the fog's mushy whiteness set everything afloat. Even our own bodies appeared to have no feet. Climbing higher still, we seemed to have mounted the Stairway to Heaven. After more than an hour of hiking blind, we got startled by a fissure splitting open the fog. Peering through it gave us a sneak preview of the Big Hole Valley. Far below, we saw a patchwork quilt of green-and-brown farmland, creased with skinny rivers. Lording over the farmland stood a monstrous thunderhead, wide enough to dwarf several mountains. Its bluish midriff formed deep purple shadows, crowned with bubbles frozen in outer space. All that hugeness was inching toward us, at a height poised to strike us in the faces. It was like viewing the cloud through a jet plane's window. Thank goodness, we were located safely to one side and a good distance away. Also, we felt glad that the cloud looked past its prime in terms of storm activity, but one could never tell. If the air temperature dropped rapidly after sundown, perhaps the cloud's vigor might be restored.

Meantime, I found myself having another daydream. This time, I journeyed into the cloud's hidden core. How might it look from the inside? Smooth? Fibrous? Turbulent and lumpy? Filled with hailstones trampolining on updrafts? When I noticed myself having such thoughts, I telepathically told the cloud, *No. Don't come over here. I do NOT want to see how you look from the inside.* Of course, I did not really believe the cloud could hear me. Nor, did I believe I could influence its approach. I just covered my bases because one never knows, and superstitious people cannot be too careful, whether it means talking to clouds or avoiding cracks in the sidewalk.

Anyhow, back in real-time, the fissure soon fell behind us, leaving nothing else to look at besides white fog. No clock-check was needed for us to know it was getting late. Our bodies knew it, and, perhaps our eyes did too, although it was hard to tell, in whiteness that faded like a weakening flashlight. With no end in sight, we were forced to start worrying about finding a place to camp. Just when it seemed like the dream might never end, the CDT's foundation shrank to 7 yards wide. Angling more steeply uphill, Heaven's staircase began to look ominous. Could there have been a worse place to hear thunder? Had it come from our left or right? Who could tell, with the sound dispersing in all directions?

One reassurance was knowing the climb could not last forever. It had to end somewhere. And yet, long after we had last seen limber pines, a few hooligans reached through the fog with their black zombie arms and tried to spook us. That's right, their color was black, not gray because of burning more recently than their peers down below.

"It's a good thing we weren't up here this afternoon," See-Hawk shuddered.

I could hear some fatigue stiffening his voice. Hoping to buoy him along, I encouraged him with cheerful reminders, "This is our last climb before reaching Wisdom...buffalo burgers...hot showers..."

"Say no more," he groaned. "I'm trying to speed up, Sunshine. Sorry, I'm just tired."

We were both feeling zonked by the time we stepped from the fog into a shock of open space. It happened all at once, like stepping out through a curtain. Before us, sat an 8,700-foot crow's nest, spanning a few acres of summit pressed against the sky. Half the summit's scattered trees were dead and the other half living, but most barely stood taller than our heads.

"Five on a scale of ten," I wagered, in terms of lightning safety.

"Seven, inside the saddle," SeeHawk replied.

Beyond the crow's nest, we saw a shallow depression, filled with taller trees that had been milled into toothpicks by another burn.

"Even though camping low is usually safer than camping high," I told SeeHawk, "personally, I'd rather camp up here than down in Domino Land."

"Really?" he muttered, thinking it might be worth hiking past the burned saddle before making camp. Then, he caught himself being a doofus, and exclaimed, "This is totally awesome, Sunshine!"

The sun had already set. The sky was still bright. While unpacking our gear, we saw the same giant cumulonimbus cloud we had seen earlier, now reappearing from a strange angle. It bloomed into a gorgeous shade of pink as other parts of the sky became streaked with orange highlights.

Once everything was pitched and cooked, SeeHawk and I sat together atop the grassy crow's nest, slurping down forkfuls of tomato-pesto pasta.

I thought while I was eating, *When will this long day ever end?*

The colorful sky answered, *As soon as you finish dinner.*
Good! I thought, *because I can't wait to fall asleep.*

However, the pot was not empty yet.

In between mouthfuls, I asked SeeHawk, "Was it really just yesterday that we left Pintlar Creek?"

SeeHawk had to think for a moment before answering, "Yes, it was."

"And, this morning that our compass went all screwy before we found a charbroiled CD-sign?"

"Plus found morel mushrooms!" SeeHawk stuck in.

"Right, oh man. We've sure gotten our money's worth, today."

Growing sentimental, SeeHawk acknowledged, "Thanks for convincing me to believe I could do this trip Sunshine."

Smiling, I agreed, "It's wonderful, isn't it?"

"More than wonderful," he emphasized. "It's totally magnificent. Like, more magnificent than I could ever have imagined. Trying to describe it would be like, like…trying to hold air in your hands. How are we going to describe this to anyone?"

"By saying it's magnificent."

"Truly magnificent."

The fog returned after we finished eating. One by one, nightfall's stars got pushed out of sight. A few odd thunderclaps rumbled toward the south. Then, quixotic silence floated us into sleep. Twice, I got awakened with my eyes closed. The first time, I saw lightning flash on my left. The second time, I saw lightning flash on my right. That was just business as usual for the Rocky Mountains. We slumbered deeply, beneath a migration of whales gliding past invisible stars.

* * *

Who could guess how early or late it might have been when SeeHawk and I awoke the next morning? Our tent looked bathed in light from all sides. If we had gotten killed in our sleep, we were waking up in Heaven. Or, more precisely, our tent had been swallowed by a low-hanging cloud.

SeeHawk lost his balance when he climbed outside to have a look around.

I lingered between the folds of our soggy sleeping bag, noticing that the garments strung on our interior clothesline had gotten wetter overnight. When I finally climbed outside, syrupy cloud vapor oozed over my shoes and hid them completely. Kicking the fog made it roll like water. Slapping created swishing patterns, which could be strained through my fingers. Blowing created puffs of steam. This was all so much fun that it was too bad we had to hurry and strike camp.

Today's agenda combined 20 miles of hiking with 25 miles of hitchhiking along a lightly traveled highway. Altogether, that was an ambitious goal to complete before Wisdom's motels and restaurants closed for the night, but we thought we could make it if we hiked briskly and did not make any wrong turns.

Heading out of camp, it felt strange to stroll down a gentle hillside without being able to see our shoes. When we dropped low enough to exit the cloud, a sunlit forest threw up its sashes and sang good morning. Glittering streams forwarded us into a confluence of valleys, whose flat dirt road matched our expectation. Everything seemed in order until a second dirt road offered us a choice.

I whipped out our literature and reported uncertainly, "DeLorme's Atlas only shows one road. Poppa Jim doesn't mention any second road, and the Book of Beans takes a different route, so…uh…could this road be new?"

Frowning, SeeHawk replied, "It doesn't look super old, but it wasn't built yesterday."

Having no other reference, I said, "Probably, we should just stick with the road we're on since it was right to start with."

"Aye-aye, captain," SeeHawk agreed.

"But, please help me focus," I added, "because we cannot afford to make ANY wrong turns today. Like, nada, zip, zero."

We continued following the same dirt road for another two minutes, before, whoops! We ran into a stick-arrow telling us to turn around.

"Well, there you go," I smirked. "This road's been dummy-proofed."

"Thanks to The Boys," SeeHawk guessed. His assumption was based upon remembering two other occasions when The Boys had scratched arrows into dirt trails, hoping to save us from making wrong turns.

In this instance, the road was so hard-surfaced that it made sense to build an arrow from sticks, rather than trying to make scratch marks visible. Nevertheless, I felt irked because come on. No Chief Navigator wants to be told they have erred on a day when they cannot afford to make mistakes.

When SeeHawk noticed my irked expression, he tried to ease the blow by suggesting, "Want to look for The Boys' shoeprints, before we jump to any conclusions?"

Liking that idea, I helped him search above and below the arrow. Unfortunately, we could not find any shoeprints, old or new. Again, that made sense, since the road's hard surface refused to even accept our shoeprints when we stomped really hard.

Thus, having no means to prove who made the arrow, I tended to think we should stick with our aim. However, I fully realized that my ego could be fooling me.

When SeeHawk saw me square up my shoulders, he timidly suggested, "It's probably time to turn around, Sunshine."

"Why?" I demanded. "Because you figure any random arrow, made by The Boys or not, probably has better judgment than me?"

"No," he rolled his eyes. "Don't be silly."

"Then, why? Because you feel sure it was made by The Boys, and you'd trust their judgment over mine in a heartbeat?"

"Again, no. Quit with that, Sunshine. I trust you like Prudential, or like my dad and my brother. I trust the arrow too, though because it probably wouldn't exist if somebody didn't know something, okay?"

"What if you thought the arrow was made by a woman?"

"What?"

"Would you still trust it like your dad and your brother?"

"Of course. What are you talking about?"

"You, giving your opinion about something you can't know since you aren't able to read maps and you don't even know what we're looking for."

"You're right, I don't."

"So why are you saying stuff that could trigger an emotional response capable of influencing my normally impeccable judgment, which is usually accurate whenever it's not being messed with?"

"Er, sorry, Sunshine. I guess I overstepped my bounds," he groaned. "Delete whatever I said. You lead the way. I promise to be fine with whatever you decide. I just want to eat dinner in Wisdom tonight."

"Me too," I agreed. "That's why this decision is stressing me out."

SeeHawk held his tongue while I took another glance through maps that told me nothing new. Like it or not, I simply had to consult my sixth sense, using willpower to screen out any distractions. After taking a deep breath, I stepped across the arrow.

SeeHawk followed me, making no comment.

Proceeding down the road, we soon rounded a curve that seemed to match our atlas. All we needed for a full restoration of confidence was one definite landmark. Unfortunately, both sideline forests surrounding the road provided no view of anything besides close-growing trees.

Eventually, I started to wish we had peeked at the road indicated by the arrow, just to know what it looked like. Then, something dawned on me that seemed critical.

"The Boys have Poppa Jim's updates," I realized. "What if they know something about these roads that we don't, and that's why they built the arrow?

"Whoa," SeeHawk replied, "that's a game-changer, Sunshine. We should definitely turn around."

"What?" I stammered. Sure, my theory made sense, but it did not prove we should turn around. Why did my partner always have to trust The Boys at the drop of a hat? Whereas, for me to convince him of almost anything usually required an argument. Feeling snubbed, I retorted, "Not so fast, buster. First, we need to finish ruling out this road, so we won't have to waste time coming back twice."

"You don't think we've already gone far enough already, to prove this is the wrong way?"

"Well…okay…maybe you're right," I conceded, "but, darn. Why does this have to happen on a day when we need to hurry?"

Retracing our steps all the way back to the stick arrow, this time, we obeyed it and turned onto the alternate road. Within minutes, we started passing clear-cuts littered with logging debris. Replanted saplings had already sprouted. Obviously, it was a logging road, and probably a new one.

SeeHawk seemed encouraged by the same observations that made me think we were going the wrong way.

Finally, I put my foot down and told him it was time to turn around.

"Again?" he reeled. "You've got to be kidding, Sunshine."

"I'm not kidding," I assured him. "And don't feel surprised because I thought it was the other road all along."

Neither of us spoke while backtracking to where the stick-arrow resumed mocking our intelligence. Having wasted one full hour, we stepped back over the arrow and retraced our steps, again rounding the curve that seemed to match our atlas. This time, we kept going until we reached a second curve, which was unmistakably the real curve shown on our atlas. In other words, we could have avoided turning around in the first place, by simply having gone another quarter-mile.

Fighting to stay calm, I glibly remarked, "Gee Willikers, SeeHawk. It looks like today's twenty-miler has turned into a twenty-four-miler."

"Can we still hope to reach Wisdom before dark?" he worried.

"Can pigs fly if they flap their ears really hard?"

Catching my meaning, he laughed, "Maybe."

A few minutes later, we passed a tiny blue-and-white CD sign nailed onto a tree, slightly above our eye level. A bit farther still, we reached a trailhead marked with a large CD-sign, fronting a several-acre meadow framed with conifer trees. Glancing all around, we could not figure out where to enter the trees.

"Number seven," I joked, indicating a situation repeated so often that we might as well just give it a number.

Fifteen minutes of searching turned up nothing more promising than two ATV ruts smashed through the grass. We decided to follow them, only to watch them deteriorate into a deer trail. Cursing and groaning, we returned to the CD-sign and spent another ten minutes scouting the meadow's perimeter. Finally, we spied a teensy weensy potato-chip-of-a-little pipsqueak CD-sign, nailed high enough up a tree to be clipped by low-flying airplanes.

It took self-control for me to simply say, "Let's start fresh and not make any more mistakes, okay?"

"Fresh as a daisy," SeeHawk nodded. "Ladies first?"

The next half hour saw us march up and down numerous inconsequential hills. Our first mistake, after starting fresh was losing the trail inside a stubbly clear-cut. Our second mistake was wasting 15-minutes figuring out where it entered another massive burn.

SeeHawk tried to keep things cheerful by reminding me about Blue Man going ballistic inside a meadow near Electric Peak. He and I enjoyed rehashing that story on frustrating days when we needed a good laugh.

Presently, though, our gloom stemmed from the burn's interior looking creepy. Its daylight seemed too golden, considering the sun's high elevation. Its unnatural silence made us feel restless.

Fortunately, everything improved after we found a signed trail-junction identifying the CDT. Being back on track helped us start appreciating the burn's somber beauty. For instance, its denuded trees had sleek silhouettes. Its naked ground looked ready for new landscaping. Nature had plans for the burn's recovery, and if its timescale disappointed human beings, then, tough luck. They would just have to wait.

Thoughts like this were keeping us engrossed when we came upon another stick arrow lying across the trail. Instead of appearing to direct traffic, this time it pointed toward a youth dressed in blue jeans.

SeeHawk noticed the boy's hand clutching a 5-gallon paint bucket and whispered into my ear, "Mushroom hunter."

Putting two-and-two together, I gasped, "Do you think he built the other stick-arrow, and it wasn't The Boys, after all?"

"Probably," SeeHawk nodded, "but, look at that. He's picking morels."

Sure enough, we saw the forager rummage underneath a burnt log, such as might spawn morels.

I gave my partner a stern look.

"Don't worry," he chuckled. "I won't ask to share his bounty. Today, we're on a mission to reach Wisdom, and that's all."

As it turned out, though, our mission got delayed by another snafu. We were expecting to leave Poppa Jim's low route at a turnoff leading up to a new high trail described in the Book of Beans. Strangely, however, we could not find the turnoff. Only after overshooting it by two miles did we realize we had mistakenly turned onto an unmapped logging road and gotten dumped onto Elk Creek Trail No. 18. At the same time, we found out we were taking an accidental shortcut to Highway 43. That was good news in terms of our hurry to reach Wisdom but, ugh. Leaving and returning to the woods in slightly different locations would insert another small gap in our continuity, albeit a very minor gap.

SeeHawk's opinion was, "We've already given up our chance for a perfect track record. This disconnect will be so minor that we should probably just accept it, quit goofing around, and get to the San Juan Mountains.'"

"Fair enough," I decided. "Maybe if we add up all the pros and cons, in this case it makes sense to accept the cards we've been dealt."

Fortunately, the Elk Creek Trail turned out to be gorgeous. Blankets of fallen oak leaves, carpeting a mature oak-and-pine forest enshrined its tumbling water. A gradual descent of several miles finally ended inside a flat meadow, whose lone occupant was a grazing bull moose.

SeeHawk noticed a bright red carabineer lying beside the trail, and remarked with surprise, "I think I saw this hanging off Redbeard's backpack."

Laughing, I informed him, "Sorry, but that's impossible, sweetie. Remember where we are? This is not the CDT. Plus, there are about a million red carabiners in the world."

"This is definitely Redbeard's," he insisted, clipping the metal fastener onto his backpack.

Suddenly, a report of gunshots scared us to a halt.

We had just reached a junction of two dirt roads. Hunting season was a few months away. Most likely, the shooter was practicing targets, but still. What if they were practicing targets on the move?

We gritted our teeth while shuffling forward, hoping to get seen before getting shot. Soon, we spied two men cleaning shotguns behind a parked pickup truck. The sight of them scared me, but I tried to smile anyway.

"Where are you two going?" one shooter bluntly inquired.

"To Wisdom," SeeHawk answered, without hesitation. "We're hiking the CDT."

My eyes told him, *Shh! Are you whacked? Don't give away our plans to hunters!* Although, I privately agreed with him that the gunmen looked harmless.

"The whosit?" we were asked again.

"The CDT," SeeHawk repeated.

Speaking more slowly, I spelled out the name, "Con-ti-nen-tal Div-ide Trail."

"Huh," the man shrugged. "Never heard of that one."

He and his friend had heard of Wisdom, though. They came right out and offered to drive us the last half-mile to Highway 43, in case walking might not get us there fast enough to hitchhike before dark.

I wanted to tell the men, no thanks. "Yellow-blazing" was strictly against our code of honor. However, it made sense to consider what might happen if we failed to catch a ride that evening. Never mind missing dinner in Wisdom. The real pitfall would be further delaying our entrance into the San Juan Mountains. Experience had shown us time and time again that even a few hours could make a difference. But, wait. What was I thinking? Bust my buttons! Fetch me some brain soap! We could not yellow-blaze. It would be unethical. Tacky. Our integrity would be ruined. Even though technically, we had already left the CDT back when we made a wrong turn, but accepting one compromise did not justify another.

Before I could make up my mind, SeeHawk stepped forth to accept the gunman's offer.

Sigh. Case closed. Now we were committed. Because who would dare shilly-shally with a pair of armed hunters?

SeeHawk went first, climbing into the pickup truck's open rear bed. We rode for four minutes before alighting onto Highway 43. Within seconds of seeing the hunters drive away, remorse hit me like a ton of bricks. Could SeeHawk and I still return to the woods, turn around, and walk back to the highway? How silly would that be? But also, how much better would we feel after connecting the dots? Although, our connectivity would break again upon returning from Wisdom at a slightly different location. So, what difference was an extra half-mile going to make?

Suddenly, I noticed a surly thundercloud descending toward us. It seemed to be growing darker right before my eyes. Either lightning was brewing or the sun was about to set. Regardless, we could not afford to waste time nitpicking over a lost half-mile. The cloud was dragging a slender tongue of rain, aiming to swipe off the mountain and lick us. If we could not catch a ride before the rain arrived, we were going to need to run for shelter. At present, though, we still had a little more time. Anxiously waiting, it helped soothe our nerves to pace back and forth, trying to stay hopeful. Occasionally, a car appeared and sped right past us, without its driver even glancing in our direction. Soon, the highway's yellow lines began to glow. The sun popped in to say goodbye. Then, it dropped out of sight for good. Right on cue, the highway's traffic virtually ceased. It was as if driving after sundown had been outlawed in Montana. The most we saw a car after that was only about once every five minutes. Then, once every ten minutes. Meantime, the approaching rain cloud started to spit forked yellow lightning. Where could we hide? Nowhere, if we wanted to keep hitchhiking. Which, however, seemed pretty futile with no more cars appearing.

Heaving a sigh, I finally told SeeHawk, "Maybe it's time to discuss our camping options."

Suddenly, a red SUV zoomed into sight. Was this our chance to be saved?

We waggled our thumbs like we wanted them to fall off.

Neither the SUV's driver nor passenger glanced in our direction.

With sinking hearts, we watched two red brake lights wink around a curve and vanish from sight.

That was all. Another opportunity lost.

"Maybe they'll come back," SeeHawk hoped.

"Ha-ha," I chortled. "Like they don't have anything better to do than pick up a couple of smelly-looking strangers."

"Don't you remember that semi who looped around to pick us up at Marias Pass?" he reminisced.

"Oh, yeah. That was a miracle, but the thing about miracles is, you can't expect them to happen twice. So, we really need to start looking for a campsite."

The rain was nearing impact, in t-minus five.

SeeHawk granted me five last minutes in which to catch a ride, before calling it quits and just finding a place to camp.

Three minutes later, fat raindrops hit the pavement. We had seen no more cars. The thunder was getting louder. Feeling utterly disappointed, both of us wrenched open our backpacks, one minute too late. The downpour hit us faster than we could deploy our ponchos.

Suddenly, coming from far down the road, a pair of headlights hurtled back into sight. Right before our astonished eyes, the red SUV whipped a U-turn, pulled over, and threw open its door. The driver and his wife waved us over. They were inviting us to jump in. We were being rescued seconds before getting drenched!

SeeHawk crowed all the way to our seats, about auspicious timing and benevolent spirits.

Once we got underway, the wife twisted around to cheerfully offer, "Would you like a beer?"

I stared into her cooler chest filled with ice-cold lager, and thought, "Heck, yes!" But, I reluctantly said, "No thanks," because I did not want her husband to get arrested for driving with an open container.

"Oh, it's okay," she reassured me. "You can drink and drive in Montana, just so long as you don't get drunk."

"No, it isn't," her husband disagreed.

"Yes, it is," she insisted. "I do it all the time, and no one ever bothers me."

Rolling his eyes, he explained, "Well, they would bother you, if you got pulled over."

Changing the subject, our hostess produced a grocery bag full of something soft, asking, "Would you like some morel mushrooms for dinner? We just went out to the forest and picked them."

Chapter 10

Wisdom

Hear me. I am tired. My heart is sick and sad. Our chiefs are dead. The little children are freezing. My people have no blankets, no food. From where the sun stands, I will fight no more forever.

— *Chief Joseph to Colonel Nelson A. Miles,*

SeeHawk walked into Wisdom hankering for some buffalo meat. He was not craving 90%-lean protein because of being a health-nut. Nor, did he have a do-gooder's appetite for hoofed animals that consume 35-lbs. less feed per day than cattle. Rather, his motive was to absorb some "good medicine" from the stars of his favorite western movies.

Buffalo had been captivating SeeHawk's imagination ever since the night we stayed in Marysville. This was because of a certain book he had read there, describing how Asian buffalo migrated through America's prehistoric forests and prairies, in company with mastodons, giant ground sloths, and giant beavers, who all went extinct while the buffalo survived. The book had cited 200,000 years as a modern estimation of how long wild buffalo withstood heat waves, snowstorms, droughts, and predation, before 30-40 million of them got slaughtered by one generation of human beings. Circa 1820 marks the beginning of when westbound frontiersmen shot virtually every herd roaming America's prairies. The spoils created giant caches of rotting bones, found by homesteaders 50 years later who sold batches of them to industrial manufacturers for $6-$30 per ton. Most of the remaining bones got distilled into charcoal used for refining sugar, ground into fertilizer, boiled into glue, or carved to make decorative buttons, combs, and knife handles.

It can be assumed that the bones being scavenged were huge because prehistoric buffalo reached twice the size of today's modern buffalo (who still look impressive, at 6 feet tall and 1-ton heavy on a livestock scale). From a genetic perspective, buffalo share ancestry with pigs, hippopotami, camels, deer, giraffes, pronghorn antelope, sheep, goats, and cows. Some of their unique talents include being able to reach snow-covered grass by shoveling with their heads, growing fur capable of withstanding cold that would kill domestic cows, rolling in the mud for defense against extreme heat and mosquitoes, and surviving without water for 3-4 days. Native Americans found countless uses for buffalo by-products, including turning their hides into tipis, bedding, clothing, moccasins, boats, drums, shields, grain bags, horse-rigging, and rope, as well as using their hooves to make glue, tails to make switches and fly swatters, manes for fans, rope, belts and stuffing, dung-chips for fuel, and bones for rendering fat. Altogether, it seems that buffalo were the Native Americans' single source for obtaining homebuilding materials, kitchen utensils, office supplies, heating fuel, transportation accessories, farm implements, and dinner ingredients.

SeeHawk had all of this in mind when he strode into one of Wisdom's two restaurants and ordered a domestic "bison burger," drenched in sweet-sour country music. Therefore, he made a big ceremony out of eating the whole thing, and even ceremoniously licked his plate.

The town of Wisdom, commercially speaking, could be absorbed in one glance. It was neither rustic enough to be called "historical," nor modern enough to offer any fast-food joints. For tourists, it was just a quick gas-and-food stop, given pizzaz by its Native American gift store. But, for the local retirement community and outlying ranches, it was the closest thing they had to a social hub.

SeeHawk and I wasted no time in booking an affordable room at the Nez Perce Motel. While checking in, we were delighted to spot an alcohol-burning soda-pop-can stove sitting in the motel's lobby. Apparently, Blue Man had left it as a gift, the same way he did in many trailside towns.

Once we got settled in our freshly painted motel room, I used its handy pushbutton telephone to call California and see how our dog and house were doing.

"Tierra's happy," house-sitter-Erik reported. "Everything's fine, except for the toilet. Brown stuff came gushing out when I turned on the washing machine. The bathroom door was closed, so I didn't see it coming until it flowed underneath the door. By then, you don't even want to KNOW what happened. Your dad and I had to call a plumber. Sorry, the job cost four hundred bucks."

When I hung up the phone, SeeHawk asked for a recap.

"Everything's fine," I said. "Whenever you leave home for six months, stuff's gonna happen."

The following morning, we heard a knock on our door and came face-to-face with Redbeard. He was rooming with Teach at Wisdom's only other motel. Constant sunburn had reddened his pink skin, adding a few freckles to his open-mouthed smile. His blue eyes looked bloodshot, but they were still dancing. His bright orange hair had developed blond highlights, whose overgrowth needed raking whenever he laughed. His whole face lit up when he saw his lost carabineer clipped onto SeeHawk's backpack.

"Where did you find it?" he gasped.

"On the Elk Creek Trail," SeeHawk recalled.

"You came that way too? Right on! Teach and I took the Elk Creek Trail because it was a shortcut to town."

"We took it because we got lost," I explained.

Redbeard said he and Teach were temporarily out of contact with String Stick and Dutch because the other two had shipped their resupplies to Salmon, Idaho. Luck willing, they were all hoping to reassemble south of Chief Joseph Pass.

SeeHawk and I expressed hope to catch the group after doing our laundry in Wisdom, but we realized it would be a long shot.

Hearing our plan caused Redbeard to perk up and ask, "There's a Laundromat here?"

"According to The Book of Beans," I replied, "and, boy, do we ever need it. Yesterday, I packed my wet clothes in with my dry clothes. Now, they're all rotting together in one bag. I'm afraid to even open it."

Redbeard chuckled grimly, "Last night I rinsed my clothes in our motel's bathtub, but the water stank so bad, they might smell worse now than before I washed them. You should taste what we filtered out of the tap. This morning, the water stank like sewage, even after we used our filter."

After Redbeard brought that story to our attention, See-Hawk and I could have sworn his Hawaiian shirt and standup shorts did smell a bit worse than when he had just been avoiding stream baths.

After bidding our jolly friend goodbye, the two of us checked out of our motel and strode back across Highway 43. Inside the same country-music restaurant that served domestic bison burgers, we ordered two ranch-style breakfasts, to enjoy with a side of month-old newspaper comics.

After breakfast, we commenced searching for the promised Laundromat. One full hour of searching uncovered nothing more than a locked apartment door. Its faded sign was an old piece of paper, onto which someone had handwritten, *Temporarily Out of Order.*

"Live and learn," I groaned. "That's what I get for packing all my wet and dry clothes into one bag."

SeeHawk voted to just stink for the next week because we needed to hurry up and start hitchhiking back to Chief Joseph Pass. However, one whiff from my laundry bag changed his tune.

"Before we give up, let me try asking around town," I told him. "You can just sit here and write postcards until I get back."

SeeHawk imagined himself drinking another cup of strong cowboy coffee, spiked with half-and-half. Mmm, yes, that sounded like a good idea. He kissed me farewell and headed back into the restaurant.

My search began at a small grocery store, inside of which three cigarette smokers were playing a game of cards. They all told me to try an RV park down the road. That was a good lead, but its laundry machines turned out to be broken. The RV park's attendant knew of a functioning laundry machine, except, someone who had its door key was out-of-town for two days. The Indian-themed giftshop's clerk could not think of anyone. Nor could Wisdom's auto mechanic, the desk staff at the motel with stinky water, a bartender in the town's only saloon, or a waiter at the town's other restaurant. Desperation seized me as I stepped into line at the post office, behind a middle-aged woman who was waiting to get her mail. It would have been rude to come right out and ask if I could rent the woman's home washing machine, but I sure felt tempted. Instead, though, I patiently waited my turn, before confirming that the postal clerk had no leads to offer.

SeeHawk was high on caffeine when I returned from my search, admitting that I had failed. He felt eager to skip town, but, of course, my above-and-beyond effort had left me in need of emotional consolation, so I let my arm be twisted, and ordered a hot-fudge-brownie sundae. When the sticky dessert arrived, just for kicks, I asked our waitress if she knew of an available washing machine.

Fifteen minutes later, SeeHawk and I stood on the doorstep of the same middle-aged lady I had almost approached in the post office!

Daisy immediately treated us like friends. She offered to do our laundry, asked us to stay for dinner, and even showed us her porcelain doll collection (ranging from old-fashioned beauties to an eye-blinking hula dancer).

Both SeeHawk and I were dressed in long johns and waist-up naked, except for my sports bra—with our second load of laundry spinning in soapsuds—when Daisy's husband pulled into the driveway.

SeeHawk did not have time to pull on a shirt before Burt strode through his front door. Imagine the brawny logger's surprise upon finding an elfin ax-murderer and half-naked crazy lady occupying his wife's kitchen. Fortunately, nobody raised a fist, and after Burt quickly recovered, he was eager to make us feel welcome.

We practically drooled while watching Daisy load her sparkly Formica table with steaming butternut squash, broiled elk for SeeHawk, and head lettuce topped with her "secret" creamy dressing (made from *Dream Whip* and distilled vinegar).

Burt talked over dinner about logging trees around the Big Hole. He described why building A-frame log fences was better than barbed wire, to avoid the problem of metal posts getting uprooted by thawing and freezing winter snow. From the standpoint of forestry, Burt knew the Big Hole like the back of his own hand. Therefore, we found it shocking to learn that he had never heard about the Continental Divide Trail.

In her turn, Daisy reminisced about having raised three children at the same time she logged trees and built fences alongside Burt, and that was not all. In addition, Daisy had spent countless years cooking and doing laundry for 100 ranch hands (P.U. and wow)!

When I spoke about the waitress who had referred us to knock on her door, Daisy replied crisply, "She's a sweet gal, but her husband? He's another kind. Works as our head of forestry. You know, one of those ENVIR-O-MENTALISTS. You can blame them for all the big fire damage you see. It's a shame they don't let loggers take over managing our forests."

I froze at hearing the word "environmentalists" pronounced like a cussword. Personally, I was opposed to clear-cutting, but I held my tongue because I had not come to Montana to stand on a soapbox. Furthermore, it was obvious that Daisy loved Nature more than a lot of so-called environmentalists, just from hearing her talk about Montana's extreme weather, wild birds, and growing seasonal vegetables in her garden. Therefore, I just politely smiled and felt relieved when Burt launched into a fun story about his friend successfully domesticating a moose.

It was early evening by the time our hosts cleared the table and urged us to sleep in their guest bedroom. We felt honored, but we had to decline because the mountains were calling and The Boys were getting ahead of us.

Low golden sunbeams shot over the Continental Divide while SeeHawk and I walked back to Highway 43. The evening's cool breeze felt harsh against our eyes. I began to miss Daisy's cozy kitchen. I shivered a little, but not from being cold. I just had no idea what to expect between Chief Joseph Pass and Yellowstone National Park.

It was obvious where to hitchhike. The best location rested beneath a big storefront mural of a melon-breasted Indian maiden, luring tourists to notice the Native American-themed gift shop. Several westbound cars lifted our hopes for a quick ride, but they all turned toward Jackson, instead of heading west. Still, we remained hopeful, until sunset flipped the same switch it had flipped the night before, and every last car vanished in one swoop. Feeling alarmed, I pulled out a black *Sharpie* pen and printed "Chief Joseph Pass" onto a scrap of paper. Unfortunately, the sign was of no use without any cars. Long golden sun rays lowered like bridges, inviting us to sky walk, rather than hitchhike, up to Chief Joseph Pass.

Finally, SeeHawk sighed, "Should we get a room?"

"Five minutes," I snapped. "This is all my fault, for making us do laundry. Please, give me a little more time to be saved from feeling guilty."

Of course, we were starting to regret having turned down Daisy and Burt's offer of lodging, but that was not the worst of it. We just felt completely done with Wisdom. I could not bear returning to the same country-music restaurant again, for another sweet-sour-sauced, You're Not On the Trail breakfast. My entire heart and soul ached to sleep underneath the stars. If only, another car would appear.

Time dragged on, while the golden sun rays inviting us toward the pass rescinded their invitations and tilted away like drawbridges.

I felt on the verge of giving up when suddenly, a cowboy strode out of the saloon across the street.

We stared him down hard.

He jumped into his pickup truck and chugged toward us. It seemed like a miracle when his truck pulled over and came to a stop. He stared at my little paper sign, bobbing up and down. *Chief Joseph Pass*, it kept repeating, like a broken record. My lips kept mouthing the words, "Please, please…" The cowboy sat and stared at my antics, neither responding nor looking away. Was he interested? Or did he just think I should get a job working at street fairs? I could not tell. He wore his hat tipped so far forward that it completely hid his eyes. All I could see was his chin and shoulders. I told myself he was probably using his hat to block out the sun, even though it had already set. I was willing to believe anything because See-Hawk and I desperately needed a ride. Trying to peek underneath his hat did not give me any clues because I could not duck low enough to see his eyes without being obvious. All the while, I kept bobbing my little sign, up and down, still mouthing, "Please, please…"

Slowly, he leaned across his truck's wide bench seat and rolled down his window to ask, "Where ya headed?"

I glanced at my hands still holding the printed words. Could he not read? Or was he too drunk to read? Let alone, too drunk to drive? Looking closer, I noticed that he seemed to be looking past me, rather than at me. It seemed like maybe he did not want to make eye contact. Perhaps, my silly behavior embarrassed him. In any case, I shamelessly begged, "Chief Joseph Pass. Can you take us there, please?"

The cowboy scooted backward, to sit straighter on his cab's bench seat.

"I'm not going there," he grunted. "Really, I just came into town for a beer and a shot. Now, I'm headed home, which is that-a-way." He pointed toward Jackson, where all the other drivers had gone.

Darn. What a letdown. I felt like I could not bear it, until, suddenly, the cowboy lifted his chin and declared with a shrug, "Aw, come on, I'll take you up there anyhow. I don't know why. Guess I'm just in the mood to be nice." He looked surprised by his own words, almost to the point of smiling, before he climbed out of his pickup truck to formally say, "Name's Rory."

I almost giggled.

When Rory stood up to his full height, he looked like a poster-perfect cowboy. With thick muscles, tightfitting blue jeans, a deep suntan, and his cowboy hat tilted just-so, he looked capable of staring a battery off Robert Conrad's shoulder. At the same time, his metallic blue eyes contained unexpected softness. In fact, while strapping our backpacks onto his luggage rack, he revealed that he was not even a genuine cowboy, but rather, a tour guide who took senior citizens canoeing and hiking in the Big Hole.

Once Rory retook his seat, he glued his eyes to the highway, started up the engine, and politely asked, "What would you like to hear?"

I saw SeeHawk open his mouth to answer. Instead of beating him to the punch, I waited in suspense. What was my fiancé going to request? Rock n' roll music? New age? Hawaiian? Bluegrass? The last thing I expected to hear him say was, "Anything country's fine with us."

Rory's head did not move. Maybe his eyes did not even leave the road. Nevertheless, it felt like he turned his head to look at SeeHawk. After letting the request hang in midair for a moment, Rory politely popped in a country music tape and went back to driving. Only once, did I catch a little smile sneaking onto his lips, when he thought I was not looking.

Our next discourse began with Rory claiming that tarps made better camping shelters than tents. He presented some good arguments, but what really got his motor humming was recounting the ambush of 800 Nez Perce Indians and their 2,000 horses at Ruby Creek, near Big Hole Pass.

"It was an early morning in August, eighteen seventy-seven," Rory began, "when an old blind Indian got up to take a pee and was spotted by an American soldier, who shot him dead."

From there, he went on to describe how that first shot had

kicked off a battle in which American soldiers shot straight into the tipis of Chief Joseph's tribal families. Their apparent motive had been resentment of the tribe's "non-treaty" status, by which the tribe had expressed refusal to give up nine-tenths of their land to fortune-seekers wanting to mine it for gold. Either the attacking soldiers did not care, or else they did not know, that the tribe had lived cooperatively with American settlers for five years prior, while peacefully tolerating encroachments made onto their land by fur-trappers, gold prospectors, farmers, and ranchers.

The battle at Ruby Creek had stemmed from a conflict, sparked in 1877 when U.S. Army General Howard ordered Chief Joseph's tribe to pack up their tipis and move to a small reservation in Idaho. Chief Joseph had replied that his people could not relocate within the specified 30 days because their livestock was scattered across a wide area, and the Snake River was dangerously high. He asked General Howard for permission to relocate during the Fall when the river would be lower. Unfortunately, General Howard refused and told his army to use force if the tribe did not leave within 30 days.

Small skirmishes ensued between individual tribesmen and local settlers before all the Nez Perce finally fled southward along the Continental Divide.

When word of their escape reached General Howard, he pursued them with an army that grew to 200 cavalrymen, 30 infantrymen, 100 scouts, horse packers, livestock, and a cannon.

This was in comparison with the Nez Perce having about 125 warriors and 675 passive members, including a large percentage of women and children.

General Howard intended to subdue the deserters by any means. He spent about 50 days chasing them from White Bird Hill, near the Salmon River, along an old Indian route called the Lolo Trail, and then southward through the Bitterroot Mountains.

The Nez Perce campaigned for mutual trust by not sending scouts to keep track of their pursuers. They hoped to inspire compassion from any witnessing settlers and other native people but, as a result of not scouting, they missed seeing a second army sneak toward their camp near Big Hole Pass. Colonel John Gibbon of the US 7th Infantry took them completely by surprise when he ordered his riflemen to fire three quick rounds into their tipis, and then launched a full battalion charge.

Anyone witnessing that morning's bloodshed would have expected the Nez Perce to surrender immediately. Instead, though, they somehow drove back the American soldiers and scared Colonel Gibbon into a retreat.

Gibbons' next strategy was to fire cannonballs into the Nez Perce camp. Nobody got killed because his arsenal arrived late. However, the Nez Perce women and children refused to flee before burying their dead and collecting their horses. Meantime, the tribe's warriors overtook some U.S. soldiers from behind, displaced them, and dug into their rifle pits. A legendary 24-hour battle saw Nez Perce fight the U.S. Army with their own weapons until the tribe deployed scouts, who learned General Howard's Army was one day away from reaching Ruby Creek. At that point, they abandoned the rifle pits and joined their fleeing women and children, who were heading eastward along the Continental Divide.

Upon reconvening, the tribe's human loss totaled 89 men, women, and children, including 12-17 warriors. They could no longer trust the American settlers, so a different attitude possessed them while fleeing through Leadore and Dubois, Idaho. When they crossed Yellowstone National Park, they were hoping to gain freedom beyond Canada's international border but stormy fall weather and constant traveling made it difficult for them to find food.

Meantime, several tussles with white settlers gave the Nez Perce a dangerous reputation. In turn, such notoriety further agitated the pursuing armies. After a five-day battle in late September, Colonel Nelson Miles overtook the tribe in northern Montana's Bear Paw Mountains. It was lightly snowing when

Chief Joseph surrendered to save his remaining women and children. Those last four-hundred and thirty-one survivors had fled approximately 1,170 miles, only to get captured 40-miles short of the Canadian border.

Rory might have shared this story with every senior citizen who ever attended his guide trips, but his enthusiastic retelling still showed how much he loved the Native American people.

After the three of us reached Chief Joseph Pass, things grew awkward. Apparently, Rory did not feel ready or willing to say goodbye. SeeHawk and I groped for adequate words while watching our Trail Angel saunter back to his pickup truck. Once he disappeared, we thought, is that it? It took a few moments for Rory to reappear, clutching four red apples and looking unwilling to be thanked. Then, he remembered some strawberry granola bars stashed inside his glove box. After settling into his driver's seat, finally Rory looked straight into our eyes for the first time, and gave us a warm smile.

* * *

During the night that SeeHawk and I camped on Chief Joseph Pass, I dreamed about feeling my fingers and toes tingle. A momentary flash of bright yellow light pushed through my closed eyelids. Thunder rumbled. Then, came silence. Sleep. Eventually, more tingling. Another flash. This time, it came from a new direction. More distant thunder. One last flash. After that, I slept soundly until the next morning.

When daylight reached in and opened my eyes, I could hardly believe how brightly the sun was shining. Was our thru-hike, finally about to start feeling like summer vacation? Could we afford to enjoy a few leisurely breakfasts? Au contraire. Such early heat could only mean one thing.

* * *

SeeHawk and I felt like we were getting a late start leaving Chief Joseph Pass. Therefore, it was frustrating to miss a critical blaze within the first hour, and accidentally climb onto the summit of Anderson Mountain. Fortunately, we got rewarded with a nice panoramic view, even if it only contained commonplace clouds and forested mountains.

After hiking back down to where we had made a wrong turn, we needed to vent some disgust. Hair pulling. Teeth gnashing. Groaning from our bellies. All of it helped us cope with seeing the blaze we had missed look obvious from a different angle.

The crest's next segment was striped with alternating meadows and conifer belts. Each meadow featured a unique ensemble of purple lupins, white mariposa lilies, yellow sunflowers, red Indian paintbrush, and yellowish-red sulfur buckwheat. On paper, a long stretch of timber following the meadows looked reassuringly flat. Therefore, SeeHawk and I were not expecting to vault a series of skyline knolls, one after the next, upon a jeep road that seemed like a glutton for exercise. Perhaps jeep drivers loved gunning their engines over giant whoop-de-dos, but not backpackers traveling on foot.

SeeHawk and I both felt exhausted by the time we entered one sunny meadow whose flowers were exclusively colored red-white-and-blue. Needless to say, we immediately thought of the American flag. I loathed politics and usually avoided the whole subject, but at that moment I found myself forgetting who had run for president eight months earlier, against George Bush.

"Gore," SeeHawk reminded me, without even thinking.

"Oh, right," I nodded.

Suddenly, a whole package of memories came rushing back. Just eight months ago, I had torn up my ballot in the voting booth and started another one, feeling indecisive.

"Geez, you wouldn't expect thru-hiking to erase a person's memory that fast," I blushed.

SeeHawk threw back his head and laughed. "Wake up, Sunshine. I was kidding about Gore. He's Bush's vice president."

Wait, what? Was SeeHawk teasing me or making an honest error?

"Nuh-uh," I corrected him. "Cheney is Bush's vice president."

"Are you sure?" he gasped.

"Totally sure. You've lost more brains than I have from thru-hiking, if you can't even remember who's leading our country NOW."

"Well, if you don't want wrong answers, then don't strain my brain in the middle of a rollercoaster ride," SeeHawk snapped.

"Don't get defensive," I retorted. "We all have senior moments. Sometimes, I forget my own phone number when I'm at home using it all the time!"

"You do?" he frowned. "That should worry you, since you've had the same number for almost a decade."

"Okay, so we're even. Now let's back to figuring out who ran against Bush."

"Why?"

"Because we clearly need some mental exercise."

"Not while we're hot, thirsty, and tired."

"Don't make excuses. If we let our brains slack, they'll become dishrags by the time we get home."

"A nice, cool dishrag pasted across my forehead would feel pretty good right now," SeeHawk imagined.

"Argh. Quit changing the subject and please help me solve this."

"I'm not changing the subject. I'm just hot."

"Okay, well, it's going to bug me until we solve it, so, do you want me to ask you again after the air cools off?"

"Why can't you ask me never and just forget about it, since this has nothing to do with thru-hiking?"

"Because it's starting to really bug me that I can't remember who ran against Bush."

"Okay, fine," he conceded. "I'll figure it out. Just, hold on a minute."

A couple of minutes passed in silence.

Finally, he said, "I'm sorry, Sunshine, I just can't think about presidents while I'm hiking. My brain is totally blank."

"Oh wait, duh!" I cried. "Silly, it was Gore!"

"Oops!" he laughed. "We forgot about Gore because of my first joke."

Falling back into silence, I wondered how much other top-drawer information had leaked out of my memory during the past month. My brain did not feel atrophied. In fact, thru-hiking required lots of precise mental calculations. Perhaps I had only forgotten about Gore due to my sympathies getting scrambled by everything we had experienced during the past month. After all, it had been emotionally confusing to repeatedly hike past ugly clear-cuts, meet happy cows who would soon be shipped to feedlots, talk with a greedy pig farmer on the Amtrak train, listen to a kindhearted laundrywoman denouncing environmentalists, and hear Rory lament about the Nez Perce Indians. My own political philosophy had always placed both Democrats and Republicans into the same narrow peapod; two dueling giants, endlessly ignoring all the superior advice provided by Nature; endlessly using the same old semantics to pit ambition against ideology. Anyhow, politics had never been my thing. Now, more than ever, during this half-year that I was spending among forces larger than myself, I just wanted to enjoy meeting all kinds of people who lived and worked near the Continental Divide. Never mind if they were loggers, meat ranchers, sport hunters, or anyone else whose beliefs differed from mine. I was thru-hiking purely for the sake of experience (and also, of course, for the cheese and crackers).

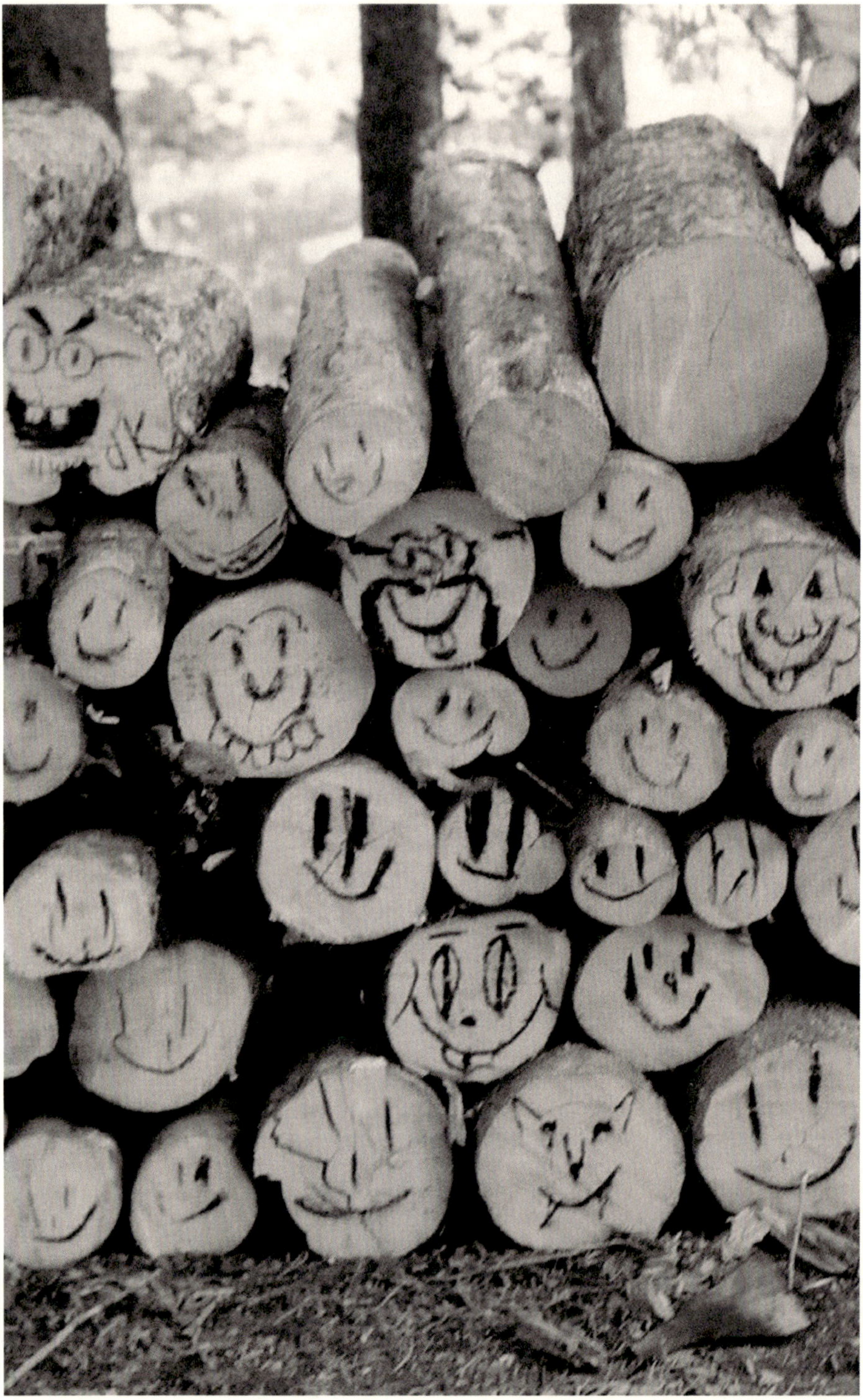

Chapter 11

Coming About

By perseverance the snail reached the ark.

— *Charles Spurgeon*

On top of Big Hole Pass, SeeHawk and I declared ourselves halfway-finished rounding the Big Hole.

I summarized our position by saying, "If this was a sailboat race, right now we'd be rounding the outside buoy of a ninety-mile loop."

SeeHawk replied, "So, you're saying we have forty-five miles left of going sideways? Yeesh. I'm not sure whether to cheer or cry."

"You should cheer," I told him, "because it's all going to be beautiful, no matter how much we sweat or how often we get lost."

"You're right, it will all be beautiful," he agreed. "Sorry for being a complainer, Sunshine. I know I made a fuss before coming on this trip, but now that we're here, I wouldn't want to be anyplace else."

"Atta-boy," I smiled. "And, of course, I'm right there with you about too much east-west when we're supposed to be heading south."

He seconded my agreement with a loud belch.

"Tea with the queen," I reminded him.

"Belch with the Welch," he fired back.

"Augh, that's disgusting!"

"No more disgusting than some of the smut you've been dishing out lately."

"Do you think we'll ever be presentable again?" I worried.

"Of course, we'll shape up when it matters," he promised. "There's just no reason to act like poodles in bear country."

We were feeling a little loopy because Big Hole Pass lacked interesting scenery, and also because nothing was going on with the weather. Basically, all we had to look at were hundreds-upon hundreds of ordinary lodgepole pine trees and stout Douglas firs, seen from a 7,000-foot crest that separated southwestern Montana from northern Idaho. The view was big and green. Pleasant, but not remarkable. The sky was overcast, but only with smooth stratus clouds that could never produce thunderstorms. We were totally safe. We had easy access to shade and shelter. The only thing we could possibly have desired was a pinch of air-softener to mitigate the Bitterroot Mountains' arid climate. Already, during midmorning, our lips felt parched. Intensifying heat was making our nostrils itch. By late morning, we could no longer smell the nearest pine trees. This seemed like a bad omen, heading into mountains that were going to become increasingly dry during the coming weeks, first alongside Wyoming's southern border, and then heading southward into the Great Basin. I began to think we ought to switch into desert mode for a while, by leaving camp earlier, taking an afternoon dinner break, and pulling into camp just before bedtime, but nope. Fat chance because, by now, daylong hiking felt like part of our own skin.

As SeeHawk surveyed the increasingly dry mountains, he suggested starting to use our water filter more often, and even treating silty water with iodine, because we were seeing more cows and fewer vigorous streams.

The southern mountains evoked a mood that diluted our sense of purpose. They felt appropriate for recreational activities like hunting and horse riding, but too relaxed to inspire athleticism for its own sake. Thus, we had to self-motivate, which, for me, meant struggling all day long not to measure the passage of time, until, finally, the clouds faded enough to guarantee it getting near dusk.

After miles upon miles of seeing nothing but trees, it felt exciting just to happen upon a scenic tent site. In addition to facing a modest overlook, it came furnished with a party-sized fire ring, pre-stocked with crushed beer cans, shredded rope, and other tidbits of human trash. Lying beside the fire ring was a pile of fresh bear scat. SeeHawk and I would normally have taken the hint and pressed on, but we had been crossing uneven terrain for miles. Whereas hiking into the dark might have doomed us to make an emergency camp, stopping where we were guaranteed us a comfortable night's sleep. Plus, we could spend our hour dinner enjoying a lovely view of treetops plunging toward a graying horizon.

I examined the scat near the fire ring closely, before concluding, "At least, it's only from a black bear and not a grizzly. I'm sure we could drive the old pooper away, just by making some noise and flashing our headlamps."

"You mean, I could drive the old pooper away, while you hide inside our tent, cheering me on?" SeeHawk teased.

"Exactly," I grinned.

Perhaps, I would have felt more inclined to look for a better campsite if I had realized how drastically Montana's 2-year drought was affecting the local bears. The triple whammy of the drought combined with an early Fall freeze and late Spring freeze was triggering berry shortages all over the Rocky Mountains. Bears were starving as far south as New Mexico, according to reports of garbage cans being raided in towns unused to having bear problems. Meanwhile, hunters were finding fewer bears in regions with robust populations. And so on, and so forth, blah, blah, blah. Yes, SeeHawk and I believed in bears, but after failing to see one during six weeks in Bear Country, we had stopped holding our breath. And yet, there is a first time for everything.

During our nightly search for tent-stake-pounding rocks, we heard a rustle in the bushes.

Freezing in place, I whispered, "Isn't it a little early for visitors? We haven't even started dinner yet."

SeeHawk whispered back, "Maybe our noble guest would like us to fix him a yummy peanut-butter-and-honey sandwich?"

I gave my partner a poke in the ribs.

Standing together in hushed mode, we listened to the rustle drawing nearer. Darn it, our camping gear was spread all over the ground. Where was our pepper spray? How did its trigger work? I had never fully understood what to pull and how hard. We had rarely worn bear spray since leaving the Bob Marshall Wilderness. Rumors had persisted throughout central and southern Montana, but, to us, the whole region did not look like a haven for predators of salmon, roadkill, and cooler chests. Nonetheless, I jumped when two hulking creatures popped out of the bushes. Surprise, surprise. It was Redbeard and Teach! Those crazy jokers. They were dressed in knitted sleeping caps and grinning like pranksters.

"We're camping over there," Teach announced, pointing through the bushes.

Redbeard emphasized, "Just so you know, we cooked dinner right where you're setting up your tent. If you're worried about bears, you might want to sleep someplace else."

"Thanks for the warning," SeeHawk replied, "but I guess it won't matter, since we're planning to cook here, too." Then, he reached into his pocket, pulled out a crumpled slip of paper, and ceremoniously announced, "I think this is yours."

Redbeard brushed aside an orange forelock and accepted a resupply schedule he had accidentally left at the post office in Wisdom.

"Thanks!" he grinned. "I was wondering what happened to that. After finding my carabineer and now this, you must think I've got holes in my pockets."

"Only as many holes as we have," SeeHawk grinned, sticking one finger through a hole in his shorts.

"Does this count?" I added, shoving my fist through a giant scissor-hole chopped out of one pant leg to take pressure off my kneecap.

Teach laughed through a watery yawn, "Well, anyway, it's great seeing you guys. We're gonna hit the sack. Good luck with the bears."

"Good luck to you, too," we waved, watching The Boys disappear into the bushes.

I got right to work simmering brown rice pasta in aromatic peanut butter sauce.

Taking a whiff, SeeHawk remarked, "Nothing could smell yummier to bears than what you're cooking tonight."

"And yet, we haven't seen a single grizzly, or even black, during six weeks of cooking where we camp," I reminded him.

Stiffening with surprise, he exclaimed, "Hey, that's my line, not yours. Aren't you superstitious about jinxes!"

"Gah!" I squealed. "Please, Spirit of the Mountain, let me take it back. We don't need to see bears. We don't want to see bears."

SeeHawk chuckled, "Don't worry, Sunshine. Bear stories get blown out-of-proportion by scared campers telling stories around campfires."

"SHH!" I scolded. "Now you're making the jinx worse. Do you realize it's almost a hundred percent odds for something with bear breath to be smelling what I'm cooking? Have you forgotten the bear poop sitting on our front porch?"

SeeHawk ignored my warning while starting to organize our next day's maps.

I needed to set his thinking straight, so I sternly quizzed him, "Can you remember what we're supposed to do if we see a bear?"

"Take pictures?" he guessed.

"NO!" Smack.

"Okay, okay," he laughed. "How about raising our arms above our heads, to look all big and mean?"

"For a black bear, yes, but not for a grizzly," I reminded him.

"Right, of course not," he agreed while starting to remove a hangnail that suddenly bothered him.

"So, how should we act if we run into a grizzly?"

"Scared," he replied, biting the hangnail with his teeth.

"Ha-ha, very funny," I glowered. "Now, will you please give me a real answer?"

"To what?"

"To how we should act if we run into a grizzly. Should we try to look threatening and scare it away?"

"Absolutely," he replied. "Er...maybe?...I mean, no."

Fuming, I snorted, "Look, if you don't want to participate, that's okay, but please, at least, tell me you can remember not to look into a grizzly bear's eyes, all right? I'm reminding you because I know that might be hard to cement in your brain since the bear is your sacred guardian-animal-thingie."

Ignoring my sloppy reference to his Amakua, SeeHawk mumbled obediently, "I understand, Sunshine. Don't ever look into a grizzly bear's eyes."

"Or a black bear either," I emphasized. "Actually, we shouldn't look into any animal's eyes because we don't want it to think we're picking a fight."

"Obviously," he nodded. "Good, so, is that all?"

"Yes, that's all."

As it turned out, though, no bear lecture had been needed, since no four-legged thieves came knocking overnight.

The next morning commenced with a short bushwhack over to Redbeard and Teach's camp. Our friends were stomping around in long underwear, sipping hot drinks and blowing frosty steam through bright pink noses. A long strand of mucus, dangling from Teach's nostril, looked disturbingly like a rubber icicle. It jiggled while he spoke and hula danced when he laughed. He could not feel the jiggle because his nose had gone numb. I thought Redbeard should be responsible for saying, "Blow your nose," but perhaps he and Teach had established their own form of wilderness etiquette; or else, maybe constant togetherness had just lulled Redbeard into not paying attention.

Once we all hit the trail together, a short descent from the overlook lowered us into a sun-speckled conifer forest. SeeHawk and I kept pace for 15 minutes before a leveler stretch of woods enabled our companions to speed ahead.

"Hey, it was great seeing you guys, while it lasted," I called after them, feeling a bit forlorn.

Before long, the enclosed conifer forest transitioned into a roomier oak forest, containing a creekbed smothered with dry leaf litter. Here and there, we passed shovel pits dug by gold prospectors who apparently had not found anything. One decaying log cabin stood watch, over a fruiting huckleberry thicket we could enjoy guilt-free because we had no idea the bears were starving.

Continuing onward with purple-stained lips, cheeks, and hands, we spied a rare northern community of Ponderosa pine trees flaunting their long needles and black-seamed tortoise-shell bark. The sound of rushing water lured us toward rapids, labeled on our map as North Fork Sheep Creek. Piles of loose rock, fallen trees, shorts-snagging willow bushes, and impenetrable shrubbery tried to muscle us away from the creek, but we tunneled right through, sometimes wondering if we had lost the CDT. Both of us felt hot and bothered by the time we reached a shady landing tiled with flagstones and clumps of beargrass. Here, the trail split in two, where, strangely, no division appeared on our maps, including USGS, Forest Service, and deLorme's atlas. Both forks more or less aimed parallel to one another. Therefore, they might have belonged to the same trail—if, for instance, one had been built as a detour around the other, due to some kind of immovable blockage. No sign was posted to give us any help. Since we could not see far into the upstream woods, we needed to put on our thinking caps.

I spent ten minutes poring through various texts and drawings, before giving up and telling SeeHawk we might as well try the left-hand fork.

He stepped into position behind me, and that is when he noticed an enormous arrow, made of whole pine logs, lying on the ground between my shoes. That's right, the arrow was not lying beside my shoes. I was literally straddling it!

"Okay, class," I declared, "so, today we've learned that huge things can be as hard to spot as tiny things."

"Which is an important metaphor for regular life," SeeHawk added, sagely.

Choosing the path indicated by the arrow, we crossed several avalanche chutes in quick succession. A dense border of willow shrubs and pine trees gradually evolved into spruce trees and firs. Near the forest's timberline, I peered through a gap between thinning treetops and saw clouds overtaking the late-morning sky. A second, wider clearing revealed a ring of blunt peaks belonging to the crest. Hiking in front, I was first to reach a ladder of short switchbacks. When I looked up from their base, I noticed the overhead clouds forming a queer spiral. Right before my eyes, its center broke open, revealing a pinhole of blue sky.

"SeeHawk?" I gasped.

He did not answer.

Spinning around, I caught him fondling a deer's antler, back inside the clearing.

When my gaze touched him, he tiredly announced, "This looks like a great place to eat lunch, Sunshine."

I hated feeling ruthless. He had every reason to demand a meal break. We had already climbed close to 3,000-feet that morning, and he was carrying the majority of our food. Even my own hunger meter was bawling. I would gladly have stopped to eat inside the clearing, if not for needing to climb right afterward. Climbing on a full stomach had never worked well for me. If we ate inside the clearing, we were going to have to stay down there until my food digested, which might force us to outwait whatever the sky's unsettled clouds had in mind. It was hard to know for sure, without a bigger view, but, one thing was certain. All of this delay sounded worse than just coaxing my partner to climb over the next high point before we ate. Therefore, I reluctantly ordered him, "Drop that deer antler, or carry it in your hand, and follow me. I promise we'll eat as soon as it's safe."

He barely had time to think, before I bolted up the switchbacks, leaving him behind.

Climbing without thinking, I paid no attention to the sky. It stood to reason that not much could change during such a short climb. After a while, though, I paused for a backward glance and felt my stomach drop. Where was SeeHawk? Surely, not still lollygagging in the clearing down below. I hollered his name and got no answer. Shoot, we needed to hurry. I hollered louder. Why was he not answering? Could he still be worshipping that confounded deer antler? Would he dare try strapping it onto his backpack at a time like this? Or had he tripped and gotten hurt because of me rushing him into the climb before he felt ready? Should I retreat back down to see if he was okay? What would happen if I went back down? Might we get stuck inside the clearing for the rest of the afternoon? That would be awful. Not necessary, either, since there was no realistic chance SeeHawk could be injured. The switchbacks were sturdy and free of debris. He was coming at his own pace, and that was okay. I needed to just keep climbing and let him catch up.

Upon reaching the Continental Divide, at 7,650-feet, I spied the very thing I had feared most. It was a black wall of rain, getting dragged toward the crest by one gigantic thunderstorm. The cloud's base was broad enough to dwarf its own lightning, making the yellow forks below look comically miniature.

My eyes traced two miles of the naked crest sideways, surveying our path to outrun the storm. Centered above that path stood Pyramid Peak, bald right on up to its 9,616-foot summit. Scattered shrubbery and fractured boulders armoring the peak's baseline offered zero lightning protection to hikers with poor timing. Did SeeHawk and I have poor timing? I sure hoped not because when the storm rammed into Pyramid Peak it was going to go berserk.

"SEEHAWK?" I shouted down the empty switchbacks.

Why was he still not answering? Had he gotten delayed by a rock in his shoe? Or needed to take a nature stop before starting to climb? Heaven help him if he was still trying to strap that frigging deer antler onto his backpack.

"SEE-HAWK!" I bellowed.

The air remained silent.

Suddenly, a wooly face popped up from beneath the lower switchbacks, looking worn out and panting,

"Phew!" SeeHawk exclaimed. "I guess you can't beat impatience. What's gotten into you, Sunshine? Ate your *Wheaties* this morning?"

I pointed toward the oncoming thunderstorm, whose rain had recently thickened into a full-blown flash flood.

"Right," he nodded. "You've got your weather-legs on. I should have known. How come you can haul ass whenever a storm's coming, but you're pretty slow the rest of the time?"

"Speak for yourself, slowpoke!" I barked. "No more stopping until we drop into the glacier bowl."

"How far will that be?"

"Two miles, give or take."

"Dang, okay."

Leaping into a sprint, I visualized towing my partner toward Pyramid Peak. We had no other choice besides staying on the trail, forward or backward, because the crest's windward edge dropped into a precipitous forest, and its leeward upslope was about to get creamed.

Midway beneath Pyramid Peak, I glanced backward and saw SeeHawk shrinking into the distance. For a moment, he disappeared behind the mountain's shoulder. There was no point in shouting for him to speed up. He could never have heard me over such a great distance. Of course, I could have stopped and waited for him to get closer, but, no. I refused to slow down because this was a critical situation, and hopefully fear of getting left behind would inspire him to move faster.

The next few minutes saw me experience a bizarre shift in consciousness, from racing the storm to witnessing my own progress, as if from someone else's body.

Meantime, SeeHawk lapsed into feeling dog tired. His backpack seemed to be ripping apart his shoulders. Bitter stomach acid splashed into his throat. He desperately wanted to catch his breath, but how could he let me know he needed a break? Instead of stopping, he forced himself to keep plugging along, as fast as two dragging legs could move.

By the time the flash flood hit Pyramid Peak, SeeHawk outdistanced it by a mere quarter-mile. Rain turned the trail into a temporary stream. Sheet lightning flickered close toward the east. Two lucky hikers were escaping by the seat of their pants. From that time onward, being distanced allowed SeeHawk and me to view the storm as harmless entertainment. We enjoyed watching it pounce with its barrel unlocked and chambers loaded. Suddenly, a blinding firebolt struck Pyramid Peak. Demonic thunder crackled overhead. The incoming cloud, being unable to climb, got squished sideways like a crashing train, Its front end started bulging toward us! There was only one thing to do. Thank heavens for adrenaline. My legs became whirling pistons. SeeHawk sprinted like his shorts had caught fire. We ran full-tilt for such a long time that it began to feel like the race would never end. Finally, we dipped into a shallow saddle whose widespread trees permitted us to catch our breath.

"How's that for excitement?" I panted. "Guess those two miles across the summit were rounded down from three-and-change."

"Three miles more than I had left in me," SeeHawk replied.

The saddle we had entered overlooked a glacier bowl, whose deep interior advertised safety. Before descending, first, we were instructed to traverse a short distance along its upper rim. Chutes of broken granite sucked our eyes 500-feet down to a yellow grass meadow, where two black-throated elk were peacefully having breakfast. The elk must have been telepathic because merely being looked at from such a great distance alerted them to scoot toward the nearest trees.

No danger was threatening the place where we had stopped, so it seemed permissible to catch our breath before leaving the saddle.

SeeHawk could barely smile when I handed him a lemon-flavored Power Bar. The valiant plugger's blood sugar had hit rock bottom. His hands trembled while tearing off half the bar for me. Drool dripped from his mouth onto his beard. He chomped his chunk in half and swallowed it like a snake. Fortunately, it only took seconds for the bar's digestible sugars to kick in. After a few moments, his lips curled into a smile.

That was my cue to make like a banana and split, with See-Hawk following close behind.

We were lucky the storm did not bulge a bit farther sideways. Otherwise, it would have felt scary to traverse above the glacier bowl's fractured interior, searching for a favorable line of descent. Wobbling boulders gripped our shoes with their nonskid lichen, while we dropped alongside Fourth of July Creek. A border of pink monkeyflowers and yellow arrowleaf groundsel paraded alongside us, pantomiming exclamations. At the bottom, we entered the same yellow grass meadow whose telepathic elk were long gone. Crossing it straightaway, we entered a fir forest whose dark interior contained a surprise. Cabin Lake had been waiting all afternoon for us to arrive. Merely touching the lake's tepid water inspired us to rip off our clothes. We swam for a long time. The ecstasy got even better during a sprinkle of warm rain.

Soak-and-eat sushi recharged our engines for one last push from afternoon into evening. Climbing alongside Squaw Mountain, we gained another 1,000-feet of elevation. At the top, we reached an unspecified 10,404-foot summit, flanked with a view of neighboring granite peaks. That was all we had time to notice before a surprisingly cold breeze scooted us onto dusty switchbacks descending past Upper Slag-a-Melt Lake. Festive pink monkeyflowers, yellow arrowleaf groundsel, violet harebells, purple veronica, and white valerian cheerfully introduced the upper lake's sibling, Lower Slag-a-Melt Lake. Stopping there, we retired beneath a crooked pine tree that covered our tent like a patio umbrella.

The lake's flatwater lay perfectly still. Today's race was finished. Serenity was now in session.

One fat log became our countertop for cooking oily tuna casserole, and, later, our bench for watching the water fade to gray. Everything remained peaceful until some tardy mosquitoes buzzed in at dusk. Hungry and rude, they divebombed our faces. Over the lake, they riled-up trout who started casting circles across its still water.

"Time to hit the sack," SeeHawk announced, slapping every inch of his arms and body in preparation to enter our tent.

"We'll need an extra-early wakeup to beat the mosquitoes," I decided, "so no map-reading tonight."

Upon retiring, we took for granted that Redbeard and Teach were camping someplace farther ahead. In actuality, though, the truth was different. After leaving us in their dust, the pair had lost track of the CDT's passage alongside North Fork Sheep Creek (perhaps failing to recognize the giant log arrow we had almost overlooked.) Becoming disoriented, their arrival to the switchbacks approaching Pyramid Peak had been much later than ours. As a result, while we sped over to and down to Fourth of July Creek, they got stuck spending two hours inside the same clearing where SeeHawk found a deer's antler. After that, they might still have overtaken us by nightfall, if not for what happened inside the clearing. Somehow, Redbeard got a wild hair up his nostril and persuaded Teach to leave the CDT. This was not because Redbeard wanted to take a shortcut. Nor, did he wish for easier terrain. In fact, quite the opposite. Redbeard's impulse stemmed from a romantic notion that hiking cross-country from Squaw Mountain to Ajax Lake might give the two friends a "real" experience of the Continental Divide. Of course, Teach had not come to Montana wishing for an introductory course in serious mountaineering. By the next morning, even Redbeard was going to wake up admitting his own foolishness. The pair had spent hours with eyes glued to their compasses, feeling rocks slip out from underneath their shoes and hearing fresh thunder boom in the wings. Upon reaching safe ground, Teach was going to swear never, ever again to repeat that adventure on any future date, regardless of whether Redbeard might beg him, pay him, or even offer to carry his backpack.

* * *

July 21 dawned with tendrils of white mist twirling off Lower Slag-a-Melt Lake's green water. The sun came up clear. The air held its breath. Nothing moved along the lake's forested shoreline, except for two human beings quickly striking camp.

"What a gorgeous day!" SeeHawk rejoiced.

"Don't trust it," I warned him. "This afternoon could still turn out like yesterday."

"Really?" he protested. "Couldn't we be going into one of those high-pressure spells you always talk about?"

"We could," I acknowledged, "but the air smells moist, so you know what that means."

A flat trail leaving Lower Slag-a-Melt Lake looked swept with a push broom. Every one of its obvious trail junctions displayed legible destination signs. Staying almost level helped our tired legs recover from yesterday's highspeed chase. In such immaculate circumstances, we felt surprised to meet six trail volunteers inspecting the CDT for maintenance needs. They were day-hikers, not overnight campers, so, presumably, not going far enough to discover the confusion near North Fork Sheep Creek (where Redbeard and Teach had lost the CDT). Also, they were Montana residents, despite looking totally unprepared for rain.

In hopes of giving them a diplomatic warning, I casually remarked, "It looks like we might get thunderstorms this afternoon."

A snicker of amusement rippled through the group.

"Of course, it looks clear now," I added, "but every morning has been like this, and we've been getting rained-on almost every afternoon."

Hearing me persist made the volunteers wink at each other, clearly enjoying my paranoia.

Don't say I didn't warn you, I thought, while SeeHawk and I waved goodbye and carried on our way.

After passing by the volunteers' parked cars, we entered a forest whose trail needed repairs right from the start. Unfortunately, this was opposite to the inspection team's aim. In fact, just 300-steps out of the parking lot, I got confused by an unsigned trail junction, which forced me to check my compass. In doing so, I noticed my face reflected in the compass's mirrored lid and shrieked.

"SEEHAWK! Why didn't you tell me I've got a giant zit?"

"What zit?" he mumbled.

"Wait a minute," I frowned. "When my face gets all purple from eating olallieberry fruit rolls, do you tell me about it, or do you just let me embarrass myself in front of people we meet on the trail?"

"Sometimes," he admitted.

Grrr.

The poorly signed trail escaping inspection made us backtrack twice, through dense woods that were heating up fast. It did not help our mood to have the air remain stagnant. Soon, we spied Big Swamp Creek trickling through a disjointed timberline. Even though the day was young, we gratefully dropped to our knees and plunged our hair into the creek's cool water. I was head-down in rapture when a woman's voice sang across the water.

"Good morning!"

Glancing up, I saw wilderness ranger Lucinda approaching. Tall and slim, she kept her wrinkle-resistant khaki uniform as tidy as the chestnut-brown braid trailing down her back. Her job was making rounds through the backcountry, destroying illegal fire rings, picking up trash, and remedying other kinds of wilderness abuse.

When I saw Lucinda approaching, I flipped back my wet hair and brightly replied, "Good morning. We're not exactly lost, but we can't find the Continental Divide Trail. Do you know where it is?"

She pointed 30-steps away, saying, "Right there."

That was all the exchange we had before Lucinda strode off toward wherever else hikers might need answers to silly questions.

Suddenly, I realized we were being offered guidance through the timberline's cryptic terrain. I grabbed my backpack and urged SeeHawk to help me chase Lucinda before she disappeared. Unfortunately, she proved to be an extremely fast climber. We were still far behind when she vanished through a high granite notch.

On top of the notch, SeeHawk and I met an arrowhead-shaped stone peak, chiseled smooth by prehistoric glaciers. The peak's backside plunged onto a slope sheathed in volcanic talus. Banisters of beargrass, slurping the sun's radiance into their lightbulb-shaped flowerheads, glowed as if installed to guide hikers down the trail.

Lucinda was nowhere to be seen. That did not matter because once we hit bottom the trail became obvious. Flat terrain helped us reestablish a steady hiking rhythm. Cumulus clouds drifting overhead bubbled into the late-morning sunlight. Were any of them slated to become future thunderstorms? Either way, we did not feel worried because seeing lightning on a regular basis was starting to help us take it in stride.

A section of the trail blazed with bright-orange paint splashes had been autographed by Joe Phillips in 1953. Poppa Jim's guidebook mentioned one of the blazes marking a 90-degree turn. Following that turn, we were warned to expect some confusion approaching Little Lake, before climbing over an adjacent saddle.

In real life, the 90-degree turn soon appeared and beyond it, the orange blazes kept going. Within minutes, we ran into an upsloping meadow whose fluted skyline presented four saddles. Vertically, the meadow's length from trail to skyline was hard to estimate. Maybe it covered one mile or even two. All the grass in between angled helter-skelter, between numerous small hills, rocky knobs, and conifer glades. Such uneven terrain could have hidden Little Lake almost anywhere.

"We can't afford to overshoot the lake," I told SeeHawk, "because we need it to show us which saddle to aim for."

Looking around, he observed, "I don't see any Trail Eighty-Seven sign or any ax-blaze."

"No kidding. That's why I need a moment to figure out where Poppa Jim started climbing."

Despite the whole scene looking fit for a Julie Andrews movie, no evidence existed of anyone previously climbing away from the orange-blazed trail.

"Could there be two ninety-degree turns, and we haven't reached Jim's yet?" SeeHawk wondered. "I mean, I know square corners are like two-dollar bills, but his directions say 'obscure' and that corner was super obvious."

"Although, the saddles we're seeing match his directions perfectly."

"But, not his missing sign and ax-blaze. Where are they?"

"Who knows? Swallowed by entropy? Stolen by aliens? It's hard to say, without having any updates."

Ignoring my implication, SeeHawk sighed, "Well, all I know is that behind us there's an obvious trail, ahead it keeps going, and uphill I see a huge meadow with no trail, that could eject us into Never-Never Land if we spend an hour climbing the wrong way. I mean, where's the lake? There are a lot of missing details, Sunshine. Maybe we should just stay on the Joe Phillips Express until we either run into another sharp corner or make sure there isn't one."

"But I'm almost positive this is where Jim started climbing," I insisted. "Why don't we just do a little test climb and see what develops? If we can't spot the lake quickly, I promise we'll come right back down."

SeeHawk narrowed his eyes. "Is that a rubber promise or an ironclad promise?"

"Probably rubber," I admitted, flashing him a grin. "So, you'd better hope we have a good horoscope today."

Just a few strides uphill, the meadow's deep grass became embroidered with alpine ferns, leafing thistles, blooming dandelions, purple lupins, yellow lupins, and pink Indian paintbrush flowers. So much eye candy vied for our attention that we kept forgetting to search for Little Lake. Also, we stopped questioning which among the four saddles Poppa Jim had crossed. The rightmost saddle looked easiest to approach, whereas all the other three were perched above sketchy-looking shale cliffs, but our map showed the cliffs having gentler backsides. Altogether, it was a difficult puzzle to solve without the missing piece, which was why we really needed to find Little Lake.

SeeHawk said nothing about my promise to turn around quickly. He just kept following me up the meadow's centerline because the terrain was open, not to mention pretty, and the climbing was easy.

After 20 minutes of seeing no water anywhere, not even a trickle, few places remained for a lake to still be hiding uphill. Coming alongside a vertical stand of trees, I got an urge to sashay over and peek through them. Part of me did not want to find Little Lake behind them. If I did, that would mean Poppa Jim had climbed something that might scare me. Although, it would also mean we had not spent 20 minutes climbing in the wrong direction, so I felt conflicted. Emerging from the trees onto a small granite balcony, I found myself perched above a shaft of deep space, closely facing the nearest shale cliff.

SeeHawk gasped when he stepped through the trees and looked 300-feet off the balcony's sharp edge. Below us stood a tower of stacked boulders, guiding our eyes down to a pretty timberline lake. The water's green shoreline was dribbled with darker green conifer trees, outwardly matted with naked gray rock. Breezes stirring the water turned into flashing yellow sequins.

"Is THAT Little Lake?" SeeHawk grimaced.

"It looks like we climbed WAY too high," I groaned.

How could we safely shed some elevation? Surely, not by rock-climbing down the stacked boulders. We needed to search for a gentler line of descent. However, before turning around, we spent a moment staring at the opposite shale cliff. Its salt-and-pepper shadows looked capable of camouflaging a trail, but our experienced eyes could not find one.

"Are you SURE that's Little Lake?" SeeHawk repeated.

Before I could respond, my eyes fell upon a black dot circling the lake's blue-green water.

"Lucinda!" I cried. "She's as small as an ant! LUCINDA!"

"Hello?" An ant-sized voice floated 300-feet upwards.

"ARE YOU ON THE CONTINENTAL DIVIDE TRAIL?"

"Yes ---- -- --- -----," the voice squeaked. "- --- lost ---. Went way down -- --- --- -----. Funny isn't --? --- hiked this ------- -- -- - -DT four -- -ive times ------, --- --- ---- ------ - couldn't find --- - ---- -- --- -ake."

Her words sounded so faint that SeeHawk could not even hear them.

I took a stab at the translation. "She's hiked this section of trail four or five times in the past, but today she had trouble finding the lake."

"Ha-ha," SeeHawk groaned. "I guess, if she got lost, we shouldn't complain."

Feeling rescued by serendipity, we both gave Lucinda a wave and watched her finish circling the lake. Once her trajectory showed us where to look, I spied a faint zigzag etched across the scree cliff's salt-and-pepper shadows. Not just a goat path, it looked like a real trail. Whoopie!

Feeling encouraged, I took another glance down the tower of stacked boulders upon which we stood. Could I feasibly crawl down them? The worst obstacle appeared to be a few tufts of beargrass, long and slick. Was my mind downplaying the danger because I wanted to take a shortcut?

SeeHawk paid no attention to where I was looking. He just turned around, in preparation to retreat.

Thinking out loud, I muttered, "This won't be dangerous if we take our time."

Alerted by my voice, he spun back around. When he saw where I was looking, he frowned so hard that a wrinkle of skin bulged between his deep-set eyes.

"Are you SURE you can get down there, Sunshine?" he demanded. "Some of those cracks look pretty deep. I'd hate to see you fall, or me either, for that matter. Plus, what about your ankles? What about your knees? Aren't they too fragile for a drop that steep?"

I did not like being reminded about having fragile kneecaps while mustering willpower for a brave move. Besides, I was enjoying feeling adventurous.

SeeHawk decided there was no way I would actually try it, and wandered off to search for a safer descent.

During his absence, I evaluated a launch point that looked reasonably safe. Squatting near as I dared, I tried to extend both arms down far enough to rest my 40-pound backpack upon a small ledge. I wanted to release most of its weight onto the ledge, shimmy down after it, and then sit on the ledge while refastening my backpack, after which I could figure out what to do next. Probably, the rest of the drop would be easier, since beginnings were always the hardest. I was formulating this scheme when SeeHawk's voice called through the trees, "I think we can get down here, Sunshine. Do you want to come over and take a look?"

His words arrived just in the nick of time. I could easily have retracted my arms, hauled up my backpack,- and gone over to join him. The only reason I ignored his summons was that I loved feeling courageous and independent. It was thrilling because, seriously, how often did I get to climb down something steep without feeling afraid?

Disregarding a twinge in my left kneecap, I cautiously lowered my backpack off the stone balcony. Soon, I felt it catch upon an interim boulder. So far, so good. The next step was wiggling from a squatting position onto my belly. Lying prone gave relief to my knees, while I extended my arm further down, toward a wider ledge where I wanted my backpack to land. Now, I found myself stuck on my belly, with one outstretched arm dangling my backpack not quite low enough. The ledge sat 2-feet lower. This created a problem because it turned out that my arm was not strong enough to pull 40-pounds back up, with my body lying flat. If I tried using two arms, I might slip into a nosedive. Therefore, I found myself stuck, facedown, with my belly stretched flat. This awkward pose prevented me from yelling loud enough for SeeHawk to hear me. If I lost my grip, my backpack was going to go tumbling down the boulders. That could not be allowed to happen, but my hand was getting tired. My arm could not stay strong much longer. Therefore, I did the only thing possible. Inch by inch, I loosened my grip on the backpack's cushiony strap and slowly let it slide through my fingers. I must have held my breath when the strap ran out of length. Quietly, it slipped free from my hand. I heard a reassuring thump. Phew. My backpack had landed on the thin ledge below. Next, however, the thing I had been dreading began to happen. Now that my backpack was far out of reach, the indifferent ledge let go of it. All my precious belongings slowly rolled head-over-tail. Upon reaching the next lowest boulder, my backpack got stuck long enough to stand up straight, before rolling down to the next lowest boulder. Horror gripped me when I saw it flip over a third time, only to fall back and rest, rocking slightly back and forth, on the brink of disaster.

When SeeHawk found me still lying on my belly, I was facing the other way, with my legs dangling into space. The plan was, hopefully, to lower my shoes onto the same ledge which had failed to hold my backpack.

SeeHawk evaluated where my shoes were aiming, and he inquired with concern, "Are you sure you can get down that way, Sunshine? I can help, if you want."

"No thanks," I grunted. "Aren't you proud of me for being brave today? Why don't you take off your backpack and follow me?"

"Be careful, sweetheart," he warned again. "Take your time. Keep a firm grip with both hands. We're not in any rush today."

But, aren't you impressed with me for trying this? I kept repeating inside my head. *Because I sure am!*

Out loud, though, I snapped, "If you're not going to follow me, then please don't bother watching. Just go find your own way down, so we can both keep moving."

Beads of perspiration were dampening my forehead. I could not glance upward because I felt afraid to look anywhere besides straight ahead. My mind remained focused until my partner disappeared. Then, the stone I had been gripping grew slippery in my hands. I grasped it harder, struggling to keep hold. It took a full minute, using extreme caution, to lower my legs as far as they could reach. Blindly tapping whatever my shoes could feel, I found a secure foothold and let go with both hands.

It felt marvelous to sink onto the receiving ledge. Now, I was committed, for better or worse.

The next, shorter drop looked equally dynamic. I decided to make small moves until I reached a lower landing from which traversing might be possible. Unfortunately, though, there was not enough wiggle room to lie down again. Shimmying was also out-of-the-question. Therefore, I just lowered my backpack, the same as before, except now with one arm grabbing an overhang because my foothold was precarious. It felt risky to extend my arm again, with full knowledge of how heavy my backpack was going to feel. A handy tuft of beargrass offered me something easier to grab, but I refused to trust it and just leaned against the precipice because beargrass could potentially break or get uprooted. Grabbing the next lowest boulder, I extended my burdened arm down as far it could reach. Again, my arm fell a little too short. I found myself caught in the same predicament, again with my backpack dangling just a bit too high. This time, the shortage was only 1 foot. I was going to need to drop my backpack again. Nervous sweat trickled down my cheeks. Serious willpower was coming into play. The boulder I was clutching felt abrasive and slippery. Relaxing my lower hand, I slowly released the cushiony strap until it began sliding through my fingers. When the slack ran out, I had to let go completely, but, at least, by then, I had minimized the distance. It was nerve-wracking to feel the strap break free a little quicker than I expected.

"NO...!"

SeeHawk was too far away to recognize where my shriek came from. When he burst through the trees, his eyes shot over the balcony.

My backpack had started slowly flipping downhill. It completed one full rotation...got checked by its impact with an out-thrusting boulder...rose again...flipped over one more time... finally, got wedged against a larger boulder, and that one did a better job of stopping its fall.

Stop! I mentally chanted, *Please.*

Defiantly, the uncooperative boulder released my backpack, allowing it to tumble back into motion. Now, it lumbered through open space, before bouncing against yet another boulder...down to the next...gaining speed from increased momentum. A patch of soft beargrass changed its execution from flops into cartwheels.

SeeHawk stood helplessly on the balcony above, spouting useless exclamations.

"Ouch!"

Thump.

"Oh no!"

BAM.

My backpack seemed destined to reach Little Lake in shreds. Several more boulders checked its fall, but only until the next boulder gave it another launch. How far was my precious purple backpack going to fall? The whole distance down to Little Lake? Into its blue-green water. Could the whole package sink out of sight before I got down there? Or get snagged by a tree standing along the lakeshore? A ray of hope appeared when the fall began to lose some momentum. My backpack froze into a standing posture...toppled forward...rose back up...fell...and, rose again, like a stage play villain fighting a slow death. When it finally hit something large enough to stop its fall, it surrendered completely, like a motionless corpse.

I scrambled down the boulders, for perhaps 120-feet.

SeeHawk lumbered down after me, dragging his beast-of-a-backpack over each protruding ledge as fast as he could manage, with its framework scraping and clanking like hand tools.

When I reached the corpse, I pressed it all over, searching for broken bones. Miraculously, nothing felt different. I could not even find any superficial flesh wounds, aside from the pulverization of some tortilla chips rubber-banded onto the lid.

Once SeeHawk joined me in realizing everything was okay, we almost giggled with relief.

I still needed a moment to collect my head, but the danger was over. We were well-positioned to take a shortcut, and nobody could lecture me about taking risks since that would have been my job.

A sideways scramble across stockpiled boulders landed us on the loose shale cliff. It felt peachy keen to join the CDT without having dropped all the way to Little Lake.

Glancing upward and seeing nobody above us stirred me to mutter, "Thank goodness, Lucinda didn't see our clown show coming down the rocks."

SeeHawk agreed, "She would have been cringing, but don't worry about offending her tender sensibilities. I'm sure spotting clowns is part of her job."

"Well, I'd rather not make her ask for a pay raise."

At 9,250-feet, we found the clown-spotter enjoying a hummus sandwich decked out with real spinach. When we sat down beside her, we must have looked envious, because she offered us each a bite. Technically speaking, it was lunchtime, but not for us. Our late-eating strategy only allowed for nibbling on energy bars, while we spent a few minutes cloud-gazing with the ranger.

Lots of new cumulus clouds were popping into the sky. A few of the biggest started bubbling suspiciously by the time SeeHawk and I got back onto our feet.

Lucinda was still enjoying her lunch break, so she remained seated and threw us a wave.

We descended from the saddle into loose cover of trees, which blocked us from keeping tabs on the clouds. After a long time descending, we emerged onto a beach framing Lower Rock Island Lake. Two darkening clouds said swimming might be risky, but shoot. The opportunity was calling. If we declined to swim, how else could we cool off before starting our next climb? Thinking fast, we dove into the lake and rushed out quicker than either of the surprised clouds could charge their zappers.

Back in climbing mode, we felt lucky to be starting fresh, because, hooey. The next 1,000-foot incline was brutal. At least, it felt brutal coming after a long morning of excitement that had drained our reserves. Thick coverage of trees promised to give us weather protection, but our gosh-darned legs seemed to have gone on strike. Without help from either adrenaline or our legs, both of us found ourselves gasping for breath. Together, we swore never again to criticize other switchbacks for being too flat, while wondering how we could suffer from climbing such flat switchbacks, with our stomachs screaming about missing lunch. Switchback after switchback prolonged our suffering until we finally collapsed onto a thinly timbered summit.

It was probably teatime when we unpackaged our long-awaited cheese-and-cracker lunch. It would have felt grand to spend a half-hour recovering from the climb, but nature only gave us five minutes. Barely did we get down more than a few swallows, before a whopping thunderclap scared us back onto our feet, frantically stuffing our pockets full of uneaten cheese-and-crackers.

The rest of the afternoon became a high-speed blur. Dwarf conifer trees scattered along the crest kept us half-exposed, with no quick means of escape. We did not feel in danger, but not safe either. A sinister-looking squall cloud crept in from the west. It boomed like a Harley muffled through earplugs. Bright yellow daggers made us squeal in surprise. Each blinding flash bouncing off a nearby tree made it look like we were dashing past runway photographers.

For a long time, the crest's elevation hardly changed. Recurring flashes kept making us wonder. Were the crest's dwarf trees giving us any real protection? Or were we just pushing our luck?

At long last, the CDT decided we deserved a break. Angling down a short drop, it released us into a soggy meadow tucked between two wooded slopes. Midway across the meadow, we leaped over Hamby Creek without blinking. Then, we needed to figure out where to aim. The meadow's bordering trees offered no clues. Our visibility was limited. There were too many choices.

SeeHawk stood by, fidgeting with his pack straps.

I rifled through our literature, finding nothing relevant.

A few minutes of wandering hither and yon narrowed down our choices, until found the exit. Then, we were in. A dimly-lit forest permitted us to stop without looking at the sky. My adrenaline had rebounded, but SeeHawk was bonking hard. He scarfed a couple of homemade energy bars, seconds before a cloudburst sent us scrambling into our rain ponchos.

The ensuing climb made us sweat so hard that it felt like we were taking warm showers. Nevertheless, we kept wearing our ponchos after it stopped raining because more rounds of thunder were advancing from the west.

Inside one small clearing, a sudden break in the trees exposed a cumulonimbus cloud that looked like an oil fire. Black and spreading, it was skewered upon a peak one-mile upwind, crowned with a luminous rose-pink halo.

Closer in the distance sat a complex valley, somewhere containing Berry Creek. SeeHawk and I needed to drop into that valley before another storm could get there first. So, where was my partner? *Come on, SeeHawk. Quit lagging and catch up.* Thunder exploded. My intestines lurched.

Huffing up behind me, SeeHawk complained, "What octane did you fill up with this morning, Sunshine? How did you climb those switchbacks so fast?"

His backpack felt murderously heavy. His legs felt like rubber. He was itching to remove his hot, sticky poncho, but the look in my eyes warned him to keep silent.

The skewered black cloud was starting to break free.

"Go FAST!" I shouted.

Dropping off the overlook, we entered a tangled conifer-oak grove that should have felt safe but just felt strange. Its convex floor seemed to push us against the treetops as if our heads might be able to break through and poke the sky. Pink lightning took turns flashing on both sides. Was it coming from two different storms? Or one double-wide storm? Suddenly, the forest's light level dropped. Dusk gave way to immediate blackness.

"The wall cloud must be right over us," I guessed.

SeeHawk halted upon a bed of crackling oak leaves and decisively grunted, "Camp."

"Yes," I nodded, with my legs going limp.

Our next race began with practiced speed.

SeeHawk flung down a pile of puzzle pieces that included our tent's thin ground cloth, spring-locking poles, and crooked tent stakes. I helped him hastily whap together the poles, unfold the tent's irregular body, and fumble with its jumbled clips and bungees. Perhaps rushing made our brains short-circuit because we suddenly found ourselves clutching a mess of twisted fabric. It took a moment for each of us to notice the other struggling. After sharing a giggle, we both quit thinking and jammed whatever remained into any open holes.

Finally, I barked, "Ready, go!"

Having practiced the same routine nightly for seven weeks, we practically had it down to a science. Tugging, shimmying, and skooching our chosen halves of the tent, we stretched parts of it into something that came looking like...what? Modern art? A tent destroyed by a hurricane?

"Damn," SeeHawk mumbled.

I stared in disbelief.

It was about to start pouring. We could smell the rain's breath. Fighting to stay calm, we quickly unclipped all the disarrayed hooks and mislocated poles.

"Relax and focus," SeeHawk ordered.

Together, we started clipping things differently, and jamming uncooperative poles into different holes, until I realized we were creating another mess.

"Stop!" I hollered.

Right on cue, we had to burst out laughing. Criminy! How else could two tired idiots cope with such incompetence?

"Can you remember how to put this danged thing together?" SeeHawk wailed. "Because, suddenly, I can't."

"Nor can I!" I confessed. "My mind is blank."

The spell was broken by an earth-shaking thunderclap, which sent oak leaves raining onto our mess of crooked fabric.

I could not even hear whatever SeeHawk said next.

"Hurry!" I shrieked.

Another loud thunderclap set our thinking straight. This time, we got the tent pitched correctly and threw our backpacks inside, seconds before a torrential squall ripped into the oak grove.

After that, everything became business as usual. An especially fine light show looked even better with our headlamps switched off.

In the midst of a noisy downpour, one lingering question moved me to speculate, "Do you think those six CDT volunteers got back to their cars ahead of the rain?"

SeeHawk replied spookily, "Only The Shadow knows, and he won't tell."

We waited for the downpour to ease into a drizzle, before cracking open our tent's breezy vestibule and boiling some water for vegetarian chili.

"I'm having fun," SeeHawk affirmed, "but we can't go full-tilt every day from dawn to dusk. Otherwise, we'll be toast before we reach Wyoming."

"Stormy weather comes in cycles," I assured him. "This cycle appears to be having its big blow-out. Hopefully, it'll be calmer tomorrow.

* * *

My prediction about getting a breather from daily thunderstorms seemed proven by the sunrise. In newborn daylight, the same oak forest which had looked demonic under siege now evoked a pastoral daydream. The change was encouraging, but SeeHawk and I could not be fooled. Even though we left camp a bit late, once underway, we locked our engines into fifth gear and never looked back.

Gentle terrain made it easy to follow country roads through a series of open cow pastures and domestic woods. We coasted right along, until the CDT decayed into disconnected segments, requiring a lot of guidebook checking and landmark spotting to stay on course. After that, the rest of the afternoon became a grind. We noticed the sun turning golden, around the same time our tired brains and legs hollered uncle. It would have been nice to pull over and make camp early, but there was one last item left on our agenda.

A short climb lifted us onto a flat escarpment huddling in a wind shadow of the Continental Divide. Its southward view was supposed to save us from getting lost the next morning, by offering us a sneak preview into a broad lake basin. We felt eager to spot the CDT's exit from the basin, while height and distance gave us an advantage. But, first things first. A cluster of historic mining cabins urged us to quit obsessing and do a little sightseeing. Only after crossing the escarpment did we smell trouble. Clearly, the lake basin's details were not going to be forthcoming. The only landmark we could recognize was a belly button of dark water resting in the middle, which had to be either Darkhorse Lake or Cowbone Lake, and we could not tell which.

"Probably it's Darkhorse," I guessed, "because look how dark it is. But anyway, what we really want to find is Cowbone Lake, because that's where the CDT takes off."

SeeHawk felt eager to help me search for clues, so I told him we were looking for a trail scaling either the basin's rear headboard or its right-hand wall. The rear headboard was a naked scree peak that looked off-limits for anyone prone to vertigo. The right-hand wall was an equally steep ridge, forming a square corner where it butted into the headboard. Both of our guidebooks provided a fair amount of detail, without making it clear to me whether their authors had taken the same route or chosen two different routes.

When I mentioned to SeeHawk that we could probably camp at Darkhorse Lake, he protested, "That place looks kind of spooky. Do we have any other choice?"

"Cowbone's not much farther," I offered, "so if we keep going, we could wake up near the base of tomorrow's climb. But I can't show you where since I'm only seeing one lake."

"Wait, a minute," SeeHawk exclaimed, remembering a certain passage of text. "Are you suggesting we could camp where a bunch of thirsty cows stampeded off the Continental Divide and fell through the ice?"

"Yeah," I nodded. "Why?"

"Ugh," he shuddered. "No thanks. I know bone broth is supposed to be healthy, but we're not that low on calcium."

Rolling my eyes, I reminded him, "The cows drowned a long time ago. Plus, we don't even know if that story is true or pulp fiction."

"Still," he insisted, "I'd rather play it safe than find cow teeth in my noodles."

"Fair enough," I chuckled. "We'll camp at Darkhorse, but let's make sure to find the exit trail before we lose this view."

The Book of Beans contained a troubling passage about deceptive CD-signs, mountaineering skills, impassable cliffs, and inconspicuous trails.

Poppa Jim's guidebook mentioned blazes disappearing, lots of deadfall, and needing to follow a compass heading.

After rereading both descriptions to SeeHawk, I asked him to mentally reverse the Book of Beans' directions and compare them with Poppa Jim's.

He stammered in response, "Why are you asking ME? I don't even know where to start, Sunshine. I mean, it's super confusing trying to match the end of one description with the beginning of another."

"I know, but we have to try," I insisted. "So, what do you think?"

"I think we should start with Cowbone Lake, but you're telling me that's Darkhorse?"

"Yes, but I'm not totally positive. Can you see another lake?"

"Nope, darn it. Is this turning into another confusing episode?"

"Not if we can piece everything together."

After another few minutes of running my eyes up, down, across, and all over the rear peak, I finally spied a hair-thin line zigzagging up its bald scree face.

"There it is!" I cried.

SeeHawk stared where I was pointing and could not see anything resembling a trail.

I should have felt glad. Finding the lake basin's exit gave us permission to quit scouting and set up camp. It had been a long, high-mileage day. Our legs were complaining and our stomachs felt hollow. I only hesitated because the trail's appearance made me cringe. In addition to scaling a steep scree peak, its switchbacks hardly showed, which meant they were probably super skinny. Also, they appeared to end 100-feet below the top. How was I going to scramble up the last 100-feet? Could trying thrust me into a replay of getting stuck on Mather Pass two years ago?

SeeHawk still had not seen any trail. Curiosity made him ask, "Do you think you're looking at Poppa Jim's route or the Book of Beans?"

"I'm not sure," I admitted. "Probably Poppa Jim's, since he would be more likely to recommend a goat trail."

"Are you saying the Book of Beans route might be better?" he hinted.

"At this point, any trail we can find might have to do."

The sun looked near setting. It was time for us to quit stalling and get moving. Pocketing our maps, I took a deep breath and hoped for everything to fall into place the next morning.

After dropping off the overlook, we had an easy time maneuvering through the lake basin's thick woods. Up close, Darkhorse Lake did not look either dark or spooky. In fact, it looked delicious. Better yet, we arrived in time a comfortable swim, beneath tangerine-orange clouds that brightened after the sun went down. Even after wriggling into our nightclothes, we still had enough daylight left to dine in style beside the lake.

The next morning commenced with filling every possible water bag up to its lid. We topped off our bellies before leaving camp, because the CDT's next convenient water source lay 24 miles away, not counting Cowbone Lake, of course.

As it turned out, though, Cowbone Lake would have been a beautiful place to camp. Its shoreline did not display any rotting cow bones, and if we had not just left camp, perhaps we might have even taken a quick swim.

"So far, so good," SeeHawk declared, "but where are the switchbacks you saw last night?"

Peeking through trees bordering the lake, we could only see slivers of the bare scree peak we were expecting to climb.

"Don't worry," I told SeeHawk, "Poppa Jim's guidebook says the trail is hard to spot from here. That's why we tried to find it last night. So, I guess, now we should try to get closer?"

"Easier said than done," SeeHawk noted, searching for a gap in the bordering woods.

"Do you have any better suggestions?"

Smiling, he answered, "Are you feeling what I'm feeling? Is it time for some 'musical fruit'?"

Catching his drift, I joined him in singing,

Beans, beans, the musical fruit.
The more you eat, the more you toot.

After going a few rounds, I answered him flatly. "Very funny, but, no. We are not going to reject Poppa Jim's trail without checking it out first. Let's see if this footpath doubles back toward the peak."

I was referring to a tidy little footpath circling the lake, which looked eager to be of service. Never mind that it aimed toward the ridge, instead of toward our anticipated climb. For lack of a better option, it made sense to follow the only show in town.

After a short distance, the lake path widened from being hiker-sized to horse-sized.

My guess was, "Maybe a trail crew came through after the Book of Beans was written and did some rerouting."

SeeHawk worried, "If we don't U-turn soon, where will we be headed?"

"Who knows?" I confessed. "Maybe onboard The Magical Mystery Tour, complete with flying pigs and mocha-fudge ice cream?"

"Great!" he grinned, "Count me in."

So, onward we went as if my theory held water.

The trail's insistence upon aiming toward the ridge eventually began to whet our interest. Its face was a mess of disorganized conifer trees, chimney chutes, overhanging bluffs, and weathered sedimentary rock. Nothing straight ahead looked welcoming to novices wearing sneakers and backpacks. I knew about chimney climbing from having once watched my ex-boyfriend Dave press his hands opposite to his feet while scaling a vertical granite tube. Which is to say, I knew better than to even think about trying it. Ditto for scaling the bluffs. They looked too crumbly and slick for the likes of me, or maybe for anyone without climbing gear and ropes. But, shoot. If I was going to avoid all the scary options, where else could we climb? There had to be another exit route hiding somewhere. Was it camouflaged, like the rocky trail Lucinda had shown us above Little Lake? If so, my hunch placed it farther toward the right, where the ridge and the lake merged close together. SeeHawk and I could easily have walked in that direction, but the footpath told us to keep aiming straight. Interestingly, though, it was subtly deteriorating from a horse-sized trail into an overgrown game trail.

Feeling discouraged, SeeHawk mumbled, "This seems...not promising anymore."

"Except," I reminded him, "the Book of Beans does tell us to expect some confusion."

"So, feeling confused is supposed to make us happy?"

"Not punch-drunk happy. Just happy whenever things don't get worse."

"Oh, boy," he groaned

The feeling was mutual, with both of us feeling a little punch drunk. The morning's bright sky was working in our favor. No more thunderstorms were forcing us to hurry. It even became fun playing trail detective, each time the trail ducked away and hid behind a concealing tree or shrub. However, the ridge gave us a wake-up call when we ran into a boulder chute undercutting its raw stone bluffs.

"Game over," SeeHawk sighed, whirling around to face Cowbone Lake.

"Hold up," I told him.

The place where we stood offered a clear, backward view of the peak now behind us. Its switchbacks should have shown like Memorex, now that its full face stood in plain sight. There were no more trees in the way, and the sunrise was hitting it from a better angle. So, where the heck was Poppa Jim's trail?

"Did you just see dust on your eyeball last night?" SeeHawk wondered.

"Maybe," I admitted, "but there's something else missing. We're supposed to be seeing a third lake."

"WHAT?" he cried. "Why didn't you mention that before, Sunshine? A third lake? That sounds important."

"I just haven't been able to imagine where it could be hiding. I mean, obviously not on the scree, and not down here either, unless it's ridiculously skinny."

"Then, where else could it be?"

Turning back around to reconsider the ridge, I mumbled, "Maybe up there, somewhere?"

SeeHawk ran his eyes up to the same crumbling bluffs and chimneys he had dismissed before. Once again, he reached the same conclusion. "I don't see any place for a lake to be hiding. This whole situation is starting to smell fishy. Do you really think the CDT could scale something that steep?"

"Not if you forced me to bet," I agreed, "but as far as the lake goes, I'm trying to be open-minded. Because remember how much trouble we had finding Little Lake?"

"That was in rolling terrain with a lot of room for lakes. Here, it would have to be a puddle."

"Maybe it is a puddle. Poppa Jim doesn't mention the size."

"All right, well, if it is a puddle, then, do you think this is where Jim started climbing? And maybe the Book of Beans author went up the scree?"

"Or else, they could both have gone up here, and just recorded different landmarks. I really have no idea."

SeeHawk's eyes darted back and forth, making comparisons like a used-car shopper. At length, he decided, "Well, if my vote counts, I'm voting for the peak because, at least, you can get a good footing on scree. All it takes is climbing fast and never stopping until you reach the top."

"That philosophy almost killed me on Mather Pass," I reminded him.

"But, it didn't kill you. It made you stronger. And, nobody's going to die, today, Sunshine. I know you can climb scree without any problem. Just focus on using your feet, not your head."

"Sorry partner," I protested, "but you'd have to light the forest on fire to get me up there unless we find the trail I saw last night, and even then, hoo-boy."

"Okay, well, if you're not going to accept my vote, then what do you recommend? Climbing straight uphill from here? Ay caramba, that even scares me! No way could I trust the talus not to slide. You can't dig your feet into talus at all."

I had not been paying attention to any talus, but now that I looked where SeeHawk was looking, I saw what he meant. So, where did that leave us? Stuck between a rock and a hard place? Suddenly, my eyes spied an inconspicuous ledge slashed across the overhanging bluffs. It looked like part of an old, washed-out trail. Growing excited, I cried, "Bet you a hundred pushups that's Poppa Jim's trail!"

SeeHawk squinted 200-feet upward and could not see any ledge where I was pointing. He responded nervously, "Easy there, Pie Eyes. Don't let desperation make you hallucinate. There's no trail up the peak, and none here either."

Resenting his inference, I lowered my gaze to a steep talus chute underpinning the ledge. Its downward end climbed out of some ankle-high shrubbery, overhanging a second talus chute, supported by a column of stacked rocks chinked with spidery crabgrass. Aside from the talus, everything else looked likely to give our sneakers good traction. Probably, the worst danger would be intimidation, since the grade was extremely steep. I thought we could fudge a respectable route if we took our time and got creative.

When SeeHawk noticed my bold expression, he hastened to repeat, "See why I prefer scree over talus, any day?"

"Nope," I disagreed. "I'll always take talus, hands down."

"That's because you don't have as much climbing experience as I do," he explained.

"Which should give my opinion more weight," I countered, "since I'll be the one to get stuck if I get scared."

"Except, you won't get scared if we climb fast."

"That might be true on a shorter slope, but here there's no way to go all the way up without stopping, so it's important to keep me within my comfort zone."

SeeHawk heaved a sigh, balled up both hands, and pretended to beat himself in the head. "I don't know how you do it, Sunshine, but you always seem to win me in these kinds of debates."

His surrender thrilled me for a moment, but I did not smile because assuming responsibility for whatever might happen to us did not feel like a win. In fact, it felt a little scary. Therefore, I just said, "Let's not commit before we do a little test-climb. If it feels safe, we'll keep going. If not, we'll turn around."

Chuckling, SeeHawk replied, "Haven't I heard that someplace before?"

Blushing, I admitted, "Unless my loveable stubborn-streak won't let me stop."

Together, we rock-hopped across a swath of polished boulders initiating the ascent. I used my trekking poles for prevention against slipping, but SeeHawk felt no need because he had better balance. Soon, we reached the uprising column of grass-chinked rocks. Their steep angle required us to climb on tiptoes. Thirty steps upward, I noticed intense heat reflecting onto my face and arms. This was before the sun had risen past breakfast height. How much hotter were things going to get on our way up? Trying to climb faster, I felt my calves tighten from staying on tiptoes. Eventually, the tightness turned into cramps, which forced me to slow down. A bit higher up, the rocks gave way to hardpacked dirt, causing my poles to bounce rather than dig in. It was not a steep enough grade for climbing on all-fours, but too steep for climbing upright, so we had to lean forward at an awkward angle. Every time I paused to recover from feely woozy, SeeHawk bent over, wheezing for breath. At one point, both of us paused together to discuss our next options.

Above and beside us stood the steep talus chute SeeHawk had been dreading. Its purplish rock flakes were stacked like poker chips spilling down the mountain. Nothing appeared to be holding the talus in place. When I kicked one flake loose it did aerial flips downhill, clinking all the way. When I stomped on the talus, thank goodness, nothing slid. Clearly, trekking poles had no relevance, but I clutched them anyway. The move had to be quick. Dashing across the slippery chute, in less than a minute I landed safely on a little patch of shrubs, which held my shoes in place.

SeeHawk came after me, bounding across the talus faster than I could blink. He landed like a paratrooper on my little patch of shrubs, forcing me to lean away so our backpacks would not collide.

A second talus chute, similar to the first but resting higher, challenged us to repeat the same drill This time, I did not bother testing for slippage. I just dashed across it pell-mell and stuck the landing.

Again, SeeHawk followed me, being careful not to say anything, for fear of interrupting my courage.

A few yards uphill, there was a whitebark pine branch dangling just out of reach. Grabbing it could help me shimmy onto a wind-sanded boulder, split down its middle as if by an ax. I wanted to wedge one hand into the split and use it to reach the branch, but the whole maneuver looked tricky wearing a backpack.

SeeHawk grew impatient and finally climbed around me. Up went one of his clubby shoes, kicking into the crack, which he used for leverage to hoist himself onto the boulder.

I wanted to follow him, but he was already wriggling out of his backpack, slinging it over one arm and saying he would return in a moment. Without waiting for any response, he vanished into a clump of higher pine trees and returned moments later, unburdened. On his way back down, he watched me debate whether to stick with my own plan, involving the branch, or try to imitate what he had done. When he got to within reach, he offered, "Want to hand up your backpack?"

Gratefully, I slipped it off my shoulders.

He whisked it away, into the upper trees.

Now, I had no excuse to keep dawdling. Cautiously, I kicked up one shoe and wedged it into the crack. Reaching one arm up, I found that I could not grab the crack without removing my shoe. Darn.

When SeeHawk returned, he looked dismayed by my failure to repeat his maneuver.

Avoiding his gaze, I grabbed a smaller knob of rock and used it to hoist both shoes into the crack. This would have made a cool "rock-climbing" pose for a photograph. However, coming unhooked from everything else besides the crack, with my body hanging in empty space, gave me a sickening feeling. Lowering both shoes, next I tried hugging the boulder and scaling it like a worm. Unfortunately, fright blocked me from attempting one critical reach, so I could not get up that way, either. Meantime, my brain grew dizzy from trying, failing, and thinking too hard. There was only one feasible alternative. Acting on impulse, I reached up and grabbed the whitebark pine branch. It felt like a cluster of straws in my hand.

"Don't DO that!" SeeHawk barked. "Trust the rock, not the branches, Sunshine."

Ignoring his advice, I clung on tight and swung my feet across the boulder. Next, scaling my trusty life rope, hand-over-hand, I landed upon the boulder and flashed my partner a winning smile.

His expression could have wilted a daisy.

Unfazed, I followed him into the small cluster of pine trees containing our backpacks. Amongst the trees sat one enormous boulder, pinned against the mountain by a sturdy pine trunk. Ooh, was that tempting. The boulder's supporting trunk had withstood countless winter avalanches and spring thaws without ever letting go. Still, I pressed and pushed before sinking my weight onto it and taking a ride. Everything felt safe. The boulder's solidity helped me feel grounded. It did not matter about having my legs dangle freely into space. I felt safe, not only because the supporting pine trunk was sturdy, but also because it blocked me from seeing anything downhill. Seriously, in all this time, I had never once looked below my shoes. As a result, I still had no idea how high we had climbed. Now, assuming our position to be roughly midway up, the farthest I dared to look in any direction was back over my shoulder, into the upper trees. Close above, I found SeeHawk standing guard. When he saw my forehead relax, he straightened his shoulders and got back to business.

"Stay put, Sunshine," he told me. "I'll climb up aways and find the safest route to the top."

I did not dare make eye contact. Experience had taught me never to surrender my sense of self-sufficiency before the hard part was over, so I kept my eyes averted while telling him, "Go ahead, but please don't take long."

His shoes made a creepy grinding noise stomping out of the trees.

I felt a little panicky after he was gone. Rivulets of sand dribbled past me, dislodged by his sneakers scraping the upper slope. Following the dribbles came unnerving silence. I was stuck on my saddle like a helpless baby bird. Needing some distraction, I traced my eyes along the tree trunk holding me up. It looked like I was riding an elephant's trunk. Riding an elephant was fun. At least, thinking it was fun allowed me to risk a quick peek around my elephant's trunk. 500-feet below, I spied Cowbone Lake. Holy guacamole! We had climbed a long way. The lake's framing boulders looked like beach pebbles. Its shiny silver water had shrunk to a polished dime. *We're going all the way*, I thought. *Whatever's left above, we'll just have to tough it out.* Unexpectedly, my eyes fell upon a second silver gleam, not far above Cowbone Lake. Was it the third lake mentioned in Poppa Jim's guidebook? If so, what could its location tell me about where Jim exited the basin? Lifting my eyes into the broader distance, I saw the scree-covered peak we had examined last evening, now from a sideways angle. Lo and behold, there were the switchbacks! They DID exist. My brain had not invented them. So, how did they look? Man, oh, man. Perhaps, we were dodging a bullet. For a mountain goat, the switchbacks looked adequate, but if Poppa Jim thought backpackers could manage them, I was forevermore going to avoid anything he called "steep."

In the meantime, though, I just wanted to finish what we had started and put this whole nerve-wracking mess behind us. Never mind whoever's route we might be following. We had a date to keep with the Continental Divide. Wyoming was waiting. Colorado was waiting. I clamped both legs around my elephant's saddle and twisted my shoulders far enough to gaze uphill. Channels of scree peeked through the intervening trees. The nearest bluffs looked crumbly and slick. There was no more vegetation above the grove where I sat.

Suddenly, a familiar voice drifted down through the air, "I think I-- -oun- - sp--, Sunshine…isn't -ny good…see if ------ --- thing better…"

"Can you see the STOCK TRAIL?" I hollered uphill. "Is it really a trail, or just some ledge?"

"Wha-?" the voice quavered. "Sunsh---, did you say something?"

"Never mind," I decided.

"WHAT? Are you OKAY?"

"YES. Never mind."

"You're OKAY?" he repeated, now sounding concerned.

"YES!"

"Where ARE you?"

"Down in the trees. Where else?"

"…WHERE are you, Sunshine? Talk to me more, so I can find you."

"I'M RIGHT where you LEFT ME."

Presently, I heard SeeHawk's shoes come crunching back down the upper slope. Fresh rivulets of sand dribbled past my hideout. Finally, his shaggy head popped up from behind an overhang 30-feet above. His cheeks were splotched with dirt. Fat globs of sweat clung to his forehead, making him look like a baking meat roast. When he saw my expression, he quickly grinned, before looking back toward his feet. The adjacent overhang swallowed him from sight. Soon, his face reappeared, looking different. Uh-oh. Why was he frowning? Had he run into an impasse? I watched him scamper a few steps sideways. Little dribbles of scree came sledding past me. Suddenly, two clubby shoes bounded onto a dirt ledge supporting the trees above me and stuck the landing. SeeHawk's poker-face was perfect. Anyone who barely knew him could have thought he was smiling.

"Come on up, Sunshine," he sang, with forced cheerfulness. "I'll wear your backpack going up this first part. There's just one little section where you might need to apply some focused attention, but I promise you'll be fine. Just keep moving fast."

I felt afraid to leave my secure little hideout. Clearly, whatever lurked uphill was not going to be easy. I took a deep breath, made up my mind, and timidly let SeeHawk coax me out of hiding.

First, he climbed down to where I was sitting. Next, he removed one of his backpack's straps, to make room for slinging my backpack onto his freed shoulder. After both backpacks hung from his shoulders like two purses, he extended a hand to help me stand up.

I gazed into his sweat-stained face and thought, *Sunshine, you can handle anything your fiancé is willing to climb wearing two backpacks.*

Out loud, I said, "No thanks."

It would have been nice to feel SeeHawk's hand touch mine, but I dared not surrender any self-sufficiency. Past experience had taught me that so doing could render me unable to regain my independence.

As soon as we stepped out of the trees, bright yellow sunlight drilled into our backs. I maneuvered around SeeHawk and struck out on my own, without volunteering any explanation. It felt reassuring to clutch my trekking poles, even though they were useless upon steep slippery rock. I felt vaguely confused. The most important goal was to finish climbing before I could lose my nerve. Marching straight uphill, I climbed shoe-over-shoe, until an overhanging boulder forced me to halt. Glancing right and left, I found myself pinned between a steep talus chute and a slippery rock chimney.

SeeHawk saw me hesitate and called out encouragingly, "Just turn left to cross the scree, Sunshine. I've already climbed most of it. You'll have an easy time, after the first part. Trust me, you'll see."

Obeying his command, I glanced toward the left and saw exactly what I feared. Dashing across the scree was going to feel like slipping through cornmeal.

"Go ahead," he urged me. "I know it looks steep. That's because it is steep, and it's also loose, but don't worry. You've crossed plenty of scree before. Don't stop moving, or even slow down. Just keep going until you reach the other side. You know it's going to slide, so just expect a little slipperiness and don't worry. You'll get across before you know it."

Ignoring his advice, I stubbornly turned around and headed in the opposite direction. Talus scared me a lot less than scree. The biggest danger in my book was always fear itself. My best chance for survival hinged upon staying within my comfort zone.

SeeHawk objected "Come BACK and TURN LEFT. You're heading the wrong way."

I aimed toward the talus I had seen from down below. If I could scale it safely, the ledge was going to receive me within 40 -feet. Up close, it really looked like an old, washed-out trail. I just needed to take charge. Stay cautious. Not wait too long.

"DON'T climb the TALUS," SeeHawk bellowed.

One stacked rock flake broke loose beneath my shoe. Well, of course. Talus was talus. Down low or up high, it made no difference. I just needed to pretend I was 400-feet lower and do the same thing I had done far below.

"Get OFF the talus," SeeHawk practically shrieked. "I know you hate scree, Sunshine, but you've got to BELIEVE me when I tell you it's safe. Just follow me, for once, okay? Please? Pretty please? NO, SUNSHINE! ACK— "

He reached out to grab me, but it was too late.

I lunged up the talus faster than he could react.

There was no way for him to catch me, wearing two backpacks.

I lunged because I expected the talus to be steep. I wanted to climb all of it faster than I could get scared. Unfortunately, my first few steps revealed the incline was steeper than it looked. Nothing down below had been quite as steep. Could I climb the whole way without losing my nerve? Hopefully so, because once I set foot on the talus, there was no turning around. Its flakes were too loose. There was nothing to grab besides my trekking poles, which just bounced off the talus, but I still had to hold them and pretend they were helping. Most important was not to think about anything besides climbing. It felt precarious to keep my backpack upright, but crawling might have sent me into a belly slide. Furthermore, the angle at which I was leaning pushed my center of gravity toward the talus, thereby holding it in place, if I was not mistaken. Although, the same leverage was also pushing me backward, or maybe trying to flip me over. My shoes could not find anything solid. Well, too bad. I needed to just keep peddling upward. Never mind the sound of dislodged rock flakes clinking into empty space below me.

SeeHawk scrambled sideways, trying to get positioned underneath the chute. He assumed I had gone crazy. He felt a little crazy, himself. Why would he even consider climbing talus when scree was available? He only followed me because he feared I might get scared and freak out. He did not realize that, for once, I had transcended feeling afraid.

I felt confident because my wits were holding solid. At least, they felt solid until both my quadriceps turned into wooden planks. Apparently, I had been climbing too fast. Unfortunately, I could not afford to slow down. Climbing steadily almost stopped me from breathing. Slowing down made no difference. My quadriceps had become useless. The only leg muscles still propelling me upward were my calves and hamstrings, flexing and pushing. Continuing to strain made my temples tingle. *Oh no*, I thought, *please don't get vertigo*. Breathing deeply, I managed another 10-steps. They felt clumsy but did the job. Suddenly, there it was! Right before my astonished eyes, I saw a blur of mental dissociation. My brain needed a moment to reengage. Then, it showed me the truth. I had reached the ledge! Safety was only a few steps away. One step. Two steps. Upward, I flung one leg. Up went the other. Shakily, I raised my body into a standing position. Slowly, I shuffled around to see where I had landed. The view on both sides made it obvious. I was standing on part of an old stock trail. Probably, it was the same stock trail down which a legendary herd of thirsty cows had once stampeded, before falling through Cowbone Lake's fragile ice. Gazing uphill from the ledge, I saw no deadly washouts. The coast looked clear for climbing safely up and onto the Continental Divide.

Suddenly, I remembered to look around for SeeHawk. Turning back downhill, I saw him laboring up the talus, poor guy. He looked stunned beyond words. With one backpack swinging from each arm, he was having a tough time defying gravity.

I watched him huff-and-puff for another full minute, before his backpack, and then mine plunked onto the ledge beside my feet.

His arriving remark was, "You can finish the climb without me if you want to."

"Er, no thanks."

I still felt dizzy. We were safe, but finishing the climb would be easier after my head cleared. Besides, it was our motto never to split up for any avoidable reason. I needed to stay put until SeeHawk stood up and gave me a nod. Once that happened, I bolted uphill like Wonder Woman reacting to a bee sting.

Precisely where SeeHawk and I reached flat ground, one huge rock cairn proved we were landing upon the Continental Divide. Or, at least, it proved we had reached the top, and that was good enough.

SeeHawk nearly wept when he grabbed me into a hug.

I needed to cry because the whole adventure safely behind us had not seemed extreme in real-time, but afterward, it gave me a shock.

Cowbone Lake looked beautiful from 9,200-feet above sea level. Its forested basin was striped with moving cloud shadows, heralding thunderstorms due to arrive on schedule.

"Lightning schmitening," I bragged.

Never mind my usual superstition about jinxes. Given everything we had just conquered, silly old lightning could knock itself out, for all I cared.

Heading away from the huge rock cairn, SeeHawk and I ran into the first of several intersecting crests mentioned in our guidebooks. Feeling wary, I pulled out our compass and reviewed the Book of Beans' mention of a four-wheel-drive track, footpath, unsigned post, hiker registration box, and occasional cairns.

Visualizing numerous details in reverse, I asked SeeHawk, "Do you think we're still more than a half-mile from the registration box?"

He answered, "Nah, this has to be our trail. Either it used to show and got erased by weather, or else no trail workers have been up here yet, except to build the cairn above Cowbone Lake."

"Okay, but if that cairn was built for the CDT, why didn't they put another one here?"

"Maybe the workers got tired and quit. I bet building those huge cairns is a lot of work. The rocks probably have to be hauled a long way."

"No doubt," I agreed. "Anyway, I think we should keep heading straight, but let's also watch out for anything resembling a registration box, footpath, or four-wheel drive track."

We watched in every direction, but all we found was a crosswise dirt road, not seeming to match anything described in our guidebooks.

"Could this be Goldstone Pass?" I speculated.

"Probably," SeeHawk shrugged.

Thinking of a joke, I asked him, "Why did the chicken cross the road?"

"I don't know. Why?"

"Take a guess."

"Because the land ahead looked hot enough to fry an egg?"
"No, silly."
"Then, why?"
"Because its mother had warned it not to stop at the drive-thru."

Soon after crossing whatever the road was, we merged onto an immaculate, manmade footpath. Its slight upgrade led us onto a freakishly isolated fin of broken lava. Partway across the lava was a very strange place to find a middle-aged man, seated all by himself, but there he was. Not wearing any hat for sun protection, and looking thoroughly exhausted, he sat beside a small daypack, which could barely have held his lunch, canteen, and rain jacket.

"Been puking my guts out since all day yesterday," he started off explaining. "I'm a little better off today, but still not able to carry my own backpack. The wife's carrying it for me. See her out there?"

He pointed toward a faraway dot, moving toward us from a great distance.

"Good lady," he beamed. "Once she delivers my pack, she'll go back for hers."

"Are you aiming to reach Cowbone Lake tonight?" I asked him. "Because if you are, keep in mind that it's pretty tricky getting down to the lake. There's no real trail to speak of. It's just a long, steep drop that's pretty challenging. Doing it twice will be gnarly for your wife. If she gets tired, you might pull in after dark."

"Oh, she won't mind," the sick husband promised. "She's a real tough cookie. Actually, we're in somewhat of a hurry to get down there. Last night, my wife tried getting water over that-a-way..." He pointed toward a dramatic downslope blanketed with rocks that looked ready to slide. "She didn't make it all the way down, though," he added, "because she didn't have a rope or nothing. So, until we get to Cowbone Lake, we're making do with what little water we have left." He waggled his half-full drinking bottle suggestively.

I eyeballed the distance between wife and husband. They appeared to have progressed only 1-2 miles since morning. At that rate, they were going to reach Cowbone Lake after dark.

"Have you thought about camping at Pratt Creek?" I suggested. "That's a water source only two miles from here. You could leave the CDT at Goldstone Pass, camp at Pratt Creek, see how you're feeling in the morning, then continue on if you feel ready to carry your own backpack tomorrow. Otherwise, maybe you could hitchhike from Pratt Creek out to someplace with a doctor if you need one."

The sick man chortled, "Thanks, but I'm sure we'll reach Cowbone Lake tonight. My wife's a tough little peanut. You'll see what I'm talking about when you meet her."

Trying not to frown, I thought, *Who's the saint who puts up with this guy?*

Ten minutes later, we met the appointed saint. She was, indeed, a peanut. Short. Feisty. And, sure enough, she did have sturdy legs. However, her husband's backpack was a monster among monsters. I seriously doubted she could drop and return from Cowbone Lake twice before any thunderstorms took shape, not to mention before the sun went down. Already, her cheeks were turning red, just from the effort of hauling her husband's mega-backpack across one mile of broken lava. She had good reason to complain, but in response to meeting us, she just extended a saintly smile.

Without hesitation, I launched into the same speech I had given her husband. When I got to the part about Pratt Lake, she lowered her eyes and thought for a moment, after which she said, "We'll see..."

I finished that conversation feeling sure of one thing. Neither the saint nor her husband was going to leave the CDT if they could help it. Oh, well. Sometimes, you just cannot change people's minds. Besides, how could I, the Queen of Stubborn, expect anyone else to be less stubborn?

Beyond the lava's end, and less than 20 miles from our next water source, SeeHawk and I sat down beneath a solitary pine tree, to eat spicy, salty, and garlicky chickpeas for lunch. Once again, we had made the mistake of packing thirsty food for a day without water refills from morning until night. We started craving water halfway through the meal and taking measured sips only increased our thirst.

While SeeHawk retired our lunch utensils, I noticed his lips twitching oddly and wondered if he wanted to kiss me.

Testing to see, I twitched my lips back at him.

He licked his lips and twitched them again.

I puckered my lips into the shape of an air kiss.

He burst out laughing.

I laughed with him, before closing my eyes to wait for the real thing. When nothing happened, I opened my eyes, and what did I see? My fiancé was pulling a ticklish hair out of his mustache!

"It's getting long," he explained matter-of-factly. "I'm going to need to shave as soon as we get home."

So much for backcountry romance.

Back on the trail, we entered a broad expanse of half-bare mountains, whose lumpy summits were flecked with old snow. The Continental Divide cut right through their midst, replicating a backbone with ribs on both sides. The afternoon's heat was becoming intense. Too bad we could not afford to drink bigger sips of water. Nevertheless, we still felt comfortable, thanks to some fair-weather clouds stirring up a lukewarm breeze. It was all fun and games until we entered a dusty forest whose interior stopped the breeze as if somebody had unplugged a fan.

Poppa Jim's guidebook warned hikers to beware of getting lost during the next few miles. We could easily see why, since the forest's interior was flat, viewless and its trees were evenly spaced. Unsigned jeep roads, meandering to-and-fro, contributed to the appearance of everything being random. Fortunately, the CDT had recently been blazed with fresh ax-cuts, strategically positioned to catch the eye of hikers.

SeeHawk felt so appreciative that he said, out loud, "Whoever blazed this trail deserves a medal. I wonder if they kept getting lost when they tried to figure out where to put the blazes."

Unfortunately, though, even the world's most fabulous blazes could not save us from growing bored as the forest stretched on and on. With its air feeling stuffy, water-rationing keeping us on the edge of thirst, and late afternoon inducing heavy glue, we needed some diversion. Therefore, it was exciting to see two sweating gentlemen burst through the trees ahead. Plotting an introduction, we tried to make eye contact, but they both had their eyes locked to GPS devices. Right before we all would have crashed, finally, the men glanced up, and when their eyes met ours they looked weirdly overjoyed.

Without even bothering to say hello, one of the pair blurted out, "Is the trail marked up ahead?"

"What?" I responded, not initially understanding his question.

Then, it sank in that GPS fixation had caused both men to overlook the big blazes SeeHawk and I had been following, and I had to swallow a fit of giggles. "You can put those GPS thingies away until you get to Goldstone Pass," I told them.

Not in your lives, two faces said, and without further comment, they disappeared into the trees.

SeeHawk and I laughed loud and long. Then, we got heckler-payback in the form of no more blazes because the forest ran out of trees.

Stepping out into the open suddenly changed everything. We found ourselves facing nature's rendition of The Yellow Brick Road. It was a wide-open crest, paved with yellow grass that descended for miles in a straight line. Its terminus met a new range of mountains, whose low entry point had to be Lehmi Pass. Roughly ¼ mile in that direction stood a giant stone cairn, playing traffic divider. Logically speaking, our trail should have aimed straight for the cairn. Instead, it simply ended where the grass began. We needed to descend cross-country from there, and, wow. What a pretty path The Yellow Brick Road turned out to be. Just a few yards downhill, its grass became packed full of colorful pink geraniums, purple fleabanes, yellow arnica flowers, white mariposa tulips, white yarrow, pink pussytoes, purple harebells, and purple Lupins. It was like dropping into an English Garden, nearly 8,000-feet above sea level.

Although the flowers were distracting, thankfully, we did not have to worry about getting lost, with Lehmi Pass staying visible in the distance. We still wanted to find the CDT, though, because trails equal speed and we needed to get water from Lehmi Pass before nightfall. Also, it would have been nice to have a trail lead us sideways, into either of the crest's bordering forests, because the sky was up to something. A little rain was falling to leeward. Occasional bolts of lightning were flashing to windward. A few passive clouds overhead looked ready to collide.

Unfortunately, when we reached the cairn, it failed to supply any kind of trail. In fact, all it seemed to be marking was a dramatic change in the crest's vegetation, from wildflowers mixed with grass to stragglier grass mixed with sagebrush. We halted above the sagebrush because, jinkies. Its brittle branches felt like razor wire. Rather than bloody our legs, we decided to search harder for the CDT, inside either of the forests on both sides. Having no clue where to search first, we decided to split up and each take a side. Curses erupted. Daylight burned. The happy ending came when we discovered a good trail heading into the right-hand woods.

Smiling with relief, we descended swiftly through a chain of small meadows enclosed by thick woods. Muffled thunderclaps could be heard toward the west. One meadow appeared to have gotten a memo from its northern counterparts, saying thruhikers were coming who enjoyed the no-exit game. Agreeing to cooperate, the meadow pranked us.

"Oh NO!" I groaned. "This is NOT a good time."

"It's late and I'm thirsty," SeeHawk complained. "There HAS to be an exit. Come on, come on. We need to reach Lehmi Pass before it gets dark."

"We'll be able to find the spring in the dark," I assured him, "but water won't matter if our brains explode before we get there."

It felt silly to keep examining the same walls of trees over and over again. A layer of smooth clouds capping the meadow was subtly darkening from silver to gray. We needed to keep moving, but what else could we do besides keep searching?

Perhaps our "French" expletives intrigued a young doe who wandered into the meadow and stopped to have a look at us. As soon as her eyes met ours? Foom! Caution scared the youngster back into the trees. And what do you know? Her departure showed us the meadow's exit.

SeeHawk spent several minutes raving about having gotten help from an "animal guide." If he still felt at all thirsty or tired, at least, he was finished complaining about it.

Late-evening redirected the sky from darkening grays into watercolor pinks. Things hummed along while we passed through more woods until the woods ended. Straight ahead, we faced a last baker's mile of The Yellow Brick Road. Lehmi Pass was waiting. Did we dare make a run for it? The danger involved a pair of short wire fences and one chain of high-voltage powerlines. We needed to walk alongside the fences and duck underneath the powerlines. Nothing else ahead stood taller than ourselves. Thankfully, the ground was dry. It had recently stopped thundering. Now, the only visible lightning was located faraway to the west.

I paused between the forest's last trees and told SeeHawk to wait for my signal.

Above the open crest loomed a cryptic mixture of agitated stratus and smooth Mammatus udders.

Lehmi Pass looked so close, SeeHawk could hardly wait.

I begged him to be patient, saying, "It's quiet now, but, you know what that means?"

"The queen just farted?" he guessed.

"Har-har. No, it means the Final Strike is coming."

SeeHawk's shoulders sagged and he croaked. "Water."

Understanding his need, I made a snap decision. "Okay, but if we're not going to wait until it's safe, let's RUN!"

Within seconds of leaving the trees, my arms started to shiver. Where had the chill come from? Was a new breeze picking up? Or had we stepped into it when we left the trees? I stopped to dig out my windbreaker jacket. After putting it on, though, I realized that wearing sleeves would impede me from checking my personal voltage meters. In fact, come to think of it, did I even feel cold? Or was I just nervous? Either way, it looked like we were getting close to camp. There was no point in deliberating about jackets. We just needed to hurry.

Partway down to the high-voltage power lines, SeeHawk directed my attention toward a gray veil of rain, turning petal pink against the darkening rouge sky. A scroll of waveform peaks, silhouetted through the veil, echoed a graceful backdrop of wavy cumulus clouds. Above Lehmi Pass, one supreme rainbow tapped a ridiculous polka-dot cloud, paying homage to a cottony cumulonimbus fringed with pink. like a dyed carnation. The Yellow Brick Road momentarily flared into an orange stripe flanked with ripening peaches. Then, the entire sky burst into every pastel color Easter has ever seen. SeeHawk and I could hardly keep hiking, for swiveling our heads back and forth, drinking gallons of beauty.

When I finally remembered to look straight upward, I noticed a strange swirl in the overhead clouds. Being near Lehmi Pass, there was no turning back.

"Sprint," I cried.

Together, we downshifted into our final race for the day.

SeeHawk was first to duck underneath the high-voltage power lines.

I held my breath while ducking through after him.

Of course, it was silly to duck, since the power lines were floating high above our heads, but one question lingered. What about the recent storm's Final Strike? Waiting for it felt like a pause between hiccups. The strike had to be coming because no thunderstorm lasting for an hour could leave the stage without taking a bow. Or could it? Was my Final Strike theory about to be disproven? I kept my ears peeled while we merged onto a graded dirt road that crookedly descended toward Lehmi Pass.

SeeHawk walked close alongside me, feeling overheated from hurrying downhill. The moment our shoes touched flat ground, he yanked off his sweaty baseball cap and let his hair breathe.

"SeeHawk!" I shrieked. "Your hair! Your HAIR!"

"My what?" he chuckled. "Oh, do I have hat head? Ha-ha, never mind. We'll be asleep soon anyway."

"No!" I gasped. "Your HAIR is up! It's STANDING STRAIGHT UP!"

He chuckled again, "Oh, that's okay. It's probably just oily. Here, let me show you how easy it is to flatten."

He dragged one meaty palm across his whole scalp, smoothing all the hair flat, and, sure enough, that did the trick. His hair took a snooze, for about one second, before it popped straight up again!

"RUN!" I shrieked.

Run? Going into our 24th-mile for the day? Both of us could barely walk.

"Just reach the trees," I begged him. "Come on. Once we get there, you'll totally be able to stop. I'll drag your backpack into camp if you want."

The trees were less than ¼ mile away.

SeeHawk did not take my warning seriously. To him, the overhead clouds looked harmless. Besides, it had not thundered for nearly half an hour. No Final Strike could be that delayed. Also, he could not see his own hair, so he had no idea what was freaking me out.

I felt anguished, watching him sluggishly bring up the rear. Should I stick with him, or run to safety?

The road dipped slightly to round a blind curve. Soon, we were only 100 yards from the trees. Then, 20 yards. Then, so close we could almost smell them, which is where a strange thing happened. Both of us simultaneously ran out of breath. It happened precisely at the same instant. We were seconds away from safety. We could almost have crawled to Lehmi Pass, and yet, both of us had to collapse over our knees.

When my eyes met SeeHawk's, hysteria erupted. We could hardly laugh for wheezing.

"Sorry for being a worry-wart," I admitted, "but your hair. Seriously, it looked like you were being electrocuted."

BANG!

Lightning struck the road, so close behind us that we almost fell over in surprise.

Ten frantic leaps carried us to safety, with a flash flood chasing us into the woods. Rain erased everything for about three minutes. Afterward came silence so deep that SeeHawk and I could almost hear each other think. Its message was clear. *Mortals beware. You must NEVER disrespect the Final Strike.*

After surviving that close call, SeeHawk had no complaints about needing to find Poppa Jim's spring after dark. It was vigorously flowing, and its water tasted delicious.

I spent his absence pitching our tent beside a pile of neatly cut firewood, upon whose ends some joker with a *Sharpie* had drawn smiles, google-eyes, mustaches, and buckteeth. Dozens of funny faces stood guard over our tent while Fate watched us sleep if such a thing existed.

Somewhere nearby, beneath the same stars, Redbeard and Teach were struggling to recover from agonizing thirst. They had hiked without water for sixteen miles after failing to locate an off-trail water source. The next morning, they were going to wake up vowing never again to let their bottles run dry, no matter what any guidebook promised in terms of reliable water sources.

Chapter 12

Perspective

If we had no winter, the spring would not be so pleasant.

- Anne Bradstreet

"Lemme pass," SeeHawk joked while elbowing me off the CDT's exit from Lehmi Pass.

It was early in the morning, but July 24 already felt hot enough to make us dream about cold streams, ice, and popsicles.

The trail leaving our campsite dipped into a saddle crossed by Captain Meriwether Lewis almost 200 years earlier. History says Lewis mistook the Lehmi River for "the great Columbia River." Therefore, imagine his surprise upon peeking over the Continental Divide. Yes, by golly. He saw another "sea of mountains" where he had expected to lay eyes upon the Pacific coastline.

Um. Clark? Ha-hem. I gotta tell you, buddy, I think you were right when you said we shouldn't have eaten those mushrooms.

In the aftermath of that guffaw, Captains Lewis and Clark enlisted the Shoshoni Indians to give them a crash course in western topography. Once comprehending the lay of the land, their Corps of Discovery continued forth, canoeing, horseriding, and walking, until they successfully reached the Pacific Ocean. The Corps overwintered in forts they built near the ocean, ate salmon up to their chins, and returned to Saint Louis, Missouri the following year. Incredibly, they arrived home having lost only one man, while crossing 7,689 miles' worth of snowbound mountains and rapid rivers, enduring extreme cold and heat, battling periodic starvation, and encountering Native Americans who were not always friendly. As a bonus, they returned with documentation of many new animal species, including jackrabbits, coyotes, prairie dogs, pronghorn antelope, bighorn sheep, Rocky Mountain goats, and grizzly bears.

SeeHawk and I could hardly imagine undertaking such an adventure. By comparison, our cushy little thru-hike seemed meaningless and easy. However, perhaps we had one thing in common with The Corps, which was taking each new challenge one day at a time.

For instance, on the morning we left Lehmi Pass, our goal was simply to reach Quartzite Spring by the day's end. All this required was putting one foot in front of the next, since the entire route consisted of signed trails and reliable dirt roads.

With July's bright sun climbing high into the sky, we started skirting small mountains whose colors flipped from green to silver in passing. Each color shift was caused by green conifer trees covering the mountains' north sides and silver sagebrush covering on their south sides, such that the color changed abruptly from north to south. Seen together from their south sides, the mountains as a group resembled green-edged silver fish scales, adding a little panache to the otherwise drab landscape.

Wyoming was a short distance ahead. As the crow flies, we could have gotten there in no time. However, on foot, we were slated to spend another 9 days completing our 3-week long, east-west-east loop around Montana's Big Hole Valley.

We had entered the southern mountains expecting a full menu of adversity. Heat. Steep terrain. Lightning. Thirst. Dirt everywhere. It was all business as usual along Montana's southern border. Therefore, we hardly blinked when a high-pressure gale smacked us to attention, near Goat Mountain. The powerful windstorm shoved us uphill, over the top, and down through a graveyard of dead whitebark pine trees, before releasing us into a green forest shading Quartzite Spring. It had been a noisy ride, but when dusk showed us a tree-sheltered campsite, a whistle blew somewhere and everything fell silent.

Quartzite Spring was a fountain of youth by thru-hiking standards. We splashed our faces clean, rehydrated our soup, and filled our mugs with cold, clean water.

Our neighbors for the night were 50 mooing and pooping forest cows, who all gathered around the next morning to watch us cook hot banana-cereal, but then ditched our scene without saying goodbye.

We had woken up early to eat breakfast in camp, before hiking nonstop along five miles of dirt roads connecting Quarzite Spring to Highway 19. Our hope was to hitchhike early enough that we could reach Leadore, Idaho before the highway turned into an oven. This scenario sounded a lot better than walking 13 miles along scorching-hot pavement, with no view of anything besides dusty mountains. Assuming success, we were hoping to fetch our next resupply box during the afternoon and return to Bannock Pass the following morning.

A billboard sign formalizing the dirt road's transition from forest to high desert said, *Leaving SALMON National Forest. Land of Many Uses.* Far to one side, we saw a shallow valley floored with bright emerald grass, which must either have been covering an oasis or receiving piped irrigation. Its backdrop of mountains could have passed for giant sand dunes if they had been white instead of brown. Even alongside the road, everything wore a thick coating of dirt, including haggard sunflowers, sinewy lupins, and sagebrush chewed into stumps by cattle.

July's long hours made the sun work overtime, but it climbed without rest until we landed inside a hard dirt parking lot, unceremoniously crowning Bannock Pass. Three small billboard signs, casting three squares of shade onto a plane of bare dirt, invited us to enjoy three personal-sized rectangles of coolness. Collectively, the signs spelled *Bannock Pass. EL. 7,672 FT. This traditional Indian route provided access from Montana's buffalo country to snake and salmon river fishing streams. Welcome to IDAHO.* One sign featured a dramatic illustration of snow-capped mountains, bearing no resemblance whatsoever to Bannock Pass on July 25. Had Idaho's park service tried to save money by repurposing a sign from Switzerland? Nah. More likely, the artist lived in Idaho year-round.

First thing after dropping his backpack into the billboards' tepid shade, SeeHawk turned around and walked to the parking lot's north end. Peeking downhill, he saw zero cars driving up or down Highway 29. Nothing was moving. It was all dead silence. Feeling instantly bored, he came back to the billboards' shade and sat down beside me.

Together, we attracted a few high-flying vultures.

Once I grew restless, I headed back into the sunlight and shuffled around aimlessly, like a pasture horse without an appetite. Shimmers of heat were starting to crinkle Idaho's brown mountains. A few token pine trees gave Highway 29 a wide berth. My eyes searched everywhere within walking distance of the highway and found no shade larger than our hideout beneath the billboard signs. Thinking about water reminded me to ration. Meals were forbidden until we reached Leadore because every entree we had left required boiling in too much water.

When my brain started complaining, I read the billboard signs again, just to do something.

SeeHawk spent the same eternity rocking back and forth from his heels to his toes. He was thinking about the movie *Once Upon A Time In The West*. Specifically, he was remembering the opening scene in which a pesky fly buzzes around an outlaw waiting for a train. Bannock Pass looked so desolate that he doubted outlaws, or even flies, would bother going there by choice.

Eventually, I borrowed SeeHawk's camera and photographed the billboard signs, just to be productive.

Meantime, he wandered away again, to relive the disappointment of seeing no cars crossing any brown horizons.

During his absence, I returned to the shade and stole a sip of water. My skin felt dry. That seemed disturbing. On such a hot morning, I should have been sweating. Another small sip seemed justified. for precaution against heat-stroke, but that was all. SeeHawk and I both needed to conserve, in case we might end up walking to Leadore.

As the minutes ticked on, malaise set in. I quit watching the highway and just used my ears. How might it sound to hear a car approach? There was no telling since no cars had come along. Occasionally, I stole another sip of water, feeling guilty but doing it anyway.

When SeeHawk finally returned from sightseeing, his face looked more relaxed. He tried to make small talk, but, Clump! The taste of dry air made his mouth shut quickly. All he could do was collapse back into his personal plot of shade.

The next 30-minutes passed like waiting for a doctor. Finally, we lost patience and marched off the pass. The parking lot sat only a few yards behind when two black SUVs came barreling over a ridge east of the pass. Holy Batmobiles! They were aiming toward the highway!

Feeling awestruck, we watched the two melting shapes solidify through a cloud of heat distortion. It was like watching a dystopic action movie. More importantly, both vehicles had empty backseats!

SeeHawk and I leaped into a wild dance. Thumb-waggles. Voiceless pleading. We did it all, while the first SUV's driver brazenly sped past us. Ditto for the second. Vroom. Vroom. Off went both vehicles into Idaho's brown mountains, with their drivers appearing not to even have seen us.

"Dang, have we lost our touch?" I worried.

Trying to stay positive, SeeHawk replied, "Maybe they both had a train to catch."

Getting ignored had been a letdown, but, at least, seeing cars gave us some encouragement. We discussed whether lunchtime might summon more traffic. One foreseeable problem with walking off the pass was that Highway 29 had an extremely narrow shoulder. Drivers speeding along might feel afraid to pick us up. Thinking along those lines convinced us to turn around and strive for patience.

I kept myself calm by pretending to drink a cold *Cherry Pepsi*.

SeeHawk slouched beside me, drinking cold *Cherry Coke*. After emptying the bottle, he still felt thirsty. A broad silver knife helped him split open a watermelon, juicy and full of seeds. The juice dripped down his chin. Maybe it would taste good with a stick of salty buffalo jerky. Suddenly, SeeHawk realized he was seeing two red cowboy shirts jouncing down a hillside one-quarter-mile away. Inside the shirts sat two horseback riders. They were aiming toward a pickup truck hooked to a horse trailer. Wait, how had we failed to notice the pickup truck?

"Payday!" SeeHawk shouted.

"Go get 'em, cowboy!" I cheered.

My partner took off running.

I stayed beside the highway, being ready, in case his absence might trigger Murphy's Law.

The red-shirted cowboys were loading up their horses. See-Hawk hollered out in greeting. Both heads turned.

I was too far away to hear anything they said. My heart pounded, while I stood near the billboards, watching and wishing.

Finally, SeeHawk came trotting back. His pace said, yes! There was no time to explain.

The cowboys were already driving their pickup truck toward Bannock Pass. From a distance, they looked barely out of high school. A blue-eyed cowgirl sitting in the back seat was probably married to the older man in the driver's seat. She wore men's riding clothes, with a white cowboy hat pulled low over her eyes and fitted snugly against her blonde ponytail.

The driver called out, when he pulled up, "Howdy!"

"Hello," I answered, not wanting to sound like a tourist with cowboy envy.

SeeHawk rejoined me, just in time to hear the driver give us a quick rundown. He could only drive us a couple of miles because he needed to stop and pick up some bulls.

SeeHawk and I locked eyes. Would a two-mile jumpstart be worth leaving our strategic position on the pass?

Six blue eyes barked, *Hurry up.*

"Okay!" I grinned.

The driver pointed toward his trailer hitch. Gulp! Wait, a minute. Was he suggesting to have our backpacks ride on the hinged metal joint between his pickup truck and horse trailer? Now, hold on there, buddy. All our hopes and dreams were stuffed inside those soft nylon pouches. If the trailer bounced and sent them flying to either side or if they fell straight down and got run over by the trailer? Holy road rash! Could we take such a risk? I almost said, "no thanks." Except, during that same moment, two flop-eared cattle dogs jumped onto the hitch like a couple of kids boarding a carnival ride. Apparently, riding the trailer hitch was a regular activity for the dogs. No leashes. No cages. No missing limbs, either. I still had the willies, but if a cowboy thought it was safe enough for his cattle dogs, then perhaps our backpacks could ride with them. Still, it was hard not to cringe while I watched our backpacks being casually slung onto the slick metal hitch. Nothing got tied down. The dogs waggled over to sniff their new traveling companions.

Next, it was SeeHawk's and my turn to climb into the pickup truck's air-conditioned king cab. At that point, we could still have jumped-shipped, grabbed our backpacks, and smothered them with apologies. Were we making a terrible mistake? Well, the alternative did not look good either, so I put on my brave face and climbed on in.

It felt exhilarating to get forced-air refrigerated for a short ten minutes. Next thing SeeHawk and I knew we were stepping onto Highway 29's skinny shoulder, somewhere near some bulls who needed moving.

The eldest cowboy told us in parting, "We'll be back in a couple of hours. If you're still here, we'll drive you the rest of the way to town."

"Don't worry," I laughed. "By that time, we should be long gone."

The first thing we did was vacate the pavement. Never mind expecting less traffic than a skunk farm. We set up shop on the highway's gravelly shoulder, just anywhere, since one patch of dirt looked as good as the next. I futzed around, molding my backpack into something between a lumpy chair and a backrest, while SeeHawk started rummaging through his pockets. The sun's heat seemed concentrated by lacking access to shade. What was that clear stuff running alongside us? Hey. Eureka! It was a stream! Except, scratch that. It was really more of a drainage gutter. The water came out of a culvert pipe tunneled beneath the highway. Still, though, what an excellent surprise! Could we drink it? Or, at least, stick our feet into it?

"No way," SeeHawk said firmly. "The acidity from all that cow pee might dissolve our toes."

Darn, but all right. We just plunked ourselves down between the untouchable water and radiating asphalt, hoping not to be there for a while.

SeeHawk passed the time memorizing pawprint illustrations from a book called *Scats and Tracks*.

I sat empty-handed, feeling hot and thirsty. My thumb stayed cocked, ready to flip an invisible cigarette lighter if any vehicle appeared, no matter its size, shape, or color. I was eager to advertise our need for a ride, but what good was eagerness without an audience?

As the minutes ticked by, my imagination traveled backward in time. I became a vintage American hippie, sitting alongside Route 66 with all my worldly needs crammed into a rucksack and my clothes reeking of freedom. I felt infinitely patient because I had no commitments and could wait however long it might take to catch a ride. A visiting breeze ruffled my ponytail. Its pillow of coolness momentarily lifted hairs off the back of my neck. Ooh, that felt good. The sky looked beautiful. It was blue like a heartache in some funny love song. My soft, sticky shoes felt rooted to the earth. No longer restless, I could have sat still for hours, enjoying heat-imposed delirium...until it dawned on me that I was in danger. Uh-oh. My blood was boiling. I needed to drink water. One measured sip restored my senses. I needed to escape. The sun was too hot. But, where could I go?

The dream. My confusion. The asphalt's dizzying heat. It all got cleaved apart when, suddenly, an 18-wheeler roared over the northern horizon, hauling a wobbling, open trailer full of gigantic boulders.

SeeHawk and I leaped backward with alarm, even though we were already clear of the pavement. No chance, in heck, could we get picked up by such a monster. Even if its driver had been crazy enough to attempt stopping, short of crashing, probably one of the trailer's stockpiled boulders would have flown out and smashed us dead. We knew all of that, but hey, it never hurts to show people that things are looking up, right? So, we flashed our thumbs-up signals, not only to the first 18-wheeler but also to a couple more coming along after it. Each succeeding giant plastered us with more dust, before careening away and thundering into oblivion.

"Well, that was exciting," SeeHawk sighed, watching the caravan's dust cloud settle.

"The Land of Many Uses," I reiterated, thinking abstractly about industry and nature.

SeeHawk went back to reading *Scats and Tracks*.

Instead of turning into a hippie again, I took a sharp look around and caught my breath. Leaping lizards! What, in the name of oversights was parked across the highway? Two horse trailers? Why had we not looked over there before? Or, more specifically, why had we not noticed two long rectangles of shade containing two men eating lunch together? Land sakes, Nelly. How long had salvation been sitting across from us?

"Must go," I announced as if sleepwalking.

SeeHawk was too absorbed in studying pawprints to bother looking up. He just mumbled absentmindedly, "Go ahead, Sunshine. I'll stay right here and keep a watch out for cars."

As luck would have it, the sandwich eaters were government employees. Too bad because their job contract prohibited driving civilians to Leadore, but, at least, they could legally share their shade.

I sat off to one side, joining the men's conversation for so long that, eventually, the red-shirted cowboys and cowgirl returned, having finished fetching their bulls.

"How ya doin'?" one government man said, in greeting to the group coming down.

"Better n' ever," replied the oldest cowboy, smiling a bit too eagerly.

"Sure y'are," the government man smiled back. His tone sounded casual, almost like teasing, but it was obvious that he meant to perform an interrogation.

"Yeah, well, you know…" the cowboy awkwardly laughed.

It seemed like he and his wife had been through this drill before. Instinctively, they squatted side-by-side, resting elbows upon the knees of their tightly-stretched blue jeans, as if they had been sitting down at a conference table. It looked like they wanted to converse with the government men at their own eye level, probably to establish some rapport. However, both the cowboy and his wife kept their hats pulled low enough to almost hide their eyes. Also, while the former looked straight into the government men's eyes, his wife kept her gaze aimed toward the ground and never looked up.

"Where are your cows?" one of the interrogators demanded.

Having anticipated the question, the cowboy confessed, "I've been having a little trouble getting them to stay put, lately." He went on to explain that his cows had been coveting a neighbor's "greener" grass. On Sunday, they had been legal, but, since, their migration path was anybody's guess.

The government man seemed less interested in anything the cowboy said than in reading his face. After enough cow questions were asked, his next topic was, "Have you sprayed for weeds?"

That question lifted a few pounds out of the air. It seemed that all four participants were united in their resentment of thistles, knapweed, spurge, and toadflax invading pastures where weeds did not belong.

I waited until the group finished speaking, before asking the cowboy and his wife if they could still give us a ride to Leadore.

Thank heavens, they said yes!

SeeHawk was still across the way, reading *Scats and Tracks*. He looked unaware of anything happening across the highway.

Did this mean he had been neglecting to watch out for cars? Who could say? Not him, since not a single car had come along during my absence.

When SeeHawk heard my summons for taking another ride in the air-conditioned king cab, he bounded across the highway like somebody had hollered, "Free tickets to Zappa."

Twenty minutes later, we arrived in Leadore, Idaho.

The older cowboy touched his hat and said to us in parting, "Whenever you get thirsty, remember that cow paths will always lead you to or from water."

* * *

An afternoon rumor flew around town, about an old lady seeing a stark-naked man peek out the door of Leadore's tiny Laundromat. Jeepers, who was he?

SeeHawk and I could guess, and sure enough. Inside a small, steamy room, we found Teach hovering over a washing machine that sounded determined to pound a hole in the floor. He flashed us a harried grin when we entered. I did not have to shut my eyes because he had gotten dressed after finishing his first load.

"Boy, are we surprised to see you!" I hollered, over the machine's deafening noise. "We thought you'd be far ahead of us by now."

"We would be," Teach hollered back, "if we didn't get lost for a WHOLE DAY near Fourth-of-July Creek. Redbeard doesn't listen to me, well enough. The whole time, I KNEW we were going the wrong way. I tell you, I've figured out how Midwesterners got stuck living in the Midwest. It's because they couldn't escape because they've got no sense of direction."

SeeHawk laughed loudest, being originally from Illinois.

Meantime, Teach launched into saying, "Yesterday, Redbeard and I ran out of water on the way to Lehmi Pass." His voice grew emphatic, "Do you know how delirious people can get from hiking sixteen straight miles without drinking water?"

"No, we don't," SeeHawk answered, feeling proud to flex his vigilance as our team's Chief Water Officer.

After recounting his adventure approaching Lehmi Pass, Teach remarked, "By the way, I talked with my mom on the phone and she's worried about you two."

"Why?" I wondered, secretly feeling flattered that she had even heard of us.

"Because she's afraid hiking the whole trail together will make you want to kill each other. She says my dad and her get along really well, but they could never stay together every minute of every day."

SeeHawk and I shared an easy laugh.

"Tell her we're fine," I assured him. "If we could hike the whole PCT together without killing each other, probably the worst we'll do on the CDT is drive each other crazy."

Having said that, it dawned on me that SeeHawk and I had not squabbled for quite some time. Did this mean we were finally working through our differences?

Teach lowered his voice to reveal, "One thing Redbeard and I have figured out is that the only times we bug each other is when somebody feels frustrated. I hate how Redbeard acts whenever he's frustrated, and he hates how I act whenever I'm frustrated. So, if either of us gets into a bad mood, we just have to split up and give each other space."

"Good strategy," I acknowledged. "Except, SeeHawk and I have a rule to always stay together, so we can't lose each other."

"Then, I guess you'll just have to keep driving each other crazy," Teach winked while stuffing his freshly washed clothes into the Laundromat's only dryer. "More power to you for being able to stay friends. I just wanted to let you know what works for us because we seem to be getting along great these days. In fact, we're getting along so well that," he dropped his voice lower, "I think we're starting to become telepathic."

"How so?" I asked him.

"Well, for one thing, we seem to magically be able to hike at the same speed, even when we're separated and not able to see each other. It's like we can intuitively sense whether to slow down or speed up. Sometimes, we even know what the other person is going to say before he opens his mouth. I'm not talking about normal stuff. Sometimes, it's really weird things the other person couldn't possibly have known."

"We've had the same experience!" SeeHawk marveled.

Dryly, I reminded him, "It doesn't take mental telepathy to know you're thinking about either water or camp time."

"Oh, yeah?" he shot back. "Well, it also doesn't take mental telepathy to know you'd like to squeeze in three extra miles."

Teach recognized his cue to exit and told us to look for him at the RV park.

Left alone with the overheated washing machine, SeeHawk and I felt guilty about taxing it further, but not guilty enough to have mercy. In went our stink pile. Plink, plink, plink. We popped in several quarters, slid the noisy coin acceptor into its sheath, and headed back out to Leadore's empty highway.

Local pedestrians said their town had two restaurants known to serve dinner. On our way to compare both window menus, we happened to notice an odd-looking fellow meandering through a gas station across the street. He seemed to be aiming toward us but it was hard to tell, because he kept sidling off course as if drunk or confused, and his head kept glancing from side to side. Gosh, was he a thru-hiker? If skinniness qualified, then maybe. If sun-bleached hair and burnt-brown legs proved it, then probably. His clothing certainly fit the stereotype. A synthetic blue t-shirt with purple nylon shorts and flimsy white sneakers outfitted him perfectly for southern Montana's heat. Also, he wore a soft nylon rucksack, slung over his shoulder like an oversized purse.

When the youth drew close enough for us to be sure, I forgot to be polite and gasped with surprise, "Wow, you sure are sunburned!"

He explained, with the zeal of being barely over twenty, "That's because I don't wear sunscreen or a hat."

Several nickel-sized flakes of dry skin, peeling off raw wounds perforating his chest, drove me to remark, "We can see that."

Not at all fazed, he announced, "My name's Boomhauer. I came here from Florida." And onward he went, describing himself to be an experienced thru-hiker, currently soloing the CDT, but temporarily traveling with a man named P.E.

When I mentioned the Book of Beans, Boomhauer went on a lark. He had been gifted the whole guidebook series by a generous relative. After skimming through it for two minutes, he had decided it was useless and tossed it into the trash!

SeeHawk and I could not resist giggling, but we had to admit, the Book of Beans had successfully guided us through many sticky situations. Our rants were mostly about just two beefs. We would have preferred getting rid of the giant photographs to save weight, and it was tough having most of the guidebooks' directions be written opposite to our aim.

Growing curious, I asked Boomhauer, "Has using only Jim's guidebook kept you on course?"

"Mostly," he said. "I've also got a compass, so I can always just aim. I'm still learning how to use it, but from what I've learned so far, it seems pretty easy. You just have to figure out how to get it to tell you north, south, east, or west."

I raised an eyebrow and skeptically asked, "What about when the trail aims diagonally to those headings?"

"I still just aim," Boomhauer insisted. "You figure, it's a southbound trail, so if you head south for long enough, eventually you'll run into the CDT."

Criminy. Whether or not that logic made sense, we had to give the young man merit points, for having reached Leadore.

"Are you strictly following the CDT?" I asked him.

Boomhauer stared at me, looking confused.

"I mean, are you trying to hike every mile of the trail?"

"Of course," he answered, "I'm doing the official trail."

Point taken. My question had been silly. Anyone could see that Boomhauer was a purist. In fact, simply breaching the subject got him started listing every single item in his ultralight possession, which was not much. Basically, it came down to one body-sized sheet of Tyvek (serving as his tarp), one hoop-supported mosquito net (his tent), one summer-weight sleeping bag, and a liter-sized water bottle. He did not carry a stove (not even featherweight like Blue Man's). Instead, he and P.E. exclusively ate cold food purchased from trailside towns. Nobody was shipping them food from home, except for maybe a rare box of cookies. Mostly, they ate potato chips, corn chips, canned tuna, cheese, crackers, and anything frosted by *Little Debbie*.

"Does eating junk food for every meal give you enough energy to feel good, when you're hiking twenty-eight miles per day?" I queried Boomhauer.

He earnestly bragged, "*Doritos* are the mainstay of my success."

"Have bears ever tried to raid your empty tuna cans?"

Shrugging, he replied, "We sleep with our food and don't have any problem. People talk about bears, but I've been on two thru-hikes before and never had a bear try to get into my tent."

SeeHawk's reaction alerted me to warn him, "Don't you dare think about sleeping with our food."

Caught red-handed, my partner grinned, "Okay, but just remember. If I didn't need to hang anything, I could use the extra time to meditate, which would put me in a better mood all day."

Getting back to interviewing Boomhauer, my next question was, "What do you wear for rain protection? Just the Tyvek you sleep on?"

"Oh no," he chuckled. "I never worry about rain. Good weather follows me wherever I go. I know it sounds crazy but I swear, it's true. I've hiked the whole AT, PCT, and CDT down to here, and never had any problem with bad weather. If you want my good luck to rub off on you, just stick near me. Good weather follows me wherever I go."

I wanted to laugh, but I held it in.

Boomhauer was being completely serious.

Next, I asked which of the CDT's two "official" routes he was planning to follow out of Bannock Pass. It was a choice between the new CDT, from Sheep Creek to Interstate Highway 15, or else an older route described by Poppa Jim.

Boomhauer thought for a moment before answering, "Jim does make the new trail sound confusing, but his old route might not count after the new trail's been cut."

SeeHawk and I shared Boomhauer's respect for the word "count." Even though we had "dinged our new truck" several times since leaving Canada, deep-down, we were still purists, which meant we wanted to strictly follow the CDT whenever possible.

"Speaking of commitment," I told Boomhauer, "we're kind of on a mission to order some dinner."

Boomhauer said he would meet us at the RV Park, and off he went, as if pushed by a shifting breeze.

Before SeeHawk and I could return to reading menus, along came P.E. prancing up the sidewalk. As soon as the slightly older man introduced himself, we could tell he was from circa New York. His lanky stature, rubbery joints, and skinny limbs said volumes about surviving on Boomhauer's junk-food diet. He had soft brown skin and curly black hair, which made him look ageless. He was not a drifter, though, because employed full-time as a physical education teacher, and he was ten years older than Boomhauer, but they did have in common past completion of the Appalachian Trail.

When I mentioned that Boomhauer claimed to be averaging 28 miles per day, P.E. confided, "Frankly, he hikes too fast for me. I'm always struggling to keep up. It's crazy. We never get any time to rest. I'd rather slow down, sometimes, and enjoy the scenery."

SeeHawk remarked, "It's no wonder Boomhauer can hike that fast since he hardly carries any weight. Is your backpack small, like his?"

"Not quite," P.E. answered. "All Boomhauer carries is a tarp, mosquito net, sleeping bag…" Etcetera and so forth. He proceeded to list off every item Boomhauer carried as if reciting a grocery list.

After agreeing to see P.E. at the RV Park, SeeHawk and I finally got around to reading one restaurant's menu. Before we could form an opinion, though, we got ambushed by three separate locals who all recommended the Sagebrush Café.

I had no idea what to expect upon walking through the restaurant's front door. Would its cook be a plump matron, pan-frying chicken? Or a corn-fed *Grizzlies* fan, chicken-frying steak? Such questions never crossed my mind, until SeeHawk and I received an enthusiastic welcome from a slender soubrette with the Cheshire Cat's smile and eyes like a wolf. Giggles burst out of the woman like bubbles. We asked her a few questions and gasped at her work ethic. Daisy from Wisdom could not have worked harder. This one-woman-army operated The Sagebrush Cafe 7 days a week, serving breakfast, lunch, and dinner with just one employee helping her cook, wash dishes, wait tables, and chat up the counter crowd. She and Daisy both deserved equal respect as ironclad vertebrae in The Backbone of America.

The Sagebrush Café's dinners came in reasonable portions. Therefore, SeeHawk and I returned the next morning having no idea that it would be dangerous to order two ranch-sized omelets with biscuits-and-gravy and hash browns on the side. Nor did we realize how long it might take for our breakfasts to arrive, with just the same two ladies servicing a full house.

SeeHawk passed the time drinking bottomless coffee.

I sipped hot chocolate.

Together, we sank our noses into month-old newspaper comics, which distracted us from the din of roaring laughter and clattering dishes.

Spiderman's enemy was getting caught red-handed when a tiny "ding" went off in the kitchen.

"That's my gravy," SeeHawk mumbled.

Not immediately catching his meaning, I asked, "What's your gravy?"

"The microwave dinged. My gravy must be hot."

When I realized what his ears had detected through all the dining room's noise, I teased him, "Is trail hunger turning you into Pavlov's Dog?"

"Right now, Pavlov's Dog wouldn't be able to match me for facedown eating," he predicted.

Within minutes, two steaming mountains of food landed on our table with a loud thud. Not even Pavlov's Dog could have finished both plates. By the time we quit trying, we had to stagger out of the café clutching swollen stomachs.

Back in the RV Park, sunlight danced across a poetic view of Idaho's silken grasslands. It felt splendid to take long, hot showers with tingly *Dr. Bronner's* peppermint soap. We dried off without realizing the soap dispenser had been filled by our PCT friends, Bob and Jane (recently missing us as they section-hiked the CDT northbound, like two opposite ships passing in the night).

Once breakfast sank below our necks, we got right to work striking our tent in preparation to leave town. Beside us sat some flattened grass, evacuated earlier by Redbeard and Teach who were already hitchhiking back to Bannock Pass. Two erect tarps still stood on the grass, respectively belonging to Boomhauer and P.E. The partners were seated together at a nearby picnic table, sorting through their latest mini-mart purchases like kids dividing Halloween candy.

Boomhauer talked while he worked, in a voice that gradually rose in pitch and became more garbled. Words left his mouth in a logical order but did not seem to make much sense.

Somehow, though, either P.E. understood everything his partner was saying, or else he just had a knack for empathy because he kept interjecting supportive remarks like, "Totally, man ... Yeah, it can go like that ... I hear what you're saying ... That's the way the ball bounces."

Finally, in a hushed whisper, I asked SeeHawk how much of the conversation he could understand.

"Not one word," he confided.

After strapping shut his ultralight backpack, Boomhauer picked it up and groaned, "Wow, that's heavy!"

He did not appear to be joking.

SeeHawk and I struggled not to openly compare the Floridian's lightweight gear and 4-day food supply with our heavier gear and 9-day food supply. It grew harder to keep silent as Boomhauer's complaints mounted, until, finally, I lost patience and challenged him to a duel.

"You want to feel heavy?" I proposed. "Set down your backpack and try lifting SeeHawk's."

Boomhauer shot back, "Yeah, I know. My backpack's REALLY heavy."

Louder, I repeated, "Yes, but try lifting SeeHawk's."

Seeming not to hear me, Boomhauer repeated, "This load is gonna be tough to carry out of Bannock Pass."

Growing exasperated, I argued, "But you've only packed four days' worth of food, not NINE like those of us who aren't resupplying in Lima. Feel the difference. I promise you'll be stoked about your pack-weight from now on."

Finally, I just gave up trying and let Boomhauer win. Good thing, too because the joke came full circle one hour later. It began with local man Ned offering to drive SeeHawk and me back to Bannock Pass. Our eyes widened as we watched a man more than twice our age fling SeeHawk's backpack into his pickup truck like it hardly weighed anything.

Once behind the wheel, Ned began sharing impressive war stories.

"You think your backpacks are heavy?" he winked. "When I was a paratrooper in 'Nam, we had to jump out of airplanes wearing two hundred pounds of gear and ammunition. Then, it was our job to search out the V.C. You wanna know scary? Spend a night in the jungle."

Deep creases etching Ned's face grew deeper with remembrance, as his consciousness traveled back in time.

"After notifying the bombers, we'd be given coordinates to rendezvous with the helicopter and get the hell out, without getting killed. I hated being involved in any effort to kill humans, V.C. or not," Ned added, for the record.

He went on to explain that it had been his code of honor to always witness whatever he and his associates did, so they would remain accountable for their actions. Also, he made clear that his reasons for going to Vietnam had been partly because our president said it would ultimately save lives, and partly because he had sworn to serve his country, without second-guessing his superiors.

The confession ended with him saying, "Vietnam was the ugliest war you could imagine. But, you know what? Fighting wasn't the hardest part. It was coming home that broke my heart. Here, we had gone through so much hell, doing what our government told us we HAD to do, and when we got home, we expected the people for whom we had risked our lives to feel proud of us, but they jeered, and shouted that we had done it all for nothing." His voice trailed off into bitter silence.

How must that reception have felt, I wondered, with so many haters being unable to see his pain? Right on the spot, I felt cured of any illusion that carrying 40 pounds on my back, hiking 20 miles per day on maintained trails, and spending less than two hours hitchhiking were burdens worthy of complaint.

The humble veteran, who still served his community as a volunteer firefighter, shared a memory from my home state.

"Back when I lived in California," he recalled, "you know how I always knew I was home? It was when we flew over the Statue of Liberty. Then, came the Golden Gate Bridge. Those were the two sights I always looked forward to, Statue of Liberty and the Golden Gate Bridge."

I had grown up seeing the Golden Gate Bridge regularly and never got a homey feeling from seeing it. Therefore, I wondered what, personally, gave me a homey feeling. Right off the bat, I knew it was nothing that could be held in my hand, like jewelry or a photograph. Nor, was it the comforting sweetness of hot chocolate, a favorite stuffed animal, an old sweatshirt, or even a cherished memory. My own anchors seemed to include smelling dry grass mixed with sweet wildflowers, feeling a warm breeze caress my skin, and basking in the shade of giant oak trees. Perhaps that explains why I enjoyed sleeping on the Continental Divide. However, I did not immediately feel at home where Ned dropped us off, on the summit of Bannock Pass.

The breeze that greeted us was a godsend because 3:00 p.m. was a dreadful hour to cross southern Montana's sunbaked mountains. Everything in the foreground looked as desolate as a party without guests. All we could hear was imposing silence.

With reality setting in, I began to wonder. Were we ever going to see Redbeard and Teach again? By now, they had to be a whole day ahead of us. We were hoping to catch them sooner or later, but as we started to climb, sluggishness hit us like a ton of bricks. Even if our backpacks were not paratrooper-heavy, they were still heavy. Also, we felt hungover from the breakfast we had eaten five hours earlier. But, shoot, we could not stop climbing and just dumbly stand in the middle of nowhere, with no shade, water, or victory in sight. Therefore, we forced our balking legs to keep slowly moving.

The route leaving Bannock Pass consisted of two parallel tire ruts, commandeered by the CDT for use as a hiker trail.

SeeHawk started groaning when the load crushing his shoulders found some tender meat and started to dig in.

I felt determined not to complain about my pack weight. Only once did I need to pause and tuck folded napkins underneath my bra straps.

Near the top of the first incline, I burst out laughing. The mountains overlooking Idaho looked like Russet potatoes.

Thinking about potatoes led me to remember a certain glass jar weighing down my backpack. Travesty of all travesties, it contained 16 oz. of processed cheese dip. Why in *Tostitos* name had I let Boomhauer's passion for junk food influence my better judgment? Truthfully, though, I could only blame myself. Cheese dip was one of my childhood fetishes. So, here I was, paying karmic tribute, by letting the plasticky orange goop weigh me down until whenever I might be able to eat it.

One moment of weakness digest me to beg, "After we digest, will you please help me out? Just a couple of bites? With nice crunchy chips?"

SeeHawk gruffly reminded me, "How many times have I told you? Cheese dip is not my thing. I've just never liked the taste."

"There's a first time for everything," I reminded him. "People change as they get older. Maybe your tastebuds have evolved since you last tried it."

"Doubtful," he grunted

"Then, would you just eat some as a favor to the nicest person you know?"

"Niceness is overrated," he argued.

"Same with abstinence."

More and more, both of us were starting to readjust our shoulder straps into crooked positions that we hoped might relieve various shoulder pains.

SeeHawk did some thinking before he blurted out, "You know, spending a whole day taking it easy in Leadore reminded me how good it feels to relax."

Say WHAT? *Whoop, whoop. Slacker alert. Release the hounds!*

Instead of giving a voice to the sirens inside my head, I calmly replied, "Are you saying we shouldn't take any more rest days until we finish crossing the San Juan Mountains?"

"Sunshine," he growled. "Give your body a BREAK!"

Reacting quickly, I laughed, "Sure, sorry. I was just kidding. Hey, look at that!"

I pointed at a brown blur, zooming across a brown valley almost straight below us. When the blur crossed our sightline, its color changed from brown to white.

"Antelope!" I exclaimed.

There must have been 20-30 gallopers in the herd. Their abrupt color shift arose from first seeing their chests and then seeing their rumps.

Feeling eager to see any antelope at all, SeeHawk demanded, "What O'CLOCK, Sunshine?"

"I don't know," I stammered. "There they go. They're almost gone. You'll just have to follow my finger next time."

Finally, he spied a white blur formed by all the fleeing rumps, seconds before it flew over a foothill and vanished.

One hour later, my partner was still yammering about the impressive speed of antelope. Luckily for me, this diversion put him in such a good mood that he consented to eat a little processed cheese dip.

At the end of the evening, we pitched camp atop a high hill, nestled against a backstop of sheltering whitebark pine trees. It would have been impossible to eat a full dinner, but we needed to lose some pack weight, so we coaxed our bloated bellies to accept creamed-spinach-and-sweet potato soup. At the same time, we watched the sinking sun touch Idaho's brown horizon.

"Someday, I'd like to watch the sun go all the way down, without ever looking away," I sighed.

"You can do that right now," SeeHawk suggested.

Laughing, I agreed, "You're right, I could."

Without further discussion, I dutifully polished off my last spoonful of soup.

Trying again, he emphasized, "I mean, you could have that full sunset experience right now, while we're sitting here."

I laughed again and got busy completing my evening camp chores.

The sky's afterglow remained bright long enough that we could read our next day's literature without using headlamps.

Finally, we kissed each other goodnight.

I closed my eyes, but, after a while, nothing happened. It still felt too early to fall asleep. Hoping to get drowsy, I shoved my head into SeeHawk's armpit, inhaled his calming pheromones, and thought about giant oak trees, green spring grass, The Statue of Liberty, and the Golden Gate Bridge.

A coyote howled at the rising sliver-moon.

Never mind whatever lay ahead. It felt good to be back in our home away from home.

* * *

Once again, during the night, I dreamed about being a superhero who could never catch the criminals I chased.

In the morning, I woke up feeling fresh and ready to hike fast...until I donned my backpack and tried to stand up straight.

When I noticed SeeHawk having the same problem, I told him, "The good thing is, starting off with nine days' worth of food means we'll feel like astronauts by the end of the week."

"You mean, thirsty for *Tang*?" he grimaced.

"Well, that too."

It felt harsh that we had to start climbing straight out of camp. Elk Mountain barely seemed to grow larger as we strained to reach its 10,194-foot summit. Thinking about the coming weeks and months, I wondered. How were we going to keep averaging 20 miles per day through progressively drier mountains, carrying increasingly heavy loads of water?

One nice reward for climbing Elk Mountain was that we got to rise above 10,000-feet for our first time on the Continental Divide Trail. Gazing eastward from the top, we saw a 10-mile chain of summits defining our next skywalk along America's Backbone. The Red Conglomerate Peaks, clustered 40 miles in the distance, flagged where we hoped to be in three days' time. Close on our right, a parallel valley's gunwale was crowned with the snow-capped Lehmi Peaks.

The next ten miles of trail were defined by a jeep track running continuously along the bald crest. Theoretically, we could descend from almost anywhere, but if lightning chased us? Step aside, ladies and gentlemen. We were going to need a fair head start to reach any cover of trees. Fortunately, Montana's weather gods seemed to be feeling kindly toward backpackers, judging by all the morning's clouds resting on both horizons.

I felt moved to suggest, "Maybe we're getting lucky because we've entered Boomhauer's fair-weather bubble."

"You're probably right," SeeHawk agreed, "since it sounds like his requests go right to the main office."

Succumbing to temptation, I could not resist adding, "So, you think we should try to stay near Boomhauer?"

"Absolutely," SeeHawk confirmed, not seeming to realize I was egging him on.

"Although, if we have worse weather luck than Boomhauer, maybe HE won't want to hike near US."

"Ooh, the old flip side," SeeHawk laughed. "That's true. Although, frankly, I think we have pretty good weather-luck, ourselves. I mean, hardly anyone besides us finished the PCT in Washington, two years ago. But, if Boomhauer feels worried about absorbing bad influences, he should definitely steer clear of those rain-magnet guys we met in East Glacier."

During the late morning, a lopsided meadow presented a good breakfast site next to a spring. We decided to sit down and eat lunch for breakfast. That way, if any storms moved in during the afternoon, we could just nibble on cold granola cereal and keep going.

Midway through eating, SeeHawk announced, "Speak of the devil!"

Looking up, I saw a sunburned Floridian approaching.

"Where's P.E.?" I wondered.

Boomhauer glanced over his shoulder and confessed with surprise, "I don't know. The last time I looked, he was right behind me. Guess it's been a while. What are you eating?"

I tipped forward my mug to show him, "Curried chickpeas with brown rice and olive oil."

"That figures," he teased. "Today, I have *Doritos* and cookies."

SeeHawk noticed Boomhauer's 1-liter water bottle looking half-empty and suggested he might want to refill it at the spring.

"Nah," the avowed minimalist shrugged. "Why carry extra, when I've already got enough to get by?"

"Because it's seven miles from here to the next water source," SeeHawk warned him.

Looking unconcerned, Boomhauer leaped to his feet, flashed us a smile, and bounded up the Continental Divide's next green incline. Within a quarter-hour, he crossed its summit and dropped out of sight.

Seconds later, P.E. appeared. He had been sweating hard from hurrying to catch up. Barely slowing down, he pointed toward the incline. It seemed like he lacked sufficient breath to ask.

"Yes," we nodded. "He went that-a-way."

"Thanks!" P.E. waved and kept going.

Toward mid-afternoon, it started to rain. By that time, See-Hawk and I had finished the whole 10-mile skywalk. We were safely below the crest and swimming in Morrison Lake. In fact, it was even better than that. We were basking in water so sinfully warm that adding a cold shower just doubled our pleasure.

After swimming, we spent a few extra moments examining the water's bizarre algae growths, colorful mineral deposits, and swirly blue snail shells. That was all the leisure we could afford, before duty's recess bell sent us packing.

At the end of a long day, we pitched camp beside a creek flowing through an open meadow. The site came packaged with relaxing dinner music, provided by a cluster of mooing cows. Less relaxing were the rubbery mozzarella clots exercising our teeth, jaws, and necks. Entertainment-wise, nothing could have been nicer than watching pink lightning zap the evening's red sky.

We slept beneath storm clouds slipping into darkness, and woke up admiring a fresh blue sky. In fact, it grew hot by the time the sun reached eye level.

Our first trailside attraction of the day was a sun-bleached cow skull, artistically nailed onto a CD-sign. We snapped a photo without ever wondering what the skull might be trying to tell us.

Soon afterward, we reached Tex Creek, whose shallow water gave us a choice between wet shoes or wobbly stepping-stones. I was busy examining the stones when a faraway voice caused me to look up. Gazing downstream and across the water, I saw two fly-fishermen, both dressed in flannels.

"---- -orning!" the shorter fisherman's voice warbled across the water. "--en -ou -et -- Harkness Lake, -an -ou te-- --- frien- -ill -e'll be there ---ight?"

"WHO?" I hollered.

"WILL," he hollered back. "--- waiting a- --- –ake for us. --- got food. Tell –im n-- -- eat it all, becau- we're al---- out of food.

B-- --- no problem because -- -as plenty. W--- you see WILL, TELL --m we-- -- --er- -onight, okay?"

"GOT IT!" I confirmed and gave him a thumbs-up.

Without further exchange, SeeHawk and I got back to business and rock-hopped across the creek.

Once we got back up to speed, my partner inquired, "What was that conversation about?"

"The fishermen are almost out of food," I explained. "They're supposed to meet a guy named Will at Harkness Lake. If we get there first, we're supposed to tell Will not to eat before they get there."

"Will's probably going to be stoked to have fresh fish for dinner," SeeHawk imagined.

"Except, it might be a late meal, since Harkness Lake is twelve miles from here, including some big climbs."

Speaking of lateness, SeeHawk and I lost the CDT just ten minutes beyond Tex Creek. The trail vanished upon a hillside crisscrossed with cow paths that all matched each other in size and appearance. The cow path we chose led us onto a partially forested plateau, where we found a manmade trail aiming in the right direction.

"This has to be the CDT," I told SeeHawk, "but I sure wish they'd have put up a sign for reassurance.

Before long, we came upon a trailside oak grove whose shade looked inviting. Stopping for breakfast, we sat upon a bed of crackling oak leaves and wetted our crunchy maple granola with water that turned to milk. Soon, we heard twigs snapping, followed by heavy footsteps coming up the cow path.

A man's voice called out, "Are you on the trail?"

From someplace closer, another voice answered, "I don't know."

SeeHawk and I looked at each other. Were we hearing the two fishermen we had seen at the creek? Should we offer them some help?

"I'm almost sure this is the CDT," I whispered to SeeHawk, "but I'd hate to influence them without being positive."

We decided to sit tight and let the men find us, thereby leaving it up to destiny. I kept expecting to hear more twigs snapping and see faces at any moment. Instead, after two moments, it seemed like the voices were gone. Uh-oh. Had both men retreated back the way they came? Or wandered off-course, due to losing track of each other? Then, a different idea struck me. What if they had found the real CDT, and we were the nincompoops following some other trail? Dread took hold, while we finished our cereal…until, finally, we heard boots crunching back up the cow path, followed by the tallest fisherman barging into our oak grove.

"Where's your friend?" I quizzed him.

He drawled like warm honey, "Taking a shit. By the way, is this the Continental Divide Trail?"

"We think so," I said.

"Let's hope so," SeeHawk added.

"Good," the fisherman grinned, visibly relaxing.

We interviewed him and learned he had traveled from Minnesota to Montana in order to help his friend backpack a short section of the CDT, on an assignment for the Continental Divide Trail Alliance. Now, the pair was headed back to Mission Control. They were going to inform team leader Will about the trail's condition in southern Montana.

"Probably Will's gonna pull into Harkness Lake right about now," the Minnesotan estimated, before twisting around to holler, "Hey! You DONE out there?"

Within seconds, we heard the hurrying man come huffing and puffing up the cow path. As soon as he appeared, both comrades fell in together, and off they went.

By this time, SeeHawk and I had finished eating, so we were able to strike breakfast quickly and catch up.

The Minnesotan, in particular, seemed glad for some lively conversation. After a while, though, we had to speed ahead, because his buddy could not keep pace with thru-hikers and we needed to stay on schedule.

Once back to being a twosome, SeeHawk and I climbed into a forested ravine checkered with broken sunlight. Its floor was a goulash of pine needles, rocks, and herbaceous greenery, snuggled inside the forest like a secret garden. We were in full stride, and getting near a timberline, when the trail we had been following for over a mile suddenly fizzled out. Why? Because we had reached the end of the line? Peering uphill, we saw a grassy crest underscoring a cloud-freckled sky. Our maps depicted the Continental Divide as a bold yellow line, which meant nothing since it was always obvious on paper. Two last minutes of climbing lifted us onto a grassy crest. Our eyes needed a moment to adjust from the forest's confinement to wide-open emptiness. We had been hoping for a red carpet welcome, but all we found was one giant stone cairn, posing against the sky like a pedestal that thought it was a statue. Also, we saw a smattering of green gentian stalks, pitted like corncobs from having dropped their flowers.

Overall, the highland ahead looked spectacularly disorganized. It was mostly horizontal, but instead of being solid, it was a conglomeration of ridges, bulging here and sagging there, like a failed soufflé. Two of its nearest landmarks included a short knoll and a tall, conical peak, neither of which stood out our topographical maps. Ditto for several half-moon cliffs, linear valleys, and a faraway string of high-voltage powerlines; they were all too insignificant or distant to show on our maps.

Feeling disconcerted, I muttered, "Houston, we have a problem."

SeeHawk cringed, not wanting to ask.

"Let's just do the Boomhauer thing for now," I decided. "We can check our maps again after we see something that really stands out."

The most obvious place to aim was around the knoll. Partway around, we lost sight of the cairn. On the knoll's backside, we ran into a surprise. Somebody had built a second cairn, precisely where the knoll blocked hikers from seeing both at once.

"Is this somebody's idea of a joke?" I complained.

Glancing back and forth, SeeHawk saw the problem. "We can't establish a trajectory, can we?"

Both of us hunted around for a third cairn.

Finally, I sighed, "Let's just keep ourselves in the ballpark, and pick up the pieces as we go."

A cool breeze cleared my head, while we proceeded generally toward everything green. During the next quarter-hour, I kept glancing backward to confirm the knoll was shrinking behind us, and it was. Well, hooray for that. Maybe our aim was nebulous, but, at least, we seemed to be getting somewhere.

One odd development was not seeing the fishermen appear behind us. What could have been keeping them? Were they stuck behind the knoll, scratching their fishing hats in confusion? Even if they were, we did not feel too worried, because the crest's open terrain was going to keep us visible, regardless.

Meantime, SeeHawk and I could hardly call ourselves leaders without establishing some kind of plan. Two diverging ridges looked promising. Both were more-or-less matched in altitude. The ridge that aimed left bordered a sidecar valley, clearly to be avoided. The ridge aiming straight ahead connected the nearby conical peak to some half-green mountains farther in the distance. I had been neglecting to use our compass, but our guidebooks seemed to have lost synchronization. A quick perusal of Poppa Jim's text produced no correspondence with the Book of Beans. Lacking Poppa Jim's updates made it impossible to know if we were following an old or new version of the CDT, assuming we were even on it. Thirdly, although Poppa Jim's guidebook provided a lot of detail, somehow we could not find any of its landmarks. For instance, where was his mentioned fence? In such open terrain, it should have been obvious. Did failing to see it mean we had merged onto the new CDT? If so, where was the Book of Beans' grassy two-track? How about its seasonal creek? Blazed trees? Signposts? No such landmarks materialized anywhere. Nothing was adding up correctly. Why was the Universe making this so difficult?

Before I could sort things out, the crest's gentle breeze exploded into a windstorm that almost snatched the pages I was holding and flung them out of my hands.

Panting with surprise, I told SeeHawk, "Forget the directions. Let's just figure out which mountain looks most likely to divide rainfall toward the east and west."

"Gadzooks, who can tell?" he shrugged. "They all have two sides."

After a moment of testing my theory, I agreed, "You're right. There are too many variables."

The only thing behaving properly was good old Helios, riding his shiny chariot across the sky. The golden god's steady progress urged us to get our act together and ignore the wind's commotion.

When we came alongside the conical peak, I glanced up and happened to spy a pimple capping its pointy summit.

"Is that a cairn?" I squealed.

Looking where I pointed, SeeHawk squinted like a raisin, trying to see the pimple.

"Why would the CDT aim way up there?" I wondered. "Who'd want to climb so high, just to come right back down on the other side?"

"Maybe for a really great view?" SeeHawk suggested.

"Better than this? How much better could the view be? We're already on top of almost everything."

It seemed like time to recheck Poppa Jim's guidebook. Deciding to risk it, I strategically faced my back toward the wind. Slowly and cautiously, I fished three folded pages out of my pocket. Covering half the text was necessary, to stop it from being spastically vibrated by the wind. All the words showing between my fingers looked blurry, through stray hairs whipping across my eyes. Hastily, I confirmed that we were supposed to climb an un-trailed mountain, by improvising switchbacks to compensate for its steepness. Well, how about that? There were not many peaks to choose from, and climbing the cone would, indeed, require improvisation. But, if Poppa Jim had climbed it, where was his missing fence?

Strengthening wind gusts prodded me to hurry up.

I folded everything away and curtly told SeeHawk, "Let's just climb a short distance and see what we find."

I knew my decision was silly. How could the CDT logically scale an isolated peak? I only got suckered because my overwhelmed brain asked my unthinking legs to take a turn at the wheel. Fortunately, it turned out that having the wind push us diagonally uphill eliminated any need for improvising switchbacks. Partway up the cone, we gained a rewarding view, which obviously did not belong to the CDT.

When SeeHawk saw me reach into my pocket, he knew we were finished climbing. Once again, I gripped the windblown pages like someone clutching money on a subway train. My eyes scanned the same jittering text I had read before, memorizing placenames and relevant landmarks. A wildcard wind gust hit while I was reading and snatched all the pages out of my hands. Wait, a minute. What happened? Oh NO! Faster than I could react, the stolen white pages shot downhill like scattering chickens.

"SEEHAWK!" I screamed. "That's our directions to Cottonwood Pass!"

He threw down his backpack and leaped into action.

There was no possible way to catch all three chickens. The gale was too powerful. Only by means of Divine Intervention could he have snatched two, before the third page skipped downhill faster than he could run.

Triumphantly returning back uphill, my flustered superhero shoved the two retrieved pages deep into my fist. Before letting go, he squeezed my fingers tightly around them. Then, he keeled over, heaving to catch his breath.

After inspecting both pages, I shakily reported, "No Cottonwood Pass, but don't worry, partner. I can get us to the pass, and from there we'll start using the pages you rescued. High-five, partner! You saved our butts, bigtime!"

I was stretching the truth, insofar as I had no idea how to utilize Poppa Jim's missing fence, grassy two-track, seasonal creek, blazed trees, or signposts, but, so what? Invisible landmarks were pretty much useless, anyway.

Cupping my hands, I shouted through the wind. "Let's traverse around from here and try the other side."

Before losing our backward view, SeeHawk glanced toward the knoll, one last time. He still could not see any fisherman. What, on Earth might they have been up to? Were they just lollygagging? That seemed unlikely, given their rush to bring Team Leader Will fresh fish for his dinner. Something else had to be delaying them. Something specific, like maybe a long lunch break? Giardia? Getting ambushed by malevolent woodland faeries? Regardless, SeeHawk and I still figured the fishermen were going to be okay, because the weather was cooperating, and the Minnesotan had seemed to know his left from his right.

As for "frying our own fish," though, it was high time for us to figure out where to aim next. Together, we circled through the wind's eye. Soon, the wind started pushing against our backs. A new view appeared. We had reached the peak's backside. Where were the missing landmarks? All we saw was a greater expanse of open green highland. That was a big letdown. Neither of us felt sure what to say.

Glancing downhill, my eyes caught sight of a thin brown line. It looked like a trail, aiming sideways to our goal. Where had it come from? Out of the sidecar valley behind the knoll? Out of *Disneyland's Magic Kingdom*? Feeling giddy, I gestured for SeeHawk to follow me downhill. It did not take long to confirm I had found a bona fide trail. Not only was it real. Furthermore, it was soft. Our shoeprints remained wherever we stepped. There were nobody else's shoeprints besides ours, so that answered one question. For better or for worse, we were not following Boomhauer. P.E. or The Boys.

"This trail just gets used by a bunch of animals," I concluded, based upon seeing a lot of paw– and hoof traffic.

SeeHawk was riding my bumper, so when I suddenly halted, he ran smack into me.

My reason for halting was to ask, "Is that a post?"

"Where?" he returned.

"Over there," I pointed toward some half-green mountains in the distance straight ahead.

Ignoring my finger, he demanded, "What o'clock, Sunshine?"

"I don't know. Noon, I guess? Or one, or something? Just, look where I'm pointing."

SeeHawk squinted hard enough to lose some eyelashes, but he still could not see anything resembling a post.

"Maybe it's just dust on my eyeball," I decided. "It kind of comes and goes, though. Maybe it's a tree trunk. Or some weird power line? It could even be a jeep track. But if I had to put down money, I'd say it's a CD-post."

"Awesome!" SeeHawk beamed. "Lead the way, Mountain Momma."

I started jogging in slow-motion and therefore failed to notice a divot that cause me to stumble and lose my balance. Trekking poles saved me, but when I looked up again, shoot. Where was the post? Had it really just been dust on my eyeball? I marched back and forth, trying to find an angle that would make it reappear.

SeeHawk tagged along behind me, wishing to have seen it in the first place.

Suddenly, a short wooden fencepost popped up beside us. Well, bust my buttons! Where had it come from? Out of a hideyhole in the uneven crest? Its location seemed fishy, but never mind nitpicking, because it looked like we had found Poppa Jim's fence! Now, if I could only tap into my reptilian memory. What did Poppa Jim want us to DO with the fence? Crawl underneath it? Follow it? Turn away from it?"

Lacking remembrance, I decided to keep following the animals' trail of choice, while, at the same time, hopefully keeping Poppa Jim's fence in sight. That strategy paid off when I spied the vertical object I had lost a while back. Sure enough, it was a post, and not just any post, either. It looked smooth and blond, like several others I had seen during the past few weeks.

SeeHawk marveled, "How could you spot something so thin from a half-mile away?"

"With eyes as good as your reflexes," I explained.

Grinning, he agreed, "I guess I do have good reflexes. But, not everyone has your x-ray vision, so what do you think? Did whoever marked this trail expect hikers to have binoculars?"

It took me a moment to realize he was joking because, seriously, binoculars would have been a big help.

As we resumed hiking, the powerful windstorm grew even stronger. Hunger kicked in, making us want to eat lunch, but we kept going because sitting down in such a wind would have been awful. Instead, we just nibbled chunks of sticky peanut butter *Power Bar*, hoping for its signature blend of rice syrup and bran to sustain us beyond Cottonwood Pass.

The crest's open terrain made it tricky to estimate how fast we were moving. Slowly but surely, the half-green mountains ahead seemed to be growing larger. When we finally reached the slim, blond post I had sighted from afar, we were able to confirm that it said, "CD." Furthermore, I spotted the next post in line, again so far away that SeeHawk could not see it.

Suddenly, I grew worried about the two fishermen. They had not been spring chickens. Could either of them see such faraway objects? Just in case they might need help, I visualized mentally towing them in our direction.

Meantime, my laboring legs began to slow down. Constantly marching into the wind was tiring. My skull felt squeezed by an ice cream headache. Sometimes, I needed to brace my trekking poles backward, for resistance against getting tipped by big gusts. My flimsy windbreaker jacket and thin hiking pants could barely keep me warm. I needed to sit down and rest my shoulders. More than that, I needed to eat lunch.

While lunging onto a low summit, SeeHawk and I got punched sideways and backward by conflicting wind gusts. A square corner redirected us toward a triangular peak standing far in the distance. I struggled to concentrate. What had our guidebooks said about the peak? Were we supposed to hike up to it, or leave the crest sooner? If sooner, where exactly? The crest now stretching in front of us could have been exited from many locations. Choosing an exit by guesswork was going to be difficult with the wind rattling our brains. Occasionally, we got lifted onto our tiptoes. Our backpacks rode upon the gale like airfoils. Altogether, there was a lot of turmoil happening at once. We might have enjoyed pausing to regroup, but sitting down in the wind would have chilled us into a stupor. Therefore, we just plunged into the next long straightaway.

A pair of giant cairns took shape in the distance. Both stood too far removed to be visually connected with the last CD-post, but close enough together to form a line of their own. If viewed like an arrow, they were telling hikers to stay high and keep aiming toward the triangular peak. However, building them must have taken a lot of work. Just one cairn, alone, could have directed hikers toward the peak. There had to be a different explanation for positioning two cairns fairly close together. Were they meant to be viewed as gateposts, inviting hikers to pass between them? If so, why had they not been positioned even closer together? Were they meant to flag two different exits from the crest?

As we drew near the first cairn, a strong hunch told me to keep going. There was a shallow saddle coming up ahead. Its low entry looked convenient for travelers coming from several directions. Was the low point Cottonwood Pass? Maybe, but if so, why were both cairns not centered around the low point, instead of positioned off to one side? Also, how could any water-loving cottonwood tree possibly grow near the dry saddle, let alone, on top of it? Altogether, the evidence seemed thin, but if we were not seeing Cottonwood Pass, where was it hiding? Behind the triangular peak?

Feeling thoroughly confused, I wanted to consult our rescued guidebook pages. I felt scared to pull them out with the wind still raging, but it needed to be done. *Take your time,* I cautioned myself. *Feel what your fingers are doing, so if the pages slip, you'll notice it.* Inch by inch, I coaxed the folded pages out of my pocket. Fighting to stay balanced, I pinched them so hard that my fingers turned white. Wasn't that silly? I was being a worrywart. Wait, no I wasn't. *Quit thinking and focus.* Each time the wind blew harder, my backpack gave me a push or a yank. Skimming through each page, I found nothing that matched what I was seeing.

Meantime, SeeHawk noticed his eardrums getting blasted. He started to prance around, mumbling things I could not hear through the wind's persistent noise.

"Please don't distract me," I grumbled. "How about if you step a little closer, so I can use you for a wind-block?"

He noticed me frowning and said something unintelligible.

I laughed because opening his mouth let the wind smash his lips into rubbery oyster shapes.

Taking one last flip through the pages, I searched for any relevant keywords like "cairn," "saddle," or "Cottonwood Pass." Unfortunately, nothing relevant appeared. The specific directions we needed were still lost. Staring holes into tomorrow's directions was not going to help.

While stuffing all the pages back into my pocket, I happened to spy 40 brown dots clustered below the saddle.

"Elk!" I cried, pointing through the wind.

The 700-lb. giants looked shrunken to the size of ants. I could barely distinguish their black turtlenecks from their dark maple bodies. The bulls' majestic racks, known to weigh upwards of 20 lbs. apiece, looked reduced to the size of whiskers. And yet, even from such a great distance, it was obvious the entire herd was on high alert. Their bodies were all stiff with readiness, waiting for the leader to issue orders.

SeeHawk's face looked equally frozen, staring in awe at the faraway creatures.

"How can they know we're here during a major windstorm?" I shouted to be heard.

Startled out of fan-worshipping, SeeHawk professed, "They have senses people don't think about because most of us don't know how to use them."

Telepathic or not, it was easy to identify who ranked as the herd's leader. He stood apart from the rest, commanding their attention merely with his presence. Somehow, even while looking away, he gave them a discreet signal which prompted them to form into a neat line and gallop toward the saddle. Partway across the saddle, though, the entire line halted. It seemed like they had run into an impenetrable force field. I squinted hard and discovered they had encountered a barbed-wire fence. Staying in single-file, with the leader going first, each elk in its turn stepped through the fence, with one rear guard protecting the back of the line. After they all got through and promptly re-aligned, they departed in formation, with the rear guard still keeping his charges safe.

"Should we follow them?" SeeHawk begged.

"Of course," I smiled, "but not because they're divine animal guardians sent to be our benevolent guides. Just because that's our trail."

A ramshackle string of erratic boulders, whose linear alignment mingled with the cairns, guided us across the herd's beaten tracks. As soon as we entered the saddle that might or might not be Cottonwood Pass, Blam! We got hit by a confluence of springboard-topography, whose vortex felt like a wind tunnel. Hunching forward, with hands clamped over our hair, we struggled to read a small wooden sign. Talk about a letdown. It did not even mention the CDT. Thinking backward, we reached a firm decision. Screw it. The saddle had to be Cottonwood Pass, anyway.

Turning onto an overgrown pack trail that angled toward the timberline, we dropped out of the wind as if jumping into a sack. One minute, it was windy. The next minute, calm. Feeling overjoyed, we regained confidence, until the pack trail vanished into a stand of tall grass.

"Oh NO," I moaned.

"Lunch," SeeHawk grunted.

For no apparent reason, I burst into giggles.

"It could be later than three, and we haven't eaten anything since breakfast," he almost sobbed. "But, let's not eat before we find Meadow Creek because I know you won't be able to digest your food until we finish getting lost again."

"Wait," I exclaimed. "How do you know about Meadow Creek?"

"Because you mentioned it this morning."

"You can remember what I read to you this morning?"

"Some of it," he clarified. "Yeah, why not?"

Instead of answering, I smiled from ear to ear. Apparently, sometimes, my fiancé actually did listen.

A few seconds later, SeeHawk exclaimed, "Hey, lookie here. A horse print."

Sure enough, he had found a procession of hoof tracks stamped through the tall grass. Following the tracks downhill, we quickly regained the pack trail we had lost, only to have it disappear again...reappear, etc....until searching began to seem foolish.

At the timberline's entrance, I paused to examine our rescued guidebook pages. They told us to follow a trail through light woods until we reached Meadow Creek's headwater, and then to climb onto a spur ridge marked with a CD-pole.

Comparing the directions with our current situation led me to suggest, "Maybe we're having trouble because that wasn't Cottonwood Pass."

SeeHawk's eyes bulged slightly.

"I mean, maybe that's why we still aren't seeing anything resembling a cottonwood habitat."

Within moments of being the naysayer, I spied an intact trail heading into the forest. Phew. Except, it looked bound for the valley's floor, whereas I thought we should stay high, to intercept Meadow Creek's headwater.

"Maybe the headwater appears lower down," I speculated. "Or maybe this trail leads to an intersection that'll take us back uphill."

"What if we never find Meadow Creek?" SeeHawk wondered.

Catching his meaning, I smiled, "Then, we'll eat lunch just anywhere, after bushwhacking for miles under attack from hungry cannibals hurling flying coconuts. But, you figure, at least heading downhill will eventually lead us to water, even if it's not Meadow Creek."

"Just like following cows will always lead us to water," SeeHawk laughed. "Okay, so tell me, what comes after Meadow Creek?"

"Poppa Jim's spur and a CD-pole."

"Those two should be obvious. We'll probably see them next time we're above the timberline, right?"

"Yes, so we shouldn't let ourselves drop too far. Which means, we shouldn't stay on this trail if it drops for too long."

"Okay, but getting back to the bushwhacking idea, are we still honoring our pledge not to do it?"

"Only when the terrain is unreasonable," I hedged.

"You mean, our pledge has loopholes?"

"Something like that."

"Got it," he nodded, looking satisfied.

As it happened, though, the trail did not end up leading us too far downhill. Instead, it led us into a thinning band of conifer trees and just stopped there. Feeling dumbfounded, we agreed it was time to enact Plan B.

Before breaking protocol, I whispered to SeeHawk, "If we find the trail quickly, we'll pretend this never happened."

Bushwhacking horizontally and upward in turns, we made slow progress, through woods full of dry brush. Eventually, we stumbled upon a disjointed game trail, blazed at odd intervals with a small pocketknife. Following the blazes, we entered a vertical clearing whose boulders framed a trickling creek. Not just any creek, it looked capable of being a headwater.

"Lunch!" I cheered

SeeHawk's face broke into a smile. However, instead of throwing down his backpack, he said, "I know we agreed to eat here, but let's wait until after we find the spur, okay?"

"Seriously?" I frowned. "Didn't you just say you were starving?"

"Yes, but I know you won't be able to relax until we find proof that we're on the CDT," he said, "and, frankly, I won't either."

"Ha-ha, so now, the shoe's on the other foot? Okay, Lone Ranger. Let's giddee up!"

Pausing to refill a water bag first, I crossed the shallow creek in two short hops, with SeeHawk following close behind.

The next stretch of woods coughed up a new game trail, once again haphazardly blazed by hunters. Thicker dry brush camouflaged the trail's broken and disjointed segments, forcing us to expend a lot of energy staying alert. We felt famished by the time we entered a narrow slot of open space, separating the timberline from an extremely steep incline covered in grass. Directly at the top sat a slice of clear sky. It was like reaching a new station in an obstacle course. *Buck-up, challengers. You know what to do from here.*

I stared up the incline, feeling silly for being scared. Any six-year-old could have climbed its soft grass without fear of falling. Never mind my historical relationship with vertigo. There was no real danger, so I refused to hesitate.

SeeHawk stayed a short distance to one side, watching me climb like a gawky insect, poles above sneakers. Soon, I felt a familiar sensation of gravity tugging me backward. No problem, I was going to be fine. The key was just to keep going, no matter what. Two-thirds of the way up, I noticed something hilarious. I could hear myself breathing! After a full afternoon of getting my ears blasted by wind, not only did my own breathing sound foreign but also, I could hear another new sound. It was the faint squish, squish of SeeHawk's sneakers compressing soft grass. Laughing in surprise, I discovered that laughter helped me avoid feeling dizzy. Truly, that was something to smile about!

At the top of the climb, we reached Poppa Jim's spur, or a semblance thereof. The expected CD-pole was nowhere in sight. Together, we turned around and took a long look backward, into the headwater valley we were leaving. From the spur's high perspective, Meadow Creek looked shrunken into a bright blue ribbon, stringing together the valley's interior trees. One prominent horse trail could be seen joining the stream at a lower elevation. Its length and solidity made it eclipse any trail we had seen inside the valley.

SeeHawk gave me a questioning look.

Catching his drift, I answered, "No, that's not the CDT. We're supposed to stay high, not get funneled downstream."

Turning back around, we started marching across the spur without knowing exactly where to aim.

SeeHawk said nothing, but I could tell what he was thinking.

"It beats me where that CD-pole is hiding," I admitted, "but we'd better find it fast, because now, I'm starving, too."

"Don't even mention food," SeeHawk begged. "Just feed me when it's time to eat."

Midway across the spur, we passed a splotch of hard snow that did not seem to realize it was July. Upon reaching the spur's far edge, we peered into a crosswise valley whose timberline seemed unnaturally low. Above the timberline stood a wall of loose scree, connecting our perch to mirroring summit that could have been the spur mentioned in Poppa Jim's guidebook.

"Which spur is it?" SeeHawk asked.

"The spur of the moment," I hedged.

"Should I spur you on to give me a better answer?"

"Only if you don't mind hearing something spurious, since I don't know which spur matches the one in our guidebook."

A faint game trail, etched across the scree, offered to ferry us from one spur to the other.

Mister Scree Lover took a hard look at the game trail, wondering if it could support our weight, and he smelled trouble. Instead of speaking, he loosened his backpack, wiggled some blood back into his shoulders, and shot me a worried look.

"Roger what you're feeling," I told him. "Everything here is not as expected."

"Do you think we should turn around?"

"WHAT?" I gasped. "No! Never. Even if this isn't the CDT, it's probably a shortcut back to the CDT."

"I don't know, Sunshine. You're worrying me," he confessed.

My partner had good reason to feel skeptical, but what were our other options? Retreating back to the grassy slot? Then, down through all the dry brush threaded with broken hunters' trails? Or, even further, back to the windblown saddle, to inspect two cairns we had ignored during our first pass? If we retreated that far, what could we gain? Descending to the horse trail we had seen heading in the wrong direction?

SeeHawk guessed what I was thinking, and it made him mutter, "I don't know, Sunshine. Are you sure about this shortcut? Even I think it looks sketchy, and I'm no chicken when it comes to crossing scree."

"But it has trees below to catch us if we fall," I argued. "Even if we go for a wild ride, probably nothing worse will happen than getting a lot of gravel shoved up our noses."

Chuckling at my nerve, SeeHawk sighed. "Okay, Curious George. If you really want to try it, then let's get moving. I don't want to eat lunch and dinner as a combo-meal."

SeeHawk stayed behind me for protection, while I gingerly stepped forward. As soon as I placed one sneaker onto the scree, it disappeared. Schoop! No more sneaker, followed by sneaker number two. Schoop! Now, all I had below my knees were lower legs with no feet.

Bringing up the rear with his heavier backpack, SeeHawk, was struggling not to collapse the game trail. Rivulets of scree kept pouring out from beneath his invisible shoes.

It was a strange way to travel, but, having left the spur, both of us felt committed to going all the way. We just needed to be patient because it was slow going, due to requiring extra effort and caution. Partway across, we encountered some fallen logs, resting 40-feet above the timberline.

"How funny," I laughed, feeling confused. "Did these trees roll uphill, or are they left over from ages ago?"

"We're crossing an avalanche-zone," SeeHawk presumed.

"Eek."

The rest of the crossing felt hairier, knowing we should probably not create any large disturbance. Nevertheless, we successfully reached the opposite spur, and gratefully stepped back onto firm ground.

Immediately on the landing, stood a barbed wire fence, prohibiting entrance into a tidy conifer forest. There was enough room near the ground to roll underneath the fence, but instead, we turned sharply and began hiking alongside it. After a short time, I spied a vertical object gleaming one-quarter mile in the distance.

"SeeHawk!" I cried. "There's the pole we've been missing!"

He could not see any pole, but it made no difference. He openly wept, because finding a CD-pole meant we had permission to eat lunch.

Ten minutes later, we reached an official-looking boundary gate, garnished with a sun-bleached cow vertebra.

"Cow bones on both ends," SeeHawk noted. "At least, southern Montana's trail crew realizes hikers go in both directions."

Before passing through the gate, we observed what the cow's vertebra might have been intended to communicate. *Warning to all you northbound hikers. This looks like a perfect place to reconnoiter, but don't expect to see where you're aiming. Happy sleuthing*!

SeeHawk and I stepped through the gate feeling lucky to have done as well as we did. The first tree heading southward rang our lunch bell. Pulling over while most local people were eating dinner, we sat in the tree's lukewarm shade and fixed a pile of sweet and drippy PBC (peanut butter, chocolate, and graham cracker) sandwiches.

The next half hour saw us effortlessly romp through a mature conifer forest. One of its giant elders bore a blaze that could have been seen across a football field but only faced a small clearing. Taking direction from the blaze, we turned onto another good trail, which carried us along for a quarter-mile, before ramming us into a solid wall of trees.

Part of me wanted to scream but, ha-hem. Not today. Screaming was for ungrateful people.

Taking a deep breath, I told SeeHawk, "It's time to go Boomhauer again. Forget following any of these trails. Let's just use our compass to find Harkness Lake."

SeeHawk frowned but he did not argue.

After punching through the trees, we crossed a perpendicular band of increasingly hilly woods. Within minutes, the woods spit us onto an open sagebrush desert, uniformly blistered with repeating foothills. The change was startling. Beneath a blue sky turning golden, we saw several flat jeep roads vanish amongst the foothills. I whipped out our compass and selected the jeep road best matching our aim. Conditions were perfect. The terrain looked easy. I was willing to bet that nothing besides human error could stop us from finding Harkness Lake.

After losing sight of the rear forest, I started expecting to see water around every bend. Soon, my expectation came true, but not in the way I had expected. Instead of reaching Harkness Lake, we started passing spring-fed cattle ponds, cascading down a series of natural terraces. Their shorelines had been trampled into ovals of gushy mud. One pond beckoned us to go for a quick swim, and, of course, we could not resist, but we decided to wade into the water wearing flip-flops.

SeeHawk sloshed in first. His progress was slow until the water touched his shins, at which point one of his legs punched through the pond's mucky floor and got swallowed up to the knee. When he lifted out his leg, flip-flop and all, it looked plastered in wet asphalt.

"Don't wade," I hollered to him. "Just toss your flip-flops and dive."

Unfortunately, he could not dive, because the water was shallow. Instead, he continued slowly marching forward, until guilt about wasting time made him turn around and slog back to shore.

"Some bath," I teased.

He stomped out of the water, wearing mud galoshes.

Still wanting to swim, I shuffled gingerly across his tracks, saying, "Behold, Grasshopper. I shall demonstrate the proper technique."

Stepping into the water, I got my toes wet, before noticing SeeHawk picking something small off his shins. Suddenly, I remembered the leech episode of *Little House on the Prairie*. That was the end of my career swimming in land-locked ponds.

Toward dusk, two tired thru-hikers wondered how long the sagebrush desert's repeating foothills might go on. Despair almost beat us to a few dusty cars, parked near a sheet of darkening water. We rubbed our eyes and stared. Could it be? Yes! After a full day of battling wind and confusion, finally, we were seeing Harkness Lake. Better yet, we were also seeing a smiling man walk up to greet us.

I spoke first, "We met your volunteer and his buddy this morning, catching some fish."

Team Leader Will looked delighted.

I had to glance away, before dropping the bomb. "If you'd like to eat that fish for dinner, not breakfast, you might want to send out a search party."

SeeHawk tried to soften my blow by adding, "Hopefully you won't need to, though, since the lights from your camp might help them find you after dark."

It did not seem necessary to trouble Will further by reporting the CDT's signage problems. He was already going to get an earful, whenever his dispatch rolled into camp.

* * *

The landscape beyond Harkness Lake vacillated between high desert and forest; hot versus cold; dry versus moist. It was almost like walking into *Burger King*, except not really because the changes happened faster than SeeHawk and I could decide what to order.

Nicholia Creek's gentle current led us from camp into a weedy marshland, flooded with beaver dams misting in cold sunlight. A short, dusty climb lifted us onto a hardpan ridge rippled with heat mirages. Doubling-up on sunscreen seemed necessary before we dropped into an open valley cradling Deadman Lake. The valley's interior felt like an oven, but its tropical-green water could have preserved an iceberg. Atop the next 8,400-foot ridge, we hiked alongside a spring-fed stream, choked full of algae nourished by the sun. Drought-tolerant sagebrush stood withering on both sides, wishing its roots could be used for walking. I plunged my hat into the stream's cool water, plopped it back on my head dripping wet, and felt refreshed for five minutes. That was how long it took for the sun to bake my hat dry as a cracker.

"What's up with all these hot-and-cold extremes?" I complained "Either the Continental Divide boils our brains, freezes our tootsies, or tries to blow us into outer space. When are we going to have one perfectly comfortable day?"

As if granting my wish, the next valley we entered embraced us in a stillness that felt like our own skin.

Feeling astonished, I cheered, "Now THIS is t-shirt weather!"

Unfortunately, it turned out that horse flies also love t-shirt weather. Swatting them with our hats only made the greedy dive-bombers dizzy. We had to resort to bare-handed slapping.

Atop a third summit, one lonely limber pine watched me implore Mother Nature, "Forget anything I've said today about perfect weather. Please send some wind. Just, not as much as yesterday."

My wish was granted on demand, by a fresh breeze shooing away the horseflies.

Feeling increasingly astonished, I complained. "It's too bad we can't pop into *Seven-Eleven* today and buy a lottery ticket."

SeeHawk chimed in, "Plus, some flypaper to hang on our backpacks, for the next time we get perfect weather."

Climbing onto a fourth high overlook, we gazed into a tremendous valley, flat and brown in every direction. Its elongated middle was scored clean-across by Road 328. Otherwise, it contained a string of power lines. That was about it. No postcard material, anywhere.

Our long descent into the valley began with a drop, through haggard sagebrush, filled with flying grasshoppers whose wings sounded like rattling maracas. Ambient dirt blurring the dry air discouraged us from looking far ahead until we spied a few hundred black specks in the distance. What were they? Slowly, over time, the specks grew into domestic buffalo. How exciting. We wanted to see them up close. Descending faster, we spooked three elk who folded around and vanished like four-legged magicians. Further downhill, we ran into a love triangle, consisting of two young humans and a dog wearing saddlebags.

"Good morning," announced the pack's young male leader. "We're hiking the CDT northbound, through Montana."

"Southbound CDT," SeeHawk returned.

"Then, I should warn you," the leader replied, "we got lost in the section you're coming to. Never even saw the trail. I think they're relocating it to a different ridge from the one described in our guidebook."

I noticed him clutching the Book of Beans and remarked, "How strange because those guidebooks you're reading are pretty up-to-date."

"Yes, except where you're headed," he corrected me. "This section of the trail's been changed so many times, whoever moved it the last time probably forgot to relocate some signs. Anyway, I'm glad we got here as fast as we did. It was partly dumb luck. Partly, smart guessing. We just chose the best-looking ridge and happened upon the CDT partway in. No telling where we'd be otherwise. The ridges between I-15 and Sawmill Creek all look the same. If you choose the wrong one, you're screwed, and there isn't any water up high."

SeeHawk threw me an uneasy glance.

Changing the subject, I asked our informant, "Can you think of any hints for finding the trail from this end?"

"Well, no," he admitted. "We weren't keeping track of southbound landmarks. That's why I'm saying you ought to pay attention."

After giving thanks for the young man's advice, I philosophically told SeeHawk, "Drink up, gentlemen. It's time to get back to work."

My partner responded nervously, "Are we worried about the water situation?"

"Worrying is for warts," I scoffed. "Besides, first, we have to even find the water shortage."

"Do you think we'll have trouble following the CDT?"

"I have no idea, but it probably won't help to be missing Poppa Jim's updates."

That remark was met with silence. Privately, SeeHawk thought to himself, *Not those confounded updates again.*

"Anyway," I went on, "the best thing we can do is carry extra water, and cross our fingers. Unless, you want to take Poppa Jim's old, low route around the unfinished high trail?"

"Are you joking?" SeeHawk frowned, "How much high scenery would we miss?"

"One full day's worth."

That was as far as our conversation got before we came alongside the valley's domestic buffalo. They were grazing peacefully inside a fenced pasture, looking comically regal with their humped silhouettes, girlish ringlets, disgruntled caveman expressions, and postures daring anyone to push them around. Little did they know their pasture rested near thousands of cached buffalo bones leftover from a historic stampede.

At the valley's end, SeeHawk led me into a meadow containing a fox's skull and a camper having a nosebleed. The next fertile woods contained a pretty tent site beside Irving Creek, from which we could distantly admire the Red Conglomerate Peaks. Dinner went down quickly, followed by starlight. I dreamed about diving into dirt, not water, and woke up finding a tick inside my shoe.

"Now, now. You fanged little tidbit of darkest evil, what are trying to warn us about, this time?" I asked our uninvited guest, before thwacking it into some nearby grass.

SeeHawk piped up and asked, "If you knew that tick meant to warn us about something, would you change anything about our plans for today?"

"Not yet," I told him, "because it's all so up in the air, I wouldn't even know what to change."

"Right," he frowned. "So, maybe I shouldn't have asked."

Tinkling summer rapids accompanied our first mile of hiking through sunlit woods. Songbirds were sharing happy stories. Tangy strawberry-apple fruit rolls tasted like Summer. Momentarily, I smelled methane gas, near Irving Creek's intersection with another, smaller creek. The methane odor coincided with a sudden change in the trail's blazes, from traditional exclamation points into bands cut fully around each trunk.

"Why did somebody ring all these trees?" I complained. "Didn't they know it might kill them?"

"Maybe that was the point," SeeHawk suggested.

We followed ringed trees for another 15 minutes, before realizing the forest was starting to look domestic.

"This must be a logger's trail," SeeHawk guessed.

Thinking the same thing, I called for a retreat.

Together, we retraced our steps back to the methane odor, and this time followed a different trail away from the creeks' junction. Before long, we entered a slanted meadow. It turned out to be the first among many square meadows, belonging to a checkerboard timber forest built from blocks of replanted trees.

"Uh-oh," I remarked, feeling my heart sink. "We must be where the Book of Beans says the CDT disappears. Now we're supposed to look for some blazes that might only be visible through binoculars. Plus, we're supposed to watch pit for bear scat and claw marks."

SeeHawk openly guffawed, "BEAR scat and CLAW marks? Seriously? Ha-ha. How about some bear sign, too, while we're at it? Ho-ho, give me a *Sharpie* and I can tell you what I'll write on that bear sign."

Good grief. Well, how could I blame him? Anyone might feel cynical after spending seven weeks in bear country without ever physically seeing a bear. Although, SeeHawk seemed to really be getting on a roll.

"BEAR SIGN?" he ranted, imitating Blue Man. "Who cares about BEAR SIGN? There's bear sign EVERYWHERE on this trail! How about giving us a compass heading, lady?"

"SHH! Don't jinx us, please don't jinx us," I pleaded.

Hoping to muzzle my partner's bravado, I reminded him that we were still in bear country.

"Bear country?" he snorted. "It's been weeks since we last saw a pile of 'bear sign.' I think all my elaborate food-hanging efforts have just been perf...er...perfluous...er, whatever that word is. I mean, there aren't even any bears here. I've just been going through the motions because people keep telling us to be paranoid."

"The word is perfunctory,'" I told him, "and even if you don't want to believe in bears, remember. It's not nice to heckle Mother Nature. You know what she does to hecklers?"

"No, what?"

"She puts castor oil in their *Chiffon*."

"Fair enough," he laughed. "Okay, okay, Sunshine. I know I'm going overboard. Sorry, It's just hard to keep hanging our food every night without seeing bears. But, I promise I'll try to take bear sign more seriously from now on. Do you hear that, Spirit of the Mountain? I'm going to take bear sign seriously from now on. The bears, I mean. We don't need to see them or read their signs. We're just here to have fun."

"Enough," I grumbled. "Come on, let's keep moving."

As it turned out, despite having a complicated appearance, the checkerboard timber forest was easy to cross. We just NEEDED to spot cairns spaced a quarter-mile apart, which was manageable for my sharp eyes.

SeeHawk took delight in exploring each meadow, especially after realizing they were littered with so many animal bones that I joked about calling him SeeBones.

"Maybe we're crossing some local mountain lion's hunting ground," he speculated.

"I'm not sure Montana has mountain lions," I said, "but it could be a super carnivorous grizzly bear."

"Or Bigfoot. Although, shouldn't that dude be getting pretty old by now?"

A quick jaunt past the Red Conglomerate Peaks revealed they were smaller than they had looked from a distance. Behind them stood an open ridge, buckling crookedly toward Sawmill Creek. Scored down its spine was a faint trail that could not be missed until it snuck away from us. Feeling alarmed, we glanced right and left, wondering whether to search some leafy woods on our left or drop into a shadowy ravine on our right. The ravine's tangled underbrush looked rife with confusion. Deciding to turn left, we spent twenty minutes having no luck, before deciding to head back onto the ridge. Having lost a bit of elevation, we regained the ridge slightly downhill, and there it was, resting in plain sight. The CDT had never changed course.

Juggling mixed emotions, we continued heading down the ridge for another few minutes, only to have the trail swerve sideways again. This time, it visibly dropped into the right-hand ravine and started weaving through some tight conifer woods. SeeHawk and I could not figure out why, since the ridge had been a comparative superhighway. Chaotic underbrush shoved us back and forth, hugging the left bank of a deep and narrow creek. Why were we getting corralled into such a mess? Had whoever built the CDT grown bored with staying on the ridge? Or had we accidentally strayed onto a side trail? At one point, where the creek's banks squeezed close together, we decided to hop from one bank to the other. Now, descending through looser vegetation, we followed a clear path down the creek's right bank, until it flattened out inside the mouth of a sandy beach.

"Well, how about that?" SeeHawk grinned.

"I'm not sure this is the CDT," I admitted, "but it does look like we're getting somewhere."

The trail's next challenge appeared simpler than it was. We needed to follow some gentle rapids through a floodplain approaching Sawmill Creek. Unfortunately, the floodplain's scalloped edge kept forcing hikers to choose between wading into the rapids or climbing around scrub brush rooted in soft sand. SeeHawk and I opted for climbing every time, only to see the CDT reappear near the water, which enticed us to trot back downhill, only to get forced back uphill, only to see the CDT reappear downhill, and so forth until we began to feel like the joke was on us.

Nevertheless, by morning's end, we successfully reached a wooden sign identifying Sawmill Creek.

SeeHawk examined some sneaker prints entering the water and confidently guessed, "These were made by a thru-hiker."

I naturally assumed, "Because they weren't wearing boots?"

"Well, that too," he agreed, "but also because any day-hiker would have taken off their shoes."

Chuckling, I pointed out, "So, now, you and I are day-hikers?"

"Sometimes," he admitted.

"Well, here goes nothing, partner," I said, peeling off my sneakers. "Are you ready to tackle the Book of Beans' high route to I-Fifteen?"

Glancing up in surprise, SeeHawk groaned, "You mean, that mess we just came through wasn't the bad part?"

"Are you kidding?" I laughed. "We're not even there yet. It's coming up next."

Taking a moment to absorb my implication, he nervously asked, "Should we consider taking Poppa Jim's low route around the unfinished trail? I'm feeling up for it. How about you?"

"I'm still excited for the high route," I told him, "but since you're our Chief Water Officer, it's really your call. I'll tell you what, though. We're about to eat one of our fancy smoked-salmon lunches. Should we put off this decision until we have full stomachs?"

"Deal," he grinned. "Just tell me where to sit."

Close beyond the creek, SeeHawk collapsed onto some soft grass, stretched out his legs, and waited for me to assemble one of our rare, smoked-salmon lunches. His eyes drooled, watching me procure the shiny salmon pouch, along with a baggie of whole-wheat crackers and a single lemon from the minimart in Leadore. Neither of us could have predicted what happened next. Right in the middle of eating, with a half-eaten cracker clutched in his hand, SeeHawk fell fast asleep!

When I saw my partner slump over his lap, my heart sank. No wonder he wanted to bypass the problematic high route that might involve water shortages. I needed to use my elbow just to wake him up. While packing away our lunch trash, I spent a moment considering our choices. It was fair to argue that religiously following Southern Montana's spotty trails had been stealing time away from our future farther south. No doubt, Yellowstone National Park was going to be spectacular. Obviously, Colorado was going to be Hiker Heaven. Even in the short term,

I could hardly wait to reach Mack's Inn, Idaho, and get a fresh start heading into Wyoming.

All these influences led me to tell SeeHawk, "Okay, Chief Water Officer, you win. Let's play it safe and take Poppa Jim's low route."

My partner looked extremely grateful, but he did not gloat, because he knew full well that I would have preferred tackling the high route.

Poppa Jim's prescribed departure from Sawmill Creek started off being green and pleasant. Only gradually did the dirt road's scenery change from dusty conifer forest to drab brown foothills. After a while of nothing improving, I started to sorely miss the doggone crest. Darn it, why had I surrendered so easily? Perhaps, a little nap was all SeeHawk had needed. He seemed to be walking swiftly along the flat road. How swiftly could he have climbed, now that he felt better? Imagining what kind of views we might have seen from the crest made me wallow in self-pity. My inner voice pleaded. *Can we still turn around?* Of course, the answer was no. It would have been cruel to push my partner past his limits, especially with an official low route offering to keep our thru-hike intact. It was time to prioritize my partner's needs, for a change, the same way he often prioritized my needs. Therefore, I needed to keep my mouth shut, and just spent the next half-hour secretly feeling miserable.

At the end of an hour spent weaving through foothills, we emerged onto flat pastureland, distantly approaching Interstate Highway 15. Everything hit home when we stepped out, into the open. My stomach felt tight. We were supposed to still be in the mountains. I asked SeeHawk to stop and we both turned around. The view that confronted us made us gasp.

America's Backbone touched both horizons. Its silhouette was an autograph painted across the sky. If any view of the Continental Divide had ever looked magical, that view was going to shine in our memories forever.

During the same moment, I candidly noticed what the two of us were trying to accomplish, and it soothed my frustrations.

Never mind if SeeHawk and I could not hold a candle to Lewis and Clark. Who cared if our new truck had suffered a few dents? My knock-knees and skinny ankles; his bulky calves and overconfident brain; those imperfections were the substance of our team. Whether or not we could eventually reach Mexico, just coming this far qualified us to feel proud.

Throwing back my shoulders, I grabbed SeeHawk's arm and cheered, "Come on, partner! Let's blow this popsicle stand. It's time to get on with seeing the San Juan Mountains."

SeeHawk slapped me a high-five and picked up his pace.

Hopefully, we were going to enjoy an easy road walk the rest of the way to Interstate Highway 15.

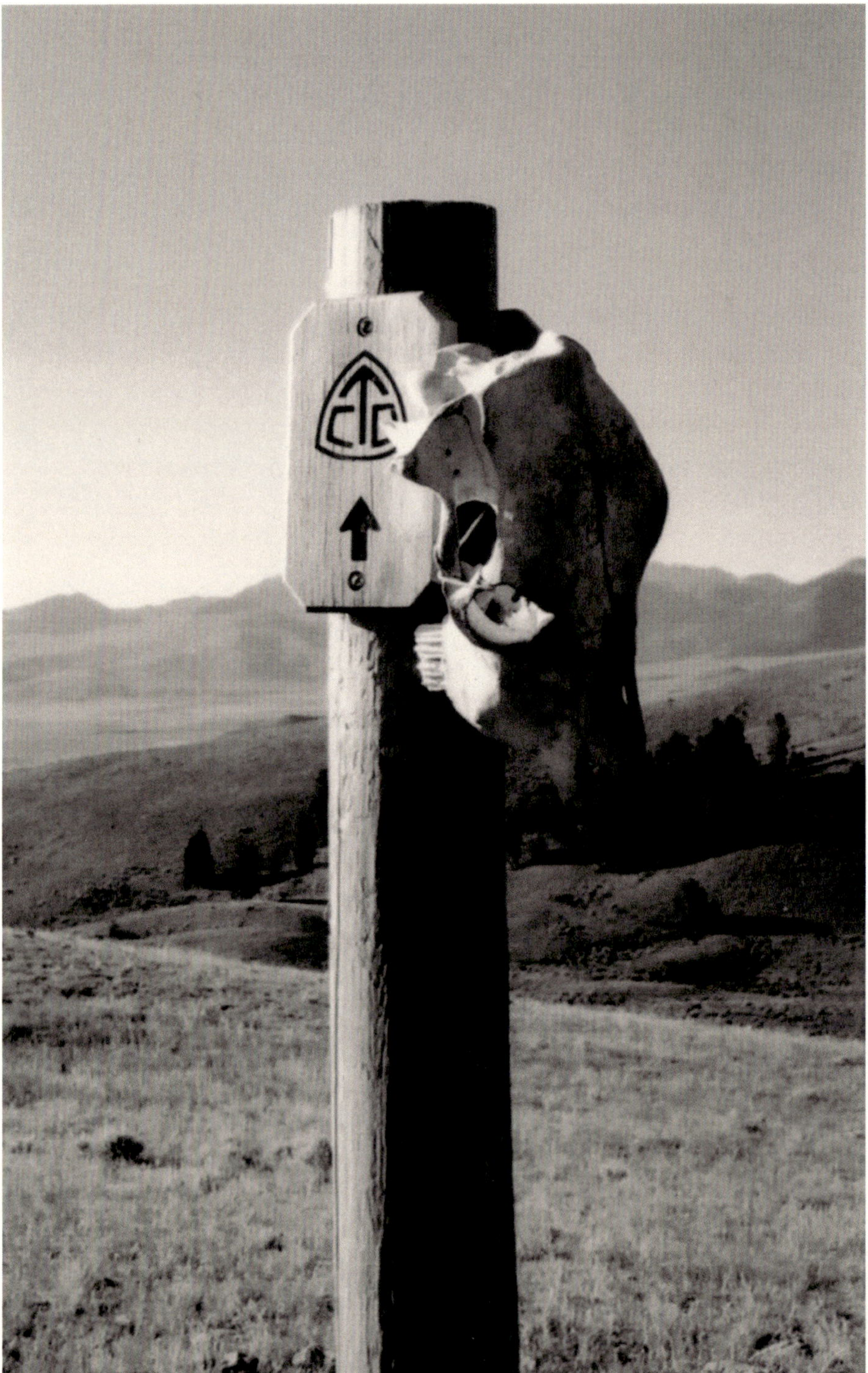
CTC

Chapter 13

Beasts

If the multitude of mankind knew of my existence, they would...arm themselves for my destruction.

— Mary Shelley's Frankenstein

    SeeHawk scowled at a dismantled cattle trough that had once been fed by an underground spring. He and I stood midway across broad pastureland separating the Continental Divide from Interstate Highway 15. Rain showers were ending on two horizons. All the sky in between held a variety of pinks, ranging from bubblegum and rouge to dark raspberry-red. A katabatic breeze, slippery and cool, kept sweeping dirt that looked dusty but felt sticky beneath our shoes. There seemed to be moisture hidden everywhere, in the clouds, in the ground, and even in the air we breathed.

    Upon stepping away from the dismantled trough, I stared at its dry perimeter, wishing, "If only we had a shovel or even a good-sized digging rock."

    Glancing sideways, SeeHawk hinted, "Or if animals could talk."

    A few muddy cows, chumming around with one oddball antelope, certainly knew where to find a cold drink, but they ignored SeeHawk's remark and just kept grazing.

    Minutes after we left empty-handed, the sky's pink afterglow started to fade. Refusing to feel discouraged, we discussed our last options for finding water that evening. The best-sounding option was a low-volume creek. Option B was a questionable-sounding duck pond. Lastly, our guidebook mentioned an odorous marsh, which probably did not deserve to be called Option C. Obviously, in all three cases we needed to worry about water quality. However, at this point, it seemed like we should count ourselves lucky if we could find any water at all. The landscape ahead looked mangy with weathered rabbitbrush and sagebrush. Its bare patches hardly showed through tight openings. A small pond or stream could easily be missed. Furthermore, we did not know whether to search for reflective water or clear water, glossy mud or pond scum, and whether it might be colored blue, silver, golden or green. Therefore, we just adopted the mindset of kids on an Easter egg hunt, determined not to miss any eggs, no matter their color or size.

Fortunately, there was no need to divide our attention between water-hunting and route-sniffing. The route was made clear by a pivotal landmark, called Pinetop Hill, proudly wearing its name on its hat. Our ultimate goal was a backdrop of mountains looming far in the distance. We could already see matchbox-sized cars whizzing along a straightaway beneath the mountains. Presumably, inside the cars were drivers blasting radio music, guzzling coffee, and gobbling crunchy snacks to help them stay awake. I could have used a little coffee myself, for defense against feeling bleary, but it did not matter. Even in a dream state, I spied our first letdown. It was an oval of cracked mud, peeking through some rabbitbrush nestled against the trail.

"Darned drought," I fretted. "Bye-bye duck pond. I guess, this means we're down to just the creek? Unless you want to count the ill-smelling marsh?"

"That's only an option if Earth gets hit by a meteor shower and all the other water dries up instantly," SeeHawk asserted. "But, hey, look who just got new batteries."

Looking where he pointed, I saw a steady gleam piercing the sunset's pink sky.

"You're right, Venus does seem brighter," I agreed. "Maybe all the women are having a wild party."

"Maybe they invited the Martians over for a kegger."

"We'll find out when Mars comes up."

"We will?"

"Yes, because if most of the men aren't home, Mars should look dimmer."

On our way through a stand of waist-high grass, I stepped into a thin sheet of water, so transparent I never saw it until my feet felt a cold splash. Realizing the significance, I happily sang, "Dinner!"

"Not so fast," SeeHawk advised.

He pointed toward a few cows grazing upstream.

"Of course," I nodded. "First, we need to perform the sniff-test."

Kneeling down, I thrust my nose toward the clear liquid and took a big whiff. Oh, my goodness. How bad was it? Truthfully, it just smelled like water.

SeeHawk's whole body sagged with relief. Nevertheless, during a moment of refilling our screw-lidded water bags, he could not resist joking about bagging cow drool.

I had to respond by shouting like Lucy. "Get some disinfectant! Get some iodine!"

After SeeHawk guzzled enough water to fill a fishbowl, he leaped to his feet and led us out of the grass. Within minutes, we discovered a patch of dry ground suitable for gripping tent stakes. That seemed like a miracle, considering our surroundings. There were not many patches of firm ground to choose from, because prairie dogs had drilled tunnels everywhere, turning all the flatland into a giant sponge.

Once our tent stood ready for occupancy, I set a pot of cow drool to boil. Then, SeeHawk and I began debating the obvious question. What could have killed thousands, if not millions, of local prairie dogs? Just before the conversation might have turned morbid, our attention got diverted by a freak accident.

My first comment was, "Now we know what happens when you boil noodles in iodine water and then add cheese and milk powder."

"*Smurf* Stroganoff," SeeHawk groaned. "Is that even edible?"

"Don't ask me," I shrugged. "You're talking to a woman who got C's in chemistry."

Both of us stared into our pot full of bright blue noodles. Would it have been ethical to dump them into some unfortunate prairie dog's vacant condo? Ethical or not, how could we bear to throw away the delicious cheddar cheese for which we had sweated and cried and tortured our dehydrator? No way, José. There was only one solution. We needed to switch off our headlamps and pretend to be eating orange noodles.

Long after twilight, the evening remained warm enough for comfortable stargazing. Far in the distance, we heard freight trains and coyotes howling in rounds.

I brushed my teeth wearing nothing but a t-shirt, which led me to remark, "Doesn't tonight seem awfully warm, considering that it's not very cloudy?"

"It does," SeeHawk agreed, "but remember that we're getting near the end of July. If this was Illinois, we'd be seeing fireflies."

"Fireflies remind me of visiting my relatives from Indiana," I reflected. "If we were there tomorrow, some firemen might come over and screw-open the fire hydrant, so kids could splash around in the street."

"When's the last time you saw a fireman do that?"

"Twenty years ago."

"Yep, that sounds about right," he nodded.

The night's late warmth continued to perplex me after we zipped our tent shut for the night. I fell asleep thinking about microclimates and thought about them again first thing in the morning.

During the hour of sunrise, nothing could be seen outside our tent. The explanation was tule fog. Opaque, white, and almost thick enough to lick, it smelled like a freezer and felt like a freezer. Our cheeks stung while rushing to strike camp. Layering up every garment we had felt like wrapping ourselves in cheesecloth, shrink-wrap, paper, tinfoil, and finally a garbage bag—all of which failed to stop us from shivering.

By the time we started hiking, it hurt just to breathe. Our noses hurt. Our throats hurt, even with hands cupped over our mouths. Perhaps the whiteness was not ordinary tule fog. It could have been a "pogonip," composed of airborne ice crystals. Regardless, its attack made speaking impossible. Therefore, we said nothing from the time we left camp until we merged onto a frontage road shouldering the Interstate Highway. Only a chest-high guardrail protected us from speeding cars whizzing past our elbows. It was creepy to see such close traffic appear as blurry shadows. Sometimes, the cars completely vanished, but we could still feel their forcefields pushing against us.

My blood sugar was starting to drop from shivering. I needed to eat something, but the frozen fruit roll stashed inside my pocket was only fit for pounding tent-stakes or beating a drum. Besides, my frozen mouth could neither have chewed nor swallowed.

During that strange interval of walking, SeeHawk noticed a golden object flashing through the fog and bent over to pick it up. When he realized what he was holding, his stiff cheeks cracked into a smile.

"Feel how heavy this is!" he exclaimed.

The shiny object was a brass surveyor's pendulum, properly called a "plumb bob."

"Nobody will ever find it here," he reasoned. "Probably it's been sitting in this cow pasture for years."

I could guess his intention, so I felt obliged to warn him, "That looks awfully heavy for doing hypnotherapy. Wouldn't your arm get tired?"

"Maybe," he shrugged.

"Are you willing to hoof it all the way to Mack's Inn?"

"Totally," he grinned. Then, on second thought, he asked, "How far are we talking about?"

"Five days, more or less."

"Okay," he nodded. "I guess that's doable. Not easy, but doable."

His mind was made up, but after one mile of carrying an extra 2 lbs. he decided Mr. Plumb Bob was not ready to leave Montana. Instead of just dropping the treasure, though, he ceremoniously hung it upon the frontage road's barbed wire fence, vowing to retrieve it during some future car trip. In other words, he doomed himself to forevermore regret having left it behind.

We crossed I-15, as the fog began to lift. Out from beneath its cover of whiteness came a two-block-long strip of defunct businesses and ramshackle houses. Our atlas said we were passing Monida. Our eyes only saw a modern ghost town, until we noticed most of the houses were equipped with satellite dishes.

Beyond the last building, we came across a junkyard heaped with industrial cisterns, retired school buses, railroad cars, damaged construction vehicles, heavy machinery, mobile homes, disemboweled car guts, conduit piping, oversized wire, fencing materials, wooden pallets, oil barrels, and other things too jumbo for ordinary recycling.

The fog had been rising all this time. Filtered sunlight was kissing our cheeks. Why could SeeHawk and I not stop shivering?

The next landmark to appear was a narrow-gauge railroad track, bordering I-15. Modern trains presently used the railroad for commerce between Salt Lake City and Butte. However, once upon a time, stagecoaches had used it for transporting visitors to and from Yellowstone National Park.

Straight in the distance far ahead, the frontage road's lifting fog exposed a new skyline full of bulky mountains.

"There's what we missed by taking Poppa Jim's low route," I informed SeeHawk.

Conflicting emotions barred him from responding.

Above the Continental Divide, a crown of backlit clouds beckoned us to climb back into Heaven's arms. More encouragement was added by a single sunbeam spotlighting our turnoff onto a perpendicular dirt road. There stood a building signed, *Sheep Experiment Station.*

Imagining the experiments, I nervously joked, "Is that where Dr. Frankenstein creates his Frankensheep?"

"Don't ask me," SeeHawk shrugged. "My dad's patients were mostly pigs, horses, and cows."

We spent the next half hour visualizing atrocities involving sheep. Thank goodness for the rescuing beauty of purple lupins, pink geraniums, and pink bull thistles, all coming alive when the fog broke open. Sunshine poured out of the sky like an opera, coaxing complex fragrances from all the flowers and sagebrush. It took another half-hour for the fog to disappear, but once it was gone, the road's exposed switchbacks heated up instantly.

Within ten minutes, SeeHawk and I switched from shivering to craving shade, cold water, and ice. Therefore, imagine our delight upon finding an unexpected freshwater spring, shaded by a few overhanging spruce trees. Everything would have been perfect, except for one problem. While reaching out to soak his hat, SeeHawk made an alarming discovery.

I stood by, feeling helpless while I watched him frantically dig through his pockets. What could he have been missing? The expression on his face told me not to ask. Several minutes passed before the truth came out.

"I can't find our maps for the CDT's next section."

"Oh! Is that all?" I laughed. "Don't worry. The next section of trail is pretty simple. I've already sort of got the directions memorized."

"No, Sunshine," he explained. "I dropped ALL the rest of our maps for hiking to Mack's Inn."

"FOUR DAYS' WORTH!" I shrieked.

Before I could say more, SeeHawk dropped his backpack and took off sprinting downhill.

"Hi Ho, Silver!" I called after him.

"Don't worry," he shouted backward. "I promise I won't come back without them. If you get bored, take a bath or something."

Late in the morning seemed early for a bath, but since nobody was around, I did as he suggested. It felt terrific to strip down and splash-bathe, for about two minutes. The zing ended when a fresh wave of clouds shot over the trees and cooled off their shade. By the time I got dressed, I was shivering so hard, I could barely retie my sneakers.

The next 20 minutes felt like an eternity. Sitting alone gave me little to do besides worry like a field mouse about having lost our maps. There was no question of returning to Interstate Highway 15. Even if SeeHawk and I could have hitchhiked to wherever wilderness maps were sold, we would have needed to buy more food before returning to the trail, thereby falling even farther behind schedule, and so on and so forth.

My teeth were practically chattering by the time SeeHawk marched back up the mountain, shouting, "Don't worry, Sunshine, I found the maps right where I dropped them. Ha-ha. Silly me."

Seeing him pop into sight gave me a surprise. Just like a month ago at Strawberry Creek, I noticed another dramatic change in his appearance. Instead of looking like a bearded salesman turned gold prospector, now he looked like a storybook version of Jesus.

With guilt on his sleeve, my partner apologized, "Sorry, I guess I got careless this morning. Usually, I stash all the maps inside my Velcro chest pocket, but today, I stuck them into a pocket that doesn't fasten shut."

"It's okay," I told him. "This is one of those days where we just have to count our blessings."

Climbing side by side, we immediately stepped from the spring's cold shade into overcast sunlight. Within a short distance, the groomed dirt road fell off and went kerchunk! In other words, it nosedived into a cavity shaped like a missing wedge of cake. Both of us stopped and stared downhill. What, in the name of road-construction guffaws? Had we missed a turnoff somewhere? Seeing no other choice, we decided to play along, and down we went. Immediately after hitting bottom, we rebounded back up, soon reaching an open summit crowned with barbed wire fencing. Presumably, the fence marked Montana's southern border. It led us eastward, through silvery sagebrush sprigged with pine trees and red Indian paintbrush. Presently, Big Table Mountain appeared in the distance. As gigantic mountains go, it was a fortress of sloppy terraces. Patchy grass spilling down the terraces was getting sheared to brown by hundreds of domestic sheep. I became so engrossed in looking at the sheep that I almost stepped on a pair of brown "horse apples." Good thing I looked down in time because, it turned out that one of little brown balls was not horse manure. It was a terrified Northern Pocket Gopher!

Retiring clouds blushed salmon-pink while SeeHawk and I polished off a whopping 24-mile day. We felt too exhausted to dread scooping water out of Rock Spring's banquet-sized stock trough. The water tasted fresh, and if it was tainted with Frankensheep's drool? Hopefully, drinking it would give us a new superpower.

After SeeHawk and I holed up for the night, I tried to count experimental sheep jumping over A-framed pine log fences. It was a weird image, but not food for nightmares, because I did not think my wild theories about sheep experimentation could ever come true.

The next morning dawned sunny and clear. Not even one rebellious cloud interrupted the blue sky. A dusty trail leaving our campsite crossed a high point where everything changed. The summit's backside dropped into an old volcanic spillway, trenched with crooked lava gullies. It was fun for us to twist and turn through the spillway's banked curves, like human bobsleds. At the bottom, though, SeeHawk and I appreciated having the forest flatten out and return to normal.

Ax-cut blazes marked an easy stroll through the next stretch of sunlit woods. We were on cruise control when our trail ran out of trees, meaning it also ran out of blazes. Poppa Jim advised following some old fenceposts, but we could not find them and that was okay. The CDT remained obvious, cutting through a carpet of soft, green grass. Soon, we got halted by a cloud of white wildflowers, but not for long. Deep within the flowers, SeeHawk spied Poppa Jim's fenceposts, mostly collapsed and leaning at odd angles.

It was challenging to avoid trampling on the flowers, while we traipsed from post to post, trying to stay on course. Eventually, we ran into a crop of waist-high grass, which hid the posts from every angle besides top-down. Fortunately, in that location, the posts started being tied together with kinky barbed wire, forming a traceable fence that separated Montana from Idaho.

"You've heard of the Tour de France?" I asked SeeHawk. "Well, now we're doing the Tour de Fence."

"Speaking in my defense," he returned, "it's getting hot. When's lunch?"

"Not until we finish digesting breakfast," I asserted. "But if you want to know, specifically? I think we could eat after passing Slide Mountain."

"Which should be how far?"

"Another a few miles."

Intensifying heat dogged us through a series of sunlit pine groves, separated by meadows whose grass kept swallowing the old broken fence. Finally, we entered one sunny meadow whose shorter grass left no place for the fenceposts to hide. So, where were they? Feeling perplexed, we stopped to take a better look around. Close on our left stood a long border of conifer trees, plunging steeply into a downhill forest. One tree sported a humongous ax-blaze, advertising switchbacks dropping into the forest. Was the blaze meant for CDT hikers? How could it be? Our guidebooks prescribed staying on the crest all the way to Slide Mountain. Moreover, we could already see a 100% scree, volcano shaped mountain looming in the distance straight ahead. Unless our eyes were malfunctioning, that silver volcano had to be Slide Mountain. Still, though, it was always possible for the CDT to take small detours without abandoning the crest. Poppa Jim's guidebook did mention some confusion involving a meadow, a left-hand turn, and the Continental Divide changing directions. In an effort to visualize how it could change, I suggested, "Maybe we've reached one of those backbone-versus-rib situations, where, if we keep going straight, we'll end up on a rib."

SeeHawk ran his eyes along the crest, and he could see why I did not sound convinced.

"You're probably right," he offered, "but let's not trust some random blaze before we try harder to figure out where the fence went."

Without further discussion, SeeHawk strode across the clearing's weather-cropped grass, aiming to seek out any hidden fenceposts.

Meantime, I confirmed that the switchbacks dropping sideways looked sturdy enough to belong to a National Scenic Trail. But, so what? Could sturdiness, alone, justify descending in the wrong direction? I felt reluctant until SeeHawk came back reporting no fenceposts and no trail, either.

It looked like dropping into the trees our best option, but before committing, I warned SeeHawk, "If we don't quickly turn back uphill or find another backbone, I'm going to hit rewind."

"Got it," SeeHawk nodded. "Our goal is to stay high. Sky-high. Pie in the sky."

"Apple pie with ice cream."

"Or huckleberry pie, yum."

"Too bad Pie Town is three states away."

"Four states away if you count Idaho."

Dropping steeply into the left-hand woods, it did not take us long to smell the familiar odor of a mistake. So, why did we keep going? Well, for one thing, after spending the whole morning following piecemeal trails, just dropping down sturdy switchbacks felt pretty satisfying. But was such satisfaction worth forfeiting 200-feet of elevation?

Both SeeHawk and I broke out of trance when we landed upon a narrow bench, from which the descending trail took off sideways. We could still see the crest, but only as a thin band of sunlight shining through floating treetops. It was time for both of us to laugh off our mistake, admit we had been slacking, and turn the heck around. Instead, though, we egged each other on. In fact, we even grew excited when the trail crossing the bench aimed toward Slide Mountain.

"So far, so good?" SeeHawk marveled.

"Shh," I scolded him, trying not to smile.

Grasping at straws, he suggested, "Maybe the CDT comes down here to detour around some kind of impasse blocking the crest."

"Or, maybe it's a hidey-hole for hikers needing a break from being chased by lightning," I proposed.

SeeHawk screwed up his nose and snorted, "Sure, why wouldn't trail-makers everywhere start adding rest stops with toilets and *Coke* machines? Ha-ha, right. There's a first time for everything."

CDT or no CDT, we followed whatever trail we were following, from the bench's dark pine-spruce woods into a brighter grove of majestic oak trees. Being old and huge, the oaks leaned heavily upon their elbows, having sprawled too far to support their own weight. Several had conspired to form a towering cathedral, whose interior was slatted with thick, yellow sunbeams. Leaf litter crunching loudly beneath our sneaker enhanced the illusion of indoor acoustics. The cathedral's exit was a tunnel of arching branches, whose self-repeating geometry looked hypnotic.

Altogether, it seemed like our gamble was paying off until the trail's extension became overgrown. Slowing down to negotiate some blockages, we started to wonder. Why would any trail crew construct more than a mile of immaculate tread, just to send hikers into a tangle of underbrush? Had we missed a turnoff somewhere? Well, even if we had, at least we were still aiming toward Slide Mountain. Deciding that was good enough, we forged onward. When the trail completely vanished, we had to make an uncomfortable choice.

"Bushwhack?" I suggested.

"Up? Or forward?" SeeHawk worried.

Above us loomed a nightmare of dry brush, stuffed into gaps between living shrubs and trees.

"Upward, as soon as we can," I decided, "but, for now? Forward."

"Do you think we should eat lunch before we get to Slide Mountain?"

"You mean, here?"

Glancing around, he conceded, "Well, no."

"Okay, good. Then, full-steam ahead."

We tried to keep smiling, but it was discouraging to constantly weave back and forth through the forest's tight undergrowth, searching on and on for a place to start climbing. Just when we felt on the verge of losing hope, voila! We stumbled upon a new trail aiming toward Slide Mountain. Unfortunately, it soon petered out, but then it reappeared, only to disappear again, and so forth, until we finally decided it was just another deer path.

Still waxing positive, SeeHawk reminded me, "Even if all we can find are deer trails, maybe one of these fakers will lead us back to the crest."

Suddenly, an awful idea struck me.

"What if we've been angling away from the crest this whole time?"

"Huh?" SeeHawk frowned. "What does angling away mean?"

"Well, instead of checking our compass, I've just been assuming Slide Mountain is still straight ahead."

Catching my implication, he deduced, "Are we talking about your rib theory again?"

"Right, based on what Poppa Jim says, we could be getting pushed diagonally off-course, without knowing it because we can't see the sun."

"Cripes, if you're right, what should we do?"

"No idea, but I hope there won't be anything super-steep between here and the CDT."

"Is it time to check our compass?"

"No, because we didn't take a heading before going into the trees."

"Then, what do you suggest?"

"Well, frankly, there's also another thing bugging me."

"Uh-oh. What's that?"

"Well, it seems like we've spent an awfully long time on Montana's side of the crest."

"Yeah, so?"

"Poppa Jim's directions only mention either staying on the crest or dropping onto Idaho's side."

"Whoa, hold the phone!" SeeHawk exclaimed. "That sounds important, Sunshine."

"Yeah, so we probably haven't been on the CDT for a while now."

"Crud, and what does that mean?"

"Maybe, we should climb back to the crest from here, and get the lay of the land before we keep going?"

Glancing uphill, my partner's eyes narrowed. There was no easy ascent visible from where we stood. Also, however, there was no point in arguing with determination, so uphill we went.

SeeHawk marched in an upright position, lunging over sinkholes and doing the limbo beneath ricocheting branches.

I monkey-climbed over the sinkholes, using my trekking poles for shields to deflect the scratchiest branches. Sometimes, I grabbed the mulch itself, which caused one large chunk to come off in my hand. Imagine my surprise, when I found myself holding a moose antler!

SeeHawk fawned over the dirty antler as if it had been cast in gold. Feeling its dead weight rest upon his arm, he gleefully announced, "THIS is the whole reason we got lost today, Sunshine!"

From that point onward, nothing could have rained on SeeHawk's parade. Never mind his trophy weighing several pounds. It fit neatly onto his backpack, which made it good enough for keeps.

"Now, let's find that crest and soak in some sunshine!" he bubbled happily.

It only took another few minutes to climb out of the trees.

Instantly, we got blinded by wide-open sunlight. The perpendicular crest was, once again, smothered in ivory-white wildflowers, surrounding another series of weathered fenceposts.

"See?" I bragged. "Who needs a compass, baby? Here's your best compass!"

Laughing, SeeHawk agreed, "I had total confidence in you, Sunshine. Sorry if it didn't seem that way. It's just hard to cope with constantly changing trails. I feel like we've done this whole state from cover to cover. Are we ready to bust out of Montana, or what?"

"Ready since last week," I agreed. "This place is starting to feel like quicksand."

Both of us sprouted rocket-boosters and zoomed toward Slide Mountain, for about 1-mile, until our tired bodies cried out for food.

SeeHawk wanted to sit down and start eating, right on the trail.

I thought we should press on until we could find some nice shade inside Slide Mountain's baseline forest.

A vote was taken and my side won.

In hopes of keeping SeeHawk motivated, I began to sing praises about every common spruce tree and purple volcanic peak visible from the trail. Which is to say, I made up a bunch of terrible comedy songs and forced SeeHawk to hear them.

Meantime, a pastoral valley took shape alongside us, steering Camas Creek's headwaters into northern Idaho. Soon, we encountered a junction of signed trails, forking off the crest in different directions. The fork signed Jones Creek Trail climbed away from our destination, so, nix to that. Another fork dropped steeply into the Camas Creek valley. We wanted to stay high and keep following the crest, but its continuation was labeled the Bear Creek Trail, which did not ring any bells. Furthermore, somebody had drawn a crude arrow on the sign, claiming the CDT descended toward Camas Creek. This claim made no sense, with Slide Mountain waiting 1-mile ahead. Feeling confused, I consulted our maps to see what was the matter.

SeeHawk watched my finger trace the CDT's curve around Slide Mountain. "If the curve starts here, instead of up ahead," I told him, "the trail would have to traverse a long way below the crest, which can't be right. Unless...if you think about it, descending would put us on Idaho's side of the crest, like Poppa Jim says. Wait, a minute. Could this arrow be pointing toward the END of Jim's Idaho section?"

SeeHawk groaned, "You're doing way too much thinking, Sunshine. Slide Mountain is right in front of our noses. It's hot. I'm thirsty. We haven't eaten lunch yet. Please, let's stick with the program and keep going."

"I want to, but since the arrow begs to differ, don't you think we should at least pop down for a short distance and see what's below, just to cover our bases?"

Gazing down the switchbacks, SeeHawk frowned, "That's a lot of elevation to lose, just for proof we're going the wrong way."

"Five minutes," I promised.

"Okay, but not one minute extra."

As it turned out, we descended for ten minutes. Five, ten, fifteen, whatever. Not until we turned around and looked back uphill did we notice a sun-bleached CD-sign, standing apart from the other signs we had left at the junction.

"D'oh!" SeeHawk frowned. "How did we miss seeing that?"

"Lesson learned," I sighed. "Breathe. Make yoga fingers. It's a beautiful day for enjoying some fresh air."

"So, the arrow we followed down here was a mistake?"

"Ha-ha, yes. Isn't it funny what people can do with ballpoint pens?"

At the foot of Slide Mountain, we mounted a forested ridge, directing us to circumvent the mountain's broad base. Not far along, we got surprised by pretty Salamander Lake hailing-us over to enjoy a scenic lunch. Its banks were smothered with frilly pink, red and yellow flowers, all shouting in unison. *Hey, look over here, hungry people! Sit down and feast your eyes!* It was hard to resist such a gregarious sales pitch, but we did not stop because drinking water from stagnant lakes always seemed riskier than drinking from streams, if we could find them.

Soon, we lost sight of the Camas Creek valley. This was partly due to our line of travel, but mostly due to entering a thicker spruce-aspen forest, which blocked our views in all directions. Shortly after becoming confined, we met another confusing junction of trails. Two of its outgoing forks both seemed unsigned, until we happened to notice a teensy-weensy, pint-sized, shrimp of a little CD-sign nailed absurdly high atop a 12-foot tall, bark-intact lodgepole pine log. Minutes later, we were still chuckling about that goofy-looking sign, when we ran into a middle-aged man, leading three younger men in our direction. All four in the group wore hard hats, carried shovels, and had bear spray holstered onto their belts, but only one was drinking a can of *Mountain Dew*.

I had to elbow my partner to stop him from staring.

"That's not yours," I hissed. "Let the poor fellow enjoy his bubbly in peace."

"Hi there," the leader introduced himself. "I'm the District Ranger of our Doo-Boys ranger district."

"Doo-Boys?" I repeated. "You mean, Doo-Bwah?"

Suddenly, I blushed, realizing I had just accused the local official of mispronouncing his own district's name.

Not at all fazed, he explained with a wink, "Guess the name might be French, but around here it's pronounced Doo-Boys. Anyway, today, we're out here fixing up the trail. I take it you two are CDT thru-hikers?"

We nodded, hoping his workers might feel encouraged by our usage of their improvements.

Leaning onto his shovel, the District Ranger elaborated, "This trail needs a lot of work, but only about thirty-or-fifty hikers come through here each year, so it's hard to get money from the government, Usually, we just make a little headway each year. This year, we're erasing all the side trails made by animals. Doesn't sound like much to accomplish, but you'd be surprised. The CDT gets a lot heavier traffic from animals than from people. Some of the animals make trails so convincing, they fool people into getting lost. That's why we're blocking the side trails with branches and putting up signs."

Reflecting upon our recent confusion, SeeHawk and I assured the crew that their service was both needed and appreciated.

The ranger looked proud to be in charge of making it happen. Also, he seemed infamous for chatting up hikers because as soon as his workers recognized a conversation brewing, they all dropped their shovels and sat down beside the trail.

On the topic of trail work, I described the CDT's condition between Rock Spring and Slide Mountain. When I mentioned hunting for fallen fenceposts, the ranger's face broke into a smile.

"You tried following THAT old fence?" he laughed. "We've been removing those broken-down posts for years. It's a big job. Nobody can do it all at once. Usually, we just take out a few posts every year."

Say what? I had to clamp my lips shut. No way was I going to mention to four committed trail workers that some hikers relied upon the posts for navigation.

SeeHawk might have spilled the beans, except, before he could comment, I silenced him with a pinch.

"Seen any bears?" the District Ranger wanted to know.

I reported hearing a couple of grizzlies bawl and bark in northern Montana. Otherwise, we had seen nothing besides scats and paw prints.

The District Ranger looked incredulous.

His companions appeared to think SeeHawk and I were either joking or suffering from amnesia.

"Seriously," I insisted, "even though one of our guidebooks keeps harping about bears, we never saw a single black or grizzly in Glacier National Park."

"Well, you're going to see them here," the District Ranger assured us.

Struggling not to look irreverent, I tried to redirect the conversation, by asking, "What's with the Sheep Experiment Station, down near I-Fifteen?"

All four locals exchanged a loaded look.

Uh-oh. Had I mentioned something top-secret classified?

Suddenly, one of the men snorted into full-blown laughter. "I have a friend who works there," he explained. "It's nothing really...er...nothing I can tell you about."

"Oh, come on," I pressed him. "You can imagine what kinds of thoughts have been going through my head."

All three laborers shared an inside-joke kind of laugh.

Not stopping there, the same worker confided, "Frankly, our sheep people don't like hikers getting routed through these woods. It invites visitors to see something that might freak 'em out. They don't want people asking questions like you're asking."

Growing more curious, I implored him, "Can't you please give me one example of something that would freak us out?"

"Oh, you know..." he mumbled evasively, looking cornered.

Half of me, naturally, assumed he was trying to fool me; but, I also wondered if he honestly felt reluctant to talk about it.

His eventual answer was, "It's really nothing I can think of off the top of my head. Just...you know...sheep stuff."

"Come on," I begged. "Please, give us one example, so we won't go into shock if we see something strange?"

At last, he straightened up and said, "Okay, well look...if you're going to see anything...it might just be something small...like, uh...maybe a sheep with a glass window in its side?"

"GLASS WINDOW!" I gasped.

"Yeah," he shrugged, trying to look nonchalant. "It's just to help researchers see into the sheep's belly. I mean, can you think of a better way to find out what it's eating?"

Okay, despite how serious the tattler looked, clearly he had to be joking. However, just in case, it was time for SeeHawk and me to stop asking questions.

After saying goodbye and getting underway, now that it had been brought to our attention, we noticed quite a few animal trails forking off the CDT. A bit farther around Slide Mountain, the trail grew increasingly steep-sided. We had to step carefully through a series of drainage gullies that were all bone-dry on the first day of August. Partway through one gully, SeeHawk spotted a suspicious pile of tube-shaped excrement.

"Speak of the devil!" he announced. "This can't be more than a few days old."

Seeing bear scat made our skin prickle, due to remembering the District Ranger's warning. We kept expecting to see fuzzy faces, big paws, and sharp teeth appear around every corner. The more scats we saw, the more excited we grew. Eventually, though, failing to see any actual bears caused us to lapse back into joking about rumor mills and campfire stories.

Meantime, the afternoon's peak heat shifted our focus to an enticing blue line drawn on our maps. We thought it would feel marvelous to take a cold swim in Ching Creek. Hurrying to get there before the day cooled off, we appreciated entering a wide trail corridor whose lack of steep edges helped us gain speed. Midway around one broad curve, we sideswiped a huckleberry thicket whose barren condition reminded us about Montana's 2-year drought. Near the curve's end, we froze in surprise.

Forty yards ahead stood a stout mother bear, poised in midstep with her paw tilted forward. Her face looked frozen as if belonging to a statue. She had splendid orange fur, a blunt black nose, and black-button eyes, which formed a hypnotic triangle.

Several yards behind her stood an unmoving cub, hiding between two massive conifer trees, quietly awaiting instruction.

Momma bear looked as surprised to see humans as we felt in reverse. Her nostrils twitched as if analyzing our conflicting aromas of garlic-and-onion sweat mixed with peanut butter and chocolate. Her head aimed toward us, but her body faced sideways, due to having stopped partway around a curve in the trail. It was obvious that she did not want to fight. She was just evaluating the situation.

After a few moments of locking eyes, I remembered to look away. The spell broke when my body turned sideways. Immediately, I heard questions spilling through my brain. *Is she a black bear or a grizzly? Can black bears be orange? Why didn't we ask the District Ranger which kind of bears are most common around here? Should I assume she's a black because her shoulders aren't humped? If she's a grizzly and she charges us, should we run or play dead? How long will she wait for us to think about all this stuff?*

Suddenly, I noticed SeeHawk's whole body facing the bear. He had not turned away because he was hypnotized.

"Look away!" I hissed.

"Oh, right," he whispered.

Slowly and cautiously, he twisted his body sideways.

Where is our pepper spray? I thought. *Inside SeeHawk's backpack? Did he pull it out when we saw all the bear scat? If I glance toward him to check, will the mother bear get spooked?*

Two minutes passed, during which nothing happened. Finally, I decided to risk peeking back into the danger zone. My eyes remained lowered, avoiding confrontation. It took nerve to glance upward and check on the bear's position. Like a whip, my eyes shot out and came back. Too fast. Nothing could be learned from such a quick glance. The second time, I rotated my head far enough to fully see the bear's face.

She had neither budged nor moved a whisker.

We were having a standoff!

Meantime, the little cub kept waiting patiently between two background trees. It looked as adorable as can be. I wished I could pet its furry little head.

Of course, I knew momma bear was going to feel threatened if I kept staring at her cub, so I turned away again. Flashbacks of our bear training from Glacier National Park kept cycling through my head—inconclusively since I did not know if we were facing a black bear or a grizzly. Meantime, I forgot to just observe the bear's body language like I would for a dog. Somehow, even though I knew momma bear was eager for us to move out of her way, at the same time it never occurred to me to actually move.

After another brief silence, by sheer coincidence, both SeeHawk and I chose the exact same moment in which to risk another peek. Consequently, it happened in unison that we both discovered momma bear had backed up several yards. Now, most of her body was hidden behind the same trees sheltering her cub. Her head and body looked more relaxed. She had decided to hunker down and wait for two hump-backed baboons to catch the hint and move out of her way. However, when she felt both my eyes and SeeHawk's hit hers at the same time, apparently the impact gave her a shock because she responded immediately. Quicker than we could think, her whole body stiffened. Then, out she came, charging toward us from between the two trees! It was a slow-motion charge. In fact, really, it was more of an amble than a charge, but still with clear intention.

Not daring to move, let alone speak, SeeHawk and I separately wondered how to react.

If momma bear kept ambling along, she was going to reach us in less than a minute. Should we run away? Or just stand there and look big? Or play dead? How could we decide, without knowing what kind of bear we had annoyed?

I decided to look away again and moved nothing else. With my back facing SeeHawk, I could not observe his reaction. Thirty seconds passed, during which I assumed the bear was still coming. When I finally ventured another peek, I noticed a galling sight. SeeHawk was staring straight at our assailant! His eyes were transfixed. He could not look away! Her wild beauty had ensnared him like a potion. This was not the beginning of SeeHawk's love affair with bears. Having spent half his life reading books about animal totems, and regarding Ursus to be his personal guardian, he had come to Montana believing he could telepathically communicate with all bear-kind. Now that one was slowly coming toward him, he was trying to tell her that we were friendly and would never harm her cub. His eyes did not blink until he heard me whisper.

"Ffft! SeeHawk!"

By this time, she was seconds from impact.

Acting in desperation, I moved my arm just far enough to poke him in the ribs. Thank goodness, that did the trick. Broken out of trance, he hastily looked away.

Both of us held our breath while waiting to hear the bear panting, or feel her fur brush against us, or see teeth reaching toward us, or whatever else might happen at biting distance. Instead, though, nothing happened. Where was she? Finally, I had to look. More cautiously than before, like a bad actor, I tried to slouch a little and slacken my face, in hopes of looking humble. Keeping that posture fixed, I slowly turned around and discovered, to my surprise, that both bears were gone! They had silently vanished. That was encouraging. Except, where had they gone? To the left? To the right?

SeeHawk and I both felt anxious, as we took a long look around, watching, waiting, and voicing private dialogues inside our own heads. *Thank you, momma bear. We apologize for being rude. We promise to scram. Please be gone.*

Finally, I allowed myself to speak, "That was close."

Cautiously, my breath returned.

It was okay to move.

We turned to face the trail.

"What a beautiful creature," SeeHawk sighed. "I sure wish I could have gotten a closer look."

"CLOSER?" I gasped. "Ack, SeeHawk, be careful what you wish for. You should be telling The Universe you don't need to see any more bears, and just feel thankful we didn't get mauled."

"Yeah, okay, right," he laughed, clearly not taking my warning seriously. "Anyway, the coast looks clear. Are you ready to keep moving?"

Physically, I felt ready, but I still had the willies.

SeeHawk chivalrously offered to be our frontman. He took a few steps forward and that was all.

In the next instant, the momma bear came bolting back out from between the two trees still hiding her cub. This time, she looked pissed! As soon as her beady black eyes met ours, I knew we were in trouble. Then, I noticed SeeHawk becoming hypnotized again. Just like before, he was staring straight into her eyes, as if making that mistake once had taught him nothing. Argh! Well, too late. It no longer mattered about making the bear angry. She was already charging us, and not just ambling. This time, it was a full-speed charge. We needed to do something, fast!

I grabbed SeeHawk's arm and yanked him backward.

Whirling about-face we fled back around the trail's broad curve. It was difficult to move fast wearing backpacks. We searched for a pullout, hoping to escape from the trail. A gap between some uphill bushes offered partial concealment.

Crouching up there together, we tried to breathe quietly, while waiting for momma bear to come racing around the corner. Ten minutes passed. No bear came. Not a sound was heard, besides our own breathing and shuffling of shoes.

Finally, SeeHawk stood up and declared, "It looks like she's given up the chase."

Nervously agreeing, I followed him back to the trail, chanting, "Fooled her once. Fooled her twice. Three strikes and we'll be out. It's time to make some noise."

We tried to keep a slow pace, but Ching Creek was waiting and the afternoon's heat was starting to cool off.

SeeHawk stayed in front as we proceeded around the trail's wide curve. Practically tiptoeing, his eyes were first to strike the giant conifer trees which had hidden both bears before we got charged. This time, nothing moved or made a sound.

When I saw SeeHawk's fingers signal an all-clear, I cautiously followed him around the corner.

He started chanting in Hawaiian, loud and deep, which made him sound both reassuring and intimidating.

We probably held our breath for a couple of minutes straight, while passing between the two trees whose bark might still have felt slightly warm, or been smudged with a little baby bear fur.

Several blind curves followed in sequence. We kept our pace slow until the trees pulled back to give us a wider view. Ahead, sprawled a good-sized huckleberry thicket.

"Bear Heaven," SeeHawk observed.

Correction, though. It was only a semblance of Bear Heaven because of its fruit being temporarily out-of-stock.

After passing through the thicket, I bluntly asked SeeHawk a lingering question. "Do you know what you did wrong back there?"

"Oh NO!" he groaned as if hearing the worst news possible. "Was I acting contrary?"

"No," I answered, feeling annoyed by his melodrama.

"Obstinate?"

"No."

"Then, what was I, sweetheart? Stupid? Broke? Irresistibly handsome?"

"NO, ding-dong. You were the guy who thinks he's immortal again. You stared straight at the bear, even after I told you to look away."

"Yep, I sure did," he agreed, without apology.

"Okay, so, I know you're not in the mood for a big lecture, but, next time, can you please look away without me asking? If not for me or for yourself, then do it for Tierra. She's expecting us to come home safely."

Hearing mention of our dog made SeeHawk concede, "Okay, Sunshine, I've got your message."

Hoping so, but wanting to make sure, I tested him by asking, "What message have you got?"

"What you just said," he confirmed.

"What did I just say?"

"Not to look away."

"TO look away," I corrected him.

"Right, TO look away."

"Good. So, now, can you please say it in a full sentence, just to insert the correct message into your brain?"

"IT in a full sentence, to insert correct message into brain," he repeated.

"For crying out loud!" I roared, "SEEHAWK, stop being a smartass. You know this is important. Please, repeat after me. Next time we see a bear, I'll look away, so it won't want to attack us."

"Next time we see a bear, I'll away, so it attack us."

"Oh, never mind," I grumbled. "Please, just remember that we aren't immortal, okay? We need to practice basic safety, just like everyone else, no matter who happens to be our Amakua."

"Basic safety. Immortal. Absolutely," he agreed.

"NOT immortal."

"Exactly, not immortal. Not being immortal is not being totally safe."

Sigh.

By the time we reached Ching Creek, the forest's hard sunspots were melting into shadows. We threw down our backpacks and got straight to work removing dusty shirts and shorts. Neither of us could wait another moment to rinse the odor of fear off our skin.

A small wooden footbridge served as a seat for dangling tired legs into the creek's deep water. Not only was the water deep, it was also tropical-green, churning like a jacuzzi, and cold enough to send shivers up our spines. Once having jumped in, we discovered the current could easily carry us downstream. Fortunately, we were both able to grab the wooden footbridge before getting swept away. However, holding onto the bridge was not easy with our bodies being tugged, so we had to keep things short. After a few delicious minutes, we climbed out, shimmied back into our dusty clothes, and dutifully hit the trail.

Toward sundown, we came across a trail register, signed the day before by Boomhauer and P.E. Two additional autographs came from Redbeard and Teach, who seemed close enough ahead that we might still catch them. Neither String Stick nor Dutch had entered their names. Why not? Later, we would learn it was because their latest hitchhiking adventure had begun with a two-hour wait to catch a ride to Lima with an I-15 driver, who then could not restart his car, obliging them to help him hail someone with a cell phone, so he could call a tow truck, and so on.

Being far removed from any such commotion, SeeHawk and I peacefully signed the trail register and continued on our way. Before long, we ran into a few hundred free-ranging sheep. Noticing that two sheep were black, with all the rest being white, I joked, "There's proof these can't all be clones from the sheep experiment station."

It took a little maneuvering to squeeze around the herd. In the process, our noses got filled with dust scented by flowering grasses, lupins, wintergreen, pine needles, cow pee, and sheep pee (which smells nothing like cow pee). Upon exiting the dust cloud, we mounted a steep ladder of switchbacks whose endpoint bore a sign saying, *U.S. SHEEP EXPERIMENT STATION. DANGER GUARDING DOGS.* There were no dogs in sight—just a gentle stream, innocently trickling through a flowery meadow.

"Camp time," SeeHawk declared, "and that's an order."

While slurping mugs full of hot corn chowder, we watched the evening's pink sky ooze into shades of purple. Slippery pesto pasta followed the corn chowder, beneath a twilight sky filled with glittering stars.

Sometime during the night, SeeHawk crawled out from under our sleeping quilt and flipped his body upside down, to rest his feet beside my head. Consequently, the first thing I saw the next morning was a smelly brisket foot staring me in the face.

A quick check outside confirmed no bears had tried to rob our food during the night. Nor had we gotten harassed by any guard dogs, nor even sheep with glass stomachs. Everything seemed peaceful in our little neck of the woods, atop the Rocky Mountains in southern Montana.

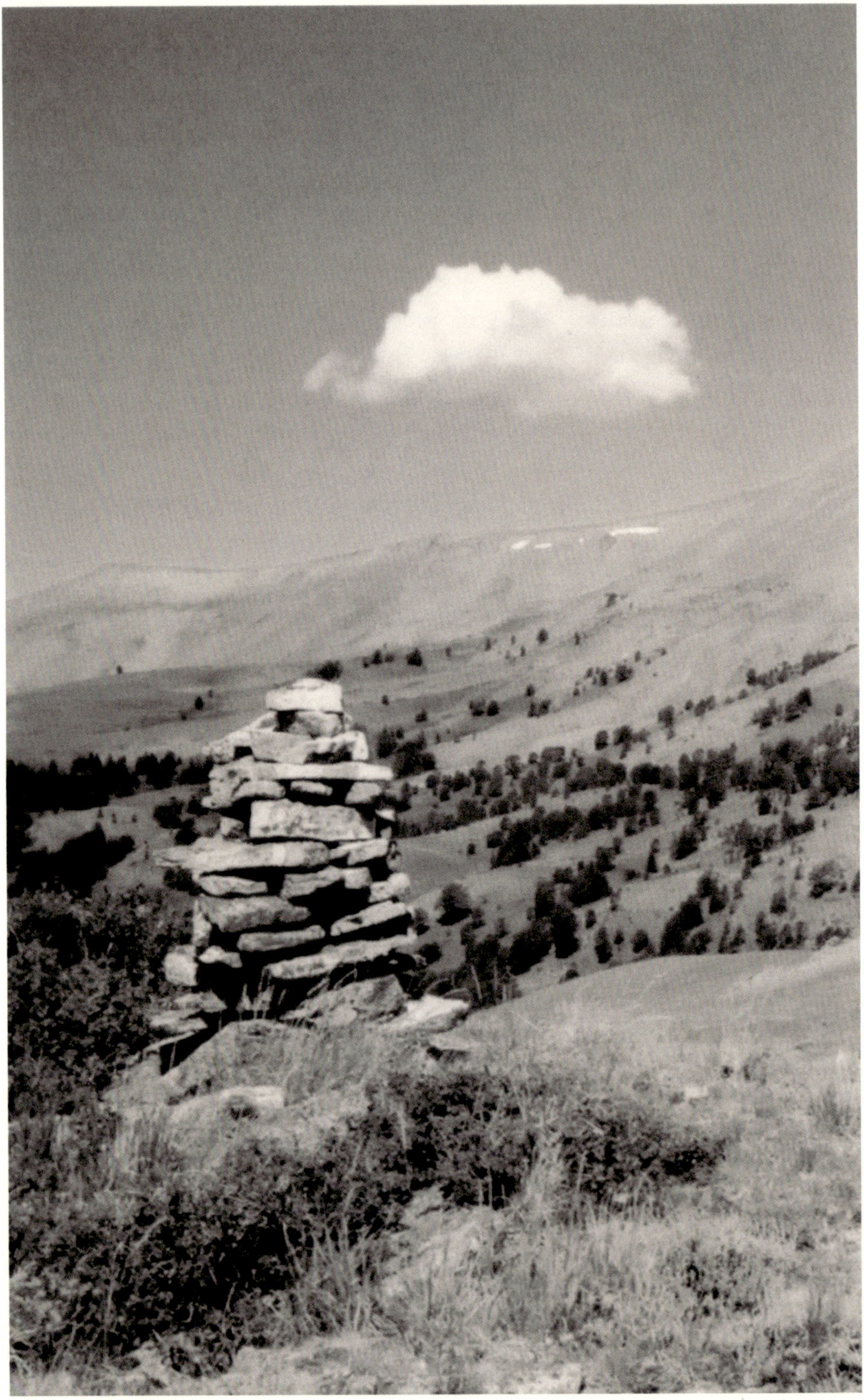

Chapter 14

One Down

The only courage that matters is the kind that gets you from one moment to the next.

— *Mignon McLaughlin*

    The morning of August 2 dawned cold enough to freeze Montana's cow pies. Even before SeeHawk and I crawled outside our tent, the cold numbed our noses and made our cheeks sting. As we set about striking camp, steam from our breath danced around our faces.
    SeeHawk muttered wishfully, "Maybe today's heat won't be as bad as we think going over Taylor Mountain."
    I chuckled, "Right, and maybe we'll find somebody selling snow cones on the summit."
    Once everything was packed, we congratulated ourselves on getting an early start. Unexpectedly, though, we had to march all over a frozen streambed, searching for the trail we had left last evening. In the process, frosty grass and ice-crusted willows soaked our sneakers, leaching water into our socks, which made our feet freeze, causing them to ache, which amplified our frustration about not being able to leave camp, which was a bad way to start the new morning.
    Once we finally figured out how to leave our camp, just stepping into a dry forest helped us feel warmer. That was in our minds, but not according to SeeHawk's keychain thermometer. The forest's shade stayed refrigerator-cold for another 20

minutes before it leaped up. Foom! That is how fast we went from shivering to wearing t-shirts and shorts.

At 8,000-feet, the CDT broke out of the trees, to mount an open summit capping the Centennial Mountain Range. Scattered purple lupines, white yarrow, pink geraniums, and yellow cinquefoil decorated the summit like cupcake sprinkles. In the distance ahead, a doughy-looking monster among dirt piles, named Taylor Mountain, commanded respect by filling the eastern skyline.

Our trail aimed straight toward the rising sun, whose low angle outsmarted our hats, forcing us to continuously squint, which slowly drained our batteries.

SeeHawk's lethargy soon reached a point where, when he went to see a man about a horse, he did not even bother unzipping his shorts. Instead, he just scrunched them up high enough to pee underneath them.

I teased him for being lazy, until I got teaser's payback, by spending the next quarter-hour wondering why my floppy sun hat could barely shade my eyes, only to realize its brim was flipped backward over my head.

The main issue weighing upon both of us was how to make our water supply last for 17 miles. Two gallons of water seemed like plenty for less than a day's mileage, but, once again, we had packed thick whole-wheat crackers with garlicky hummus for lunch.

Even before reaching the first of two big climbs, SeeHawk's concern spiked to a point where he raised an eyebrow when I peed for the second time that morning.

I felt a little guilty, myself when I saw a trail of clear liquid, rather than yellow liquid, trickle between my sneakers.

"Maybe you're right about me drinking too much," I conceded. "From now on, I'll try to take smaller sips."

But wait, come to think of it—sure, I was squatting, but I had not yet started peeing. Wasn't that strange? Where was the liquid coming from? Uh-oh! Leaping aside, I traced it backward and discovered something awful. When SeeHawk and I had decided to stop, I accidentally rested my backpack upon my water bag's bite-valve, pinching-open the valve, which let everything out.

For some reason, hearing a lot of humorous adjectives woven into my confession did not tickle our Chief Water Officer's funny bone.

Instead, he moaned, "You drained your water AGAIN, Sunshine? We'd better hike fast until we reach our next water source." Keeping in mind, he said this while gallantly pouring a little water from his drinking bag into mine.

Poppa Jim's guidebook cautioned southbound hikers to examine Taylor Mountain from a significant distance. The reason was to identify one among two ascending dirt roads, before losing sight of them at close range.

When I read that the roads contained switchbacks, I snickered, "Lightning-shaped roads for a lightning-prone mountain, isn't that funny? The mountain comes with a warning label."

Of course, I said this without knowing that lightning had actually chased Redbeard and Teach off Taylor Mountain, just the day before.

"Anyway," I told SeeHawk, "it doesn't look like there's going to be any lightning before we get over the top."

SeeHawk raised a fist and started tapping his head.

"Gah, sorry!" I laughed. "Knock on wood."

"Can you see the two roads?" he asked.

"No," I admitted, shielding my eyes to get a better look. "They must be the same color as the mountain, or really thin, or washed-out or something."

"Dang," he replied. "If your sharp eyes can't see them, Poppa Jim must have eyes like an eagle."

"Then, he's a mixed breed," I joked, "since he seems to also have legs like a mountain goat."

"Plus, his last name's Lupus."

"Right, he's a three-in-one animal, like the shapeshifters in your fantasy novels, and I bet he can let off a good howl, too."

A slight descent approaching the mountain surprised us with a tiny oasis of pine trees. Inside their shade, we reviewed Poppa Jim's description of the two roads we were supposed to have sighted from afar. His directions were simple and the terrain looked obvious but we still resolved to count every turn along the way.

Upon reaching Taylor Mountain's broad base, we chose the only dirt road we could find and launched into our first serious climb of the day. Expecting no shade on the way up, our mood remained sober as we began counting, "First left, eight-point-three...first right, eight-point-five..."

Tiny sweat beads popped through my skin. It looked like I was frying. Next, came itching. The air felt extremely dry. It would have been nice to splash my arms with a little cool water, but nope. Rationing was mandatory until we crossed Taylor Mountain and the next peak afterward. I could hardly wait to finish both climbs, and truck-on down to Blair Lake for a nice afternoon swim.

"Second left, eight-point-seven...second right, nine-point-oh..."

SeeHawk regarded every word I spoke to be a tragic waste of saliva. Eventually, he got fed up and snapped, "Don't count out loud for my benefit, Sunshine. If you talk less, you'll be able to drink less."

Ignoring his rebuke, I kept on reciting, "Third left, nine-point-two..." Huff. Puff. "...Help me pay attention. We're getting close to nine-point-four..." No way, no how, was I going to miss seeing the dirt road's transition to a better dirt road. But, oops! Somehow, my count went too high, causing me to realize we had overshot our mark.

"Focus," SeeHawk chanted.

Together, we dropped back downhill, soon reaching a forked road junction that should have been obvious to anyone with eyes.

By strange coincidence, in the same location, a blustery wind pounced from out of nowhere. The air temperature dropped, but that was all. No change appeared in the sky's fluffy clouds.

Poppa Jim's guidebook mentioned an old mining prospect coming up soon, which sometimes held water after heavy rainstorms. We dared to hope, but all we found was an empty hole, not even containing gold. This letdown set me to wondering. Had Montana's 2-year drought depleted aquifers and creeks as far south as Wyoming's Great Basin, where water shortages could be dangerous, instead of just a nuisance?

More than one hour after starting to climb Taylor Mountain, it looked like we were finally getting near the top. The mountain's highest switchback was extremely long, cutting across its forehead like a prominent worry wrinkle. Near 9,650 -feet, we had to blink to make sure we had not slipped into a dream. Sure enough, the vision was real! Way, high up there, a herd of about twenty cows stood grazing near the summit. When our approach spooked them, they all scuttled into a tizzy and followed their alpha leader onto the road in front of us, forcing us to "chase" them if we wanted to keep going.

Soon, a passing hawk spied Taylor Mountain having a parade and swooped down to circle above the cows.

Probably, the bull in front knew his harem was unfit for nonstop trotting, but his bullish personality would not let him change course. SeeHawk and I might have found ourselves tripping over fallen heifers, if not for the old patriarch finally receiving an epiphany and realizing that he, and all his sweeties, could just pull over to let us pass.

It was a comical moment when SeeHawk and I marched by the old fellow and saw him contemplating his own genius.

"That's one big step for cow-kind," SeeHawk laughed. "Although, I bet if we came back tomorrow, he'd need to solve the same problem all over again."

Meantime, seeing the parade break up caused the hawk to ditch the cows and start circling over us.

"Do we look tastier than beef?" I cringed, feeling hunted by the predator's hungry gaze.

"Check out that awesome wingspan," SeeHawk gushed, feeling blessed by the acrobat's majestic beauty.

As a threesome, our little parade bumped into another surprise upon finishing the climb. There was a mad-dog windstorm sandblasting Taylor Mountain's summit. The hawk got blown straight out of sight. Our hats almost followed. We grabbed them just in time.

The summit was crowned with a giant stone slab, seeming to hold up the sky like a stadium's top bleacher. If not for fear of getting blown into eternity, we might have climbed onto the bleacher and gazed across northern Idaho. Instead, we just crouched inside its wind-shadow, looking back upon seven miles' worth of familiar mountains, including Slide Mountain, Big Table Mountain, and even the pointy Lehmi Peaks.

I wanted to say something profound, but all I could think of was an old cigarette slogan, *You've come a long way, baby*.

SeeHawk broke a short silence by asking, "Can you remember all the places we camped last week?"

"Are you kidding?" I chortled. "I can't even remember where we camped last night."

"In the meadow by the sheep sign," he said.

"Oh, right!" I laughed. "Thanks because I seriously forgot, and it's only been a few hours."

Talking further revealed that neither of us could remember more than two campsites we had occupied since leaving Leadore. Was our memory loss caused by fatigue? Dehydration? Overheating? Or were we just traveling too fast for our brains to store everything?

Life seemed good inside the bleacher's wind-shadow, but we could not afford to slack. Battening down our eyelids, we charged back into the wind's strongest current. It helped to row our trekking poles like oars. Bracing them sideways gave us resistance against getting pushed off-course. Fortunately, the summit turned out to be small. Within a few minutes, we dropped onto Taylor Mountain's backside, feeling as if we had only taken a little hayride through the Jetstream.

Back in relative calm, the CDT descended toward a whole new experience. It began with exiting Taylor Mountain upon a tailfin of purple lava talus, which snaked downhill like an ancient ruined staircase. Nothing held the talus in place besides inertia and a few gnarled tree roots. Ahead, the tailfin faced a panoramic view that made us keep stopping to feast our eyes.

We were hoping to see something dramatic appear in the direction of Yellowstone National Park. Instead, we saw the surrounding landscape dramatically fall away. It happened on both sides of our aim, where twin saddlebags, each 3,000-feet deep, exposed the tailfin beneath our feet like an after-dinner T-bone. Each saddlebag contained a broad, flat desert, showcasing one central lake. To the left, that showpiece was Upper Red Rock Lake—a small blue jewel ringed with bright green grass—which looked exotic because its colors were extreme. To the right, Island Park Reservoir filled a much bigger space, shimmering through the heat like a holographic mirage.

With everything ahead embodying desolation, I curiously asked SeeHawk, "Would you ever want to hike the CDT again, someday?"

Instead of answering, he pointed toward the right, saying, "Can you believe that's the world's largest caldera?"

Fixing my attention upon Island Park Reservoir, I watched its bluish-silver aura leak into the desert's shimmering heatwaves, creating an illusion of water with no edges. Far in the background, the snow-capped Grand Tetons gleamed like shiny milk teeth, begging to be admired. Our future looked exciting, but, first things first.

"Are you feeling stoked for Montana's final exam?" I asked SeeHawk.

"Final exam?" he repeated.

"The big test to see if we're ready to tackle three more states."

"We still have another big climb left? I thought Taylor Mountain was today's Big Daddy."

"No silly. I'm talking about tonight's bushwhack over the crest into Idaho."

"Oh, fiddlesticks, the b-word," he groaned. "Any time I hear you say 'bushwhack' nowadays, I'm quaking in my boots."

"Exactly," I chuckled. "So, can you guess where tonight's b-word will start?"

"Uh...maybe at the starting line?"

"Ha-ha, very funny. Yes, at the starting line. Go pat yourself on the back, Mister Smarty Pants. But can you also guess the name of what comes AFTER the starting line?"

"Let's see, maybe some four-letter words, if we have to do the b-thing?"

"You're a pill today, Smothers. Yes, I suppose we might utter a few profanities. But, my point is, if there happens to be a SIGN marking the trail out of here, can you guess what it might say?"

"Wilderness Boundary. Proceed at Your Own Risk?"

"GAHH! Forget it. End of discussion."

"No, no, Sunshine. I'm all ears. Go ahead and lay it on me, if you must."

"Okay, here goes," I smiled. "Drumroll please?"

SeeHawk faked a drumroll.

"Ladies and germs, may I present, Ta-Dah! Hell Canyon."

"Ouch," my partner cringed. "So, we're going from the frying pan into the fire?"

"Yes, but not an oil fire. I'm sure it'll be easy. Plus, our reward for finishing the final exam will be a big gravel road dropping straight to Mack's Inn. And, if we finish quickly, we might get to eat blueberry pancakes for breakfast."

"What if we flunk and take a long time?"

"Well, if Mack's Inn has an *I-Hop*, I suppose we could eat pancakes for lunch or even dinner."

"Okay, I'm in," SeeHawk grinned. "By the way, speaking of Hell Canyon, do you know how to make Holy Water?"

"Um...no."

"You boil the Hell out of it."

Without another word, my goofy partner sped down the talus like he could already smell pancakes.

Once we landed upon solid ground, the CDT led us through a web of dirt canyons trapping the sun's heat like pizza ovens. We felt tempted to guzzle our last dregs of water, but experience told us to make them last. We could not afford to take any water source for granted, even if it was a full-blown lake.

Beyond the last pizza oven, a hardpan dirt road guided us down to a horse pasture where our next climb began. The noontime sun was fixed overhead. We had not eaten lunch. Our shoelaces felt tight from heat-induced swelling. Our shoulders felt ready to go on strike. Union rules called for a smoke-break, but never mind. We just started climbing. Onward and upward, maintaining a steady rhythm, we lost track of time and pretty much stopped thinking. In one straight shot, we gained 600-feet. Was the climb already finished? Gosh, well, hooray! Now, we could eat lunch. Except, what did we see from atop the summit? Payday! There was Blair Lake, resting 200-feet below. Its blue-green water looked delicious. Better yet, it looked ripe for swimming. We just needed to get down there quickly.

"You search left, while I search right," I told SeeHawk.

Both of us reconvened within minutes, not having found any footpath, jeep road, or even a cairn to indicate where people started descending toward Blair Lake. Clearly, it was time to put the lake on hold and start eating, but, ugh. Could we really relax sitting up in the heat, masticating garlicky hummus and crackers, with a lake in plain sight calling our names?

Feeling desperate, I lowered my legs through a small summit notch and groped around with my shoes, trying to find something sticky. A steep cornice caught my shoes and held them securely, allowing me to squat into a ready position. Using the cornice for a slide, I glissaded down to the kind of loose scree that normally scared me, stood up, and kept going. Scree-skiing was so much fun that if a chairlift had offered to take me back up, I would have done it all over again.

SeeHawk skied down behind me, singing, "I am Pierre, the French backpacquer. I love women. I love French wine. I love talking in a French accent."

Once hitting bottom, he and I made a dash for Blair Lake. It took about one second to yank off our shoes and sink four bare feet into the lakeshore's cool grass. A margin of gloppy mud barely slowed our tumble into the lake's tepid water. It felt heavenly to float on our backs, with algae tickling our tummies and flossing sock-lint from between our toes. After we got dried off, whatever we unpacked for lunch slid down the hatch like weasels on a water slide.

SeeHawk checked his wristwatch and cautiously reported, "It looks like we've finished lunch at seven p.m. That leaves three hours for us to finish Montana's final exam. What do you think?"

"I think, therefore I am," I answered. "But, about Hell Canyon? I think we can push our curfew up to dark, if necessary, because the canyon isn't supposed to be dangerous. It's just a test of what we can hack, in terms of traveling cross-country."

Several thin streams fanned through a watershed heralding Hell Canyon's entrance. Its muddy banks were streaked with yellow dandelions, red Indian paintbrush, purple asters, and pink geraniums.

Surveying all the flowers inspired me to hope, "Maybe Hell doesn't match what it says in the Bible."

SeeHawk happily agreed, "Maybe whoever named the canyon just didn't want to share it."

I took a deep breath, before pulling out our compass. This moment was exciting. Even as a kid, I had always loved taking final exams.

Our most obvious target was a high gap separating two forested walls. I established a compass bearing before starting to climb, but it was easy to just follow Hell Roaring Creek. The worst challenge was trying to squeeze through a mob of bordering willows. Gradually, SeeHawk and I found ourselves getting pressed against the water. High overhead, a ribbon of sky subtly turned pink. We cracked a few jokes about burning our feet. In went our shoes. Brr, they got soaked. Then, we cracked jokes about Hell freezing over. The creek's central current was choked full of willows. We could only make progress by paddling and splashing through the willows like dogs. Finally, we decided to just look for another option, because jungle-grade bushwhacking was too exhausting.

A steep embankment appeared on our right, hinting that perhaps we could bypass part of the creek. Was its angle too steep? I felt intimidated, but the climb would be short. Furthermore, it was covered with soft sand, promising firm support if we kicked good footholds.

SeeHawk went first, marching kick over kick until he reached some shallow divots pressed into the sand.

"Look who we're following!" he exclaimed. "These kick-holes were made by String Stick and Dutch."

I felt like asking how he could tell. To me, the divots looked totally shapeless. Anyhow, I decided to take SeeHawk's word for it, so I could enjoy thinking that following String Stick meant we were walking in Poppa Jim's footsteps.

Atop the embankment, we ran into a stock trail paralleling Hell Roaring Creek. Whether or not it was the CDT, it looked promising, until it led us straight into a barricade of twiggy shrubs. Groping around for an opening, we soon located a hidden passage through which we could keep going. The only downside was having Hell Roaring Creek prank us during our absence. As soon as we emerged from the shrubs, we discovered the creek had ducked out of sight, behind a thick border of trees.

"Playing hide-and-seek, now, are you?" I teased.

SeeHawk shot me a worried look.

"Keep the faith," I told him. "We're on the closest thing this area has to a cow path, so it'll eventually lead us back to the water."

Together, we continued following the stock trail around a blind curve buried in vegetation. Once it straightened back out, Hell Roaring Creek popped back into sight, grinning like a magician wearing different clothes.

"What happened?" SeeHawk stammered.

"Maybe one of the Five Chinese Brothers got thirsty?" I ventured.

Somehow, the creek had instantly expanded from a thin stream of water into a mighty floodplain. This made no sense, considering that creeks usually expand downstream, not upstream. Of course, increased width did not necessarily need to go hand-in-hand with a greater volume of water. In fact, from where SeeHawk and I stood, we could not even see any water, between thousands or millions of willow shrubs smothering the whole works.

Ironically, the stock trail viewed the water's disappearance as a cue to drop back toward the floodplain. Its landing point was a grassy meadow dotted with white saxifrage and yellow arrowleaf groundsel. Patches of exposed dirt confirmed that String Stick and Dutch had crossed the meadow, heading upstream. SeeHawk and I planned to follow their lead, but within a few steps, we spied our meal ticket peeking through some woods close ahead. It was a spacious campsite, equipped with a dangling paint bucket used to protect campers' food from squirrels and marmots.

July's long twilight inspired us to build a rare cooking fire, sending up sparks into the starry sky. Our last chore of the night was loading everything smellable into the campsite's handy paint bucket. After that, we happily fell asleep, thinking our final exam was off to a good start.

Exit stars. Enter new morning.

SeeHawk and I could almost smell pancakes when we opened our eyes. The sooner we could reach Mack's Inn, the sooner we could order breakfast. A pile of flapjacks drowning in butter, maple syrup, blueberries or blueberry-flavored corn syrup, or even *Mrs. Butterworth's*, was calling our names. Striking camp in a hurry, we returned to the meadow we had left last night, only to have its trail end within 100 yards.

"This is NOT a good way to start off the morning," I complained.

SeeHawk stroked his wooly beard, saying, "Maybe most horse packers turn around after occupying the campsite."

"Okay," I agreed, "but even so, where are String Stick and Dutch's footprints?"

SeeHawk helped me search the meadow through and through, but we could not find any evidence of our friends continuing into the upper canyon. Groaning and grumbling, we quit searching and blundered upstream, until we found a skinny footpath that matched our aim but showed no evidence of anyone else's foot traffic.

I vented some frustration by hollering at Montana, "Smooth move, *Ex-Lax*. I get why you're hiding our friends' footprints. This final exam does not allow cheating."

Higher upstream, Hell Roaring Creek shrank into a skinny headwater, crammed between willow thickets. Detours were possible but the incline's complex terrain made them interesting. For instance, one adjacent meadow was vertically striped with shallow lava gullies jutting down to the water's edge. Opposite the meadow stood a spruce-pine forest that looked too steep for efficient travel. Mostly, SeeHawk and I stayed alongside the creek, wading back and forth through its ankle-deep water, between rickety side-climbs through narrow lava gullies.

Traces of the old stock trail reappeared in places, testifying that a small percentage of horse riders did venture into the upper canyon. Above and upstream, we could see the canyon's vertical stone walls reaching gothic proportions. Each next choice began to feel critical. We perceived no warning before Hell Roaring Creek jackknifed through a slickrock gash that bent its water sideways. Poppa Jim's guidebook said the water was destined to reach the Gulf of Mexico, via the Red Rock, Beaverhead, Jefferson, Missouri, and Mississippi Rivers.

When SeeHawk heard me speak about the Mississippi River, he concluded, "So, if I drop in a pine needle here, it should eventually float down to my friend Shearm, in Louisiana?"

Falling in love with the idea, he selected an appropriate pine needle, mumbled some sacred Hawaiian chants, and ceremoniously dropped it into the creek's gentle current. Together, we watched the little token of friendship float downstream.

Finally, SeeHawk asked, "What comes after the spring?"

"Look up there," I pointed

Above a mile of rising treetops sat a crown of electronic gadgets servicing the Federal Aviation Administration.

"If I'm not mistaken," I told SeeHawk, "that's Sawtell Peak."

"You mean, that's our finish line?"

"If I had to bet on it."

"Cowabunga!" he grinned. "Let's quit farting around and

rock-and-roll, baby. I smell blueberry syrup coming out of the microwave."

Just in the nick of time, I noticed my partner preparing to leap from one wet slickrock bank to the other.

"Wait!" I shrieked. "Before you sprain an ankle, let's think about this first. We can't just barge into the forest without knowing where to aim. It might contain lava gullies that don't show from the outside."

Feeling some wind leave his sails, SeeHawk silently pouted.

"Why don't we stay on this side of the creek until we find a better entrance?" I suggested. "That way, we'll be able to see the FAA equipment until it's time to go in, and then our aim will be perfect."

With obvious reluctance, my partner admitted, "Once again, your noodle beats my motor drive, Sunshine. Besides, you're right about this not being a good place to cross."

Continuing upstream, we searched for any kind of official entrance, or blazed tree marking the opposite forest. After finding neither, I caved in and agreed to go Boomhauer, without even bothering to take a compass heading.

The progress we had made going upstream enabled us to cross the creek in one leap. When we glanced up from the landing, we found ourselves too near the forest to look over its trees one last time, so we had to guesstimate where to aim for the FAA equipment. Luckily, we were able to hike blindly through the trees for 20 minutes without blundering into any lava gullies. The next surprise came when we happened into a half-acre clearing, floored with purple lava talus. Peeking into the clearing from above stood several volcanic crags, unsuccessfully masquerading as Sawtell Peak. Of course, SeeHawk and I could not be fooled, since none of them were crowned with FAA equipment.

Lowering my gaze to a huge talus cairn, centered in the clearing, I squealed, "This is the PASS! We did it, partner! We made it to the top without getting lost in Hell!"

SeeHawk laughed, but he did not look bowled-over. After all, Montana's final exam had been pretty straightforward, if not always easy.

Refusing to calm down, I went on exclaiming, "Do you know what this means? WE'RE FINALLY ABOUT TO LEAVE MONTANA!"

At least, that was my assumption until we started searching for the clearing's exit.

"Oh, no. Not this, again," SeeHawk groaned.

We searched everywhere. Across all the thick-layered talus, around the clearing's edges, and even into the trees, we searched. There was no jeep road. In fact, we could not even find any terrain that looked favorable for jeeps. Dang, how frustrating. Was it time to employ the b-word and just make our own way over Sawtell Peak? The lava crags watching us from above said, no. We needed to find Poppa Jim's missing jeep road. It was sure to exist because his directions were always accurate.

SeeHawk helped me reexamine every yard of the clearing a second time. We circled around and around, revisiting areas we had already ruled out. Eventually, we just jumped around like apes.

"It's got to be right under our noses," I wailed. "Are we getting karmic payback for stepping on too many ants?"

"No, I don't think so," SeeHawk replied. "We probably just need to remove our pancake goggles and focus."

"Focus?" I repeated. "How much harder can we focus?"

My head felt ready to explode. The harder I stared, the more confusing everything seemed. My brain just could not take it anymore.

Suddenly, SeeHawk shouted, "Here it IS, Sunshine! Here's our ticket to IDAHO!"

Sure enough, his finger pointed toward a faint depression scooped across the talus, which could only be seen by squatting down low with the sun at a perfect angle.

"High-five, partner!" I laughed. "You've earned a squirt of whipped cream on your pancakes!"

Clasping hands, and with great ceremony, we prepared to step from Montana into Idaho. But wait! First, our attention got diverted by something tiny and white poking out of the big stone cairn. What could it be? Taking a closer look, we discovered it was a folded scrap of paper. Carefully opening fold after fold, we pressed our heads together and read its neatly handprinted message...

Dutch, where are you? I've been waiting for an hour. Now I'm thinking you already came through here. Are you heading down to Mack's Inn? Hope I guessed right. See you there. - String Stick

GLOSSARY OF TERMS

Cairn: Rocks stacked into a small or large pile, to mark a cross-country route or inconspicuous trail.
Corn Snow: Granular springtime snowpack formed as a result of thawing and refreezing.
Crag: Upward thrusting protrusions of rough, weathered rock.
Gaiters: Knee-high sleeves worn around lower legs to keep rocks and snow out of shoes.
Glacier: Year-round accumulation of snow large enough to creep by means of its own weight and gravity.
Krummholz: Trees dwarfed to the size of shrubs by extreme conditions at high elevations.
Scree: Loose, slippery gravel sloughing off crumbling stone.
Section-Hiker: Backpacker completing all or portions of a long trail in a disjointed fashion, broken up over time.
Slack-Pack: Hike part of a trail unburdened, with somebody driving one's gear forward.
Swale: Shallow trough cutting through a gently sloped or flat landscape.
Switchbacks: Zigzagging tread cut across a steep mountain, for ease of climbing.
Talus: Accumulation of flat stone discs fractured off a mountain by erosion.
Tarn: Small mountain lake filled by broadly draining snowmelt rather than any visible creeks.
Trail Angel: Someone who unexpectedly provides assistance to backpackers.
Thru-Hiker: Backpacker aiming to complete a long journey in linear fashion, from start to finish.
Vitamin I: Ibuprofen.
Yellow-Blaze: Get driven on wheels around sections of a hiking trail.

HISTORICAL REFERENCES

The Great Divide, Time-Life Books, 1973
Copper Camp, Writers Project of Montana, Riverbend Publishing, 2002
Lewis and Clark, Frank Burd, Publ. John Hinde Curteich Inc., 2001
Scats and Tracks of the Rocky Mountains, James C. Halfpenny, A Falcon Guide, 1998
Beyond Backpacking, Ray Jardine, Adventure Lore Press, 2000